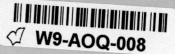

GULF OF MEXICO
CARIBBEAN SEA
CUBA, HAITI, DOM. REP.
Sugar
Tobacco
Coffee
Manganese
EXICO
otton
etroleum
ead
offee
opper
CENTRAL AMERICA
Coffee
Bananas
Cacao
VENEZUELA
Petroleum
Coffee
Cacao
Iron Ore
COLOMBIA
Coffee
Petroleum
Gold
ECUADOR
Cacao
Coffee
Bananas
BRAZIL
Coffee
Cotton
Cacao
Wood
Rubber
Iron Ore
PERU
Cotton
Sugar
Lead
Petroleum
Copper
BOLIVIA
Tin
Lead
Zinc
PARAGUAY
Wood
Cotton Fiber
Quebracho
CHILE
Copper
Nitrates
Iron Ore
Sheeps Wool
URUGUAY
Wool
Cattle Products
Wheat
ARGENTINA
Cattle Products
Wheat
Wool
Corn

Governments of Latin America

WILLIAM W. PIERSON

Professor of History and Political Science
University of North Carolina

FEDERICO G. GIL

Professor of Political Science
University of North Carolina

McGRAW-HILL BOOK COMPANY, INC.

New York Toronto London

1957

GOVERNMENTS OF LATIN AMERICA

Library of Congress Catalog Card Number 56-8861

IV

50005

THE MAPLE PRESS COMPANY, YORK, PA.

PREFACE

There has been a marked increase in the study of the governments and politics of Latin America by political scientists in the United States in recent years, reflecting the increasing importance of this area in world affairs and particularly to this country. Many colleges and universities have recently instituted courses on the subject in the departments of political science, although formerly such instruction was usually left to the historians. An increasing number of political scientists have turned their attention to Latin America, resulting in a growing number of excellent monographs and special studies. Nevertheless, we are still heavily indebted to historians for our knowledge of Latin-American institutions. Because of the close economic and political ties of the United States and Latin America, and the growing cultural exchange between the two areas, we may anticipate that study of the government of Latin America, as well as other aspects of its civilization, will continue to receive increasing attention in this country.

There is a vast and meritorious literature relating to the government and politics of Latin America written by Latin Americans. These studies have usually dealt with the institutions and political practices of the country of which the author was a citizen. This literature contains many studies of the constitutions, institutions, jurisprudence, public administration, social legislation, suffrage, political parties and electoral practices, government and business, the rights of citizens, or other aspects of the government of a single country. Until recently relatively few works on comparative government were written by native authors. Formerly it was often said that a citizen of Latin America was likely to be better informed on the governments and politics of Europe than on those of neighboring states. He had few means to acquire the latter information, except by travel and observation. Fortunately the situation in this respect is changing, for during the past two decades an increasing number of studies of comparative government in Latin America have appeared.

A single volume dealing with the governments of the twenty Latin-American republics poses difficult problems of scope and method of treatment. One plan is to treat each of the countries individually, which has the merit of simplicity and ready identification of the information concerning each state. If fully carried out, however, this plan would require twenty volumes or monographs. In time, perhaps, studies of this type and number will be published. There will still be needed, however, a single-volume treatment of the several governments, and the choice must be made between the treatment of each country individually and separately, or a topical and comparative treatment. Each of the authors has experimented with both methods in teaching the subject. After years of teaching the subject country by country, we abandoned this approach in favor of the topical and comparative method. We have now had six years' experience with this plan, which we believe is superior for the following reasons: First, when we followed the plan of the separate treatment of each country, we were never able in the time limits of a quarter or semester course of instruction to complete the survey of all. Secondly, the separate treatment left largely to the student the difficult—and sometimes too difficult—task of formulating his or her synthesis or comparison. Thirdly, we have come to the conclusion that in a survey course many subjects and phases may be better studied topically and comparatively than by a country-by-country examination. Some examples of these subjects, in our judgment, are Church and state relations, the courts, dictatorship and personalism in politics, political parties, women in politics, social legislation, problems of political stability, and federalism and unitarism as forms of political organization. We think these are sufficient reasons for the adoption of the plan we have followed. At the same time we are aware that much information concerning particular countries needs to be presented, and this we have done either in the text or in footnotes.

Among other questions as to content and scope of treatment is that of whether or not to attempt an analysis of the colonial institutions and administration established and practiced by Spain and Portugal. Undoubtedly competent studies of both empires are available. Our decision to include in this volume a brief consideration of the colonial background was due to the conviction, shared by many, that a knowledge of the colonial heritage is essential to the student's understanding of later developments. Likewise our study of the struggles for independence is for the purpose of affording information concerning many political experiments and concerning the origins of many political problems and ideas of significance for the subsequent era.

We have sought to avoid special emphasis. Attention is, for example, given to constitutions, but not without awareness that there may be and

GOVERNMENTS OF LATIN AMERICA

McGRAW-HILL SERIES IN POLITICAL SCIENCE

JOSEPH P. HARRIS, *Consulting Editor*

ADRIAN · Governing Urban America: Structure, Politics, and Administration
ADRIAN · State and Local Governments
BONE · American Politics and the Party System
CHRISTENSON AND MCWILLIAMS · Voice of the People: Readings in Public Opinion and Propaganda
FERGUSON AND MCHENRY · American Federal Government
FERGUSON AND MCHENRY · American System of Government
FERGUSON AND MCHENRY · Elements of American Government
FIELD · Governments in Modern Society
FRANK · Cases on the Constitution
GOSNELL, LANCASTER, AND RANKIN · Fundamentals of American Government: National, State, and Local
GOSNELL, LANCASTER, AND RANKIN · Fundamentals of American National Government
GROSS · The Legislative Struggle
HAAS AND WHITING · Dynamics of International Relations
HARTMANN · Basic Documents of International Relations
HOLLOWAY · State and Local Government in the United States
MANGONE · A Short History of International Organization
MCCLOSKY AND TURNER · The Soviet Dictatorship
MILLETT · Government and Public Administration
MILLETT · Management in the Public Service
NEUMANN · European and Comparative Government
PIERSON AND GIL · Governments of Latin America
POWELL AND PARKER · Major Aspects of American Government
PRITCHETT · The American Constitution
PRITCHETT · American Constitutional Issues
RIEMER · Problems of American Government
ROCHE AND STEDMAN · The Dynamics of Democratic Government
RODEE, ANDERSON, AND CHRISTOL · Introduction to Political Science
SVARLIEN · An Introduction to the Law of Nations
TURNER · Politics in the United States: Readings in Political Parties and Pressure Groups
TURNER AND VIEG · The Government and Politics of California
VANDENBOSCH AND HOGAN · Toward World Order
WALDO · Ideas and Issues in Public Administration: A Book of Readings
WILSON · The American Political Mind
WILSON · Police Administration

has been much difference between the formal constitution or the written instruments of government in evidence and the real and operative constitution of fact. Both are proper subjects of study. Again, the role of personalism (*caudillismo*) in politics and the many appeals to violence and revolution as ways of political action have been of much importance in Latin-American history and have, despite all the diversity in detail, followed certain patterns. We have given full recognition to these influences, but we have also been interested in evidence of respect for legality and for what Woodrow Wilson called "the orderly processes of constitutional government."

Finally, it has been our desire and plan to give priority and whenever feasible controlling emphasis to the opinions of Latin-American writers concerning problems, issues, and practices of government and administration. While we are indebted to foreign opinion and scholarship—to many pioneering achievements of excellence and worth—we have thought that a special effort should be made to ascertain and present the views, contradictory as they often are, of Latin Americans concerning their own governments.

It has been our steadfast purpose to write a just and objective appraisal of government and politics of Latin America. Both of us feel that the fulfillment of such a purpose requires of those attempting it travel in the countries and long acquaintance with the people. One of us has visited thirteen of the countries, with more than one visit to four of them; the other is a native of Cuba and has traveled in fifteen of the countries. Both of us have visited Spain and Portugal.

WILLIAM W. PIERSON
FEDERICO G. GIL

CONTENTS

Chapter 1: LATIN AMERICA—PEOPLES, LAND, AND RESOURCES

The term "Latin America" and the most commonly used substitutes, "Hispanic America" and "Ibero-America," refer in a geographic sense to the lands reaching from Cape Horn to the northern border of Mexico. The insular states of Cuba, Haiti, and the Dominican Republic are included. The term in the form of an adjective (i.e., "Latin-American") has served to designate or classify various activities, peculiarities, achievements, and characteristics of the peoples residing within these territorial areas. In these senses, it may be considered to have somewhat the same connotation as the adjective "European" when applied to the several peoples and territory of Europe.

Those employing the expression "Latin America" as implying either an ethnic or a linguistic unity are mistaken in such usage, since neither of these unities exists. To be sure, the countries emerging from the Spanish empire have Spanish as the official language. Portuguese is the official language of Brazil, and French is that of Haiti. Indian languages are still spoken in some of the continental states. As to ethnic composition of the population, it is well known that the Spanish American countries have as race stocks descendants of Spanish settlers, Indians, Negroes, immigrants, and those of mixed blood. Similarly Brazil has descendants of Portuguese settlers, Indians, Negroes, immigrants, and the mixbloods. But there are countries with no Indians, such as the insular republics and Uruguay. There are some countries with very large Indian populations—Mexico, Central America (with the exception of Costa Rica), Ecuador, Peru, Bolivia, and Paraguay; while the precentage of Indians in the population is smaller in Brazil, Colombia, Panama, Chile, Argentina, and Venezuela. Brazil, Cuba, and Haiti have a large number of Negroes, while Argentina, Costa Rica, Guatemala, Honduras, and Mexico have relatively few. Furthermore, the distribution of Spaniards and of immigrants has been uneven. An ethnic factor not always understood by foreigners is that the Indians of Latin America represent many different families and significantly different cultural types. The Indians in history have shown radically different aptitudes for the assimilation of alien culture and for political and social participation.

"Latin America" may be used by those entertaining the idea, perhaps the ideal, that at some future time the presently separated states will be politically united, in one state or, if not in one, in two or three. Those favoring and expecting this outcome might argue that historical origin, colonial background, language, religion, racial affinities, community of interests and dangers, and similarities in culture will induce here, as they have elsewhere, political unification. Various plans of union or federation, embracing in scope the whole or parts of Latin America, have been proposed; some of them have been tried. Among the notable experiments have been Gran Colombia (1820–1830), the Federation of Central America (1823–1839), the union of Haiti and Santo Domingo (1821–1844), and the thwarted union of Peru and Bolivia (1836–1841). A dozen or more efforts have been made for the renewal or partial renewal of the Federation of Central America. All attempts at the unification of two or more states have so far failed. If the intense spirit of nationalism prevalent in many—perhaps in all—of the republics is kept in mind, the hope for political unification seems illusory. In fact, the thesis concerning the community of ties will not stand close examination.

If political unification is impracticable—and the facts so far seem to justify that conclusion—cooperative sentiments and action in diplomatic, economic, and cultural relations are quite different possibilities. Although the Latin-American countries have not always presented a united front in international congresses or relations, groups of them in unison have made impressive demonstrations of capacity for cooperation. The term "Latin America" has a general, but not very precise, meaning in international relations as representing the interests and sentiments of the governments and peoples concerned.

Population and Its Distribution

The map shows certain peculiarities in the distribution and concentration of population, especially in the continental areas. In South America, a concentration occurs in territory near the sea. To be sure, there are some notable exceptions, the most important of them being the north-central *pampa* and the Tucumán district of Argentina, the Andean highlands of Peru and Bolivia, southern Paraguay, the interior plateau of Ecuador, the Antioquia and Bogotá areas of Colombia, and the eastern fork of the Andes running through Venezuela. In North America the heavily populated regions are the central plateau of Mexico, the highlands of Guatemala and El Salvador, the intermontane region of Costa Rica, and

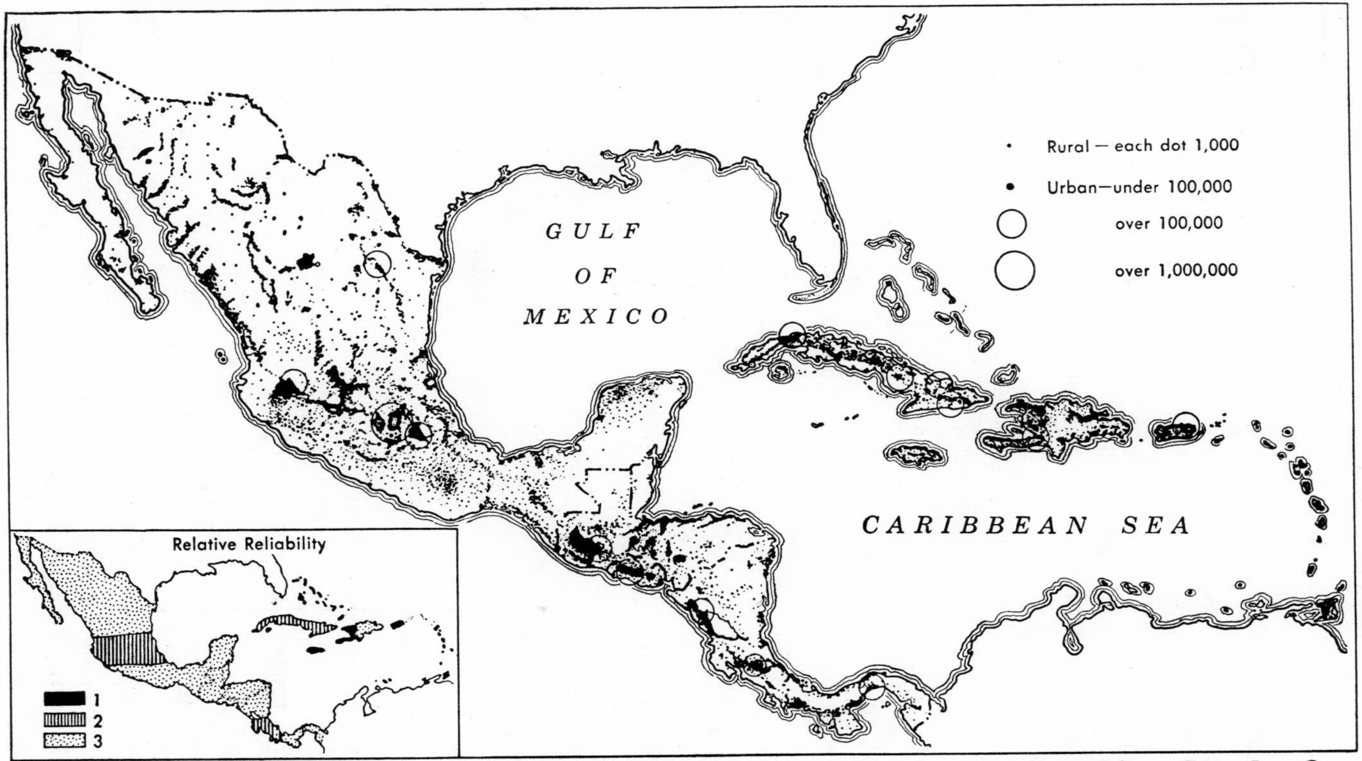

Figure 1. Population of Hispanic North America. SOURCE: Preston E. James, *Latin America,* New York, Odyssey Press, Inc., Copyright, 1950, pp. 742–743.

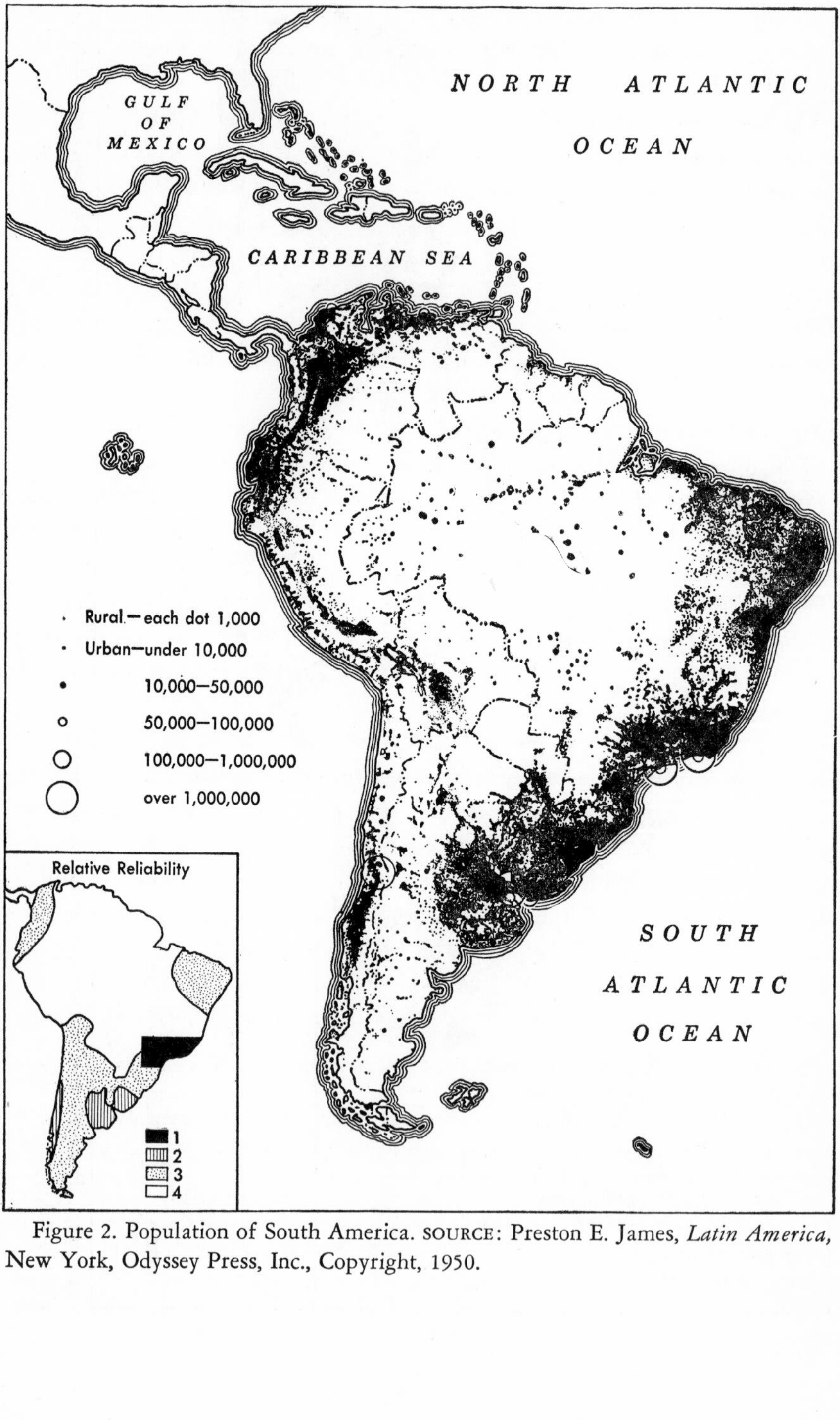

Figure 2. Population of South America. SOURCE: Preston E. James, *Latin America,* New York, Odyssey Press, Inc., Copyright, 1950.

the "depression" or lake region of Nicaragua. Vast stretches of land in the llanos of Venezuela, the Amazon valley, the lowlands of Bolivia, and the plateau of Patagonia are sparsely populated.

On the continent, there has been a definite choice of people to live in the highlands in order to escape tropical heat. It has been observed that "in the United States, over three-fourths of the people live on plains less than 1,000 feet in elevation, while in South America only one-third so live."[1] Since 65 per cent of the land surface is below 1,000 feet in elevation, it is not surprising that the heaviest concentrations of populations on the plains or lowlands are to be found south of the Tropic of Capricorn in Uruguay, Argentina, and the central valley of Chile. This preference for the highlands does not obtain in the island countries, nor is it true of Nicaragua, as has been said.

The growth of cities and the trend toward urbanization are important factors in the population. Latin America now has five cities with populations estimated at a million or more—Buenos Aires, Rio de Janeiro, Mexico City, São Paulo, and Santiago. Buenos Aires, with more than five million inhabitants, is ranked fifth in population among the cities of the world. In addition to these five, there are thirty-nine cities having 100,000 to 1,000,000 inhabitants.[2] In several countries the importance of the cities has given added strength to movements in favor of a greater measure of municipal home rule. However, the growth of the cities in population has in some countries caused forebodings and led to studies of agrarian problems in relation to population. Do the big estates, the methods of agricultural exploitation of the soil, and the treatment of agricultural labor impede the growth of the rural population? Would a plan of redistribution of lands be a solution? These are some of the unsolved questions concerning population trends.

The desire to attract settlers from the outside was often expressed during the time of the wars for independence and during the nineteenth

[1] R. H. Whitbeck and Frank E. Williams, *Economic Geography of South America* (3d ed., New York, McGraw-Hill, 1940), p. 13.

[2] Preston E. James, *Latin America* (rev. ed., New York, Odyssey, 1950), p. 7. It is interesting to note that many of the capitals are located in the highlands—La Paz, 11,910 feet; Quito, 9,350; Bogotá, 8,350; Mexico City, 7,870; Guatemala City, 4,877; San José, 3,870; Tegucigalpa, 3,200; Caracas, 3,040; San Salvador, 2,155; and Santiago, 1,710. São Paulo, capital of the state of the same name, is 2,500 feet above sea level, and Belo Horizonte, capital of Minas Gerais, is 3,000. Buenos Aires, Montevideo, Panama City, Havana, Port-au-Prince, and Ciudad Trujillo are located at seaside and Managua at lakeside. See W. L. Schurz, *Latin America* (New York, Dutton, 1942), p. 16.

century. This desire led to the creation of public agencies to promote immigration, to concessions of lands to companies or individuals commissioned to bring in settlers, to promises of religious toleration, and to the adoption of generous naturalization laws. During the first half century of independence, Argentina and Brazil adopted immigration policies which merit our study. Brazil, under both its emperors, arranged for and administered the settlement of several "colonies" or groups of immigrants from Europe. But the most systematic ideas and plans to this end came from Argentina. There two thinkers, Alberdi and Sarmiento, formulated principles which the government and people came to accept.

Alberdi, in the famous treatise *Las Bases,* written prior to the convention which framed the constitution of 1853, proposed and defended the thesis that to populate the land would be to govern it, civilize it, and enrich it. He thought that, with an enlightened immigration policy and with fair treatment of new settlers, people from Europe, especially from northern Europe, would come. They would, he predicted, bring with them ideas about education to which they were accustomed, they would favor better means of transportation and communication, they would cultivate the soil in accordance with modern agriculture, and they would favor the importation of machinery and industry. The constitution affirmed some of these principles, and later laws were adopted and treaties negotiated, guaranteeing to immigrants rights to acquire property, civil rights, and religious liberty. With such rights assured and with the laws justly and equally administered, Alberdi had confidence that the new citizens would fully and promptly be incorporated into the political life of the country. With the development of one of the most excellent immigration services, large numbers of foreigners came to Argentina. Although many of the newcomers were seasonal migrants and although some who came with intention to settle later returned to their former homes, of the 2,000,000 immigrants who came between 1856 and 1900, 1,200,000 remained. It is estimated that prior to 1930, 6,300,000 people had entered the country. It was estimated, also, that of the immigrants who remained, 1,300,000 were Italians and 1,025,000 were Spaniards.[3] This is known in Argentina as the "re-Europeanization."

Other countries have received settlers from the outside and there have been from time to time campaigns similar to that led by Alberdi. Many other countries have organized agencies for the promotion of immigration. Brazil and Uruguay have shared the experience of "re-Europeanization."

[3] This latter estimate was made in 1924. James, *op. cit.,* pp. 315–316.

The countries which have received the largest increments to the populations from immigration have been Argentina, Brazil, Uruguay, Cuba, and Mexico.

Many of the prophecies of Alberdi were fulfilled, but in some countries problems were caused by the presence of large numbers of foreigners, especially when they were concentrated in location and when they continued to employ the language of the country of origin. The assimilation of such people, who followed different customs and who lived somewhat apart in cultural and social isolation, was slow and difficult, causing some misgivings.[4]

Indian and Negro Elements of the Population

A study of the composition and characteristics of the population would lead the student into many fields of interest and inquiry, such as those of social classes, cultural and economic status, mixture of races, birth and death rates, and many other matters of concern to statisticians, anthropologists, and sociologists. In some of these areas of interest, differences of opinion are so divergent that generalization is hazardous. The definition of terms and the principles and methods employed in making classifications of people are important since they affect the conclusions that are drawn.

The last point is illustrated by the problems of classification of people according to race. The three better-known methods of principles are (1) by blood, somatic, and physiognomic or cranial measurements; (2) by sociological judgments of customs, education, social status, and standards of living; and (3) by the language habitually spoken, especially by the "mother" tongue. The statistics of classification based on any one usually differ from those based on any other.

Another factor may be the changes in definition of terms. The terms "creole" (*criollo*) and "mixblood" (mestizo) are and have been used with varying signification. In the colonial period the term "mestizo," within the Spanish dominions, usually signified the descendant of parents one of whom was Spanish and the other Indian. In time, with further

[4] Professor Emilio Willems reports that between 1824 and 1840 probably 200,000 Germans entered Brazil, but that the number of those who left is not known. He estimates that between 1827 and 1939 the immigration to the State of São Paulo was 2,439,490, of which 950,963 were Italians, 425,546 were Portuguese, 387,769 were Spaniards, 186,769 were Japanese, and 38,122 were Austrians. "Immigrants and their Assimilation in Brazil," in T. L. Smith and A. Marchant (eds.), *Brazil: Portrait of Half a Continent* (New York, Dryden, 1951), pp. 206–224.

mixtures, blood percentages were calculated and given designations thought to be appropriate.[5] Certainty was not always possible, and such terms, if they continued in use, had popular rather than scientific meaning. Also, in time, the term "mestizo" became generic in significance and in some countries was expanded in scope to embrace persons having a percentage of Negro blood.

TABLE 1
POPULATION CLASSIFICATION OF MEXICO

Race	Number	Percentage
Census of 1921		
Indians	4,180,022	24.16
Mesti-Indios	8,504,820	59.33
Whites	1,404,804	9.80
Foreigners	245,124	1.71
Census of 1940		
Indians	1,486,717	7.56
Mesti-Indios	1,458,368	7.43
Mestizos	7,268,920	36.98
Mesti-blancos	9,263,172	47.13
Whites	176,375	0.90

SOURCE: J. E. Iturriaga, *La estructura social y cultural de Mêxico* (Mexico, 1951), pp. 95–96. Cf. Jorge L. Tamayo, *Geografía moderna de México* (Mexico, 1953). According to the latter, "Indian" means a person who speaks only an Indian language; by "Mesti-Indio" he means one who speaks both an Indian and the Spanish language, but who adheres to Indian culture and folkways; the "mestizo" speaks Spanish, but in clothing, footwear, and habitation shows many characteristics of the Indian; and the "Mesti-blancos" speak Spanish, do not wear Indian clothing, and do not in general adhere to aboriginal culture.

Since some countries have adopted linguistic and sociological norms in making their census reports and for the purpose of making racial classifications, the new definitions and principles have caused noteworthy readjustments in statistics. In Mexico, the new methods of classification were adopted after the census of 1921. A comparison of the racial classi-

[5] The Spanish ethnologist José Pérez de Barradas, in *Los mestizos de América* (Madrid, 1948), listed fifty-eight words pertaining to mixtures called "primary," i.e., mixtures of two bloods, and forty-five terms designating "secondary" mixtures, i.e., of three bloods—European, Indian, and Negro. See J. Ycaza Tigerino, *Sociología de la política hispanoamericana* (Madrid, 1950), pp, 122–123.

fications according to the census of 1921 and according to that of 1940 is shown in Table 1.

A recent estimate of the total number of Indians living in the Western Hemisphere, which was based upon data collected during the decade following 1940, gave the figure 16,211,630, of whom 539,837 were said

TABLE 2
INDIAN POPULATIONS*

Country	Number	Percentage
Argentina	50,000	0.38
Bolivia	1,650,000	50.00
Brazil	1,117,132	2.70
Chile	130,000	2.58
Colombia	147,300	0.91
Costa Rica	4,200	0.64
Ecuador	1,000,000	40.00
El Salvador	348,907	20.00
Guatemala	1,820,396	55.44
Honduras	105,732	9.54
Mexico	5,427,396	27.91
Nicaragua	330,000	23.90
Panama	64,960	10.90
Paraguay	40,000	4.16
Peru	3,247,196	46.23
Venezuela	100,000	2.79

* These statistics were taken from J. E. Iturriaga, *La estructura social y cultural de México* (Mexico, 1951), p. 103. Cf. Donald D. Brand, *The Present Indian Population of Latin America*, Latin-American Studies, University of Texas, ser. V. His numbers are 6,525,000 for Mexico, 3,915,000 for Peru, 2,452,000 for Guatemala, 2,138,000 for Bolivia, 1,949,000 for Ecuador, 1,281,000 for Brazil, and 1,270,000 for Colombia. For countries with less than a million, he gives 754,000 for Paraguay, 498,000 for Chile, 453,000 for Venezuela, and 274,000 for Argentina. He defines the "Indian" as 75 per cent pure in blood.

to live outside of Latin America. It is assumed that this was an estimate of "pure-blooded" Indians, but a definition of such an Indian was not given. Table 2 shows the statistics as they relate to Latin-American countries.

Estimates of the Negro or negroid elements of the population are again uncertain, and the definition of terms is variable. A general estimate made in 1950 gave the number of Negroes in Latin America as 30,000,000, out of a total population of 162,000,000. Of the Negroes,

19,000,000 were residents of South America. The distribution according to countries, as calculated by another specialist, is as follows: Brazil, 17,360,200; Haiti, 3,300,000; Cuba, 2,249,000; Dominican Republic, 1,700,000; Colombia, 952,200; Venezuela, 443,000; Mexico, 225,000; and Panama, 233,200.[6]

All the countries having large numbers of Indians—Mexico, Peru, Guatemala, Bolivia, Ecuador, and Brazil—have offices within ministries and special services which have to deal with Indian affairs. These offices and services deal with a variety of matters, not always the same, such as health, education, lands, communication, and marketing.

In some of these countries, during the twentieth century, there occurred a remarkable increase of interest in Indians, signalized by ethnological and anthropological research, and by efforts to assimilate those living in cultural and political isolation. Indian arts, manners and customs, folklore, and languages were studied with unaccustomed enthusiasm. There were those who spoke and wrote about the Indians as a social asset, actual and potential, rather than a liability to be tolerated; there were those who praised and magnified qualities attributed to them. For a time there was considerable strength in a movement which has been called "Indianism." In this way, the "forgotten man" of previous times was "rediscovered."

Much has been written about the manners, customs, and characteristics, regarded as strong or weak, and about values of different race elements of the population of Latin America. Opinions, favorable or adverse, have been expressed about each in turn. Of special concern to the theme being considered in the present section is the interest in the mestizo manifested in current literature and politics. The numerous group of "pathological" writers of the late decades of the nineteenth century and the early years of the twentieth commonly expressed pessimism about the mestizo, as well as about the Negro and the Indian.[7] Some of these writers were doubtful of the power of education and of improved economic opportunity

[6] W. S. Woytinsky and E. S. Woytinsky, *World Population and Production: Trends and Outlook* (New York, Twentieth Century Fund, 1953), pp. 51–52. See Donald D. Brand, *The Present Indian Population of Latin America,* Latin-American Studies (University of Texas, ser. V, 1953), pp. 48–55.

[7] By "pathological" writers is meant that group who have written about the alleged weakness of Latin America in politics, economics, and culture. They explained many problems in terms of these weaknesses or "ailments." Their opinions will be noticed later from time to time. An analysis of some of these opinions is found in W. W. Pierson (ed.), "Pathology of Democracy in Latin America: A Symposium," *American Political Science Review,* vol. 44, no. 1, March, 1950.

to change the traits which were assigned categorically to these several race types. Any change for the better from whatever cause, if it occurred at all, they thought, would come about slowly.

A marked change of opinion respecting the mestizo has occurred during the last generation. Some may continue to debate certain assumptions employed in value judgments of this racial group: (1) that the mixture of two races tends to perpetuate the weaknesses of both parent stocks; (2) that such a union tends to produce in the offspring the virtues and strengths of both races; and (3) that the mestizos, like other persons, show individual differences, without certainty as to prediction of character and aptitude. The current writers, of whom the Mexican philosopher and educator Vasconcelos was an early leader, have recognized the mestizo as presently or potentially the preponderant factor in the population of nearly all the countries of Latin America. Some think that the formation of their peoples is and will be a progressive process of *mestización,* as they call the mixing of bloods and cultures. In this process the pure-blooded Indian and the pure white will be absorbed—as, indeed, will be the "pure" mestizo—in further mixtures. In the well-known book of Vasconcelos, *The Universal Race* (originally published as *La Raza Cósmica*), the prophecy of a race of mestizos was based not only upon a biological or blood union, but a blending of cultures. Some of the writers agreeing that this prophecy is in process of consummation, consider that at least in some countries, such as Mexico and Brazil, the natural fecundity of native peoples will provide for growth in population without reliance upon immigration. Some of this group of writers think that Alberdi's plan of re-Europeanization is wrong in premises and contrary to a proper respect for Latin America's culture and destiny.

Some Geographical Factors

Latin America presents many physiographical and climatic contrasts, such as those between mountains and plains, deserts and jungles, areas of drought and those of light rainfall or of unusually heavy rainfall. Vasconcelos used the phrase "nature in a tempestuous mood" with reference to Mexico, and Subercasseaux that of "mad geography" (*geografía loca*) with reference to Chile. Bolívar once wrote that overcoming the mountains and the tropics would be future triumphs of man through science. Nature in Latin America has interposed many obstacles to travel and communication and to the exploitation and utilization of resources. It has also provided some of the most difficult, perplexing, and persistent problems of government.

The area is about eight million square miles, approximately three-fourths of which is within the tropics. It has been estimated that, of the land mass of the continent of South America, 40 per cent has an elevation above sea level of less than 600 feet and 65 per cent has an elevation of less than 1,000 feet. On the other hand, 6 per cent has an average elevation of about 10,000 feet. The great central plateau of Mexico embraces 15 to 20 per cent of the entire territory, and its elevation ranges between 6,000 and 8,000 feet. The western sierra, stretching from Oaxaca to Arizona, has a mean altitude somewhat above 10,000 feet, whereas the eastern sierra, bordering the Gulf of Mexico, has an average elevation of about 6,000 feet.

Elevation in tropical Latin America in respect to climate counteracts and "compensates" for latitude. Because of the moderating effects of altitude upon climate in tropical and equatorial regions, the areas ranging from 3,000 to 7,500 feet above sea level are the most densely populated. Such regions were the centers of the great Indian civilizations, the mysterious exception being that of the Mayas. Health, energy, and industry were and are favored by such locations.

The contrasts in physiographic and climatic features are perhaps equaled by the unevenness in the distribution of certain natural facilities for commerce. For example, the better harbors in South America are located on the Atlantic coast, while those on the Pacific side are in the main open roadsteads, requiring breakwaters or other constructions for the protection of shipping. This distribution is reversed in Central America and Mexico, with most of the good harbors located on the Pacific side. The distribution of rivers and river systems in South America is uneven, with all the great river systems flowing into the Atlantic Ocean. No streams of importance for commerce are found on the Pacific side, with the possible exception of the Guayas River in Ecuador.

A climatic feature showing extremes of difference is that of rainfall. In South America, much of the land is swept by prevailing winds from east to west, which means that many of the regions east of the great mountain ranges are better supplied with rains than those to the west. There are exceptions to this generalization. A study of the map showing rainfall, according to a modification of the Köppen system, will reveal these exceptions. Attention is directed to the area of heavy rainfall in southern Chile and to some areas that are arid or of light rainfall in eastern parts of South America.

The dominant physical feature is the series of mountain chains, the

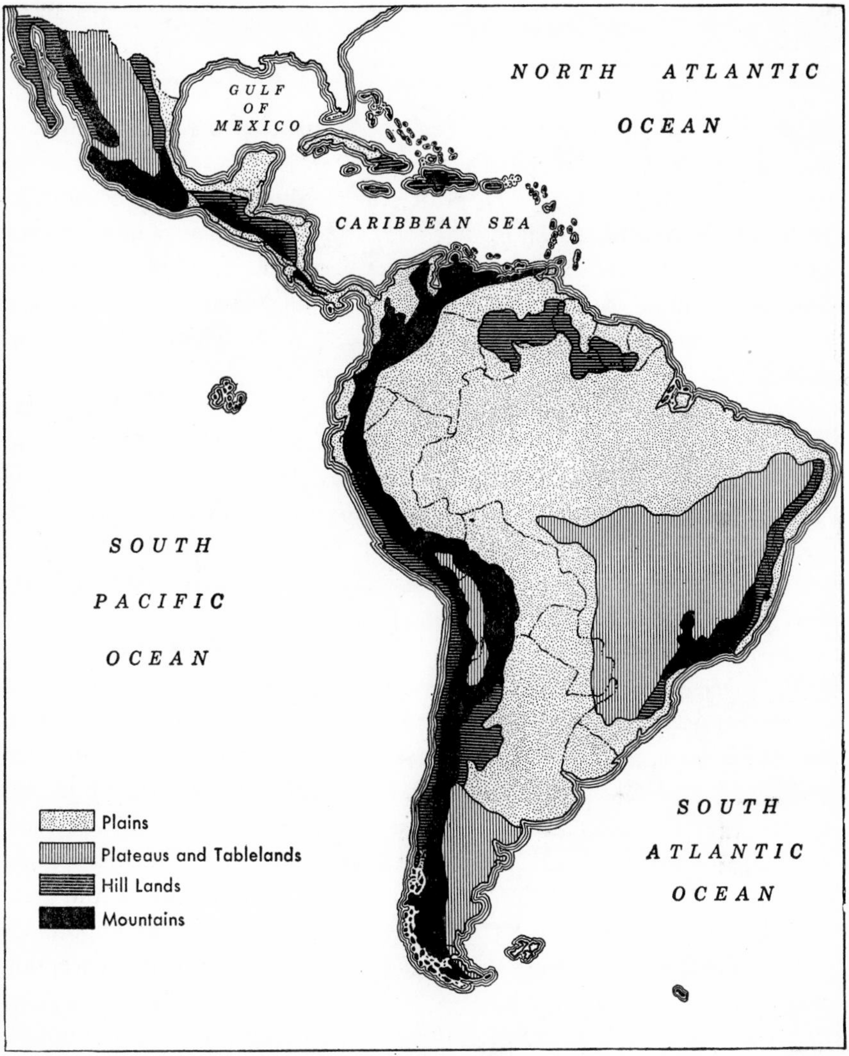

Figure 3. Principal classes of land forms. SOURCE: Vernon C. Finch and Glenn T. Trewartha, *Elements of Geography,* New York, McGraw-Hill, 1949.

longest in the world, extending 7,000 miles throughout the length of Latin America. The Andes of South America are, next to the Himalaya, the loftiest mountain range in the world. In this vast mountain range, there are numerous volcanoes, active or extinct, and earthquakes or temblors are frequent. In South America this formidable barrier has few passes, and these have an elevation of 10,000 feet or more. There are

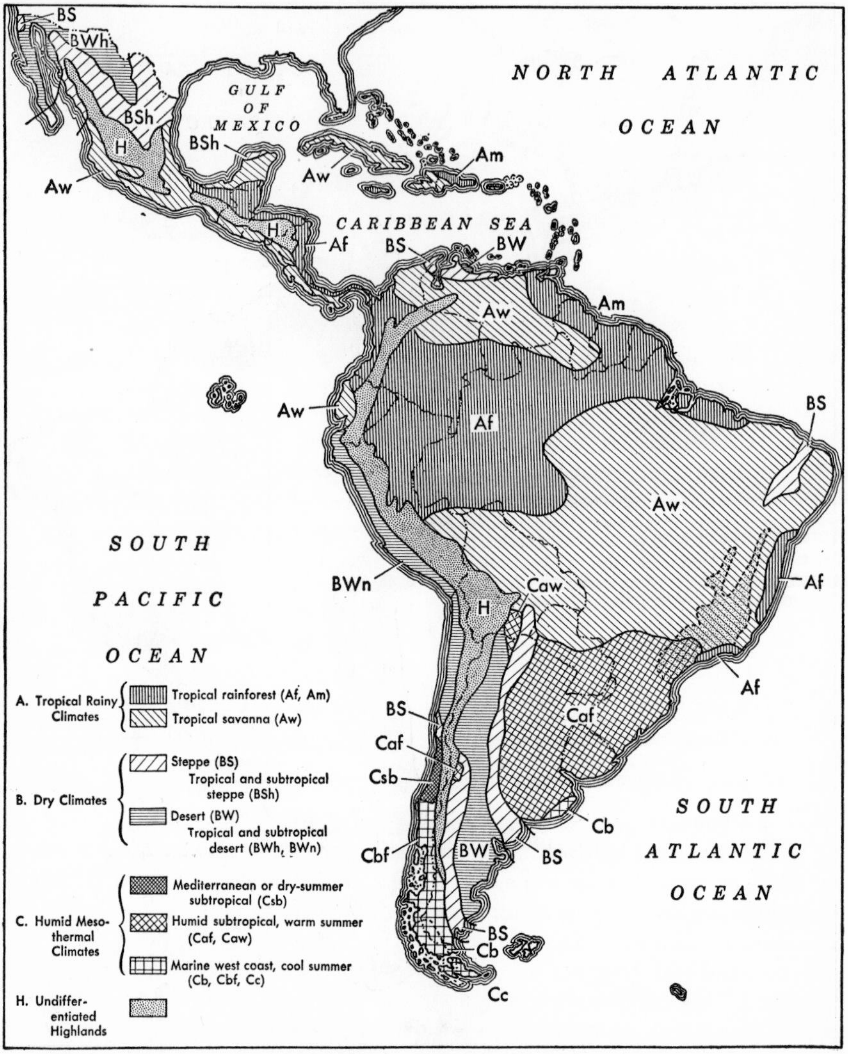

Figure 4. Climates of Latin America. SOURCE: Vernon C. Finch and Glenn T. Trewartha, *Elements of Geography,* New York, McGraw-Hill, 1949.

other mountainous regions in southeastern Brazil, in southern Venezuela, and in the Guianas.

In Table 3, information is offered concerning areas and population of Latin-American countries.

Many great natural resources of Latin America are located in remote and isolated places, difficult of access, and have been exploited only at

TABLE 3*
POPULATIONS AND AREAS

Country	Area	Population
Argentina	1,079,965	17,108,000
Bolivia†	419,470	3,990,000
Brazil	3,288,383	52,645,479
Chile	296,717	5,930,809
Colombia†	447,536	11,477,495
Costa Rica	19,695	803,084
Cuba	44,164	5,870,904
Dominican Republic	19,332	2,135,872
Ecuador	171,874	3,383,654
El Salvador†	13,173	2,179,249
Guatemala	42,042	2,788,122
Haiti	10,204	3,111,973
Honduras†	44,880	1,365,605
Mexico	763,944	25,791,017
Nicaragua†	57,143	1,057,023
Panama	28,575	805,285
Paraguay†	157,047	1,405,627
Peru†	482,258	8,405,000
Uruguay	72,153	2,353,000
Venezuela	352,143	5,400,000
Total	7,810,698	158,007,198
For comparison:		
United States	3,022,387	150,697,361

* Some of these data are estimates, without factual accuracy claimed. In some items, there are discrepancies in the literature. The variance in the estimates of area is explainable with reference to some entries because boundary disputes are as yet unsettled, and with reference to some others geodetic surveys may not have been completed. These explanations do not account for all discrepancies. An interesting case of deviation in estimates of area is that of El Salvador, varying from that of 7,225 to 13,176 square miles. Variations in estimate of the area of Bolivia range from 416,040 to 708,195; that of Peru from 482,257 to 697,600. Less radical variations appear in many of the other estimates.

†Territory in dispute.

‡Estimate of territory in dispute.

great expense. The Cerro de Pasco copper mines of Peru, the nitrate industry of Chile, the petroleum industry of both eastern and western Venezuela, and the banana culture in eastern Honduras are good illustrations. There are vast deposits of iron ore in Brazil and Venezuela, but both are distant from other materials essential to the production of iron and steel, such as coal and limestone. Another illustration might be found in the problems of rice cultivation in the Chiclayo cluster of oases on the northern coast of Peru. The growing of rice there requires an expensive and organized system of irrigation. Not only does this system of irrigation necessitate careful administration by public authority, but the costs of production and transportation do not in ordinary times permit the rice so grown to compete with rice produced in the Orient, a fact which in turn calls for a protective tariff. Latin America is well supplied with potential hydroelectric power, but many of the better sources of such power are located in places remote from the centers of population and industry, and some of these isolated power sites present engineering problems which are expensive to overcome.

The successful exploitation of natural resources located in regions difficult of access may entail complex operations requiring large outlay of capital. These circumstances lend themselves to corporate endeavor and to organization of the kind called "vertical." By this term is meant that such an industry may require, in transportation facilities, both shipping and railway services; in staff, many different levels of proficiency; in its management, a concern not only with finance, production, marketing, labor, legal and public relations but with health services, physicians, nurses, hospitals, schools and teachers, recreation, playgrounds, theaters, and a miscellany of other facilities such as hotels, mercantile establishments, and police. Some of the operations of such an industry may be carried on in more than one country before the products are ready for the market, e.g., the disposition of the high-grade iron ore extracted by the Bethlehem Steel Corporation at El Tofo and Cruz Grande in Chile.

Given these general contrasts, geographical sectionalism may well have significant political and institutional influences. Some examples of sectionalism might serve as a basis of subsequent thought about them.

Colombia, Venezuela, and Ecuador. Colombia has four major geographical zones or regions: (1) the high center, stretching from Pasto and Popayán to the confluence of the Cauca and Magdalena Rivers, including in the area the large cities of Bogotá, Medellín, and Antioquia; (2) the Pacific coast and the valley of the Atrato River; (3) the Caribbean coastal plains, with the cities of Cartagena, Barranquilla, Puerto Colombia, and Santa Marta; (4) the southeastern lowlands. The marked differences between the two river valleys and within the Pasto, Antioquia, Medellín, Bucaramanga, and Cúcuta areas might suggest other subdivisions.

In Venezuela, we have a good example of a geographical sectionalism which has been identified with the more important and prolonged political regimes—the llanos and Valencia with that of Páez, the *oriente* and Cumaná with that of the Monagas brothers, Coro with that of Falcón, Caracas and Valencia with the rule of Guzmán Blanco, Guárico with that of Crespo, and the Andean provinces with the governments of Castro and Gómez. This list of geographical sections omits the island of Margarita, the Maracaibo area (Zulia), the large and sparsely populated region south of the Orinoco, and the Amacuro delta, which have not as yet produced a national leader of comparable power. It might be emphasized that the bulk of the population resides in the mountainous and upland region which stretches from the Gulf of Paria in the east to the junction of the mountain chain with the main cordillera of the Andes at San Cristóbal in the state of Táchira.

Ecuador has pronounced geographical sectionalism in its western lowlands, the high Andes, and the eastern lowlands. The first two of these sections have internal variations in surface configuration, climate, and resources. The western lowlands have territory with heavy rainfall and areas that are arid or semiarid. The chief products of the western region are cacao, coffee, ivory nuts from the tagua palms, *toquilla* fiber from the jipijapa palms for hats, cotton, and fruits. Approximately one-fourth of the population lives in this territory. The highland sector is made up of two ranges or chains of the Andes with an intervening plateau. The passes permitting entrance from the coast are above 11,000 feet in elevation. On this plateau live about two-thirds of the population, engaging mainly in subsistence farming and stock raising. Here is located the famous "avenue of volcanoes," with Chimborazo being above 20,000 feet in altitude. The eastern Andes have not been crossed by railroads or by improved highways, and the trans-Andean lowlands, in dispute with both Colombia and Peru, are a region that is distinct and isolated, dependent on mule trains for transportation and communication with the rest of the country.

Peru and Bolivia. Peru has three major regions: (1) the coastal plains, traversed by more than fifty small rivers, utilized for irrigation; (2) the central *altiplanicie* or cordillera crossed by railways at the highest elevation above 15,000 feet; and (3) eastern Peru, which slopes downward to lowlands. The central highlands, 200 to 250 miles wide, constitute about 40 per cent of the territory of the country. Although a variety of minerals is known, copper, silver, vanadium, and petroleum are most important in commercial value. The highlands, the home of the great mass of the Indians of Peru, are also important for agriculture and stock raising.

Bolivia, formerly known as Upper Peru, is now an inland state. Although its cities were way stations along the ancient overland trade route which in colonial times led from Peru to Buenos Aires, its isolation has historically endured because of the formidable natural barriers to communication. The extraordinary variety and richness of the mineral resources have been the attractions causing the conquering Spaniards and later others to undergo the risks and hardships imposed by nature. The lofty plateau, or *puna,* of about 40,000 square miles in area is the seat of three-fourths of the population. Here and in the bordering mountains mining operations of importance are conducted, with tin, copper, silver, bismuth, and lead being the principal minerals exploited. Here, also, are the chief agricultural and cattle-raising enterprises. The eastern slope of the Andes, known as the *yungas,* with a heavy rainfall and abundant forests, is an undeveloped resource of the country. It is as yet sparsely occupied. Even less so are the lowlands, to the east and north, drained by tributaries of the Amazon. These lowlands comprise more than one-half of the territory of the country. The cities of the Altiplano, La Paz (11,910 feet), Potosí (13,780), and Cochabamba (8,435), are among the highest in elevation.

Chile. This country is a special case of the influence of geography upon institutions and form of government. Yet it has a highly differentiated geography and climate. Its major regions are the desert of Atacama in the north, with rich nitrate deposits and other mineral resources; the central agricultural valley, which is the home of 90 per cent of the population; and the rainy southern region of forests and grazing lands. This last region consists of many islands, a narrow coastal strip, the Strait of Magellan, and the larger part of Tierra del Fuego.

The narrow, compact central valley has been described as "the heart of the Chilean nation"; it is fertile and is blessed with mild climate. It has farms for wheat and other cereals, orchards, vineyards, and livestock enterprises. This concentration of population and of agricultural activities has been generally regarded as a strong geographical influence in support of a centralized, unitary form of government.

Argentina, Paraguay, and Uruguay. The student of Argentine regionalism might think of the great city and port of Buenos Aires on the one side and the rest of the country on the other—the city or *porteño* interest versus the provinces—and this would be to consider, historically, one of the most persistent conflicts in politics. The major historical and geographical sections include the city and province of Buenos Aires; the *litoral* provinces of Santa Fe, Corrientes, and Entre Ríos, the last two sometimes called "mesopotamia"; the Chaco, in the north; the northwest territory from Mendoza to the Bolivian border, with its many oases, arid plains, and mountains; and the Patagonian territories to the south. *La pampa*—or, as it is sometimes called in English, "the pampas"—consists of about 250,000 square miles and includes most of the province of Buenos Aires, parts of Santa Fe, Córdoba, and the former province of La Pampa. It is in this broad plain that the bulk of the Argentine population resides, and it is here that cattle raising and wheat cultivation have attained impressive development. Here are located many industrial plants occupied with the processing of animal and grain products. This region has been profoundly affected by the re-Europeanization process.

Uruguay, smallest of the South American republics, represents in its land a continuation of the southern hills of Brazil and the transition to the alluvial plain bordering the La Plata river system. It is for the most part a rolling, hilly plain, with some forests, no mountains, and little barren land. Excellent grazing is afforded for sheep and cattle. Wheat, corn, and flax are cultivated, but Uruguay is predominantly a pastoral country. It has a truly "temperate" climate, without extremes of temperature, a sufficient rainfall, and a terrain without barriers to communication and transportation.

The inland state of Paraguay has two main divisions: that east of the Paraguay river, consisting of upland plains which rise in elevation to form the Paraná plateau; and the region west of the river, known as the Chaco, which is wooded marshland, subject to annual floods. The eastern portion, with mild climate and varied topography, is the seat of the majority of the population.

Brazil. This vast country, containing nearly one-half of South America, has an unusually large proportion of its area that is actually or potentially productive; it has a wide diversity of natural resources. Many geographical regions may be identified. Also, several "frontiers" or areas have been identified with certain interests and industries, such as dyewoods, sugar and tobacco cultivation, cattle raising, cotton culture, gold and diamond mining, coffee culture, and rubber extraction. In several of these activities Brazil has experienced a curious rise to world leadership and a subsequent decline of relative position, except in the production of coffee.[8] Each of these activities has had a regional incidence with accompanying social, economic, and political consequences.

It has been stated that "the greater part of the Brazilian territory is made up of highlands."[9] A notable escarpment borders the sea, from Bahia (Salvador) southward, reaching a height in some places of nearly 3,000 feet and is in places surmounted by mountain ranges reaching an elevation of 8,000 or 9,000 feet. Aside from the Brazilian highlands south of the Amazon and the Guiana highlands north of it, the large areas of lowland are those of the upper Paraguay and upper Amazon. Most of the rivers which drain the Brazilian highlands have their sources in the central or southeastern part of the highlands, some of them near the crest of the escarpment. These rivers, with a few exceptions, flow into the Amazon or La Plata systems. All of them descend over margins in falls or rapids. The São Francisco River, one of the exceptions mentioned, rises in the southeast, flows northward parallel to the coast, turns eastward, and after the falls of Paulo Afonso descends to the Atlantic.

The major geographical sections are as follows:

1. The northeast, reaching from Bahia around Cape São Roque to about São Luiz on the coast, encloses two parts, the one densely populated and engaged in diversified agriculture, the other less populous and often called a "calamity area."[10]

2. The southeast, including the heavily populated states of Espírito Santo, Minas Gerais, São Paulo, and Rio de Janeiro, and the Federal District, with several mountain ranges and with two rivers (the Paraíba and the Rio Doce) which break through the escarpment, is a center of agricultural, mining, and pastoral pursuits.

3. The south, composed of the states of Paraná, Santa Catarina, and Rio Grande do Sul, through which the escarpment runs to the city of Porto Alegre, and thereafter with a series of coastwise lakes and lagoons, has three main clusters of population numbering about 8,000,000 people.

4. The north, composed of the states of Maranhão, Pará, Amazonas, and the territories of Amapá and Rio Branco, has 40 per cent of the national domain and about 10 per cent of the population.

[8] J. F. Normano, *Brazil: A Study in Economic Types* (Chapel Hill, N.C., The University of North Carolina Press, 1937).

[9] James, *op. cit.,* p. 357.

[10] F. W. Freise, "The Drought Region of Northeast Brazil," *Geographical Review,* vol. 28, pp. 363–378. Floods have at times been no less damaging in this region.

5. The central west is composed of the states of Goiaz and Mato Grosso, and the territories of Guaporé and Acre.

Brazil has one of the world's greatest reserves of iron ore, and there are important stores of manganese, quartz crystal, copper, lead, chromium, nickel, zinc, and industrial diamonds. Low-grade coal is mined in Rio Grande do Sul and Santa Catarina. Many sites for hydroelectric power are available.[11] Industrialization is already far advanced in the state of São Paulo and has attained great development in Minas Gerais, Rio de Janeiro, and Rio Grande do Sul.

Central America and Panama. A general description would be that of a narrow coastal plain or lowland on the Pacific side, the highlands—with intermontane basins or plateaus—and a broader belt of lowlands on the Caribbean side. This generalized description would require serious qualifications. There are the depressions in Panama—the location of the canal route—and in Nicaragua. The Pacific band of lowlands is interrupted in El Salvador. The concentration of population in Nicaragua is in the lowlands, despite the availability of upland areas. The mountain ranges and folded structures found south of the Nicaraguan depression run in a northeast and southwest direction, whereas to the north the mountains and high valleys run west to east. The entire shore line and bordering lowlands on the Caribbean have a heavy rainfall, ranging in averages from 80 to 200 inches.

Mexico. The five major divisions of this country are as follows:

1. The Pacific northwest, composed of Lower California, Sonora, Sinaloa, and Nayarit, is sparsely occupied and has slight rainfall.

2. The northern plateau, reaching northward from the 22-degree line of latitude to the international border and lying between the two sierras, contains approximately 40 per cent of the domain and about 20 per cent of the population.

3. The central plateau, with its numerous basins such as Mexico City, Puebla, Toluca, Jalisco, Guanajuato, and Morelos, comprises about one-sixth of the national territory and is the most populous part of the country.

4. The gulf coast and the Isthmus of Tehuantepec.

5. Southernmost Mexico, comprising four states, contains 12 per cent of the area and 14 per cent of the population.

[11] One of the extraordinary plants is at Cubatão (Santos) where water from a reservoir created by damming the headwaters of the Tiete River is piped to the Atlantic side of the escarpment and dropped to turbines from a height of 2,378 feet.

Mention was made of several land depressions which are known as bolsons, such as those of Mapimí and San Luis Potosí in the north. Such a land depression, usually without external surface drainage, means that a lake at one time existed. If the lake has dried up or has been drained, the salts deposited may or may not mean that a region of unusual fertility has been left or that mineral resources of value may be found. The difference between the central and northern plateaus is not immediately and abruptly defined, and the southern parts of San Luis Potosí, Zacatecas, and Durango form a zone of transition. The depressions of the north are lower in altitude than those to the south.

Mexico, along with Brazil, Argentina, and Chile, is undergoing industrialization. Iron and steel products are manufactured at Monterrey; food processing, chemicals, beverages, textiles, and oil refining are items of industrial development at Mexico City. Other industrial centers are located at Puebla, Cuernavaca, and Orizaba. The great majority of the people are occupied with agriculture and cattle raising.

Cuba, Haiti, and Santo Domingo. The island of Cuba has three mountainous divisions: the western with the Sierra de los Órganos and nearby highlands, extending through the provinces of Pinar del Rio, La Habana, and a portion of Matanzas; the Alturas de Trinidad in Las Villas or Santa Clara; and the high Sierra Maestra and other ranges of the extreme east in Oriente. Separating the first two mountainous groups are the plains and marshlands, known as the Llanuras de Colón and the Ciénaga de Zapata. Between the Trinidad–Sancti Spíritus and the Sierra Maestra are the plains and terrace lands of Camagüey and the central valley of Cuba. In the Oriente area, there are the important basins of Santiago and Guantánamo and on the northern shore the isolated city and section of Baracoa. Since Cuba has an equable climate and fertile valley lands, the population is concentrated in the lowlands, with the exception of the Llanuras de Colón and the marshlands. Another exception is that of the densely populated Vuelta Abajo, in the southern piedmont of the Sierra de los Organos, famous for the cultivation of fine tobacco.[12] Supplied with numerous and excellent harbors, with railways and improved highways, and a productive soil, Cuba has a varied industry and agriculture, unusually great land use, and a relatively crowded population. Every province produces sugar, rice, and fruits; several grow tobacco or coffee or henequen or all of them; and several have cattle raising, mining, and cacao production as industries.

[12] L. Marrero, *Elementos de geografía de Cuba* (Havana, 1944); S. Massip, *Estudio geográfico de la isla de Cuba* (Havana, 1925).

The minerals chiefly exploited are manganese, copper, nickel, and chromium.

The sharp contrasts and variety characteristic of Latin America are demonstrated arrestingly in the island containing the republics of Haiti and the Dominican Republic. The surface configuration may be summarized as follows: There are three mountain ranges, in confused arrangement, but running in a generally east-west direction, with the highest being the central cordillera summits, reaching 10,000 feet above sea level. Between each range of mountains and the next, there is a lateral plain, the northern known in the Dominican Republic as the Cibao. The southern, known in Haiti as the Cul de Sac, has a saline lake in a depression below sea level. There are many intermontane pockets, which are densely populated, several shore-line plains of great agricultural value, and the relatively wide plain extending along the southern coast of the Dominican Republic. With a surface so diversified, there is variation in climate, rainfall, and vegetation and consequently in industry.

Some Economic Factors

Aside from mining and handicrafts, the productive portion of Latin-American people has been until recently chiefly occupied with agriculture and cattle raising. With the products of its mines and oil wells, its meats, grains, fruits, sugar, coffee, and forest resources, Latin America has bought from abroad manufactured goods, machinery, the mechanisms of transportation, drugs and many chemical products, textiles, and luxury articles. The economy has depended upon the ready sale of its agricultural, animal, and mineral products in foreign markets. With greatly expanded production and competition after the middle of the nineteenth century, a favorable and even balanced trade was contingent upon many unstable factors. It was threatened by the fluctuations of foreign-market demands, war interruptions, financial depressions, restrictions of economic nationalism, and many minor hazards. All Latin-American countries engage in some form of subsistence agriculture, but few of them have a sufficient diversification to meet the demands and needs of local consumption or the requirements of healthful nutrition. Most of them have imported, and some still import, staple foodstuffs, many of which they are capable of producing themselves. This condition results in the main from the one-sided or specialized agriculture which devotes acreage and energy to the production of a few crops for export.

Latin America has been well known for the production and export of primary or raw materials. At first these products were shipped before any processing or refinement and classification were undertaken; some still are marketed in that condition. Very significant changes have occurred with reference to some exports with the establishment within Latin America of meat- and grain-processing plants, grinding and refining plants for sugar, domestic classification of coffee and fruits, and oil refineries.

Another stage was the acquirement on a limited scale of modern means of transportation and communication in the form of railways, streetcar lines, and telegraph, telephone, and cable lines. Apart from Argentina, Uruguay, Cuba, and perhaps Paraguay, there were difficult and often perplexing engineering problems in construction and operation of railways; in several countries there were health and sanitation problems. For these forms of transportation and communication, foreign capital and materials, shipping, engineering skill, and operative techniques were necessary; local law and cooperation were needed. The construction of railroads across the Andes encountered stupendous difficulties. The transcontinental line from Chile to Argentina, opened to traffic in 1910, crossed the divide through a great tunnel at an elevation of 10,512 feet; the central railway of Peru reached—106 miles from the coast—an elevation of 15,680 feet. The high costs of construction, the necessity of importing rails, rolling stock, and most of the materials for bridges and repairs, the shortage of fuel, the heavy costs of maintenance, and the fact that freight haulage was mainly one way (that of goods to shipping port) made the railroads a hazardous economic venture. Indeed, it has been claimed that Latin-American railroads were a "political rather than an economic enterprise." Government subventions and concessions, guarantees of income, capitalization and stock manipulation, and scandals gave rise to many charges of unfairness and lack of good faith on the part of governments and companies. Often the foreign stockholder, receiving reduced dividends or none, complained that the government was unfair, and the Latin-American public, charged high rates by railroads that were poorly maintained, complained of exploitation. Despite the rather remarkable record of achievement in construction, Latin America is by way of comparison inadequately supplied with railway transportation. By 1930 the total mileage was 76,360 miles, as against 249,309 for the United States. The countries most amply provided with this utility were Argentina, Uruguay, Brazil, Chile, Mexico, and Cuba.

In the twentieth century came the efforts to secure improved highways for motorized vehicles and to obtain airplane routes and services. Comparatively speaking, Latin America is, despite notable constructions, behind the United States and Europe in road mileage. In respect of highways, especially all-weather hard-surfaced roads, the expense of building is comparatively greater since the materials are scarce or difficult to assemble or have to be imported. Meantime all the systems of transportation known to Latin-American history—human carriers, pack trains, trails, rivers, railways, improved highways, and planes—are in use. Probably much research is needed to ascertain the kind of transportation facility that is feasible and economically supportable in any given state and locality.

One of the generally recognized features of the economy, having very significant social and political influences, has been the large-estate system of land tenure—a system inherited from the colonies, but extended after independence. The new or enlarged estates were established through grants or sales of the public domain, as in Argentina and Mexico; from sales of expropriated church lands, as in Mexico; or from encroachments upon Indian lands, as in Mexico, Bolivia, and Peru. Along with the big estates, there was the social and legal institution of peonage, designated under a variety of names. This system of labor was based primarily on permanent indebtedness of the worker to the landlord. The older relationship of landowner to agricultural worker was semifeudal, softened and humanized by mutual rights and obligations which had a traditional sanction. Although there is in some countries a survival of some features of this older relationship, peonage and the old-style hacienda have undergone many changes. Absenteeism on the part of landowners, the great increase in demand for the products of the farm and ranch, the industrialization of many properties, the substitution of contract labor, and the use of tenancy and sharecropping in some countries brought about many changes in law and practice respecting peonage. In some places the bonds were tightened; in others they were moderated. In some countries, peonage was abolished. Despite the fact of the big estate as a common feature, there have been countries, such as Costa Rica, Colombia, and Honduras, wherein small properties were to be found in number. The vastly important efforts in Mexico to break up some of the big estates in order to distribute lands in small holdings, the movements in several countries to clothe property holding with a social and public function, and the movements to abolish peonage will be studied later.

Another significant feature of Latin America was monoculture, defined as one-sided or specialized economy. Leading examples are the specialization in the production of nitrates and copper for Chile, sugar and tobacco for Cuba, tin for Bolivia, bananas for several Central American countries, coffee for Brazil, and wheat and animal products for Argentina. In some countries this specialization went so far that production of subsistence foodstuffs did not meet the demands of the local market for essential supplies. Specialization in production would be safe if the demand were steady, if commerce were free, and if there were something like international division of labor, but it is highly vulnerable if there are war interruptions, international depressions, and effective competition—all of

TABLE 4
RELATIVE IMPORTANCE OF TRADE OF VARIOUS AREAS, 1938–1948
(Percentage participation)

Exports	1938	1946	1948
Latin America	100.0	100.0	100.0
South America	75.7	76.6	77.1
Argentina	23.8	25.8	24.9
Brazil	27.2	21.3	18.0
Chile	8.2	5.0	5.0
Colombia	4.7	4.4	3.9
Venezuela	10.6	10.4	17.4
Central America	3.3	2.5	2.6
Mexico	11.4	8.6	7.3
Caribbean	9.6	12.3	12.6
Cuba	8.3	10.4	10.8

SOURCE: Taken from Simon G. Hanson, *Economic Development in Latin America* (Washington, D.C., The Inter-American Affairs Press, 1951), p. 423.

which were to come after 1914. The hard lessons of the last forty years were to cause many thoughtful Latin Americans to know of the risks of reliance on one or a few export products. If Latin America is seriously to take account of the world situation and the experiences of other countries, as well as of its own experience since the First World War, the indicated solutions would be diversification of production, industrialization, and the attainment of a greater measure of economic self-sufficiency. Some countries are trying to apply these remedies, but old habits of production are not easy to change. The methods of effecting the changes are likely to cause radical and violent differences of opinion. Given favorable conditions, monoculture has been profitable; it is still widely prevalent.

Foreign trade of Latin America during the present century has experienced not only the vicissitudes of wars and depressions but the changes due to competition from other areas, to scientific achievements in producing substitutes for some of its primary materials, and to its own progress in diversification and industrialization. Year by year there have been

TABLE 5
MARKETS FOR EXPORTS AND SOURCES OF IMPORTS
(Percentage participation)

	1938	1946	1948
Markets for Exports			
United States	32.3	40.2	38.0
Continental Europe	30.6	21.0	24.9
United Kingdom	17.5	12.2	11.9
Canada	1.1	1.5	2.0
Latin America	6.3	13.0	8.8
Africa	0.5	2.2	1.1
Asia	1.6	2.8	2.4
Oceania	0.1	0.1	0.1
Other	10.0	7.0	11.4
Sources of Imports			
United States	33.8	59.2	59.1
Continental Europe	35.9	9.6	12.6
United Kingdom	12.1	6.2	8.9
Canada	1.0	2.2	2.0
Latin America	9.2	18.1	10.9
Africa	0.3	0.7	0.3
Asia	5.4	1.1	1.3
Oceania	0.1	0.1	0.1
Other	2.2	2.8	4.7

SOURCE: Simon G. Hanson, *Economic Development in Latin America* (Washington, D.C., The Inter-American Affairs Press, 1951), p. 424.

changes in the volume and character of exports and imports. Normally about one-half of the Latin-American exports have gone to European markets and about one-third to the United States. It is significant that since 1938 more than 80 per cent of Europe's total imports from Latin America has usually come from South America. Cuba, Mexico, and Central America have sent less than one-fourth of their exports to Europe; Brazil sent about one-half and the west-coast countries of South America slightly more than one-half; whereas Argentina, Uruguay, and Paraguay sent more than two-thirds of their exports to European markets.

Trade among the Latin-American countries up to the time of the Second World War had been a relatively unimportant percentage in their total commerce. In 1938 the estimate was that less than 10 per cent of the imports of these countries came from within the region, with little of manufactured goods being included in the exchanges. During the war, however, the percentage rose to more than one-fourth of the total imports (1943), with the countries which had become relatively industrialized—Argentina, Brazil, Mexico, and Chile—finding a market for their manufactured products within the region. Some Latin-American manufactured products during the war entered the United States market. The gains encouraged expansive hopes for the future, but the increases were not permanent. When peace came and the more experienced and industrialized countries returned to competition, the percentage of imports from fellow Latin-American states began to decrease. By 1948 the figure for these imports had fallen to about one-ninth of the total imports. A corrective for this trend toward reduced trade within Latin America may be the treaties or agreements between countries, such as those concluded by Argentina with certain neighbors regarding reciprocal exchanges.

During the present century and especially within the last two decades, scientific explorations have dispelled the former idea that Latin America was lacking in iron-ore resources. The "reserves" of this ore have been found to be of high quality and of unexpected magnitude in indicated tonnage. The most promising findings were located in Chile, Mexico, Brazil, and Venezuela, with lesser discoveries in Colombia and Peru. Most of the scientific exploration was undertaken by the Bethlehem Steel Company and the United States Steel Corporation. The former has been engaged in important developments in Chile and Mexico, and both were active in Venezuela.[13] Quantity production for export has already developed in Mexico and Chile, amounting in the former to 1,200,000 tons (1947) and in the latter to 1,700,000 tons.

Using iron ore as raw material for the production of pig iron, steel ingots, and finished steel products plants have been constructed and are in operation in Chile, Brazil, and Mexico. In 1953 Brazil produced 872,000 tons of pig iron, over a million tons of steel ingots, and 810,000

[13] For a report of the discovery in Venezuela by United States Steel, see T. W. Lippert, "Cerro Bolívar; Saga of an Iron Ore Crisis Averted," *Journal of Metals and Engineering,* February, 1950.

tons of finished steel. Argentina, with a new plant under construction at San Nicolás, has mills which depend for raw material upon scrap and imported billet. New plants are being opened in Colombia (Paz de Río) and Peru (Chimbote). It is estimated that in 1952 Latin America produced 1,500,000 tons of steel. The prediction has been made that, with the development of transforming and assembly plants and with growth in steel and iron production to capacity, it will be possible for some countries in the near future to reduce imports of machinery, tools, motors, railway equipment, and the like.

Latin-American industrialization, formerly by some considered impractical because of assumed lack of certain basic resources, technological

TABLE 6

DISTRIBUTION OF LATIN-AMERICAN IMPORTS, BY SOURCE
(In millions of dollars)

Source	1951	1952	1953
United States	$3,638	$3,337	$2,850
Europe	2,905	1,750	1,500
Canada	197	277	200
Japan	89	49	100
Other sources	361	687	550
Total	$6,380	$6,100	$5,200

SOURCE: United Nations, Department of Economic Affairs, *Economic Survey of Latin America 1953* (New York, 1954).

skill and experience, and capital, has made astonishing progress in Argentina, Brazil, Chile, and Mexico. Important advances are being made in Cuba, Colombia, and Peru. The manufacture of textiles, cement, rayon, iron and steel, wood pulp and paper, chemicals, pharmaceutical products, foodstuffs, leather goods, and ceramics has reached large proportions since 1938. The claim was made in 1947 that Brazilian industries were supplying 60 per cent of the needs of the country. Although many of the ingredients for drugs, rayon, paints, the materials for rubber tires, and parts for machines were still imported, the assembly, the finishing process, and the marketing were accomplished by domestic agencies. This development was regarded as a step toward self-sufficiency and diversification. These enterprises received tariff protection which virtually assured the local market to domestic producers. Some countries by reason of governmental restrictions have a "managed system of importation." The controlling part of government in this process of industrialization will be examined later. It might be said here, however, that this practice adds to the burdens of governments already occupied with other problems and issues, such as irrigation and water control, the development and distribution of electrical power, education, labor, housing, road construction, and the raising of the standard of living. As the effects of public decisions are carried out and the process of industrialization advances, commercial exchange is affected in character and in volume.

The chief commodities imported by the United States from Latin America in 1953 were coffee, sugar, copper, lead, zinc, tin, bananas, petroleum, iron ore, cacao, oil seed and vegetable oils, tobacco, wool, hides, and fibers. The principal exports of the United States to Latin America were machinery and vehicles, metals, chemicals, nonmetallic minerals, foodstuffs, textiles and fibers, wood and paper, and inedible animal and vegetable products.

TABLE 7
UNITED STATES INVESTMENTS IN LATIN AMERICA (1950)
(In millions of dollars)

Country	
Argentina	$ 356
Brazil	644
Chile	540
Cuba	642
Mexico	415
Panama	348
Total	4,867
Field of investment	
Agriculture	$ 520
Mining, smelting	628
Petroleum	1,408
Manufacturing	780
Public utilities and transportation	1,042
Trade	243

SOURCE: *Foreign Investments of the United States* (U.S. Department of Commerce, 1953).

The chief economic factors and trends in Latin America, then, are production for export and monoculture, an expensive transportation system made up of both ancient and modern methods which is mainly geared to an export economy, the big-estate system and the plans of agrarian reform, and the ideas and policies of industrialization. These economic factors are closely related to such problems as the low standard of living for the masses, the low purchasing power of the masses, and movements for the organization of labor. They are also powerful influences in politics, revolutions, dictatorship, and efforts to secure democracy in government.

Some Sociological Factors

According to sociologists, there are large segments of population, especially Indians, which are not yet "incorporated" in society and live in cultural and political isolation, despite recent educational, labor, and social legislation. The large, though varying, percentage of adult illiterates in the population is a handicap to efforts at making representative government operate successfully. Because of the high value placed on the individual and personal leadership, there is a disposition to vote for the man rather than the party or the platform—a disposition which supports the *caudillo* or dictator system.

Again, it is often claimed by sociologists that Latin Americans suffer from apathy or cynicism toward government. But there is the seeming contradiction of many political parties and factions, much discussion of politics by the press when no censorship is imposed, and much patriotic and nationalistic fervor—all requiring adherents. The attitude is often to be encountered, which is supposed to have been entertained in Spain, that the government—and the Church, too—is something imposed, something to be borne, about which little is to be done except in those upheavals that come from time to time. Perhaps this explains what apathy there may be.

Some writers emphasize the overdevelopment of family loyalty, nepotism (*filhotismo*), and extranatural kinship (*padrinazgo*). Many, thinking that an active middle class is a necessary safeguard and defender of self-government, believe that a middle class in Latin America is either nonexistent or ineffectual. Some write of the prevalence of both petty and large-scale graft in both society and government.

On the side of positive values, great significance should be given to the increasing group of intellectuals. In their wide interests and their literary productivity, they have shown a remarkable versatility. The wide variety and large number of publications led Professor Chapman, in 1927, to remark facetiously: "The amount of material on the republic of Cuba already reduced to writing is, of course, more than one man could read in ten thousand years."[14] Professor Crawford's *A Century of Latin-American*

[14] Charles E. Chapman, *A History of the Cuban Republic* (New York, Macmillan, 1927), p. 657.

Thought—now unfortunately out of print—analyzes the ideas of forty-four authors, whose published works number 320 volumes.[15] This book has much significance for the student of Latin-American political theory, although it is not limited to that subject. In it, information can be found about the impact of independence upon the Latin-American mind, the quest for guidance from foreign writings and institutions, the effort to attain intellectual independence as a corollary of political independence, the conflict between the "black" and the "white" legends, the conflict in attitudes toward the United States, the influences of positivism and Latin-American contributions to that system of thinking, spiritual reactions against materialism, developments in philosophy, and contemporary ideas of social justice. The student of Latin-American political thought should take account, in addition, of the important contributions in such areas as international arbitration, jurisprudence, dictatorship, and relations of church and state.

There are, furthermore, many humanistic works in both prose and verse, some of them having enduring merit and some the quality of genius. This is true, also, of art and music, with the latter having the characteristic counterpoint of poignant sadness against a lively spirit of joy.

One of the social assets, about which some Latin Americans write, is the strong love of personal liberty, which endures in spite of the tyrannies that have on occasion been imposed. To some this regard for liberty and individualism offers resistance to sumptuary regulation by church and state; to some it affords an obstacle to social discipline in affairs necessitating cooperation. It is recognized, however, that great social value is placed upon custom, proper form in conduct and relations, the claims of family, and the ties of friendship. Individualism is, therefore, subject especially to the extralegal regulations of custom. The second social asset has been called the "unwritten social constitution," and this seems to mean a heritage of faith and hope enshrining rights of life, liberty, home, and religion. A writer has declared that this "constitution" cannot "be easily trapped under the microscopes of history" in order that it be examined critically and evidentially, but it is in the oratory and in the statesmanly thought of many Latin Americans one of the imponderable social forces.

Later it will be shown that in all the new political constitutions of Latin America, government is given a social function with reference to such

[15] William Rex Crawford, *A Century of Latin-American Thought* (Cambridge, Mass., Harvard University Press, 1944).

matters as childhood, the family, old age, and labor. In some, property has a social function and obligation. With these provisions and the legislation implementing them, there has been much social planning.

Finally, some write of Latin Americans as having "come of age," as having attained intellectual independence of Europe and the United States, as having made realistic studies of themselves, and as having in recent years shaped laws and institutions to their own conditions, both sociological and geographical.

BIBLIOGRAPHY

Alberdi, Juan Bautista, *Las bases y puntos de partida para la organización política de la República Argentina,* many editions, the first published in Valparaiso, 1852.

Arciniegas, Germán (ed.), *The Green Continent: A Comprehensive View of Latin America by Its Leading Writers,* New York, Knopf, 1944.

Dagnino Pastore, L., *Geografía industrial argentina,* Buenos Aires, 1944.

Hanson, Simon G., *Economic Development in Latin America,* Washington, D.C., Inter-American Affairs Press, 1951.

Harris, Seymour E. (ed.), *Economic Problems of Latin America,* New York, McGraw-Hill, 1944.

Hudson, William Henry, *The Purple Land That England Lost,* London, 1885.

James, Preston E., *Latin America,* rev. ed., New York, Odyssey, 1950.

McBride, G. M., *The Land Systems of Mexico,* American Geographical Society, Research Series, no. 12, New York, 1923.

Manito, O., and J. J. Nágera, *Geografía física de América y de la República Argentina,* Buenos Aires, 1938.

Marrero, L., *Elementos de Geografía de Cuba,* Havana, 1944.

Massip, Salvador, *Introducción a la geografía de Cuba,* Havana, 1942.

Nash, Roy, *Conquest of Brazil,* New York, Harcourt, Brace, 1926.

Romero, E., *Geografía del pacífico,* Mexico, 1949.

Schmeider, O., *Geografía de América,* Mexico, 1946.

Vivó, J. A., *Geografía de México,* 2d ed., Mexico, 1949.

Whitbeck, R. H., and Frank E. Williams, *Economic Geography of South America,* 3d ed., New York, McGraw-Hill, 1940.

Wythe, George, *Industry in Latin America, New York,* Columbia University Press, 1945.

Chapter 2: COLONIAL INSTITUTIONS OF SPAIN

The object of this and the subsequent chapter is to analyze and describe briefly the salient features of the govermental system of the Spanish and Portuguese colonial empires. The treatment of the government and society in the Spanish colonies is the longer, because their legislation, administration, and institutions were the more highly developed and systematic. In both chapters the effort has been made to give an appraisal of the colonial heritage. The influences of that heritage have been persistent, but frequently they have been the subject of recurring issues in the politics of modern Latin America. A study of colonial government is therefore a proper and useful background for that of the present governments of these countries.

At the time of the discovery of America, Spain was in process of achieving national and political unity. Through the marriage of Isabella, queen of Castile, and Ferdinand, king of Aragon, these two ancient kingdoms were united, but each retained its political and administrative identity, its own laws, assemblies, and many other institutions. The fact that Isabella had provided the financial backing and legal authorization for Columbus's enterprise explains the political subjection of the American colonies to the crown of Castile. The laws and institutions of Castile were projected into the New World, thus shaping decisively the structure and character of early Spanish American institutions.

Castile at the end of the sixteenth century had what was called an absolute monarchy, in that power in each of the great branches of government, secular and clerical, was concentrated in the crown. Privilege—whether of the noble or the church or the municipality—became less and less a check on royal power. The crown liberated itself from the feudal limitations of the Middle Ages, and Castile was perhaps better prepared than any other European country at the time to take advantage of the opportunities offered by a colonial empire. The Indies were treated as the direct and exclusive possession of the crown, as separated kingdoms united with those of the Iberian Peninsula "under a common sovereign, bound to Spain by the dynastic tie."[1]

[1] Clarence H. Haring, *The Spanish Empire in America* (New York, Oxford

At an early date it was announced that the laws and institutions of the Spanish Indies were to be patterned after those of Castile, and to a very remarkable degree this principle was carried out. But the New World, so vast and complex, presented diverse geographical, racial, social, and economic characteristics. On the continent, especially in Mexico and Peru, the Spaniards found long-established political and social institutions which in some cases were continued under colonial rule. The crown decreed that the juridical customs of the Indians should be respected as long as they were not opposed to the interests of Spain, and thereby new elements came to exert influence upon the development of institutions.

Frequently local conditions made impractical an application of Castilian law and practice. It was necessary to evolve both principle and practice especially designed to meet local circumstances and interests. These "laws of the Indies" were formulated either in the mother country or, in times of emergency, by officials in the colonies.

The laws of the Indies had certain characteristic features. They were, in the first place, laws for the specific case. Legislation decreed experimentally for concrete cases was later made general. Although the mother country made an effort to give institutions a uniform structure, the forces of local reality prevailed, and institutions similarly designated and described acquired different features according to region and environment. On occasion the mother country sought to deal with the trivial problems of the small community as well as with the political issues affecting the large viceroyalty. Moved by distrust of colonial officials, it resorted to a multiplication of instructions and orders which tended to confuse and delay the administrative operation.

But above all, the laws of the Indies were inspired by religious feeling. The conversion of the Indians and the defense of the faith were among the main objectives of colonization, and these motives were reflected in legislation. Many laws were drafted by theologians rather than by jurists, and political problems were resolved in the light of ethics and religion at the risk of jeopardizing economic or social interests, whether of the colony or of the mother country.[2] This fact could explain the contradiction between law and reality which at times was observable in the administra-

University Press, 1947), p. 7. Professor Haring's work is an excellent and systematic description of government in the Spanish colonies.

[2] José M. Ots Capdequí, *Manual de historia del derecho español en las Indias* (Buenos Aires, 1945), pp. 329–333.

tion of the colonies. In many cases too great an effort was made to defend the accepted spiritual values with laws of difficult if not impossible application.

Although uniformity was sought and although many sacrifices were made to obtain it, rigidity was not an unvarying characteristic. Much flexibility existed in the system, as becomes evident to any careful examiner of documents. It must be also emphasized that transplanted institutions acquired new features of local origin. Spain, aware of differences in interests and circumstances of the several colonies, embodied this knowledge in operating certain institutions. Examples of legislation authorizing variations in administration are numerous.

Institutions of Imperial Control

Spain evolved the elements of a plan of administration which within half a century was refined into a system of imperial control. In this process Spain did not borrow from other nations but relied on its own experience. This experience had been gained in governing territories and peoples conquered in the war with the Mohammedans. Many of the offices and institutions of the colonial system had already been employed in the reconquest of the mother country, and the terms used in Castile to designate them were later applied to their counterparts in America.

The House of Trade. As the number of expeditions to the New World increased and with it the volume of colonial affairs, a chief administrative agency for the regulation and promotion of commerce with the Indies was created for this purpose. This new agency was the Casa de Contratación or House of Trade established in Seville by a royal decree of January 20, 1503.

Thus appeared the earliest institution in Spain created specifically for the government of the American colonies. The agency was at first composed of three officials entrusted with the task of supervising all the merchants and ships that carried goods and passengers to and from the New World and seeing to it that all laws and ordinances relative to navigation, emigration, and trade were enforced. This agency has been described as "at once a board of trade, a commercial court, and a clearing house for the American trade." It received and cared for all the gold, silver, and precious stones due the royal treasury from the mines of America. It was in charge of outfitting and provisioning ships, purchasing supplies of all kinds, and receiving all goods sent from the Indies to Seville, which was the only port in Spain opened to the American trade.

In addition, it performed the duty of registering all persons and merchandise sent to and from the colonies. The Casa also had jurisdiction of civil and criminal matters having to do with colonial trade and navigation. With characteristic paternalism, the functions of the various officials were precisely described in the laws regulating the operations of this agency.

Under Charles V the organization, powers, and personnel of the Casa grew steadily, but the original purpose of controlling all trade and travel to and from the Indies was retained. The three original officials became the heads of departments in what had become in effect a government ministry, and they had the services of numerous clerks and secretaries. The great administrative reforms introduced by the Bourbon kings in the eighteenth century brought about the decline of the once-powerful House of Trade by depriving it of its most important functions. It was moved to Cádiz in 1717 and finally abolished in 1790 after a distinguished existence of 287 years.

Another institution designed to lighten the work of the Casa was established in 1543. The Consulado de Sevilla, as it was called, was a guild of merchants of Seville engaged in the colonial trade. It was represented by officials elected every year by the indirect vote of the Seville merchants. The main functions of the so-called consulate were to settle all civil suits between members of the guild, to see that their common interests were protected, and to issue rules and regulations for its own procedure. It was located close to the Casa, and the relations between the two were always close and cordial. The establishment of the Consulado relieved the House of Trade of all civil cases between merchants. The legal procedures were simpler and more expeditious than those of the ordinary law courts. Having been moved to Cádiz at the same time as the Casa, the Consulado disappeared with it in 1790.

The Council of the Indies. The creation by Charles V of the Council of the Indies, the counterpart in colonial administration of the Council of Castile, was an act of enduring importance which rounded out the system of imperial control. The establishment of this institution was the result of an evolution rather than a sudden decision on the part of the crown. After several trials with temporary groups of advisers, Charles V decided in 1524 to create the Royal and Supreme Council of the Indies to act in matters relating to the colonies in general accordance with its model the Council of Castile. Its authority extended to practically all fields of government action: legislative, financial, military, ecclesiastical, commercial, and judicial. No other council or royal agency could interfere with its activities. The Council served as the body expressing the commands of the king, who was the source of authority in the colonies.

As was explained earlier, the House of Trade had the immediate supervision of all commercial and economic matters of the colonies and in executive matters of this kind it had a fairly free hand. However, even in this field, principles of policy and laws were determined by the Council of the Indies, and in legislative and judicial matters the House of Trade was subject to its veto.

As a legislative body the Council prepared, with the approval of the monarch and in his name, all the laws and decrees related to administration, taxation, and policing of the overseas dominions. The king consulted with it in the determination of the territorial divisions of the empire. It held broad powers of nomination of royal officials, corresponded with them once they were in office, and kept watch over their conduct. Supervision of all ecclesiastical affairs, including nominations to important clerical offices and approval of papal letters, was also a matter for consideration by this body. Its judicial functions were those of a court of appeals in suits originating in the colonies, but it also served as a court of first instance in all cases arising in Spain related to the Indies. It also made the arrangements for the judicial review of the conduct of an official at the end of his term (*residencia*) and for the visits of inspection which were ordered from time to time. Not less important were the censorship powers which fell within its jurisdiction. Without its approval no book dealing with the New World could be printed in Spain or in the colonies, and its permission was needed for the importation of any books into America.

A chief function of this Council was to give legal expression to the principles and ideas formulated by the monarch, but its influence upon legislation was considerable. Its major responsibility lay in the execution of those laws. In time the legislation adopted by the crown and the council, by its complexity and variation to fit local conditions, became contradictory. Efforts to systematize and codify it, carried on during more than a century, resulted in the monumental compilation of colonial legislation known as the Recopilación de Leyes de los Reynos de las Indias, published in 1681. This code contains digests of 6,400 laws, arranged in nine books, divided into chapters (*títulos*). It is still an indispensable subject of study for those with an interest in present-day Spanish American law.

In the eighteenth century the once powerful Council declined in importance. With the introduction of a system of cabinet members and the appearance among them of a secretary or minister of marine and the Indies, the Council was deprived of the greatest portion of its former powers other than its judicial prerogatives. It remained as an advisory body. In 1812 it was abolished by the Cortes of Cádiz, and although it was reestablished by Ferdinand VII after his restoration, this revival was brief. It disappeared finally by a law of March 24, 1834.

Administrative System in the Colonies

The first royal representative in America was Columbus, who had been given by the famous Capitulaciones de Santa Fé, which was the contractual agreement with the Catholic Kings, the titles of admiral, viceroy, governor, and captain general in the lands he expected to find. Columbus was the first "lawgiver" in the Indies. By virtue of the patrimonial nature of his title, he was more than a royal representative; he was a governor enjoying the broadest powers.[3]

It is often stated that the discovery, conquest, and colonization of America were enterprises of a popular nature, meaning that, in the early period, private enterprise prevailed over official state action. The legal bases of all expeditions were the *capitulaciones* or contracts with the crown; these were reminiscent of the Castilian town charters of the Middle Ages. In each of the regions being colonized the contracts given the respective explorers constituted the first source of law. However, despite private enterprise, the influence of the crown was pervasive even at this early stage. The conquistador always took possession of the land in the name of the sovereign of Castile. The decisions of the magistrate appointed by the conquistador could be appealed to the king's court. Many clauses of the contracts embodied provisions for the welfare of the Indians and related to the spiritual objectives of the colonization.

Columbus's contract was never fully honored by the crown and was the subject of prolonged litigation. This and other contracts led to efforts in courts and before the Council of the Indies to recover royal prerogatives at the expense of the rights of holders of such instruments. These curtailments or abrogations of contract were not in all cases arbitrary or unjustified, since some of the holders failed to fulfill their obligations. The

[3] For the text of the Capitulaciones de Santa Fé accompanied by an interesting study of Columbus's rights and privileges, see Alfonso García Gallo, *Los orígenes de la administración territorial de las Indias* (Madrid, 1944).

so-called private phase of colonization declined during the sixteenth century.

Viceroys and Captains General. The earliest experiments in colonial government were conducted in Española or Santo Domingo, which remained the center of Spanish authority for several years. Later, the first viceroy appointed to rule over the Spanish dominions was sent to Mexico. In 1535 Antonio de Mendoza became the viceroy of New Spain with jurisdiction over Mexico or New Spain, New Galicia, Central America, the Antilles, and (after the conquest by López de Legazpe) the Philippine Islands. In South America the first viceroy was appointed for Peru in 1542 with his capital in Lima; this official was granted jurisdiction throughout Spanish South America. In the eighteenth century new subdivisions were made in these two vast areas into which Spain had divided the Indies. In 1718 the northern part of South America became a separate administrative division with the creation of the viceroyalty of New Granada. In 1776 another viceroyalty was carved out of the original jurisdiction of Peru to constitute the viceroyalty of La Plata, with its capital at Buenos Aires and extending westward from the mouth of the Río de la Plata to the Andes.

These viceroyalties were subdivided into extensive subordinate areas. The earliest such subdivisions were the provinces which were administered by a governor, although the precise title varied. Subsequently in some parts of the empire two or more provinces were politically associated and placed under the administrative supervision of a captain general or a president.[4] The captains general had a relative independence, and viceregal authority over them was vague and of a supervisory nature. In the reign of Charles IV there were four captaincies general: Cuba, Guatemala, Venezuela, and Chile. The powers of the captains general increased toward the end of the colonial era.

Viceroys and captains general were technically the supreme authorities within their jurisdictions as the direct representatives of the crown. They were the chief civil officers and military commanders, the secular heads of the Church, and they exercised supervision over the administration of justice and finance. At times, as a consequence of the vast distance

[4] The title "captain general" is confusing, since it refers to both a military rank and an administrative office. The title of "president" refers to an official residing in a province in which an *audiencia* (an administrative and judicial tribunal) was located. The presidencies existed in those combinations of provinces located within the jurisdiction of an *audiencia* but not in the capital cities, where viceroys and captains general resided.

Figure 5. Viceroyalties in Latin America about 1800. SOURCE: A. C. Wilgus, The Development of Hispanic America, p. 189. Copyright 1941 by A. Curtis Wilgus. Reproduced by permission of the publishers, Rinehart & Company, Inc., New York.

separating the colonies and the mother country and the urgent nature of certain administrative problems, the viceroys had to make decisions without guidance from the high organs of government in Spain. They were authorized to modify royal orders and even suspend them altogether when circumstances made it advisable.

Provincial Executives. The vast areas designated as viceroyalties or captaincies general were subdivided into smaller political jurisdictions headed by functionaries known as *gobernadores, corregidores,* or *alcaldes mayores.* These subdivisions were created without following any uniform system in their geographic distribution and nomenclature. All three types existed in the two large viceroyalties, the only difference being that a *gobernador* ruled a district generally larger than the region under the authority of a *corregidor* or an *alcalde mayor.* The areas under command of the *gobernadores* were in general sparsely populated frontier regions which called for a strong personal authority in the interest of public order and military defense. These officials exercised within their jurisdiction broad judicial and political authority and generally combined with it ample military powers.

Provincial executives were responsible to the *audiencias* in matters of justice and to the viceroys or captains general in administrative affairs. They also acted at times as fiscal agents in the collection of revenue, and as vice-patrons with delegated authority over ecclesiastical matters. In their extensive judicial functions they served as courts of appeal in the most important cases decided by municipal courts, the ultimate appeal being made to the *audiencia.* Relations between the municipalities and these officers were close and frequent, giving rise to many charges of encroachment.

Indian villages and towns which paid tribute to the crown were similarly organized into districts over which were designated *corregidores de pueblos de indios.* These officers were especially charged with the duty of protecting and promoting the welfare of the Indians in addition to exercising the political and judicial authority of their counterparts in the Spanish communities. More than an official, the corregidor was to serve as a guardian or tutor of the Indians living within his district. He was to protect them against abusive practices of the white settlers, to respect their customs provided that these were not against Christian principles, and to reprimand them with kindness for their excesses. In spite of the special care supposed to be taken in the selection of persons entrusted with such delicate functions, corrupt practices and abuses occurred. These officials often became the oppressors rather than protectors of the Indians. They subjected the natives to many illegal exactions, forcing them to undersell their products and to buy unwanted articles at unreasonable prices. Commonly they used their authority to compel the Indians to provide personal services of various sorts without giving them the remuneration provided by law. The frequent abuse of their power by these officials was at times the cause of Indian revolts.

Significant reforms in the colonial system were made by the Bourbon dynasty during the eighteenth century. One was the establishment of administrative areas known as intendancies (*intendencias*). An institution borrowed from France, the intendancy was first tried in the New World in Cuba in 1764, and after several other experiments, it was extended throughout the colonies by 1790. The system as finally established, however, was not uniform. The functions of the intendants differed according to regions governed by the laws of establishment.

The intendants enjoyed wide judicial, administrative, and financial powers and were directly subject to the king with respect to the last-mentioned activity. Their most important function was the collection of royal revenues. The special duties were of a varied nature: the promotion of agriculture, industry, and commerce; the development of irrigation and cattle raising; the supervision over water supplies, markets, mints, bridges, and inns; the inspection of troops; and the inspection of depots.

The new system provided for greater uniformity and centralization of functions in provincial administration and undoubtedly resulted in betterment of conditions in the colonies. Its major fault lay in the fact that in most cases the creole or colonial Spaniard was excluded from the opportunity to acquire experience in these offices.

The Audiencias. After the political failures of Columbus, the crown took the first step toward the creation of a more elaborate administrative system with the establishment in 1511 of the first *audiencia* in Santo Domingo. This institution was to play a prominent political and judicial role in America.

The *audiencia* was primarily a judicial tribunal, but it is important to emphasize the fact that from the beginning this institution became in the colonies something more than it was in Spain. In the mother country the term had only the meaning of a tribunal or court of law, and such was its primary significance in America. However, in the New World, it was invested in addition with a number of functions other than judicial ones. Furthermore, each *audiencia* had local characteristics and powers.

Figure 6. *Audiencias* in Colonial Spanish America before 1550. SOURCE: A. C. Wilgus, *Latin America in Maps,* New York, Barnes and Noble, 1943, p. 114.

All these tribunals had a common superior, the Council of the Indies; their general powers were prescribed in the same code, the Recopilación; and they were all supposed to have the same rank and importance. In practice, however, the viceregal *audiencias* of Mexico and Lima were tribunals of greater significance. The viceroys, also presidents of these bodies, had the right to send orders to the lesser *audiencias* within their jurisdictions, which were bound to obey them. Therefore, although theoretically they exercised equal authority in their own territory under the Council of the Indies, there was actually a degree of subordination to the viceregal administration.[5]

Briefly described, the colonial judiciary was composed of the highest court of appeals, the king, as represented by the Council of the Indies; the *audiencias,* as the highest court within the colonies; the *gobernadores, corregidores,* and *alcaldes mayores* with jurisdiction at the provincial level; and the local courts (*juzgados*) as the principal courts of first instances. This system was supplemented in the colonies by a series of special tribunals, such as the ecclesiastical courts, the military tribunals, commissioned investigators, and the courts established to hear only cases related to the cattle industry. There existed besides other administrative courts such as the merchants' guild, the miners' guild, the custom house, and the mint courts. Each one of these had a jurisdiction of its own in cases which belonged to its respective field.

As a court of law the *audiencia* acted as the supreme tribunal in the region committed to its charge. Appeals from the minor courts were brought before it, and in most cases its decisions were final. It sat in judgment on acts of viceroys or presidents when appealed to by someone affected. It took an important part in the conduct of investigations, revising the decisions of the judges appointed to conduct them or enforcing them. The nonjudicial functions of the *audiencia,* without precedent in the courts of Spain, included supervision over inferior judges, investigation of the treatment of Indians, collection of tithes, wide ecclesiastical authority, and limited legislative powers. Politically it acted as an advisory council to the viceroy or captain general who presided over it. An indication of its preeminence is shown by the fact that it often assumed control of the government in case of death or removal of the chief executive.

The Fiscal Service. The bureaucratic structure of the colonial exchequer

[5] The *audiencias* of Santo Domingo (1526), Mexico (1527), and Lima (1542) were the centers from which most of the others were established. The other tribunals were established in Panama (1535), Santiago de los Caballeros de Guatemala (1543), Guadalajara or New Galicia (1548), Santa Fe de Bogotá or New Granada (1549), La Plata or Charcas (1559), San Francisco de Quito (1563), Santiago de Chile (1609), Buenos Aires (1661), Caracas (1786), Cuzco (1787), Puerto Rico (1831), Havana (1835), Puerto Príncipe (transferred from Santo Domingo in 1797), and Santiago de Cuba (1835).

was not complex and suffered few changes until the introduction of the intendancy system in the eighteenth century. In each important city of the colonies royal officials were in charge of the collection of revenues. These officials exercised certain judicial functions, having jurisdiction in first instance of all fiscal suits. The way in which they were ordered to perform their duties furnishes a good example of the deliberate Spanish policy of diffusing responsibility, as well as of the distrust by the crown of its servants where money was concerned. Every entry in the exchequer books had to be attested by all the officials, every deposit had to be made before all of them, and all communications had to be signed by them together. The funds of each district were deposited in the royal chest, which had several different locks, to each of which one of the officials had a key.

The offices were filled by sale to the highest bidder, and the incumbents were bound to certain restrictions, such as depositing bond and making inventory of all their possessions. They were also obliged to transmit their accounts periodically to the Council of the Indies and to submit to that body a detailed report every three years.

The tax structure in the colonies was the result of the accumulation of taxes created to meet specific purposes but continued indefinitely. Finally, the machinery for their collection and administration became unduly complex and costly, a situation which has persisted in some of the Latin-American republics to this day.

The Municipalities. The local unit of political organization in the colonies and the only one in which the residents participated was the town council known as *cabildo* or *ayuntamiento*. Much study had been devoted to the *cabildo* in an effort to measure its influence and define its place in the perpetuation of Spanish colonial institutions in the later political life of Hispanic America. The colonial *cabildo* has become a subject of considerable controversy. Some have regarded it as an institution of power, as a training school for future democracy, as the sole institution which in any real degree was independent of imperial control, and as the basis of later federalism. Others, however, have considered it as a weak institution, oligarchical rather than representative and democratic, and have denied the validity of its pretensions as a school for future self-government. They have been skeptical of the claim that it was a forerunner of federalism.

The fact is that the *cabildos* did not all develop or exercise the same degree of power. Some of them were strong, just as others were comparatively weak. Many factors entered into this result. Some cities were isolated, having poor facilities of communication, a fact which prevented efficient supervision and ready interference; some had a citizenry of particular individualistic assertiveness; some were situated in agricultural areas which, as compared to the mining areas, were neglected by Spain; and some had their political and social character affected by the ease or difficulty with which the Indians were conquered. Between such extremes of circumstances and nature lie the explanations and causes of strength and weakness.

In Spain the municipalities had formerly enjoyed a very considerable measure of autonomy in the management of their affairs, and although they had lost many of their freedoms during the sixteenth and seventeenth centuries, the forms and tradition of autonomy had survived. The golden age of city home rule—the twelfth, thirteenth, and fourteenth centuries—was the time when the influences of sectionalism stamped upon the Spanish character its seemingly ineradicable individualism. There were differences in the *cabildos* arising from variations in the policies and practices of the several governments of medieval Spain and from the greatly varied customs of the complex ethnic groups and geographic sections of the Iberian Peninsula. The cities, new and old, won privileges, in varying degrees, during the wars of reconquest against the Mohammedans and in the bitter feudal struggles between the kings and nobles in which they gave aid to one or the other side.

Therefore, the Spanish brought to America no institution so old, none so rooted in their hearts, as the *cabildo*. Three considerations, however, should be kept in mind in considering this transplantation of municipal institutions. Many Spanish cities were given, as we have just mentioned, special rights in the reconquest of Spain from the Moors; similarly, cities were founded and given rights in the conquest of America from the Indians. Secondly, the colonization of the New World was under way before the forces of centralization in Spain had destroyed municipal autonomy there. The dead and dying city life of Spain seemed, under these circumstances, to have a sort of renaissance in America. Thirdly, wherever in America there was any considerable grouping of the natives and former citizens of any Spanish city, or any concentration of members of any one of the Spanish ethnic units, they sought to establish in their new homes the governmental system and the political customs which their own race and city had had in Spain.

The *cabildo* consisted of a council of *regidores* (councilmen) and one or more magistrates (*alcaldes*) whom the council elected together with various minor officials. In the very earliest days all these officials were popularly elected. This early practice gave way to a system of annual elections, on the first of January, when the retiring council elected their successors from among the resident citizens. Later, after 1620, the offices of councilman were offered for sale or were filled by appointment. These changes were, however, not uniformly carried out. Following the installation of the *cabildo,* it usually proceeded to elect from its own membership or from the citizenry certain administrative officials such as the herald or municipal standard-bearer, the chief constable, the public trustee, the inspectors of weights and measures, and the legal agent.

The law of 1620 relative to the sale of offices of the council had a dispiriting effect upon municipal life and ideals. It was ordered that in the awarding of the office, after bids had been made in public auction, consideration should be given to men of capacity and, whenever possible, to original settlers and their descendants. The fact was, however, that in the opportunity for gain, officeholding having been made a business, ideas of duty, patriotism, and good administration were often abandoned.

Another phase of municipal government in the colonies was the town meeting (*cabildo abierto*) to which the entire body or a part of the resident citizenry was invited or summoned. These meetings were held to deal popularly with matters and situations unforeseen by the law, to adopt policies in time of crisis, to raise troops, to receive important information and communications, to give notice of new taxes, and for other purposes. Proceedings were of an advisory nature, and decisions, if any were reached, were not necessarily binding upon the municipal council.

The powers and duties of the *cabildos* were political, judicial, economic, social, and religious. The two magistrates (*alcaldes*) were judges in civil and criminal cases, and the council as a whole acted as a court in such cases as were taken to it on appeal from the magistrates. On the other hand, as a council, the *cabildo* legislated for local needs, subject to the annulment of the higher authorities. The political powers and activities of the council included the control of the police, the administration of public works, and the inspection over jails and hospitals. It admitted persons to its citizenship and could withdraw this status. It was an organ of communication between the people and the royal government. Its chamber was the place for the verification of credentials and the reading of royal decrees. It had partial control of the local militia, and one of its duties was to aid in the protection of the frontier. On the death of a governor, one of its members was supposed to succeed to his authority, although this was of little significance, for there was usually a lieutenant to take the governor's place, and if not, the *audiencia* was likely to grasp the command. On occasions, the municipal council was the medium for the expression of public will in opposition to misrule. There are dramatic instances in Paraguay, Upper Peru, and New Granada when the *cabildos* led armed resistance to royal officials.

In addition to the powers actually exercised, there were potential powers belonging to the council. Should royal government collapse under misfortune or disaster, the *cabildo,* being a self-perpetuating body and close to the people, might become the instrument of popular sovereignty and might, by common law, come into the legitimate authority of the state.

The economic powers of the municipality included the administration of certain funds, limited powers of taxation, and health regulations. It had the duty of protecting the food supply and the power of fixing prices. It distributed or allotted town lots and sometimes also lands, and it granted building licenses.

Although the list of its powers is impressive, the *cabildo* was in final analysis an inferior agent executing the orders of a superior power. There were instances, such as the death or delinquency of higher officials, when it exercised real powers, but these were exceptional. The *cabildos* were uniformly weak in financial resources; all new taxes had to receive royal approval, and much of the income had to be spent in church festivals and political celebrations.

Means of Control: Residencia and Visita

The difficulties of ruling such vast territories as the American colonies, situated at great distances from the mother country, and of effectively controlling the royal bureaucracy presented an ever-recurring problem to the crown. Abuse of power was not unusual, and dishonesty and incompetence were frequently present, rendering inevitable distrust on the part of the crown. The *residencia* and the *visita,* both well-rooted institutions in Castile, became the most efficient instruments of control used by Spain in the prevention or correction of these evils. In addition there were required both regular and extraordinary reports from the different classes of officials. The right and duty of independent communication with the crown or the Council made these different classes of officials spies upon each other and critics of conduct.

The *residencia* was the judicial review of the conduct of an official made at the expiration of his term. In charge of the procedure was a special judge, appointed by the crown or by its representatives in the colonies. This judge, on reaching the town in which the investigation was to be conducted, issued a proclamation concerning the opening of the procedure, and anybody was free to appear before the court to give evidence or make charges. After giving the official who was being investigated an opportunity to defend himself, the judge prepared his report, pronounced sentence, and sent all proceedings to the Council of the Indies or the local *audiencia.* Though officials could be excused from the *residencia* by royal dispensation, it seems that a waiver of it was extremely rare.

The *visitas* or visitations differed from the *residencias* in that they could be ordered at any time while the *residencia* could only come at the expiration of the term of an official. The *residencia* was ordinary and inevitable; the *visita,* extraordinary. The latter might refer to any problem, whether that of an individual or that of the country or province. These inspections were instituted without notice. There were general visitations to an entire viceroyalty or captaincy general and specific visitations for the purpose of inspecting the conduct of an individual official. The power of a visitor general was according to specification. During the time of his inspection his authority could be supreme and over that of the existing officials. All findings and corresponding charges were sent by the inspector to the Council of the Indies, accompanied by a detailed report of the procedure for ultimate approval by the crown. Only the crown and the Council could determine the final action to be taken as a result of the visitation.

The question of whether these two institutions contributed to good government is debatable. Serious criticisms can be made, stressing their defects and specifically emphasizing the waste of energy, money, and time involved. It appears that the system may have often discouraged initiative on the part of the colonial officialdom, and thereby retarded the development of the colonies. Both institutions undoubtedly had virtues and represented the desire of the crown to maintain efficient and honest administration in its overseas possessions. If the results did not always conform to the theory, this discrepancy was due mainly to the peculiar conditions of the empire.

The Church

During the colonial period the clergy occupied as prominent a position in America as it had in the mother country. In the colonies the legal principles which regulated its relationship with the civil authorities were known as the Royal Patronage of the Indies (Real Patronato de las Indias). Secured through concessions from the papacy, this control of patronage became one of the most jealously protected prerogatives of the Spanish kings. Many aspects of it remained the source of controversy at the end of the colonial period. Through the Royal Patronage, the government had control of the clerical personnel, subject to some limitations. During the entire colonial period the crown sought to extend and strengthen this prerogative.

The essential feature of the Royal Patronage was the right of presentation, i.e., the power of the monarch to name a candidate for any vacant ecclesiastical office to the Pope for canonical installation. Installation of prelates by the Pope became a formality, and candidates often assumed office on the authority of royal credentials without much concern for the consent of Rome. The king exercised extensive jurisdiction over the ecclesiastical affairs of the colonies, and in a sense the Church was converted into a branch of Spanish colonial administration. It served the crown in upholding colonial rule, and at the same time it was an effective agency for transmitting to the New World the civilization of Spain.

The Royal Patronage also included the right to collect tithes. In return for this papal concession the crown was obligated to assume the expenses incurred in the maintenance and propagation of the faith. Civil jurisdiction over ecclesiastical matters sometimes invaded the realm of spiritual affairs, giving the king quasi-pontifical authority. However, it must also be noted that the crown fulfilled its commitments with zeal and that the propagation and maintenance of the Catholic faith in far distant lands were impressively achieved by the remarkable crusading spirit of the Spaniards.

Delegation of the privileges of Royal Patronage was approved by the Pope, and the king left many of its functions to the viceroys and other high officials in the colonies. Through the mediation of these officials the right of presentation was exercised, churches were established, and schools, hospitals, and charitable institutions were administered.

The crown had the power of permitting or forbidding the admission to the colonies of all papal documents and their circulation there. Also royal approval was required for all decisions of the Church councils.

It is advisable to distinguish between the control of appointments of the religious personnel, which was the essence of the Patronage, and the many other aspects of the relationship of Church and state. In spite of the extraordinary control exercised by the government, the Church always maintained much independence in purely ecclesiastical matters. For one thing, once a cleric was appointed, tenure was permanent. The crown could only transfer an offending priest to a post of less importance. If it is true that there was civil control over some affairs of the Church, it is equally true that a high degree of dignity was given to the clergy. These honors and privileges were always zealously upheld by the state.

The serious issue of politicoecclesiastical relations was that of restraining the influence and power of the Church in the economic sphere. In many colonies the ecclesiastical establishment was a heavy economic burden. The vast wealth of the church represented by revenue-producing lands, by capital loaned at interest, and by rentals from church-owned buildings posed a serious problem. The acquisition by the Church of much of the best land, secured by means of benefactions, purchase, or foreclosure, aggravated the concentration of land in the control of a few. The amount of church property has been variously estimated. According to Alamán, in Mexico at the close of the colonial period it consisted of one-half of the total value of all productive real estate.[6]

The Church was granted the right to hold property in its right, receive bequests, and engage in economic enterprises. It was entitled to a special court in which its members were judged. The property holdings, subventions, and exemptions gave to the Church a formidable economic power, The wealth of the different branches of the Church was represented not only in buildings and objects employed for spiritual purposes but also in tithes and first fruits, which the clergy was entitled to receive at the source on agricultural and pastoral properties. Perhaps the worst feature of this accumulation of wealth by the clergy was the fact that ecclesiastical lands were under the right of mortmain and therefore could never change owners or be redivided and distributed; thus the size of these properties could only increase.

The Church performed a valuable role as a banking and credit institution. There were no banks in Spanish America until near the end of the colonial period, and the Church partially supplied the service. It lent money at low interest rates and was a lenient and just creditor. Loans to landowners passed in some cases from generation to generation, and some real estate mortgages were by agreement considered "irredeemable." The landowners depended in large measure upon Church loans for their working capital.

[6] Lucas Alamán, *Historia de México* (Mexico, 1849–1850), vol. I, p. 67.

In missions, in the arts, and in the maintenance and support of all educational and charitable institutions, contributions of the Church should be given recognition. "Virtually all of the social services of the community in colonial days were the peculiar and exclusive domain of the clergy. They created and managed the schools, hospitals, and asylums. They administered the numerous pious funds established by devout laymen or ecclesiastics."[7]

Something must also be said regarding the Church's control of certain functions which are today clearly within the realm of the civil powers. The control of cemeteries and of the registry of marriages and births became an issue of great significance in the republican period. An understanding of the relationship between the Church and the Spanish state is essential for a clear comprehension of this and many other serious problems of a religious nature experienced by the Latin-American republics since the end of the colonial era.

The Labor System

The problem of the supply of labor was one of the earliest and most complicated which the Spanish colonial administration attempted to solve. After the first Indian rebellion in 1494, Columbus enacted legislation imposing a tax on all Indians between the ages of fourteen and seventy. This tax was to be paid quarterly and consisted of a small amount of gold or cotton. If the Indians were unable to pay in this manner, they were permitted to do work as a means of satisfying the tax. When in 1499 after a revolt by the colonists an agreement was reached, one of the conditions of peace was that they be given allotments of Indians to work in their service. This marks the beginning of the system of distributing Indians for labor purposes (*repartimiento*). From 1499, apparently it was the practice to require Indians either to pay the tribute or to perform labor. Subsequently legislation enacted in 1503 legalized the forced labor of free Indians, although attempting at the same time to curb irresponsible exploitation. The application of this legislation led to the establishment of the encomienda, which for some time served as a foundation of colonial economy. The encomienda was a concession, conferred by royal favor, of a number of Indians to a preferred Spaniard. The grantee assumed the obligation of instructing the Indians in the Catholic faith and the

[7] Haring, *op. cit.*, p. 192.

elements of civilization and of defending their persons and property. In return the Indians paid their protector a tribute or worked for him.[8]

The institution became in practice a subterfuge for slavery, and it took many years of protest and agitation before its worst feature, the right to use the services of the Indians, was abolished. Indians were assigned by written deeds, in lots of perhaps fifty or a hundred, to individual Spaniards who could use them as laborers on their lands. Wages were nominal and instruction limited to rudiments of religion. A gradual decline of the native population during the sixteenth and seventeenth centuries was the result of the system. The crown then undertook a more direct control of the allotment of forced labor, which led to the rise of a wage-earning class among the Indian population, especially in the mines and in the Spanish communities, and to the development of the system of contract labor for unskilled workers.

In view of the religious forces involved in the Spanish conquest of America, the conquerors did not remain indifferent to the various moral problems posed by the exploitation of the Indian peoples. The question of the legal status of the Indian was one which occupied the attention of the theologians and jurists of Spain. The discrepancy between the crown's policy toward Indians and the reality of their lot was brought into the open by the Church in its role of guardian of the spiritual phases of colonization. Influential clerics censured the colonists for their oppression of the natives and started agitations at the court for public recognition and protection of the rights of the Indians. These efforts resulted in the adoption by the crown of a series of measures designed to alleviate the wrongs committed. This humanitarian legislation did not have the desired effect, since enforcement of it was opposed by public opinion and established customs. There were serious revolts in the colonies. High officials were sent out to enforce the decrees, and new *audiencias* (in Lima and Guatemala) were established with the same purpose. In Peru, aversion to the "New Laws" of 1542 caused a bloody civil war, and in Mexico the promulgation of most of the decrees was withheld for fear of a rebellion. The result was compromise and the continuation of the encomienda as an institution. The forced-labor system was, again, an inevitable result of the

[8] The encomienda system, like many other institutions, had its origin in Spain. During the reconquest of the peninsula, when Christian warriors were slowly winning back their lands from the Mohammedans, the monarch often rewarded them and some of the great clericomilitary orders by distributing the lands of the conquered and granting tax-collecting concessions.

peculiar conditions in the colonies. However, in 1549, a royal order prohibited the substitution of personal service to the holder of an encomienda in lieu of tribute. Enforcement of this prohibition marked the end of the encomienda as a system of forced labor. All tributes were paid in money or kind and not in personal service. Although the institution was not definitely abolished until the eighteenth century, it became almost exclusively a system of tribute after 1549.

The Commercial System

In the economic administration of its colonies Spain adopted and perfected the mercantilist policies and practices which were current in sixteenth-century Europe. The idea that self-sufficiency and national power could not be attained except through a protectionist or monopolistic policy and that the precious metals alone constituted wealth was by no means original with Spain. However, Spain became the leader in applying these ideas, and the rest of Europe was the imitator.

The early commercial policy of Spain, judged by the standards of the time, was relatively liberal. Later, however, the crown imposed restrictions and taxes. In the middle of the sixteenth century both export and import duties were set in the ports of Spain, and export duties were added in the colonies. The increasingly high prices of imports from Spain placed an excessive burden on the colonists, and they exercised an unfavorable influence in the development of colonial trade. Goods sent to the Indies included the products that the colonies were not allowed to or could not produce, such as hardware, oil, wine, textiles, garments, and (in early times) cattle. The chief cargoes to Spain included raw materials from the fields and mines, such as coffee, tobacco, cotton, cacao, timber, salt, copper, tin, gold, silver, and precious stones.

The two Andalusian ports of Seville and Cádiz were the only ports legally authorized and enjoyed all the incidental benefits. The efforts of other cities to participate in colonial trade were unsuccessful because of the opposition of the merchants of Seville, whose influence was powerful, and also because of the greater ease in administering the commercial system. This policy of closed ports had its counterpart in the Indies, where only three harbors were permitted to trade directly with Spain: Veracruz, Cartagena, and Nombre de Dios in Panama.

Intercolonial trade was subject to restrictions and in some cases, especially between New Spain and Peru, was strictly prohibited. The crown saw this restricted-port policy as the only way to enforce its economic

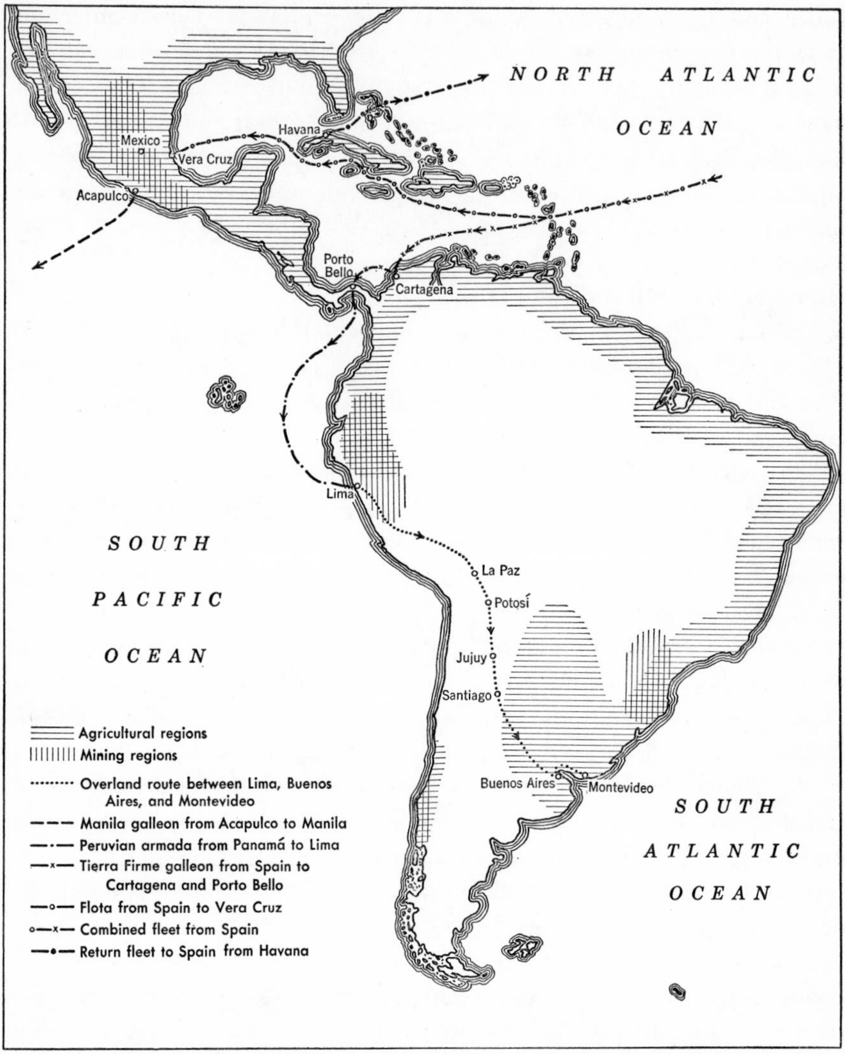

Figure 7. Trade centers and routes in Colonial Spanish America. SOURCE: A. C. Wilgus and Raul d'Eça, *Outline History of Latin America,* New York, Barnes and Noble, 1943.

regulations, and it is fair to say that the restrictions were urged not only by merchants in Spain but in many instances by businessmen in the Indies as well.

The enforcement of policy in all phases of commercial intercourse was the responsibility of the Casa de Contratación or House of Trade at Sevilla. The Casa, to assure effective enforcement of the closed-ports policy and to protect Spanish vessels from predatory raids, adopted in 1543 the fleet or convoy system, which operated for nearly two hundred years. Two fleets, one for Mexico and the other for Panama, averaging some seventy ships each, customarily sailed once a year in either direction. Each fleet had an armed convoy, and routes and schedules were carefully regulated. The cost of the system was defrayed by a special tax on imports and exports. The famous fairs of Jalapa and Portobelo, which served as the official markets of the Indies, began when the fleets arrived at their respective ports. News of the arrival of the ships was circulated through the colonies in time for goods to be brought for exchange to the fair sites. The fleets carried back to Spain the shipments of gold and silver from Peru and Mexico, and the consignment to the crown of royalties from the mines and pearl fisheries.

This system tended to work to the advantage of the small but powerful group of merchants, members of the Consulate of Seville. Prices were determined by agreements between the agents of Seville and the chief importers in the colonies, and great profits were obtained by the large firms which supported the system.

Among the most serious weaknesses of Spain's economic administration were the heavy burdens placed upon the colonists. However, customs duties, sales taxes, and other exactions were not the only burdens of commercial activity. Spain's enemies also contributed to the weakening of the system. Dutch, French, and English pirates and freebooters were numerous and never ceased to harass the Spanish communities by raids. Their attacks upon shipping were both damaging and profitable. The illegal trade carried on by both foreigners and Spaniards was perhaps even more damaging than freebooting. Contraband trade was conducted in many cases with the complicity of colonial authorities. It became inevitable owing to the lack of adequate military protection and to the failure of the mother country to produce and supply enough goods to satisfy colonial needs. It was only natural that the colonists welcomed an opportunity to secure goods at lower cost and that the merchants would find it profitable to engage in contraband trade. The value of all this illegal trade probably exceeded that of the legitimate commerce.

In the eighteenth century many drastic changes were introduced in the system, which had become both unprofitable and corrupt. After a long process of decadence and some attempts to revitalize it, the fleet system was abolished in 1789. The monopolistic trading corporation, used by the Dutch and the English, came into high favor, especially in the early part of the century. In 1743, a work was written in Spain which eventually caused significant changes in economic policy. It advocated drastic reforms, such as the distribution of land to Indians, the training of Indians as farmers and artisans, the extension of agricultural credits, the reduction of taxation on colonial trade, the reduction of custom duties on foreign goods, the organization of an overseas mail service, and measures to restrict the Cádiz monopoly.[9] Some of these ideas were incorporated in legislation. By the famous act of 1778 free trade within the empire was extended to all the American provinces except Mexico and Venezuela, and by a series of decrees enacted during the following years, reduction of duties was granted and a list of tax-exempt articles was allowed. The main object of all these measures was to promote greater volume in trade, lower prices, and greater prospect of successful competition with foreign shippers.

This economic freedom naturally caused far-reaching effects in the colonies. Business was increased in volume, prices were lowered, and the demands in colonial markets were more adequately satisfied. Contraband became less profitable. The monopoly enjoyed by the Seville-Cádiz group was broken, and a new class of merchants appeared in Spain and in the colonies. The grant of freedom of trade within the empire stimulated a desire of extending that freedom to international trade.

Education

Just as political and economic institutions of the mother country were brought and adapted to America by the colonists, the culture of Spain was likewise transplanted in full to the New World. This projection of culture was in part the function of the education which was provided by both public and private means. Through such agencies as the missions, the encomiendas, the municipal councils, the religious orders, and the schools and universities, and by the combined action of church and state, Spain was successful in this effort. In every field of creative endeavor Spain provided the skilled workers, and through their accomplishments the indelible pattern of Spanish civilization was imprinted on the colonies.

Spanish legislation did not ignore education. There are numerous illustrations which serve to show the intent of the crown to make available some educational facilities to large segments of the population. There were serious efforts to educate the Indian, and the Church made attempts

[9] José Campillo y Cossío, *Nuevo sistema de gobierno económico para la América* (Madrid, 1743).

to train and utilize native teachers in spreading European civilization and Catholicism. It is true, however, that educational policies reflected the aristocratic spirit of colonial society and were mainly designed for the benefit of the upper classes.

The wealthy class, Spaniards, creoles, and upper-rank mixbloods (mestizos) received their education in church schools or from private tutors. The arrival of the Jesuits in Mexico in 1572 gave impetus to the development of higher education. They opened schools in the viceroyalties of Mexico and Peru, and by the time of the expulsion of the order, there was a Jesuit school in every large colonial city.

The first formal act creating a university in the New World was a papal bull of 1538 chartering that of Santo Tomás de Aquino in Santo Domingo, but this institution did not function as a university for a good number of years thereafter. The universities of Mexico and Lima were created by both pontifical and royal action in 1551; the former opened its doors in 1553, and the latter was provided with adequate funds in 1571, the date for the beginning of its effective existence. These universities, as well as the others established later, had the typical structure of medieval institutions with four schools (*facultades*)—arts, law, theology, and medicine—and were empowered to grant the bachelor's and master's degrees. Twenty-six universities were founded in Spanish America. Six ranked with Lima and Mexico as major universities; the others were really colleges empowered by papal or royal authority to award higher degrees. These institutions enjoyed a large degree of autonomy and jealously guarded their prerogatives and special jurisdiction.

The class distinctions of colonial society, reproduced in universities, resulted in a denial, confirmed on occasions by law, of admission to those of mixed blood. The creoles made up the majority of the students, and members of this class were eligible to chairs in the faculties. Professorships were considered as a distinction and an honor, and the faculties were composed of churchmen, lawyers, judges, and government officials. These institutions, much as modern Latin-American universities, were basically professional schools which left general instruction in the liberal arts to the secondary schools authorized to award the bachelor's degree. Many of the above-mentioned features can still be found in institutions of higher learning of Latin America, especially those features related to administration, autonomous status, professional character, and composition of faculties.

Through succeeding generations theologians, jurists, naturalists, poets, and artists gave to colonial society its intellectual distinction. Some notable writers were of mestizo or Indian origin. Taking into account the obstacles to publication and the limited opportunities and facilities for education, a remarkable literary production of historical, ethnological, geographical, and religious studies was accomplished. The influence of French thought was felt during the eighteenth century. A notable scientific revival began in Spain and extended itself to the colonies. The works of the Encyclopedists, of Bacon, Descartes, Copernicus, Grassendi, Boyle, Locke, Condillac, Buffon, Voltaire, Montesquieu, Rousseau, Lavoisier, and Laplace were read and circulated in secret.

Society

In the colonies class differences carried differentiation in legal status, and these legal distinctions were supplemented by customs that became somewhat rigid. Laws were designed to promote and preserve divisions of class and race. To such class distinctions as prevailed in Spain was added a system of social stratification based on race and percentage of Spanish blood, and customarily the several strata were differentiated as to privileges and opportunities. However, whether the Negro or the Indian or the mixture of the two was of lowest social status was not determined uniformly in all the colonies.

Baron von Humboldt mentioned the existence of seven castes in the Indies: (1) Spaniards born in Europe; (2) Spaniards born in America, called creoles (*criollos*); (3) mestizos, descendants of white and Indian; (4) mulattos, descendants of white and Negro; (5) zambos, descendants of Indian and Negro; (6) Indians; and (7) Negroes.[10] This list, of course, did not exhaust the possibilities and blood mixtures. In some of the colonies persons of mixed blood were called by the generic name of *pardos;* in Venezuela, this group, toward the end of the colonial era, represented about half the population.

Spaniards and creoles were almost exclusively the persons of distinction and wealth. These two groups constituted the upper crust of society, well above the position held by inferior groups, and the distinction was recognized by law. The numerous groups of the half-breeds, which steadily increased because of the relatively small number of women immigrants from Spain, always strove to place themselves among the whites. The

[10] Alexander von Humboldt, *Political Essay on the Kingdom of New Spain* (4 vols., London, Longman, Hurst, Rees, Orme, and Brown, 1811).

Spaniards of European origin (*peninsulares*) were a privileged class by reason of migration and residence in the colonies, not because they had been in Spain members of the aristocracy. As officials, they enjoyed positions of dignity and importance, without responsibility to the local population. In spite of the fact that the law made no distinction between them and the creoles, only on rare occasions did the latter rise to the high administrative ranks. In business enterprises the competition of industrious and hardworking immigrants from Spain often resulted also in the displacement of the creoles. These immigrants came to control most of the trades; they often became owners of great landed estates and mines.

The creole aristocracy was based on wealth as well as social status. It was composed of the descendants of the conquerors and rich landowners who had been given a title or an honorary office. The preferences of these aristocrats in the choice of a career were the legal profession, the higher clergy, and the armed forces. Fond of titles and honorific posts, the wealthy creole was constantly seeking both. Usually such a person endeavored to create an entailed estate (*mayorazgo*) with its attached privileges. Not always too sure of their purity of blood, the creoles took great pains to prove it by means of long and expensive genealogical investigations. A considerable number who claimed to be creoles with pure Spanish blood were in reality mestizos. It was possible to obtain from the crown through a special procedure a dispensation which in effect reclassified the person involved. These special patents or licenses were not only used as dispensations for the mestizo to change his status, but they were also used as devices to secure for him the right to participate in trade, to wear certain apparel, and to carry an umbrella.

Another class which enjoyed special privileges was that of the Indian nobility or native aristocracy. The hereditary Indian chiefs were treated with special considerations, since it was Spanish policy to encourage their survival. Colonial law authorized transmittance of chieftaincies (*cacicazgos*) by inheritance. The chiefs were exempt from taxes imposed on other Indians, and legally although not socially they were on a footing of equality with the whites. Some Indian chiefs were rewarded with titles of nobility.

Below the European and the creole were the rank and file of the population, with Indians and mestizos occupying a slightly higher social level than Negroes and mulattoes. Some Indians lived very much to themselves either on reservations or in their own villages. They often governed themselves, preserving their traditional ways of living. The majority however, lived in semiservitude, being exploited by the whites in spite of the protection afforded by colonial laws. There were occasional revolts, but only in a few instances did these rebellions assume serious proportions.

The legal and social status of the mestizo was far inferior to that of the whites. The latter looked with suspicion and fear at the rapid development of a mixblood class and up to the eve of independence were opposed to the social ambitions of the mestizos. Although half-breeds were appointed to minor ecclesiastical and state posts, most of them were found in the group of small farmers and stewards; in the large cities they formed a lower middle class of lesser shopkeepers and artisans. They were handicapped by status and by the considerable number of illegitimates among them. During the wars of independence, many mestizos enlisted in the army to escape the stigma inflicted upon their class.

Negroes and zambos composed the lowest class of society, and in some places the mulattoes were placed with them. This group included Negroes who were out of bondage, and they were numerous. The freedmen were subject to many restrictions. They could not appear in the streets after dark, carry weapons, or occupy public offices, and they had no access to the craft guilds. Spanish law, however, looked after the welfare of the slave, and many detailed regulations of a humanitarian nature were issued concerning them.

Although in the early stages of colonization some of the lesser nobility of Spain came to America, the crown encouraged also a different type of immigrant. Among the latter were farm laborers and artisans, and a sizable number of settlers of this type came to the colonies. The artisans were to play a significant role by reason of their membership in the powerful guilds (*gremios*).

The stratification of colonial society was to continue. Perhaps its persistence was more prolonged on the western coast of South America and in the most isolated areas of the Spanish domains. The legalization of such stratification passed with the colonial era, but it continued in social customs for a long time after independence was attained, and in some places still persists.

A Comparison

In appraising the possible impact of colonial institutions and practices upon contemporary government, it may be helpful to note the principal features which distinguished Spanish colonization from that of England. Differences in institutions, motives, objectives, human elements, and policies may well account for the diversity of the end product. The English and the Spanish colonial systems are often compared to the disparagement of the work of Spain, but it must be remembered that comparisons can be sometimes misleading because of the unlike and even contrasted social processes of the colonies in North and South America. Only in the case of the Spanish West Indies and the English plantation colonies in Virginia and in South Carolina were conditions nearly similar; a fair counterpart to the Spanish system cannot be found in the English settlements of the north Atlantic seaboard. In the Spanish possessions the transmission of European culture and civilization was achieved by the establishment of imperial domain and not, as in the case of English America, by the growth of little settlements of immigrants acting on their own impulse. Therefore one must be aware, before attempting dangerous generalizations, that there are many other factors, geographical and historical, which are to be taken into account if differences between Latin America and the United States are to be explained in scientific fashion. The purpose of this brief comparison is to emphasize the significance of preindependence institutions in the historical development of both Americas.

As we have seen, Spain, at the time of the colonization, was an autocratic monarchy, usually described as "absolute," which had achieved triumph over nobles and municipalities, and which had made the Church its ally and instrument. Spain could and did establish imperial institutions responsible to itself alone. If it established colonial governments with an elaborate system of checks and balances, jurisdictional autonomy, and granted to towns and guilds a limited measure of self-government, it did so by choice or acquiescence and not by any mandate from a superior authority. England, on the other hand, although very far from having a democratic system, had sown, by the seventeenth century, the seeds of democratic institutions, and it was in the process of becoming a limited monarchy. During the seventeenth century parliamentary supremacy, the Bill of Rights, habeas corpus, and the beginnings of the cabinet system and of party government were to be adopted. "The rights of Englishmen" were guarantees which colonials claimed as well as residents of the mother country. Charters became to some areas constitutions governing the colonial corporation, limiting both the colony and, constructively, the home government. The English colonies of all classes of North America had, by far, the greater opportunity for experience in self-government.

There was also a difference in basic objectives and motives. For the

Spaniard, animated by religious zeal and military ardor, the New World offered opportunities to conduct a crusade to convert infidels, to engage in the adventures of conquest, and to gain wealth. Both the zeal and the desire of adventure went parallel with the search for mineral riches. The Englishman, dissatisfied with conditions at home, was more intent upon finding refuge in the colonies from religious or political persecution. Because mineral wealth was not found, the English colonies began as agricultural settlements, with commerce and minor industries coming later. Although Spain was not entirely indifferent to the establishment of agricultural colonies, Mexico and Peru with its gold and silver had superior attraction.

Again, the differences between the native populations found in the New World must be noted. The indigenous element in the English area of colonization was at a low stage of civilization. Being primitive, it offered resistance but no conflict of cultures; it was occupied but little in the exploitation of the soil. On the other hand, the large masses of Indians in Spanish America—highly organized in Peru and Mexico in so-called empires—influenced European culture in considerable measure, and mixed with the newcomers creating new castes. The Spaniards were to live with the Indian, use him, and convert him. The natives were from the start regarded as subjects of the Spanish crown, whereas in the English colonies they were generally treated as independent nations—friends or enemies, as the case might be. The relations of English colonial governments to them were diplomatic rather than those of ruler and governed.[11] Left in the main to take their chances in a sort of struggle for existence, they were either exterminated or pushed back. In the Spanish domains survival of the Indian was of concern to the settlers, since he supplied the labor force that was needed for the exploitation of mineral resources. As to the European settlers, the strict regulation as to immigration imposed by the Spanish crown was in striking contrast with the general indifference of the English government as to what sort of people went to the colonies. The policy of exclusion of foreigners was maintained to the downfall of Spain's rule on the mainland, although some exceptions were made.

Some policies were common to both countries. Both followed colonial theories that were universally accepted at the time. The idea that a colony exists for the benefit of the mother country was the main principle adopted by all colonizing nations. When it came to the enforcement and

[11] Edward Gaylord Bourne, *Spain in America* (New York, Harper, 1904), p. 253.

practical application of such theories, it became evident, however, that Spain, because of its power and suitable conditions at home, was capable of practicing them and carrying them to conclusion. England, by the force of circumstance, allowed the colonists to exercise a large measure of self-control. This and the participation of local residents in colonial government resulted, in the British colonies, in the accumulation of wide political experience before emancipation. In Spanish America, on the other hand, there was a near monopoly of high administrative posts held by *peninsulares*. The creole, lacking practical knowledge of public affairs, took the hard road of political apprenticeship after becoming independent from the mother country.

The Colonial Heritage

The system of colonial government briefly described in this chapter remained in existence for over three centuries of Spanish domination in the American colonies. Many of the features of this system have endured to become conditioning elements in the structure of contemporary government in Latin America, although institutions may have been stripped of former powers and original functions. The *audiencias,* shorn of all consultative and administrative attributes, still function in some countries as strictly judicial bodies. Court procedures have undergone only minor changes since colonial days. The intendancies are partly preserved in the provincial structure of some of the independent republics. The *cabildos* fell into decline later, but their traditions continue to influence municipal government decisively. Colonial means of control have influenced contemporary constitutional devices aimed at preventing corruption and maladministration in government.

These facts are only thought-provoking examples of the potential effects of the colonial past. One must refer to historical antecedents if he is to have a clear understanding of contemporary problems such as that of the relations of Church and state. A real comprehension of present political institutions depends in some measure upon acknowledgment of colonial influences. Such Latin-American contemporary political phenomena as the dominant position of the executive and the resulting weakness of the legislature and the judiciary, the lack of any real local self-government, the tendency to depend upon outside elements to solve problems, and the excessive red tape and burdensome bureaucracy may then be convincingly explained as resulting, if only in part, from habits and traditions established by colonial domination.

BIBLIOGRAPHY

Altamira y Crevea, Rafael, and others, *Contribuciones a la historia municipal de América,* Mexico, 1951.

Arboleda Llorente, José María, *El indio en la colonia,* Bogotá, 1948.

Ayala, Francisco J., *Iglesia y estado en las leyes de Indias,* Seville, 1949.

Bagú, Sergio, *Economía de la sociedad colonial,* Buenos Aires, 1949.

Bourne, Edward Gaylord, *Spain in America, 1450–1580,* New York, Harper, 1904.

Cunningham, C. H., *The Audiencia in the Spanish Colonies as Illustrated by the Audiencia of Manila, 1583–1800,* Berkeley, Calif., University of California Press, 1919.

Fisher, Lillian Estelle, *The Intendant System in Spanish America,* Berkeley, Calif., University of California Press, 1929.

———, *Viceregal Administration in the Spanish American Colonies,* Berkeley, Calif., University of California Press, 1926.

Haring, Clarence H., *The Spanish Empire in America,* New York, Oxford University Press, 1947.

———, *Trade and Navigation between Spain and the Indies in the Time of the Hapsburgs,* Cambridge, Mass., Harvard University Press, 1918.

Lanning, John Tate, *Academic Culture in the Spanish Colonies,* New York, Oxford University Press, 1940.

Mecham, J. Lloyd, *Church and State in Latin America,* Chapel Hill, N.C., The University of North Carolina Press, 1934.

Miranda, Jose, *Las ideas y las instituciones políticas mexicanas (1521–1820),* Mexico, 1951.

Moses, Bernard, *The Establishment of Spanish Rule in America,* New York, Putnam, 1907.

Ots Capdequí, José María, *El estado español en las Indias,* Mexico, 1941.

———, *Las instituciones sociales de la América española en el período colonial,* La Plata, 1934.

Pereyra, Carlos, *La obra de España en América,* Madrid, 1920.

Priestley, Herbert Ingram, *José de Gálves, Visitor-General of New Spain, 1765–1771,* Berkeley, Calif., University of California Press, 1916.

Ruíz Guinazú, Enrique, *La magistratura indiana,* Buenos Aires, 1916.

Simpson, Lesley Byrd, *The Encomienda in New Spain,* Berkeley, Calif., University of California Press, 1950.

Smith, Robert Sidney, *The Spanish Merchant Guild. A History of the Consulado, 1250–1700,* Durham, N.C., Duke University Press, 1940.

Zavala, Silvio, *Filosofía de la conquista,* Mexico, 1947.

———, *New Viewpoints on the Spanish Colonization of America,* Philadelphia, University of Pennsylvania Press, 1943.

Chapter 3: COLONIAL INSTITUTIONS OF PORTUGAL

In 1500, a fleet under the command of Admiral Pedro Alvarez Cabral sailed from Lisbon to continue the enterprise begun by Vasco de Gama and to establish more firmly the Portuguese domination of India. Whether by designs not yet fully known or by reason of a plan to avoid the storms then supposed to frequent the Cape of Good Hope, the fleet sailed westward across the Atlantic. On April 22 land was sighted, and thus, "accidentally," Brazil was discovered.[1]

Cabral took possession of the land and continued his voyage to India, after sending one ship back to Portugal with the report of his "discovery." Although subsequent expeditions explored the coast of Brazil, Portugal, with its energy absorbed in the colonization and exploitation of the Orient, neglected its American possession for some thirty years. Its public enemies and competitors and private adventurers of various nationalities had by 1530 prowled along the coast of Brazil in search of wealth or places of possible settlement. The corsairs of the French, half traders and half pirates, were perhaps the most persistent of the interlopers. The Portuguese government took action in 1530 and sent Martím Affonso de Sousa in command of a strong expedition to oust them. In 1532, Sousa established the first permanent Portuguese settlement in the bay of São Vicente, known today as Santos. While Sousa was in São Vicente, John III made the decision to colonize the entire Brazilian coast and projected in 1533 the system of captaincies (*capitanías*) as the means of accomplishing the plan.

The Donatario System

By the first donation, the coast was divided into fifteen captaincies, which were distributed among twelve of the leading noblemen. Each received land extending 50 leagues along the shore and indefinitely to the west or to the boundary marked by the Treaty of Tordesillas. The *donatarios* or grantees were invested with economic and political powers. These powers were of a feudal nature, similiar to those in vogue in the Azores Islands, and were to be transmitted through hereditary succession.

[1] Jonathas Serrano, *História do Brasil* (Rio de Janeiro, 1931). In this work account is taken of the speculations as to the objective of this voyage.

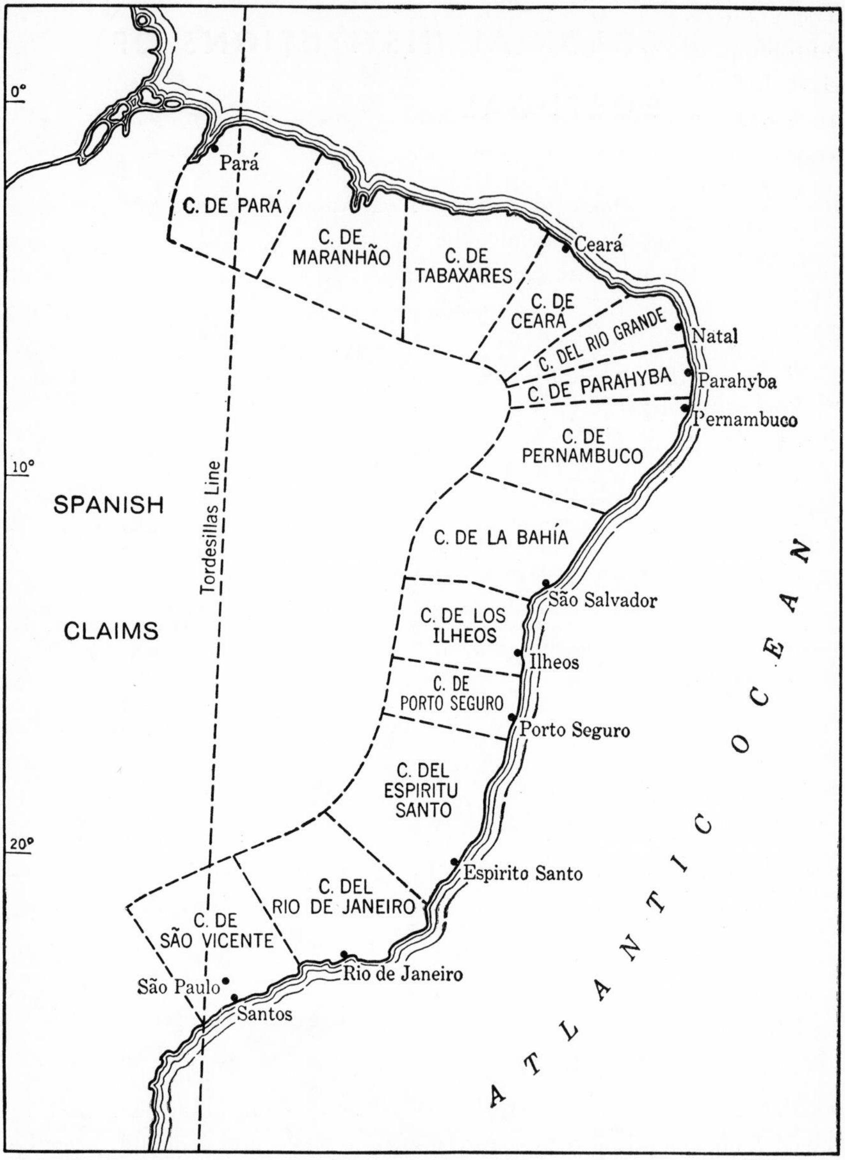

Figure 8. The *capitanías* of Brazil. SOURCE: John Francis Bannon, *History of the Americas,* New York, McGraw-Hill, 1952, vol. I, p. 136.

The grantees were also governors, empowered to charter towns, to administer justice, and to bestow land grants. They were authorized to enslave Indians and to sell a number of them in Lisbon; they were given 10 leagues of territory along the coast as personal estates. In return they assumed the obligation to defend and colonize their *capitanías* on their own account. All powers not specifically granted to them in the charters were reserved to the crown. In some cases these charters contained rights reserved to the colonists. For example, the territories of the captaincies were "places of asylum," and no person taking refuge there could be prosecuted for previous crimes.

By 1549 many things combined to rouse Portugal to a clearer perception of its responsibilities toward Brazil. The captaincy system had failed to accomplish the purposes for which it had been created, because of the territorial extension of the grants, the scattered settlements, the lack of mutual defense, and liability to attack by the enemy—the Indian and the foreign freebooter. Few of the grantees had the means and resources needed for such an enterprise. Some of them did not even attempt colonization of their captaincies; some others tried and failed. The distance from Portugal and the lack of a coordinating center which could direct the colonizing effort were also factors which contributed to the failure. In spite of all these difficulties, some grantees established proprietary colonies and laid foundations of certain institutions which endured. However, the captaincy system was considered a failure, and in 1549 the crown decided to abolish most of the political rights of the *donatarios*. It was decided to name a governor general to whom these political powers were transferred. The territorial divisions of the country were maintained. The grantees who had been partially successful were allowed to retain most of their economic rights. In the future new captaincies were to be added, and the surviving features of the system were retained until the eighteenth century.

There are those who have found in the captaincy system the germs of the federative principle in Brazil. Oliveira Lima sees the fundamental principle remaining more or less operative during the colonial era and even after independence, and he considers that efforts and policies in favor of centralization failed to destroy these territorial divisions and to induce the people to forget the tradition of autonomy associated with them.[2] Those who have shared this view pointed to the facts that (1)

[2] Manuel de Oliveira Lima, *The Evolution of Brazil Compared with That of Spanish and Anglo-Saxon America* (Stanford, Calif., Stanford University Press, 1914), pp. 55–56.

each of the captaincies lived its own life, more or less independent of its neighbors and with little interference from the royal representatives long after there were no *donatarios* left in Brazil; and (2) the local administrators of the captaincies maintained their independence of the governor general or viceroy.

The Governor General

In accordance with the new scheme the captaincy of Bahia was bought to serve as seat of the central government. Thomé de Souza, a talented administrator with long experience in Asia and Africa, was the first governor general. Other officials were appointed to complete the reorganization of the colonial government: a chief judge (*ouvidor geral*) in charge of justice, a superintendent of finance (*provedor mor*) in charge of tax collection and fiscal administration, and a military official (*capitão mor*) entrusted with coastal defense. These offices continued to be the important branches of colonial administration through most of the colonial era.

The powers of the governor general, derived from the king, were to secure cooperation of all the captaincies in common defense, to curb abuses by the *donatarios,* to act as the king's fiscal agent, and to mediate between the colonists and the captains.

Labor System

The labor supply was perhaps the most difficult problem. The native population of the Portuguese domain was at a different stage of development from that of the Spanish possessions of Peru and Mexico. The Brazilian Indians, whether belonging to the Tupi-Guarani linguistic family who inhabited the coast or to the Tapuias of the interior, were at a nomadic level of civilization. They were not organized in "empires" as were the Indians of Mexico or Peru, and there were in Brazil no evidences of the "city culture" with an elaborate social and political organization like that found in some Spanish areas.[3] As it has often been said, the Spanish conquest was facilitated by the existence of a native ruling class which already exercised autocratic control. The Portuguese did not find the same advantageous conditions in Brazil.

They were also handicapped by the smallness of the population of the mother country. The population of Portugal in the fifteenth century has

[3] Alexander Marchant, "The Unity of Brazilian History," in T. Lynn Smith and A. Marchant (eds.), *Brazil: Portrait of Half a Continent* (New York, Dryden, 1951), pp. 41–42.

been estimated at about one million inhabitants. As Gilberto Freyre says, the Portuguese counterbalanced this weakness with their remarkable mobility and their capacity to adapt themselves to new environments. The encouragement of the mixture of races and the tolerance of foreigners in the population afford some explanation of the ability of the Portuguese colonists to adapt themselves readily to different conditions. At any rate, in Brazil, Portugal again demonstrated the aptitude of its people for living in harmony with alien peoples.[4]

Portugal transferred to Brazil its concept of labor. The institution of slavery had long existed in a country which also was actively engaged in the slave trade. In America the Indians were to the Portuguese a part of the wealth to be exploited. Slave hunting was carried on with skill and cruelty. When disease and much fighting decimated the tribes which inhabited the coast, the Portuguese settlers went after the Indian in the interior. Portugal's policy with regard to enslavement of the Indian was not so clearly defined as that of Spain. It was only during the period of Spanish domination of Portugal that Indian slaves were declared free, but even then emancipation was not generally enforced.

The Paulistas, or natives of São Paulo, sold Indian slaves to the agricultural areas. They penetrated the interior, and brought back Indians who were distributed along the coast. The number of Indians enslaved by the Paulistas reached the hundred thousands, according to accounts of the Jesuits.

The Negro slave, however, was always preferred by the Brazilian planter. The government encouraged this importation, since it controlled trading posts (*feitorías*) on the coast of Africa and the trade was profitable. The Portuguese legislation concerning Negro slavery, like that of Spain, was humanitarian in many respects. It made emancipation possible, with the result of a large free Negro population in Brazil.

Society

A society evolved which was hybrid in its composition, and agrarian in occupation, one which utilized slavery as its economic base. This society developed more by reason of individual and family initiative than by direction and control of government, and it was dominated by the rural or semirural family. This colonial family combined a variety of social and economic functions which included that of "political command in the

[4] Gilberto Freyre, *The Masters and the Slaves: A Study in the Development of Brazilian Civilization* (New York, Knopf, 1946), p. 24.

form of an oligarchy." This was a stratified society with social distinctions similar to the ones developed in Spanish America but distinguished by the lack of any bitter racial prejudices. Calógeras mentions the following classes: the *reinões,* born in Portugal; those other Portuguese born in Brazil and equivalent to the Spanish American *criollo;* the mestizos, or half-breeds; those with an Indian-Negro or Indian-mulatto mixture; and, at the bottom of the social scale, the Indian and Negro slaves.[5] A free proletariat composed of Negroes, Indians, poor whites and mixtures may be added.

In Brazil the enormous estates of the interior were ruled by the landowners from their mansions (*casas grandes*) very much in the feudal manner. In the sugar-raising areas the sugar mill (*engenho*) was a feature of the estate. The great planters (*senhores d'engenho*), like those of Pernambuco, constituted a colonial aristocracy. Each *engenho* was a patriarchal and self-sustaining community. About the manor house there was always a village containing all the workshops and other facilities that the sugar mill required.[6]

The Church

Six Jesuits came to Brazil with Thomé de Souza. Their activities and those to be associated with them exerted a profound influence on the country. The Jesuit group was headed by Father Manuel de Nobrega, of whom a historian said "there was no individual to whose talents Brazil is so greatly and permanently indebted."[7] The Jesuit missionaries utilized education as the cornerstone of their system, and they accomplished the task of conversion of the Indians. They established numerous schools for both races. Despite opposition among the settlers they carried on a campaign against enslavement of the Indians. Thus the regular clergy aided greatly in achieving the spiritual ends of colonization. Besides the Jesuits, other orders like the Capuchins, Benedictines, Franciscans, Mercedarians, and Carmelites shared in the missionary work. State and church relations were highlighted in the question of Indian slavery by the many conflicts between settlers and missionaries, particularly the Jesuits.

The secular Church was organized in Brazil shortly after the estab-

[5] João Pandía Calógeras, *A History of Brazil* (Chapel Hill, N.C., The University of North Carolina Press, 1939), p. 26.

[6] Roy Nash, *The Conquest of Brazil* (New York, Harcourt, Brace, 1926), p. 125.

[7] Robert Southey, *History of Brazil* (3 vols., London, Longman, Hurst, Rees, Orme, and Brown, 1810–1819), vol. I, p. 53.

lishment of a central seat of government. About the same time, the crown obtained the rights of patronage. Thus, the Portuguese government exercised control of all ecclesiastical personnel as had its Spanish counterpart. In contrast with the Spanish colonial Church, however, the religious establishments in Brazil, with the exception of the Jesuit order, did not represent a comparable economic force. Ecclesiastical policy in Brazil seemed to have been more lax than in the Spanish Indies, and there are not many evidences that sustained efforts were made to assure religious unity by the exclusion of heretics and non-Catholics. There was never set up in Brazil a separate Tribunal of the Inquisition, and inquisitorial authority was not seriously exercised in the colony.

We might conclude with Oliveira Lima that "the pleasant memories of the eminent services rendered by the clergy to Brazilian civilization might well account for the generous treatment given the Church at the time of its separation from the State dictated by the republican provisional government in 1890."[8]

Foreign Influences and Intervention

Thomé de Souza and his successors up to 1572 had to concern themselves with the problem of keeping out foreign intruders. The French were the most determined in their colonizing efforts. In 1555 they established a settlement on an island in the bay of Rio de Janeiro. The Portuguese were not able to expel them until Mem de Sá, third governor of Brazil, assisted by the Jesuits, organized a successful attack. The failure of the French settlement in Rio did not prevent further French incursions during the next fifty years; at the end of that time, however, they were terminated. The English were also interested in Brazil and were active in trading along the coast. At times they attacked Portuguese settlements, but they were never successful as colonizers except in British Guiana.

A new era began for Brazil in 1580 with the union of Portugal and Spain during the reign of Philip II. Philip was satisfied to govern Portugal and its colonies through Portuguese laws and Portuguese officials. The most important governmental reform of the period of Spanish domination was the creation in 1604 of the Conselho da India, a counterpart of the Council of the Indies in Spain. It prepared the laws for Brazil, supervised colonial affairs, and exercised judicial functions. Brazil gained some benefit from Spanish rule by expanding its frontier at the expense

[8] Manuel de Oliveira Lima, *Formación histórica de la nacionalidad brasileña* (Madrid, 1918), p. 35.

of Spain. On the other hand, the destruction of the Armada in 1588 increased greatly the danger of foreign attack against the colony.

The union with Spain involved Portugal in a long conflict with the Dutch which was to have significant consequences for Brazil. Dutch capitalists established the Dutch West India Company with the purpose of organizing attacks on the Spanish commercial monopoly in America. The place selected for the Company's first enterprise was Brazil. The first invasion, against Bahia, ended in failure; but a new attempt, this time on Pernambuco, in 1630, was successful. It marked the beginning of Dutch control over the richest area of Brazil, extending from the São Francisco River almost to the Amazon. The Dutch remained in control of this region for almost twenty-five years. Joan Mauritz, Count of Nassau-Siegen, the first Dutch governor, was a statesman and administrator who, during the seven years of his rule, introduced important administrative reforms. He rebuilt the city of Olinda and encouraged trade by forming the tradesmen into companies and removing many commercial restrictions. A reorganization of the sugar industry was undertaken with success. Since Holland was at that time perhaps the leading trading nation in the world, Brazil benefited considerably from its direct ties with the best markets of Europe. Brazilians were given a share in the tasks of government, although higher administrative posts were reserved for the Dutch. Joan Mauritz followed a liberal policy as to religion, giving the Catholic Church freedom in religious matters and in the administration of its property. His policy of religious toleration attracted many Portuguese Jews to Pernambuco.

Brazilians outside the Dutch area, and some within, were hostile. Symptoms of unrest within were evident as early as 1641. A few years later the Dutch faced a formidable rebellion led by Brazilian planters and supported by the clergy, and later in 1654 they were expelled. This war of the Brazilians for independence from foreign domination had far-reaching effects. It was an opportunity for a union of whites, Indians, and blacks against a common enemy, and in their common struggle germinated the seed of autonomy. It was not Portugal that fought against Holland but Brazil, and Brazilians of all colors and races participated in this war of liberation. After the final victory, representatives of the four classes of the population were decorated and given titles. Portuguese rule was restored but without much help or encouragement from the mother country.

Despite the local initiative in the war against the Dutch and the participation of the several classes in it, few changes in colonial administration occurred. The territories recovered from the Dutch were formed into two areas, Maranhão and Pará, each under the rule of a *capitão mor.* The tendency during the period was toward a stricter administration and the development of greater power by the central government in Bahia. The most important effect was in the development of sentiments of self-confidence and pride.

Local Government

In many respects Brazilian local governments resembled the Spanish-American municipalities. These corporate bodies were, in their character and to a certain extent in their composition, representative, especially in the early colonial period. At the time of the colonization the cities in Portugal had lost privileges formerly secured in the wars against the Moslems, but in Brazil the municipal corporation was endowed, for a time, with some elements of autonomy which resisted the authority of *donatarios,* governors, and viceroys. Like the Spanish-American *cabildos,* the Brazilian municipalities varied in prestige, in importance, and in strength or weakness. Their "democratic" or "undemocratic" character is again debatable.

The governing body was the *senado da câmara* or city council composed of lifetime, or hereditary, or elected officials, who were the chief merchants, landowners, and professional people of the community. This body, which enjoyed extensive powers in many local affairs, derived its main influence from the practice of sending representatives to Lisbon to make their desires known to the king and to strive for desired legislation or to complain against royal officials. Freyre and some other students of Brazil emphasize the power of the rural landlords (*senhores de engenho*) as opposed to the lesser power of the municipal councils, but they suggest that the situation was different in the new population centers created by the gold rush where municipal authority had more substance.

Another form of local government originated from the powers exercised by the *capitão mor.* These officials, originally naval commanders, later became heads of political districts on land. They became assistants to the governors of the captaincies and municipalities and were endowed with wide administrative and military authority. Though their powers were specified in instructions, they disregarded the legal limitations. They were charged with enforcement of the law, acted as judges in the levying of the militia, and furthermore, were given extensive economic powers. The *capitãos mores* interfered in court trials, meddled in ecclesiastical affairs, and acted as the despotic rulers of their communities, thereby becoming the real political bosses of their districts. A third form of local government was that of the Indian villages and missions controlled by the Jesuits or other religious orders.

Economic and Political Frontiers

It will contribute to the understanding of changes in governmental institutions which were introduced in a later period to examine some nonpolitical factors bearing upon them. It is in order, therefore, to mention briefly the expansionist process as it involved the geographical and economic frontiers of Brazil.

The Portuguese, during the sixteenth century settled only on the coastal areas. The march westward and the penetration of the Brazilian backlands or interior (*sertão*) began on a full scale in the next century. From the north, starting from Pernambuco or Bahia, slave hunters, prospectors, and missionaries led the march toward the west, occupying the valleys of the São Francisco and Parahiba Rivers. In the south, São Paulo became the center of expansion, and the Paulista mestizos were the pioneers of the frontier movement. As it is often said, the expansion of Brazil was a movement to bring the economic frontiers of the country to its political boundaries.[9]

This penetration was accomplished by the *entradas* and the *bandeiras.* The first were exploring, slave-hunting, or mine-prospecting expeditions which operated not too far from the coast. The term *bandeiras* is generally used to designate the expeditions which affected, during the seventeenth and eighteenth centuries, the conquest and occupation of territories already explored. The discovery of gold in Minas in 1693 provided a new impetus to the penetration of the interior; the prime motive had been, until then, slave hunting. Further expansion occurred at the expense of Spain. When the Treaty of Madrid was concluded between Spain and Portugal, it established approximately the configuration of present Brazil. *Bandeiras* and Jesuit missions had almost tripled the extent of the colony. Later, in 1777, the Treaty of San Ildefonso confirmed these boundaries with the exception of some Portuguese losses in the south.

[9] J. F. Normano, *Brazil: A Study of Economic Types* (Chapel Hill, N.C., The University of North Carolina Press, 1935), p. 2. The best work on Brazil's moving frontier is perhaps Basilio de Magalhaes' *Expansão geográphica do Brasil colonial* (São Paulo, 1935).

Brazilian economy in the colonial period experienced marked fluctuations with consequent effects on the political and social systems. During the seventeenth century Brazil was the greatest producer of sugar in the world, but later it lost its supremacy to the West Indies and Europe. The

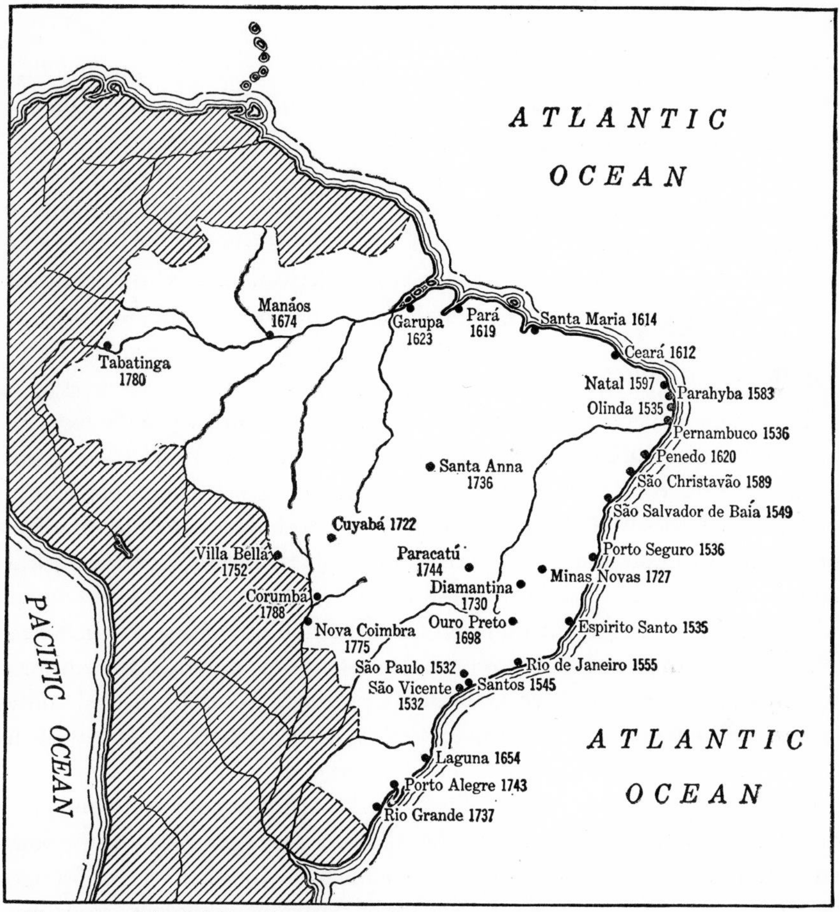

Figure 9. Colonial Brazil. SOURCE: John Francis Bannon, *History of the Americas,* New York, McGraw-Hill, 1952, vol. I, p. 329.

decline of the sugar industry and the discovery of gold and diamonds in the interior were causes of a shift in economic strength from Pernambuco and Bahia to the mining regions of Minas Gerais. Thousands of people, Portuguese and foreign, came every year into the mining area, and this great immigration populated a region which previously had been sparsely occupied. A civil war broke out between Paulistas and immigrants from

Europe (*emboabas*) which was won by the newcomers and led to political changes such as the creation of new captaincies general in São Paulo and Minas Gerais.

The gold rush continued when other rich mines were discovered in Matto Grosso and in Goiaz. An even more important discovery took place in 1729 when diamonds were found along the tributaries of the São Francisco River. New and populous cities resulted from the sudden influx of immigrants; some of the agricultural areas and seaboard towns suffered a decline in population.

The change in leading products moved the economic frontier of the country during the colonial period, just as it was to move it again during the independent era. The sugar and plantation economy had been the basis of economic leadership of Bahia and Pernambuco. This status was lost as a result of the discovery of gold and diamonds.

Commercial Policy

The trade policy of Portugal was framed in accordance with mercantilist ideas of the period. Brazilwood, tobacco, salt, diamonds, and other products were royal monopolies, and industries which could have competed with those of the mother country were forbidden. In spite of these restrictions, certain aspects of this policy were relatively liberal. Until 1649, any Portuguese ship was allowed to go to Brazil, and foreigners were allowed to engage in trade on the condition of paying certain taxes. The union with Spain in 1580 brought restrictions and effective enforcement of such legislation with the development of contraband trade on a large scale. Smuggling, in turn, led to the establishment of a convoy or fleet system by the government.

The need of Portugal for friends and allies after regaining its independence from Spain resulted in a breakdown of the exclusionist policy and in the granting of important commercial concessions to foreign nations, especially to England. The basic principle, however, remained unchanged; and Brazilian trade continued to be channeled through the mother country until the royal family established its residence in Brazil in 1808.

Eighteenth-century Changes

The newly developed mining wealth of Brazil caused further changes in administration. The establishment of the captaincies general of São Paulo and Minas Gerais, already mentioned, was followed by the setting up of additional territorial units as the population increased. At the middle of the century it was evident that the center of political life had shifted to the south, and the colonial government became mainly concerned with the economic development of the growing captaincies of Goiaz, Matto Grosso, and Minas Gerais. A step was taken to unify Brazil in administration. The instrument of unification was the Act of 1763 which raised the colony to the status of a viceroyalty and established the new capital in Rio de Janeiro. This act resolved any doubts by declaring the supremacy of viceregal authority over that of the provincial governors. Thus, the adminstrative shift from Bahia to Rio de Janeiro, the outlet for the products of the mines, completed the cycle started by the opening up of the interior.[10] The change had been preceded by the creation of a ministry in Portugal in charge of colonial affairs.

This unification of Brazil as well as all the reforms introduced in colonial government in the period 1750 to 1777 were undertaken under the administration of the able Marquis de Pombal, minister of King Joseph I.[11] Many writers have speculated as to the possibility that several nations might have risen in Portuguese America instead of one had Pombal not adopted these unification measures.

The reforms adopted were also designed to improve the financial and judicial phases of administration in an effort to eradicate corruption in government. A new court or Relação, patterned after the tribunal in Bahia, was set up in Rio in 1751. The jurisdiction of this court extended over thirteen vast and important districts in the south. At the same time, Pombal regained the captaincies for the crown by buying them from their owners. Compensation was given in the form of quitrents or lands. A new compilation of laws (1754–1757) resulted in a code of thirty-nine volumes. The practice of three-year appointments of governors and other high colonial officers was ended.

In the field of trade, the concept of the monopolistic trading company returned to favor. Pombal himself created the Pará-Maranhão Company in 1755. This company promoted the rapid growth and development of products like rice and cotton in that region. A similar company was created for Pernambuco and Parahiba, but it conflicted with local interests and became extremely unpopular. These companies were created as parts of a serious effort to regain for Portugal a share of the considerable pro-

[10] Calógeras, *op. cit.,* p. 17.

[11] For a good treatment of Pombal's administration, see Antonio de Sousa Pedroso Carnaxide, *O Brasil na administração pombalina* (São Paulo, 1940).

fits made by English merchants who had long held many advantages in the colonial trade. Both companies were abolished in 1779 after Pombal's fall from power. The abolition of the system of convoy in 1765 was a move in the direction of more freedom of trade.

The century witnessed a reform which was designed to equalize all castes and colors in one body politic. The emancipation proclamation of Pombal in 1756 prohibited Indian slavery under any pretexts and specifically stated that Indians were to be governed by the same laws applying to all Portuguese subjects. Certain features of this proclamation are cited as evidence of Pombal's intention eventually to abolish all forms of slavery in Brazil, including Negro slavery, which was abolished in Portugal in 1773. The measure practically disbanded the Jesuit missions, a step which was completed with the banishment of the Jesuit order from Portugal and the colonies in 1759. The legal equalization of the Indian did not free him, however, from more refined forms of exploitation.

Comparison of Portuguese and Spanish Institutions

From this brief analysis of Brazilian colonial institutions it may seem evident that, although the Portuguese evolved an imperial system, it presented a far less systematic uniformity in patterns of administration than the one used by Spain in its colonies. It might also be said that the Portuguese system, while affording greater flexibility than its Spanish counterpart, was proportionately less efficient.

In fact, the two systems presented some similarities which have often been noted. In Portugal, as in Spain, legislation was enacted which was found to be impractical in America and was ignored by the colonial officialdom. An extensive bureaucracy developed in both empires. A virtual monopoly of higher and responsible government posts was held by the *peninsulares* and *reinões* in both cases.

However, the differences are striking. Some have called attention to the limited cultural development of colonial Brazil as compared with the Spanish colonies; others have pointed to the differences in the development of cities and towns or have stressed the seemingly stronger substance of the municipalities in Spanish America.[12]

For one thing, Portuguese colonization was much less characterized by the religious motive. Willingness to live with the Indian, to assimilate him, and to teach and convert him to the true faith were qualities of the Spaniard. The idea of religious assimilation of the Indian was also felt

[12] Marchant, *op cit.,* pp. 42–47.

by the Portuguese, but it was a much less driving motive in government. It is significant that Jews played an important role in Brazil's colonial development. This element was viewed by the Portuguese in a tolerant manner, while it always encountered the hostility of the Spaniards. In the colonization of Brazil there was a franker admission and toleration of enslaving practices. This was accompanied by a candid encouragement and acceptance of miscegenation.

Portuguese colonial society showed less discrimination of either a legal or a social character based on blood stratification than in the Spanish colonies. This should not be construed as meaning that colonial Brazil did not have a class society but rather as meaning that there existed an informal and social discrimination, rather than a systematic and legalized plan. In fact, the Portuguese recognized many shades of racial mixtures, and terms related to the degree of these mixtures are more numerous and elaborate in the Portuguese language than in Spanish.

In their commercial policy the Portuguese trade system was far less exclusive than that of the Spanish and gave much more ready access to foreigners, especially British nationals. The long-standing alliances between England and Portugal might well account for this fact.

BIBLIOGRAPHY

Buarque de Hollanda, Sergio, *Raizes do Brasil,* 2d ed., Rio de Janeiro, 1948.

Calmon, Pedro, *Espírito da sociedade colonial,* São Paulo, 1935.

Calógeras, João Pandía, *A History of Brazil,* trans. and ed. by P. A. Martin, Chapel Hill, N.C., The University of North Carolina Press, 1939.

Freyre, Gilberto, *The Masters and the Slaves: A Study in the Development of Brazilian Civilization* (originally published as *Casa Grande e Senzala*), New York, Knopf, 1946.

Hill, Lawrence F. (ed.), *Brazil,* Berkeley, Calif., University of California Press, 1947.

Magalhães, Basilio de, *Expansão geográfica do Brasil colonial,* Rio de Janeiro, 1935.

Malheiro Dias, Carlos, *Historia da colonização portuguesa do Brasil,* 2 vols., Oporto, 1921.

Morison, S. E., *Portuguese Voyages to America in the Fifteenth Century,* Cambridge, Mass., Harvard University Press, 1940.

Nash, Roy, *The Conquest of Brazil,* New York, Harcourt, Brace, 1926.

Oliveira Lima, Manuel de, *The Evolution of Brazil Compared with That of Spanish and Anglo-Saxon America,* Stanford, Calif., Stanford University Press, 1914.

———, *Formación histórica de la nacionalidad brasileña,* Madrid, 1918.

Oliveira Vianna, F. J., *Evolução do povo brasileiro,* 3d ed., São Paulo, 1938.

Ricardo, Cassiano, *Marcha para Oeste,* 2d ed., 2 vols., Rio de Janeiro, 1942.

Smith, T. Lynn, and A. Marchant (eds.), *Brazil: Portrait of Half a Continent,* New York, Dryden, 1951.

Southey, Robert, *History of Brazil,* 3 vols., London, Longman, Hurst, Rees, Orme, and Brown, 1810–1819.

Varnhagen, Francisco Adolpho de, *História geral do Brasil antes de sua separação e independencia de Portugal,* 3d ed., 5 vols., São Paulo, n.d.

Wernek Sodre, Nelson, *Formação da sociedade brasileira,* São Paulo, 1944.

Chapter 4: POLITICAL INDEPENDENCE

During the period from 1810 to 1826, the Spanish and Portuguese empires in America, which had lasted for three centuries, were broken up; Spain lost all its continental possessions and Portugal lost Brazil. Earlier France had lost Haiti, but during these years, in 1821, the island, previously known as Española, was united under a single government. These momentous events had causes, both immediate and ultimate, which differed in influence and effect upon regions and localities. The ultimate causes refer to discontent and criticisms that were of long standing; the immediate ones were current and precipitated the wars of independence. Both sets of causes of the dissolution of the Spanish empire will be summarized first. Those which led to the independence of Brazil and Haiti will be treated afterward.

1. One of the long-standing causes of dissatisfaction with Spanish rule was the antagonism between the European-born Spaniards and the creole class. A virtual monopoly of the higher officers was enjoyed by the *peninsulares*. The viceroys, captains general, governors, the upper fiscal agents, the bishops and the upper clergy, the military officials above the rank of colonel, and the special investigators were with few exceptions from this class. Its members, especially those who were officials, enjoyed social privileges that were invidious. This system left only the lower brackets of official service open to creoles, who found barriers in their way, subordination as their role, and inferiority their rank in society. This cause of discontent was significant, especially in South America, since leadership in the revolution came from the creoles.

2. There were long-standing economic grievances due to the extreme form of mercantilism that was adopted. The system favored large profits on a small turnover which, without supplying commodity demands or satisfying commercial interests, artificially increased prices. The inconveniences and indirection of communication in matters of trade were sanctioned and continued in order to have relative ease in control, inspection, and defense; but they tended to place legalized commerce in a strait jacket. Smuggling and contraband were made inevitable. A taxation system was evolved which was both inefficient and inequitable. Charges of corruption in fiscal administration were probably exaggerated and on

occasion were unsubstantiated but they were recurrent. Although Spain might reasonably have claimed leadership in the reform of mercantilism in the eighteenth century the reforms moderated and altered the system but did not abolish it. When the struggle for independence came there were outspoken charges that the commercial system was designed for the exploitation of the colonies in benefit of the mother country. The very reforms adopted probably contributed to the consciousness of economic grievances. Some of the colonies predominantly agricultural or pastoral in their economic pursuits were neglected as compared to others having rich mineral resources. Two of these "neglected" areas, La Plata (Argentina) and Venezuela, became foci of revolution.

3. The political, social, and ecclesiastical system, with its severe restraints on liberty, its censorship, its inequalities, its stratification of society, and its antiquated practices, was subject to the charge of tyranny. As to the reality of this tyranny, opinions differ now, and they differed at the time of the wars of independence. It is a fact, however, that those who drew up declarations of grievances indicted Spain for despotic misrule.

4. The mother country was charged with responsibility for keeping the colonists in intellectual isolation and ignorance. Despite the large number of universities and educational establishments founded and operated, and despite some literary and scientific activities by colonials, Spain had encircled its empire with a sort of "iron curtain" to shut out influences thought to be inimical to orthodoxy and loyalty. To some writers the expulsion of the Jesuits (1767), who were leaders in education, was both a political and cultural blunder, whereby a probable support of imperial loyalty was converted into a critic.

5. The legislation and policies of the Bourbon kings and Spain's participation in the Enlightenment of the eighteenth century led to a relaxation of certain restrictions. The censorship became less strict, travel abroad by colonials was permitted, and there was some introduction (sporadic and clandestine as it was) of foreign thought. Certain foreign influences worked to cause a change in colonial sentiments. The example of the United States in the attainment of its independence with outside aid, despite the opposition of the foremost naval power in the world, was an influence of great weight. The political ideas professed and the institutions adopted in the United States were also strong influences, but they were perhaps secondary to the force of example. The political ideas and theories of the French Revolution and of the Napoleonic period were attractive and provocative sources of revolutionary thought, upon which

many were to draw. Great Britain not only provided its rich political lore, but by many was regarded as a possible ally and support in obtaining independence. Several of the future leaders in the struggles for independence—including Miranda, Bolívar, San Martín, O'Higgins, Nariño, the Carrera brothers, and Belgrano—had traveled and studied abroad. They and others of similar experience were media, in public or in secret, of the communication of foreign thought and of criticism of the colonial system.

6. There were precursory movements, some taking on the character of insurrections or revolts, some that of conspiracy, and some that of incitement to a war for independence. It would be a matter of controversy as to when these movements began, since some writers would project them far back in colonial history. For our purposes, the period from 1780 to 1810 is taken because it is immediately previous to the active struggles for independence and because it coincides with the career of the man who was called "the Precursor," Francisco de Miranda. During these years he made repeated efforts to enlist foreign aid in revolutionizing the Spanish colonies in America and at least two efforts to incite revolution. The story of his travels, his adventures, his mission, his near successes, and his vain efforts to incite revolt is a sort of epic. Although he was unsuccessful in his plans, he made many of his fellow countrymen and some foreign governments aware of the grievances of the colonies and conscious of Latin America as a factor of the future. In addition, some would list the uprising of Indians in Peru under the leadership of Tupac Amaru (1780), the conspiracies such as that of Gual and España in Venezuela (1797), and the influences of the expeditions of the British to Uruguay and Argentina (1806–1807).

Undoubtedly there were grounds for complaints and discontent on the part of mestizos and other mixblood people and on the part of Indians, although these groups and the Negro slaves were relatively inarticulate. There would have been some doubt as to who their real enemy would be—whether the Spaniard or the creole.

A continuing controversy has been that between the critics and the defenders of Spanish colonial system, between the so-called "black legend" and the "white."[1] On the one side, it has been claimed that Spain in the conquest of the New World conducted a Christian crusade and accom-

[1] Cf. J. Juderías y Loyot, *La leyenda negra; estudios del concepto de España en el extranjero* (Barcelona, 1917); and *La leyenda negra y la verdad histórica* (Madrid, 1914); J. V. Lastarria, *Investigaciones sobre la influencia social de la conquista i del sistema colonial de los españoles en Chile,* in *Obras completas,* 1st

plished a work of civilization by means of sound legislation and by good administration and practical social policy. By the other side of the polemics, starting with Las Casas, it was held that the conquest was a brutal work of violence and exploitation, that the good features of legislation were more often than not unenforced, and that the imperial and local administrations were faulty and retarded progress. This dispute—probably without the possibility of scientific resolution, since impressive data may be assembled in support of each contention—has continued to our own times.

Such fundamental causes of discontent were not at work uniformly throughout the Spanish empire. In Argentina and Venezuela, for example, the antagonism between creole and Spaniard was strongly active, whereas this irritation was either absent or weak in Chile. Again, economic discontent was widespread in Argentina and Venezuela, but this factor was not of paramount concern in Chile and New Granada. The Indian and his interests were to play a significant and tragic part in the early phases of the conflict in Mexico, but they were of relative unimportance in South America. Again, in Mexico, the Church and clerical personalities were highly important throughout the revolution, but in South America the Church did not have an equally decisive influence on the course of these events. The unevenness in effect of the causes of discontent may have contributed to the regional character of the struggles for independence.

The immediate causes giving occasion or precipitating revolutions for independence affected both empires simultaneously, but with quite different results. The events and influences of the French Revolution, the European coalition and intervention in France, the wars and diplomatic policies of Napoleon, the international blockades, and the Continental system were factors in the background. There were repercussions of the revolutionary era in the New World—such as the transplanting of some revolutionary institutions in the French colonies, the insurrections in Haiti, the loss of Trinidad to Great Britain in 1797, the loss of Louisiana to France in 1801, and further relaxation of Spanish commercial restrictions. Then, by way of enforcement of the Continental system, there was developed Napoleon's great design with reference to the Iberian

---

ser., vol. 7 (Santiago, 1906–1909); C. Parra Pérez, *El régimen español en Venezuela* (Madrid, 1932); Mariano Picón Salas, *De la conquista a la independencia* (Mexico, 1944).

peninsula, in which Spain was duped and victimized. By a secret clause of the Treaty of Fontainebleau (1807), Spain agreed to allow French troops the right of transit over Spanish territory in order to attack Lisbon. Should this invasion of Portugal occur and succeed, that country was to be dismembered.

In 1807, by secret agreement, the British promised to provide armed escort for the royal family and court of Portugal if removal from Lisbon to Brazil was deemed advisable. In advance of the appearance of the French troops, this dramatic and significant transfer of the royal household and of the administrative agencies of the government was undertaken. The prince regent, Dom João, and his associates arrived in Bahia in January, 1808.

The possible transfer of the seat of the Spanish monarchy to the Western Hemisphere was considered, but if the Spanish government ever seriously thought of this move, those in authority waited too long. In the meanwhile, the French policy as to Spain evolved in rather obscure stages, but the expansion of the sphere of military occupation and the declarations of the field commanders gave indications of the intervention to come. A conference was held at Bayonne, with representatives of France and Spain and with both Charles IV and his son Ferdinand in attendance. In the midst of many intrigues and scandals, and under many pressures, Charles abdicated in 1808 in favor of his then popular son. Later retracting this abdication, Charles was induced to renounce the throne and to transfer his sovereign rights to Napoleon. Ferdinand, who had been proclaimed king of Spain, was forced to endorse his father's actions and became a technical prisoner in France. On June 6, Napoleon proclaimed his brother Joseph as king of Spain and the Indies. The imposition of this intruder (*el Rey Intruso*) provoked a popular resistance which was the expression of outraged nationalism.

At first this resistance was municipal in organization, with local juntas or councils as units of authority and leadership. This action was in conformity to the ancient theory by which, in the event of such a disaster as the capture and imprisonment of the king and of invasion, the cities and their *cabildos* became residuary legatees of sovereignty, authorized to govern provisionally, to resist conquest, and to act as trustees of royal interests until the captive monarch could be restored. It was therefore with the assumption of legality that the cities organized themselves and combined to form the Junta Central Gubernativa del Reino which on January 30, 1809, was located at Seville. The central Junta declared the colonies to be integral parts of the Spanish monarchy, entitled to send deputies to Spain. This was an appeal for cooperation and aid in a joint effort in behalf of Ferdinand.

In January, 1810, the central Junta made an important and perhaps mistaken decision. It transferred its authority to a regency of five members, which was to be even less successful in resisting the French. This new agency offered further bids for colonial support. Among them were proposals of changes of status for the colonies and for colonials, promises of some measure of autonomy, and an invitation to send representation to a national parliament (Cortes). The further victories of French arms in Spain caused the regency to take refuge on the island of León in the Bay of Cádiz.

The several outbreaks of violence and the conspiracies occurring in different colonies, prematurely aimed at revolution, have given occasion for rival claims as to the time and place of the first movement for independence. The prestige of the imperial authority was on the wane because of the events that occurred in Europe after 1808, the timid and vacillating leadership of colonial governors in the last years of the continental empire, and the missionary efforts of precursors such as Miranda. Nevertheless, the spirit of loyalism and the habit of obedience were still strong. A "watchful waiting" policy, in order to ascertain the course of events in Europe, seemed to have been adopted. The central Junta of Spain was regarded as legally constituted, and it was given substantial support, especially in money and supplies. As long as it lasted, the colonies remained in a formal sense faithful, despite the fact that some groups were restive and made plans for independence. The regency was regarded in a distinctly different light. Its legitimacy was questioned, and its actions regarding the colonies were viewed with disfavor or indifference. The arrival of the news that the regency had taken refuge on the island of León and that continental Spain had been lost to the French was made the occasion in Venezuela, Argentina, Colombia, and Chile for actions out of which the wars for independence emerged. This succession of events is made clearly manifest in the proclamation issued by the provisional Junta of Caracas on April 20, 1810. This dignified statement declared that the regency was illegal and claimed the right to "erect in the bosom of these countries a system of government, . . . exercising the powers of sovereignty which have fallen upon the people, in conformity with the very principles of the ancient and wise constitution of Spain . . . ."

Thus the French invasion of Portugal and Spain and the subsequent events (1807–1810) are considered as immediate causes of crises preliminary to the launching of struggles for independence in Spanish America.

Regional Character of the Struggles for Independence

The Spanish colonies did not unite in a common effort to win independence. In certain cases, it was not clearly evident that independence was the goal. In the very beginning, with a profession of loyalty to Ferdinand VII, those who engaged in any struggle sought to substitute a local junta for the existing Spanish administration; the struggle was a local one.

The chief centers of military and political activity were located in southern South America, northern South America, and Mexico. These regions had distinct leadership, responded to different motives and principles, and fought their wars with different degrees of success. Even within these regions, unity and cooperation could not be assured. In Argentina and Paraguay, the war effort having started, there was no restoration of Spanish control. All the other countries—if such they may be called at this stage—experienced "reconquests" or restorations of Spanish control, in some cases more than once. As between these regions, there was no common time schedule for declarations of independence or for the adoption of constitutions. There were no joint negotiations for purchases of supplies and munitions or for recognition and alliances. During the decade 1810–1820, there were only casual and perfunctory diplomatic exchanges between regional powers.

Within each of the geographical areas of South America, important relations and ties were established. In the south, there was the expedition from Argentina to Paraguay in 1811, followed by a convention between the two. Much more important in consequences was the part of Argentina in the liberation of Chile, the brilliant military exploit of San Martín in the crossing of the Andes, and the cooperation of the two countries in the campaign in Peru. In the north, many ties were established between Venezuela and New Granada. One of Bolívar's great state papers, the Cartagena Manifesto of 1812, was an appeal for aid in the liberation of his country from the iron rule of Monteverde. The aid given was to be repaid later by Bolívar's difficult but decisive crossing of the northern Andes and the victory of Boyacá. Ecuador was to be liberated by the army of Bolívar. An important development in these intraregional relationships was the formation of Gran Colombia—the political union of Venezuela, New Granada, and Ecuador.

In the second decade, 1820–1830, momentous changes occurred. These may be summarized as follows: (1) the coalescence of the northern and southern movements for independence in South America following the dramatic interview of Bolívar and San Martín at Guayaquil in 1822; (2) the participation of the Colombian army in the liberation of Peru and Bolivia; (3) the negotiation of certain treaties of alliance and arbitration (1822); (4) the development of the doctrine of *uti possedetis juris* of the year 1810; (5) Latin-American consideration of President Monroe's message of 1823; and (6) the holding of the international Congress of Panama of 1826. The status of Latin-American countries was partially formalized by acts of recognition by the United States, Great Britain, and Portugal. There occurred what some have called the beginnings of Pan-Americanism.[2]

In Mexico, during the years 1808–1809, there were some indications that Mexico might have its own junta, but with a continuation in office of the existent officialdom, acting in opposition to the French and in defense of Ferdinand VII. This movement developed under the leadership of the *cabildo* of Mexico City and the towns of New Spain, with the possible cooperation of Viceroy Iturrigaray. It has been claimed that the viceroy had ambitions to head the new government, possibly with himself as monarch. The plan was opposed by the *audiencia* and the resident Spanish element. In an extraordinary event (September 15, 1808) the viceroy was deposed and replaced by Garribay, through irregular choice of the *peninsulares*. A period of confusion ensued, marked by intrigues, the activities of secret societies, changes in the viceregal office, and the development of factionalism among the loyalists. The survivors of the Valladolid conspiracy, now under the leadership of Father Miguel Hidalgo, parish priest of Dolores, early in 1810 planned a rebellion. Disregarding the *cabildo* as an institutional means of giving legality to the effort, Hildago and a small band issued on the morning of September 16, 1810, the Grito de Dolores for independence under the banner of "Our

[2] Domingo Amunátegui Solar, *La emancipación de Hispanoamérica* (Santiago, 1936); Joseph B. Lockey, *Pan Americanism; Its Beginnings* (New York, Macmillan, 1926); W. R. Shepherd, "Bolivar and the United States," *Hispanic American Historical Review,* vol. 1, 1918; William S. Robertson, *The Rise of the Spanish American Republics* (New York, Appleton-Century-Crofts, 1918); Francisco J. Urrutia, *La evolución del principio de arbitraje en América* (Madrid, 1920).

Lady of Guadalupe," patron saint of the Indians. Thus a member of the clergy called Indians—and Mexicans too—to a racial and national war, the purposes of which included expropriation of Spanish-owned property and the hope of the redress of ancient grievances. The emergent issues over the ensuing eleven years—themselves the subject of much controversy—were political, personal, clerical, and vaguely social. When the Spanish revolution of 1820 occurred, the loyalist cause seemed victorious in Mexico. With a return to the constitution of 1812 projected, a political realignment was caused resulting in the Plan de Iguala—the first of the long series of "plans" in Mexico—composed of twenty-three articles. The most significant provisions offered three guarantees: (1) the Roman Catholic religion as the only faith to be tolerated, (2) independence under a monarchical form of government, and (3) the union of all Mexican citizens without distinctions of race. On the basis of these guarantees, the forces of Iturbide and Guerrero were united as the Army of the Three Guarantees. Independence was easily attained, and with it Mexico proceeded to revolutionize Central America and later to participate in the Congress of Panama.

The Legal Basis of the Revolutions in South America

The procedure in general corresponded with that followed in Spain, 1808–1809, in that local government was established through the instrumentality of the *cabildo.* The council of the capital city, with the endorsement of the open town meeting (*cabildo abierto*), was the usual agency for the deposition of the incumbent colonial officials. The next conventional step was the establishment of provisional juntas which, while representative of the *cabildo,* usually included some other interests and organizations. Later representatives of other *cabildos* were admitted, forming a central junta to act for the colony or "state." Further steps might be the call for an election of an assembly or a constitutional convention, such as occurred in Venezuela and Colombia in 1811. The emphasis on the city not only conformed to Spanish precedent but reflected the fact that the *cabildo* was the center of creole leadership. Nevertheless, since a single *cabildo* had no jurisdiction over others of the same colony, some form of cooperation between cities had to be evolved.

It was soon manifest that the *cabildo,* even if it were that of the capital city, was not aptly designed for the government of an entire country, whether in time of war or peace. The disharmony between cities, the ineffectual arrangements for concerted action, and the localism of some cities in reference to policy eventually caused the *cabildos* to play a diminishing role in the struggles for independence. Ultimately they were to yield to military necessity and to future dictatorial regimes—some superseded under law, some overcome by force, and some abolished. Nevertheless, they had played a memorable part in starting the train of events leading to independence.

Character of the Wars and the Development of Political Factions

The opposing forces in the wars, 1810–1826, were not simply those of colonials against Spaniards. Among the loyalist forces there were in all sectors a large number of colonials of American birth. In South America the royalist leaders and commanders took the initiative in recruiting for military service members of social classes which had hitherto not participated in affairs of importance. In Mexico, the "patriots," especially under the leadership of Hidalgo and Morelos, from the beginning enlisted Indians and mestizos—a fact which probably caused a majority of the creoles to remain loyal. The creoles in South America, who furnished the initial leadership of the revolution, were as a class divided in allegiance. At the outset, and even after expeditionary forces were sent from Spain in 1815, the armies and garrisons stationed in the colonies were inadequate in numbers for prosecuting a full-scale war in such extensive territories. Spanish authorities not only mustered into service creole loyalists, but in South America they yielded to the strong inducement to enroll recruits without regard to previous social status. Whether from choice or necessity as a war measure, patriot governments and leaders, in turn, enlisted soldiers from the various social classes.

These several considerations, especially the fact of a large percentage of colonials in the Spanish military personnel, form the basis for the significant, but still controversial, description of the wars for independence as "civil wars."[3]

This thesis was supported by Bolívar's sad and angry statement (1812): "Our divisions, and not the Spanish army, brought us back to slavery . . . ; the internal factions, which, in fact were the deadly poison which carried the country to its tomb." And again (1814): "It seems that

[3] Cf. Laureano Vallenilla Lanz, *Cesarismo democrático* (Caracas, 1919). The first essay is entitled "La guerra de emancipación fué una guerra civil." He estimates that a majority of the field forces of the royalist armies was made up of persons born in the colonies. This estimate takes account of the forces sent from Spain in 1815.

Heaven, to grant us at one time humiliation and pride, has permitted that our conquerors be our own brothers, and that our brothers only may triumph over us . . . Your brothers and not the Spaniards have torn your bosom, shed your blood, and set your homes on fire and condemned you to exile."[4]

Some reservations have been offered to acceptance of this thesis as being generally applicable. Still, the "civil war" character of the struggles, where it developed, prolonged the strife, made the wars more frightful, and contributed to the bitterness caused by the trials of those charged with treason and giving aid to the enemy. It was to leave the problem of the reincorporation of the loyalist into republican society and politics.

All these countries suffered economic distress during these war years, with production reduced or halted, without large reserves in the treasury, and with the labor system of the colonial period no longer enforced. Very commonly the field armies had to live off the country. Undoubtedly great difficulty was encountered in the effort to feed, transport, and clothe armies in countries which were distracted, divided in loyalty, and exhausted.[5] The requisitions, forced loans, and confiscations suffered by the civilian population were in proportion to the insatiable needs and appetites of the armies.

In the prolonged wars, with divergent choices in policy and principles under discussion, and with conflicting judgments as to responsibility for success and failure, factionalism in politics appeared and grew. Political leaders in the new Latin-American communities showed an unexpected gift for political theory and commentary, and for the formation of institutions, but not always for agreement. There was also the disposition to look abroad and to imitate, without that practice being a contribution to unity. What these peoples had to do in order to achieve independence and what they would do with independence once they had obtained it were questions before all the inchoate countries, and some of the answers gave rise to the early political parties.

As to the form of government, there were choices to be made between monarchy and republicanism and between the federal and unitary types of organization. Convinced advocates of each were to be found. The vested interests, especially the Church and the clergy and the great landowners,

[4] The quotations are from the "Cartagena Manifesto," in Vicente Lecuna and H. A. Bierck (eds.), *Selected Writings of Bolívar* (New York, The Colonial Press, 1951), pp. 21 and 81.

[5] Eloy G. González, *La ración del boa* (Caracas, 1908).

sought to preserve and protect in the new regimes their old privileges, but they did not always present a united front. The new army as a political force was to emerge from the struggles for independence as a formidable power—and it, too, was subject to division. Likewise, the aspiring and newly self-conscious members of the lower classes were to have divergent opinions. No single scheme of classification of these factions would accurately and fully represent the political alignment in every state. The following classification, applicable to Mexico, is suggestive of party lines in some other countries: monarchists versus republicans; unitarists versus federalists; conservatives versus liberals; clericals versus anticlericals; the military versus the civil power. Even with reference to Mexico, this classification does not specifically take account of the pro–United States group, the pro-French faction, the Masonic societies, and the divisions among the monarchists.

These wars were immortalized by many acts of heroism and deeds of sacrifice and valor, which in time became legendary; they were conducted under difficulties which sorely tested nobility of character and persistence of will. Marked by a civil-war character, by much dissension and factionalism, the winning of independence was an achievement of a high order in both military and political action. None the less, internal revolution and the *coup d'état* became means of political action, and some governments were converted into dictatorships.

The International Status of the Spanish American States

The wars for independence had been brought to a conclusion by the decisive battles of Boyacá (1819), Carabobo (1821), Pichincha (1822), and Ayacucho (1824) and by the absorption of the belligerent forces operating in Mexico in the Army of the Three Guarantees under the Plan de Iguala (1821). With the capitulation of the royalist forces in the island of Chiloé and the evacuation of the fortresses of Callao, Puerto Cabello, and San Juan de Ulúa (1826), military activities had been suspended according to a series of truces. There was no general treaty of peace and no recognition by Spain. Some of the new states had exchanged recognitions, and Brazil had recognized certain countries by 1821. Recognition of Gran Colombia and Mexico in 1822, Argentina and Chile in 1823, and Brazil and Central America in 1824 by the United States was in time followed by recognition by Great Britain of Argentina and Colombia in 1825 and Mexico in 1826. Under the friendly but pressing mediation of Great Britain, Portugal had granted recognition to Brazil in 1825.

The British gave formal recognition to Brazil in 1827. These several acts of the British had been accompanied by treaties of amity and commerce. France, after signing a treaty of amity and commerce with Brazil in 1826, which at the same time granted recognition, adopted in 1830 a policy of negotiating further treaties of this character, the first being with Venezuela in 1832.

These actions and treaties were of high importance in giving "international status" to the new countries. So long, however, as the mother country withheld recognition from the Spanish American states and so long as European intervention in support of the possible restoration of Spanish control was a matter of diplomatic speculation and of concern to governments and public opinion, these countries were on the "margin of international life."

In the decade 1820–1830, during which the new countries faced serious dangers, foreign and domestic, there were in their situation elements of both strength and weakness.

1. First among the influences in support of independence were the acts of recognition by some states and the treaties of commerce.

2. The developing opposition of the British government and people to European intervention in the interest of Spain may be considered as protection. English naval strength and diplomacy (1822–1827) were factors of significance in the support of independence.

3. The message of President Monroe to the Congress of the United States in 1823, later to be known as the Monroe Doctrine, was for more than a century to be of importance in inter-American and international relations. The two most famous passages of the message have to do with future colonization and with interference of European powers in the Americas. First, President Monroe wrote:

> In the discussions to which this interest had given rise, and in the arrangements by which they may terminate, the occasion has been judged proper for asserting as a principle in which the rights and interests of the United States are involved, that the American continents, by the free and independent condition which they have assumed and maintain, are henceforth not to be considered as subjects for future colonization by any European powers.

Separated by many paragraphs, the second passage came:

> In the wars of the European powers in matters relating to themselves we have never taken any part, nor does it comport with our policy so to do. . . . With the movements in this hemisphere we are, of necessity, more immediately con-

nected, and by causes which must be obvious to all enlightened and impartial observers. . . . We owe it, therefore, to candor, and to the amicable relations existing between the United States and those powers, to declare that we should consider any attempt on their part to extend their system to any portion of this hemisphere as dangerous to our peace and safety. With the existing colonies or dependencies of any European power we have not interfered and shall not interfere. But with the governments who have declared their independence and maintained it, and whose independence we have, on great consideration and on just principles, acknowledged, we could not view any interposition for the purpose of oppressing them, or controlling in any other manner their destiny, by any European power, in any other light than as a manifestation of an unfriendly disposition toward the United States.

Still later in the message, there was the much-ignored passage: "It is still the true policy of the United States to leave the parties to themselves, in the hope that other powers will pursue the same course."

4. A principle had been formulated concerning territorial domains and jurisdiction. This was the principle of *uti possedetis juris* of the year 1810, under which the new states could assert rightful claims to the territory possessed in 1810, the year in which many of them began their struggle for emancipation. Claims and rights under this principle might not and did not have definitive grounds for undisputed settlement, but the principle was accepted as a basis of negotiation and arbitration.

5. Certain countries, with skill and energy, made diplomatic efforts to regularize their positions. Argentina, Chile, Peru, and Mexico were active in this way, but it was the work of Bolívar and his associates that was more comprehensive in scope and more enduring in influence. This program embraced such objectives as the negotiation of treaties of alliance and friendship, arbitration of disputes, interstate acceptance of the principle of *uti possedetis,* proposals of the league of the new states for defense against outside attack, and the holding of an international congress. Upon Bolívar's initiative and on the eve of the battle of Ayacucho, the invitation was issued to the then existing states of Latin America to send delegates to a congress to be convened on the Isthmus of Panama. Great Britain, Holland, and the United States were then or later added to the list. As finally formulated, the purposes of this congress were to form or renew treaties of alliance; to consider the expediency of a joint effort for the liberation of Cuba and Puerto Rico; to consider means of giving effect to the declaration of President Monroe; to establish the rights of nations, then in controversy, especially those of countries

at war and those which were neutrals; to pronounce a policy as to the slave trade; and to declare what should be the relations with Haiti.[6]

The Congress of Panama resulted in little positive achievement. Indeed, the four conventions to which the delegates agreed were ratified by only one power, Colombia. But the Congress became a precedent for future congresses of American states and was one of the originating causes of later Pan-Americanism. Meantime, it was regarded as an outward demonstration of the will of these new states to continue to be independent.

Despite these elements of strength, there were serious liabilities and weaknesses in the situation. Political disorders affected nearly every country, amounting to anarchy in some. All faced economic difficulties, with finances and rehabilitation everywhere a problem. These hazards of independence will be more fully analyzed in the next chapter.

Immediate Effects of Independence on the Colonial Heritage

The period of the struggles for independence (1810–1830) was the time of the first efforts at liquidation of the colonial system in government and society. Although some measures were premature, visionary, and drastic, some were in time accepted as definitive and as verifiable steps in progress. Some changes were opposed as being contrary to the valid traditions and best interests of the people. A list of some of the reforms adopted will indicate their diversity and significance: (1) abolition of the Inquisition; (2) extinction of the Indian head tax (*tributo*) and the undermining or abolition of slavery; (3) abolition or the reduction in power of the *cabildo;* (4) restriction of the judiciary to the administration of justice; (5) extinction of the guilds or reduction in their rights; (6) withdrawal in many cases of legal support to the caste stratification of society; (7) opening of countries to international trade; (8) encouragement of immigration and the adoption of naturalization laws; and (9) abandonment in the administrative systems of many checks and balances. In this period there was the beginning of Latin-American anticlericalism. In all countries, with the possible exception of Brazil, the army emerged with greatly increased political power. In Spanish America, there were evidences of continued sentiment in favor of monarchy. Experiments with monarchy in Mexico and Haiti, however, had been short in duration and

[6] Several other objects were entertained by delegates and officials. Among them were proposals of a congress that should meet periodically and a recognition of the principle of *uti possedetis.* See Lockey, *op. cit.,* pp. 321–338.

unsatisfactory. The monarchs involved in these experiments had been native-born, which left open to debate the possible advantages of monarchy with an imported dynasty. The course of events and the circumstances favored the republican system, in spite of the disorders in society and the defects in that form of government. Monarchy in Brazil was a different matter, since in that country it was a product of historical continuity and since a traditional dynasty was already in residence.

There were already indications of the thought that independence would be incomplete if it were limited to matters political and institutional. In time this thought was going to develop into a campaign for intellectual independence as a corollary of political independence—i.e., a campaign for freedom from colonial traditions.

Independence of Brazil

It will be recalled that in 1808 Dom João, regent of Portugal, arrived in Brazil. With him came the royal family, the court, and many others, estimated at 15,000 persons. In the midst of a tumultuous welcome, swayed by British advice, he announced a series of reform measures, including the decree which opened Brazil to the trade of friendly countries and which abolished at a stroke the remaining features of the commercial monopoly enjoyed by the mother country. An order was issued repealing the restrictions on industry; and by edicts a printing press, the Bank of Brazil, a powder factory, a public library, and naval and military colleges were established. An organic act of historic importance was that of 1815 by which Brazil was made an equal member of the "United Kingdom of Portugal, Brazil and the Algarves," thus abolishing the technical status of colony. To the new "Kingdom of Brazil," as the country was with increasing frequency called, were invited immigrants —not only workers for agriculture and industry, but men of science and the arts. Dom João became king in his own right in 1816.

These extraordinary facts—the transference of a royal court to the New World, and the government for a time of a European country from American shores—were to have decisive consequences for both Brazil and Portugal. For Brazil, there was to be not only an intellectual, economic, and scientific renaissance but an awakening of nationalistic self-consciousness and patriotism, dedicated to a determination to retain in time of peace the advantages that had been granted. For Brazilians, also, there was the excitement of participation in international affairs, such as the war with France, the invasion of French Guiana, the "reconquest" and annexation of Uruguay, and the possible intervention in the course of the struggle for independence by the former Spanish colonies.

But all was not well with the reign of King John. In Portugal there was a demand for his return, and opposition was expressed to the reform by which Brazil was elevated to equality with the mother country. The Portuguese—both those at home and those living in Brazil—acted with singular lack of wisdom and practical sense. In Brazil all too often they acted the role of parasites; at home many sought to reduce Brazil to its former colonial status.

In Brazil a revolution centered in Pernambuco broke out in 1817 and was suppressed with difficulty and severity. This revolution not only was a protest against administrative abuses but, according to some evidences, reflected a demand for a republican organization of government.

A more serious crisis developed in 1820 as a consequence of the revolution that broke out in Portugal and swept the existing government out of power. The immediate results were the convocation of a Cortes, the effort to frame a constitution, and the insistent demand that the king return to Portugal. These events at first caused a favorable reaction in Brazil. A response was made to the invitation for Brazil to send representatives to take part in the Cortes. There were again some violent commotions, which were put down with force. During this crisis, King John was hesitant to take positive action. He did send his son and heir, Pedro, to Lisbon. After having hastily and perhaps prematurely pledged that his father would accept the constitution which then was only partially framed, Pedro returned to Brazil. King John, disturbed by the commotions that were growing in Brazil and by the prospect of the loss of Portugal, decided to return to Lisbon, leaving Pedro as regent.

The Portuguese Cortes adopted several measures whose implication, if not avowed purpose, was to place Brazilian administration under direct responsibility to the government at Lisbon. It then commanded Prince Pedro to return to Portugal. On receiving a petition from Brazilian patriots that he stay, Pedro decided (January 8, 1822) to remain. This decision in effect placed him in revolt and in leadership of a movement which eventually became separatist in object. The role of Pedro in this period, 1820–1822, is still a subject of controversy. He had been identified, probably from conviction, with those seeking a constitution and certain reforms that were regarded as liberal. During the critical months from January to September of 1822, he was constrained to join those favoring independence, whether from conviction or not. There is the tradition, not evidentially established as fact, that King John encouraged Pedro to lead the movement for independence should events indicate the wisdom and inevitability of such a development. Such circumstances did occur, and on September 7, 1822, independence was declared in the Grito de Ypiranga. On October 12, Pedro was proclaimed Emperor. Although a technical state of war ensued, the Portuguese garrison was compelled to surrender and to leave for Europe, and although naval maneuvers and demonstrations caused some tension, diplomatic exchanges continued between the estranged parties. This situation, having many complications and being the occasion of many intrigues, was resolved by a series of treaties by which in turn Portugal and Great Britain gave recognition to the Empire of Brazil.

Brazil's independence, achieved in a very different manner from that of the Spanish American states, was relieved of the long-continued bitterness that marked the relations between Spain and its former colonies.

Revolution in Haiti and Santo Domingo

The colony now known by the name of Haiti felt promptly the impact of the French Revolution. In a society rigorously stratified, in which the Negro slaves outnumbered all other persons by almost ten to one, and in which the system of slavery has been very generally condemned for its brutal severity, the events in France were calculated to cause a social upheaval. This likelihood was enhanced by the dissensions among the whites and between whites and free mulattoes. Haiti had an *ancien régime* of its own.

France tried the experiment of admitting colonial representatives of the States-General and other legislative bodies. Also it authorized the colonists to form assemblies of their own and within limits to frame constitutions. It remained to be seen whether or not the colonies would fully participate in the advanced principles and methods of the great revolution. Before this question was answered, war between France and England was declared and with it there occurred the invasion of Haiti by General Whitelocke. As a way of securing aid against the British, the French on August 29, 1793, freed the slaves. Already scenes of unrestrained savagery had begun to characterize an interracial conflict, with responsibility for this frightfulness shared by all parties. The area of the conflict was expanded to include the whole island, since the Spanish part was ceded to France in 1797. A series of leaders rose to prominence, including Toussaint L'Ouverture, Dessalines, Pétion, and Henri Christophe.

The colonial status, so far as local pretension was concerned, was altered in 1804 to that of "republic" and to that of "empire" (1805–1806). The ensuing "republic" was divided, and in 1811 in northern Haiti a "kingdom" was established under Henri Christophe. Under the leadership of President Boyer, in 1821, the island was reunited. This tie was continued until 1844. In 1825, France granted conditional recognition of independence.

BIBLIOGRAPHY

Amunátegui, M. L., *Los precursores de la independencia de Chile,* 2 vols., Santiago, 1909–1910.

Amunátegui Solar, Domingo, *La emancipación de Hispano América,* Santiago, 1936.

Angell, Hildegarde, *Simón Bolívar: South American Liberator,* New York, Norton, 1930.

Basadre, Jorge, *La iniciación de la república,* Lima, 1929.

Belaunde, Víctor Andrés, *Bolívar and the Political Thought of the Spanish American Revolution,* Baltimore, Johns Hopkins Press, 1938.

García Samudio, Nicolás, *La independencia hispano-americana,* Mexico, 1950.

Herrera, Luis Alberto de, *La revolución francesa y sud América,* Valencia, 1909.

Lecuna, Vicente, and H. A. Bierck, *Selected Writings of Bolívar,* 2 vols., New York, The Colonial Press, 1951.

Lockey, Joseph B., *Pan Americanism: Its Beginnings,* New York, Macmillan, 1920.

Madariaga, Salvador de, *Bolívar,* 2 vols., Buenos Aires, 1947.

Mancini, Jules, *Bolívar,* Paris, 1912.

Masur, Gerhard, *Simón Bolívar,* Albuquerque, N.M., University of New Mexico Press, 1948.

Miranda, José, *Las ideas y las instituciones políticas mexicanas,* Mexico, 1952.

Mitre, Bartolomé, *Historia de San Martín y la emancipación sud-americana,* 3 vols., Buenos Aires, 1887–1888.

Moses, B., *South America on the Eve of Emancipation,* New York, Putnam, 1908.

Oliveira Lima, Manuel de, *O imperio brasileiro, 1822–1889,* Rio de Janeiro, 1929.

Parra Pérez, C., *Historia de la primera república,* 2 vols., Caracas, 1939.

Paxson, F. L., *The Independence of the South American Republics,* Philadelphia, Ferris and Leach, 1903.

Picón Salas, Mariano, *De la conquista a la independencia,* Mexico, 1944.

Robertson, William S., *The Life of Miranda,* 2 vols., Chapel Hill, N.C., The University of North Carolina Press, 1929.

———, *Rise of the Spanish American Republics,* New York, Appleton-Century-Crofts, 1918.

Shepherd, W. R., "Bolívar and the United States," *Hispanic American Historical Review,* vol. I (1918).

Urrutia, Francisco J., *La evolución del principio de arbitraje en América,* Madrid, 1920.

Vallenilla Lanz, Laureano, *Cesarismo democrático,* Caracas, 1919.

Vejarana, J. R., *Orígenes de la independencia sur-americana,* Bogotá, 1925.

Ycaza Tigerino, J., *La independencia hispanoamericana,* Madrid, 1947.

Chapter 5: FIRST GOVERNMENTS AND CONSTITUTIONS

The new Latin-American states experienced many difficulties in establishing stable governments and in resolving differences in opinion and aims among political factions. They suffered internal disorders during the time they were seeking independence. The decades immediately following 1820, often called the "middle ages," in many of the countries were times of extreme political instability.

Political and Economic Hazards of Independence

In the states which emerged from the Spanish empire, the removal of the mother country as a common enemy severed a bond of cohesion, and divisive forces in thought and action had even freer reign. There had already been instances of successful revolutions against governments in office, followed by at least temporary acceptance of the new order and on occasion the adoption of a new constitution. The defeated in these civil wars were treated in a variety of ways. Often political prisoners were treated with cruelty. Sometimes participants were forgiven according to agreements by which military activity was ended; sometimes individuals were executed, either summarily or after trial; sometimes members of the defeated party were banished. Eventually, amnesty was likely to be granted.

The point most insistently made by writers concerning this period in the political history of Latin America is that this was a time of anarchy in which revolutions were frequent. In Venezuela alone, it has been estimated that fifty civil disturbances occurred between 1820 and 1830, although many of them were of minor importance. Following the downfall of Iturbide as emperor in 1823, it has been said that chaos began in Mexico; struggles arose between the forces of liberalism and reaction, between those who favored the federal form of government in imitation of the United States and those in favor of centralization patterned after the French plan of internal organization, and between dictators and would-be dictators.[1] As Emilio Rabasa has well said,[2]

[1] H. I. Priestley, *The Mexican Nation: A History* (New York, Macmillan, 1923), p. 257

[2] Emilio Rabasa, *La organización política de México* (Madrid, 1913), p. 1.

> In the twenty-five years following 1822, the Mexican nation had seven constituent congresses which produced as positive works one *acta constitutiva,* three constitutions, one *acta de reformas,* and as consequences: two *coups d'état,* various uprisings in the name of popular sovereignty, many revolutionary plans, a multitude of riots, and an infinity of protests, petitions, manifestos, declarations, and of whatever trouble discontented genius has been able to invent to promote disorder and to incite the minds of men.

Mexico may be an uncommon example of the variety of organizations promoting disorders, but not of the frequency and gravity of them.

A contributory cause of revolution and unrest was the delay in reaching a firm decision as to the form of government to be adopted. In spite of the unsatisfactory experiments with monarchy in Mexico and Haiti, the debate persisted in many countries between advocates of monarchy and those in favor of a republic. Where republics were established and survived, there were stormy disputes between the federalists and the unitarists and between the liberals or radicals and the conservatives.

Despite the fact that this initial period of instability was not without constructive significance, the issue was sooner or later to arise as to how orderly government under law could be established. The resolution of this issue was often to prove temporary, and some countries were again and again to resort to revolution. Studies of the ecology, or geographical distribution, of revolutions demonstrate the frequency and number of these outbreaks.[3]

Another provocative issue was whether or not there should be a break with the colonial heritage and its multiplied influences in law, political practice and administration, education, religion, and society. Were the new states to try to abolish this heritage by drastic acts or to liquidate it item by item through gradual process, or to conserve it intact? Perhaps no consistent answer was to be expected. Attempts to bring about sweeping changes which affected the status of one or more of the great established interests, such as the Church and the big estates, incurred their bitter opposition.

Again, it should be emphasized that these new countries, with the

[3] See J. Ycaza Tigerino, *Sociología de la política hispano-americana* (Madrid, 1950), p. 157. He states that Bolivia had more than seventy revolts between 1825 and 1898. In that period there were thirty presidents, six of whom were assassinated. In Paraguay, only six presidents were able to serve for the entire legal term. In Nicaragua, within a period of fourteen years there were twenty-three executives. Data of similar import could have been supplied for several other countries.

Figure 10. Latin America after the Wars for Independence. SOURCE: John Francis Bannon, *History of the Americas,* New York, McGraw-Hill, 1952, vol. I, p. 536.

possible exception of Brazil, tended to place a premium on military leadership. Some have explained the dominance of the military leader or *caudillo* as a resulting product of the long wars of independence, but this phenomenon occurred in some countries which did not suffer long continuance of such conflicts. *Caudillismo,* a striking characteristic of Latin-American governments, has been due to numerous factors, and will be the subject of later consideration. Military rule and the evil consequences alleged to be products of it inevitably led to proposals and campaigns for the control of government by civilians and for the supremacy of the civil power over the military. This rivalry was often described as a struggle between "personalism" and "legalism" in government—although personalism was not solely characteristic of a military regime nor was a respect for legality necessarily the unswerving policy of a civilian administration.

Independence also brought economic problems. In the first place, the new states, especially the Spanish American, lost whatever incidental compensations colonial mercantilism afforded in the way of market rights in the mother country, in the provision of mercantile shipping, and in the contribution by the mother country of some of the costs of defense. Secondly, the labor system had undergone radical changes. The abolition of the Indian *tributo* had removed an incentive to work. Further changes followed in the countries which emancipated Negro slaves. In the distractions and upheavals of war, the colonial craft guilds—the *gremios* and *cofradías*—lost continuity and prestige. Thirdly, while the new freedom opened some opportunities in foreign trade, agriculture, and industry, these new states for the time being were inadequately prepared for a self-supporting economy. The financing of the war brought fiscal burdens and problems with which few if any of these countries were able to cope successfully.

On the favorable side of the ledger, however, was the belief (not always justified) that the former colonies possessed vast and unmeasured wealth in resources that awaited development and exploitation. Credit and loans from foreign bankers were at first easily obtainable. Obviously, one way of financing a war was to secure loans from abroad; and one way of promoting recovery and prosperity after war was to attract foreign investments. Both ways were resorted to when feasible. Chile, for example, was able to float a loan in England for a million pounds sterling even before the British recognized that government; and British investments in Mexico before 1830 were estimated to have been more than seventy million dollars in amount. Loans were made not only to national governments, but to municipalities and provinces. Debt charges, both on interest and principal, quickly became a problem for the countries concerned. Payments in some cases were not forthcoming, credit suffered, and bankruptcy befell some money lenders.[4]

The Early Constitutions

The first constitutions of these countries, although not always observed in letter or spirit, are important because they indicate the political traditions and aspirations, political movements, and reflect grave controversial issues which developed. Many leaders of the cause for independence had knowledge of institutional developments in the United States and France and of the currently accepted procedures in framing constitutions. The translation by Nariño of the French declaration of the "rights of man and of the citizen" and that by Pombo of certain of the important state papers of the United States—including the constitutions of Maryland, Massachusetts, and Virginia, the Articles of Confederation, and the Constitution of the United States—contained examples and principles on which the Latin Americans were to draw. The process of the framing, promulgation, and ratification of constitutions had been set forth in French works. Leaders of opinion and members of constituent bodies were ready and able to discuss, in the form of projects or action programs, such items as the constituent assembly, preambles, frames of government, separation of powers, territorial jurisdiction, citizenship and suffrage, bills of rights, and amendment procedures. Although some of the early governmental charters were provisional and comparatively crude and imperfect instruments, the new states proceeded quickly to formulate written constitutions in complete form.

In 1811 Venezuela, after five months of consideration, adopted a constitution which was an astonishing achievement in political science. The framing of this document was accomplished with a great show of reason and in proceedings of dignity. The record of this convention would have been creditable to a people of longer experience in self-government. In 1812, the Spanish constitution, which was to have much influence, was adopted. In Mexico, in 1812–1813 and intermittently later, this constitution was placed in formal effect within the territory under royalist control. As progress was made toward independence, the new countries

[4] J. Fred Rippy, *Latin America in World Politics* (New York, Appleton-Century-Crofts, 1942).

adopted written constitutions following the precedents of the United States and France. Usually these charters were framed by a constitutional convention, with promulgation by decree of the government with or without ratification. Latin America appeared to have adopted the idea of Abbé Sieyès that the constituent assembly embodied the sovereignty of the people.

There was in many minds the notion that good laws make good people and that people are like the clay in the hands of the skillful potter—to be molded. Some enthusiastic theorists, under the guidance of such thinkers as Rousseau, Mably, and Condorcet, perhaps merited the disdainful description of Bolívar that "far from consulting the codes which could teach the practical science of government [they] followed the maxims of well-meaning visionaries who imagining republics of the air tried to reach political perfection, presupposing the perfectibility of mankind." Quite often, however, there were realists who warned against the hasty adoption of political doctrines of other countries and who urged that the character of the people and their lack of experience in self-government ought to be kept in mind.

Some individuals drafted projects of constitutions such as the one outlined by Miranda, the Precursor. Juan Egaña, in Chile, prepared in 1811 an elaborate and complete constitution composed of 254 articles and accompanied by fifteen "illustrations" explaining diverse topics considered in it.[5] In addition to his Angostura Discourse, which gave advice as to a possible constitution, Bolívar on invitation submitted a complete charter for Bolivia and sent with it a lengthy explanation. San Martín drafted a constitution for Peru in 1821. In Mexico, Fernández de Lizardi, under the name of "the Mexican thinker," prepared a remarkable project of a constitution, with a commentary in dialogue form, which reflected his deep interest in education, the Indians, pauperism, the land, popular superstitions, and the rancors which divided his people.[6] Joaquín Infante prepared a project of a constitution for Cuba in 1811 or 1812, while residing in Caracas.[7] The conventional agency for the formulation of con-

[5] Luis Galdames, *La evolución constitucional de Chile, 1810–1925* (Santiago, 1925), vol. 1, pp. 225 ff. for a résumé, see J. V. Lastarria, *Bosquejo histórico de la constitución del gobierno de Chile,* in *Obras completas* (Santiago, 1906–1909), vol. IX, pp. 93–107.

[6] J. J. Fernández de Lizardi, *El pensador mexicano* (Mexico, 1940).

[7] *Proyecto de constitución para la Isla de Cuba,* edited with commentary by S. Key-Ayala (Caracas, 1928). The text of this project, with brief comment and editorial notes, appears in Andrés M. Lazcano y Mazón, *Las constituciones de Cuba* (Madrid, 1952), pp. 981–1021.

stitutions, however, was the constitutional convention, regularly or irregularly chosen.

Venezuela's Constitution of 1811. It has been generally assumed that the framers of this instrument were influenced by the United States and France. Gil Fortoul concluded that the influence of the United States was the greater in that it pertained to the federal system, whereas that of France was in the main limited to the bill of rights and to certain rhetorical expressions and humanitarian postulates.[8] Parra Pérez wrote that the provisions relating to the Venezuelan congress and to the organizations of the treasury, money, national defense, commerce, and administration generally were "copied, we might say translated, from those of the Constitution of the United States."[9] Although the Venezuelan executive power was exercised by three persons who alternated in the presidency, the attributes of this power were also copied from the Constitution of the United States. There was even more pronounced similarity in the attributes assigned to the judiciary. The Venezuelan charter departed from its guiding influences in declaring that the Catholic faith was the religion of the state and the only one to be publicly professed. Other important deviations were the system of indirect elections and the composition of the senate. The latter was to be based on population, with one senator for each 70,000 people and an additional one for fractions over 30,000.

An interesting innovation was that the provincial legislatures were empowered to recall members of the congress and name others to replace them.

The chapter devoted to the rights of man was divided into four sections under the following titles: "The Sovereignty of the People," "The Rights of Man in Society," "The Duties of Man in Society," and "The Duties of the Social Body." There was an echo from France in the provision that "no one is a good citizen if he does not observe the laws faithfully and religiously; if he is not a good son, good brother, good friend, good husband, and good father of the family." A clause was adopted that, "governments being instituted for the welfare and happiness of men, society should give aid to the indigent and unfortunate—and instruction to all the citizens." Many special privileges, especially the *fuero eclesiástico,* and titles of nobility were abolished. The constitution was to be ratified by the people of the provinces.

[8] José Gil Fortoul, *Historia constitucional de Venezuela* (2d ed., Caracas, 1930), vol. 1, pp. 220–221.

[9] C. Parra Pérez, *Historia de la primera república de Venezuela* (Caracas, 1939), vol. II, p. 133.

Briefly stated, the "bases of the federative pact" in the general constitution were that each province reserved and enjoyed its sovereignty, liberty, and independence in all that was not delegated to the federal authority; new provinces might be added or formed from those already existent, and they would enjoy equal autonomy; to the federal government was committed jurisdiction over foreign relations, the common defense, the preservation of the public peace against internal commotions and external attacks, foreign commerce and that between the provinces, the army and navy, treaties and alliances, the declaration of international war and the making of peace, the imposition of federal taxes, and legislation concerning the general interests of the confederation. This constitution recognized the principle of the separation of powers into the categories of legislative, executive, and judicial. The system of juries was adopted in principle for cases involving criminal law. The federal government was empowered to guarantee to the provinces the republican form of government, provided that the provincial constitutions were not contrary to that of the country.

The Constitution for the United Provinces of New Granada (1811). Despite the disorders and strongly separatist sentiments then prevailing in several parts of Colombia (then called New Granada) in 1811, a constitution providing for a federal form of government was adopted. It was provisional, awaiting "a better occasion and a more tranquil time" when the constitution might "regulate definitively the interests of this great people."[10] The document dealt in detail with the problem of "common defense" and with the rights and obligations of the provinces. Only one organ of the federal government, the congress, was established, although the congress was authorized to create courts. Three years later in 1814 an amendment providing for an executive branch was adopted. A plural executive of three members elected by the congress was provided. The three were to serve together under a chairman who served for a period of four months. Until 1814, therefore, the congress held the executive power in its own hands. Thereafter, the executive power was subordinate to it. This arrangement was changed in 1815 in favor of a single executive, also chosen by the legislature.

In this distinctive and highly original document, the provinces guaranteed to each other their independence, sovereignty, and the republican form of government. They named the delegates to the congress, paid their salaries, and could recall them at will. In addition to the right to legislate

[10] William Marion Gibson, *The Constitutions of Colombia* (Durham, N.C., Duke University Press, 1948), p. 9.

in matters of local interest or in those not expressly delegated to the federal congress, the provinces had the right to formulate their own civil and criminal codes.

The Spanish Constitution of 1812. This constitution, drafted by the Cortes of Cádiz, had a profound influence on Spanish America, especially the northern countries.[11] Several colonials served as imperial representatives, officially or unofficially, and participated actively and significantly in the framing of the instrument. The constitution was proclaimed in some parts of the empire then under the control of royalist forces. It was placed in at least nominal operation from 1812 to 1814, and again briefly in 1820.

Many provisions in this Spanish constitution were later incorporated in the Latin-American constitutions and greatly influenced the ideas of the constitutional framers in the New World. The sections most commonly followed were those defining the nation and citizenship, declaring the religion of the state, locating sovereignty, describing territorial jurisdiction, defining the powers and functions of the several organs of government, and outlining the process of adoption and formulation of laws.

One feature of the Spanish constitution was the elaborate scheme of indirect election of members of the Cortes or parliament, which was later copied in several of the Latin-American constitutions. The citizen-voters in each parish selected an elector for each 200 citizens, and these electors met in a district meeting to select provincial electors. These subsequently met and elected the members of the parliament.

Among the powers of the Cortes were those of proposing and enacting of laws, interpreting them, and repealing them when necessary; fixing the budget and levying taxes; establishing a general plan of public education; and protecting the freedom of the press.

The constitution provided for a standing committee of the Cortes composed of seven persons chosen from its own membership. Serving while the parliament was not in session, it was to watch over the observance of the constitution and the administration of the laws; it could in its own right convoke the parliament in extraordinary session; and it had

[11] A copy of this constitution may be found in *Documentos para la historia de la vida pública del libertador* (Caracas, 1875), vol. VII, pp. 621–653. The date was Mar. 18. According to the published list of signers, deputies from the colonies of the Philippines, Cuba, Mexico, Venezuela, Peru, Argentina, Guayaquil (Ecuador), Honduras, New Granada, Costa Rica, Nicaragua, Guatemala, Puerto Rico, Santo Domingo, and Uruguay participated. The constitution contains 384 articles distributed under ten titles.

certain duties relative to the convocation of the newly elected and succeeding Cortes. It was to make reports to the parliament at the first ensuing session.[12]

First Mexican Constitutions. The famous Constitution of Apatzingán of 1814 was really a provisional decree, awaiting the time when "the nation, free from the enemies who oppress it, may dictate its constitution."[13]

TABLE 8
NUMBER OF STATES AT CERTAIN CRITICAL DATES

	Number of states
1826	
States in existence: Argentina, Bolivia, Brazil, Central American Federation, Chile, Gran Colombia, Haiti, Mexico, Paraguay, Peru	10
1828	
Uruguay added	11
1830	
Gran Colombia discontinued. New states: Ecuador, New Granada, Venezuela	13
1839	
Central American Federation discontinued. New states: Costa Rica, Honduras, Guatemala, El Salvador, Nicaragua	17
1844	
Dominican Republic added	18
1898 (1902)	
Cuba added	19
1903	
Panama added	20

Nonetheless, it was a constitution in the full sense of the word, since it covered the fundamental principles which were characteristic of such instruments. The style and organization followed French models. Some of the principles affirmed were the sovereignty of the people, the con-

[12] An example of the early use of this institution is to be found in a decree of the Angostura congress of Venezuela, Jan. 13, 1820. It established a *comisión permanente* composed of seven persons chosen from its membership which during the recess period should act in urgent affairs, terminating those pending, watch over the fulfillment of laws, and guard the rights of the people. In addition to these general functions, this body should examine the expenditure of public funds; it might make concessions of public lands; it might resolve doubts concerning the meaning of laws; it might in cases involving great interests of the state summon the congress in extraordinary session; and it might hear certain cases against officials. *Ibid.*, pp. 172–173.

[13] J. Sierra, *Evolución política del pueblo mexicano* (Mexico, 1950), p. 114. José Miranda in his *Las ideas y las instituciones políticas mexicanas* (Mexico, 1952), pp. 349–352, offers Rayón and Morelos as projectors.

tractual origin of the state, representative government, separation of powers, and religious unity. The form of government was to be republican and unitary. Of the organs of government, a much-criticized feature was the plural executive. This body of three members, having equal powers and alternating in office each four months, was described by Sierra as being "incessantly renewable" and as a "stupendous error." It was de-

TABLE 9
DATES OF INDEPENDENCE

Country	Declaration of independence	First constitution
Argentina	July 9, 1816	1819
Bolivia	Aug. 10, 1825	1826
Brazil	Sept. 7, 1822	1824
Chile	Jan. 1, 1818	1819
Colombia	July 16, 1813	1811
Confederation of Central America	Sept. 15, 1821	1823
Costa Rica	....	1839
Cuba	Apr. 20, 1898	1902
Dominican Republic	Dec. 1, 1821	(1821); 1844
Ecuador	Dec. 11, 1811	(1812); 1830
El Salvador	....	1839
Gran Colombia	....	1821
Guatemala	....	1839
Haiti	Jan. 1, 1804	1805
Honduras	....	1839
Mexico	Sept. 28, 1821	1814; 1824
Nicaragua	....	1839
Panama	Nov. 4, 1903	1904
Paraguay	June 11, 1811	1813; 1841
Peru	July 21, 1821	1823
Uruguay	Apr. 19, 1825	1830
Venezuela	July 5, 1811	1811

nounced as a weakness by Morelos at the time of his trial in 1815, but earlier he had favored it. It reflected the prevailing suspicion of a strong executive and of long tenures. The congress was the dominant power, empowered to enact, interpret, and repeal legislation; to choose the executive and members of the supreme court; and to name field commanders of the army. The members of congress were chosen by means of an elaborate scheme of indirect elections, a system seemingly taken from the Spanish constitution of 1812. Another feature was a special court of seven members to judge retiring officials in *residencia,* thus perpetuating a colonial institution.

This first Mexican constitution had a brief life. It is to be questioned whether it had an effective influence beyond the territory controlled by the followers of Morelos and whether it survived his death.

During the years 1821–1823, Mexico underwent a "transition" in which occurred the decisive developments of the Plan de Iguala (February 24, 1821), the Treaty of Córdoba (August 24, 1821), independence and the empire of Iturbide (May 18, 1822, to February 19, 1823), and the republic (April 8, 1823). A constituent congress was convened on November 7, 1823. Federalism was favored as the liberal and "republican" form of government, and this system was embodied in the preliminary *acta constitutiva* (January 31, 1824) and in the constitution of October 4, 1824. The choice was made after a notable debate between Father Mier and his fellow priest, Ramos Arizpe. The latter, as champion of the federal system, was the author of the preliminary draft and the principal contributor to the completed constitution.[14]

In such features as the powers of the central and local governments, the separation of powers and the attributes of each, and the veto power, the constitution was definitely an imitation of that of the United States. The presiding officer, in the closing session, summoned the spirits of Franklin and Washington to look upon "some men who had followed in their footsteps." However much the model was followed, there were differences in both detail and principle. An example of a difference in detail was that the executive officials—president and vice-president—were to be elected by the state legislatures for a term of four years and they were to be ineligible for immediate reelection. Another was that of a committee, composed equally of deputies and senators, which when the congress was not in session should guard the observance of the constitution, approve or disapprove recess appointments, and convoke the congress

[14] Ramos Arizpe, priest and lawyer (1775–1843), had been chosen a delegate to the congress of Cadiz and had submitted a famous report to that body on the four eastern "interior provinces" of Mexico. By some this was regarded as hostile to centralism. After the restoration of Ferdinand VII, he was imprisoned for nearly six years. See Miguel Ramos Arizpe, *Discursos, Memorias, e Informes,* with biography and notes by V. A. Robles (Mexico, 1942). There is a translation of his report in Latin-American Studies, University of Texas, ser. XI. After his return, he became acquainted with Stephen F. Austin and Joel R. Poinsett, who influenced him in favor of federalism.

in extraordinary session. The constitution omitted a bill of rights and paid little attention to social reform. On the other hand, it preserved religious intolerance and retained the *fueros* for church and army. Although the door was not closed to changes providing guarantees of individual rights and social reforms, the framers evidently did not feel the time opportune to act upon them. Far from blind imitation of the United States, the authors of this constitution demonstrated no merely superficial knowledge of democratic and federalist theories. Whatever its merits and future inspiration for such constitutions as those of 1857 and 1917, this charter did not end the conflicts which continued to plague the government.

Early Argentine Constitutions. The long delay in the adoption of a formal constitution in a country which did not experience reconquest by Spanish arms was due to the wide divergence of opinions as to the form and functions of government.[15] In 1812, however, when the government of the so-called first triumvirate was overthrown, one charge against it was that it had failed to provide for a meeting of a constitutional convention. The successor, also a triumvirate, did call such a body, which met in 1813. Although this "constituent assembly" did not adopt a constitution, it enacted a series of organic measures aimed at the establishment of independence and at the abolition of some features of the colonial system. The executive branch was reorganized, under a single executive known as the "director" of the united provinces. Argentina's first constitution was adopted in 1819 by legislative enactment. It provided for a strongly centralized government, headed by a director who was to be chosen by the congress. This constitution, embodying principles favored by the province and city of Buenos Aires, was unacceptable to many of the other provinces. Some of them declared their independence, while some others were disposed to join Artigas of Uruguay. Although the constitution operated in Buenos Aires, disorders amounting to anarchy prevailed. The government of Buenos Aires changed hands eight times during the fateful year of 1820. In the political confusion of the times, there were proponents of monarchy, of centralization under the hegemony

[15] The steps in the evolution of a constitutional system as traced by Segundo V. Linares Quintana were: (1) the Junta Superior; (2) order of the Junta providing for the organization of provincial juntas, Feb. 10, 1811; (3) *reglamento provisorio,* Oct. 22, 1811; (4) *estatuto provisional,* Nov. 22, 1811; (5) constituent assembly, 1813; (6) *reglamento provisorio*, Dec. 3, 1817; (7) constitution of 1819; (8) constitution of 1826; (9) *pacto federal,* 1831; (10) constitution of 1853. *Gobierno y administración de la república argentina* (Buenos Aires, 1946), vol. I, pp. 159–195.

of Buenos Aires, of federalism with provincial autonomy under *caudillo* chieftains, and of doctrinaire democracy. Argentina entered into its "middle age" of civil wars.

From 1820 to 1825, the political situation in Argentina was that of union in name only, with the provinces in fact autonomous. Treaties between provinces provided bases according to which "Argentina" existed in a status that is sometimes described as *de facto*. Such was the "Treaty of the Quadrilateral" by which Buenos Aires, Entre Ríos, Corrientes, and Santa Fe should give each other mutual aid and should recognize the complementary principles of nationalism and provincial autonomy. The government of the province of Buenos Aires, under the enlightened leadership of Martín Rodríguez, Las Heras, and Rivadavia—especially the last—established internal order and adopted a series of reforms of a political, economic, military, ecclesiastical, and social character. Among these were the abolition of the *cabildo,* the suppression of tithes and the *fuero eclesiástico,* the foundation of the University of Buenos Aires, a famous land law, and a plan of colonization. This set of progressive measures placed the province in singular contrast to the rest.

In spite of the opposition or indifference of some provinces, a constituent congress was called in 1824, and from its work eventually emerged the constitution of 1826. Although this instrument provided for a unitary system, it recognized the provinces and guaranteed to them certain rights in the administration of local affairs. Nevertheless, it was vigorously attacked by those who favored a federal form of government.[16] The most objectionable feature, perhaps, was that the president was empowered to name the governors from lists selected by the respective "councils of administration" of the provinces.

The life of the constitution of 1826 was short. It was followed by civil war, the war with Brazil, the tragic interlude of Dorrego, and the rise to power and dictatorship of Rosas. It was superseded by the Federal Pact of 1831, which lasted as the basic charter of the Argentine confederation until 1851.

Chilean Constitutions. Progress in adopting a permanent charter in Chile was slow, owing to the adverse fortunes of war and widespread dissensions. A provisional instrument was proclaimed in 1812, which sketchily outlined the institutions of government, giving executive powers to a junta of three persons and legislative powers to a senate of seven and to the *cabildo* of Santiago. With liberation assured at Maipo and with the

[16] Carlos Sánchez Viamonte, *Historia institucional de Argentina* (Mexico, 1948), p. 167.

declaration of independence (1818), there was a demand for a constituent assembly. This was met by a decree naming a commission to prepare the project of a provisional constitution. This instrument was ratified in a plebiscite and was promulgated (October 23, 1818). In one passage the government (dictatorship) of O'Higgins was legalized. To him, as Director Supremo, was entrusted military control, the collection and expenditure of public funds, the direction of foreign affairs. A check on his powers was supplied in the requirement that he report to a senate, of five members, named by him. This body was granted legislative powers and the guardianship of the constitution. The colonial system of administration, courts, and municipal government was left intact. The bill of rights, reflecting the influence of Egaña, was diffuse and idealistic. It contained passages relative to the duties as well as rights of man.[17]

The government of General Freire brought forth the constitution of 1823, the work chiefly of Egaña. It provided for administrative centralization, a weak executive, and a relatively strong senate of aristocratic composition. It firmly authorized the guardianship of custom and morals by government. It expressed the faith that good laws could make men virtuous. This charter was of short duration. The clash between the Director and the congress, which was made certain by the provisions of this constitution relative to the distribution of powers, was not only a contest for power but an occasion for controversy over graver issues then disturbing Chile—internal order, credit and solvency, religious toleration, liberalism and federalism. The congress of 1826, under the guidance of the brilliant José M. Infante, declared for the federal system. After consultation with the provinces, a federal constitution was formulated, but never formally adopted or applied to the country at large.[18] Although federalism continued during the next generation to be urged by liberals as a way of progress, it did not retain popularity. Opposition to political disorders, the ascendancy of the planter and mercantile interests, and the rise to leadership of Diego Portales were influences favorable to centralization. These forces, supported by geography, gave victory to the conservative party.

Meanwhile, a constituent congress adopted the constitution of 1828, for which the newly arrived Spaniard, José J. de Mora, was chiefly

[17] Ricardo Donoso, *Las ideas políticas en Chile* (Mexico, 1946), pp. 51–52.

[18] Galdames, *op. cit.,* p. 732, calls this championship of federalism by Infante and later by Lastarria a "noble illusion." The aspirations for liberty, democracy, and justice and the advocacy of municipal autonomy, associated with the campaign for federalism, might continue, but the geographical and moral unity of the country, according to Galdames, "was the basis of Chile's force and progress."

responsible. For conciseness, symmetry, and logical arrangement it is an admirable document. On the matters then in dispute, it provided that the Catholic religion was to be the only one to be publicly exercised, but that no person was to be molested for private opinions; that the provinces were to have autonomous assemblies but were to be administered by intendants named by the president from lists presented by the assemblies of the provinces; and that the president, elected indirectly, was to serve for five years and to be ineligible for immediate reelection. The executive, although placed under some restrictions, was given sufficient powers for effective administration of public affairs. These provisions justify the idea that this constitution was a compromise. There were, however, several social reforms projected. The prospect of their enforcement was one of the causes of the civil war which resulted in the success of the conservatives and the inauguration of the "autocratic republic."[19]

In consequence of the success of the *pelucón* or conservative party in 1829, Chile adopted the constitution of 1833. This was done deliberately and after much discussion. A committee chosen to formulate a project worked during a recess of the convention and was occupied with the task for a year. In fact, several projects were submitted. Those attributed to Gandarillas and Mariano Egaña were the ones chiefly considered.[20] Neither one of these projects was adopted, but that of Egaña was the more influential as a basis of a text.

The constitution provided for a unitary form of government. Sovereignty was to reside in the people, and the powers of government were limited to those delegated to it. A congress of two chambers, with the deputies chosen directly and the senators indirectly, was provided. Suffrage was limited by the requirement of ability of the voter to read and write, although this restriction was not to become effective until 1840. Property qualifications were required for members of the congress.

[19] *Ibid.*, pp. 767–777. Galdames has a lengthy footnote in which he analyzes the divergent view of the constitution of 1828. See F. Errázuriz, *Chile bajo el imperio de la constitución de 1828* (Santiago, 1861); J. V. Lastarria, *Obras completas* (Santiago, 1906–1909), vol. I, p. 202; and C. Gay, *Historia de Chile* (Paris, 1854), vol. VIII, p. 116.

[20] Mariano Egaña was the son of Juan Egaña. A recommendation, similar to one his father had made in 1811 and in 1823, was that the senate should be the guardian of public morals, education, and the administration of law. It had some resemblance to the "moral power" recommended by Bolívar in his Angostura Discourse. Egaña also suggested that a number of ex officio senators should be appointed by the executive and that the president of the country should preside over the senate.

The framers had as a principal object the preservation of internal order, and to this end they created a powerful executive. The president was chosen for a term of five years and was to be eligible for an additional term. As "supreme chief of the nation," he was charged with maintaining public order in the interior, guarding the observance of the constitution and laws, and securing the country against foreign attack. He could appoint and remove at will ministers, counselors of state, diplomats, intendants, and governors. In the event of domestic commotion, on authorization of the congress or, when it was not in session, of the council of state, he could declare a "state of siege" in the areas affected whereby certain of the constitutional guarantees could be suspended. Also, the congress might concede to him extraordinary powers, although they must be specified in nature and limited as to duration. During the ensuing forty years, the powers of the executive were without an effective counterweight.

This constitution as originally drafted offered few norms relative to the administration of justice. Spanish private law and both the military and ecclesiastical *fueros* were left unchanged. It was declared that the right of administering justice belonged to the courts, which the law should establish, and that neither the executive nor the congress should exercise judicial functions.[21]

The suppression of provincial assemblies and the appointment by the president of all important officials having to do with local government left Chile with an extreme degree of centralization. The territorial divisions were the province, headed by an intendant; the department, by a governor; the subdelegation, by a *subdelegado;* and the district, by an inspector. These officers constituted a sort of political hierarchy. All were appointive, and each was responsible to and removable by the next highest in the scale. The intendants were constitutionally regarded as the president's "natural and immediate agents." The elective councils of municipalities had a narrowly restricted set of powers, and any action by them could be disallowed on grounds of being contrary to the interests of public order.

Additional and noteworthy features of this constitution were the following:

1. A standing committee (*comisión conservadora*), composed in the beginning of seven members of the senate, was named by that body from its own members to be in session during the recess of the congress. Its

[21] Galdames, *op cit.,* pp. 947–950.

duties were to watch over the observance of the constitution and the laws, to make representations to the president concerning these matters, to approve or disapprove certain presidential appointments, and by an amendment adopted later to report to the congress at the next session. By an amendment, this committee became representative of both houses.

2. The congress was authorized to declare an *estado de sitio* or state of siege. A notable divergence in interpretation was to develop concerning this power. Were all constitutional guarantees suspended by it? Was this action comparable to the suspension of the writ of habeas corpus in England or the United States? Did this action signify that any statutory law as well as any constitutional guarantee might at the discretion of government or on express authorization of congress be suspended? Much time was to pass and many controversies were to occur before these issues were resolved.

3. A council of state composed of the ministers, two members of the judiciary, one member of the clergy, a general of the army, an officer of the treasury, two former ministers or diplomats, and two former administrators of local government was established. Among its duties was that of making suitable nominations for both permanent and ad interim appointments to judicial and ecclesiastical positions. Despite the moderative functions originally conceived for this body, the council was thought of as a support for rather than a check on the executive.

4. The power to interpret and construe the constitution was vested solely in the congress.

This constitution, with numerous modifications, remained in force until 1925. Thirty-eight years were to pass before an amendment was to be adopted. Under this instrument, Chile was to acquire a reputation for stability. The primary object of the framers and of those who supported this constitution was that of maintaining internal order. Secondary to this aim, and consonant with it, was that the interests and control of the aristocracy should be conserved. As an operative instrument of government, this constitution was to evoke quite contradictory appraisals.[22]

Central America. The Captaincy General of Guatemala, which had been annexed to Iturbide's empire, took an important step in organizing a government of its own in 1823, a time from which is usually dated the beginning of the Federation of Central America. On July 2, representatives of the five provinces declared that they formed a "national constituent assembly and that in it resides the exercise of sovereignty."

[22] *Ibid.*, pp. 962–970.

Through provisional regulations this body immediately announced the establishment of a government with legislative, executive, and judicial branches. A constitution was to be framed, pending which the existing laws—such are were not incompatible with independence—would be observed. The new republic was called "The United Provinces of the Center of America."

The formulation of the constitution was a slow process. The completed document was published on November 22, 1824; it was ratified and placed in formal operation in 1825.

The new "Federation of Central America" was to have a "popular, representative, and federal" form of government; and all power not conferred on the federal authorities was to belong to the "states." The state religion of the federation was to be Catholic. Slavery and the slave trade were abolished. The electorate, after the manner provided in the Spanish constitution of 1812, was to act indirectly through three stages. The parish was to choose electors, one for each 250 inhabitants, to form a district convention. This latter body, in turn, was to choose delegates, one for each ten members, to a departmental convention, which was empowered to vote on president and vice-president, members of the congress, and members of the supreme court.

The legislative body was the subject of a novel arrangement. According to the letter of the constitution, it was unicameral, being designated as the "chamber of representatives." But there was to be a senate, composed of two members for each state. It shared the legislative power in that it voted on nearly all classes of legislation, but originated none. It was to remain continuously in session and to act as a council to the executive. It was charged with the functions of guarding the observance of the constitution and the laws, of preparing lists of nominees for possible appointment, and of convoking the chamber in extraordinary session. Another interesting provision was that the president was instructed to consult the chamber of representatives as to the interpretation of laws and to consult the senate about the administration of them. He was to consult the senate about the negotiation of treaties and about the conduct of foreign affairs but was not bound by the advice given.

In alleged cases of treason, venality, and grave offenses in discharge of duty, provisions were made for trial either before the supreme court or before a special tribunal which was to be named by the senate.

It is to be noted that the veto power was vested in the senate, not the president. Within ten days of the receipt of a measure from the congress, the senate was under the obligation of returning it. It could refuse approval on the ground that the act violated the constitution or it could refuse because it considered the act unsuitable for the country. An act returned with either of these objections, if repassed by a two-thirds vote, became law. If the act involved taxation, the congress had to repass it by a three-fourths vote.[23]

Several writers, including Bancroft and Moreno, have asserted that this constitution was modeled after that of the United States, but a close analysis and comparison indicates that the differences were more significant than the similarities. Possibly the example of the United States led to the adoption of a federal form of government, but even on this point one writer has contended that it was due rather to the strong sentiment for autonomy which prevailed in most of the provinces.[24] The curious organization of the legislative power was unexplained by contemporary writers, and subsequent commentators have offered conflicting explanations.[25]

The Imperial Constitution of Brazil. This instrument went into effect March 25, 1824. Having forcibly dissolved the convention which was drafting a constitution and having appointed a special commission over which he presided, the emperor may be said to have granted this charter.

Four powers were recognized: the legislative, the moderative, the executive, and the judicial. Of these, the "moderative" requires special analysis, since it was declared the key to the political organization. The moderative functions were vested in the emperor and embraced the following rights: naming the senators from lists chosen by the provinces; convoking the general assembly in extraordinary sessions; sanctioning the decrees and resolutions of the general assembly; approving or suspending the resolutions of provincial councils; proroguing the general assembly and dissolving the chamber of deputies; naming and removing ministers

[23] For a copy of this constitution, see *Digesto constitucional de Costa Rica,* pp. 29–51. (This volume was prepared by the Colegio de Abogados in 1946 under the editorship of Marco Tulio Zeledón.) The constitution contained 211 articles, arranged under fifteen titles.

[24] R. Facio, *Trayectoria y crisis de la federación centro-americana* (San José, 1949), p. 62.

[25] See Adolfo Posada, *Instituciones políticas de los pueblos hispanoamericanos* (Madrid, 1900), p. 129. He considers the plan to have been a "hybrid, between the bicameral and the unicameral." Cf. Justo Arosemena, *Estudios constitucionales sobre los gobiernos de la América Latina* (Paris, 1878), vol. II, p. 426; and L. Moreno, *Historia de las relaciones interestatuales de Centro America* (Madrid, 1928), pp. 57–58. Arosemena thought the arrangement *sui generis;* Moreno considered that it was a way of guarding against dictatorship.

of state; and granting pardons and amnesty. Included in this power was the right to suspend judges against whom complaint had been made, provided that a hearing was granted to the accused and an investigation made by the council of state. In a general sense, the moderative power conferred on the emperor the duty of seeing that all the powers of government worked in harmony. In addition, the emperor had the usual "executive" powers. The senate was composed of lifetime members. There was a chamber of deputies, popularly elected in indirect process, having a term of four years. The general assembly had the power to enact, interpret, suspend, and repeal laws. It was, therefore, the guardian of the constitution. The judiciary, composed of judges and juries for both criminal and civil cases, was declared to be independent. Exclusive of the ministers of state, there was a council of state whose members, not exceeding ten in number, served for life.

Other features of this constitution were a lengthy and liberal bill of rights, retention of the institution of the *residencia* and of the town councils, and the suspensive veto. The limited autonomy of provinces was enlarged by changes made in 1834 and 1840.

The Uruguayan Constitution of 1830. The framers of this constitution had the benefit of earlier instruments such as those of the United States, of Spain (1812), of Argentina (1826), and of Chile (1828), and influences from these sources were plainly evident. This constitution had the admirable conciseness, the logical organization, and the clarity in statement of principles that characterized the Chilean document. Since it endured until 1919, the features which have attracted most attention should be examined. First, it suppressed the colonial *cabildos* but failed to provide an adequate substitute with sufficient powers to perform functions of local importance. Secondly, the constitution has been criticized as having given too much power to the executive, but the text of the document does not warrant this assumption. The excesses in the exercise of executive powers have been held as abuses of power.[26] A feature to which much attention has been paid by Uruguayan writers and statesmen relates to Article 53, which conferred on each chamber of the general assembly the right to summon ministers before it to ask for and receive such reports as were deemed proper. This authority was developed into the right of interpellation and censure. Thirdly, by Article 96, the supreme court was empowered to judge all infractors of the constitution, but by Article 152, the legislative branch was granted the exclusive right to

[26] P. Blanco Acevedo, *Estudios constitucionales* (Montevideo, 1939), pp. 50–51.

interpret and expound the constitution. Other less controversial features were the provisions denying to the president and to senators the right of immediate reelection and that declaring that the executive and the members of the supreme court should be chosen by the congress.

The Bolivarian Constitutions. In many letters, state papers, and discourses Simón Bolívar gave expression to ideas and principles he thought suitable for incorporation in constitutions of Latin America and especially of the countries he had liberated. Although a soldier, experienced in both defeat and victory, he was always more than an active field commander; he was an administrator of government, a leader of opinion, and a framer of institutions. On several occasions, he turned from battle to bring to bear in civil affairs his versatile abilities as orator, statesman, theorist, and lawgiver. As constitution maker, he was to suffer vicissitudes in fortune as well as to make contributions of lasting importance to his people. Of enduring fame are the Cartagena Manifesto (1812), the Jamaica Letter (1815), the Angostura Discourse (1819), and the Constitution for Bolivia (1826). Of much importance to students of Bolivarian thought is the Provisional Statute of 1817.[27] So, too, were his comments of the Cúcuta constitution of 1821. The first of these state papers—the Cartagena Manifesto—was an explanation of the collapse of the first Venezuelan republic and, by implication and affirmative statement, an indication of a proper system of government suitable at that time to the new and inexperienced state. The disaster which overtook the first republic was caused, he held, not by the power of royalist arms, but by the weakness and incompatibility of the government set up in 1811. It was an impressive demonstration of the importance of the form of government and of the need that the form be appropriate to the character and experience of the people and to the circumstances.

For Bolívar's positive thought about constitutions and forms of government, the most important statements were offered in the Angostura Discourse and in the project of a constitution for Bolivia. Before analyzing his recommendations, it would be well to summarize some of his general ideas, which embraced history, economics, and sociology as well as politics. At Angostura, he issued a warning that long continuance of power in the hands of the same person may mean the end of democratic government and that in such prolonged tenure lie the origins of usurpation and tyranny. Complete authority and absolute liberty are reefs on

[27] See C. Parra Pérez, *Bolívar: Contribución al estudio de sus ideas* (Paris, 1929), pp. 58–69.

which republics have foundered. Yet he believed in republics, with liberty and political equality for citizens. But, he argued, "Absolute liberty invariably lapses into absolute power." The basic principles of a republic "should be the sovereignty of the people, division of powers, civil liberty, and the abolition of monarchy and privileges." He also warned against too much faith in systems, since experience has shown how difficult it is to govern men by laws alone. Back of governments, civic virtues must be cultivated, industry must be fostered, popular education must be encouraged and supported, and the many racial types must be fused into a nation through unity and political equality. Otherwise codes and systems of government may have little influence upon people and society. He hoped for a government which would result in the greatest measure of happiness and the maximum of social security and political stability. For the goal to be attained, the powers of government and the liberty of the people have both to be restricted. The organs of government, separate in organization, should severally be sufficiently strong to accomplish the purposes for which they were created and invested with functions. With governmental organs given functions limited by law, the popular will must be moderated. Skeptical about systems of political thought, Bolívar declared: "We must never forget that the excellence of a government lies not in its theories, not in the form or mechanism, but in its being suited to the nature and character of the nation for which it is instituted."

In his Angostura Discourse he favored a unitary or centralized organization of government as being more simple, expeditious in action, and suitable to the people. It is perhaps just to say that his arguments for this form are not as strongly expressed as those against federalism. He argued that the executive power should be vested in a single individual, chosen by the people or by their representatives.[28] This executive office should be clothed with ample powers to accomplish with vigor and dispatch the objects committed to it. He upheld an independent judiciary as a remedy for the abuses suffered by colonial people from the Spanish courts. Bolívar, so far, favored a forthright and real separation of powers instead of a partial separation or an interlocking of powers under a scheme of

[28] Some writers hold that in the Discourse Bolívar favored a lifetime tenure for the president. See Parra Pérez, *Bolívar,* pp. 78, 97. See also Gil Fortoul, *op. cit.,* and Gerhard Masur, *Simón Bolívar* (Albuquerque, N.M., University of New Mexico Press, 1848). The latter holds that a life term was not urged in the Discourse. This is believed to be the correct opinion.

checks and balances. With respect to the legislature, he would have a chamber of representatives which was to be the "voice of the people." His proposal concerning a senate was in favor of a hereditary body, which should be a politically neutral counterweight to the elective chamber.[29] Future senators were to be prepared for their service in a school specially designed for them. The senate would be a means of reconciling the rival powers of the government and the people; it would not only be "a bulwark of liberty, but a bastion of defense, rendering the Republic eternal."

Another innovation was the fourth or "moral" power, modeled upon the Areopagus of Athens and the censors of Rome. This organ was to watch over the education of the young; to promote the national enlightenment; and to denounce ingratitude, lack of patriotism, idleness, violations of the constitution, and acts against public decency.

Neither the hereditary senate nor the moral power, both criticized as impractical and undemocratic, was adopted by the congress; but many of the remaining recommendations were approved and became operative in Venezuela and later in Gran Colombia. The Congress of Angostura adopted (May 24, 1819) a lifetime tenure for members of the Senate and also made the bishops honorary members. This principle of life membership was of short duration, since the constitution of Cúcuta of 1821 established a term of eight years, with half of the membership renewable each four years.

On invitation of the state which was to bear his name, Bolívar in 1826 drafted a proposed constitution and sent with it a lengthy explanation and defense. This constitution was adopted, although with numerous modifications. It contained a number of unusual features which

[29] In a letter to Guillermo White, May 26, 1820, Bolívar wrote: "As regards *my* senate, let me say that it is neither an aristocracy nor a nobility, with the former possessing the right to command the Republic and the latter enjoying obnoxious privileges. The function of my senate is to temper absolute democracy and to adjust the format of an absolute government to that of more moderate institutions; for today it is an accepted principle of politics that an absolute democratic government is as tyrannical as any despot; hence, only a hybrid government can be free. How would you have me temper democracy except with an aristocratic institution? Since we must not cross the monarchic with the popular form of government that we have adopted, we should, at least, make a place in the Republic for one permanent body to insure stability. Without stability, any political principle becomes corrupt and terminates in selfdestruction." Vicente Lecuna and H. A. Bierck (eds.), *Selected Writings of Bolívar* (New York, The Colonial Press, 1951), vol. I. p. 227.

have caused much discussion and great diversity of opinion. One such provision was the division of the supreme powers of the state into four branches: electoral, legislative, executive, and judicial. In defense of this provision, Bolivar wrote:[30]

> The project of the constitution for Bolivia is divided into four powers, having added one more without thereby complicating the classical division of each one of the others. . . . It has seemed to me not only suitable and useful, but also easy, to grant to the immediate representatives of the people the privileges which the citizens of each department, province, and canton can most desire. No object is more important to a citizen than the election of his legislators, magistrates, judges, and priests. The electoral colleges of each province represent their own needs and interests and serve as agents of protest against the infractions of the laws and the abuses of the magistrates. I would be bold to say precisely that this representation arises from rights which the local governments enjoy in federal states. In this way a new weight has been placed in the balance against the executive; and the government has acquired more guarantees, more popularity, and new titles in order that it stand out among the most democratic.

The legislative branch consisted of three chambers—the tribunate, the senate, and the censors—with the tribunes serving for four years, the senators for eight, and the censors for life. The congress, as a whole, named the president in the first instance, confirmed the choice of vice-president, and participated in the choice of certain other officials. The purpose of such a legislative organization was to avoid conflicts and deadlocks such as had occurred in the more conventional scheme. To this end the functions of the respective chambers were clearly specified. The tribunes should have the initiative in the matters of the territorial division of the republic, taxation and expenditures, coinage of money and issuance of currency, weights and measures, declaration of war and peace, citizenship and naturalization, and grants of general pardon. The senate should have the attributes of forming codes and courts, repressing infractions of the constitution, proposing lists—to be submitted to the censors—of judges, archbishops, and prelates, confirming nominations of prefects, governors, and corregidors, and adjusting matters pertaining to the Patronato. The censors had the functions of guarding the fullfillment of the constitution, the laws, and public treaties; of charging before the sen-

[30] Vicente Lecuna (ed.), *Documentos referentes a la creación de Bolivia* (Caracas, 1924), vol. II, p. 312. For text of the project and of the letter to the congress, see pp. 311–355.

ate executive officials for such infractions, of impeaching the vice-president, of adopting acts concerning the press and printing; of encouraging the arts and sciences; and of decreeing public honors.

The vice-president and the ministers were granted the privilege of attending the sessions of the congress, of debating issues, but not of voting. Acts adopted by the tribunate were sent to the senate and on being approved were submitted to the executive for promulgation. In the case of disapproval by the senate—and of persistence in the disapproval—the act was to be sent to the censors for final action. Acts originating in the senate were to be sent to the chamber of censors, just as those originating in the censors were to be sent to the senate. In either of these cases, when concurrence was not obtainable, the act went to the tribunes. All acts were to be submitted to the president, who could consider them during a ten-day period, before the end of which he might return them, with a statement of opinion, recommending that they be considered anew. Acts to which the president objected might be decided by a plurality of the members of the congress meeting as a whole.

Perhaps the most famous recommendation was that of a president who should have a lifetime tenure. The president was to nominate the vice-president, who under normal circumstances would succeed. It is to be noted that the congress was to confirm the choice of the vice-president. This official, instead of being a figurehead, was to be head of the administrative service and, in this capacity, was to acquire experience in the management of public affairs. He was to sign, along with the appropriate ministers, all acts of the executive branch. In case the vice-president was unsatisfactory, the president could remove him, but in the case of acceptable service, he would succeed the president as if in a hereditary scheme. By this device, elections involving the succession in the executive branch would be avoided. Elections of this kind were regarded as the scourge of republics, producing anarchy, which is the "luxury of tyranny and the most immediate and terrible danger of popular governments." According to Bolívar, the faculties given to the president were the same as those granted to the president of the United States. It would seem, however, if the recommendations are taken in a strictly literal sense, that the powers would be less, especially in such an important political matter as the naming of personnel. For a president who was to be "the center of the public authority and the guarantee of stability"—in fine, "the most sublime inspiration in the republican order"—Bolívar strangely left him without the means of acquiring influence.

The judicial branch was to be independent, with the judges serving during good behavior. In the system of the administration of justice, the use of juries was recommended in criminal cases.

The internal organization was to be centralized, with departments administered by prefects, provinces by governors, and cantons by corregidors. These officers were to be chosen by the senate from lists submitted by the electoral branch. The adoption of this plan and its practical application would have meant that the executive would have had little control of internal administration.

Bolívar made no recommendation of a state church. Nonetheless, there were recommendations concerning the nomination and "presentations" of important church officials.

The Liberator offered a set of guarantees of the rights of individuals and of corporate groups, but these were brief in statement and devoid of philosophical speculation and dogmatism. Provision was made for suspension of these guarantees in periods of emergency.

This very remarkable project of a constitution was, with modifications, adopted by the congress. The number of the modifications was somewhat greater than the commentators have suggested. In fact, there were thirty-one modifications, twelve additions, and three suppressions of articles. Among the additions the best known is the establishment of a state church.

The constitution lasted only two years. In several important proposals it was inconsistent with Bolívar's earlier statement of principles. It is remarkable and inexplicable that he should have proposed a weak and a virtually plural executive, without the power to select the administrative officers and subject to numerous legislative and judicial restraints. The life term for the president was clearly in contradiction to the fears he had solemnly expressed about long continuance of power in the same person. Despite his previous advocacy of a strong central government, it is doubtful whether his plan in this constitution provided for effective control over the internal administration of the country. Aside from issues of consistency, the main weaknesses were the complexity of institutional structure and the unsuitability of the constitution to the country and people.

During the years 1825–1828, in order to consolidate the peace and to preserve the fruits of victory, to meet the dangers of the international situation, and to secure and maintain orderly government, Bolívar conceived the idea of an Andean federation of the countries which he had liberated. He thought that the Bolivian constitution was adaptable to this purpose. As the plan was unfolded and refined, there was added the proposal of federation in a different form. Of many variations of this proposal, the final seems to have been that of a federation of seven entities: Bolivia, Arequipa, Lima, Ecuador, Cundinamarca, Cartagena, and Venezuela. Thus Peru and New Granada would each be divided into two parts. The jurisdiction of the local governments would include all political affairs except foreign relations and war. The constituent states with their separate governmental structures would be unitary in organization.[31] This plan was never realized in fact.

The last phase of Bolívar as a proponent of constitutional principles was his part in the so-called Gran Convención of Ocaña in 1828. This constituent assembly met at a time when his health was in decline and when the partisanship of factions was so strong that unity of action was improbable and constructive action of any kind unlikely. The Colombian union was drifting toward separation; monarchy, dictatorship, federalism, and separation were being advocated. Disorders occurred in some areas. Some of his critics have thought that Bolívar faltered, did not exercise leadership in the convention, became pessimistic, was willing to compromise only after compromise was too late, and in the failure of the convention wound up a dictator. To be sure, the situation was difficult and still remains obscure to fair-minded students.

In his message to the convention, Bolívar drew a dismal picture of the situation in the country: The government was badly constituted, with an executive power which, instead of being strong, was subordinate to the legislative, judiciary, and the municipalities. There was a disordered, inequitable, and unproductive economy. There were factionalism, anarchy, and lack of peace and security. His remedy: "Give us a government in which the law will be obeyed, the courts respected, and the people free; a government that shall see that the general will and the commandments of the people do not go unheeded."[32]

At first, he held that the people wanted a "provisional government, empowered to preserve and organize the Republic." This was regarded by opponents as meaning government by Bolívar, and they would have none of it. Later on he seems to have accepted for Gran Colombia some elements of his previous plan for the federation of the Andes. This would have been a federation of three "districts" or states, with each of these

[31] Víctor Andrés Belaunde, *Bolívar and the Political Thought of the Spanish American Revolution* (Baltimore, John Hopkins Press, 1938), pp. 290–293.

[32] Lecuna and Bierck (eds.), *op cit.,* vol. II, p. 683.

districts to have a unitary or centralized government, but with the three united for certain purposes. Such a solution was not to be, and the convention broke up in failure, without either side's being able to muster a majority.

Federalism versus Unitarism

Many writers, orators, and statesmen of Latin America have from time to time professed the idea that the institutions of a country should be suited to the character of its people—their experience, capacity for self-government, and political culture—and to its economy. Instead of being imported and thereby artificial, it was argued that institutions should be an evolutionary outgrowth of local conditions. What may be properly borrowed from abroad in the interest of progress should be compatible with the realistic possibilities of practical use and application by the people who receive the foreign influence. These considerations have a significant bearing upon the controversies now being reviewed.

The partisans of federalism and unitarism, in turn, made the effort to show the suitability of their proposed institutions to people and local conditions. The protagonists of federalism made a determined effort to show that the system was deeply rooted in history. They argued that in Spain, under a common crown, various "states" or kingdoms which were previously independent enjoyed after unification local rights; that there had been a tradition of municipal home rule, which had been effectively realized in the colonies; that the Spanish colonial administration had been in fact decentralized; and that geographical sectionalism existed in most of the governmental divisions of the empire. Furthermore, they pointed out that some of the new countries—notably Argentina and Venezuela—had, only a short time before independence, been administratively unified under a viceroy or captain general.[33]

Those favoring centralization attacked this case at several points. They claimed that the Spanish respect for local custom and administrative practices could not be justifiably called autonomy. The tradition of municipal home rule, they argued, was a matter of sentiment and infrequent application rather than a historically sound basis for federalism, with which they considered the countries that emerged from the Spanish empire to be unacquainted.

Undoubtedly sentiments in favor of federalism were, in the beginning of the struggle for independence, strongly developed in such countries

[33] F. Ramos Mejía, *El federalismo argentino* (Buenos Aires, 1889).

as Venezuela, New Granada, and Argentina, as they were in Mexico at the beginning of the republic. This popularity was in large measure due to the influence and example of the United States.[34] The example of the United States could be and was used, however, as an argument against federalism. In that country, it could be pointed out, federation united former colonies which had been separately established and administered, whereas Latin-American federation was to divide what had been previously united.[35] Such arguments were offered at one time or another in countries like Argentina, Colombia, Venezuela, Mexico, and Brazil.

In some parts of Latin America, federalism was identified with liberalism. It was argued that the autonomy of provinces was a counterbalance to oppression by a central government and thereby a possible guarantee of liberty. This identification of federalism with a "liberal" program was persistent in Mexico, where it was associated with a series of "plans" in which attacks were made on the vested interests of the army, the landlords, and the Church. In other plans social reforms were promised, and they on occasion became associated with the concept of federalism. A somewhat similar identification occurred in Colombia. Federalism did not necessarily carry any such implications in fact or in theory. In Argentina it has not been supposed—especially by its critics—to mean any of them, but rather the autonomy of the provinces meant the rule of a local *caudillo* who might be in alliance with the vested interests, who was alleged to favor the perpetuation of "barbarism," and who was an example of personalism or dictatorship in government.

One of the most consistent opponents of federalism was Bolívar, although he was not opposed to it in principle. "The federal system, although the most perfect and the most capable of providing for human happiness in society, is, nevertheless, the most contrary to the interests of our infant states," he wrote in the Cartagena Manifesto. His arguments against the adoption of this system by Latin America were (1) its lack of suitability to a people inexperienced in self-government and newly

[34] Justo Arosemena, *op. cit.*, p. 51, holds that the *Junta de Cartagena* in 1811 in favoring federalism did not make any allusion to the United States. For contrary opinion, see J. P. Restrepo, *Historia de Colombia* (Besancon, 1858), vol. VIII, p. 124. Also, Gil Fortoul, *op. cit.*, p. 218; C. Parra Pérez, *Historia de la primera república de Venezuela,* vol. I, pp. 129 ff.

[35] José de la Vega, *La federación en Colombia* (Madrid, Editorial-América, n.d.), p. 14. Citing Cuervo, *Apuntaciones críticas sobre el lenguaje bogotano,* p. 331, he held that in Colombia the constitution makers had not made *e pluribus unum* but *ex uno plura* their motto; instead of uniting, they were dividing.

emancipated from despotism, and (2) its weakness and complexity in structure, which made it a poor instrument for the conduct of war and for effective action in maintaining internal peace and which facilitated internal factions by its dualism and decentralization. He felt that many intellectuals of his and other Latin-American countries, imbued with and beguiled by ideas derived from classical Greece, France, England, and the United States, were visionaries and favored chimerical republics of their imaginations. On several occasions he gave expression to realistic observations concerning his own people who lived in wide territorial domains, without ready means of transportation and communication, without adequately developed agriculture and industry, without ethnic solidarity, divided by racial animosities and class prejudices. For them, the federal system was neither an appropriate nor even a possible form of government. In the Angostura Discourse, he appealed directly to Montesquieu for the opinion that laws and forms of government should be suited to the people for whom they are established; they must take into account the physical conditions of the country, climate, character of the land, location, size, and mode of living of the people; they should be in keeping with the religion, resources, number, commerce, habits, and customs of the inhabitants. Against an unsuitable federalism, he upheld the idea of an indivisible and centralized republic.[36]

BIBLIOGRAPHY

Arosemena, Justo, *Estudios constitucionales sobre los gobiernos de la América Latina,* 2 vols., Paris, 1878.

Belaunde, Víctor Andrés, *Bolivar and the Political Thought of the Spanish American Revolution,* Baltimore, Johns Hopkins Press, 1938.

Blanco Acevedo, P., *Estudios constitucionales,* Montevideo, 1939.

Borja y Borja, Ramiro, *Las constituciones del Ecuador,* Madrid, 1951.

Fernández de Lizardi, J. J., *El pensador mexicano,* Mexico, 1940.

Galdames, Luis, *La evolución constitucional de Chile,* Santiago, 1925.

Gibson, William Marion, *The Constitutions of Colombia,* Durham, N.C., Duke University Press, 1948.

Gil Fortoul, José, *Historia constitucional de Venezuela,* 2d ed., 2 vols., Caracas, 1930.

[36] The leading champions of federalism of this period were José Miguel Infante of Chile, Miguel Ramos Arizpe of Mexico, Camilo Torres of Colombia, and Manuel Dorrego of Argentina. The leading unitarists were Juan Egaña of Chile, Rivadavia of Argentina, Nariño of Colombia, and Mier of Mexico.

James, Herman G., *The Constitutional System of Brazil,* Washington, D.C., Carnegie Institution, 1923.

Lazcano y Mazón, Andrés M., *Las constituciones de Cuba,* Madrid, 1952.

Matienzo, José Nicolás, *El gobierno representativo federal en la República Argentina,* Madrid, 1917.

Moreno, L., *Historia de las relaciones interestatales de Centro América,* Madrid, 1928.

Parra Pérez, C., *Bolívar, contribución al estudio de sus ideas políticas,* Paris, 1928.

———, *Historia de la primera república de Venezuela,* 2 vols., Caracas, 1939.

Posada, Adolfo, *Instituciones políticas de los pueblos hispano-americanos,* Madrid, 1900.

Rabasa, Emilio, *La constitución y la dictadura,* Mexico, 1912.

Recasens Siches, L., *Latin American Legal Philosophy,* Cambridge, Mass., Harvard University Press, 1948.

Robertson, W. S., *Hispanic-American Relations of the United States,* New York, Oxford University Press, 1923.

Rowe, L. S., *The Federal System of the Argentine Republic,* Washington, D.C., Carnegie Institution, 1921.

Sánchez Viamonte, Carlos, *Historia institucional de Argentina,* Mexico, 1948.

Shaw, P. V., *The Early Constitutions of Chile, 1810–1833,* New York, Chile Publishing Company, 1931.

Vega, José de la, *La federación en Colombia,* Madrid, Editorial-América, n.d.

Zum Felde, A., *Proceso histórico del Uruguay,* Montevideo, 1919.

Chapter 6: DICTATORS AND REVOLUTIONS

Latin Americans have had a very general interest in dictatorships and revolutions and in the course of their history have seen much of both. Probably at no one time have they all been entirely free of dictatorship. Some countries have been governed by dictators during the major part of their history.[1] Some writers have held that the origins and causes of dictatorships are to be found in the history and customs of each of the races that compose the population. Many think that the use of dictatorship as a form of government has not ended.

DICTATORSHIP

Latin-American writers have given much attention to dictatorship. The very considerable literature relative to the subject may readily be divided between apologies and adverse criticisms. Some defend a particular dictator, usually a contemporary one, while others defend dictatorship as an institution providing the only adequate and realistic solution of the disorders supposed to be characteristic of Latin-American politics. Other writers have denounced the misdeeds and misgovernment of particular dictators, and there are books and essays which objectively condemn—as strongly as may be done anywhere—dictatorship in general as an evil in itself which stands in the way of liberty, democracy, justice, and civilization.

Latin America has had many types of dictators. If one could depict the careers of all the men who have essayed this role, an amazing and diversified spectacle would be afforded. This task has been attempted by presenting case studies of types, as in Bunge's *Nuestra América.* There have been dictators, however, who cannot be classified according to type and who approach in this respect the unique. Such was Santa Anna, stormy petrel of Mexican politics from 1823 to 1855, dramatic and spectacular

[1] Of several examples, we shall mention the following: Mexico, prior to 1910, had three principal dictatorships—Santa Anna, Benito Juárez, and Porfirio Díaz; Guatemala, prior to 1944, had Rafael Carrera, Justo Rufino Barrios, Estrada Cabrera, and Jorge Ubico; Paraguay, prior to 1870, had Francia and the two López, father and son; Venezuela, prior to 1935, had Páez, the Monagas brothers, Falcón, Guzmán Blanco, Crespo, Castro, and Gómez.

in action, nine times in the office of president, inglorious in war, unstable in politics and character. Although often given the opportunity, he was never able to consolidate power on an enduring basis. Why he was so long tolerated and how, having merited disapproval, he could time after time regain support and office have not as yet been convincingly explained.

One type of dictator was the temporary ruler, who was strong enough to use power to the point of extravagance and tyranny but was weak enough to become the ridiculous instrument of those who exploited him and the public for their own ends. His tenure was brief, and his story is of interest to the "historian of anecdote and of the temporarily notorious."[2]

The schooling, whether formal or not, of dictators who lasted for an extended period was a hard and a competitive one, which often produced men of intelligence if not of learning, men of action, firmness, shrewdness, and sound judgment. Some of them were undoubtedly rude and ignorant, and some remained so; but some, like Páez of Venezuela, came to have something of statesmanship and a regard for law and respectability. The Argentine philosopher Alberdi admitted that sometimes inferior and unlettered men are ennobled and prepared for management of important affairs through experience. He wrote: "To govern ten years is equivalent to a formal education in politics and administration."

There was the cruel and bloody dictator (*caudillo sangriento*), who with corps of spies and informers instituted a reign of terror. Among many who have borne the stigma of this classification the names of Rosas of Argentina, Estrada Cabrera and Ubico of Guatemala, Zelaya of Nicaragua, and Machado of Cuba would be included.

One would find, also, the feudal overlord, constantly but sometimes capriciously at work forming alliances, now favoring and now punishing, and ever and again setting his possible rivals against one another so that by dividing he continued to rule.

Another type was the soldier of reputation and even of personal heroism, who delighted in feats of arms and in leadership of the army in battle and who in rare cases might regard the emoluments of office with indifference, as Crespo was represented to be.

One might find, as another type, the bigoted dictator who was fired by religious zeal and who with agencies which have been compared to the old Inquisition sought to invest the Church with control of thought and

[2] Of one of these caudillos of brief tenure, Vargas Vila remarked, "He enters into chronology, he does not belong to history."

conduct. Such was García Moreno of Ecuador, who had been a professor and a teacher of the natural sciences.

There was the fairly common figure of the constructor of internal improvements and memorial buildings. There was also the so-called enlightened dictator who was active in carrying out a constructive program in education, the arts, industry, commerce, and culture.[3]

Such a system of government has not in the past necessarily rested and does not in the present century depend upon a forceful seizure of power, or upon arbitrariness and cruelty in the use and abuse of power. Yet some or all of these manifestations of conduct and attitude may be in evidence, and many dictatorships originated in revolutions. A dictatorial regime may rest upon legal elections or upon the use of plebiscites, it may respect constitutional procedures and sanctions, it may effectively serve the interests of a party, and it may verifiably assert claims of acting in benefit of national interests, patriotism, and culture. Such a regime may exist without the dictator's being continuously in possession of office.

In 1890, the critics of the Roca–Juárez Celman regime in Argentina gave the following analysis:

> The national life is paralyzed as regards the functioning of its regular organs. An absorbent centralism, such as the most fanatical defenders of the unitary system would not have imagined, has been substituted for our constitutional forms. The president of the republic exercises *de facto* all the sum of public power; he has in his hands the reins of municipal power, the key of the banks, the tutelage of provincial governments, the voice and vote of members of the congress, and even makes use of the judicial power; he discharges moreover what is called the headship [*jefatura*] of the dominant party. The president exercises

[3] Raul Carrancá y Trujillo, *Panorama crítico de nuestra América* (Mexico, 1950), pp. 162–163. He writes: "Not all, notwithstanding, offered the same characteristics. There is an enormous distance between the brutal and the refined; between the bloody and the progressive; between the semisavage Páez and Guzmán Blanco, cultivated and observer of good form; between the Indian Carrera, who did not know to what use to put the watch sent to him to time his arrival at the cathedral for a celebration of his triumph, and another Indian, Juárez, the follower of Comte and sincere republican; between the alcoholic and reckless Melgarejo or the blood-thirsty Rosas, and the ascetic Francia or the mystical García Moreno; between Artigas and Lavalle, chivalrous fighters; Santa Cruz, trusting in Providence and lover of colonial ceremonials, and Santander, assassin without greatness; between Facundo Quiroga and Porfirio Díaz. For some, primitive violence. For others, refined astuteness."

[4] José Luis Romero, *Las ideas políticas en Argentina* (Mexico, 1946), pp. 189–190. This statement was issued as a campaign document by a political party.

de facto extraordinary powers to which the constitution refers when, having in mind antecedents sadly notorious in our public life, it provides that those who propose such powers in favor of a governor are to be considered as infamous traitors to the country; and these extraordinary powers . . . have been delivered to the chief of the executive power.

This passage is quoted to show in what ways a presidential regime, chosen in a manner accepted as legal, had been converted by abuse of powers (according to its critics) into a dictatorship.

With such variation in type and basis, an inclusive definition of dictatorship having historical support of fact is scarcely possible. Since dictatorial governments may be legal in origin and in operation, such expressions as "presidential government" or "constitutional president" are used not merely by way of euphemism but as synonyms for dictatorship. Broad, indefinite, and flexible meanings have been given to the term "dictatorship." Latin Americans may think—as some have—of Jackson, Lincoln, the two Roosevelts, and even Woodrow Wilson as dictators. They may consider such men of magnetism as Clay, Blaine, and Bryan as "civil" *caudillos.*

The writers of the generation following independence and those of the late decades of the nineteenth century offered a variety of explanations of dictatorship.[5] Those of the early twentieth century, while recognizing a certain evolution in dictatorship and advancing psychological and sociological interpretations, concluded by differentiating types.[6] Contemporary writers, less given to detailed explanation, but keenly aware of the ability of dictators to clothe policies and deeds with the language of democracy and to identify their regimes with the cause of the masses, especially with that of organized labor, continue to recognize variety, even if some of them condemn all forms of dictatorship.[7]

If variety and differentiation occur, some similarities may also be found. There are traceable the outlines of a common pattern of dictators in the ways they have risen to influence and finally to power, in some of the

[5] Among these might be mentioned Sarmiento, Alberdi, and Ramos Mejía (Argentina); Lastarria (Chile); Montalvo (Ecuador); and Florentino González (Colombia).

[6] Among these would be Ayarragaray, Bunge, Colmo, and Ingenieros (Argentina); Argüedas (Bolivia); Vargas Vila and Pérez (Colombia); Arcaya and Vallenilla Lanz (Venezuela); and García Calderón (Peru).

[7] Among these would be Vasconcelos and Rabasa (Mexico); Ycaza Tigerino (Nicaragua); Díaz Sánchez, Betancourt, and Rondón Márquez (Venezuela); and Haya de la Torre (Peru).

characteristic policies for the consolidation of power and the elimination of enemies, in the conduct of administration, and in the process by which they have been overthrown. These common elements remind some students of some of the famous dictatorships in the history of other peoples —of Pisistratus, Dionysius, Caesar, and Napoleon. One would find in a study of each of these men as ruler an imperative demand for order; an effort to secure better administrative service, as in the collection of taxes; a reliance on military support; a building program—roadways, bridges, monuments, and public works; a foreign policy calculated to arouse patriotism; and some one specially favored policy, such as the grant of opportunities to an oppressed class, the encouragement of prosperity, or the expansion of the national domain. These famous dictators were intolerant of criticism and inclined to limit popular participation in public affairs. And there is marked similarity in the process of attaining power and in that of losing it. Such reflections have given rise to the speculation as to whether or not the Latin-American types of this government partake of a world order of dictatorship.

A recent writer states that "the career of the typical *caudillo* offers three climactic moments: that of his fascination of the people, that of the establishment of his political domination by force, and that of the consolidation of his power to the point of unlimited rule. Primarily all reveal in the leader an instinct for personal predomination; of this order is his professed willingness to stake his life in performance of civic duty, his cult of heroism, his presumptuousness and authoritarianism, his daring turbulence in opposition."[8] In the first phase of the rise to power, the aspirant acquires by fascination, or daring, or oratory, or money, or otherwise a local following. He is nearly always willing to fight to secure and retain this support. The bond between leader and followers is usually called "prestige," by which is meant those qualities and powers of magnetism and communicable suggestion that characterize leadership. These supporters become his people (*gente*).[9] To some writers these personal followers become the retainers of a chieftain, comparable to the old feudal vassals or liegemen of medieval times. This local chieftain is sometimes called in southern South America a *caudillo de pago,* and the locality of his influence is a sort of fief. The second stage occurs when he establishes leadership over a group of neighboring *caudillos,* thereby becoming

[8] Carrancá y Trujillo, *op. cit.,* p. 160.

[9] P. M. Arcaya, *Estudios sobre personajes y hechos de la historia de Venezuela* (Caracas, 1911), p. 36.

a sectional or regional chief.[10] Thirdly, in the role of liberator or avenger or restorer, he challenges the central authority and, after a contest which may take years and which may terminate in a revolution, wins. In the fourth stage, as *caudillo nacional,* leader of a group of regional *caudillos* and of the country as a whole, he must consolidate his power by making agreements with possible foes or by suppressing them. This may result in cleavages and consequential struggles and may be a bloody "mopping-up" procedure, but with victory order is established and personal devotees are placed in office.

As the dominant dictator he develops his own style and manner of government. In ratification, elections may be held and a new constitution may be adopted. Once the system crystallizes, little variation or deviation in method is expected. A period of rule, more or less extended in time, ensues. Resistance may develop, and it may become recurrent. A dictator has an important decision to make as to how he will forestall or meet opposition. In the last phase, he may lose prestige and "touch" with his followers; he may have to yield to a new and successful revolution which may have run the same course as that by which he rose to power. Or he may grow old and die in office, and again the country may traverse the same course, since not all dictators have been able to pass on their office through natural inheritance or political bequest.[11]

Some dictators have shown a Macchiavellian skill in meeting opposition, whereas others have encountered difficulty or have succumbed to counter-revolution. Men such as Portales of Chile, Castilla of Peru, Guzmán Blanco and Gómez of Venezuela, and Díaz of Mexico exhibited great capacity in this respect. A remarkable example of this ability to deal with enemies was that of Guzmán Blanco.[12] Although a series of revolts or counterrevolutions occurred, the dictator was able to prevent a combination of opposing leaders. Through the elimination of General Matías Salazar, former friend and a hero of earlier conflicts, he was able to crush a revolt and consolidate his power and prestige.[13] Careful prepara-

[10] For an interesting consideration of the *caudillo de pago*, see A. Zum Felde, *Evolución histórica del Uruguay* (3d ed., Montevideo, 1945), p. 167.

[11] Some notable exceptions may be noted as the Monagas brothers in Venezuela, 1846–1858; the "Meléndez dynasty" of El Salvador, 1913–1927; and the "López dynasty" of Paraguay, 1841–1870. In addition to transfer of power to kinsmen there is the case of "imposed" candidacies by means of which an incumbent administration seeks to control the succession.

[12] His period of ascendancy in Venezuela was 1870 to 1889. He was the son of Antonio Leocadio Guzmán, one of the founders of the Liberal party.

[13] R. Díaz Sánchez, *Guzmán, elipse de una ambición de poder* (Caracas, 1950).

tion was made for the campaign, including the purchase of such an improved weapon as the Springfield rifle, and this was followed by the drafting of a fully documented statement of causes and events relative to the conflict and its outcome. The one was a guarantee of military success, and the other was designed to make the consequent act of punishment an act of justice rather than of vengeance. Defeated and captured, Salazar was tried and executed, becoming thereby a "dike against the anarchy of the time."

General Porfirio Díaz (1877–1880, 1884–1911) in Mexico was one of the most adroit in dealing with the enemies of his rule. Some he bought with favors and offices, some were banished or driven into exile, some were inducted into the military service, some were defeated or killed in battle, and some were assassinated. He was a past master in the game of "divide and rule." The opposition press was subjected to various embarrassments and fines; some editors were assassinated, and some newspapers were suppressed. Elections were controlled—if intervention was necessary—by intimidation and fraud.

General Juan Vicente Gómez (1909–1935) of Venezuela, with the aid of a loyal and efficient army, was usually able to crush his opposition before it passed the stage of incipient activity. Leaders of opposing groups were imprisoned or took refuge abroad. Finally he disarmed the populace and forbade the possession of certain types of firearms. The discussion of politics was forbidden in public places. Road barriers enabled the authorities to keep a check on the movement of people.

The government of Guzmán Blanco may serve as an example of the fact that the time of the consolidation of his power—the *septenio,* 1870–1877—was also that of the development of the most significant policies as statesman, "reformer," and "civilizer." The later periods in office showed refinements and realization of earlier policies rather than the initiation of new ones. In the first period occurred the humiliating conquest of the Church. Then notable economic and fiscal reforms were accomplished or started. Then was begun the construction of many public works, railways and highways, and monuments—including some to himself. Then were enacted laws relative to gratuitous and compulsory

---

p. 550. Salazar, a man of humble origin, had been a teacher, bullfighter, and barber. The "federal war," 1859–1864, had "drawn him out of anonymity" and had given him the reputation of a valiant soldier. The author holds that he was enticed into opposition and conspiracy by Felipe Larrazábal.

education, and then was initiated the movement for the introduction of French culture.

This outline of the process of attaining power, the ways and means of consolidating that power, the early formulation of policies of a characteristic nature, should be considered as a suggestive basis of comparison.

The present generation of Latin Americans is no stranger to this manner of government. In the Caribbean area alone, it has witnessed governments, classed as dictatorships, by Jorge Ubico (1930–1944) in Guatemala, Hernández Martínez (1931–1944) in El Salvador, Carías Andino (1932–1948) in Honduras, Anastasio Somoza (1937–) in Nicaragua, Trujillo Molina (1930–) in the Dominican Republic, and Fulgencio Batista (1952–) in Cuba. In the careers of these men may be found examples of many of the differences in dictatorial rule which have been pointed out and along with them some new variants. There have been cases of comparative mildness and progressiveness, of terrorism and the sinister use of Gestapo-like police forces, of several instances of *continuismo* in the extension of tenures, and of two dramatically successful uses of the general strike as a means of overthrowing certain dictators—a device employed by Cuba in 1933 in terminating the rule of Machado. The use of machine guns, airplanes, tanks, and other arms of modern warfare has been associated in at least three instances with repressive methods that were old in technique.

Explanations of Dictatorship by Latin Americans

Commentators have advanced widely varying explanations of dictatorship for more than a century, with some of the greatest minds engaged in the task, such as Bolívar, Alberdi, Sarmiento, Lastarria, Montalvo, Arcaya, Ayarragaray, and Vallenilla Lanz. In Latin America historians, political scientists, sociologists, economists, psychologists, pathologists, lawyers, poets, novelists, and the unclassified group of pamphleteers have written about the subject, and the end is not yet. Foreigners of many nationalities have joined in the effort. In the following analysis, chief reliance is placed upon Latin-American writers. Individual writers, of course, have not necessarily limited themselves to a single explanation, and some might properly appear as exponents of more than one set of causes or explanations.

1. One explanation of Latin-American dictatorships emphasizes the heritage of the races. Spaniard, Portuguese, Indian, and Negro, it is maintained, have in their respective histories recurrently employed

violence as a method of political action and have been accustomed to subjection to a chief or *caudillo* or cacique, whose rule was similar to a dictatorship. Many who held this general opinion attach blame to the colonial system for its perpetuation of racial weaknesses and for the heritage of social, political, and economic problems which provided incentives for revolutions and anarchy leading to dictatorial rule. Many who emphasize race as a decisive factor acknowledge indebtedness to such writers as Taine, Le Bon, Renan, Sighele, Spencer, and Gobineau. The followers of Taine constituted at one time what might be called a school, which was designated *tainista.*

The central thesis of this explanation is that certain races in the mass have customs and habits—such as the disposition to anarchy and submission to personalist and dictatorial rule—which result from a long evolution and constitute a sort of patrimony. These traditional customs and habits are changed only slowly, if at all. Although this group does not deny the possibility of progress of the peoples concerned from this cultural and political stage, its members do not think that such a change has yet occurred.

2. Closely related is another group of writers which also has used psychology, sociology, and anthropology in a series of studies of the pathological causes of dictatorship. This group emphasizes race as an important factor in the explanation of existing society, conditions, and practices. They also attach significance to customs, mainly bad, for which the colonial system was in part responsible. Latin-American peoples, they claim, suffer from long-continuing weaknesses and ills including such traits or habits as apathy, indolence, verbosity, arrogance, exaggerated sense of dignity, theatrical sense of the heroic (*heroicidad*), and impulsiveness. Such conditions as political anarchy or disorder, personalism in government, instability of and indifference to constitutions, big estates and monoculture, the ascendancy of generals and *doctores,* and the overlarge percentage of illiterates are the "symptoms" of a "sick people" (*pueblo enfermo*) needful of the treatment of a wise physician. In the style of the Spanish thinker Joaquín Costa, men like Alvarez, Bunge, Colmo, Argüedas, Ingenieros, Mendieta, Zumeta, and Pérez have employed the terminology of medical science, with the people as a sick patient undergoing prognosis and diagnosis, the prescription of remedy, and treatment. Political therapy and political surgery, as the case may suggest, are offered as cures for the ills of the body politic. Instead of waiting for the slow process of social evolution to operate, they would

apply scientific remedies in the form of political therapeutics.[14] Distasteful as the idea might have been, the successful application of such a plan would probably require a dictator.

3. In a third classification might be placed the many writers who have seen in the lack of general education and in the high percentages of illiteracy an explanation of political conditions and of this problem of *caudillismo*.[15]

It has been generally admitted that Latin America is relatively backward in popular education and that the percentage of illiterates has been and continues to be unduly high. The ratio of illiterates ranges among countries from as low as about 20 per cent to as high as perhaps 80 per cent. The assumptions are, of course, that a populace poorly educated and with a large portion unable to read would not be likely to take an intelligent part in politics, would not have an informed sense of rights and civic responsibilities, would not have a reasoned opinion of a system of government under law, and would not give a convinced and sustained support to such a system. Such a populace, it has been contended, resorts under stimulation to impulsive political action, is susceptible to recruitment in support of a magnetic and forceful *caudillo,* and is swayed by prejudices and superstitions. On the other hand, expansive and generous hopes have been expressed of benefits to the state from popular education, as have been evidenced by the slogans "to govern is to educate" (*gobernar es educar*) and "to educate is to redeem" (*educar es redimir*). It has been argued that education is a means of overcoming and altering racial customs which militate against the civil disorder and of remedying pathological ills. It should be noted, however, that Latin America has had many notable and devoted educators, that all governments give support—whether adequate or not—to public education, and that some governments use education as a means of political action in support of public order—of the kind officially endorsed.

It should also be stated that some deny that the lack of general edu-

[14] Cf. W. W. Pierson (ed.), "The Pathology of Democracy in Latin America: A Symposium," *American Political Science Review,* vol. 44, no. 1, March, 1950.

[15] "Popular education is the genesis of the liberty of nations." Enrique Pérez, *Vicios políticos de América* (Paris, n.d.), p. 99. Earlier (p. 91) he had written: "We have believed that the ignorance of our multitudes, aggravated by the negligence of our governments, is responsible in a ratio of at least 50 per cent that we have not been able, after a century of independence, to resolve our political and economic problems. The other 50 per cent of that responsibility falls on the vices which the colonial system left rooted and on atavistic defects. These last we have cultivated rather than corrected."

cation and the prevalence of illiteracy, although deplorable in themselves, are important as an explanation of revolutions and dictatorship. They point with some irony to the fact that most if not all dictators have had the support of some members of the intelligentsia and that this support has sometimes been expressed in terms of adulation. Some refer to the fact that dictatorships recently existed in Italy and Germany, countries with little illiteracy.

Some who maintain that the lack of education has been a primary cause of dictatorship, and that provision of education would be a preventive, have urged education in health and nutrition, in the trades, arts, and agriculture, in good government and citizenship. An education has been proposed that is suitable to the economic, social, and racial status of the individual. Many plans have been urged for new orientations in the education of professional men and businessmen, the clergy, lawyers, engineers, and planters. Some of these proposals have from time to time been put into practice, and great importance has been attached to these experiments.

4. Another explanation is that political and economic feudalism is the fundamental cause of *caudillismo* and dictatorship. One encounters this idea in some of the most famous and now classic treatises, such as those by Sarmiento and Alberdi. This idea may draw upon and make a special application of the racial heritage, such as was done in Sarmiento's *El Facundo* and the *Conflicto y armonías de las razas en la América.* Some exponents of this thesis take account of the *caudillo* as a horseman of the range lands—*gaucho*, *llanero*, *vaquero*—about whom clings a multiform and romantic legend of daring individualism. Out of such human material soldiers of fortune, revolutionists, and leaders in politics were made. Whether the future dictator was reared in the rural part and later became acquainted with the ways of urban life or was a city dweller who had to learn the customs of the *campo* or countryside, there was the problem for the national *caudillo* of blending rural and urban interests, since he was the medium of communication of these divergent factions. The careers of Quiroga, Rosas, Páez, Guzmán Blanco, and Saravia show the interaction of these influences. It can be said that the great estates, *haciendas* or *estancias,* which were and in some cases still are self-sufficient, isolated, and quasi-feudal communities, were political and economic units with the landlord or some political chief in control. These ranches became fruitful sources of *caudillos,* and on them were recruited supporters who might constitute units of fighters and voters.

This feudalism has had in history several aspects, such as that of the relation of landowner to the agricultural worker or to the worker on a cattle ranch, that of the relation of the *caudillo* to his follower, and that of the chief *caudillo* to the subordinate ones.[16] It is held that the social practices growing out of the *compadre* relations of individuals and the scheme of extranatural kinship known as *padrinazgo* informally but powerfully aid and abet this kind of feudalism.

A feudalism somewhat similar to that obtaining in medieval times in Europe and to that of modern Japan is said to have been operative in Argentina in the era of Rosas, who has often been called "el Señor Feudal." Organizing his own army recruited from the Gauchos of the great plantations and ranches and combining the cattlemen and salt-beef exporters into an informal but effective corporation, he ruled the province of Buenos Aires and later the country according to a "feudal" plan and economy, as if it were an estate. *Caudillos* like López, Quiroga, Bustos, Ibarra, and Aldao were associated and sometimes allied "feudal governors," who were eventually weakened or destroyed by rivalries among themselves. Some were humiliated and some assassinated.[17] Many writers of other countries have emphasized feudal causes of dictatorship, but Rosas is perhaps the best illustration. Not many dictators, like Rosas, were great landowners before elevation to power, although many became *hacendados* afterward.

5. Several of the explanations of dictatorship have given more or less consideration to economic causes and conditions. Those who have offered this interpretation have not been in agreement either as to data presented or as to principles and conclusions. Some of these are here presented as illustrative. First, there has been extreme unevenness in the distribution of wealth. The propertied and wealthy minority is offset by the great mass of the relatively poor and propertyless, without a middle class intervening

[16] Cf. José Ingenieros, *La evolución de las ideas argentinas—la restauración* in *Obras completas,* vol. 15, pp. 95–197; J. M. Ramos Mejía, *Rosas y su tiempo* (2d ed., Buenos Aires, 1907); A. Saldías, *Historia de la confederación argentina* (2d ed., 5 vols., Buenos Aires, 1892); A. Zinny, *Historia de los gobernadores de las provincias argentinas* (Buenos Aires, 1879–1882), vol. 1.

[17] Ingenieros summarizes some of the common policies: all entrusted the conduct of foreign relations to Rosas; he subsidized the subordinate *caudillos* with money and military supplies; each of the *caudillos* was sovereign in his *feudo* so long as he went along with Rosas; his powers and theirs were personal and irresponsible; all had flags, could coin money, and establish interior customs or tariff rates; Rosas guaranteed with his military power the stability of his friends. *Op. cit.,* vol. I, p. 425.

or with only a small middle class.[18] Then, the basic native industry has long been that of agriculture and stock raising, marked by the common and crucial feature of the big estate. The concentration of land ownership tended to increase in the nineteenth century, even in the disposal through grants, concessions, and sales of the public domain and by reason of the encroachment upon or confiscation of Indian communal properties. The spread of small property holdings (*conuco* and *colonia* are among several terms), independently owned, existent in some countries, has been offered as a panacea of social reform.

Excessive dependence upon foreign capital is another economic factor which has been used to explain the prevalence of dictatorships. Suffering a decline after independence, mining was revived with foreign capital and technical skill. Foreign capital was also invested in railways and other rapid-transit operations, mines, petroleum, meat- and grain-processing plants, banking, and various engineering activities. Furthermore, the long-supposed dearth of resources for heavy industry, such as coal and iron, caused dependence upon foreign sources of supply. Manufactured commodities, luxury articles, munitions, textiles, machinery, medicines, and many foodstuffs were imported. Producing in the main raw materials and exporting the surplus over the requirements for subsistence, many Latin-American countries were peculiarly dependent upon world markets and prices for prosperity. Outside economic crises or depressions caused financial repercussions, hard times, and revolutions. Relations with foreigners and foreign governments, the status of aliens and alien property, loans, claims, interventions, and "economic imperialism" had varying political influences—sometimes promoting dictatorship. How far these countries were to go in seeking foreign assistance in financing their industrial and economic development, to what extent they were to welcome the foreigners and to continue to treat them justly, and in what ways and on what bases of policy they were to repel such participation and ownership in the national interest were issues of grave importance. The aroused nationalist sentiment has often led to unfriendly regulations and expro-

[18] The above statement might be considered the thought of older writers. For a different opinion, consult the nine monographs bearing the general title of *Materiales para el estudio de la clase media en la América Latina* issued as *Publicaciones de la oficina de ciencias sociales* of the Pan American Union (Washington, D.C., 1950). For other works, see J. M. Quintana Pereyra, *La redención de la clase media* (Bogotá, 1936); R. MacLean y Estenós, *Clases sociales en el Perú* (Lima, 1941); R. Alarcón Pino, *La clase media en Chile* (Santiago, 1947). These works affirm the existence of such a class.

priation of foreign properties. Although some dictators were active promoters of the entrance of foreign capital, other dictators, prospective and actual, campaigned against "economic imperialism" in the name of patriotism.

Meantime, specialization in production, monoculture, staple or single crops—i.e., a one-sided or specialized economy—made some countries dependent on foreign markets.

Some objectionable features of foreign enterprise in Latin America have been the subject of repeated criticisms. Among the chief targets of criticism have been the acquisition of undue privileges through concessions, favors, and exemptions; the exploitation of native labor; aid to particular political factions, for which the price may have been further favors; interventions in local politics in order to protect interests already acquired; and the fact that foreign interests remained foreign, especially in that corporate profits and dividends were in whole or in large part sent out of the country. That foreign interests might lend material support to a dictatorial regime which was favorable to them was in the nature of things to be expected. Certainly foreigners have often joined in the homage and adulation rendered to the successful dictator. Other sources of complaint were the claims of foreigners for injury, which were sometimes supported by their governments.

Labor conditions and practices have undergone radical changes in Latin America. For a long time, labor on the great estates, with the features of peonage, low wages, and low standards of living, and the system of contract labor in the mines were thought of as obstacles to the growth of democracy and as contributory to dictatorial government. Although the bonds between the *patrón* and peon, long of a semifeudal character, were intimate and often friendly, they were to become objects of attack. Later, with the increased demand for production and for labor, with the progressive industrialization of the hacienda, and with the tightening of the bonds of peonage, relations between worker and landowner were weakened and became less friendly. Formerly indifferent to the cause of labor, some dictators underwent a change and espoused its interests. The self-consciousness of Latin-American labor once awakened, the progress of its organization was rapid. It found an ally and a leader in the new order of dictators.

6. Political scientists may be said to constitute a separate school of thought concerning dictatorships, but they have advanced differing explanations. One division has emphasized the conflict between personalism

and legalism in government. Florentino González, of Colombia, and Múñoz Tébar, of Venezuela, are good representatives of those who regarded personalism as the basic factor. *Personalismo i legalismo* (1890), by the latter author, discounted the influences of race and heredity as being necessarily controlling in a nation's life. He held that "the character of men depends on the education they receive" and that by education, national customs, civilization, and political practices it could be changed. From these postulates he proceeded to assign, as a chief difference between Anglo-Saxon and Latin American, the predominance of legalism on the one side and personalism on the other. By this he meant the difference between a government of laws and one of men, between a government in which law is supreme and respected and one under the arbitrary rule of dictatorship.

Lanz Duret, after having analyzed opinions of well-known contemporary writers, concluded that "the solution of all the political and juridical problems of Mexico will not be satisfactorily found unless Mexico might come to establish a regime of legality, a true state of law which might bring to an end the arbitrariness and abuse in our practices of government." He held that the Mexican revolution (1910–1947), while causing many social and economic improvements in benefit of the masses, had as yet failed to bring about political progress toward freedom under law. "Without the conquest," he wrote, "of the principle of legality, Mexico will remain stationary."[19]

Although this thesis has been supported by a rich documentation, its weakness lies in the ready ease by which personalism and dictatorship may be legalized. *De facto* governments have exercised constitution-making powers. Congresses have often in advance conferred legislative functions on the executive or have validated such exercise after the fact. Constitutions may provide for the grant of extraordinary powers, states of siege, and suspensions of guarantees. The ordinary functions of the executive may be so ample through constitutional provision that personalism in government is legalized. If the grant of total powers (*suma del poder*) was in itself legal, then all acts of the executive were legal.

Political scientists have found two conditions to prevail in nearly all the countries. First, the formal constitutions rarely correspond fully or coincide with the real and operative ones. For example, the conventional plan of a separation of the supposedly coordinate powers and departments

[19] Miguel Lanz Duret, *Derecho constitucional mexicano* (4th ed., Mexico, 1947), pp. 16–18.

of government has not prevented the almost universal ascendancy and supremacy of the executive. In one country, Chile, the congress for a time (1891–1924) exercised independence and control; versions of a parliamentary system have been tried in Chile, Uruguay, and Venezuela. Uruguay is making an interesting experiment with a plural executive. But, in general, the legislative power is secondary and in some cases subservient to the executive.

The second condition is that political parties or factions have frequently been personalist. The names—liberals, conservatives, centralists, federalists, radical democrats, progressives, socialists, communists—have not always represented the purposes and principles of parties.[20] A designation like Colorados or Blancos, terms used in Uruguay, would be equally identifying. To be sure, the indictment that real political parties are lacking is extreme and inaccurate, as will be shown later.

7. The next and last of the comprehensive explanations to be analyzed is that of the so-called "realists," who regard dictatorial government as it has developed the alternative to anarchy and the threat of social disintegration. As García Calderón put it, "Dictatorship appears to me the only regime adapted to the uncertain existence of to-day. The good tyrant is the ideal of the natives of the tropics—that is, the energetic civilizer who imposes order, who prevents social disintegration, who develops industries and commerce. European kings, conquering feudal anarchy and the conflict of races with a strong hand, formed nations: our dictators, when they have not been exponents of illiterate barbarism, have realized an equal work. No one who analyzes American history can safely discount the fact that Rosas and Portales, Rafael Núñez and García Moreno, Castilla and Santa Cruz were rude agents of progress and peace."[21] To some others, like Vallenilla Lanz, the Latin-American countries have been condemned to a turbulent life, and the dictator becomes a social necessity.[22] If political disorders result in subordination to a chief, it is hoped that he will be a good one, as well as a strong one. The possibility that the contrary may occur is readily admitted. The people must take the chance

[20] "Do not try to find complications of pure social interests," wrote Ayarragaray, "in the technique and genius of our primitive politics, because once stripped of its adventitious externals, the sentiment which generates all party action is adherence to the *caudillo*. . . . And as in reality there is no organic government, no political system, *tyranny, disorder, liberty, regeneration* is a man, or when several, a limited group of men." Lucas Ayarragaray, *La anarquía argentina y el caudillismo* (Buenos Aires, 1925), pp. 139–140.

[21] Prologue to Pérez, *op. cit.*

[22] Laureano Vallenilla Lanz, *Cesarismo democrático* (Caracas, 1919), pp. 188–222.

as to whether the dictator will be good or bad. It is sometimes also admitted that good and enlightened dictatorship may make people insensible to its nature and lead them to forget that "an Augustus may be succeeded by a Tiberius." The "good" dictator, however, has it within his opportunity and power to inaugurate a regime of "democratic Caesarism," as Vallenilla Lanz put it, or "democratic dictatorship," as Rabasa phrased it. There is the possibility that the dictatorship may be fully legalized.

Conclusion

Such are some of the explanations offered by Latin-American writers. The number must be large in response to the multiplied phases of this manner of government. In the midst of so much contradiction, one might conclude that dictatorship is only relatively "good" or "bad." There is too much wrongdoing, both potential and actual, in the system to permit of apology and too much verifiable service to social stability to permit of an all-inclusive censure. One weakness ineradicably associated with both good and bad dictators is the human nature of the ruler. In time, he grows old. Society—if it is so addicted—must endure the pains of giving birth to a new one.

Various adjectives have been placed before the term "dictatorship," either by way of description or classification. Notice has especially been taken of "legal" and "democratic" dictatorship. During the era of Porfirio Díaz, much was written about "scientific" dictatorship or the application of certain positivist principles to the government of Mexico. There is, also, the sinister classification of "disguised" dictatorship. Dictatorial rule in the interest of any favored ideology is a possibility, particularly when government of this kind is in the interest of a class, whether it be that of a wealthy oligarchy or a proletarian class or organized labor. The newly recognized middle class—itself of debatable existence and stability—may become, as some have predicted, an agency of "bureaucratic" dictatorship, for which the term "creole fascism" has been coined. So, too, in the mid-century choices between communism as interpreted by Latin America and "plutodemocracy" as allegedly drawn from the United States may become identified with a special kind of dictatorship. A Latin-American version of *falangismo,* or a dictatorship fashioned after Franco's Spain, is a possibility in the thought of some writers, related or not to the foregoing choices. Some, also, have suggested that these adjectives are catchwords which do not disguise the older forms and methods of dictatorship.

Some Latin-American writers have found a principle which differentiates their dictatorships and limits them. It may be admitted that formal constitutions present no insurmountable obstacle to this type of government, but it is held that there is the unwritten "social constitution" of tradition, thought of as a heritage of these peoples, which sets up intangible barriers to unrestricted exercise of personal power. They remind us that neither in Spain nor in Portugal, even in the heyday of the Inquisition and autocratic government, was absolutism to be confounded with sustained tyranny. Spaniards especially were able to reconcile absolutist government with a considerable measure of intellectual freedom and individualism. The *siglo de oro* in literature, art, historical writing, science, and navigation was also the century of autocracy in government. From medieval times, the Caesarist principle, "The prince is unrestrained by law" (*princeps legibus solutus est*) was repudiated. Instead, the principle was accepted, as formulated by Saint Isidore of Seville in the seventh century, that "the princes themselves are also bound to live according to their own laws" (*principes tenentur et ipsi vivere legibus suis*). Individualism, the home and family, and religion are, as some Latin Americans are fond of saying, "primordial elements and foundations" of freedom, the social order, and civilization. They are bulwarks against sustained encroachment by dictators.

It should be reemphasized that these seven explanations, although they have been presented separately for identification and analysis, are not mutually exclusive. It would be possible, perhaps, for elements and data from all to be synthesized in an exposition of causes, although there would necessarily be great variation in the order of presentation and the relative weight in importance given to the several factors.

REVOLUTIONS

The Spanish and Portuguese languages have many words signifying extralegal and violent means of securing or attempting to secure political action or change.[23] These terms distinguish, often in subtle manner, between efforts as to degree of importance and success. The range of dif-

[23] In Spanish there are such words as *asonada, revuelta, cuartelazo, levantamiento, sublevación, motín, montonera,* and *sargentada.* In addition, it is frequently a practice to give a popular name to a revolution, such as *la reivindicación* and *la aclamación* in Guzmán Blanco's time. The recent and successful uprising of Batista in Cuba was called the *madrugón* or "dawn movement." In Portuguese, one may find terms like *alvorôto, assuada, insurreição, levante, motim, quartelada, rebelião, revolta, sublevação.* Both languages have *golpe de estado.*

ferences in meaning is wide, reaching from the small-sized riots and barrack mutinies to full-dress civil wars and social revolutions. The term "revolution," used generically, may be misleading, but here we employ it with reference to extralegal action in politics, violent or capable of becoming violent in method, by which an attempt is made to change the control of the existing government. All these countries have had this experience, some of them many times. Although some countries have been supposed to have attained stability and to be committed to the "orderly processes of constitutional government" in making changes, revolutions are still for all of them possible ways of political action.

By the foregoing, it is not meant that revolutions are so habitual as to be endemic. Opposition parties have won at the polls. Contested elections have been settled peacefully, as in Chile and Uruguay. Serious efforts have been made to protect the secrecy of the ballot and to guarantee a fair count of votes. Laws have provided for proportional or minority representation. Nonetheless, it is a fact that revolutions have occurred and do occur.

We are not here concerned with theories and traditions relative to the "right of revolution," although thought has been given to them in Latin America; we are occupied here rather with the fact of revolutions. We are not concerned with questions about the severity or mildness of punishment meted out to participants in unsuccessful revolutions or with the readiness or obstinacy of governments in granting amnesty to political offenders.

Some alleged causes of revolutions are familiar, almost to the point of being routine. Opposition parties do not always accept the results of elections and abide by the decisions of official majorities. The government in power, in control of election machinery, often tries to determine and assure the choice of its successor—a practice called "imposition." Under the device of *continuismo,* an existent government may have its tenure prolonged. Misgovernment and corruption, the frustration of popular aspirations, violations of the constitution and the laws, and unsatisfactory conduct of foreign relations are commonplaces in items of complaint. Even with such a bill of particulars in the indictment of the existing administration, a successful revolution may have as its chief purpose the satisfaction of the personal ambitions of its leader and the interests, material and partisan, of the supporting faction. Some revolutions may be devoid of any constructive results.

Many legal issues may arise from circumstances caused by revolutions.

To what extent, if any, are the acts of revolutionary governments or *de facto* regimes to be regarded as legal or to be subsequently legalized? Latin-American writers and jurists have taken account of foreign works which have been occupied with such matters. Of such books, one that is often quoted is that of Judge Constantineau of Canada. In his commentary, for a person to be recognized as an official *de facto* three conditions are necessary: (1) the office occupied must have a *de jure* existence; (2) the person in question must be in possession of the office; and (3) he must hold the office under color of title or authority, i.e., under the appearance of legality. "Color of authority" presupposes some form of election or authorized nomination. Possession of an office or control of a government by a faction without any authorization is usurpation. The person or persons exercising power, without color of title, as usurpers, may act, but the acts are "null from whatever point of view."[24]

European thought has taken cognizance of the right of revolution—either in redress of abuse of power or in order to effect a change in the ruling party and in the form of government—and of the fact of revolution. Some writers take account of the fact that, in consequence of revolution or of political crisis, the regularly constituted authorities are deposed and a revolutionary group takes control of the government. The ideas of Jèze and Herrfahrdt concerning the legal and political status of such revolutionary governments are often consulted.[25]

In Latin America, along with efforts to establish distinctions in terminology, objections have been raised to the term "government *de facto.*" It is correctly held that the term "government" embraces all organs—legislative, executive, and judicial—whereas revolutions may alter the personnel of one, usually the executive branch. Of course, some revolutions have swept all branches of the established government out of office, making a clean sweep; such an outcome may become the case of an "authentic" revolution and the government that is set up may be considered a government *de facto.* With agreement that the term is loosely employed, there is, notwithstanding, the phenomenon of the temporary government which is the product of revolution and which has a defective title in law. To this government, even if the regular judiciary is un-

[24] Albert Constantineau, *Public Officials and the "de facto" Doctrine* (Toronto, 1910).

[25] Gaston Jèze, *Los principios generales del derecho administrativo* (Madrid, 1928); Heinrich Herrfahrdt, *Revolución y ciencia de derecho* (Madrid, 1932).

disturbed and even if the legislative branch is suspended, the designation of *de facto* is customarily given.[26]

Certainly, the successful revolution often brings into operation this *de facto* or provisional government. The preceding administration has been vacated, and the new and possibly temporary administration may be placed in office by employing the means whereby vacancies in the governing personnel are legally supplied. In this case the temporary government is a means of transition to the time when the leader of the revolution is elevated to office. It is within the possibility of the circumstance for the revolutionary government, therefore, to fit itself in a technically correct sense into the framework of the existent constitution. Such a manner of succession has occurred in Mexico. A claim might be made that the continuity of law has been preserved. These devices and the accommodation of revolution to formal law are not always practical and expedient. The fact of revolution and the establishment of a *de facto* regime present some difficulties and embarrassments in both theory and law. They may or may not be eased by international recognition or by its denial.

A doctrine concerning *de facto* governments of revolutionary origin has been sought. It may be that the supreme court of Argentina has supplied it. As is well known, in 1930, General Uriburu overthrew President Irigoyen, and thereby Argentina had the first revolution effecting a change in the federal government after a period of forty years. Winning an easy triumph and in command of the situation with forces sufficient to assure peace and order, Uriburu promised that the provisional government would maintain the supremacy of the constitution and requested the supreme court to recognize that government. Four days after the revolution was launched, the court issued an *acordada.* It is worth while to analyze this statement of doctrine, in which it was held (1) that the provisional government was in possession of military and police forces, necessary to ensure order, to protect life and property of persons, and that it had declared its intention to maintain the supremacy of the constitution and laws; (2) that the court[27] had already declared that it would give validity to the acts of functionaries *de facto,* despite legal deficiency of title to

[26] See Leonardo Viola, *El gobierno de facto y su responsabilidad* (Buenos Aires, 1935).

[27] The court referred to the judgment *In re Moreno Póstigo* reported in *Revista de jurisprudencia argentina,* vol. 24, p. 154. The court had the leading case of *Baldomero Martínez y Manuel Otero* (1865) as a possible precedent, on which two constitution makers, Justices Carril and Gorastiaga, sat.

office, in protection of both public and private interest; (3) that the government *de facto* might exercise the powers which the constitution confers on the executive branch, and that its right to do so might not be questioned before the court with success; (4) that the government *de facto* might not exercise judicial powers; (5) that the government *de facto,* in principle, lacked legislative powers but might exercise such powers when necessity required or to accomplish certain ends of the revolution, provided that these legislative functions were limited to an "indispensable minimum"; (6) and that the government *de facto* was a transitory government, between "two constitutional governments."

It has been pointed out that the *acordada* of 1930 was action by the court without a case at law between parties before it and that the action taken was tantamount to a judgment before such a case arose. To some others, this was an act of recognition—a political act. There is the opinion that such an *acordada* is contrary to the constitution. With such recognition consummated, a question might be: What is the effective and practical difference between a *de facto* and a *de jure* regime?

Thirteen years later, in 1943, another revolution occurred, this time against the government of President Castillo. Although this revolution was definitely military as to the elements and leadership involved, there was confusion in the public mind not only concerning what had occurred but concerning what was implied by the revolution and who was to be the leader. General Rawson was first designated as provisional president, but after two days in office he relinquished his powers to General Ramírez. The confusion in the public mind was continued because of the confusion in policy that developed in the new government. Without internal agreement, rivals for influence sought advantage and followed opportunist policies. Out of this diversity, the following developments were to emerge for Argentina: continued neutrality; nationalist hostility to foreign-owned industries; intervention in the provinces; interference with universities, the press, and labor unions; a prolonged state of siege; terrorism and concentration camps; severance of diplomatic relations with the Axis powers (1944); and the growing influence of Juan D. Perón.[28]

Meantime, on the first day in office of the Ramírez government, the re-

[28] Ramírez was forced out of office on February 25, 1944, by the GOU—letters standing for "Government, Order, and Unity"—an organization which behind the scenes exerted the real power. The successor was General Edelmiro Farrell, a compromise choice, who was thought of as a safe and unambitious man. He held office until the election of 1946 and until the inauguration of Perón, the successful candidate, whom he had favored.

quest for recognition was made to the supreme court, and this petition was granted.

In this revolution, the provisional government differed from the relatively mild and quasi-legal measures of the predecessor of 1930. There was a prolonged "state of siege" in detriment of guarantees to individuals. It has been claimed that the independence of the courts was invaded and that judges were removed without cause. On being asked for an advisory opinion concerning the proposed creation of a new court of appeals, the supreme court receded behind the doctrine of the separation of powers and declined to express a judgment without a case before it. The court did say, without reference to the utility of the proposed court of appeals, that the creation of such a tribunal would exceed the powers of a *de facto* government. An interesting pronouncement was made by the provincial court of Entre Ríos that for a government of revolutionary origin to be considered *de facto* it was necessary for it to pledge itself to maintain the supremacy of the constitution and the laws. In an important case, the supreme court stated:[29]

> It is undoubted that the *de facto* government has all the powers [*facultades*] which the national constitution grants to the constitutional executive power and thus the court has established in previous cases. It is undoubted, also, that the executive power can not exercise judicial functions, arrogate to itself jurisdiction of pending cases, or reopen those already decided. The contrary would be to concede to the *de facto* government extra-ordinary faculties, and those who would consent to them would incur the anathema of Article 29 of the constitution.

In these considerations, the precise line of demarcation between permissible exercise of legislative power by the provisional government and the exercise that would be forbidden was not drawn, but the exercise of legislative powers was said to be limited. Pleas of necessity, of needful efforts to avoid chaos, and of powers necessary to attain the purposes of the revolution would be heard, but the limits of action were not defined. The general principle, perhaps, was that a *de facto* government—unless it created its own organic law—does not have greater power than a *de jure* government, nor can the legislative decrees issued by provisional governments affect in detrimental fashion rights and guarantees.

[29] See *Municipalidad de la Capital y Carlos M. Mayer.* Also Segundo V. Linares Quintana, *Gobierno y administración de la república argentina* (Buenos Aires, 1946), vol. I, pp. 93–106; and S. M. Dana Montaño, *Principios de derecho público* (Santa Fe, 1937), p. 136.

Unquestionably, the court was in a difficult position; legal continuity in a time of revolution is at best precarious. Both in 1930 and in 1943, the court was open to certain criticisms. In effect, it had recognized revolution and had legalized certain results thereof, which were in themselves political acts. It had granted to a *de facto* government the powers of a *de jure* government, provided that the new regime observed the constitution and the laws. Had it granted more power? It had expressed an opinion without a case before it. Its own position of independence had been subjected to grave risks.

Another variant in revolutionary procedure occurs when the provisional government in charge of a country assembles a constitutional convention. In this case, the revolution may frame its own organic law and may incidentally legalize the acts of its own *de facto* government. A new era may thus in a juridical sense be introduced, and the revolution may in fact become a source of law.[30] This important outcome has occurred with sufficient frequency in Latin America that this possible relationship of the constituent power to revolution is familiar. In such a case, an abrupt break in legal continuity may have occurred.[31]

BIBLIOGRAPHY

Alberdi, Juan Bautista, *Del gobierno en Sud América,* in *Escritos póstumos,* vol. IV, Buenos Aires, 1895–1901.

Alvarez Suárez, Agustín E., *Manual de la patología política,* Buenos Aires, 1899.

———, *Sud América, ensayo de psicología política,* 2d ed., Buenos Aires, 1933.

Arcaya, P. M., *Venezuela y su actual régimen,* Washington, D.C., 1935.

Argüedas, A., *Pueblo enfermo; contribución a la psicología de los pueblos hispano-americanos,* 2d ed., Barcelona, 1910.

Ayarragaray, Lucas, *La anarquía argentina y el caudillismo,* 3d ed., Buenos Aires, 1935.

Bunge, Carlos O., *Nuestra América,* Buenos Aires, 1918.

[30] I. González Rubio, *La revolución como fuente de derecho* (Mexico, 1949).

[31] For a consideration of "the right of revolution" from the point of view of legal theory, morals, and history, see Felipe Tena Ramírez, *Derecho constitucional mexicano* (2d ed., Mexico, 1949), pp. 79–88. One thought advanced is that the validity of a revolution is not to be found in its legality but in its success. The law which it may contribute—i.e., a new constitution—may be imposed upon an unwilling people. This imposed constitution, enduring for a time and gaining acceptance with enforcement, may be considered to have received "tacit ratification," as did the constitution of 1917 (p. 88).

Carrancá y Trujillo, Raul, *Panorama crítico de nuestra América,* Mexico, 1950.
Colmo, Alfredo, *Los países de América Latina,* Madrid, 1915.
———, *La revolución en la América Latina,* 2d ed., Buenos Aires, 1933.
Constantineau, Albert, *Public Officials and the "de facto" Doctrine,* Toronto, 1910.
David, H. E., *Latin American Leaders,* Inter-American Biographical and Library Association Publications, ser. 1, New York, H. W. Wilson, 1949.
Díaz Sánchez, R., *Guzmán, elipse de una ambición del poder,* Caracas, 1950.
García Calderón, Francisco, *Latin America: Its Rise and Progress,* London, Fisher Unwin, 1913.
González Rubio, I., *La revolución como fuente de derecho,* Mexico, 1952.
Ingenieros, José, *La evolución de las ideas argentinas,* 4 vols., Buenos Aires, 1918.
———, *La sociología argentina,* Madrid, 1913.
Jane, L. C., *Liberty and Despotism in Spanish America,* New York, Oxford University Press, 1929.
Mendieta, S., *La enfermedad de Centro América,* Barcelona, 1910.
Montalvo, Juan, *Siete tratados,* Paris, n.d.
Múñoz Tébar, J., *Personalismo i legalismo,* New York, 1890.
Pelliza, M. A., *La dictadura de Rosas,* Buenos Aires, 1894.
Pérez, Enrique, *Vicios políticos de América,* Paris, n.d.
Pierson, W. W. (ed.), "Pathology of Democracy in Latin America: A Symposium," *American Political Science Review,* vol. 44, no. 1, March, 1950.
Rabasa, Emilio, *La constitución y la dictadura,* Mexico, 1912.
Sánchez Viamonte, Carlos, *Revolución y doctrina de facto,* Buenos Aires, 1946.
Sarmiento, D. F., *Conflicto y armonías de las razas en América,* Buenos Aires, 1883.
Vallenilla Lanz, Laureano, *Cesarismo democrático,* Caracas, 1919.
Viola, Leonardo, *El gobierno de facto y su responsibilidad,* Buenos Aires, 1935.
Ycaza Tigerino, Julio, *Sociología de la política hispanoamericana,* Madrid, 1950.
Zumeta, Carlos, *El continente enfermo,* Lima, n.d.
Zum Felde, A., *Evolución histórica del Uruguay,* 3d ed., Montevideo, 1945.

Chapter 7: CONSTITUTIONAL DEVELOPMENTS SINCE 1833

The observation has often been made that the Latin-American states frequently change their constitutions. Fifteen countries have adopted new constitutions since 1940. Examples of such frequency are ready at hand: that of Ecuador and Peru with seventeen constitutions each, and that of Venezuela with twenty-three. Nonetheless, it should be remembered that some countries have had such instruments endure for long periods of time, e.g., Argentina, 96 years (1853–1949); Chile, 92 years (1833–1925; Uruguay, 89 years (1830–1919); Costa Rica, 69 years (1871–1940); Colombia, 70 years (1886 to the present); Mexico, 60 years (1857–1917).

In the case of Venezuela—the country having had, it is believed, the greatest number of constitutions—the disposition has been to draft new constitutions rather than to amend current ones, just as it has been the practice to replace old statutes when changes were desirable by the enactment of new ones. There, also, it has been the habit of new political regimes to adopt new constitutions rather than to run the risk of loss of prestige by operating under the instrument identified with an opposing and defeated party. These ideas and practices, however, are not the prevailing ones. Several other countries—like Argentina, Chile, Colombia, Guatemala, Mexico, and Uruguay—on frequent occasions amended their constitutions.

One opinion frequently expressed in Latin America is that formal constitutions do not operate in fact. A contemporary writer states that "if we focus the problem of the evolution of political forms from the juridical point of view we will have fallen into the most vacuous and inoperative of abstractions, without contact with reality," and he concludes that "an effective constitutional evolution can not be claimed for our nation."[1] This writer thinks that institutions and changes made in them are "eponymous"—i.e., their designation and character are derived from the name and personal power of the executive or ruler who made them. The alternation of anarchy and dictatorship—the one producing the

[1] J. Ycaza Tigerino, *Sociología de la política hispanoamericana* (Madrid, 1950), pp. 153 ff.

TABLE 10

DATES OF LATIN-AMERICAN CONSTITUTIONS*

Country	*Dates of constitutions*
Argentina	1819; 1826; 1831; 1853 (1860, 1866, 1880, 1898); 1949
Bolivia	1826; 1831; 1834; 1839 (two); 1843; 1851; 1861; 1880; 1931; 1937; 1938; 1945; 1947
Brazil	1823; 1824; 1834; 1891; 1934; 1937; 1946
Chile	1811; 1812; 1814; 1818; 1822; 1823; 1826; 1828; 1833; 1925
Colombia	1811 (two); 1819; 1821; 1830; 1831; 1843; 1853; 1858; 1863; 1886
Costa Rica	1825; 1839; 1844; 1847; 1848; 1859; 1869; 1871; 1949
Cuba	1901; (1928, 1934, 1935); 1940
Dominican Republic	1821; 1844; 1858; 1866; 1868; 1872; 1874; 1875; 1877; 1878; 1879; 1880; 1881; 1887; 1896; 1907; 1908; 1924; 1927; 1934; 1942; 1947
Ecuador	1812; 1821; 1839; 1843; 1845; 1851; 1852; 1861; 1869; 1878; 1884; 1897; 1906; 1929; 1945; 1946
El Salvador	1824; 1841; 1864; 1871; 1872; 1880; 1883; 1886; 1939; 1950
Guatemala	1824; 1851; 1879; 1945
Haiti	1807; 1811; 1820; 1843; 1849; 1859; 1860; 1867; 1874; 1879; 1889; 1918; 1929; 1932; 1935; 1939; 1944; 1946
Honduras	1825; 1839; 1848; 1865; 1873; 1880; 1894; 1904; 1908; 1924; 1936
Mexico	1814; 1824; 1835; 1841; 1843 (1844); 1857; 1917
Nicaragua	1825; 1838; 1848; 1854; 1858; 1893; 1898; 1905; 1911; 1913; 1939; 1951
Panama	1904; 1940; 1946
Paraguay	1813; 1844; 1870; 1940
Peru	1823; 1826; 1827; 1834; 1839; 1855; 1860; 1867; 1879; 1880; 1920, 1933
Uruguay	1830; 1917; 1934 (1942); 1952
Venezuela	1811; 1819; 1821; 1830; 1857; 1858; 1864; 1874; 1881; 1891; 1893; 1901; 1904; 1909; 1914; 1922; 1925; 1928; 1929; 1931; 1936; 1947; 1953

* The dates shown in parentheses are those of amendments.

SOURCE: Adapted from Ramiro Borja y Borja, *Las constituciones del Ecuador* (Madrid, 1951), pp. viii–x.

other—has been, it is claimed, an unsurmounted obstacle to the effective practice of constitutionalism. This interpretation, if taken in its literal meaning, would indicate a forthright contradiction between the constitution as fundamental law and the government in practice.

Undoubtedly, constitutions have on occasion been violated with impunity, altered according to political caprice and interest, and superseded without regard to the ways of legal amendment and revision. The displacement of the Cuban constitution of 1940 by General Batista in 1952 and the substitution by decree of a "provisional statute" have had parallels in other countries. If successful revolutions may at will exercise the "constituent power" and legalize themselves and if such regimes may thereafter disregard the constitutions of their own making, it is difficult to escape the conclusion that formal constitutions under the circumstances mentioned are a species of farce and are lacking in political realism.

The contrary view, likewise extreme, holds the idea and ideal of the constitution as supreme law, in fact and theory. This is the thought mainly of jurists, and there are many of them. Some writers of constitutional history would accept this view, with the reservation that, although constitutionalism in Latin America may on occasion be given the same dignity and operative significance that it has received in some other quarters of the world, there have been interruptions and breaches in the continuity of constitutional law. Some have argued that under legal or "constitutional" dictatorship there has been observance of fundamental law. Others would state that in the political history of Chile after 1833 there was during a long period of time a partial and significant corespondence between the formal and the real constitution. Other examples have been offered in support of the idea of an operative constitutionalism conforming to theory.

There is, also, the intermediate position, which holds that neither of the foregoing opinions is a valid interpretation but that the truth lies somewhere between them. This view makes use of the distinction between the formal and the real constitution, which is familiar to political science. The situation may occur wherein some provisions of the formal constitution may be inoperative or unfulfilled and wherein the real constitution may supply governmental features, services, and even operative principles not included in the formal. The differences between the two are partial, not complete. This compromise view is well stated by a Spanish observer:[2]

[2] Vicente Herrero, *La organización constitucional de Iberoamérica* (Mexico, 1944), p. 15.

However great may be the discrepancy between the written texts and the real constitutions, there is no doubt that the former have aspired to carry into the practice of political life an ideal, and although the spirit of the written constitutions may be violated, the fact that their letter is preserved is to a certain degree a "homage paid by vice to virtue," a recognition of the vitality of those ideals for a more or less numerous part of the population. In the second place, although practice departs much from the spirit which is imbued in constitutional provisions, the exterior lines of the state structure established in them are customarily maintained intact. It may not be discounted that many effective dictatorships exist and have existed in Ibero-America, but in general they maintain the constitutional façade. Although the only power which exercises real influence in political life may be the executive, this does not mean, ordinarily, the abolition of the other constitutional organs. The majority of the dictatorships conserve at least the outward appearance of the democratic political organization provided in the constitutions. And, however limited the real power of the parliamentary organs and the independence of the judiciary may be, such organs do exercise frequently a more effective function than that of the registry of the will of the autocrat and in such instances they constitute at least potentially the germ of a real power.

Before attempting to analyze the main developments in modern constitutions, note will be taken of some reasons which militated against their operative effectiveness. First, many constitutions adopted during the century following independence contained principles and institutions imported from abroad, foreign to Latin-American experience, customs, and even interests. Secondly, some constitutions contained features in advance of the times in which they were adopted. Some of these items might have been thought of as currently impractical, but as goals for the future. Providing remedies regarded as needful, these constitutions relied for application upon legislation to be enacted later. The subsequent implementation might never come, thus confirming the idea of unreality of the constitutions, but there have been cases of the gradual and effective fulfillment of such mandates. Thirdly, new constitutions have frequently been framed in consequence of victory in civil war. Often the triumphant faction inserted into the fundamental law its own special aspirations and its partisan program of change. With the passage of time and the accession to power of a different party, support of these aspirations and programs may have weakened or even may have been converted into opposition. In the latter circumstance, a process of undermining the constitution may have started and have succeeded. Fourth, Latin-American political literature has had many references to an assumption that the formal constitution is accompanied by an unwritten "social constitution." We have already alluded to this "social constitution" as a valued heritage in which the Americas, Spanish and Portuguese, share. Positively, it has "primordial principles" giving protection to the rights of personal liberty, the family, the home, and personal religion. Although it chiefly emphasizes the rights of individuals and traditional rights of groups, this social constitution may take cognizance of inequalities and take into account the existing conditions in politics. The effort to make a formal constitution operative has been in part a problem of its accommodation and adjustment to the social constitution.

Although the disposition to imitate foreign institutions and to import principles from abroad has diminished, the other characteristics persist and are influential. The combined effect of such influences is to prevent complete adherence to the formal constitution. But it must not be assumed that Latin-American constitutions are entirely unrealistic. The precise degree and extent of observance or disregard of fundamental law varies widely.

Important Constitutional Features

In this section an analysis will be made of distinctive provisions and innovations to be found in constitutions adopted after 1833. Among the many constitutions involved, perhaps special importance should be attached to that adopted by Argentina in 1853, that by Mexico in 1857, those by Venezuela in 1858 and 1864, that by Colombia in 1886, and that by Brazil in 1891. The constitution of 1917 in Mexico ushered in a new era which will be treated in a separate section.

The State of Siege. The emergency powers, variously called the "suspension of guarantees" or "grant of extraordinary powers" or "state of siege," were constitutionally sanctioned to meet grave dangers caused either by foreign wars or by domestic commotions. Usually, these powers included the suspension of certain guarantees, the temporary detention or exile of persons, and the sequestration of property. With experience, doctrines concerning these powers were formulated and expanded. These powers were to enable the government not only to defend the public safety in the midst of crisis and actual danger but to meet an anticipated crisis or danger without waiting until it was actual. The "preventive" or "anticipatory" state of siege was placed in use, and for it authorization was demanded. That partisan use of these extraordinary powers for the defeat of political opponents in an election was possible made such use bitterly controversial. Prolonged extension of the time of a state of siege as a means of the perpetuation of an incumbent government was another factor in dispute. Other controversies arose as to the scope of powers that might be legitimately used in the state of siege.

Concerning the propriety of granting extraordinary powers to the government to meet dangers arising from invasion or foreign war or from internal disturbances, when real, there has been little or no discussion. The scope and duration of these powers, assuming the grant to have been properly made, have been debated. It is with reference to the misuse of these devices and powers that objections have arisen. However this may be, every Latin-American constitution grants such powers in some form.[3]

Of the circumstances which justify the use of these extraordinary remedies—foreign attack and domestic disturbances—the first offers little or no difficulty in interpretation. "Domestic disturbances" cover a wide range of actions in which treasonable conspiracies and subversive activities as well as violent outbreaks are included. In the great majority of cases, declarations of the state of siege are justified on grounds of domestic disturbance rather than foreign attack.[4]

The organ of government usually authorized to grant this extraordinary power is the congress, with the executive empowered to issue a declaration only when the legislature is in recess. In the latter case, there is commonly the restriction that the executive must consult with and secure the approval of a council or of the *comisión permanente*—if such a body exists. The president must give an account of his actions to the congress at the next session or call it into extraordinary session.[5] The congress may approve or suspend a declaration by the executive.

In the four countries of federal organization, the declaration of a state of siege or of its equivalent is an exclusive power of the general government.[6]

[3] In Argentina, Brazil, Bolivia, Chile, Haiti, Panama, and Paraguay the term used is "state of siege"; in Costa Rica, Cuba, El Salvador, Honduras, Guatemala, Mexico, Nicaragua, Peru, and Venezuela it is that of "suspension of guarantees"; in the Dominican Republic it is "state of national emergency"; in Ecuador it is "extraordinary powers"; and in Uruguay it is "measures of security."

[4] In Argentina prior to 1943, of twenty-nine declarations of the state of siege, only one was on grounds of foreign attack.

[5] Of the twenty-nine declarations of the state of siege in Argentina, referred to above, fourteen were by executive decree.

[6] The claim was made that this was a concurrent power, enjoyed in Argentina by provinces as well as the federal government. A controversy developed between Sarmiento, then governor (1863) of the province of San Juan, and Rawson, minister of the interior, because Sarmiento as governor had issued a declaration

The legal effect of a state of siege is the suspension of some of the guarantees. The guarantees subject to suspension are not specified in one group of countries, of which Argentina is an example, whereas in another group, of which Cuba is an example, they are precisely listed. In the countries of the first group, the declaration is interpreted as affecting rights of personal security. If property rights are affected, the usual effect is that of a temporary cessation of the owner's control and use. Permanent loss of control and use would depend upon other legislation and judicial proceedings. The judiciary is not ordinarily affected by the operation of a "state of siege" other than by having its jurisdiction of certain classes of cases suspended. Legislative immunities are supposed to be exempt from encroachment.

The prolongation of the state of siege has been especially condemned. Several have lasted for more than a year. One of the longest on record was that declared by President Laureano Gómez of Colombia at the time of his inauguration in 1949, which lasted until the overthrow of his government in 1953. During some of these prolonged states of siege, entire countries were subjected to emergency powers.

Some countries have attempted to curb abuses and the exercise of extraordinary powers by specifying the rights which might be suspended and by requiring that the congress should be promptly convened. Such was the effort of Cuba when it drafted the constitution of 1940. Only the guarantees relative to criminal procedure, habeas corpus, freedom of the press and of speech, petition, and assembly could be suspended. If the state of siege was imposed by presidential decree, the congress must be called into session within forty-eight hours to ratify or deny approval of the declaration. The suspension of guarantees may not extend beyond forty-five days. Although there is a trend in favor of adoption of such restrictions relative to the exercise of extraordinary powers, such efforts, despite all the precautions taken, have had little efficacious effect. Instances of abuse of these powers are numerous. A recent commentator has justly said: "The state of siege is probably one of the institutions which has suffered a most profound distortion in its application to the extreme of becoming, at times, a refined method of subversion and an efficient way for the violation of the constitution.[7]

---

of a state of siege in the province. For details, see Guillermo Rawson, *Polémicas con Sarmiento* (Buenos Aires, 1928), pp. 21–42.

[7] Segundo V. Linares Quintana, *La desnaturalización del estado de sitio como instrumento de subversión institucional* (Buenos Aires, 1946).

Several variants or substitutes for the state of siege have been adopted. One, supposedly less drastic, was introduced in Argentina in 1949, called the "state of prevention and alarm" (*estado de prevención y alarma*). This device places extraordinary powers at the disposal of the president in case of internal disturbance which is not so serious as to warrant the declaration of a state of siege. This device may be used by the executive almost at will. A difference is that persons arrested while it is in force do not have the option of voluntary exile as against imprisonment, which is available to them under the state of siege.

The Parliamentary System. The countries which have adopted a form of ministerial or cabinet responsibility to the congress thought of it as a means of preventing or reducing the dominance of the executive power in government. Experiments with the parliamentary system, in some form, occurred in Brazil (1824–1889), Bolivia (1931–1938), Haiti (1806, 1843, 1859, 1867, 1874), Honduras (1925–1931), Uruguay (roughly after 1875), and Venezuela (under various constitutions between 1870 and 1953). This system, in use throughout the time of the Brazilian empire, left no important traces of influence upon the republic. It is doubtful if the system had more than a formal and procedural operation in Bolivia, Haiti, and Venezuela, where technically a minister censured by vote of congress was forced to resign. There is little evidence of the effectiveness of this requirement in any of these countries. This requirement was embodied in the constitution of Honduras of 1924, and was applied on several occasions during the administration of President Mejía Colindres (1928–1932).[8]

In Chile, during the period from 1891 until 1924, a full-fledged parliamentary system, modeled upon those of France and England, was in operation. It justified the designation of the period and the country as the "parliamentary republic." Despite the fact the interpellations and censure of ministers occurred at various times after 1843, it was the victory of the "congressionalist" forces in the civil war of 1891 that ensured the employment of the system. By means of the responsibility of ministers to the congress, interpellations, censure, delays in approving budget bills, and obstructionist measures, the predominance of the legislative branch was achieved. A law concerning municipalities and another given the name of "parliamentary incompatibilities" contributed to the further weakening of presidential powers. The first ended for the time

[8] William S. Stokes, "Parliamentary Government in Latin America," *The Evolution of Latin American Government* (New York, Holt, 1951), pp. 458–459.

being control of elections by the executive; the second prevented office-holders appointed by the president from becoming candidates for seats in the congress and thus removed a means of securing support or the administration in that body.[9]

Frequently, the criticism was made that cabinets were unstable.[10] The existence of multiple parties required the formation of blocs in order to secure majorities. Occupied with the task of the formation of these unstable combinations, the congress was charged with neglect of the country's pressing problems, the need for administrative reorganization and social reform. Among the popular convictions current in 1924 was the opinion that the parliamentary system had become sterile. Following the revolution of 1924 and the failure of the military factions to agree upon a program, Arturo Alessandri, powerful orator and dynamic leader, was returned to the presidency. He led the country in the adoption of the constitution of 1925. Among other drastic changes, this instrument reestablished a strong executive and deprived the congress of the right to remove ministers by votes of censure.

Behind the modified parliamentary system, such as has been evolved in Uruguay, there is a well-rooted tradition. It was without the support of any definite provision of the constitution of 1830, and it was by liberal construction that the congress acquired during the second half of the nineteenth century the rights of interpellation and censure. In another place reference is made to the reform movements led by José Batlle y Ordóñez in favor of a plural executive and of strengthening the authority of the legislative assembly. Under constitutions adopted in 1917 (becoming operative in 1919) and in 1934, the executive, however composed, could choose ministers from the membership of the assembly. By adopting a resolution of censure, the congress could force the resignation either of the cabinet or of particular ministers. The president could dissolve the congress and call for a general election. Under the constitution of 1934, if the newly elected assembly should sustain the vote of censure, both the president and the cabinet were obligated to resign. Under Uruguay's latest constitution (1952), ministerial responsibility is retained. Votes of censure are taken in joint sessions of the houses. A vote adopted by a ma-

[9] Luis Galdames, *A History of Chile* (Chapel Hill, N.C., The University of North Carolina Press, 1941), pp. 363 ff. Cf. Ricardo Donoso, *Desarrollo político y social de Chile desde la constitución de 1833* (2d ed., Santiago, 1942).

[10] Mario Bernaschina, *Síntesis del derecho constitucional chileno* (Santiago, 1944). He records that from 1886 to 1924 Chile had 138 ministries.

jority of the total membership will force the resignation of the minister or ministers affected by it. The provision for dissolution of the congress and for a general election was omitted.

The Cuban constitution of 1940 introduced what some have called a "semiparliamentary" system, but which others have preferred to call a "conditional presidential regime."[11] Its champion, the jurist José Manuel Cortina y García, called it a "restricted parliamentary system."[12] Under the plan, the president may freely choose his cabinet, drawing its members from either house of the congress, although not limited to congressmen. The cabinet as a body was headed by a prime minister, of the president's choice. The cabinet, individually and as a whole, was responsible to both the president and the congress. A petition signed by one-third of the membership of either house constituted a motion for an interpellation which must be voted upon within eight days. After a debate of not more than fifteen days, a motion of "lack of confidence" must be voted upon immediately. The issue of confidence is raised in a single chamber and settled by it. This does not preclude the other chamber from taking up the issue. A vote of lack of confidence to be valid must have an absolute majority in the chamber involved. Cabinet crises are "total" or "partial" according to the number of ministers involved in the censure. If it affects the prime minister or more than three other ministers, it is total; all others are partial. Ministers censured must resign within forty-eight hours. There are several restrictions set forth in the constitution, designed to prevent instability. A vote of confidence may not be taken for at least six months after the appointment of a cabinet; a question of confidence may not be raised within the last six months of a presidential term; a motion of lack of confidence which has been voted down may not be raised in the same chamber for a year. After a total crisis, a question of confidence may not be again raised for a period of six months. Two partial crises are equivalent to one total crisis for purposes of this restriction. The president may not reappoint to the same portfolio a minister who has been forced to resign.

The cabinet or council of ministers may itself raise the question of confidence. In such cases the issue must be discussed and decided immediately.

[11] Ramón Infiesta, *Derecho constitucional* (Havana, 1950), pp. 291–292.

[12] José Manuel Cortina y García, *Exposición de motivos y bases para la reforma de la constitución* (Havana, 1930). His plan was substantially adopted by the convention of which he was a member.

The Cuban plan gave the congress the power, under restrictions, of forcing the resignations of ministers, but it did not give that of controlling the policy of those who succeeded. It is too early to pass judgment on the merits of the creation of the post of prime minister, but it is possible that, if the plan is revived and continued, this official may serve as an effective "liaison agent" between the executive and the congress. The opportunity of members of the congress to serve in the cabinet may have the value of emphasizing party organization and influence. Although this plan of ministerial responsibility achieved some modest victories, it encountered obstruction and was ignored by the erratic Grau San Martín administration (1944–1948) and languished during that of Prío Socarrás (1948–1952). With the restoration (1955) of the constitution of 1940, it is an open question as to what will occur with reference to the plan during the forthcoming administration of General Batista.

Latin-American Versions of Federalism. Four countries have adopted the federal form and have in a formal sense adhered to it—Argentina (1853), Mexico (1857), Venezuela (1864), and Brazil (1891). Colombia under constitutional provisions (1853, 1857, and 1863) adopted federalism by stages, being for a time partly unitary and partly federal. The experiment with federalism, after experiencing many vicissitudes, civil wars, and dictatorships, was ended with the victory of Rafael Núñez in 1885.

The question has been raised as to whether or not these countries are federal in fact. An answer depends on the definition of federalism which one adopts. The committee which framed the project of the Argentine constitution of 1853 wrote: "The federal system of government means the co-existence—harmonious and coordinated—within the same territory of two orders governmentally different: the federal or central government and the provincial or state or local powers." It went on to state that "each province retains its sovereignty and independence, and the choice of its magistrates is effected exclusively by the free will of its inhabitants." Nonetheless these provinces are members of "the same family and they have a government which embraces all, represents them in foreign affairs as composing a nation, guards their welfare and progress, and protects them as well in the enjoyment of their own peculiar institutions as in their security and independence."

Extensive studies of the federal system have been undertaken in some of these countries. In Venezuela, where the system as locally operated is often called "nominal," the government of Guzmán Blanco sponsored the plan of publishing in translation a "collection of the writings of the most famous publicists of the United States of the North." In 1879, four volumes were published, entitled *Federal Law,* and consisting of a translation of the writings of John C. Calhoun.[13]

Whatever the values of such studies and however sound in theory the conception of federalism may have been, these countries have not usually been judged as "working examples of federal government."[14] Is there a fixed pattern or standard definition of the federal form of government? Some Latin Americans argue that a comparative examination of federal governments would show "distinct gradations within an extensive scale" instead of uniformity.[15] Those asserting this idea do not necessarily maintain that Latin-American countries have been either consistent or faithful in applying their own theories of federalism.

Some of the most important and distinguishing features of federalism, as developed in the four countries having that form of government, may be summarized as follows:

1. Residuary powers. By some it is thought that the general government in the federal system should have delegated powers and that all others should be reserved to the local governments or to the people. This is not the case either in law or in fact in Venezuela, and it is not in significant degree the case in any of the others. Guarantees of rights are found in the federal constitutions, with judicial action in relation to them usually a matter of the exclusive jurisdiction of federal courts. Suffrage and election laws have generally been acts of the federal congress.

2. Federal districts. Such districts for the location of the capital and the central agencies of the federal government were established in each country. Their creation and location were controversial issues in Argentina and Mexico, especially in the former. The distinctive feature was that the districts were given representation in the lower house of the congress with

[13] *Derecho federal* (4 vols., Caracas, 1879). The translator was Juan Ignacio de las Armas. It was a translation of a portion of the Crallé edition of the works of Calhoun. The fourth volume of the translation ends with a speech by Calhoun in 1838.

[14] K. C. Wheare, *Federal Government* (New York, Oxford University Press, 1947). He thinks that overcentralization, intervention by the central governments in the affairs of local governments, some amendment procedures, and operative practices have been contrary to the "federal principle." By this principle, he means "the method of dividing powers so that the general and regional governments are each, within a sphere, coordinate and independent." (p. 11)

[15] Segundo V. Linares Quintana, *Gobierno y administración de la República Argentina* (Buenos Aires, 1946), vol. 1, p. 229.

voting privileges. Later all four countries allowed the district to be represented in both houses.

3. The territories. Some of the federal states allowed "territories" to be represented in the lower house with the right of voting, although these territories were kept under strict administrative surveillance of the federal authority.

4. Codes of law. The great codes of law—civil, criminal, mercantile, and procedure—which were adopted by the federal government were, with the temporary exception of Mexico, to be operative throughout the territory of the respective countries.

5. Federal intervention in the local governments. In Argentina, Brazil, and Mexico, the power of intervention by the federal government in the local governments—provinces or states—was constitutionally sanctioned. The provisions conferring these powers and the practices that developed varied sharply, but in each case the question arose as whether or not the autonomy of the local government was left at the mercy of the central authority. This item will be treated more fully later.

6. The sharing of federal revenues. In Venezuela, the taxation powers of the states were limited, and as a recompense the "constitutional subsidy" (*situado constitucional*) was provided, whereby the states, the federal district, and the territories have an assured share of the federal income, which is distributed on a proportional basis according to population. A merit claimed for this plan was the avoidance of dual taxation. In some countries constitutional or statutory measures were adopted specifying that certain percentages of the revenue should be allocated in aid of local government for special purposes.

7. Public education. All the federal governments came to have control over and budgetary responsibility for public education at all levels except the elementary school. Even this school, to an increasing degree in most of the countries, was to become subject to the control and support by the general government.

8. The federal congress. In Mexico there has been the interesting grant to the state legislatures of the right to initiate measures in the federal congress. In this country, during the period 1857 to 1874, there was the experiment with a unicameral congress.

Federal Guarantees to Local Governments. This a matter of such importance in three of the countries that a special section has been set apart for its consideration.

In the United States there is the guarantee of a republican form of government to each state and along with it a promise of protection against foreign invasion and, on application, against domestic violence. Of the four which adopted "federal guarantees," two Latin-American countries went much farther than the United States in theory and practice, one adopted the idea in part, and one rejected it in whole.

In Argentina, in Article 5 of the constitution of 1853, each province was authorized to adopt for itself a constitution having the "representative republican system," in accord with the "national constitution." Each province must have a system of courts, municipal government, and primary education. Having such a constitution and administrative services, the federal government guaranteed to each province the "enjoyment and exercise of its institutions." In Article 6 it was declared (1860), "The federal government may intervene in the territory of the provinces to guarantee the republican form of government or to repel foreign invasion; and on request of the constituted authorities to sustain them or reestablish them if they have been deposed by sedition or by invasion from another province." That Argentina should have gone farther than the United States was held proper by Estrada, since the need was greater. Unlike the states of the United States, the Argentine provinces did not have a militia of their own.[16] He argued that the United States in 1867–1876, after the War between the States, had done most of the things which had been done in Argentina under the name of intervention. Although aware of opinions that federal interventions in the provinces were undermining the federal system, he defended interventions as a legitimate use of constitutional power to maintain order in a society "constantly agitated by disturbances."[17]

In the important commentary by González Calderón, a distinction was drawn between "reconstructive" and "executive" interventions. The first occurs when the republican form of government is "subverted" and when a remedial program of reconstruction becomes a part of the intervention. The second relates to the relatively simple tasks of restoration of dispossessed provincial authorities.[18] The second type may merge into the first, however, since conditions that caused the "executive" kind of intervention might interrupt the "enjoyment and exercise" of local institutions.

Argentina has not been so much troubled by the difficulty of defining

[16] José M. Estrada, *Curso de derecho constitucional* (2d ed., Buenos Aires, 1927), vol. III, pp. 152–153.

[17] *Ibid.*, pp. 387–389.

[18] J. A. González Calderón, *Derecho constitucional argentino*, vol. III, pp. 548–550; R. Bisán, *Derecho constitucional argentino y comparado* (Buenos Aires, 1940), p. 132.

the "republican form of government." Estrada wrote and spoke somewhat dogmatically to the effect that this form of government meant that political power shall not be seated in a privileged class of persons or in a single person. More definitely, he held that when any one of the organs of government—legislative or executive or judicial—rises against the others and impedes the exercise of constitutional functions the republican form is lost. González Calderón summarized the characteristics of a "representative republican form" required or implied by the Argentine constitution as follows: (1) *sovereignty of the people* and "liberty of the suffrage"; (2) *responsibility of officers;* (3) *publicity* of acts of government; (4) *limited tenure* of elective officers; (5) *separation* of governmental powers; and (6) *civil equality* of all persons before the law.[19]

The supreme court of Argentina, following that of the United States, has taken the position that federal intervention is a political act. Citation was made of the cases of *Luther v. Borden* and *Texas v. White,* among others. In the leading case of *J. M. Cullen v. B. Llerena,* in a dissenting opinion, Justice Varela said: "Although the constitution has not given the judicial power the authority to resolve conflicts between the national government and the governments of provinces, it can never be pretended that the constitution has imposed on them [the provinces] the duty of respecting without recourse the political measures of the federal government which may be contrary to the constitution. . . . "[20] This dissenting opinion, submitted in 1893, seems later to have been abandoned by Varela, and the Argentine court has steadfastly refused to review cases involving federal intervention. The "federal government"—the political departments and chiefly the executive—has used a free and a high hand in the development of the powers of intervention.[21]

Which branch in Argentina exercises the power of the "federal government" in initiating and administering an intervention in a province? Despite controversies, the greater weight of opinion strongly affirms that this power resides in the congress. This contention is supported by general construction and specifically by Article 67, section 28, which stated, "It belongs to congress: . . . To make all laws and regulations which

[19] González Calderón, *op. cit.,* p. 518.

[20] *Fallos,* vol. 53, pp. 420 ff. The dissenting opinion is cited in Luis R. Longhi, *Génesis del derecho constitucional e historia constitucional argentina* (Buenos Aires, 1946), pp. 631–635.

[21] See Luis H. Sommariva, *La intervención federal comparada con la norteamericana y la suiza* (Buenos Aires, 1935); and Gonzáles Calderón, *op cit.,* pp. 485–573.

may be suitable for putting into execution the foregoing powers and *all others* granted by the present constitution to the government of the Argentine nation."[22] In the absence of any general legislation covering intervention, it might be expected that congressional authorization must precede every intervention, but a practice has developed which empowers the president to decree an intervention during the recess of the congress. Presidential actions, allegedly in emergencies, became precedents, until executive intervention by decree became a *fait accompli.* It would now be possible to find doctrinal argument in support of such action. Formerly it was expected that the president would submit a report of the intervention to the congress at its next session, but since 1907 this has ceased to be a requirement.

It is the judgment of González Calderón that, while the president may during a recess of the congress decree an intervention of the "executive" character, on request of the local authorities or without it in some circumstances, every "reconstructive" intervention should be subject to the exclusive authorization of the congress.[23] However this may be, as an observer, he would readily admit that in practice interventions by executive decree have been more numerous than those by congressional authorization —and that the disproportion tends to increase. It is his opinion, as well as that of some others, that the constitutional purposes have been subordinated to partisan political aims, that the "federal guarantee" has become a means of federal control rather than aid and protection, and that the role of the executive in the enforcement of the "guarantee" expands and that of the congress diminishes in significance—all to the detriment of federalism.

It is commonly believed that President Irigoyen, who took office in 1916, introduced a new object in the federal interventions— and with it a new abuse of power. Not only did he intervene twenty times, but one of these interventions was the longest on record up to that time. The principal object was to remove the opposition party from control in the provinces, and intervention was the device. When a valid excuse was not found, it is believed that the president fomented trouble in the provinces. Such a charge was made by Joaquín V. González in 1921 in a speech before the senate. He went on to say that Irigoyen "has abandoned the

[22] This statement would seem conclusive. González Calderón (*op. cit.,* p. 551) so considers it, but this opinion is contested in R. Bielsa, *Derecho administrativo* (Buenos Aires, 1947), vol. III, pp. 186–188.

[23] Gonzáles Calderón, *op. cit.,* p. 569.

channels of the constitution and has erected himself, in virtue of his own theories, as arbiter of the existence, the liberty, the autonomy, the functioning of the powers of the provinces. He has gone farther: he has gone so far as to disavow the character and norms which from the beginning have existed and have ruled among the powers of the federal government."[24]

The procedure in a federal intervention has become stereotyped in official style. The president issues a decree or proclamation and appoints an agent—formerly called "interventor," now "federal commissioner"—who becomes for the duration the head of the provincial government. The letter of instructions is his provisional constitution, which he carries into effect by force if necessary. The use of armed force is the exception; since these interventions have the military strength of the federal government to support them, they are usually accepted passively. Among the powers granted are those of dismissing officeholders, sometimes in all branches, and replacing them with persons of the president's party. Existing legislation may be suspended, and new legislation may be enacted by decree. The commissioner may or may not respect existing constitutions or laws. Until 1891, it was the practice to respect the provincial judiciary, but this department has also been set aside on occasion during the intervention. The termination of an intervention is subject to decision of the president and the congress.[25]

The "federal guarantee" in Brazil's constitution was stated (1891) in negative terms: "The federal government may not intervene in the affairs pertinent to the states except: 1) To repel foreign invasion, or invasion of one state by another; 2) To maintain the federal republican form; 3) To reestablish order and tranquility in the states upon the request of their respective governments; 4) To insure the execution of federal laws and judgments." There is a difference of opinion as to whether Brazil intended to adopt as a model the federal guarantee of the United States or that of

[24] Joaquín V. González, *Estudios constitucionales* (Buenos Aires, 1930), vol. III, pp. 66–67. Similar charges had been made in the past, especially against President Mitre, but the criticisms of Gonzáles carry weight because of his renown. Professor Austin F. Macdonald, in his *Government of the Argentine Republic* (New York, Crowell, 1942), p. 171, points out that General Uriburu, in 1930, on ousting this same Irigoyen utilized the power of intervention for similar purposes. He made a sudden and complete change in provinces governed by the opposition by intervening in twelve provinces within a single week.

[25] For a case study of an intervention, see Macdonald, *op. cit.,* pp. 185–188. The author points out that more than 150 federal interventions in provinces have occurred.

Argentina. It would seem that it was the more indebted in both theory and practice to Argentina. Brazil was to follow both in declaring that the determination of the nature of a republican form was a political question. Some of the same controversies as to what branch of the "federal government" should exercise the power of intervention occurred. Brazil introduced the novelty of the "federal republican form," without any clarification having been effected thereby. The nature of the republican form has not been interpreted with any significant contribution. Attention has rather been directed to the word "maintain." Here the reasoning of Barbalho has been noted:[26]

> The lack or cessation of the government in a state, a duality of governors or legislative bodies constitute a veritable suspension, violation, or deprivation of the republican form. In like manner, political conflicts between the various authorities of a state when they embarrass or destroy the constitutional action of any one of them. These are, therefore, cases for federal intervention . . . .

In the Vargas constitution of 1937, Article 9, the president's power was more frankly exposed. The interventor received his powers directly from the president. The executive was in his own discretion empowered to intervene to repel invasion, reestablish order, and administer the state whenever any organ, for whatever reason, ceased to function. The chamber of deputies was empowered to authorize intervention for the reorganization of finances of a state which had suspended the service of its debt for two years, and to assure the republican form of government, presidential government, and constitutional guarantees. Further, the president at request of the supreme court would intervene to assure the execution of federal laws and court decisions.[27]

In the constitution of 1946, the power of intervention was further refined. Articles 7 through 14 deal with the subject. The power was again vested in the "federal government" and the authorization stated negatively. The seven objects were to maintain national integrity, to repel invasions, to put an end to anarchy, to guarantee the free exercise of all the state organs of government, to assure the execution of judicial decrees and

[26] Quoted in Herman G. James, *The Constitutional System of Brazil* (Washington, D.C., Carnegie Institution, 1923), p. 18. The work of Barbalho is his *Constitução federal brasileira* (São Paulo, 1902); cf. *Intervenção nos estados—documentos parlamentares—1891–1921* (14 vols.).

[27] F. J. Legón, *Carácter y contenido de la constitución brasileña de 1937* (Montevideo, 1938).

decisions, to reorganize state finances, and to assure the observance of certain principles. Among these principles were those relating to the republican form of government, to the independence and harmony of branches of government, to the prohibition of the immediate reelection of certain officials, to municipal autonomy, and to guarantees of the independence of the judiciary. The supreme court and court of elections may request an intervention, as well as the states. In cases other than those in which the supreme court or the court of elections requests an intervention, the president must ask the approval of the congress. If the congress is not in session, the president must convoke it in extraordinary meeting. The congress alone may by law decree the intervention to reorganize state finances and to secure the observance of the "principles" (Article 7, clauses 6 and 7).

The "federal guarantee" of Mexico is limited in scope. Article 122 of the constitution states: "The powers [i.e., the organs of government] of the Union have the duty of protecting the states against every external invasion or domestic violence. In each case of internal insurrection or disturbance they will lend a like protection when requested by the legislature of the state or by its executive if the former should not be in session." The omission of a guarantee of the republican form—which in Argentina and Brazil has been a fecund source of centralization—has never been explained. Herein is found a notable difference. In section 5 of Article 76, a mechanism of federal intervention was supplied. The senate was given the exclusive power

> to declare, when all of the constitutional organs [*poderes*] of a state may have disappeared, that the occasion has arrived for the naming of a provisional governor, who shall call for elections conformable to the constitutional laws of the state itself. The appointment of the governor shall be made by the senate from a list proposed by the president of the republic, with approval of two-thirds of the members present, and in the recesses by the *Comisión Permanente,* conformable to the same rules.

In section 6 of the same article, the senate was further authorized to resolve political questions that may arise between different organs of state government, when any of them appeals for this purpose or when by reason of a conflict of arms the constitutional order in a state is interrupted. The senate in the resolution of such problems will be guided by the federal and state constitutions. The congress was empowered to pass a regulatory law respecting matters involved in both these sections.

It is the opinion of some commentators on constitutional law that Article 122 has been a dead letter. It is the further opinion of many such writers that Article 76 has been so abusively interpreted that its protective and sustaining intent and its respect for established institutions and law have been disregarded.[28] The uses to which Article 76 has been put, the expansion of powers granted to the federal congress in sections 10 and 16 of Article 73, and the interpretation of Article 14, whereby the supreme court reviews by way of *amparo* the decisions of state courts, have been the three chief means of centralization at the expense of the states. In the exercise of intervention in the states, despite the role assigned to the senate, the action and power of the executive branch have been controlling. The executive, through his "secretary of government" and the use of military force, has exerted a power of intervention that is not different in character and effect from that of Argentina, although the legal basis has been radically different. Although for a generation a single dominant party has been in office, internal differences within that party have provided incentives for sweeping changes in personnel. Thus, after the break between President Cárdenas and former President Calles, there were interventions in states having pro-Calles governors. The executive may take the initiative even before the senate or the state has invoked any clause of Article 76. In many of the proceedings, the phrase "disappearance of the constitutional organs of the government of a state" has a merely euphemistic significance. As one commentator puts it "the advance of centralism goes on violating precepts and smoothing the way, without scruples of legality."[29]

The Comisión Permanente. This institution of a "standing committee" of the congress, operating during recess periods, has been regarded as of exclusively Spanish origin.[30] According to common practice the *permanente,* as it is often called, is elected by the congress from its membership before the close of a regular session. Some countries have never established this institution; some had it at one time and later abandoned it; some have restored it; and two, Mexico and Uruguay, have had it since the organization of republican government. Venezuela provided for it in 1819, later abolished it, and restored it under the constitution of 1947.

[28] Felipe Tena Ramírez, *Derecho constitucional mexicano* (2d ed., Mexico, 1949), pp. 126–127.

[29] *Ibid.,* p. 127.

[30] Cf. *ibid.,* pp. 333–341. Tena Ramírez holds that the probable origin of the institution was in the Cortes of Aragón and that it dates from the thirteenth century. It was a feature of the Spanish constitutions of 1812 and 1931.

Chile had what was called the *comisión conservadora* from 1833 to 1925, abolishing it as of the latter date. Now, six countries—Cuba, El Salvador, Guatemala, Mexico, Panama, and Uruguay—have such a committee in some form.

The chief arguments in favor of the "permanent committee" are that for some purposes the continuity of the legislative branch can be maintained, that some types of government business or administration can be transacted without waiting for the next regular session of the congress, and that the committee can act as a check on the executive by way of guarding the observance of the constitution and the laws. The merits of these claims have been questioned. Opponents have argued that the committee discharges no useful or indispensable functions and that it has not restrained the executive.

Two of the countries give a narrowly limited function to this committee. In Panama, it is solely an advisory body to the executive, if he requests such assistance. In Cuba, under the constitution of 1940, a *comisión permanente* is established in that part of the document dealing with the "state of emergency." Whether this body acts only in times of emergency is debatable. The other countries give greater formal and actual importance to this institution. In El Salvador, according to the constitution of 1950, the *permanente* of nine members has the functions of acting on matters left unresolved by the assembly, of calling the congress into extraordinary session, of framing projects of new legislation for later consideration, of deciding liability of members of the assembly to judicial action for alleged crimes, and of performing other duties assigned to it by the assembly.

In Guatemala, the assembly before terminating the ordinary session elects from its membership eight persons, who with the president of the legislative body make up the permanent committee. Its chief functions are to decide whether any of the immunities or privileges of members of the congress have been violated and whether certain officials have violated the laws in a way warranting a case against them; to act in matters left pending by the assembly when it adjourned; and to convoke the assembly in extraordinary session when the national interests demand such a call.

In Uruguay, this body is composed of four senators and seven members from the chamber of representatives, with minority representation from the former and proportional representation from the latter. It is charged with guardianship of the observance of the constitution and the laws; in case of violation it may admonish the executive power and if a second admonition is unavailing in a matter of grave importance, it may convoke the congress in extraordinary session; it may grant or withhold its assent in all the matters assigned to it by the constitution and the laws. The right to admonish or criticize (*hacer advertencias*) has been of great importance in Uruguayan history. On it rests one of the claims that the chamber of representatives has a constitutional right to censure the ministers. The *permanente* enjoys the right to summon ministers and many other officials before it to obtain information and reports.

The Venezuelan constitution which went into effect in 1947 provided for a "permanent committee" consisting of the president and vice-president of the congress and of twenty-one members, chosen on a basis of proportional representation. It was temporary, since the constitution of 1953 abolished the institution.[31]

In Mexico, the permanent committee is composed of twenty-nine members, fifteen selected by the chamber from its membership and fourteen by the senate from its members. No scheme of minority or proportional representation is prescribed, and the absence of such representation is a weakness. Of the formal powers, perhaps the most important is that of calling the congress into extraordinary sessions. Among the special duties of the committee during a recess of the senate is that of nominating from a list submitted by the president a provisional governor for a state in which "the constitutional powers" may have disappeared. In case of a vacancy in the office of president when the congress is in recess, the committee is authorized to name a provisional president and to call the congress into session. It will then be the duty of congress to confirm this choice or name another. Although an executive chosen by the committee will not serve for more than thirty days, that period of time may be of much political significance. Another important power conceded to the committee is that of authorizing—again by a two-thirds vote—a suspension of the individual guarantees (Article 29).

This institution, in Mexico, has produced a sharp divergence of opinion. It is condemned by certain writers because minorities are not represented; because, although made up of members of congress, its functions are not legislative in nature; and because some of the functions are either unimportant or useless.[32] Others doubt the wisdom of empowering this body

[31] For an account of the installation of the *permanente* and a report of its activities, see the *Diario de Debates,* Apr. 4, 1948 (Caracas).

[32] Tena Ramírez, *op. cit.,* pp. 330–341. At one stage, he describes the *Permanente* as "un órgano insignificante."

to convoke the congress in extraordinary session and of vesting in it the vastly important role of naming, even temporarily, the chief executive.

It is obvious that the merits of the permanent committee as a sort of interim legislature and legislative watchdog exist, in practice, only so far as its parent body, the congress itself, is a truly independent body. If the latter is dominated by the executive branch, this committee is a useless mechanism. If, on the contrary, the legislature is one which is jealous of its prerogatives and can defend them effectively, the *permanente* can serve its purposes of maintaining the continuity of legislative action and of keeping the executive within the boundaries of its authority. Unfortunately, the latter case is not as yet common in Latin America.

The Modern Constitutions

In the twentieth century, and more specifically after 1917, political thought in Latin America as expressed in many constitutions adopted, as well as in political writings, underwent new orientations and emphasis. The imitation of foreign models, which had already declined to some degree, was still farther to diminish, and the tendency in many countries was in favor of institutions of indigenous origin. It can be said that the framers of new Latin-American constitutions were groping toward a more realistic basis of political thinking in terms of their own environment and peoples. Nonetheless, modern constitutionalism represented an effort to keep pace with the fast-changing and complex economic and social conditions of the times. In many cases, the new constitutions contain social and economic programs to be subsequently applied, and which require the enactment of complementary legislation.

In recent decades Latin America has experimented with innovations in governmental structure and operation. Cuba's semiparliamentary plan and optional forms of municipal rule, Uruguay's trial of a bifurcated executive branch (1919) and its recent scheme of a plural executive (1952), and Brazil's plans for services in public administration are examples of Latin-American willingness to undertake experimentation.[33]

A Cuban, Juan Clemente Zamora, in analyzing the political theories which inspired the modern Latin-American constitutions,[34] stated that

[33] Russell H. Fitzgibbon, "Constitutional Development in Latin America: A Synthesis," in Russell H. Fitzgibbon (ed.), *The Constitutions of the Americas* (Chicago, University of Chicago Press, 1948), p. 10.

[34] Juan Clemente Zamora, "New Tendencies in Latin American Constitutions," *Journal of Politics*, vol. 3, pp. 277–278, August, 1941.

during the last hundred years the legal system which guarantees the inviolability of private property and which prohibits the interference of the state in the economic activities of the individual has served to secure to the few the concentration of wealth and economic power.

He adds that

the concept of the state as a phenomenon of a predominantly social spirit supersedes the concept of the state as an essentially juridical entity; just as the doctrines of the natural rights of men and the social contract have been discarded, . . . A new concept has appeared whereby the state and the law enjoy the rational justification of their existence in proportion to the measure in which they contributed to guarantee, to facilitate, and to ameliorate the general conditions of the entire body politic.

In the opinion of this writer, modern constitutionalism in Latin America is aiming at

the assurance of a greater amount of justice in social relations and a guarantee to each individual of a greater opportunity in his pursuit of happiness.

In accordance with the preceding doctrine, the most significant innovations of the new constitutionalism are the following:

1. Private property is conceived as having a social function, which implies that individual rights related to it can be subjected to limitations, including that of expropriation when demanded by the social welfare. This concept of property is embodied in practically all the contemporaneous constitutions of Latin America. The first to adopt it was the Mexican constitution of 1917; the essence was embodied in the celebrated Article 27.[35]

2. Protection and organization of labor results in limitations on the traditional right of freedom of contract. Featured in all the recent constitutions are provisions incorporating protection of the inalienable right to work, minimum wages, maximum working hours, insurance against disability, old-age benefits, unemployment and accident insurance, prohibition of child labor, recognition of labor unions, the right to strike, and the employer's right of lock out.

[35] According to this article the state owns primarily all land and water within the national boundaries, but it can transfer title to private interests. The state is authorized at times to impose limitations on the use of property subordinating it to the public welfare. This very extensive clause outlines a power to control many aspects of property and recognizes several forms of land ownership—private, communal, and corporate.

3. The labor clauses are accompanied by others which regulate social security and establish social-welfare services, protect the family, promote cooperative enterprises, and encourage low-cost model housing. The idea that every man owes something to society, implied in the obligation to work, results logically in a reciprocal responsibility of society to look after the life and welfare of every one of its members.

4. Economic and political nationalism is manifested in various forms such as protectionist measures relative to production, restrictions on foreign immigration of both labor and capital, and limitation to citizens of the right to work. This intensely self-conscious nationalism finds its expression in constitutional limitations on the activities of foreign interests and enterprises. The objective of these measures of nationalistic protection is the establishment of each country as a self-sufficient economic unit, politically independent.

5. Significant progress has been made in public administration, although not in all countries. A few of the newest constitutions have seriously attempted to supply the foundations for the development of a professionally trained civil service.

These constitutions are generally very long. Among the most extended ones are the Cuban constitution of 1940, with 286 articles, and those of Nicaragua, Mexico, and Uruguay. This length comes from the inclusion of an excessive amount of detail and from a faulty technical organization. Arrangement of subject matter is often far from perfect; contradictory provisions are sometimes present. The resulting lack of unity and coherence is also due to the conception of the constitution as not one law but rather a series of laws formulated, but not amalgamated, by the will of constituent assemblies.

The Mexican Constitution of 1917 and Its Influences

The Querétaro Constitution of Mexico paved the way for the new constitutionalism. Although a product of the Mexican situation, this document was concerned with conditions of interest to all the Latin-American countries, and while reactions to it were neither uniform nor immediate, it was to be a positive influence upon all those who advocated political, economic, and social reforms. It might be said that few constitutions have been written in Latin America since 1917 which fail to show some degree of inspiration by it.

After a few chaotic years which followed the fall of the Díaz dictatorship in Mexico and the beginning of the revolution of 1910, the regime of Venustiano Carranza undertook to fulfill its promise of a new constitution. Carranza's proposal was for a charter which emphasized political democracy rather than social reform. Leaders like Mugica and Jara of the Jacobinos Obregonistas or radical followers of General Álvaro Obregón, however, threw their power and prestige against the Liberales of Carranza, and as a result Mexico enacted an instrument giving formal expression to new and revolutionary ideas. This constitution served not only as the basic law of the land but also as a program of reforms to be carried out in future phases of the "revolution." It is significant that this constitution antedated European efforts to incorporate the new ideas. In later years, conspicuous constitutional changes were made in Latin America. In the period 1933–1940 innovations of significance were introduced in Peru (1933), Cuba, Brazil, Uruguay, and Haiti (1934), Guatemala (1935), Colombia and Venezuela (1936), Brazil (1937), and Bolivia (1938). The Uruguayan constitutions of 1919 and 1934 were also pioneers in constitutional development toward the embodiment of social and economic legislation.

The memorable features in the Mexican constitution of 1917 are those already pointed out as characteristic of modern Latin-American constitutional law—nationalism, the concept of property as a social function, land reform, and labor legislation. In addition, Mexico's program includes provisions relative to clericalism, popular education (establishing bases for federal intervention in education), and political democracy. Some of them, such as the anticlerical clauses, were strictly not innovations but expansions of ideas included in the law of 1857. The featured provisions, such as Article 27, which started the new theory of property, or Article 123, called by some Latin-American labor's Magna Charta, represented radical departures from traditions and became sources of inspiration to the rest of the continent. Despite the fact that its implementation is not yet completed and despite the adoption of many amendments, this constitution stands as an original instrument, which is well on the way to becoming a significant tradition in the evolution of Latin-American constitutionalism.

The Cuban Constitution of 1940

More recent and also significant for many novel features and for its efforts to cope with political problems on an indigenous basis is the Cuban constitution of 1940. This document, whose provisions indicate the same interest in social reform and the desire to protect the interests of workers, represents a prudent compromise. The moderate tone of this constitution resulted from a collaboration of class interests represented in the constituent assembly and from the pressures of political circumstances. The peculiar alliances within the convention caused some of the compromises and middle-of-the-road solutions.[36]

The Cuban constitution of 1940 deserves careful attention. It embodies a semiparliamentary scheme which may afford an answer to those seeking effective ways to control executive excesses or abuses of power. It is too early to say whether or not this device is destined to be more successful than previous Latin-American experiments with the parliamentary system. The constitution also makes provision for optional forms of government at the municipal level, establishes the foundations for a tribunal of accounts, authorizes a special court of constitutional and social guarantees, and includes technical improvements in public administration. Some of these novel clauses were implemented and the corresponding institutions created in subsequent years. Its provisions for social and economic legislation greatly amplified the concept of "general welfare" and enlarged the functions of government in this field of activity. Some of these clauses had never before appeared in a constitution. The Cuban document has, undoubtedly, exerted influence upon each of the Latin-American constitutions drafted in the last decade, such as those of Venezuela and Guatemala, to mention only two examples.

Supremacy of the Constitution and the Recognition of the "Constituent Power"

Most treatises on constitutional law assert the principle of the supremacy of the constitution as the source of all lawful power. The corollary would be, in logic, that all law emanating from government must be in conformity with the constitution. If the constitution legalizes dictatorship and invests government under it with the totality of power, the issues con-

[36] For an interesting discussion of the influences behind the Cuban constituent convention, see Juan Clemente Zamora, "Tratado de derecho constitucional, *I*," *Universidad de la Habana,* vol. 21, pp. 43–97, January–June, 1947. Professor Zamora points out that, on one side, the dyed-in-the-wool conservatives such as the Demócrata Republicano party were political allies of the leftist Auténticos, while on the other hand, moderate conservatives such as the Liberal, Nacionalista, and Demócrata parties were aligned with extreme radicals like the Socialista-Popular (Communist) party. He maintains that this ideological melee prevented any sharp struggle between left and right and resulted in moderate and discreet formulas.

cerning supremacy are obviously resolved. But the striving for a jural society—perhaps the hallmark of civilization—carries with it in modern times many limitations on authority, the separation of powers of government, and rights and guarantees for individuals and groups of people. The laws of Latin America embody such ideas, and both legal and political theory have held constitutions to be the "law of laws." No ordinary act of legislation or any administrative decree could rightly alter the constitution. Changes in fundamental law could be made only by the constituent power.

All the Latin-American constitutions came to provide processes for amendment or revision. On occasion, these processes have operated, and changes have occurred with strict observance of the law. However, most of the changes and new constitutions resulted from revolutions rather than from the use of legal means of revision. All the constitutions of Mexico—like that of the United States, it might be said—were revolutionary in origin. In orderly societies, constitutional changes, partial or complete, are ideally and legally made in accordance with the methods provided for that purpose in the extant constitution. In revolutionized societies, this principle of "legitimacy" has not been observed and, under some circumstances, could not be observed. Recaséns Siches, the Spanish jurisconsult, thinks that the constituent power "is superior to the established law and is not tied down by any positive form."[37] It would seem that he distinguishes between the power to amend and the "constituent" power of remaking or revising the constitution.

Issues as to the "legality" of certain constitutions adopted during revolutions and by revolutionary means have been raised. The fact remains that Latin America has adopted constitutions in this manner, and that such laws have had a sharply varying history, with acceptance or nonacceptance being a practical kind of norm. The "constituent power" as an unregulated and unlimited power has been challenged in theory. The continuity of the "social constitution" and the respect for those universal principles of justice and liberty which might be called "natural law" are, perhaps, the most effective protections against unrestrained "constituent power" of successful revolutions.[38]

In Argentina, the foregoing considerations had an important place in the thoughts of those opposed to the government of President Perón and

[37] L. Recaséns Siches, *El poder constituyente* (Madrid, 1931), p. 77.

[38] Cf. Segundo V. Linares Quintana, "Introducción al estudio de la teoría del poder constituyente," *La Ley,* Dec. 6, 1951.

to the constitution of 1949. Perón was overthrown in 1955 by the Revolución Libertadora, aimed at "suppressing all vestiges of totalitarianism in order to reestablish the rule of law, morals, justice, liberty, and democracy." One of the steps taken was the restoration of the constitution of 1853.

Amending Processes

In almost all the countries special congressional majorities are required for valid approval of amendments as well as for their ratification in the cases when this action is the responsibility of the legislature. In some cases the laws specify periods of time which must elapse before an amendment may be adopted.

In general, the executive is given little or no participation in the amending process, and the president cannot exercise his veto power in such cases except in Nicaragua. In practice, however, such denial to the executive of a share in the amending process does not prevent a strong president from exercising a decisive influence. Examples are numerous of presidents who, seeking extensions of their terms, have succeeded in obtaining constitutional changes authorizing them to remain in office. Such tailor-made amendments, which are examples of what is called *continuismo* in Latin-American politics, always presuppose a compliant or servile legislature. Although legal, they are considered a misuse of the amending power.

A practice which is characteristic of Latin America is that of giving constitutional rank to certain laws which are not part of the constitution but which are protected against modifications other than those made by the same procedure employed for constitutional amendments. These laws (*leyes constitutivas* or *leyes constitucionales*) exist in Honduras, El Salvador, and Nicaragua. In Honduras and El Salvador the laws dealing with printing, agriculture, elections, *amparo,* and the state of siege are "constitutive laws," while in Nicaragua those of *amparo,* elections, and martial law are considered in this category.[39]

Efforts are made in some countries to protect specific provisions against amendment. Clauses dealing with reelection or duration of terms of certain public officials may be changed only by means of a far more complex procedure than the ordinary amending scheme. Guatemala, for instance, requires in such cases approval by a two-thirds vote of the

[39] Honduras (Art. 199); El Salvador (Art. 172); Nicaragua (Art. 323).

members of congress in two distinct and consecutive legislative sessions, and ratification by a constituent assembly which cannot meet until six years elapse (Article 206). In Cuba, approval by three-fourths of the total membership of congress and ratification by two-thirds of the total number of registered voters is required in similar cases (Article 286). In Bolivia and Nicaragua, amendments to the provisions in question do not enter into effect until a following term, in order that they may not benefit the incumbent officials.

In Peru under no circumstances may provisions dealing with the prohibition of the reelection of the president and vice-president or with the duration of the presidential term be amended. Sanctions are provided against those who may attempt such amendment (Article 142). In Guatemala, those who make proposals against the principle of "alternability" (no reelection in the office of president) are guilty of treason (Article 133).

Since there is no general pattern concerning the amending process in Latin America, the following is a description of a few of the most interesting and novel methods. Starting with the federal republics, we find that in Argentina the constitution may be amended in part or in whole. The need of reform is declared by congress, requiring a two-thirds vote of the members present, but the amendments do not become effective except by action of a convention called for that purpose (Article 21). A special law provides sanctions against those who in any manner advocate methods or systems which, by use of force, aim at the suppression or change of the constitution or any of its basic provisions. This law provides for sanctions against those who organize or direct groups which aim at those ends.

In Brazil, proposals for amendments are made by one-fourth of the members of either branch of the legislature or by a majority of the state legislatures. The proposed amendment is then considered by congress, and it must receive a majority vote in two successive legislative sessions. However, if the amendment is approved by two-thirds of the total membership in each house, it needs no other action to become effective (Article 217). No amendment may be legally made while the country is under a state of siege, and reforms which would abolish the federation or the republic are prohibited.

It must be noted that the methods adopted by the four federal republics are varied. As can be concluded from the preceding paragraphs, in Brazil the states are not given the power to prevent the amending of the constitution, and in Argentina, the provinces are given no participation at all in the amending process. In Mexico and Venezuela, on the other hand, the procedures resemble somewhat that in use in the United States.

Among the unitary states, Chile utilizes a semiflexible arrangement. The proposed amendment is subjected to the same procedure as an ordinary bill, with three exceptions. The proposal needs to be approved in each chamber by absolute majority. Then, the two chambers in joint session, sixty days after such approval, vote on it without debate. The president may then suggest modifications or corrections. If these are approved by both chambers the proposal is returned to the chief executive for its promulgation. If, on the other hand, the presidential suggestions are rejected, the proposal is returned to the president, who has, if he desires, the opportunity of consulting the people by means of a plebiscite concerning the points in disagreement, within a period of thirty days (Articles 108 to 110).

The methods adopted in Uruguay and Cuba are the most original and elaborate. For one thing, in both these countries voters are given positive participation in the process of constitutional reform. The Uruguayan system provides among several courses of action for amendments by the initiative of 10 per cent of the registered citizens by means of a proposal sent to the congress and submitted to popular decision at the next election. Congress may present substitute proposals in joint session, and these are submitted to the people together with the popular proposal. The Cuban system also allows the people by petition to initiate consideration of an amendment. Proposals must be made by at least 100,000 voters before congress, which meets in joint session and within thirty days, is required to call a constituent convention or a referendum, as the case might require.

The practical effect of such restrictions in the amending process as have been described may be questioned. History shows that, in many countries, all these precautions nearly always fall short of preventing changes in the constitution if such alterations are sought in earnest by those in control of power. Subservient legislatures and constituent assemblies may contrive to eliminate obstacles to constitutional reform. In other cases the more drastic step of abrogating the existing constitution altogether may be taken by revolutionary or *de facto* governments which then proceed to frame a new constitution. It is also true, however, that generally such dictated constitutions are short-lived and that reestablishment of the former law, when it was held in high esteem, may occur sooner or later. The Cuban constitution of 1940, for example, enjoys such a prestige in that country that, although suspended in 1952, it was restored following a return to normal political conditions.

BIBLIOGRAPHY

Bernaschina, Mario, *Síntesis del derecho constitucional chileno,* Santiago, 1944.

Bisán, R., *Derecho constitucional argentino y comparado,* Buenos Aires, 1940.

Borja y Borja, Ramiro, *Las constituciones del Ecuador,* Madrid, 1951.

Donoso, Ricardo, *Desarrollo político y social de Chile desde la constitución de 1833,* 2d ed., Santiago, 1942.

Gil Fortoul, José, *Historia constitucional de Venezuela,* 2d ed., 2 vols., Caracas, 1930.

González, Genaro M., *Apuntes sobre doctrina política de la constitución mexicana,* Mexico, 1947.

González, Joaquín V., *Estudios constitucionales,* 3 vols., Buenos Aires, 1930.

Herrero, Vicente, *La organización constitucional en Iberoamérica,* vol. 18 of *Jornadas,* 1944.

James, Herman G., *The Constitutional System of Brazil,* Washington, D.C., Carnegie Institution, 1923.

Larraín Zañartu, J. J., *Derecho parlamentario chileno,* 2 vols., Santiago, 1896.

Legón, F. J., *Carácter y contenido de la constitución brasileña de 1937,* Montevideo, 1938.

Linares Quintana, Segundo V., *Tratado de la ciencia del derecho constitucional argentino y comparado,* 2 vols., Buenos Aires, 1953.

Macdonald, Austin F., *Government of the Argentine Republic,* New York, Crowell, 1942.

Machorro y Narváez, Paulino, *La evolución constitucional y administrativa de Mexico,* printed in *Revista do Instituto Histórico e Geográphico Brasileiro,* special issue, vol. 1, Rio de Janeiro, 1925.

Matienzo, José N., *El gobierno representativo federal de la república argentina,* Madrid, 1917.

Pasquel, Leonardo, *Las constituciones de América,* 2 vols., Mexico, 1943.

Rabasa, Emilio, *La constitución y la dictadura,* Mexico, 1912.

Sommariva, Luis E., *La intervención argentina comparada con la norteamericana y la suiza,* Buenos Aires, 1935.

Stokes, William S., *Honduras: An Area Study in Government,* Madison, Wis., University of Wisconsin Press, 1950.

Tena Ramírez, Felipe, *Derecho constitucional mexicano,* 2d ed., Mexico, 1949.

Urrutia, Manuel A., *Intervenciones del gobierno federal en las provincias (1853–1903),* Buenos Aires, 1904.

Vega, José de la, *La federación en Colombia,* Madrid, n.d.

Chapter 8: INDIVIDUAL RIGHTS, CITIZENSHIP, AND ALIENS

Liberty is a political ideal cherished presistently and characteristically by the people of Latin America. Consequently, guarantees of individual rights are considered essential provisions of all constitutions. The general terms used to designate these bills of rights are varied. In Argentina they are under the heading of "rights, duties and guarantees of personal freedom," while they are simply entitled "individual guarantees" in Mexico and in Costa Rica, and "rights and guarantees" in Bolivia. In all the constitutions which were drafted after the First World War, in addition to the traditional rights, there are also to be found substantive provisions dealing with social and economic guarantees, and concerning the family, public health and welfare, labor, and education. In this chapter treatment will be limited to the usual traditional guarantees. The "social and economic" bills of rights, because of their special significance, will be dealt with elsewhere.

Bills of Rights

The essential rights of man which are common to all Latin-American constitutions are listed below with references to particular points of interest.

Equal Protection of the Law. Uruguay's constitution, on declaring that all persons are equal before the law, specifies that no difference may be recognized among them other than that of talent and virtue (Article 28). The Cuban constitution forbids any discrimination for reason of sex, race, color, or class, and any other type of discrimination in disparagement of human dignity (Article 20). Racial discrimination is prohibited also in Venezuela (Article 46). Titles of nobility are generally denied, and there are still retained in some countries clauses abolishing slavery.

Physical and Intellectual Liberty. With great variety in style of expression fundamental rights are guaranteed such as those of "life, honor, and security," nonretroactivity of penal laws, the right of asylum for political crimes, and security against search and seizure. Included in this group are the usual rights of persons accused of crime. The writ of habeas corpus exists in almost all the countries. Prior to 1949 this was not expressly mentioned in the constitution of Argentina, but it was developed by legislation on the basis of Article 18 of the constitution of 1853.

Capital punishment is prohibited in several countries, except for crimes committed by members of the armed forces and for treason or espionage in time of war with a foreign country. In Argentina the death penalty is prohibited in all political cases (Article 29). In Bolivia it is applicable only in cases of parricide, murder, and treason (Article 25).

Among the most cherished rights of a people are those of freedom of speech and of the press. These guarantees exist in all the countries although with variants in the restrictions imposed on them. They all agree on prohibition of those expressions which are damaging to the honor of persons, the social order, and public peace. In the majority of the countries censorship is specifically forbidden, and generally no books, films, periodicals, or publications of any nature can be suppressed without court order. Freedoms of scientific research and publication, artistic expression, and education are commonly provided.

Freedom of Movement. The right to enter or to leave the national territory and the right to change residence without other limitations than those established by laws are guaranteed in most countries.

Freedom of Conscience. Every Latin-American constitution guarantees the freedom of conscience and of worship. However, the laws of five countries declare Roman Catholicism to be the official state-sponsored religion.[1] In Uruguay tax exemptions are established in favor of churches of any denomination. On the other hand, the Mexican constitution, reflecting a strong anticlerical stand, does not recognize religious corporations as having the right to acquire, possess, or administer real estate. Furthermore, it also declares that buildings for the practice of religion are the property of the nation, represented by the federal government, and those wishing to worship must do so in their homes or in churches "which will always be under supervision of the authorities" (Article 24).

Rights of Assembly and of Association. These are also protected everywhere. The right of petition is included in most countries. In Cuba, for instance, every person has the right to direct petitions to the authorities and to have such petitions considered and resolved within a period of forty-five days. At the expiration of this period, if the petition is not resolved, appeal can be made to superior authority (Article 36). In Mexico, written answers to all petitions must be given by public officials.

[1] Argentina, Art. 2; Bolivia, Art. 3; Costa Rica, Art. 76; and Peru, Art. 32.

The petitioner must be notified of the decisions as soon as possible (Article 8).

Some unusual provisions are found in Latin-American bills of rights. In Brazil, for instance, the organization, registration, and functioning of any political party or association whose platform of action may be contrary to the democratic system is prohibited (Article 141). The Communist party was declared illegal in Brazil on the basis of this provision. The Uruguayan law expressly forbids the establishment of entailed estates (Article 9). In Ecuador and in Venezuela, the individual is guaranteed "the right of not being forced to declare, for any purpose, his political convictions or religious beliefs" and the right not to be molested for those beliefs that he professes (Articles 187 and 39, respectively). It is interesting that the right of revolution is recognized in El Salvador whenever the principle of "alternability" of the presidency is violated. The exercise of such right of revolution, however, does not affect, in theory, the existing laws. Its effects are restricted to the removal of government officials (Articles 5 and 175).

The practical value of these bills of rights is, of course, relative. As it has been pointed out, the tradition of personal freedom is well established among the peoples of Latin America. In spite of their devotion to the cause of freedom, however, there is probably no country which at one time or another has not experienced conditions under which the guarantees of freedom have been systematically ignored and the bill of rights turned into an ineffectual nicety of the constitution. It is also true, nonetheless, that in almost all the Latin-American nations there have been periods during which the laws have been strictly observed, the people have had absolute liberty to express their opinions, and the government has been respectful of individual freedom. It seems clear, then, that the effectiveness of the bills of rights is dependent upon the nature of the administration entrusted with its enforcement, as well as upon other political conditioning factors.

Political Asylum

All the recent constitutions include some provision dealing with the subjects of extradition and political asylum. The principle generally accepted is that extradition shall not be granted for political offenses or "crimes of opinion." In Honduras, this principle applies even though the consequences of the political offenses may be a common crime. Some countries specifically state that their territory shall be a place of asylum for all who are persecuted for political reasons, and that if the expulsion of such persons is decreed on legal grounds, they shall not, in any case, be returned to the country where they had been persecuted.

Observance of the right of asylum is a well-established practice in Latin America. It implies the right of a person persecuted for political reasons to seek refuge in the embassy of a foreign country and to request the protection of that country. Political asylum is generally respected as a fair and almost sacred rule in the game of politics. It is understandable that it should be so, since, under the unstable political circumstances that often prevail, those in power today might need protection tomorrow. Consequently, cases of governments' refusing to grant guarantees of safe-conduct to political refugees are rare.

Perhaps the most widely publicized case of political asylum in recent times was that of the Peruvian leader Víctor R. Haya de la Torre who, during a revolt in 1948, took refuge in the Colombian embassy in Lima. He was forced to remain in seclusion in this embassy until 1954 because the Peruvian government refused to admit that he was not a common criminal. Only after a long and sometimes bitter international dispute, involving other nations besides Peru and Colombia, was Haya de la Torre permitted to leave Peru under safe-conduct.

In the same year the revolution which overthrew the administration of President Jacobo Arbenz in Guatemala set new records in the practice of the right of asylum. Latin-American embassies in Guatemala City were overcrowded with scores of refugees and were confronted with serious problems of food and sanitation. It is claimed that 306 persons took refuge in the Mexican embassy alone. Approximately 450 more were residing in other embassies. There were efforts on the part of the revolutionary government to obtain custody of President Arbenz and his ministers on the ground that they were common criminals. However, after weeks of negotiations with foreign diplomats, the governing junta decided to issue guarantees of safe-conduct, and the group went into exile in Mexico.

Nationality

The basic principle regulating citizenship in most of Latin America is that which determines nationality by place of birth. Although adopting this doctrine of *jus soli* the Latin-American countries permit many exceptions to it, and the *jus sanguinis* principle is used so as to allow children of nationals born abroad to acquire the nationality of their parents. A few of the republics, notably Colombia, Ecuador, Haiti, and El Salvador, utilize the *jus sanguinis* as the main principle. Persons born in these countries may acquire the nationality of their parents, but again the laws provide for many exceptions. Therefore, although one principle is given preference, exceptions are allowed to permit the application of the other in all the countries, with the exception of Haiti. In the nations following the *jus soli,* exceptions are made which favor children born abroad of national parents, while in the states that follow the *jus sanguinis,* the doctrine of *jus soli* is applied to children of aliens domiciled in the country.

Children born abroad of nationals are citizens by birth provided they meet other requirements. Only Mexico, Panama, and Venezuela, among the group of nations following this practice, prescribe no special qualifications. Establishment of residence is necessary in eleven countries. Option in the choice of nationality in case of children born abroad of nationals is permitted by Argentina, Brazil, and the Dominican Republic. It is also possible, under some conditions, in Honduras, Guatemala, and Nicaragua.

Naturalization Procedures

The conditions required of persons applying for naturalization vary according to countries, but they include common criteria: residence for a specified period of time in the country of which the person expects to become a citizen; some expression or proof of political allegiance to the adopted state; the renunciation of former nationality and the pledge to abide by the laws; knowledge of the language of the adopted country; and proof that the person is self-supporting and will not become a public charge.

The required period of residence ranges from one year in Costa Rica and Ecuador to the maximum of ten years, which is required in Brazil. Some countries require the applicant to state that he believes in democratic government and that he does not belong to any group with ideas that are incompatible with democratic principles (Argentina, Brazil, Ecuador, Chile, Guatemala, Uruguay, and Paraguay). Proof of good behavior and moral character is also necessary in some countries (Costa Rica, Ecuador, Guatemala, Honduras, El Salvador, Mexico, and Uruguay). Renunciation of the former nationality and an oath of allegiance to the adopted country are prerequisites in sixteen countries. Knowledge of the language is a requirement in most states. A few require, in addition, some knowledge of basic constitutional principles. Applicants must be capable of supporting themselves by their knowledge of some trade or profession, or by holding property, in Brazil, Ecuador, Paraguay, and Uruguay. Other countries require them to have some remunerative occupation.

Some significant changes were introduced in Argentina's naturalization procedure in 1949. It was proposed at that time that the Constituent Assembly amend the law of 1853 so as to include a statement to the effect that aliens, upon completion of two years' residence, must choose between applying for naturalization or abandoning the country. Adoption of this proposal would have marked a reversal of traditional Argentine immigration policies. It was substantially modified in the final draft. At present, foreigners may by petition become naturalized if they have resided continuously for two years in Argentina. They acquire nationality automatically after five years of continuous residence, unless they expressly indicate another preference.

Naturalization in most countries is not granted automatically even though all the requirements established by law are complied with. On the contrary, it may be denied for reasons of national interest, and the authorities enjoy discretionary powers to grant or to deny citizenship. However, in Uruguay and in Chile, a person who, after meeting all requirements, is denied naturalization may appeal to the courts. The discretionary power was widely used during the two world wars to deny citizenship to enemy aliens, although their naturalization was possible with proof of loyalty to the country of adoption.

Several of the Latin-American countries include in their naturalization laws provisions especially favoring persons born in Spain or in the other Latin-American countries. In Colombia, for instance, Spanish Americans and Brazilians by birth may appear before the municipal authority and declare their desire to be officially registered as Colombians. They become citizens without having to follow the regular nationalization procedure. Natives of the Central American republics may acquire citizenship of one of the other republics in that area by procedures much simpler than those which must be followed by other foreigners. In Costa Rica, for example, nationals of the other Central American countries who have resided for at least one year in that nation become citizens by declaring before the civil registrar their intention of so doing. Native-born Spaniards and all Latin Americans may do likewise, provided they have resided in the country during two years prior to the date of their declaration. Portuguese nationals may become citizens of Brazil after one year of residence, a much shorter period than that required of all other foreigners. Service in the armed forces may facilitate naturalization for certain aliens, as is the case in Brazil or Colombia. In some countries, the residence requirement is reduced or waived entirely in the case of foreigners married to citizens. Naturalization through marriage is possible in some countries simply by proving the fact of marriage; in others, by complying with shorter residence requirements.

The political rights of naturalized citizens are somewhat restricted with relation to the holding of public offices. To be elected president, vice-president, or senator, citizenship by birth is required in all countries. Citizenship by birth is required in a few countries of congressmen and high judicial officials. Also it is common practice that the rights pertaining to legal citizenship may not be exercised by foreigners until a certain period of time has elapsed after receiving their naturalization papers. That period is two years in Paraguay, three in Uruguay, five in Argentina, and ten in Haiti. In countries which follow this practice, possession of citizenship for an even longer term may be required of naturalized persons before they may be elected to the lower house of the legislature.[2]

Aliens

After the emancipation, a generous and liberal attitude toward the foreigner was common to all the Spanish American countries. Legislation adopted with the purpose of attracting and protecting immigrants placed the foreigners in a more privileged position than in other parts of the world. Foreigners were put on the same level with nationals in regard to juridical, commercial, and in general all other rights except those of a political nature. Aliens were granted all the individual guarantees and were also given juridical status equal to that of citizens. Argentina granted to aliens the enjoyment of all the civil rights of citizens, and permitted them to engage in industry or trade, to possess real estate and purchase or dispose of it, to freely practice their religion, and to make wills and marry in accordance with the laws. They were not bound to accept citizenship or to pay extraordinary taxes. If naturalized, foreigners were free to render or refuse military service during a period of ten years from the day of their naturalization. These ample legal guarantees were further strengthened by the vesting of the power to decide cases involving aliens in the federal judiciary. General principles of this kind, included in the

[2] Departing again from earlier practices, Argentina now requires candidates for deputy to have been fully qualified citizens for ten years in the case of naturalized persons.

Argentine constitution of 1853 and followed by laws applying them, caused that country to be placed in high rank as a receiver of immigrants. Its example in this respect was influential in other countries of Latin America, and continued to be so without significant modification throughout the nineteenth century and beginning of the twentieth.

Since the First World War the presence of considerable numbers of foreigners in the various countries has led to the establishment of restrictions upon the civil rights that they may enjoy. These restrictions have been directed against those aliens who could not be readily assimilated, and have gone hand in hand with the newly born nationalist policies and the strong desire to protect nationals from foreign competition in labor, business, and other economic activities. All countries have given thought to possible methods of regulating the racial composition of their populations and of eliminating undesirable competition, and inaugurated attempts to select immigrants through the use of quota systems. The underlying motive in the change of policy which these measures involved was clearly the awakening of a strong desire to establish among all inhabitants the sense of nationality. The new concept of property as a social function, adopted by modern "social constitutionalism," also caused new restrictions to be imposed upon foreign persons and enterprises.

Restrictions upon Aliens. Although all the countries recognize the general principle of equality of civil rights for nationals and aliens, most of them impose certain restrictions and limitations on foreigners. A restriction found in all countries is that aliens may not interfere in any way in the political affairs of the country. Violation of this principle may result in expulsion of the alien without judicial process, on order of the executive.[3] Foreigners are prohibited in some countries from being chosen to positions of authority in labor unions. In two countries, Panama and Haiti, aliens are forbidden to engage in retail trade. The laws enumerate specifically the persons who may carry on this type of trade.[4] No foreigner may join a political party in Brazil, Colombia, Costa Rica, or Venezuela, and he is prohibited from intervening in any manner in domestic politics. Infringement of this law may result in imprisonment for the offender. Certain rights, such as freedom of association, are

[3] Mexico (Art. 33); Nicaragua (Art. 25). Exception is made in Nicaragua if the alien is married to a Nicaraguan or has had children by a Nicaraguan.

[4] On the other hand, in Peru and other countries, all trade activities are regulated by local law, but the right of the foreigner to engage in commerce may be determined by the law of his own country.

limited when they involve the alien in political activities. In some states aliens are not permitted to own periodicals of a political nature. Likewise they may not be permitted to serve as editors of such publications.

Although there are constitutional provisions protecting the foreigner from discrimination in regard to wages, benefits, or working conditions, other laws have established, in fact, a preference for native workers. In Mexico, nationals have preference over aliens under equal circumstances for all concessions and for all government jobs, offices, or commissions in which citizenship is not required. All enterprises in Peru must employ 80 per cent of the nationals, and the same percentage must be kept in respect of salaries paid to employees. This rule applies to professions as well as to industry and commerce. Similar nationalization of labor laws (*leyes de nacionalización del trabajo*) exist at present in most countries. In Uruguay, although the ratio of wage earners who must be nationals for all enterprises is not fixed, all large concerns are required to hire from 60 to 90 per cent nationals. In Venezuela, at least 75 per cent of the workers and employees must be citizens, and all foremen and employees dealing with the workers must be Venezuelans. At least 85 per cent must be citizens in Chile, and it is mandatory that 85 per cent of the payroll must go to nationals. The Mexican percentage is the highest of Latin America, since it is required that 95 per cent of the employees must be Mexicans. The requirement, however, does not apply to managerial personnel. In Cuba, half of all personnel must be Cuban citizens. Half the payroll must also go to nationals. It is obligatory to fill all vacancies with citizens, and in case of reduction of the labor force, alien workers must be discharged first.

Policies concerning foreign technical and managerial personnel vary according to countries. In Peru and Uruguay, there are no restrictions on the admission and employment of technicians and managerial staff. In other countries, such as Mexico and Brazil, personnel of this kind may be used by business concerns if there are no citizens available with the proper qualifications. Cuba also permits the use of foreign technicians under the same circumstances, but they are allowed to remain in the country for one year only and are required to train nationals to take over their positions. The one-year permission can be extended to two more if it is proved that no replacement of Cuban nationality is available.

In some countries 80 per cent of all teachers must be nationals, all courses must be given in Spanish, and only citizens are qualified to teach certain subjects such as history and civics. In Panama instruction in foreign languages may not be given in private educational institutions without authorization of the government. In Cuba, instruction in Cuban literature, history, geography, and civics can be given only by native-born citizens. Textbooks used in these courses must be written by authors who have the same qualification.

The exercise of the liberal profession by aliens is also regulated in every country and the recognition of academic degrees issued by foreign institutions as well. In Guatemala, no degrees are officially recognized other than those granted by the state university of San Carlos. However, foreign degrees may be validated by satisfying the requirements (*incorporación*) fixed by law, which include general examinations. This validation of foreign degrees also applies to native-born citizens who study abroad, and who on their return must meet the legal qualifications.

Professionals have in some countries, such as Cuba, the obligation to join the official organization (*colegio*) in their field before they are permitted to practice. Special statutes determine the structure and functioning of these bodies. Citizenship may be required in order to become a member.[5]

Restrictions of the activities of foreign professionals are much less strictly applied in the case of educators. A number of foreigners may be found on the faculties of universities and other institutions of higher learning. In fact, an exception favoring the teaching profession is specifically indicated in the constitution of Uruguay, which states that citizenship shall not be required for professorships in these institutions (Article 76).

Alien Property. The most significant limitations on the rights of aliens are in matters affecting property. The status of aliens before the courts of the country and the various restraints upon diplomatic intervention in their behalf are two striking features of Latin-American law which are closely related to property matters. Of course, in most countries foreigners are generally on an equal basis with nationals in all matters concerning property and cannot claim any special privilege. But, in addition, many countries have established severe restrictions on the use of diplomatic claims by declaring that no foreign person may appeal to his government for diplomatic intervention in his defense, except in the event of a denial of justice. A court decision unfavorable to the foreigner is not necessarily to be construed to mean that there has been a denial of

[5] Membership in professional organizations entitles the holder to many privileges, such as retirement pensions.

justice and that resorting to diplomatic representation is justified. In some countries, neither citizen nor aliens may, in any case, claim from the government indemnity for damages and injuries to their persons or their property caused by revolutionary factions.[6]

Very frequently it is required that, in any contract between the state and aliens or in any concession that may be granted in favor of foreigners, there must be included a clause containing the express submission of the latter to the laws and the courts of the country as well as formal renunciation of all diplomatic claims. Furthermore, even though it may not appear in the contract, this clause is considered automatically included in each case. By this means it is established that any doubts and controversies which may arise over the contract and which are not amicably solved by the contracting parties will be decided by the courts of the country in accordance with its laws, without giving rise, for any reason, to foreign claims.

The right of aliens to own property is, under certain circumstances, specifically restricted in some countries. In Peru, no foreign government or institution may acquire ownership of any part of the national territory. In Guatemala, all deposits of hydrocarbons may be exploited only by the state, by Guatemalans, or by Guatemalan companies. In Mexico only citizens or Mexican companies may obtain lands, waters, and their appurtenances or secure concession for the exploitation of mines, waters, or combustible minerals. The government, may, however, grant these rights to aliens, provided that they agree before the ministry of foreign relations to consider themselves as nationals with respect to the properties involved and not to resort to the protection of their government. Failure to comply with this agreement results in loss of the properties, which revert in that case to the nation. These principles were included in the famous Article 27 of the Querétaro Constitution. They led, it should be remembered, to a long and bitter conflict between the Mexican government and some foreign nations—among them, the United States. This conflict began shortly after the constitution went into effect and lasted for several decades.

It must be pointed out that in all countries the volume of legislation dealing with aliens is considerable. In Cuba, for example, in the period from 1925 to 1944, forty-eight laws, decrees, decree laws, and resolutions related to matters affecting aliens were put into effect. In nearly every country there is a "law of aliens" (*ley de extranjería*) which embodies

[6] El Salvador (Art. 17); Guatemala (Art. 20). Also Venezuela (Art. 24).

regulations concerning those persons. The enforcement and administrative operation of these laws are generally entrusted to a special agency. Registration of all foreigners within a certain number of days after arriving in the country is required, and each must obtain an alien registration card without which it is unlawful to undertake any activities. He may be required to report periodically in order to have his card renewed. No foreigner is allowed to undertake any permanent remunerative activity without the proper visa and compliance with these requirements.

To sum up, regulations of the kind described indicate general acceptance of certain policies on the part of the states of Latin America. These policies are the recognition of the rights of aliens as to person on a footing of equality with those of nationals; the embodiment in constitutions of the idea that disputes shall always be settled according to law administered in the courts of the country in which the alleged injury to rights occurred; as a corollary of the latter, the mandatory renunciation by the alien of the diplomatic intervention of his government in his behalf; and the right to impose restrictions upon the foreigner's ownership or use of property.

Nationalism and Foreign Enterprise. The principles listed in the preceding paragraph, and especially the idea that each country has the full right to decide for itself the political, social, and legal issues involved in property tenure, have been generally accepted by all nations. In the case of Latin America, however, past experiences of foreign enterprises have given rise to the view that the exercises of these rights should be accompanied by effective guarantees that the expropriation or nationalization of private property held by aliens should always be subject to due process of law and should be accompanied by fair compensation. It is true that this principle is accepted in most of the laws and that confiscation is proscribed, but it is also true that fear on the part of foreign enterprises that their rights will not be adequately protected when the time comes has resulted in an understandable reluctance to expand their investments. The most pressing problem facing industrialization in Latin America may very well be that of how its just desires to protect its economic and political independence from undue influence and interference by foreign interests can be reconciled with the equally justified wishes of the alien capitalists to have their investment safeguarded and to receive fair returns from them.

In this connection it must be noted that Argentina has gone farther than most countries in the regulation of the procedure of expropriation on a constitutional basis. The amendment of 1949 provided that "the price of expropriation of public service concessions shall be the original cost of the property pertaining to the enterprise, less amounts that have been amortized during the time elapsed since the granting of the concession, and excesses over a reasonable profit, which shall also be regarded as repayment of the invested capital" (Article 40). This method for determining compensation was included as a consequence of the adoption of the principles that public services belonged originally to the state, that for no reason may they be alienated or concession granted for their exploitation, and that those which were in private hands should be transferred to the state, through purchase or expropriation. Even before this was embodied in the constitution, the Argentine government had conceived an ambitious program to put under native ownership the chief foreign-owned industries of the country. In fulfillment of this program the government accomplished the nationalization of the Central Bank (1946), the purchase of the nation's telephone system (1946), the nationalization of the British-owned railroads (1947–1948), and the repurchase of the Argentine foreign debt (1947).

Foreign enterprise may also be excluded from some activities by the fact that the government may exercise a tight monopoly of certain industries or may even be in competition with private enterprise in others. In fields such as insurance, imports, manufacture and sale of alcoholic beverages, fuels, cement, oil refining, power and telephone service, railways, port services, telegraph service, commercial radio, and fertilizers, the government of Uruguay has assumed monopolies, while in others it is in a position of competing with private business. The Brazilian government is increasingly participating in industries like steel and chemicals. Through the celebrated state development entities (*corporaciones de fomento*), other governments are sharing more and more in industry, as is the case with Colombia and especially with Chile. The Chilean government has a monopoly of exports of nitrate and iodine through a public corporation in which private capital has some participation, but it has reserved for itself the production and refining of petroleum, and it controls the nation's railway system.

In some cases, the alien entrepreneur has seen his business ventures limited by restrictions imposed on the participation of foreign capital. In Chile, for instance, there are special restrictions on ownership for coastal shipping, air transport, and insurance. In Peru, a majority of the shares of an insurance company must be controlled by citizens, as well as a majority of seats in the board of directors. Not less than 75 per cent of the shares must be held by Peruvians in the case of shipping, while in the oil industry one-fourth of the shares must be offered locally. Similar restrictions exist in Colombia where 51 per cent of the stock of air lines must be owned locally, and coastal shipping is reserved to Colombians or companies owned 60 per cent by domestic capital.

Other laws may also affect the interest of aliens by establishing regulations covering the transfer of earnings and capital, by imposing specific burdens on all remittance of income outside of the country, or by levying special taxes on income of foreign enterprises. In Argentina, foreign insurance companies are subject to a higher tax rate than local companies, and special taxes are imposed on foreign concerns in transportation, the movie industry, and press services. The sending of income abroad is also subject to special imposts. In Cuba, there is in general no tax discrimination, but foreign companies may be subjected to a special tax on their gross receipts if profits of the local branches show that they are lowered as a result of intercompany dealings. The capital required for foreign insurance firms is higher than for locally owned companies in Mexico, and mining corporations pay income taxes on a higher basis than other enterprises. The foreign-owned oil industry in Venezuela operates on the basis of what seems to be a satisfactory arrangement with the government under the terms of which 50 per cent of the net profits go to the state in the form of taxes.[7]

As may be seen from the conditions described, the liberality and generous spirit which were characteristic of the early policies toward foreigners have been converted in recent times into restrictions that tend to discourage foreign enterprises in Latin America. There are circumstances in some countries which make it difficult for the foreign investor to maintain operations. Discriminatory and burdensome taxation, added to the highly restrictive labor and social legislation, has led in some cases to the same result as expropriation. The fact is that, although greatly indebted to the foreigner for the industrialization that has occurred, Latin America is at present moving toward nationalization of enterprises of this kind.

Whether this is a wise policy or not is a much-debated issue in Latin America. There are some who have warned their countrymen of the grave risks that are being taken in destroying the confidence of private capital

[7] For an excellent analysis of the problems of foreign investing in Latin America, see Simon G. Hanson, *Economic Development in Latin America* (Washington, D.C., The Inter-American Affairs Press, 1951), pp. 369–421.

from abroad. They reason, and rightly so, that this capital is indispensable if the process of economic development is to be carried out. There are others who emphasize the fact that Latin America is still dependent on foreign sources for the supply of basic materials for its own industry. On the other side, there are the extreme nationalists for whom the ideal of economic independence is worth any price. It is to be hoped that, somehow, a just and middle way can be found to reconcile legitimate nationalist objectives with the need of improving the climate of investment. One encouraging factor has recently entered the picture. This is the marked change from the attitude and philosophy under which private capital operated in those countries in the past. Most if not all of foreign enterprises in Latin America are working, at present, toward the objective of identifying their interests with those of the country and integrating themselves with the community. This new policy includes the acceptance of native-born talent at top-level positions, strict compliance with social and labor legislation, an effective public relations program, and—what is most important—a hands-off policy with regard to politics.

BIBLIOGRAPHY

Alsina, Juan A., *La inmigración en el primer siglo de la independencia,* Buenos Aires, 1910.

Baudon, Héctor R., *Estado de sitio,* Buenos Aires, 1939.

Carrillo Flores, A., *El nacionalismo de los países latinoamericanos en la postguerra,* Mexico, 1945.

Donoso Torres, Vicente, *Reformas constitucionales,* La Paz, 1947.

Fayt, Carlos S., *Los derechos del hombre y sus garantías constitucionales,* Buenos Aires, 1945.

Fitzgibbon, Russell H., "Constitutional Development in Latin America: A Synthesis," *American Political Science Review,* vol. 39, pp. 511–522, June, 1945.

Jaffin, George, "New World Constitutional Harmony: A Pan Americanadian Panorama," *Columbia Law Review,* vol. 42, pp. 523–573, April, 1942.

Jefferson, Mark, *Recent Colonization in Chile,* New York, American Geographical Society, 1921.

Lazcano y Mazón, Andrés M., *El habeas corpus constitucional,* Havana, 1948.

Linares Quintana, Segundo V., *La desnaturalización del estado de sitio como instrumento de subversión institucional,* Buenos Aires, 1946.

Oliveira Vianna, F. J., *Evolução do povo brasileiro,* 3d ed., São Paulo, 1938.

Pereda, Diego de, *El nuevo pensamiento político de Cuba,* Havana, 1943.

Rouzant, Adolfo R., *Las garantías constitucionales de la libertad civil,* Rosario, 1940.

Sánchez Viamonte, Carlos, *Manual de derecho constitucional,* Buenos Aires, 1945.

Siberio, Jorge, "El funcionamiento filosófico-político de las cláusulas de reforma de la constitución," in *Temas de derecho constitucional,* Havana, 1947.

Tovar, A. V., *La ciudadanía y los derechos políticos,* Mexico, 1952.

Zamora, Juan Clemente, "Nuevas orientaciones en materia constitucional," in *Los partidos políticos y la asamblea constituyente,* Havana, 1939.

Zorraquín Becú, Horacio, *El problema del extranjero en la reciente legislación latinoamericana,* Buenos Aires, 1943.

Chapter 9: THE EXECUTIVE

All the Latin-American countries establish in principle separation of political powers on some basis of division, and all constitution makers have been cognizant of the classical theories of separation. In practice, however, the separation of powers is not rigidly observed. With the passage of time, despite some notable attempts to the contrary, the trend has been toward the dominance of the executive. There have been many efforts to prevent the "subjugation" of the legislative branch by the executive, but they nearly always have been unavailing.

Deviations from the Principle of Separation of Powers

In some extreme cases, there has been for a time the suppression of one of the organs of government, as, notably, that of the legislative branch in Brazil during the Vargas period (1937–1945) or that in Guatemala by Castillo Armas in 1954. This complete exercise by one person or branch of the powers of two of the conventional departments of government is the subject of the classical warning of Montesquieu that liberty is thereby extinguished. Many constitutions may and do pronounce against this union of powers. But there may be exceptions which, act by act and stage by stage, become the rule.

Some important exceptions which by constitutional authorization or by custom permit deviation from the principle of separation must be considered. Generally speaking, such deviations have resulted in the increase of powers in the executive department. Many states provide for the suspension of guarantees and for the "grant of extraordinary powers." Does a suspension of guarantees confer any legislative powers on the executive? Does such a suspension extend the sphere of administrative action? May the congress delegate to the executive legislative powers? A consideration of the questions in a case study may be illuminating, and the development of thought and practice in Mexico is chosen as an illustration.

The constitutions of 1857 and 1917 in that country embodied the principle of separation, and both provided exceptions. Articles 29 and 49 (50, in the constitution of 1857) carry these exceptions, and they are closely related. In Article 29, suspension of guarantees may be granted "in cases of invasion, grave disturbance of the public peace, or in any other case which places society in great danger or conflict." Article 49 has to do with the concession to the president of extraordinary powers (*facultades*) considered by the congress necessary for him "to meet the situation." In 1876, a case arose in which it was contended that the powers granted by the congress to the executive in the event of a disturbance of the public peace were limited to an extension "to greater amplitude" of administrative action. The complainant here contended that congress could not transfer its own powers of legislation to the executive. The district court, through Judge Landa, made a distinction between a concession of the whole legislative power and that of a partial delegation. The first would be an abdication and a change in form of government, but a concession of legislative powers for the purposes sanctioned in Article 29 of a partial extent for temporary duration would be valid. Shortly thereafter, in 1877, the supreme court ruled that the congress might not confer legislative power upon the executive.[1] This conclusion rested upon the text of the constitution and upon the record of consideration and action of the constitutional convention of 1846. However, in 1879, a new member of the supreme court, Justice Vallarta, who was to have a profound influence upon Mexican jurisprudence, induced the court to reverse itself and return to the Landa position, holding that the delegation of a partial and temporary authority to legislate was not a merging of the organ of legislation with the executive. In time, by use and misuse of the arguments of Landa and Vallarta—that the partial delegation of legislative power to the executive for a limited period of time did not involve a union of "organs" of government—the successful effort was made during the Díaz dictatorship to legitimatize such a delegation in time of peace. Among the indictments of the Díaz era, by the opponents of the dictator, was that he had usurped the powers of the congress. In the constitutional convention of 1917, an effort was made to secure a clarification whereby such abuses would be forbidden, but this attempt failed. Article 49, as adopted, aside from causing much controversy as to its meaning, left the matter of granting extraordinary powers to the executive in the same position it had occupied in the Díaz period. During the following twenty years, there was "notorious and systematic violation of the constitution," with the congress surrendering to the executive powers belonging only to itself. The supreme court "was not able and did not seek to defend the constitution, but bowed to the situation, declaring constitutional the delega-

[1] *Amparo* of Faustino Goribar. Cited by Felipe Tena Ramírez, *Derecho constitucional mexicano* (2d ed., Mexico, 1949), pp. 184–185.

tion made in such circumstances."[2] These practices continued until 1938, when an amendment, urged by President Cárdenas, was adopted. The amendment was the addition of a clause to Article 49, reading, "In no other case shall extraordinary power of legislation be granted to the executive." The reference to "no other case" means "in no other case than that covered in Articles 29 and 131"[3] This amendment tends to correct the faulty expansions of the Landa-Vallarta theses and to limit the grants of extraordinary powers to occasions of emergency and to matters of economics. Whether or not the change of 1938 will stand has been questioned. By some it is argued that the prohibition of such grants in peacetime is not realistic with reference to the political situation in Mexico.[4]

In some other countries, the use of legislative power by the executive is most commonly associated with the issuance of decree laws (*decretos-leyes*). Generally speaking, a considerable part of the laws is enacted in Latin America by presidential decree rather than by the normal legislative process. There is a difference in both theory and practice among the countries as to legislation by presidential decree, however similar the general results may be. Is such an exercise of power by the executive a usurpation? Is it to be justified, whether authorized or not by any delegation, by the argument of necessity in meeting an emergency? Is it by constitu-

[2] Tena Ramírez, *op. cit.*, p. 193.

[3] Article 131 states that the congress may authorize the president to increase, lower, or suppress tariff rates and to create new rates; to restrict or prohibit importations, exports, and transit of products; and to "realize whatever other purpose in benefit of the country" having to do with the national economy. These executive measures will be submitted to the congress in the next message on the budget for approval. See the 1953 edition of the Mexican constitution issued by *Editorial Porrúa.*

[4] Some attention in Mexico has been directed to practice in the United States in matters of the exercise of "war powers"—inherent in the executive branch or granted by the Congress—and the administrations of Lincoln, Wilson, and F. D. Roosevelt have been studied in this connection. Lincoln's use of "war powers"—often without congressional grant—was not so much to the point of their interest; such use might be considered as a case of "dictatorship." Wilson sought and obtained extensive powers for the duration of the war. Mexican thinkers have argued that in no case was "legislative power" included in any of these grants. On the contrary, the grants consisted of an expansion of administrative power. Mexican writers were keenly interested in grants of power in time of peace during the era of the New Deal to enable the executive to cope with the economic crisis of the great depression. Among these powers granted were those which were considered to be legislative. They have taken note that such grants, in 1935, were declared unconstitutional by the Supreme Court. See Tena Ramírez, *op. cit.*, pp. 182–183.

tional or statutory recognition a power properly exercised in normal times and thereby a breach of the doctrine of separation of powers? May the congress invest the executive with powers to legislate by delegation previous to the issuance of decree laws or by validation of them subsequently?

In Argentina, for example, the executive is recognized as having delegated powers of issuing decree laws. To be sure, some of these *decretos-leyes* may depend upon later approval by the congress. The courts do not distinguish, as to source, between laws passed by congress and those proclaimed by the executive. The congress is at liberty to delegate its powers. If this is done, it is a political decision. The courts will decide cases involving constitutionality of either class of legislation, without regard to source. They have declared their interest to be the substance. The political justification or utility of decree laws may be that of necessity in meeting some kind of emergency, but the legal justification is a delegation prior to or a validation subsequent to the issuance.[5]

It is not certain what juridical character may be assigned to these decree laws—even within particular countries. Certainly, law by decree occurs in Argentina, Brazil, Cuba, Bolivia, Colombia, Ecuador, Nicaragua, Panama, and Paraguay. An example of constitutional recognition of the decree law is found in Nicaragua, where the executive may issue them. It is true that the congress may approve or disapprove them. Further, the supreme court is instructed to respect them, presumably when they are constitutional. Panama authorizes the legislative branch to invest the executive with powers to issue decree laws in times of emergency. Such decrees—even of a temporary character—must be approved by the congress when it meets. Paraguay grants to the president the power during recess of congress to issue decrees having force of law (*decretos con fuerza de ley*) provided they are approved by the council of state.

Thus some constitutions have given formal recognition to the decree laws; practice and custom have in some countries given a sanction to them not only for emergencies and for *de facto* governments, but for such decrees in times of peace; likewise, some courts by upholding or by invalidating them have definitely recognized them as possible sources of law.

Even if there is a requirement of subsequent approval by the legislative branch, the executive in the countries affected has become a sharer in legislative power. When this restriction is not in effect, the legislative

[5] For a careful consideration, see Rafael Bielsa, *Derecho administrativo* (4th ed., 4 vols., Buenos Aires, 1947), vol. I, pp. 343–357, and his *El estado de necesidad* (Buenos Aires, 1946), pp. 68 ff.

capacity of the executive is indisputable, and the president becomes the principal lawmaker.

Some countries have made interesting attempts to modify the doctrine of the separation of powers in the interest of redressing the imbalance in favor of the executive. The Ecuadoran constitutions of 1945 and 1946, breaking with tradition, designate "functions," not powers or branches. These charters emphasize coordination of functions rather than separation. Perhaps unrealistically, the Ecuadoran constitutions give formal supremacy to the legislative over the executive and the judicial "functions." The organ entrusted with the task of this highly emphasized coordination is the council of state. This body investigates the constitutionality of executive and legislative actions, performs some legislative duties when congress is not in session, and settles conflicts of jurisdiction that may arise among administrative agencies.[6] The constitution of Cuba embodies another concept of the functions of the three branches of government. In Article 138, after stating that the executive power is vested in the president with the council of ministers, it adds that "the president of the republic acts as the directing and moderating power." He is also "the major force that must contribute to national solidarity." This provision may be criticized as ill fitted to the Cuban "semiparliamentary" regime under which the executive continues to have much of the power associated with the purely presidential system. This fact, it has been noted, makes it highly improbable that he can fulfill the duty of serving as a national moderator.[7]

The Uruguayan Experiments

Several interesting experiments have been initiated in Uruguay. Some features may be considered as evolutionary. Others occurred in times of international crises or civil wars, in times of economic depression, and in the midst of social and constitutional changes—situations which may well have enhanced the difficulty of adoption and application. One of the evolutionary reforms was that designed to develop the constitutional right of interpellation into a modified scheme of ministerial responsibility; another change involving prolonged controversy was the adoption of a plural or collegiate executive. Both looked toward a restriction of the powers of the executive branch.

It is of interest that a powerful executive and a civil *caudillo* of great

[6] George I. Blanksten, *Ecuador: Constitutions and Caudillos* (Berkeley, Calif., University of California Press, 1951), pp. 83–85.

[7] Ramón Infiesta, *Derecho constitucional* (Havana, 1950), pp. 250–251.

prestige, José Batlle y Ordóñez, became a determined leader in a movement to limit and even to abolish the power of the president in government, by placing that power in a plural body. Twice president (1903–1907, 1911–1915), Batlle, after consolidating his power through military victory over the fabulous *caudillo gaucho* Saravia in 1904, pacified his distracted country and led in the adoption of a remarkable series of liberal and moderately socialistic measures.[8]

Between his two terms in office, Batlle made a visit for study in Europe, giving especial attention to the government of Switzerland. In 1913, through his journal, *El Día,* he caused consternation and divided his own party by proposing the collegiate executive. The chief arguments for this change were that the traditional presidency was endowed with autocratic and almost absolute powers; that this office in the hands of one person placed the country at the mercy of a good or bad man; that it inspired ambitions and provoked civil wars, causing many of the internal troubles and disorders of Uruguayan history; that the plural executive was more in accord with liberty and republican government because it suppresses the power of an individual; and that with decisions being made by a commission of nine, instead of one man, arbitrariness and error would be diminished, since nine would be less likely to err than one. The opposition argued that the collegiate executive was an imported, foreign plan, without historical roots, and was contrary to the history and experience of the people; that this type of executive could be converted into an oligarchy; that it would destroy the unity of executive action and that long arguments, customary in a deliberative body, would cause delays to the detriment of the country; and that the history of plural executives—triumvirates, directorates, and councils—gave no assurance of its being satisfactory.[9]

The election of members of the constitutional convention in 1916 was a defeat for Batlle, but the constitution placed in effect in 1919, probably because of the threat that he might again run for the presidency, caused some of his ideas to be adopted. This charter provided for a president and for an elective council of administration of nine members, on which the minority should be represented. The traditional powers of the executive were divided. The new council was to have jurisdiction of such matters

[8] J. Zavala Muñiz, *Batlle: héroe* (Mexico, 1945), pp. 247–248. For the significance of the battle of Masoller (1904), see A. Zum Felde, *Evolución histórica del Uruguay* (3d ed., Montevideo, 1945), pp. 227–232.

[9] Zum Felde, *op. cit.,* p. 235.

as public instruction, public works, finances, labor, industries, agriculture, charities, and sanitation. It was to appoint and control the ministries associated with these activities. The president was to appoint the ministers of foreign affairs, war and navy, and of the interior. He was charged with the maintenance of order and retained administrative powers in the strictly political branches of government. Although opinions differ widely concerning the results of this plan, this vertical partition of administrative executive powers lasted for fifteen years. It appears that administrative action was retarded without compensatory improvement.

In the presence of economic depression and political unrest, President Gabriel Terra (1930–1938) converted his government into a dictatorship, which he promised would be temporary pending the establishment of a new constitution. The new instrument, ratified in 1934, abolished the administrative council and reintegrated the executive powers. The president's ministry was to have minority representation. A novelty of doubtful justification was that the two major political parties should have equal representation in the senate. Under Terra's successor, Baldomir (1938–1942), the administrative council was for a brief period restored. Amendments to the constitution were adopted in 1942, one of which abolished the equal representation in the senate.

With the adoption of the "new" constitution of 1951, Uruguay returned to the plural executive. There was during these four decades both the active and the posthumous influence of Batlle y Ordóñez, his fellow Colorado (but opponent), Gabriel Terra, and the distinguished leader of the chief opposition party, Luis Alberto Herrera, of the Blanco or Nationalist party. The discussions and the action taken (1950–1951) concerning the collegiate executive were accompanied by the concurrence of the congress, the repeated and extended consideration in the press, and the referendum to the people. Whether or not a "deal" was made between the major parties, there was democratic action.[10]

The change was the result of an effective agreement between the Colorado party, led by the incumbent president, Dr. Andres Martínez Trueba, and Herrera, the veteran leader of the Blancos, himself six times a candidate for the presidency. The reform was ratified in a plebiscite by a vote

[10] For a study of the constitutional changes of 1951, see Russell H. Fitzgibbon, "Adoption of a Collegiate Executive in Uruguay," *The Journal of Politics,* vol. 14, no. 4, pp. 616–642, November, 1952. Cf. also E. Rodríguez Fabregat, *Batlle y Ordóñez, el reformador* (Buenos Aires, 1942); S. G. Hanson, *Utopia in Uruguay* (New York, Oxford University Press, 1938); Zavala Muñiz, *op. cit.;* P. Blanco Acevedo, *Estudios constitucionales* (Montevideo, 1939).

of 232,076 to 197,684 on December 16, 1951. By it the executive became the National Council of Government, composed of nine members, six from the party having the largest vote, and three from the minority party of the largest vote. A scheme of proportional representation may by law be applied, and any minority within these major factions may secure membership provided it polls more than one-sixth of the vote. The president of the Council, chosen from the representatives of the majority party, serves for one year under a plan of rotation. Five members may act for the Council. A ministry of nine persons remained to be appointed by the Council. They are removable by the Council without prejudice to their liability to censure by the general assembly. The collegial principle was applied to the provincial governments (departments).

The substitution of the collegiate for the single executive will doubtless cause problems of relationship of that branch with the congress. Article 147 established the firm power of the chambers to pass political judgment on the ministers of state. In joint session a resolution of censure can be adopted. Censure when adopted by an absolute majority of the general assembly (Article 148) will require the resignation of the minister or ministers affected. These changes made by Uruguay may be watched with interest by other Latin-American states which are faced with the perennial problem of how to restrict the powers of the executive.

It is to be concluded from this brief consideration that Latin America has reached no common conclusion as to the issue of separation of powers. Some seem to regard the principle as the constitutional basis of liberty and of limited government. Others veer toward a possible extreme of presidential ascendancy. The issue is recurrent and full of lively interest, and it is to be expected that the countries will engage in further experimentation.

The Office of President

As it has been already indicated, the executive branch holds the controlling power in government and politics in nearly all the Latin-American countries. The dominant role played by the chief executive in all governmental processes, and the resulting subordination to which the legislative and judicial branches are relegated, is the most salient feature of Latin-American government.

A Latin-American president exercises political, administrative, legislative, and, on occasions, judicial powers. He is the administrative and executive chief of the government in law and in fact. The legislature is usually pliable to his suggestions and seldom shows effective independence. He may exercise powers of taxation in extraordinary circumstances, and, as we have seen, he may use his ample authority to issue, not only administrative directives and regulations for the execution of the laws, but decrees which are substantive legislation. The judicial branch, although in general more independent than the congress, is also in most countries vulnerable to presidential opinions and influences. The cabinet is merely an instrument of his will. He has in practice an almost unrestricted power of appointment and removal of administrative officials. He exercises certain direct and indirect powers of a controlling effect in local government. In addition, the president is commander in chief of the armed forces, and, by grant or assumption, he is often the holder of extraordinary powers by which, with legal sanctions, he may exercise force as a political weapon. Both the military and the extraordinary powers are peculiarly significant in Latin America. Together they constitute a factor in the operation of government. At times, the president exercises arbitrary power, either by choice or by compulsion of circumstances, sometimes according to law, but often regardless of it. In such cases, the president becomes the government.

It was perhaps in the nature of things that the Latin-American countries should be characterized by the supremacy of presidential power. The authoritarian tradition of the colonial era, requiring obedience to the personal rule of viceroys and captains general, inspired the only system of government with which the peoples had any experience and familiarity. After the emancipation, new forms and institutions were more readily accepted if they embodied ways of thinking and habits that were ingrained by the course of centuries. The extent to which habits can be rooted in simple and uneducated people was in 1944 brought to our attention in Mexico by a curious document. It was a petition of a group of Indian residents of a small community, located not too far from the capital, which had been sent by mail to Manuel Avila Camacho, then president of the country. On the envelope, preceding his name, there appeared the solemn title "His Most Serene Highness." This, however, was not the only anachronism, for the style and spirit of the letter were identical with that of a communication which might have been addressed, two centuries ago, to the viceroy of New Spain. The people of the newly born republics were too inexperienced or too backward to undertake experiments in government with any reasonable expectation of success. In addition, the abuse of new freedoms often resulted in libertinism, and the resultant disorder made it imperative to concentrate authority in the hands of one man. Bolívar himself had foreseen this trend and had accepted it as the only alternative to chaos and anarchy. It is well to remember that the basic political problem of Latin America in the early part of the republican period was one of getting along in an orderly or semiorderly way. The pressing issue of establishing an "orderly society" took precedence over all others. Thus, in many ways, strong presidential government was the inevitable outcome of historical antecedents and political circumstances.

The influences of tradition and of conditions prevailing at the time of independence are not, however, the only factors which determined the role assigned to the executive in the scheme of government. Other elements have combined to make the pattern of executive dominance the main characteristic of Latin-American government. Among them are the constitutional grants of powers to the executive, together with their interpretation and application; the highly centralized schemes of public administration with broad appointive powers for the president; the important part the army plays in politics; the conception of the presidency that a large portion of the people have; the nature of the party system; and the new economic responsibilities of the executive. A few comments concerning each of these factors should be in order.

Constitutional Powers. It must be emphasized that, although part of the supremacy of the executive is derived from extralegal sources, a very substantial part of it is prescribed by the basic laws of the several countries. Most of the constitutions give a broadly inclusive foundation to the presidency in the governmental system.[11] A reading of the powers of the president in the various constitutions will be convincing proof that their framers intended to make the office a powerful one. The powers and responsibilities are more broadly stated than, for instance, in the constitution of the United States.[12] In addition, political practices (i.e.,

[11] See J. G. Guerra, *La constitución de 1925* (Santiago, 1929), p. 336. Also Osvaldo E. Miranda Arenas, *El jefe de estado en las constituciones americanas* (Santiago, 1944), p. 31.

[12] Chief differences of the Latin-American constitutional foundations of the executive branch as compared with those in the United States constitution are the detail with which qualifications for the office of president are set forth; the predominance of the system of direct popular election, but with some local variants; the omission of the vice-presidential office in some states; the detail with which the composition and functions of the cabinet are prescribed; the permission given, in some countries, to cabinet members to participate in the proceedings of the congress; the explicitness of the principle of nonreelection and the elaborate provisions relating to the removal of the president and to the regulation

what the president does with his office) tend to further expand his constitutional authority. It is, then, necessary to examine not only the powers that are constitutionally granted but also any divergences that may exist between the laws and the actual practice.

With reference to the legislative functions of the president, it has been already noted that legislation considerable in volume and in importance is proclaimed by presidential decree rather than by the process of congressional enactment. "Legislation by decree" is common in all Latin America with the possible exception of Uruguay, where decree laws have not been frequently used. Examples of legislation emanating from the executive branch are numerous and significant elsewhere. The income tax was imposed in Mexico by executive decree, and codes of civil and criminal procedure were put into effect in the same manner. Even the annual budget is on occasion issued by executive order in this country, but Mexico is not in this respect an exceptional case. In 1880 and 1888, the Honduran congress authorized the president to legislate in matters of police, finance, war, public instruction, development (*fomento*), and court organization. Full authority was granted to the chief executive in 1906 to prepare "certain codes and laws."[13] In Cuba legislation by executive decree has at times reached considerable proportions. Under the Grau San Martín administration (1944–1948) more than three thousand decrees were issued in one year (1946), while only twenty laws were passed by the congress.[14]

The part played by the president in the ordinary lawmaking process is also important, since in most countries he is authorized to initiate legislation in the form of bills (*proyectos de ley*) submitted to the congress. In fact, it is his exclusive prerogative in some items to propose legislation dealing with the budget, to create new administrative positions, to increase government salaries, or to change the organization of the armed forces.[15] This power to initiate legislation is freely used by the president. In Honduras, from 1896 to 1941, approximately 26 per cent of all bills

---

of succession, and to the grant of emergency powers. See Ethel M. Crompton, "The Executive Office in the Latin American Constitutions," *Southwestern Political Science Quarterly,* vol. 1, pp. 380–396, March, 1921.

[13] William S. Stokes, *Honduras: An Area Study in Government* (Madison, Wis., University of Wisconsin Press, 1950), p. 287.

[14] *Bohemia,* June 15, 1947, p. 69.

[15] Such is the case of Brazil and Chile. See constitutions, Arts. 67, cl. 2, and 45, respectively.

presented to the congress originated with the executive branch. During this same period 93 per cent of all the legislation proposed by the executive was enacted by the congress. In twelve separate years the legislature enacted every proposal that was presented to it by the president.[16] The case of Honduras may well be an extreme example of congressional subservience to executive direction, but it is not unique in Latin America.

The president may, of course, veto the laws that congress submits for his signature. The majority of the countries have adopted the item veto, the time during which the president may veto a bill varying from eight days to ten.[17] The Cuban system provides for a device intended to prevent the "pocket veto" as it occurs in the United States. If congress recesses within the ten days following the reception of the bill by the president, he is unable to kill the measure by merely failing to take action. In such cases, the executive must inform the congress within forty-eight hours of his intention to use the entire period allowed for the consideration of the bill, so that the legislature may continue in session if it so desires (Article 137). Latin-American presidents, however, seldom resort to the use of their veto power, since control of the legislature secured through political means makes it unnecessary for them to veto legislation.

In the exercise of his constitutionally vested power to issue decrees necessary for the execution of legislative acts or of powers expressly delegated to him by the congress, the Latin-American president often decides upon matters of policy which rightfully belong to the legislative branch. The ordinance power (*potestad reglamentaria*) is the essence of the broad administrative authority of the executive. By it, the president frames regulations to supplement the laws enacted in general terms by the congress. The various types of executive orders (*decretos, reglamentos, ordenanzas,* and *instrucciones*) used for this purpose are theoretically limited to implementing and applying existing laws made by the legislative body. In practice, however, the president may use his ordinance

[16] Stokes, *op. cit.,* p. 287.

[17] There are some unusual features of the veto power in Colombia. The chief executive is allowed a variable period in which to return a bill, according to the length of the proposed law: six days, if the bill has a maximum of fifty articles; ten, if it contains from fifty-one to two hundred articles; and up to fifteen days if it is longer. The president's veto can be overridden by an absolute majority of the members of each legislative chamber. If the president objects to a bill on the grounds that it is unconstitutional, and congress still insists on its passage, the bill is sent to the supreme court, which must render an opinion within six days (Arts. 86 to 88, 90).

powers in such a fashion as to make changes which affect not only the form but the spirit of the laws as well. The trend, evidences of which may be found in other countries besides the Latin American republics, has transformed the rule-making power into substantive authority to legislate.

The authority to declare a state of siege is, of course, of great importance among the constitutional powers of the president. The exercise of such extensive powers as are inherent to this institution contributes in large measure to giving the executive a privileged position. As we have seen before, there is little doubt that the state of siege can become a mighty weapon in the hands of a strong president. In addition, presidential use of the process of intervention in the federal republics has greatly strengthened executive hold on provincial or state affairs.

The president's power to spend money augments and enhances his authority. The control which he usually exercises over the budget may rest on constitutional grants or on acts of the congress, or it may merely be the result of political techniques of domination. Although the process of preparing and adopting the budget is the standard method universally employed, the president's emergency powers allow him to direct, by means of decrees, the spending of large sums in excess of those authorized by the congress. As a rule, once the president has secured emergency powers, he can legally divert public funds from the original appropriations. It is possible for him, in some countries, to allow deficiencies in the budget provided that he accounts for them to congress at the end of the fiscal year. This is never too difficult a task if the president controls, as he often does, an effective majority in the legislature. In some countries, the congress may even authorize the president to decree, on his own authority, in case of grave emergency such as war or invasion, collection of taxes one year in advance. In any case, presidential control of the public treasury, like other powers designed for times of emergency, is found to be in most countries a frequent practice rather than an exceptional measure. Furthermore, it must be noted that the nature of the tax system in most of the Latin-American republics gives a major portion of the public incomes to the central government. This makes all other political units in the governmental system dependent upon the national government for funds. Considering that the president is the chief bestower of favors because of his ample financial powers, it is easy to conclude that this situation results in enhancement of his prestige and influence.

The President as Chief of Administration. All the constitutions have elaborate provisions concerning the administrative powers of the president.

In a scheme of public administration which is in every country highly centralized, the president has, as it would be expected, unusually ample powers of appointment. He is, of course, empowered to appoint ministers and other public officials. He can also remove appointive officials at his discretion, with the exception of those who are removable by impeachment only. Civil service regulations and merit systems exist in a few countries, but in general there is little to restrict the president's power to appoint and remove at will almost the entire personnel of the national administration.

In Colombia, Chile, Ecuador, Panama, and Venezuela, the chief executive appoints the local governors. In Central America, control of local governments by the president has always been a feature of the political system. The governor (*jefe político*) of each department (province) is a presidential appointee in all the Central American republics, and in Nicaragua, all municipal officers are also appointed by the executive every two years. Municipal laws are subject to approval by the president. In addition, he has control of the local police. The local units of government have been traditionally considered in this group of countries as a part of the nation's administrative structure. Therefore, their control and regulation by the national executive has been generally accepted in their systems.

Among many other administrative duties assigned to the president is the power to negotiate administrative contracts for the performance of services and the execution of public works. Although, in some countries, it implies the obligation to give account to the congress, this authorization contributes, generally as much as the appointing power, to the enlargement of presidential influence as the main dispenser of public favors, and it is always a useful political weapon.[18]

Justices of the supreme court are appointed by the president in several countries. In Mexico, the appointments need to be approved by the Senate, while in Chile the president selects appointees from a list of five persons submitted to him by the supreme court. In Cuba, such a list is prepared by a special electoral college. In other countries, such as Colombia, where the appointment of judges falls to the legislature, the president, in some cases, submits to it the list or panel of candidates.

Role of the Army in Politics. Soldier-presidents have always been common in Latin America. Approximately one-third of the total number of

[18] See J. D. Moscote, *Introducción al estudio de la constitución* (Panama, 1939), p. 186.

presidents in Ecuador have been military men. At the time of this writing, the presidents of twelve of the republics are army officers. But even in the countries with civilian presidents the chief source of the government's power is usually the army. A president remains in office only as long as he commands the support of the armed forces, for revolutions invariably start in the barracks of the military. It is by groups and juntas of army officers that presidents are often made and unmade. A president must keep the army satisfied and united in his support if he wants his administration to survive. Often patriotic and well-meaning presidents have to devote all their time and energies to keeping from being overthrown, and their programs of constructive action must be postponed in favor of survival.

There is a definite relationship between the phenomenon of *caudillismo* and militarism, although not all major *caudillos* have been military men. The ranks of the army have produced, however, more than their share of famous *caudillos*. This flair of army men for politics has been explained sometimes as being a much-needed outlet for activity, somewhat similar to the "creative urge" which seizes the artist. According to this explanation, political activity is an escape from the tedious and routine life of the barracks.[19] Others have pointed to that sententious political maxim, frequently cited in some countries, which reads: "The last step in a military career is the presidency of the republic."[20]

Whenever the army abandons its camps and marches against the presidential palace to take over the government, it invariably does so under the righteous pretext of defending the liberties of the people or of putting an end to corruption. On assuming its self-appointed role of savior of the country, the army always pledges itself to return to its normal functions as soon as things are again in order, corrupt politicians have been swept away, and justice has been done. This promise to return the government to civilian hands rarely turns into reality, for in the majority of cases, a curious process takes place. At first, power may be shared by the components of a junta, which may include some civilians as adornments. Eventually, however, one of the army officers, by reasons of personal ability or because of a strong personal following among subordinates, or both, emerges as the "strong man." He may or may not become himself provisional president, but in any case his candidacy and electoral victory

[19] Kurt Conrad Arnade, "The Technique of the Coup d'Etat in Latin America," *United Nations World*, vol. 4, no. 2, pp. 21–25, February, 1950.

[20] Blanksten, *op. cit.*, p. 36.

are assured if, and when, the *de facto* regime considers that the time has come to hold elections and to secure the trappings of legality. With slight variations this process has occurred in the past in all the countries. It has repeatedly taken place in recent years in Argentina, Venezuela, Peru, Panama, Guatemala, and Cuba.

The case of Peru might be typical. In October, 1948, a group of high army officers seized control of the government from constitutionally elected President José L. Bustamante. The head of this military junta, General Manuel Odría, assumed the title of provisional president, promised elections at an early date, and proceeded to rule solely by decree. After consolidating its power, the government scheduled elections for 1950. Parties in the opposition were declared illegal, and General Odría, running for the presidency unopposed, was elected with 80 per cent of the vote for a six-year term.

Another interesting case is that of Venezuela, a country which had been unusually plagued throughout its history by barracks revolts. Certain episodes in this history clearly show how important a part is played by the armed forces in the national life. The Venezuelan army was chiefly responsible in 1945 for the success of a revolution which established a seven-man junta dominated by civilians (only two were army men) and backed by the Democratic Action party, the largest organized political force in the country. This government, strengthened by wide popular support, undertook a comprehensive program of political, economic, and social reforms. Elections were held in 1947 for delegates to a constituent assembly, which drafted what was probably the most democratic constitution in Venezuela's history. General elections were held later, and an internationally famous novelist and leader of Democratic Action, Rómulo Gallegos, won an impressive victory in what all impartial observers agreed was a fair contest. During the three years between the revolution of 1945 and President Gallegos's inauguration in 1948, civilians and military men of the provisional junta worked harmoniously together, and the government received the support of the armed forces. However, shortly after the inauguration of the new president, serious differences developed between Gallegos and several army officers. The officers demanded six posts in the cabinet, so as to have a stronger voice in policy decisions. On the refusal of the president to accept these terms, a three-man military junta took over the government and sent Gallegos into exile. The constitution was suspended, a state of siege was declared, and the majority party was officially declared subversive. After the assassination in 1950 of the head of this junta, another member, Colonel Marcos Pérez Jiménez, became Venezuela's new "strong man." In fulfillment of promises made four years earlier, elections for a new constituent assembly were held in 1952. The largest party having been declared an illegal organization, the opposition was reduced to four very small parties with varied political platforms. The junta felt confident that its candidates could win in an honest election. The outcome, however, was surprising. Early electoral returns indicated that an overwhelming defeat seemed to be in the making for the government-sponsored candidates. After a few hours of scrutiny, the victory of the opposition was certain, but before the scrutiny was completed, the military "junta" declared a state of siege, and suspended all election bulletins and news communiqués. Two days later came the official announcement that the government's "Independent Electoral Front" had won the election. The hand-picked constitutional assembly confirmed Pérez Jiménez as president in January, 1953, and three months later completed the task of writing a new constitution.

The role of the army as a major factor in politics and the extensive use of force as an instrument of political action are, of course, due to many and varied causes. Some of these have been already discussed in the chapter dealing with dictatorship and revolution. It might be sufficient to recall at this time that the rise of the military class was one of the most momentous although regrettable effects of the wars for independence. It must also be remembered that a low standard of living, often at the level of mere subsistence, is to be found among the Latin-American peoples. Their concentration in the struggle for the basic necessities of life has permitted, by default, political control to fall in the hands of those who are able and willing to resort to force in order to secure and to maintain that control. Other factors, such as illiteracy, isolation and localism, and the traditionally narrow base of the economies of these countries, have also contributed to the development of praetorianism.[21]

As far as constitutions are concerned, all of them expressly confer upon the president the title of commander in chief of the armed forces. He has the power of organizing and distributing the armed forces as he may find it proper in times of peace or war, and in some countries he has the authority to fix the number of such forces. Of course, he has the power to appoint, with the consent of the senate, the high-ranking personnel of the army and the navy. The grant of military power is usually much

[21] Russell H. Fitzgibbon, "Executive Power in Central America," *The Journal of Politics,* vol. 3, no. 3, pp. 297–307, August, 1941.

more detailed and substantial than in constitutions of other countries outside Latin America.

The President as the Great Father. In all the Latin-American countries, but especially in those with great masses of Indians or mestizos, the rural population, if not the sophisticated inhabitants of the large urban centers, are inclined to think of the president as the great wise father somewhat as the Russian peasant of the czarist era thought of his emperor. This role of the benevolent, understanding, but at the same time all-powerful great father is sometimes forced upon the president by a series of circumstances. As one writer puts it, sometimes "there is an implicit submissiveness, a bending of the head, which unconsciously forces upon the president the exercise of arbitrary power. Only the president can make a final decision. No other power is final, no other authority is absolute. He who would govern must also rule, or he will not be able to govern."[22]

This popular conception turns the presidency into an all-consuming job and makes the lot of a Latin-American executive a not too enviable one. In his role of father of the country he must exercise his authority in person and not through intermediaries. He must attend in detail to all matters, important and unimportant, and make all decisions, or else he might run the risk of losing his prestige and with it of finding his authority gone. He must manage all the political and administrative life of the nation and must intervene in almost every transaction between the people and the government. He must receive callers from all walks of life. A typical calendar day of presidential appointments includes a list of visitors who are fairly representative of a cross section of the country. One of the present authors once sat for several hours in a presidential antechamber, waiting to be received by the chief executive of one of the Latin-American republics. Although it was past midnight, a large group of people were still waiting for their turn. Because of the natural friendliness of Latin Americans, there were animated conversations among them, and it was not too difficult to find out the nature of the business which had taken each of them to the presidential palace. Among the group there was a committee of textile workers which intended to present to the president their side of a certain labor dispute, a delegation of party leaders anxious to obtain the president's approval of a slate of candidates for a local election, a widow who had some difficulties col-

[22] Frank Tannenbaum, "Personal Government in Mexico," in Asher N. Christensen (ed.), *The Evolution of Latin American Government* (New York, Holt, 1951), p. 417.

lecting her government pension, a group of businessmen interested in modifications of some bothersome customs regulations, and a sprinkle of job seekers.

How versatile the talents of a Latin-American president must be is well illustrated by the following anecdote told by Galo Plaza, the young and dynamic president of Ecuador from 1948 to 1952, who holds in that country the distinction of being the first president in 28 years who was able to complete his term of office. During the taking of the 1950 census in Ecuador a large number of Indians of a culturally remote community refused to cooperate with the authorities. There were some disturbances, and census officials were bodily attacked. On being informed of this situation, President Plaza flew to the scene and spoke to the Indians, explaining what the census meant in order to dissipate their fears. Only after the president promised to remain among them during the enumeration did the community agree to submit to it and to answer the questions of the census takers.[23]

Nature of the Party System. The strong personalism inherent in Latin-American politics and the absence of genuine party government have also contributed to strengthen the position of the president. A normal course of party growth has been lacking in most countries, and the logical result of personalism has been a tendency of parties to split into factions, each following a different leader. As it is only to be expected, parties have become in many cases tools at the service of personal political ambitions. Party organization is usually controlled by the inner group, loyal to the leader or *caudillo,* and candidates are normally hand-picked. Naturally, such control is intensified when the party is in power and its leader becomes the chief of the government. It would indeed be rare if any attempts were made to challenge his authority as "grand elector" to select candidates and to decide upon all party policies.

New Economic Responsibilities. An appreciable increase in the range of governmental responsibilities has taken place in recent years as a consequence of significant developments and activities in the economic field. The increase in the functions of government has given new impetus to the growing power of the presidency by investing this office with the authority to manage a great part of the economic affairs of the country. Nationalization programs and ambitious plans for economic development have resulted in the establishment of important government agencies

[23] Galo Plaza, *Problems of Democracy in Latin America* (Chapel Hill., N.C., The University of North Carolina Press, 1955), p. 35.

which exercise general supervision over the economy. In most countries the congress has played a secondary role in the creation of administrative agencies and in the general expansion of government services. It has been the responsibility almost entirely of the chief executive to undertake reforms in the administrative system whenever they became necessary. The agency entrusted in Argentina with the management of the government-owned oil industry was established by presidential decree in 1922. It was not until ten years later that its existence was formally recognized by law.[24] Important phases of industrialization programs on a large scale, such as Argentina's five-year plan, have been invariably placed under control of the executive branch. Administrative agencies, government-owned corporations, and mixed corporations have been erected and entrusted with the control and direction of government investments. The growth and ramifications of governmental operations have therefore contributed to some degree to the aggrandizement of the powers of the chief executive, who, in many cases, has become arbiter of the economic life of his country.

Methods and Techniques of Control. A large measure of authority not vested in the president by law is, nevertheless, in his hands as a result of his political powers. The methods and techniques employed by presidents in the exercise of political controls are numerous and varied. As far as the cabinet is concerned, there is no doubt about its complete subordination to the president. Ministers are his choice and they serve at his pleasure. Their appointments need not be submitted to legislative confirmation. The absence of any need for any controlling device seems obvious in this case. However, to keep the legislative branch as a subservient body does require the utilization of some political weapons. Among these, the president's control of the electoral machinery which allows him to select the members of the congress is the chief instrument. It has been said of Argentina that it "is almost impossible for any member of the president's party to be elected to congress without presidential consent.[25] This situation is by no means unique, but on the contrary, is of common occurrence in Latin America. In addition, since each chamber of the congress is the judge of its own elections and passes on the credentials of newly elected members, the president simply sees to it that the right persons are seated. Presidential control of the selection of

[24] Austin F. Macdonald, *Government of the Argentine Republic* (New York, Crowell, 1942), p. 204.

[25] *Ibid.*, p. 205.

candidates for the congress accounts in part for the weak action of the legislative branch in the defense of its prerogatives.

Furthermore, there are at the disposal of the president varied controls over legislative activity. He not only calls special sessions of congress but, in some countries, also extends regular sessions beyond the usual period prescribed by the constitution. The president's power to open sessions of the congress in Argentina has permitted the chief executive to determine, in practice, when those sessions shall begin. The doctrine and custom hold that congress may not begin its session until the president appears and reads his message. The net effect of this Argentine practice is that the president may postpone all congressional activity until such time as he considers it convenient.

It must also be remembered that through his appointive powers the president is the chief dispenser of patronage. The basis of every political machine in Latin America is the spoils system, as it is elsewhere. Control over government positions is given to congressmen as a reward for loyalty and service to the president more than to the party. A congressman's influence over patronage is in direct proportion to the degree of his friendship with the president. Naturally, this is not characteristic solely of Latin America, but it carries perhaps in this area more significance than in other countries as an instrument of presidential domination.

With regard to the judiciary it should be said that, as a rule, there is little presidential interference in the lower levels or in matters which are exclusively judicial. It is possible, however, for the upper courts to be subject to presidential influence for political purposes. Means are not lacking by which a strong president may assure a certain amount of subordination on the part of the courts. The president's power of appointment extends in many countries to the inferior courts as well as to the upper reaches. In Chile, the president appoints judges of the courts of appeal from panels prepared by the supreme court. Similar authority is enjoyed by the president in Guatemala, Haiti, Paraguay, and Peru. The chief executive in Argentina appoints all judges of the inferior federal courts with the consent of the senate. It must be noted also that, even in countries where judicial appointments are a prerogative of the legislature, it is still possible for the president to fill vacancies in the judiciary when the congress is not in session. A Latin-American president may also transfer judges, order an exchange of posts, and under certain circumstances secure their removal on grounds of ineptitude or maladministration. Transfer of judges has often been used by the president as a powerful weapon to ostracize or to force the resignation of members of the judiciary who are known to hold adverse views to the administration by transferring them to remote and undesirable posts. President Perón, who assured control of the supreme court by having four of its five justices impeached and convicted by congress, made indiscriminate use of this power in his vigorous campaign to subjugate the Argentine judiciary. After the adoption of the new constitution of 1949, the Perón administration was able to achieve its goal of complete submission of the judiciary. By interpreting the usual requirement of senate confirmation of judges as applying not only to future appointments but also to those already made and confirmed in the past, the president secured in a few months the dismissal of more than seventy anti-Perón federal judges, some of whom had been on the bench for over twenty years. The senate simply refused to confirm their appointments.

State and local governments, already susceptible to influences and pressures because of lack of vigor and financial independence, may also be, in practice, completely controlled by the president. Thus, in Mexico, although the senate has sole authority to decide upon the legality of state elections, it is the president who in reality has the final word by means of his control of congress. In 1935, the Mexican senate, on the insistence of President Cárdenas, removed the governors of Sonora, Sinaloa, Guanajuato, and Durango. In more recent times, President Alemán in two years secured removal of six governors whose personal loyalty was doubtful. At other times, the president may resort, in cases of political crisis, to the technique of intervention under some pretext. Federal controls and "interventors" who take the place of the regular state officials are often employed by the president. Resort to this device has been frequent in Argentina and Brazil. The late President Getulio Vargas of Brazil was much adept to its use especially during the early and dictatorial part of his long administration. Thus, in 1937, he removed all state governors from office with the exception of one. On that occasion he was so determined to establish federal control that all state legislatures and municipal councils were dissolved at his orders.

Another method of executive control is censorship of the press and of other media of public information. A press monopoly can be made possible by a number of government pressures. In Perón's Argentina, for example, one such pressure was derived from the control of scarce newsprint by the government trade agency which for several years had charge of importing and distributing it. A more important source of pressure on the press may be through the threat of application of special laws punishing disrespect for government officials. One of the most famous applications of the law of disrespect (*desacato*) in Argentina was the arrest and trial in 1950 of a well-known newspaper editor in Salta. This man was sentenced to six years of imprisonment for criticizing the president. Argentina, however, is not the only country in which the press has been hamstrung. The Inter-American Press Association, which is the organized voice of press freedom and an effective force for an unfettered press, has in recent years denounced the governments of Bolivia, Colombia, the Dominican Republic, Paraguay, Peru, Nicaragua, and Venezuela, for various forms of interference. The influence that a growing independent press may have in forming public opinion was well demonstrated at the time of the Brazilian political crisis which culminated in 1954 with the suicide of President Vargas. The fiery and crusading articles against government corruption published by *Tribuna da Imprensa,* a Rio de Janeiro daily, were partly responsible for an upsurge of public opinion against the administration. Subsequent events involving a clash between the armed forces and the president resulted eventually in his resignation and ultimate tragic death.

Another instrument of control which is sometimes utilized by dictators and strong presidents is the organization of a corps of secret agents and paid informers who are directly at their command. These secret bodies have instituted in some countries a reign of terror and have been responsible for many atrocities. Two famous examples are the notorious *mazorca* established by Rosas in Argentina, and the *porra* of the Cuban dictator Machado. Another famous dictator, Juan Vicente Gómez, developed in Venezuela a very elaborate spy system during the twenty-seven years of his rule. This system, which functioned at home and abroad, efficiently prevented any public criticism of the government and kept Gómez's enemies under close surveillance. An additional although indirect source of control over the political life of the country is through the controlling interest that the president may have in certain public monopolies of basic commodities. The Dominican dictator Trujillo has monopolized for many years the salt and tobacco industries as well as most forms of insurance. He has sometimes used his privileged economic position to destroy his political enemies.

Conclusion. We have seen how many conditions and devices have combined to make government in Latin America mostly presidential government. The immense power vested in the executive office by virtue of law or of political custom necessarily makes a strong president of every Latin-American chief of state. If he fails to use the powers that are at his disposal he will not last long in office. There can be no such thing as a weak Latin-American president. Only the president can give stability and permanence to the government, and if he is not willing or not strong enough to do so, then he is overthrown. Or if the president does not rule, it is because he is merely a front for some *caudillo* or strong man who is the real power. The period of Mexican history known as the Callismo, or personal government of Plutarco E. Calles, furnishes a good example. Despite the fact that Calles held no office after the expiration of his four-year presidential term in 1928, he continued to manipulate the affairs of the nation and to control them completely until 1934. It was by him and not by the three nominal presidents which Mexico had between 1928 and 1934 that all decisions were made. In 1934, Calles's control was finally challenged. A strong and popular leader in his own right, Lázaro Cárdenas, who was elected with Calles's blessing, managed then to rescue the powers of his office after a spectacular showdown with the "maker of presidents."

Weak presidents cannot have a place in systems which are exposed to the disintegrating and atomizing pressures of so many different forces. A recent case exemplifies the serious damages that an apathetic and weak administration may inflict upon the entire political processes of a country. After Cuba's twelve years of constitutional normality and orderly elections since 1940, President Prío Socarrás's erratic and weak, although well-meaning, administration (1948–1952) caused the country to fall into political confusion bordering on chaos. The result was an army revolt in March, 1952, led by General Batista, the former "strong man" of the island and "master of the *coup d'état,*" which swept out the legitimate government and instituted a personal dictatorship.[26] Much of the responsibility for this interruption of Cuba's political progress should be placed on President Prío for having failed to perform forcefully his role as leader of the nation and of his party. Through vacillation and apathy he permitted the political scene to become so confused that by 1952 a revolt became almost inevitable. All that a willing and bold leader had to do, in General Batista's own words, was "to pick up the reins of power which had been cast into the mire."

[26] See J. Losada, "Batista: Master of the Coup d'Etat," *United Nations World,* pp. 31–35, April, 1953.

STRUCTURE AND ORGANIZATION

All constitutions prescribe qualifications, both negative and positive, which must be met by those who occupy the office of president. A requirement common to all is that of nationality by birth, with Mexico demanding that the president be not only a native Mexican but also of native parentage. Citizenship, residence for varying periods, and age requirements are also common conditions. In two countries, Argentina

TABLE 11
THE EXECUTIVE BRANCH*

Country	Consecutive reelection	Term, year	Minimum age	Vice-president or *designado*†	Council of state
Argentina	No	6	30	Vice-president	No
Bolivia	No	4	35	Vice-president	No
Brazil	No	5	35	Vice-president	No
Chile	No	6	30	Neither	No
Colombia	No	4	30	*Designado*	Yes
Costa Rica	No	4	30	2 vice-presidents	No
Cuba	No	4	35	Vice-president	No
Dominican Republic	Yes	5	30	Neither	No
Ecuador	No	4	35	Vice-president	Yes
El Salvador	No	6	30	Both	No
Guatemala	No	6	35	Neither	No
Haiti	No	6	40	Neither	Yes
Honduras	No	6	30	Vice-president	No
Mexico	No‡	6	35	Neither	No
Nicaragua	No	6	25	*Designados*	No
Panama	No	4	35	2 vice-presidents	No
Paraguay	Yes	5	40	Neither	Yes
Peru	No	5	35	2 vice-presidents	No
Uruguay	No	4	35	Neither	No
Venezuela	No	5	30	Neither	No

* All countries have a single chief executive except Uruguay which has a National Council of Government. Qualifications included in the chart for Uruguay apply to members of the plural executive. In each case the president (or council members) is elected by direct popular vote.

† Countries shown as having neither vice-president nor *designado* use other systems of succession that establish the order in which a number of officials are called upon to fill the vacancy.

‡ The president cannot ever occupy the office again.

and Paraguay, the president must also belong to the Roman Catholic Church. In Paraguay he must "meet the moral and intellectual requirements which qualify him to occupy the office" while in El Salvador he must "be of known honesty and learning."[27]

Among the negative qualifications the most significant are the provisions which prohibit reelection. Presidential reelection for one or more consecutive terms is prohibited in all Latin America except the Dominican Republic, Paraguay, and (since the constitutional reform of 1949) Argentina. A strong tradition against reelection has developed in Mexico since the revolution of 1910, and the Querétaro Constitution adopted the principle that a president, after his term expires, cannot ever occupy the office again "under any circumstances or for any reason."[28] Other provisions in some countries prohibit the election of those who occupy the office of *designado* (those appointed to succeed the president in case of vacancy) and of those serving as acting president at the time of the election or during the six months preceding it. In the Central American states, persons who are close relatives of the incumbent executive and those who are chiefs or participants of revolutions and *coups d'état* are also barred. Cabinet members, supreme court justices, clergymen, or military men in active service are also excluded in some countries.

Although the principle that a chief executive cannot succeed himself is almost universally accepted in Latin America, it is not always observed. A notable phenomenon has been the practice in some countries of what is known as *continuismo,* by means of which the presidential occupant manages to continue in power by securing enactment of some exceptional legislation, or by arranging for the election of some successor acceptable to him. In the latter case, even though the president has nominally retired to private life, he still may remain as the power behind the throne. If he chooses the other course of action he may secure the suspension of the constitutional ban on reelection by a plebiscite or by decision of a constituent assembly, or, in some cases, by support of a personally loyal and friendly legislature. The political history of the Caribbean and Central American republics supplies abundant examples of such practices, but the occurrence of this phenomenon is by no means restricted to this area.[29]

[27] Paraguay (Art. 46); El Salvador (Art. 66).

[28] Art. 12.

[29] For a discussion of *continuismo,* see Russell H. Fitzgibbon, "*Continuismo* in Central America and the Caribbean," *The Inter-American Quarterly,* vol. 2, no. 3, pp. 56–74, July, 1940.

Recent developments in South America indicate that the use of such devices is not geographically limited.

Modes of Choice

All Latin-American presidents are, at present, chosen by direct vote of the people in a universal and secret ballot. Countries which formerly employed some indirect method of election, similar to that used in the United States, such as Argentina, Brazil, or Colombia, have abandoned it in recent years and have adopted the direct system. There are, however, some interesting variations. In Cuba, for example, the counting of votes in presidential elections is done by provinces. The candidate obtaining the largest number of votes in each province receives a number of "provincial votes" equal to the total of senators and representatives from that particular province. The candidate accumulating the largest total of "provincial votes" throughout the country is elected. A weakness of the system is that the candidate who receives the largest popular vote is not assured of election, for another candidate may have secured the largest number of "provincial votes." The device, then, seems to complicate unnecessarily and to no apparent advantage the simple system of direct elections.[30]

An exceptional mode of choice is provided in all countries, to be used in case no candidate obtains the necessary majority and in the event of a tie. In such instances, the majority of the countries resort to a decision by the congress. In Chile, for instance, if the count fails to show a majority, the full congress shall elect one from among the two candidates who have received the highest number of votes. The election is by secret ballot and decided by more than half the votes.[31] In Ecuador, if there is a tie in the votes of the legislators when the election is thrown to the congress, the decision is by lot.[32] In Costa Rica if no candidate is elected on the popular election, a second or runoff popular election among the three candidates who have received the largest number of votes is held. If in the first or second election the two highest candidates obtain an equal number of votes, the oldest of two is considered elected.[33]

[30] Art. 140.
[31] Arts. 64, 65.
[32] Art. 84.
[33] In order to be elected, a candidate must receive more than 40 per cent of the votes cast.

Term of Office

Seven Latin-American countries have a four-year presidential term: Bolivia, Colombia, Costa Rica, Cuba, Ecuador, Panama, and Uruguay. A five-year term is used in five countries: the Dominican Republic, Paraguay, Peru, Venezuela, and Brazil. The other eight republics—Argentina, Chile, El Salvador, Guatemala, Haiti, Honduras, Mexico, and Nicaragua—provide for a six-year term of office.

Presidential Succession

In Argentina, Brazil, Costa Rica, Peru, Ecuador, Bolivia, Cuba, El Salvador, Honduras, and Panama a vice-president is elected at the same time and in the same manner as the chief executive. An amendment made to the Peruvian constitution in 1936 provided for two vice-presidencies. Two vice-presidents are also elected in Panama and Costa Rica.

Colombia and Nicaragua use the system of *designados,* under which officials who have the same qualifications required of presidential candidates are appointed by the congress as the president's successors, for brief terms. El Salvador has in addition to the vice-president three *designados* appointed by the congress.

Various other systems are used in the rest of Latin America. In Mexico, if the vacancy occurs in the first two years of the term, the congress elects a provisional president by absolute majority and with a quorum of two-thirds of its members. The legislature then proceeds to issue a call for the election of a president to conclude the term. If the vacancy, however, occurs in the last four years of a term the procedure is the same, with the exception that there is no call for elections, and the person elected by the congress will serve for the rest of the term.

Guatemala has abandoned the system of *designados* and the established order of presidential succession in use is that of the president of the congress, the two vice-presidents of that body, and the chief justice of the supreme court. In other countries, such as Chile, the members of the cabinet—their order of precedence being specified by statute—will take the place of the president. In absence of all these officials, the president of the senate, that of the chamber of deputies, and the chief justice will be called, in that order, to fill the vacancy. *Designados* and presidential successors other than vice-presidents do not serve out the term in question, and a call for elections is issued within the period prescribed by the constitution.

The single vice-president is in all countries the presiding officer of the senate. The two vice-presidents of Peru, however, do not have that function and have no specific duties. It should be noted that in this country, at the end of his term, the president becomes automatically a member of the senate for one term.[34]

The Council of State

Such a body exists in Colombia, Ecuador, and Paraguay with varying functions and powers. In Colombia it is a supreme consultative body for the government in matters of administration, although its opinions are not necessarily binding on the president. In that country it also prepares bills and codes to be presented to the congress and discharges the functions of a supreme tribunal of administrative litigation. The Ecuadoran council of state, made up of representatives of the three branches of the government, the armed forces, and two private citizens elected by the congress, acts not as an advisory body but rather as a supervisory agency entrusted with vigilance over the constitutional order. It has some legislative powers when the congress is not in session, and like its Colombian counterpart it acts as a court in administrative cases. In Paraguay, the council of state is both an advisory and supervisory body, since it assists the president in economic matters and in international relations, and it also approves the decrees issued by the president. Members of this council are representatives of the government and of business, industry, the army, the Church, and educational institutions.

The Cabinet

Provisions relating to the composition and functions of the cabinet are found in all the Latin-American constitutions. Some of the older constitutions specify the exact number of cabinet members and indicate their titles. The present trend, however, is not to specify its composition. Such an innovation was introduced, for example, in the constitution of Argentina in 1949 and defended on the grounds that the growth of governmental action should not be prevented by any constitutional barrier.

As we have already seen, the president has the power to appoint his ministers and to remove them freely. No legislative confirmation of their appointments is required in any of the countries. However, it is possible for the congress in some countries such as Cuba, Ecuador, Venezuela, Peru, Uruguay, or Bolivia, where some form of parliamentary respon-

[34] Art. 155.

sibility exists, to record votes of censure against cabinet members and, under certain circumstances, to obtain their separation from the cabinet.[35] In Uruguay, the freedom of the president (prior to the 1952 reform) in the choice of his ministers was restricted by law to those "citizens who are able to depend on the support of their parliamentary faction," although he could in any case distribute four ministries among persons in the ticket of the party that elected him.[36]

In all countries, with the exception of the Dominican Republic, the appropriate member of the cabinet is required to attest the acts of the president with his countersignature before they can become effective (*refrendo ministerial*).

The number of departments making up the executive branch as well as the nature of their functions varies from country to country. In a small state, such as Honduras, there are six departments, each under a minister and an undersecretary: *Fomento* (Development) which includes Agriculture and Labor, Government (including Justice, Sanitation, and Charity), War, Finance, Public Education, and Foreign Relations. The list of Cuban ministries is fairly representative of the more common executive departments to be found in Latin America. The cabinet in that country is composed of the Prime Minister, the Secretary of the Presidency, twelve ministers (each head of a department), and ministers without portfolio (not more than four). The departments under their charge are State, Justice, Government Treasury, Public Works, Agriculture, Commerce, Labor, Education, Sanitation, Communications, and National Defense.

The ministry of interior (or government) is common in Latin-American countries. Resembling its French counterpart, this department has many important functions. It is usually charged with the maintenance of public order and may exercise supervision of the internal administration. It may be directly responsible for the management of the federal capital and the territories, as in Argentina. It may exercise control over the police and other law-enforcement agencies, and it is the agency of the national government which on occasions intervenes in state affairs. It is usually in charge of the administration and enforcement of electoral laws, and it supervises all phases of the election process. In Ecuador it is given control of the government printing office, and in Argentina it directs other activities such as postal savings or civil aeronautics. The supervision of

[35] See Chap. 10, pp. 260–261.
[36] Art. 162.

political relations assigned to this department and its participation in electoral affairs generally make it a key post in the national administration of every Latin-American country.

The ministry of education performs such functions as administering the school system, promoting anti-illiteracy campaigns, development of the arts, and maintenance of libraries, museums, and laboratories. It is important because it generally commands a substantial part of the national budget. Two ministers of recent creation, those of labor and national economy, have increasingly gained significance in Latin-American cabinets. All these departments are in general subdivided into smaller units known by various denominations. There is little uniformity in the structure of these units as between countries, and in general, there is no systematic plan of organization extending to all services of administration.

There are numerous administrative agencies which enjoy a degree of autonomy or which, although assigned to a ministry, operate more or less independently. They are sometimes called "autonomous entities." These agencies, established either by laws of congress or by presidential decrees, have their roles, functions, and powers specified in detail by such laws. No organizational uniformity is found among these agencies other than the preference for the administrative control by a board. The establishment of such independent or semi-independent agencies has an extended history of development in some countries, such as Argentina.[37] In recent years the use of such agencies has greatly increased. As is to be expected, efforts on the part of governments to meet new economic problems which resulted from the two world wars gave impetus to this trend.[38]

As in the United States, the heads of the various executive departments are directly responsible in all matters of policy to the president. Each cabinet member, has, of course, a legal responsibility, and may not violate the law, but the political responsibility for all actions that his ministers may take rests with the president alone. As has been noted, there exists a limited degree of parliamentary responsibility in at least eight of the Latin-American states, and in others such as Argentina or Brazil ministers may be summoned by the congress to explain matters of importance.

Aside from the provisions dealing with cabinet responsibility to the legislative branch, some countries establish the principle of individual and collective responsibility of ministers. In El Salvador the president and

[37] See Macdonald, *op. cit.,* p. 224.
[38] For details and examples, see Chap. 16, pp. 403–405.

his ministers are collectively responsible for the acts they authorize. In Ecuador, the cabinet shares responsibility with the president if he violates the constitution. In similar fashion the principle of criminal responsibility for offenses committed by cabinet members is specifically recognized in some countries. In Colombia, ministers are responsible for offenses committed in the exercise of powers delegated to them by the chief executive.[39]

Powers and duties of ministers are both political and administrative. They may include the following: to comply with and to enforce the constitution and the laws; to prepare bills, regulations, and decrees, and to propose them; to countersign the laws and documents authorized by the president, except those appointing or removing ministers; to attend sessions of congress, to report to that body, and to answer questions; and to serve, in general, as an organ of communication of the administration with the congress.

The cabinet as a body is designated in some countries as the council of ministers, and its functioning is regulated in all the most recent constitutions. The Cuban constitution, for example, devotes to its regulation an entire chapter composed of thirteen lengthy provisions.[40] It is obvious, therefore, that in Latin America the cabinet has a legal existence, powers, and responsibility as a body. In some cases—at least in theory—it may be something more than a part in the machinery of administration and consultation which assists the chief executive.

Presidential Responsibility and Immunities

Clauses relating to the responsibility of the president can be found in some constitutions. They state that the president is responsible to the congress for acts or omissions that violate the constitution or the laws, and they provide the procedures to be followed by those who make charges against him. In most countries the president cannot be prosecuted or tried for common crimes except with the previous consent of the senate. In Chile the president may be accused only during his term of office or within the six months ensuing. During this latter period he is required to remain in the country.[41]

The usual procedure of impeachment with slight variations or different

[39] El Salvador (Art. 77); Colombia (Art. 135); see also Blanksten, *op. cit.*, p. 94.

[40] Title XII, Arts. 151–163.

[41] Chile (Art. 39, cl. 1). A similar provision applies to the members of Uruguay's plural executive (Art. 172).

nomenclature is used for removal of the president in all the countries which have a bicameral legislature. The general pattern is for the lower house—upon charges being preferred against the president—to appoint a committee of investigation. The committee reports to the house, and upon a vote of two-thirds of its members, the case is presented to the senate for trial. The senate has no option but to hear the case. When the time arrives this legislative body converts itself into a court presided over by the chief justice of the supreme court.[42] This system is essentially the one used in Argentina, Bolivia, Brazil, Colombia, Cuba, Chile, the Dominican Republic, Ecuador, Haiti, Mexico, Nicaragua, Peru, and Uruguay.

On the other hand, in Costa Rica, Guatemala, Honduras, and El Salvador, all with a single legislative chamber, this body may declare by two-thirds vote whether or not there are sufficient grounds for proceeding against the president and bringing him before the supreme court in order that he may be put on trial according to law. In Panama, however, the National Assembly (congress) may not only take cognizance of charges against the president but also pass judgment in the case.[43] In that country as well as in a few others an identical procedure of impeachment is applied to other public officials, such as ministers, judges of superior courts, diplomatic agents, and others.

A majority of two-thirds is necessary to convict the president in all impeachment cases described. The penalty, in case of conviction, involves removal from office, to which may be added disqualifications for holding public office indefinitely or for a specified period. The person convicted may, of course, after removal be brought before the ordinary courts like any other citizen if he has committed an indictable offense.

Because of the dominance of the executive branch, impeachment of a president has taken place only on rare occasions in Latin America. Although there are a few instances in which presidents have been removed through this procedure, these cases are exceptional, and in most countries no president or vice-president has ever been impeached. Such is the case of Argentina where only a few persons have been impeached in all its history, and none of these were occupants of the presidency. In Cuba, on the other hand, President Miguel Mariano Gómez was removed in 1936, when "strong man" Batista brought pressure to bear in congress and impeachment procedures against him were instituted. President Gómez

[42] In Cuba, all supreme court justices are members of the tribunal which is organized for this purpose (Art. 122, cl. 1).

[43] Art. 119, cl. 1.

was convicted on the charge of undue interference with the legislative branch. It must be noted, however, in this case that President Gómez was never in full possession of all the powers of his office. Many of these powers remained in control of chief of the army and "president maker" Batista. When it came to a showdown, the latter was able to manipulate a personally loyal majority in the congress. It was then a case of the legal and nominal chief of state versus the real power—the president in fact. The most recent case of impeachement was the conviction in 1955 of Guizado, acting president of Panama, on charges of complicity in the assassination of his predecessor President Remón. Guizado was not only removed from office but also sentenced to six years of imprisonment after trial before the national assembly.

BIBLIOGRAPHY

Amadeo, Octavio, *El presidente argentino,* Buenos Aires, 1917.

Demicheli, A., *El poder ejecutivo (del Uruguay): génesis y transformaciones,* Buenos Aires, 1930.

Echeverría, Buenaventura, *Derecho constitucional guatemalteco,* Guatemala, 1944.

Hambloch, Ernest, *His Majesty the President: A Study of Constitutional Brazil,* London, 1935.

Herrera Guerrero, Héctor V., *La división de poderes en la constitución de 1917,* Mexico, 1946.

Lazcano y Mazón, Andrés M., *Las constituciones de Cuba,* Madrid, 1952.

Linares Quintana, Segundo V., *Gobierno y administración de la República Argentina,* 2 vols., Buenos Aires, 1946.

Llana Barrios, Mario, *El juicio político; estudio constitucional historico-político,* Montevideo, 1942.

Merino Darrouy, Luis, *Evolución del poder ejecutivo en Chile,* Santiago, 1949.

Morales Elizondo, Oscar, *El principio de la división de poderes,* Mexico, 1945.

Naon, Rómulo S., *Los ministros: su carácter y función constitucional,* Buenos Aires, 1915.

Pereda, Setembrino Ezekial, *El poder ejecutivo,* 4 vols., Montevideo, 1918–1923.

Stuart, Graham H., *The Governmental System of Peru,* Washington, D.C., Carnegie Institution, 1925.

Villa Gonzalez, León, *El principio de la división de poderes en nuestras constituciones,* Mexico, 1942.

Zeledón, Marco Tulio, *Lecciones de derecho constitucional,* San José (Costa Rica), 1945.

Chapter 10: THE LEGISLATURE

Although the constitutional systems of Latin America have entrusted the legislature with the power to enact laws and to determine public policy, the congress, in reality, is not the center of the political life of these nations. As we have seen in the preceding chapter, the executive rather than the legislative branch holds a position of preeminence. Logically, the weakness of all legislative assemblies and their inferior prestige and authority as compared to those enjoyed by the president are the consequence of the almost omnipotent role that the legal systems and political customs have assigned to the executive branch. However, weak legislative bodies are also partly the result of such factors as the nature of the class system, defective electoral processes, and the fragmentation and fluidity of organized political groups. These factors combine to make the theory of legislative supremacy nothing more than fiction in Latin America.

Historical circumstances may also have contributed, to some extent, to congressional weakness. The fact that there never existed important deliberative bodies in colonial days and the lack of any parliamentary tradition may, perhaps, account, in some measure, for this defect. It may also be true that, in many instances, the congress by its factional quibbling and lack of responsibility has incurred an unfortunate stigma and is regarded with good-humored contempt. This causes the people to look to the chief executive for order and leadership and to condone presidential usurpation of authority. Thus, the president often assumes a major role in the determination of legislative policy with the tacit consent of the people and of the members of the congress.

Despite the validity of these observations, it would be unjust to conclude that all Latin-American legislatures have failed to fulfill their constitutional mandates. Some congresses were not rubber-stamp bodies, e.g., those of Chile in the period of the "parliamentary republic," 1819–1925; of Uruguay under the constitution of 1917; or even of Honduras from 1927 through 1931. On the contrary, they were independent, properly elected deliberative assemblies which challenged effectively the ascendancy of executive authority and participated actively in the determination of national policies.

The effectiveness of all Latin-American legislatures is handicapped by some common defects. The legislative powers of the president being so ample, the scope of congressional functions and authority is necessarily restricted. The relative brevity of the congressional sessions tends to lessen the efficacy of the legislative as a check upon the other two branches of government. In nine countries the executive alone has authority to call congress into special sessions. In many cases the legislature is to be concerned exclusively with such matters as might be included in the presidential summons. The lack of parliamentary experience frequently prevents the attainment of compromises and the ironing out of differences which are so necessary to all legislative chambers. Legislators engage in bitter controversies which often lead to personal encounters involving physical violence. A defeated minority sometimes chooses to abandon the floor rather than to accept compromise. In addition, there is always a strong tendency to depend upon direction from the executive in the enactment of legislation.

Latin-American political scientists have been well aware of these defects. In fact they have been, in general, more severe than foreigners in their criticisms, for they have indicted their legislatures not only for inefficiency and irresoluteness but also for acting too often against the public interest. Searching for correctives, some writers have stressed the need for a reform of congressional organization. Among the modifications that have been proposed are the reduction of the number of members; the establishment of advisory committees and technical counseling at the service of legislators; the determination of a fixed period for the approval of certain types of legislation; and the division of the legislative task into two phases—one session devoted to research, preparation, and drafting of projects, and another for the actual enactment of those projects into law.[1]

Many of the conditions generally ascribed to the congress in Latin America may vary sharply and distinctly not only between the various nations but within individual countries. In Argentina, for example, Carlos S. Viamonte refers to three distinct periods in the history of the congress: the first phase extends from the *cabildo* of 1810 at the outset of the independence to the Constituent Congress of 1853, the second period from this date to 1912, and the third from 1912 to the present time. During the first period the Argentine assemblies reflected the restlessness and troubles caused by the revolution for independence and by the press-

[1] See, for instance, Jorge S. Oría, *Ficción y realidad constitucional* (Buenos Aires, 1946), pp. 213–216.

ing problem of national organization. The great debate of the period was that of federalism versus unitarism. The second period, from 1853 to 1912, was an era of institutional development. The prestige of the legislature was increased by the enactment of the codes and the organic laws which gave the country a legal system. The legislatures of this era frequently demonstrated independence by resisting vigorously any encroachment of the executive branch, and in this they were generally supported by public opinion. The third period of development was significant by reason of the participation of the masses in the electoral process and the formation of new political parties which soon gained representation in the congress as a result of electoral reforms. The tone of the legislative branch was then set by the activity of parties of a popular nature, previously excluded as a result of corrupt electoral practices, and by the appearance of new problems of social and labor significance. Viamonte, on appraising the role of the congress in his native country, observes that toward the end of the second period this body was nearly always a subservient instrument of the executive, and further notes that it became finally a "courteous reunion of oligarchs who never debated ideas but who argued politely over their own private interests." The congress of the third period was a much less educated body but more representative of the elements of society than its predecessor. He noted, however, that after 1916 the legislature became again an "officialist" organ, inclined to complacency and insensitive to the feelings and the desires of the people. He finds, that, although there is popular representation, there may be now even greater subservience to the executive than in the past. The so-called "labor parliament" which swept into power in 1946 was certainly popular in composition, and yet it was a docile instrument in the hands of President Perón.[2]

Lawyers have traditionally been predominant in Latin-American legislatures, but there are also other professionals among their members such as physicians, engineers, journalists, and university professors. Generally speaking, one can distinguish several categories among legislators. There are, in the first place, the professional politicians for whom politics (*hacer política*) is just a way, if rough, of making a living. They are the political bosses, who, in large or insignificant scale, as the case might be, operate their own machine, and who change party affiliation with great ease and expediency. It is from this group that, in general, a president recruits the

[2] Carlos Sánchez Viamonte, *Historia institucional de Argentina* (Mexico, 1948), pp. 191–195.

core of his supporters in the congress. There are also the wealthy landowner, the big industrialist, and the promoter, who aspire to sit in congress not because of political ambition but as a matter of business sense and convenience. They become perennial senators or representatives, and they are almost exclusively concerned with watching over their vast economic interests and those of their associates and protecting those interests from damaging legislation. As a rule, this type of "politico" encounters no difficulty in finding a safe place in the ballot. Most political parties are willing to hand him the nomination in return for a generous contribution to the party chest.

More recently a new type of legislator has appeared in most countries. He represents economic groups which only recently have become influential such as labor unions or farm organizations. The rise of new nationalistic parties and the increasing political significance of labor have thus affected the nature and composition of legislative assemblies. These parties, competing for power with the older traditional groups of conservatives and liberals, have gained legislative representation and, in some cases, control of the congress. This has not necessarily resulted in the much-needed development of legislative vigor and independence, but at least it has turned new congresses into bodies which are more representative of the popular will than their predecessors, which often represented only the interests of a ruling oligarchy.

CONGRESSIONAL ORGANIZATION

Four of the republics of Central America (Costa Rica, El Salvador, Guatemala, Honduras), Panama, and one state in South America (Paraguay) have adopted a unicameral legislature; all the others provide for the bicameral form. In countries with a federal form of government, as in the United States, the upper chamber represents the major political subdivisions of the union, and the lower chamber represents the people. It is obvious, however, that the bicameral structure is not related to the federal system. In fact, the only reason for the use of bicameralism in unitary countries is to provide for discussion and approval of laws at two distinct times and by different chambers. Those who advocate the adoption of the unicameral system contend that neither this feature nor the older age of the members of the upper chamber is any assurance that better legislation is attained. There no longer exists in Latin America, they further argue, the aristocratic type of society which would justify in

TABLE 12
THE LEGISLATURE

Country	Upper chambers*		Lower or single chamber†	
	Representation	Term, years	Representation	Term, years
Argentina	2 for each province 2 for capital	6	1 for each 100,000 inhabitants	6
Bolivia	3 for each department	6	105 deputies	4
Brazil	3 for each state 3 for Federal District	8	1 for each 150,000 inhabitants	4
Chile	5 for each "provincial group"	8	1 for each 30,000 inhabitants	4
Colombia	1 for each 190,000 inhabitants	4	1 for each 90,000 inhabitants	2
Costa Rica	...	...	45 deputies	4
Cuba	9 for each province	4	1 for each 35,000 inhabitants	4
Dominican Republic	1 for each province 1 for Santo Domingo District	5	1 for each 60,000 inhabitants	5
Ecuador	2 for each province 1 for each of 2 Oriente provinces and the Galapagos Islands 12 "functional" members	4	1 for each 50,000 inhabitants	2
El Salvador	...	...	3 for each department	2
Guatemala	...	...	1 for each 50,000 inhabitants	4
Haiti	21 senators elected by departments	6	37 deputies elected by *arrondissements*	4
Honduras	...	...	1 for each 25,000 inhabitants	6
Mexico	2 for each state 2 for Federal District	6	1 for each 150,000 inhabitants	3
Nicaragua	16 senators-at-large	6	42 members-at-large	6

TABLE 12 (*Continued*)

Country	Upper chamber*		Lower or single chamber†	
	Representation	Term, years	Representation	Term, years
Panama	....	...	1 for each 15,000 inhabitants	4
Paraguay	....	...	1 for each 25,000 inhabitants	5
Peru	50 senators	6	150 deputies	5
Uruguay	31 senators-at-large	4	99 deputies-at-large	4
Venezuela	2 for each state 2 for the Federal District	5	1 for each 40,000 inhabitants	5

* In all countries the upper chamber is the Senate or Chamber of the Senate.

† The lower chamber is known as the Chamber of Deputies or Representatives in states with a bicameral system. However, the single legislatures of the other six countries are known by various other titles.

unitary states the existence of the senate. It is also pointed out that even in those countries with a federal plan, bicameralism has not achieved its objectives. Often the states of the union have their interests defended more effectively by their deputies in the lower house than by those who represent them in the senate.

The Lower and Single House

Elections. Members of this branch of congress or of the unicameral legislatures are chosen by direct popular vote in all the countries. In some, a system of proportional representation is used. Representatives are elected by direct vote in Cuba from each of the six provinces which are given representation in proportion to their population. In Brazil, representatives are elected by the states, the territory of Acre, and the Federal District. They are chosen in a similar manner in Uruguay, by departments, with each of these having at least two representatives.

A feature of the Latin-American systems is the practice in Brazil, Mexico, Colombia, Venezuela, Uruguay, Paraguay, El Salvador, and Panama of choosing alternatives (*suplentes*) or substitutes at the same election.[3]

[3] The institution of the *suplencia* seems to be of Spanish origin. It appeared for the first time in the Cádiz constitution of 1812. Its merits are questioned, since

In Honduras, in case of permanent absence of a deputy, a substitute is appointed by the congress to complete his term. In the Dominican Republic the law provides that vacancies be filled by the respective chambers which choose a substitute from a list of three names presented by the political party to which the former deputy belonged. If the party fails to submit a list the chamber is free to appoint any person. Total membership of the lower house varies from 304 in Brazil, which has the largest body, to 34 in Nicaragua.

Terms. The terms of members of the lower house range from one to six years. A term of four years is found in Brazil, Chile, Uruguay, Bolivia, Cuba, Haiti, Guatemala, Costa Rica, and Panama; two years in El Salvador, Colombia, and Ecuador; three years in Mexico; five years in Venezuela, Paraguay, Peru, and the Dominican Republic; and six years in Argentina, Nicaragua, and Honduras. In some countries, such as Brazil, Peru, Venezuela, or the Dominican Republic, the terms of representatives are not staggered and there is complete renewal of the lower house at every election. In others there may be partial renewal every second year, as in Cuba, Bolivia, Guatemala, or Argentina. In two countries, Mexico and Guatemala, reelection of any member of the legislature to the next succeeding congress is prohibited by constitutional provision.

Qualifications. Citizenship and the full enjoyment of civil and political rights are common qualifications required for election to the lower house. Only native-born citizens are eligible in eleven countries,[4] but elsewhere naturalized citizens can be elected as deputies or representatives provided they have resided continuously in the country for a specified period counted from the date of naturalization. This residence period may extend from four to ten years. The minimum-age requirement is twenty-one years in Brazil, Costa Rica, Chile, Cuba, Venezuela, and Guatemala; while the rest of the countries establish a minimum of twenty-five, with the exception of the Dominican Republic where a deputy must be thirty years of age.

In the majority of the countries the constitution provides that certain persons are ineligible to serve in either branch of the legislature. Members of the armed forces and the clergy, government officials, citizens who hold

---

members of the lower house supposedly represent the entire nation and not just their districts. Election by districts is merely a technical device to maintain their number in proportion to the population.

[4] These are Bolivia, Brazil, Ecuador, El Salvador, Guatemala, Haiti, Honduras, Mexico, Nicaragua, Paraguay, and Peru.

contracts with the government, debtors to the Treasury, and close relatives of the president and of members of the cabinet are frequently excluded. A common provision is a declaration that the office of congressman is incompatible with any other office remunerated by the state, province, or municipality or related with any agency supported wholly or partially by public funds. However, in several countries this provision does not apply to university staff members with teaching functions. Thus, in Cuba, professors in an official institution may qualify for election to the lower house. Similar exceptions are also operative in Chile, the Dominican Republic, Guatemala, Honduras, Nicaragua, Paraguay, El Salvador, and Uruguay. This exception is generally justified on the grounds that teaching positions are obtainable only by competitive examinations, a procedure which excludes risks of coercion or favoritism by the administration. Furthermore, it is argued that such persons possess technical and specialized knowledge which can be used by the congress in the public interest.[5]

The Upper House

Elections. At the present time, all fourteen countries with an upper chamber elect their members by direct popular vote. Those with a federal scheme of government and several countries with a unitary form provide for equal representation for each state or province. Another group of states apportions senatorial seats on the basis of population. It should be noted that the capital city and the federal district are always represented in the membership of the senate. Thus, in Argentina, Mexico, and Venezuela, two members for each state or province and two for the Federal District are elected; in Brazil, each state and the Federal District elect three senators.

In Nicaragua ex-presidents become lifetime members of the senate, and in Peru the outgoing chief executive becomes a senator for one term. The Venezuelan upper house includes four members chosen at large, who represent minorities which received a certain percentage of the total vote but which failed to elect any candidates by states. A distinction is made in Ecuador between "functional" and "provincial" senators. Thirty-three senators, popularly elected, represent the provinces and the Galapagos Islands. In addition, there are twelve "'functional" senators, who are not popularly elected but chosen by economic, professional, and occupational groups and who represent these interests. Cultural groups such as the universities and labor unions, agricultural associations, and other similar

[5] Ramón Infiesta, *Derecho constitucional* (Havana, 1950), p. 225.

organizations are given representation in congress by this device. The "functional" senators are in turn of two kinds: national and regional. Four of the twelve are "national functional" senators, and they represent the sectors of public education, private education, journalism, scientific and literary organizations, and the armed forces. The other eight are "regional functional" senators and are equally divided between the two major regions of the sierra and the coast. They represent the interests of industry, labor, agriculture, and commerce in each of those regions. They are chosen by electoral colleges designated by the economic or occupational group entitled to representation.

"Functional" representation has existed in Ecuador since 1929, and is defended as an institution well fitted to political reality. It is claimed that it serves two fundamental purposes within the governmental scheme of that country: it gives an added protection to forces such as the land-owning class, the army, and state educational centers; and it contributes, in addition, to maintaining the necessary balance of power between the two major regions which compose the republic.[6]

In some of the countries, such as Mexico, Colombia, Venezuela, Ecuador or Uruguay, alternatives (*suplentes*) are also chosen for each incumbent senator, and these are called upon to fill a seat if it becomes vacant before the next election. In the upper chambers of Argentina, Bolivia, Brazil, and Chile, staggered senatorial terms are used, as in the United States. In the rest of the countries an entirely new senate is chosen at one time. The most numerous bodies are those of Brazil and Colombia, with sixty-three members each, and the smallest that of Nicaragua, with only fifteen senators.

Terms. Senatorial terms range from four years (Colombia, Ecuador, Uruguay, and Cuba) to eight years (Chile, Brazil). A six-year term is used in Argentina, Mexico, Peru, Bolivia, Haiti, and Nicaragua. In Venezuela and the Dominican Republic senators are elected for five years. Members of the senate can be reelected to the next succeeding congress in all the countries except Mexico.

Qualifications. The requirements of citizenship are about the same as those provided for membership in the lower house, but the age requirements are higher, the usual rule being thirty or thirty-five years.

In Cuba in addition to the usual qualifications senators must not have belonged to the armed forces in active service during the two years

[6] George I. Blanksten, *Ecuador: Constitutions and Caudillos* (Berkeley, Calif., University of California Press, 1951), pp. 105–107.

immediately preceding their nomination. In Colombia, a senator is required to have occupied one of certain offices (president, *designado,* member of the congress, cabinet minister, chief of a diplomatic mission, governor of a department, justice of the supreme court, councillor of state, attorney-general, or comptroller-general), or to have been a university professor for five years, or to have practiced a liberal profession as possessor of an academic degree. In Nicaragua senators must be of "secular status." The Mexican list of qualifications is more extensive than any other. In addition to the common conditions, the person may not be a member of the federal army or may not hold a command in the police or the rural constabulary in the district from which he is elected for at least ninety days preceding the election. A similar disqualification applies to heads of the executive departments and supreme court justices unless they resigned ninety days prior to the election. State governors cannot be elected in a district under their jurisdiction even if they resign their office. Ministers of any religious denomination are also excluded.

Officers of the House and the Senate

As a rule, the officers of the lower chamber include a president, one or two vice-presidents, one or more secretaries, and in some instances, a treasurer and a comptroller. These officers compose the steering committee known as the *mesa directiva.* The presiding officer and the other members of this *mesa directiva* are generally chosen in the house by a plurality of votes for a term of one year, and they may be reelected. In Mexico, however, officers of both chambers are elected at the last meeting of each month to serve during the following month. This committee usually prepares the legislative calendar and exercises general supervision over the activities of the house. The presiding officer may in some countries have the important power of appointing the members of the permanent or standing committees. In nearly every republic the president also exercises the powers of recognition of speakers, restriction of debates, keeping of order, and decision of points of order.

The organization of the senate is very similar to that of the lower house. In countries where there is a vice-president, he invariably presides over the senate, but he has no right to vote except in case of a tie. In all other countries, a presiding officer and one or two vice-presidents, who serve in case of absence or disability of the president, are elected by the senators. An interesting innovation made in the new Uruguayan constitution of 1952 is that the president of the senate and of the general assembly (congress) shall be the member of the leading party who received the most votes at the election.

The steering committee of the senate usually determines the order of legislative business and names the members of the regular committees. In some countries, such as Uruguay, members of the standing committees are appointed by the president of the senate, but they are subject to approval of the total membership.

The congress of Honduras furnishes an example of the organization of unicameral legislatures. The Honduran congress elects a president, a vice-president, two secretaries, and two prosecretaries. The presiding officer may, if he chooses, exercise a great deal of control over the legislature by making use of such discretionary powers as those of regulating the duration of the sessions, recognizing speakers, and appointing the standing committees. The rule has developed of designating as president of the congress a person closely identified with the chief executive and his policies. The Honduran system does not allow the opposition any representation among the officers or the committees of the congress. The evils derived from this despotic control exercised by the majority party and by the presiding officer overbalance by far the advantages of expediting legislative business.[7]

Standing Committees

There exist in every legislature a number of regular or standing committees created by the rules of the house and the senate. The role played by these committees in the legislative process is of great significance since, as a rule, the bulk of legislation originates in them. Only occasionally are major changes made before enactment of important bills as reported by these committees. The number and nature of the committees vary according to countries. There are nineteen in the chamber of deputies of Argentina and eleven in the senate, and in each committee political parties are represented in proportion to their strength. Committee members are appointed in the house by the presiding officer, but the real appointive body is in practice the party caucus. Committees are not required to report on any bill unless they so desire, except in the case of the budget bill which, the rules specify, must be discharged within one month.[8] On the

[7] William S. Stokes, *Honduras: An Area Study in Government* (Madison, Wis., University of Wisconsin Press, 1950), pp. 271–275.

[8] Austin F. Macdonald, *Government of the Argentine Republic* (New York, Crowell, 1942), pp. 255–259.

other hand, in most other countries, committees are obligated by the rules to report on every bill, so as to prevent any "burying" of proposals.

In Mexico the number of committees is the same in both houses. Members are elected for three years by a special committee in which each state is represented by one member designated by the state's delegation (*diputación*). Bills must always be reported by the committees. In Bolivia, congressional committees must not only report on all bills, but on certain proposals a report must be made within a specified number of days.

The Ecuadoran "Legislative Committee"

In Ecuador, in addition to the regular committees of both chambers, a "legislative commission" is provided for by the constitution, which is authorized to prepare bills for amendment or interpretation of the constitution, and some general bills. Its bills are not referred to any of the regular committees of either house, but are presented directly to a joint session of congress for action, and upon passage go to the president for promulgation. The commission is composed of one senator named by the senate; one deputy chosen by the lower house; one representative of the executive department appointed by the president; one representative of the judiciary selected by the supreme court; and the dean of the faculty of jurisprudence at the Universidad Central of Quito, as an ex offico member. These persons and two alternates for each are named for a four-year term and may be indefinitely reelected. They must meet the same qualifications as those elected to the senate. Legislation prepared by this body is acted upon by a joint session of the congress and not by either chamber acting separately. Furthermore, such legislation requires approval by two-thirds of those present, but, once passed, it is not subject to presidential veto.[9]

Other Committees

Investigating committees are also used, and their existence is recognized by constitutional or by statutory law. These are, of course, short-lived committees which disappear as soon as their report is made to the parent body. The authority, scope, and methods of such committees have been the subject of controversial debates in some states. In Argentina, for example, the chamber of deputies in 1941 passed a resolution creating a committee

[9] Constitution of Ecuador, Arts. 77, 78. See also Blanksten, *op. cit.*, pp. 115–116.

to investigate anti-Argentine activities, which was granted specially delegated authority to receive the assistance of the armed forces, to violate the home and the secrecy of correspondence, and to order the arrest of persons. It is of interest to note that when the investigating committee requested assistance of the police to enter and search homes, the chief executive refused to extend such aid on the grounds that such a request was unconstitutional. The chamber of deputies in turn declared that the committee had acted within its proper boundaries and recommended that it exhaust all actions before the other two branches in order to make possible the fulfillment of its mandate.[10] All efforts of the committee, however, proved futile in view of the determined boycott of the executive branch.

In addition, a certain number of party committees are found in every congress. These may include congressional campaign committees, policy committees, patronage committees, and others.

Sessions of Congress

In most countries constitutional provisions fix time limits for legislative sessions. This is significant in view of the fact that all countries have attempted to strengthen the legislative branch of the government in recognition of the positive danger of domination by the executive and of the need of assuring a balance of power among the three "powers." In Cuba, El Salvador, and the Dominican Republic the congress meets twice in every year. In all the other countries there is one annual session. The duration of the legislative sessions ranges from two months in Ecuador and Nicaragua to nine in Uruguay. In most countries, however, legislative sessions may be extended. In Venezuela the congress may stay in session for another ninety days by a favorable vote of two-thirds of the members of congress on the initiative of either of the chambers or of the chief executive. In Mexico, on the other hand, the period of the legislative session may be shortened but never extended.

As has been mentioned previously, the constitutions also provide for the call of extraordinary or special sessions of the congress. In some of the countries the chief executive has the exclusive power to call congress in special session. In others, such a privilege may be exercised either by the

[10] *Diario de Sesiones de la Cámara de Diputados,* 1941, vol. II, p. 283. Cf. Segundo V. Linares Quintana, *Gobierno y administración de la República* Argentina (Buenos Aires, 1946), vol. I, p. 300.

executive or by the presiding officer of the congress upon request of the majority, as in Chile, or of two-thirds of the members, as in Ecuador and in Honduras. Some of the countries which use the permanent committee give this power to that body. In some countries the congress, whenever assembled in extraordinary session, is limited to dealing exclusively with those matters that have been the subject of the convocation. Such is the case in Argentina and in Nicaragua. It is also true in Chile unless the special session was called at the initiative of the congress itself.

Parliamentary Procedure

Foreign precedents and customs, especially those of the United States and France, have exerted some influence on the development of Latin-American parliamentary practices. Often the writings of well-known North American, or British, or French authors are cited by congressmen in support of a certain parliamentary point. The rules generally declare that a quorum is constituted by a half plus one of the membership of the respective chamber. They also prescribe how often the chamber meets and impose penalties, in some countries, on those members who are absent from a certain number of meetings without proper authorization.

Joint Sessions

Meetings in which both houses of congress sit together are held for various purposes besides those of a ceremonial nature. Joint sessions are required in Brazil to inaugurate the legislative session, to issue common rules of procedure, to receive the oath of office of the president and vice-president, and to consider a bill over the president's veto. Joint sessions have a special significance in Ecuador in view of the extensive list of matters which, by constitutional prescription, require consideration of the congress meeting as one body. This list includes the amendment of the constitution; the formal proclamation of the president-elect and vice-president-elect; acceptance or rejection of the president's resignation; the decision to declare the chief executive physically or mentally incapacitated; the election of justices of the supreme court and other high officials; the enactment of the national budget; the approval of presidential appointments requiring congressional consent; the grant of extraordinary powers to the executive or the withdrawal of such powers; and the examination of the actions of cabinet ministers and censure of such actions.

Congressional Immunities

All countries recognize in general the inviolability of the legislators for their opinions and votes. Congressional rules usually place certain limitations upon language used in debate, and members may be reprimanded if they violate such regulations.

The scope of parliamentary immunity from arrest in some of the Latin-American countries is very broad, as stated by the supreme court of Argentina, "for peculiar reasons that are native to our own society and for motives of state."[11] It was felt by the drafters of these constitutions that ample safeguards were indispensable if the members of the legislature were to be adequately protected against abuses of the executive branch.

One group of countries extends such an immunity over the entire congressional term of office; others limit this privilege to the duration of the legislative sessions and a period before and after; while a third group regulates the subject in a special manner. Countries of the first group, such as Argentina, Bolivia, Brazil, Costa Rica, Cuba, Haiti, Panama, Paraguay, Uruguay, and Venezuela, follow the principle that legislators are immune from arrest from the day of their election until the expiration of their terms unless surprised *flagrante delicto* (in the actual commission of the crime), and even in this instance notice must be given immediately to the respective chamber. Neither can legislators be indicted on a criminal charge except with the authorization of the body to which they belong. In such cases decision is made by the votes of two-thirds of the members.

Among the countries in the second group the Dominican Republic establishes congressional immunity only during the duration of the legislative sessions. The other countries extend the immunity for a period which varies in each case, before and after the legislative sessions.

Mexico is a good example of a third group of states. In this country the members of congress as well as supreme court justices, cabinet ministers, and the attorney general are liable for common crimes committed during the time of their office, and also for those that they may commit in the discharge of their duties. The chamber of deputies acting as a grand jury (*gran jurado*) decides, in cases involving a common offense, by an absolute majority, whether there are sufficient grounds for proceedings against the accused. If the decision is a negative one, such

[11] Case *In re Tabanera, Fallos,* vol. 119, p. 305. See Linares Quintana, *op. cit.,* p. 291.

proceedings are discontinued. The so-called "official offenses" are tried by the senate, acting as a grand jury, upon previous accusation made by the lower house. The senate's decision in such cases requires a majority of two-thirds, and the only penalties that it can impose are those of loss of office and disqualifications for holding any other for a certain period.[12]

It is not surprising that the remarkably broad basis of parliamentary immunity has led to many misuses and abuses in almost every country of Latin America. Some have shown awareness of such dangers and in recently drafted constitutions have attempted to prevent abuses of congressional immunity by restricting such privileges. The earlier constitutions of Cuba, for example, vested in the congress the power to authorize the arrest or prosecution of any of its members, but they did not make it mandatory for the legislature to answer in any way the writ by which the courts request the authorization. The results of such a system were shown by the large number of cases in which each chamber had chosen to take no action on the judicial request and by the number of petitions which had been formally rejected. During the period from 1902 to 1920 the record shows that, of 372 writs received by the congress, in only one case was authorization granted.[13] This situation prompted the Constituent Assembly of 1940 to take a special interest in the matter. In the course of the debate one delegate stated that, in thirty-nine years, up to 1,261 crimes had been committed or presumably committed by legislators under congressional immunity. This figure included 2 murders, 9 homicides, and 265 libel cases, the rest being misdemeanors. With reference to libel suits, he pointed out that in many cases they had involved the use of a "delegated immunity," as when a congressman serves as nominal editor of a newspaper and in practice transfers his personal immunity to other persons who are writers or owners of the publication.[14]

The constituent convention, in order to remedy these abuses, voted that if the senate or the chamber of representatives fails to decide upon the requested authorization within forty days after the opening of the legislature such an authorization is understood to be granted. It was also provided that in all cases the decision of the congress must be taken for

[12] Arts. 108, 109, 111.

[13] Infiesta, *op. cit.*, p. 235.

[14] Andrés M. Lazcano y Mazón, *Constitución de Cuba (con los debates sobre su articulado y transitorias en la Convención Constituyente)*, (3 vols., Havana, 1941), vol. III, p. 79. See also Evelio Tabío, *La inmunidad parlamentaria* (Havana, 1947), p. 22.

acknowledged cause. A similar action was taken by the Venezuelan Constituent Assembly of 1947, in deciding that the respective house will, in every case, reach a decision within five days counted from the session in which it received an account of the facts.[15]

Disciplinary Power

This power is generally vested in each chamber by most of the constitutions. It may include measures ranging from reprimanding or calling a member to order, or censuring him, to the extreme disciplinary measures of expulsion. In some countries these actions may only be taken by a two-thirds vote of the members. Somewhat related to the disciplinary power is the authority of each chamber to compel members to attend its sessions. In Uruguay, where neither chamber may commence its sessions unless more than half its members are present, the minority may meet for the purpose of compelling absent members to attend under penalties which they may prescribe.[16]

In some countries the functions of senator and deputy are obligatory. Such is the case in Ecuador where, in addition, legislators cannot resign without permission of the respective house at the risk of losing their citizenship for two years. Other countries, such as Argentina, Cuba, or Chile, may expressly permit the resignation of members of the legislature. In general a simple majority is sufficient to accept voluntary resignations although a two-thirds vote is required in a few states.

FUNCTIONS OF CONGRESS

To carry out its functions the congress is endowed in all the countries with particular powers of a legislative, directoral, constitutive, electoral, and quasi-judicial nature.

In the determination of the general power to legislate there is usually included the authority or duty to enact codes and laws of a general character;[17] to levy and collect taxes, duties, imposts, and excises that may be

[15] Cuba (Art. 127); Venezuela (Art. 146).

[16] Art. 110.

[17] However, attention must be called to the fact that many constitutions have provisions empowering the congress to enact any other laws that it may consider necessary in the public interest, or that may be necessary to execute provisions of the constitution. Such clauses may be considered similar to the famous "implied powers" clause of the United States Constitution.

necessary for the general welfare; to discuss and to approve the national budget; to approve loans, with the obligation in some countries of voting the revenues necessary for the payment of interests and amortization; to coin money and to fix the standard of weights and measures; to enact laws for the regulation and promotion of domestic and foreign commerce, and for agriculture and industry as well as for the protection of labor, old age, maternity, and employment; to establish uniform rules for obtaining citizenship; and to regulate the communication services. In some countries special majorities are required for the approval of those laws dealing with certain economic matters.

The power to declare war and to approve treaties of peace is also common to all the congresses. A vote of two-thirds of the total membership of the congress is required for approval of treaties in most countries, although in a few an absolute majority of the full membership is sufficient. A curious provision in Bolivia authorizes the legislative branch "to exercise the right of influence" over diplomatic actions or international commitments negotiated by the executive.[18] No occasion for an interpretation of this clause has ever arisen, and there is no evidence that the congress has ever attempted to interfere with the executive's conduct of foreign relations.

The power to fix the number of the armed forces or of the militia and of regulating its organization is generally included, as well as authority to permit the entry of foreign troops into the national territory. In Uruguay the congress has the power to refuse or to allow the sending of troops abroad. In such cases if authorization is given by the congress this body must also fix the time for their return to Uruguay.[19]

Among the electoral functions of the congress is that of scrutinizing the votes for president and vice-president. In many cases, however, the congress simply declares the election of each of these officials in view of the certificate transmitted by the supreme electoral body which exists in some countries. Of course, the task of electing a president or a vice-president may fall upon the congress under certain circumstances. It may be entrusted in some instances with other electoral powers such as the selection of supreme court justices and other important officers. In Honduras, the legislative and not the executive department has the power to appoint supreme court judges and members of the superior tribunal of accounts, although it has been noted that the electoral function in such

[18] Art. 58, cl. 16.
[19] Art. 85, cl. 12.

cases is of a somewhat artificial character, since in practice the chief executive submits nominations to the leaders in congress.[20]

An important formal power of the congress is that of giving or withholding approval of appointments that are made by the president. Consent of the upper chamber is needed in many countries for appointments of ambassadors and ministers. Almost everywhere, approval is also required for appointments of high officers of the armed forces. It should be mentioned also that in countries where the state has the right of presentation in the filling of high ecclesiastical offices, as in Bolivia or Peru, the congress participates in the exercise of such functions.[21]

The quasi-judicial functions of congress relate to the impeachment proceedings against the president and other officials which have already been described. Other judicial powers assigned to the legislative department may include the authority to punish for contempt. In a majority of the countries the congress also participates with the president in the exercise of the pardoning power by passing bills of general amnesty.

Despite the strong "presidentialism" of Latin-American systems, the executive and administrative powers assigned to the legislative branch are always in theory, if not in practice, very significant. Congressional scrutiny of the president's actions has given theoretically to the legislature an important share in many executive functions. Aside from the participation in the appointment of high officials, in the making of treaties, the power to prescribe executive and administrative duties by the issuance of regulatory legislation, and the possibility of investigations, the Latin-American congresses may be vested by law with the power to call cabinet ministers and to question them about their activities or with authority to censure them for their actions.

In a majority of countries the congress can compel cabinet ministers to appear and answer questions. Without distinguishing at this time between countries which have some form of parliamentary responsibility and those which do not, it can be said here that such a power may be used by the legislatures of Argentina, Bolivia, Brazil, Colombia, Cuba, Ecuador, El Salvador, Guatemala, Honduras, Mexico, Nicaragua, Panama, Peru, Uruguay, and Venezuela. Ministers are permitted to attend the meetings of congress, in most countries on their own initiative, and they can participate in the debates. The general rule is, however, that they do not vote, since they are not members of the legislature. If they are legis-

[20] Stokes, *op. cit.*, pp. 283–284.
[21] Bolivia (Art. 71, cl. 8); Peru (Art. 123, cl. 14).

lators, their congressional rights are suspended by the fact of their appointment to the cabinet.

Other potential if not operative powers of congress to check executive control and to assure its share in policy making are illustrated by the case of the Dominican Republic. There the legislature may interpellate cabinet members and has the authority to examine and to approve each year all acts of the administration. The results of such interpellations or disapproval are not specified, and there are no instances on record of the use of such power.[22] Similar provisions establishing the right "to censure the conduct of the executive" exist also in Honduras and Nicaragua. It is well known, however, that in these republics the decisive influence of the president is so strongly felt through the whole legislative process that it renders such provisions inoperative.

THE LEGISLATIVE PROCESS

The Latin-American systems do not restrict the privilege of introducing bills to the members of the legislature, but rather they give ample opportunities to the other branches and organs of the government to participate in the initial phase of lawmaking. Proposals of laws may be introduced by any member of the legislative chamber or by the executive directly or through his ministers. In Ecuador bills may be introduced with the support of at least three members of either one of the three "functional" branches. Supreme Court members may represent the judiciary for the introduction of legislation. Resolutions and declarations may also be introduced by any member of the congress, and the procedure is much the same for any type of proposal. In Colombia, bills may be presented by any congressman or by a cabinet member, but the lower house has exclusive power to initiate legislation raising revenue, and bills dealing with the administration of justice are initiated by one of the special standing committees or by a cabinet member. In Uruguay, bills may be presented by any member of congress or by the executive, but the latter has exclusive initiative on matters concerning the national debt and the creation of public offices and services. In other countries the judicial branch is given authority to originate proposals dealing with justice and judicial procedure. In the group of states where the judiciary does not enjoy this privilege it still plays a significant part in lawmaking, e.g., in Honduras, where the congress often transmits bills to the supreme court

[22] Art. 33, cl. 19, 20.

and requests its advice on their constitutionality before assigning them to a committee.[23] Also in Colombia, justices of the supreme court may participate in debates on legislation concerning civil law and procedure. In Cuba legislation may be initiated not only by members of the legislature, but also by the executive, the supreme court, the supreme electoral tribunal, and the tribunal of accounts on matters within their competence. The Cuban system also includes the method of popular initiative and allows the introduction of bills by at least 10,000 qualified voters. The state legislatures have in Mexico the right to initiate laws or decrees in the federal congress.

The procedure regarding passage of a bill through the legislative chambers is usually to be found in the *leyes de relaciones* and the rules of those bodies. Bills must be presented in writing with the signature of the author or authors to the secretary, and the presiding officer proceeds then to assign them to the proper committee. As we have noted before, committees are in some countries forced to consider proposals or to report on them under special circumstances. Each house keeps a legislative calendar on which bills are placed as they are discharged by the various committees, but party leaders usually decide in informal conferences questions of precedence and indicate the preference to be given to proposals.

In Honduras a bill is discussed article by article in three separate readings, and members can speak a maximum of three times on any point, with the exception of the author, who is not under any restriction.[24] Proposals receive two readings in Argentina, and only on the second can items of the bill be discussed separately. As a rule, on presentation of the committee's report members representing the committee's majority and minority respectively are given an opportunity to present their views. In countries where three readings are prescribed, the second and the third are simply reduced to a reading of the bill by title only, and the real debate is confined in practice to the first meeting. There is also the possibility in most countries that the congress may, by a special majority, decide to discuss a proposal after only one reading. Although it is not a common occurrence, legislative rules in some countries permit either branch of the legislature to transform its total membership into a committee of the whole for specific purposes. This permits consideration of proposed legislation under less formal procedures.

[23] Stokes, *op. cit.*, p. 276.
[24] *Ibid.*, p. 276.

Voting may be by voice or show of hands. It may also be by rising, or it may be by each member answering yes or no as the role is called. The Cuban congress uses two additional ways of voting: secret voting by depositing written ballots, which is used in the lower house for the election of officers; and voting by white and black balls (*por bolas*), which is used by the senate when acting in judgment on the conduct of officials or whenever the decision requires a two-thirds vote. In addition to these conventional modes of voting, modern electric voting machines have been installed in several Latin-American legislative halls.

Approval of bills is by an absolute majority except when specified otherwise by law. In Cuba a distinction is made between ordinary and extraordinary laws. The organic laws,[25] those indicated as such in the constitution, and any other to which the congress may give this character are extraordinary. All other laws are ordinary. Extraordinary laws require for their approval a majority of the total number of members of each house. Ordinary legislation can be approved by a majority of those present.

In Honduras, a member of the congress may request that a bill be reconsidered after it has been approved by the majority. Concurrence of a two-thirds vote is necessary in such cases in order to reopen the debate and to take a new vote.

In countries with a bicameral system, after a bill has been approved by one chamber it passes to the other. In Cuba, once a bill is approved in one house, it is referred to the commitee on style for its final drafting. It is then printed and distributed among the members within twenty-four hours after its approval, and finally it is sent to the other chamber or to the president, as the case may be.[26] As a rule, no bill that has been rejected completely by either one of the legislative chambers may be introduced again during the same legislative session.

Compromises between the Houses

A conflict arises when, after a bill is passed by one house, the other returns it with additions or amendments. This conflict may be solved by several methods. In Argentina, if the chamber in which the bill originated rejects the amendments proposed by the revising chamber, this body may

[25] Among the organic laws are those dealing with the civil service; the executive and judicial branches; the tribunal of constitutional and social guarantees; the electoral courts; the tribunal of accounts; and the municipalities.

[26] Ley de relaciones (Oct. 25, 1946), Art. 20.

insist on its modifications by a special vote of two-thirds, in which case, the other chamber may reject it only with a two-thirds majority. A similar plan is used in Chile, although there a mixed committee composed of an equal number of members of each house is appointed to work out a compromise. In Venezuela, Ecuador, Bolivia, and Uruguay the method of holding a joint session is used to decide the problem. A third method is employed by Cuba and also by Haiti, which consists of the use of conference committees to adjust disagreements between the two chambers. In Cuba, a conference committee composed of five senators and five representatives is formed in order to conciliate the divergent views of the two houses. If the committee fails to agree, the proposal is considered rejected. If, on the contrary, it agrees to a formula, its reports is submitted for discussion and approval in both chambers, but no amendments can be made to it. The report must be approved by both houses.[27] The practice for solving legislative differences in Brazil is that of holding joint sessions of the appropriate standing committees of both chambers.

Approval and Publication of the Laws

Proposals, after having been approved in the form already described, are transmitted to the president. Two more steps must be taken before a bill becomes law: its promulgation or sanction by the president, and its publication. As we have seen in the preceding chapter, the president may, of course, reject the bill by using his veto power. If he approves it, he signs it and orders it to be published. The act passed by the congress and approved by the president is then printed in the official publication known as *Registro Nacional, Registro Oficial, Diario Oficial,* or *Gaceta Oficial,* according to the country. It is only after the bill has appeared in this official periodical that it becomes law. In Cuba, for instance, the civil code in Article 1 provides that "the laws will go into effect three days after their publication in the *Gaceta Oficial de la República* unless otherwise provided in their text." The Spanish civil code established a period of twenty days under the same conditions. In all cases, the law in question has no validity despite congressional and presidential approvals until this other requirement is fulfilled. Despite the frequency with which the terms "promulgation" and "publication" are indiscriminately used,[28] it

[27] *Ibid.,* Arts. 22 and 23.

[28] See Linares Quintana, *op. cit.,* p. 308; Andrés M. Lazcano y Mazón, *Las constituciones de Cuba* (Madrid, 1952), pp. 327–329. For definitions of these terms see Rodolfo Rivarola, *Diccionario manual de instrucción cívica y constitucional argentina* (Buenos Aires, 1934).

can be said that both phases are invariably found in the legislative process of every Latin-American country. The legislative function is completed with the approval of the executive and the implied ordering of the law's enforcement, or promulgation; publication serves the purpose of making the law known to the people.

BIBLIOGRAPHY

Christensen, Asher N., "The Role and Organization of Legislative Assemblies in Latin America," in Asher N. Christensen (ed.), *The Evolution of Latin American Government,* New York, Holt, 1951.

Donoso, Ricardo, *Desarrollo político y social de Chile desde la constitución de 1833,* Santiago, 1942.

Estrada, José Manuel, *Curso de derecho constitucional,* 3 vols., Buenos Aires, 1927, vol. III.

Jiménez de Aréchaga, Justino, *El poder legislativo,* 2 vols., Montevideo, 1906.

Lanz Duret, Miguel, *Derecho constitucional mexicano, y consideraciones sobre la realidad política de nuestro régimen,* 4th ed., Mexico, 1947.

Linares Quintana, Segundo V., *Las incompatibilidades parlamentarias en el derecho argentino y comparado,* 2 vols., Buenos Aires, 1942.

———, *Legislación y asistencia técnica,* Buenos Aires, 1935.

Matienzo, José Nicolás, *El gobierno representativo federal en la República Argentina,* Madrid, 1917.

Mayer, Jorge M., *Las comisiones parlamentarias de investigación,* Buenos Aires, 1936.

Mijares Palencia, José, *El gobierno mexicano: su organización y funcionamiento,* Mexico, 1936.

Rabasa, Emilio, *La organización política de Mexico. La constitución y la dictadura,* Madrid, 1917.

Rodríguez Pineres, E., *Táctica parlamentaria,* Bogotá, 1937.

Romero, Miguel, *El parlamento. Derecho, jurisprudencia, historia,* 2 vols., Buenos Aires, 1902.

Tabío, Evelio, *La inmunidad parlamentaria,* Havana, 1947.

Chapter 11: THE ADMINISTRATION OF JUSTICE

THE DECALOGUE OF EVERY GOOD JUDGE

The judge should be studious of the science of law and of human psychology, virtuous, discreet, just, honest, not vicious, courteous, not proud or envious, performer of his duties, upright and not a doer of acts which are forbidden to him and to others; since only by uniting these qualities will he be able to deserve the sympathy of the society which chose him to do justice to his fellow citizens and which in its turn judges him according to the position in which he places himself; he will be judged by humanity according to his acts either as a good judge or as a bad judge, in the first case he will merit the esteem of all, and in the second, degrading himself, he will degrade the justice which he represents.—Andrés Maria Lazcano y Mazón, President, Sala de la Audiencia, Havana

Introduction

All Latin-American countries establish the judiciary as a separate organ of government. In a formal sense, the courts are independent in the exercise of their functions, with obedience due only to the law. The constitutions of Bolivia, Cuba, Nicaragua, Panama, and Venezuela declare this independence explicitly. All specify that the judges of the courts shall be lawyers who have exercised their profession for a period of time, thus giving formal assurance of technical competence. The courts as administrators of justice are in political theory and by constitutional mandate the protectors of human liberty and the guardians of both individuals and collective interests at law. They are in the majority of Latin-American countries also guardians of the constitution itself.

Foreign Influences on Jurisprudence

It is well, at the outset, to emphasize the heritage in these countries of Roman law. Many of their eminent jurisconsults would agree that the Romans "fixed for all time the categories of judicial thought."[1] In the civil law—in relation to persons, things, and acts—the Roman law has

[1] E. Cuq, *Les Institutions juridiques des Romains,* quoted by José Santiago Rodríguez, *Elementos de derecho romano* (Caracas, 1928), p. ix.

come to be "a part of modern civilization," as an Argentine has written. Studies in Roman law are standard courses in the law schools of Latin America, ranging in duration from two to four years. The law of these countries bears ineffaceably the seal of this source.

In Spanish America, the multiplied influences of the mother country are pervasive in the civil, criminal, mercantile, and procedural law. A code of commerce promulgated in 1829 by Spain was to have, along with the Ordenanzas de Bilbao, an abiding influence on mercantile law. Likewise of great serviceability and influence was the Redacción del Código Civil de España by Gorosabel in 1832. In the civil and criminal law codes, the Spanish influence has been partially displaced by that of France and Italy. The Code Napoléon and the civil code of Italy of 1864 in both form and substance had, in these fields of law, a powerful influence. The effect, according to repeated expression of opinion, has been to produce a blend of systems, with a result which has not always been coherent and consistent. In countries of federal organization, especially in Argentina and to a less degree in Brazil and Mexico, there has been the influence of the United States in the field of constitutional law.[2] The developments in theory and practice of judicial review of legislation have in some countries been influenced by the United States.[3]

In one of the early cases following the adoption of the constitution of 1853, the supreme court of Argentina declared,[4]

Nothing induces one to believe that the authors of our Constitution, on sanctioning the articles which make reference to the federal jurisdiction, might

[2] Segundo V. Linares Quintana, "Comparisons of the Constitutional Basis of the United States and Argentine Political Systems," *The University of Pennsylvania Law Review,* vol. 97, April, 1949.

[3] M. Dana Montaño, *Las ideas políticas de José Manuel Estrada* (Santa Fé, 1944), p. 18. Professor Montaño records an extraordinary number of translations of works by writers of the United States during the period 1855–1880, including those of Story's *Commentaries* (translated by Calvo and Cantilo), Kent's *Commentaries* (by Carrasco Albano), Curtis's *Origin and Adoption of the Constitution of the United States* (by Cantilo), *The Federalist* (by Cantilo), Whiting's *War Powers* (by Rawson), Lieber's *Civil Liberty* (by Manso), Pomeroy's *Executive Powers* (by Varela), Tiffany's *Government and Constitutional Law* (by Quiroga), and Wilson's *Congressional Government* (by Belín).

[4] *J. C. Gómez v. La Nación, Fallos,* vol. 2, p. 44. There is much evidence in Juan A. González Calderón, *Derecho constitucional argentino* (2d ed., 3 vols., Buenos Aires, 1923), relative to the influence of the United States on Argentine jurisprudence, in case law, in commentaries, and in constitutional derivation. Citations of works written in the United States and of cases decided in the United States are frequent in court opinions and in briefs of lawyers.

have had in mind Spanish legislation; rather, on the contrary, it is an evident truth that they thought only of imitating the Constitution of the United States in this particular, as they did in the rest, with very few variations; and thus it is to the principles incorporated in that same Constitution and to the jurisprudence of those states to which one should go in order to know the scope of this jurisdiction which did not have proper precedents among us.

Examples of the influence of the jurisprudence and constitutional theories of the United States upon Argentina and Mexico are in the doctrine of the separation of powers, the abstinence of courts from the decision of political questions, the expansion of the sphere and function of government through use of "implied powers," the interpretation of the "republican form of government," the theory of "concurrent powers," and theories of dual taxation.

In civil law, certain countries were definitely influenced by France. The civil code of Haiti in 1825, that of Bolivia in 1831, and that of the Dominican Republic in 1844 were drawn almost wholly from the Code Napoléon.

Code Making in Latin America

The several standard or classified fields of law have their respective codes, such as civil, criminal, and mercantile. There are codes of procedure (*procedimiento* or *enjuiciamiento*) for each of these branches. Country by country, these distinctive codes have had their evolution, and with their formulation and explanation are associated the names of many distinguished jurisconsults, either in the role of drafters or as commentators. The names of Andrés Bello of Chile, Vélez Sarsfield of Argentina, Teixeira de Freitas and Clovis Bevilaqua of Brazil, and Aranda, Acosta, Sanojo, and Dominici of Venezuela, are especially renowned. Some of the countries have frequently amended or revised their codes, with the intent of modernizing them or of reforming them in the light of criticisms.

Many codes have been largely copied from those of other states, but whether one country has profited from the labors and experience of another has been a debatable issue. Bolivia at one time adopted the civil code of Bello, of Chile, but did not place it in operation. The civil and commercial codes of Argentina were adopted by Paraguay. There is evidence that the Chilean code strongly influenced the first civil codes of Venezuela, Uruguay, and Honduras. In Honduras, the prevailing influences have been those of the civil codes of Spain and Chile. Out of 258 articles of the present code of Honduras, 206 are literally the same as corresponding articles in the Spanish code and 185 are the same as the Chilean code of 1855.[5]

It seems that code making, however, has been a national endeavor which has not necessarily been influenced by the line of action and thought adopted by other Latin-American countries. An exception might be made as to more recent and special codes having to do with mining law, labor law, and social law. In most of the countries these codes—general and special—have been accompanied by a literature of commentary and exposition.[6]

In Mexico, although the power was definitely conferred on the federal government to formulate and issue a penal code, such a power with reference to a civil code and a code of civil procedure was in doubt. It was held that, in accordance with section 1 of Article 104 (1857), the judicial power had authority to decide controversies that might arise from the application of federal laws and that in consequence, by implication, it must take into account the measures necessary to make these laws operative. Such measures would, it was argued, properly include these codes.[7]

In Brazil, the historical basis of law—civil, criminal, and commercial—is the Ordenaçoes Philippinas of Portugal. In time these ordinances were to be displaced by codes, but the process was slow and uneven. The first code was that of criminal law (1830), followed by a criminal-law code of procedure in 1832. The commercial code of 1850, although having a distinctly original flavor, was much indebted to France. The civil code, a project repeatedly entrusted to one person after another, was not formulated as a systematic body of law until 1899. This code became famous and a subject of much controversy. It was not formally adopted and placed in effect until 1917. The delays in the formulation and adoption of the civil code caused the insertion in other codes of matter

[5] William S. Stokes, *Honduras: An Area Study in Government* (Madison, Wis., University of Wisconsin Press, 1951), p. 109. He cites L. Mejía Moreno, *Práctica del derecho civil hondureño* (Tegucigalpa, 1934).

[6] The dates for the adoption of civil codes by the several countries are as follows: Argentina, 1869; Bolivia, 1831; Brazil, 1917; Chile, 1855; Colombia, 1876; Costa Rica, 1886; Cuba, 1889; Dominican Republic, 1844; Ecuador, 1860; Guatemala, 1877; Haiti, 1825; Honduras, 1880; Mexico, 1870; Nicaragua, 1867; Panama, 1902; Paraguay, 1876; Peru, 1852; Salvador, 1860; Uruguay, 1868; Venezuela, 1836 (code of civil procedure), 1862 (first civil code).

[7] Felipe Tena Ramírez, *Derecho constitucional mexicano* (2d ed., Mexico, 1949), p. 110.

more properly belonging in a civil code. Foreign influences have been manifest in many features of Brazilian law. Portugal, Spain, France, England, Switzerland, and Germany have individually in one or another branch of law had a contribution to make.[8] An example of British influence was the presence in the code of criminal procedure of 1832 of the writ of habeas corpus. This writ in time was broadened to protect rights other than those of personal and physical liberty. The confusion occasioned by such a widening of the scope of the writ led lawyers to demand a limitation of it to the traditional purpose. A new writ, that of *mandado de segurança,* was created to protect personal and even property rights. It has been described as a "unique feature."[9]

Some countries may designate a law or a collection of laws as a code. For example, in 1875 Chile adopted a law, subsequently modified many times, called the Código Orgánico de Tribunales (COT). Uruguay has a Código de Organización de los Tribunales y de Hacienda (Law No. 9164). In Cuba, in 1929, there was adopted a Código Notarial, whereas in that country a Ley Hipotecaria (1893) is in reality a code of mortgage law. Likewise, there is a Ley Orgánica del Poder Judicial (1909) which might be considered a code.

International Private Law

In the field of international private law—sometimes designated as the "conflict of laws"—domestic legislation, the civil code, and the commercial code may have interacting influences affecting property, contracts, mortgages, bills of exchange, matrimony and divorce, and general business transactions. Many international conferences have considered these matters. Of especial importance are the treaties of Montevideo (1888–1889) which were ratified by Argentina, Bolivia, Paraguay, Colombia, Peru, and Uruguay, where they have the force of law. There is also the Bustamante Code, approved at Havana in 1928 and ratified by the great majority of American countries, although some accompanied ratification with reservations.[10] In these difficult matters of private law, some principles proceed

[8] Cf. Clovis Bevilaqua, "A cultura jurídica no Brasil," in *Revista do Instituto Histórico e Geográphico Brasileiro,* special issue, vol. 9, pp. 317–358, 1922.

[9] A. Marchant, "Politics, Government and Law," in T. L. Smith and A. Marchant (eds.), *Brazil: Portrait of Half a Continent* (New York, Dryden, 1950), pp. 374, 380.

[10] For a copy of this code, see Antonio Sánchez de Bustamante, *Manual de derecho internacional privado* (Havana, 1939), pp. 485–563.

from international instruments and some from the civil and commercial laws of particular states.[11]

Structure of the Judicial System

The highest court is usually designated the "supreme court of justice." Bolivia, Chile, Ecuador, and Paraguay call it the "supreme court." Haiti, Cuba, and Brazil use the term "tribunal." Venezuela until recently called it the Alta Corte Federal y de Casación, but the constitution of 1947 designated it the "supreme court of justice." This odd designation of the Alta Corte Federal y de Casación had historical explanation. For many years, between 1880 and 1904, Venezuela had two high courts, the Alta Corte Federal and the Corte de Casación, a system to which it returned in 1953.

In all countries the provisions of the constitution respecting the judicial branch are supplemented by legislation. The judiciary act or *ley orgánica del poder judicial,* as it is commonly entitled, implements the constitution.

The composition of the supreme courts and the tenure of members vary sharply. Some constitutions leave the determination of the number of members to the legislative branch. As established, the number of members ranges from three in Paraguay to thirty-one in Cuba. Tenure in Argentine, Brazil, Chile, Mexico, Cuba and Peru is for life or good behavior. In Bolivia, Haiti, and Uruguay the tenure is ten years; in Ecuador, Honduras, and Nicaragua, six years; in Paraguay and Venezuela, five years; in Costa Rica and Guatemala, four years; and in El Salvador, three years. In Uruguay judges of the appellate court have life tenure, while that of judges of the supreme court is ten years. In the new constitution of Costa Rica (1949) judges are considered reelected unless congress decides otherwise by a vote of two-thirds of the entire membership. In Colombia, where life tenure is supposedly provided, this tenure seems to be contingent upon reelection (Articles 143 and 144). In general, the constitutions provide that, while tenure is secure for the term specified, judges are subject to impeachment.

Not only is the professional competence and experience safeguarded, as has been noticed, but requirements as to citizenship and age are generally specified. Almost all the constitutions declare that the judicial

[11] For a general consideration of this matter, see Manuel Garcia Calderón, *La capacidad cambiaria en el derecho internacional privado* (Lima, 1951). The author explains the five patterns of law and practice observed by American countries, including the United States.

office is incompatible with the exercise of any other public function. Some of the countries expressly deny eligibility to members of the clergy.

The majority of the countries provide for the selection of members of the highest court by one or both of the other branches of the government, rather than by popular election.[12] There are three prevailing modes of selection, with many variants in detail:

1. Nominations may be made by the executive, with or without advice, and confirmed by the senate or the congress. This plan is adopted by Argentina, Mexico, Panama, Paraguay, and Peru. Some may require that the president submit a list from which a choice is made, and some may require that presidential nomination be previously approved by a council or other body. In Brazil the president names, with approval by the senate, the members of the supreme tribunal, but usually on nomination of the court itself. In Haiti, the members are appointed by the president. In the countries where the presidents nominate court members and the senate ratifies, it is a matter of common complaint that ratification is a matter of course, with dissent on the part of the senate very rare.

2. The members may be chosen by the congress. This plan may take the form of the nomination of a list by the senate with election by the chamber of deputies, as in Bolivia. The congress elects the members in Guatemala, Honduras, Nicaragua, El Salvador, Uruguay, and Venezuela.

3. Chile, Colombia, Cuba, and the Dominican Republic have special plans of selection. In Chile, a vacancy is filled by the president from a list of five individuals nominated by the supreme court, provided that the two eldest members of the Corte de Apelaciones figure in the list. In Colombia, by a statue of 1924, six members of the court are named by the senate and six by the chamber of deputies. The plan of Cuba calls for a special electoral college composed of four members of the supreme tribunal, three lawyers named by the president, and two members of the faculty of law of the University of Havana. The president of the republic will, on advice of the council of ministers, submit nominations from the list of names prepared by the college to the senate for ratification.

[12] Many of the countries have from time to time changed the methods of selection. For example, Mexico has had at least four modes of choosing the membership of the supreme court: (1) election by the state legislatures (constitution of 1824); (2) popular election, by indirect process (constitution of 1857); (3) election by the congress on nomination of the state legislatures (constitution of 1917); (4) nomination by the president with confirmation by the senate (amendment of 1928). Lanz Duret contends that under all these modes of selection the influence of the executive was paramount.

TABLE 13
SUPREME COURTS: MEMBERSHIP, TENURE, AND APPOINTMENT

Country	Members	Tenure	Mode of appointment
Argentina	5	Life	Nominated by president; confirmed by senate
Bolivia	10	10 years	Nominated by senate; elected by chamber
Brazil	13	Life	Appointed by president on approval by senate
Chile	13	Life	Appointed by president from list submitted by the court
Colombia	12	5 years	Six elected by each chamber, from lists submitted by president
Costa Rica	17	4 years	Elected by congress
Cuba	31	Life	Nominated by president from list by an electoral college; confirmed by senate
Dominican Republic	7	5 years	Appointed by senate
Ecuador	15	6 years	Elected by congress
El Salvador	19	3 years	Elected by congress
Guatemala	7	4 years	Elected by congress
Haiti	9	10 years	Named by president
Honduras	5	6 years	Chosen by congress
Mexico	21	Life	Nominated by president; confirmed by senate
Nicaragua	5	6 years	Elected by congress
Panama	5	10 years	Nominated by president; confirmed by congress
Paraguay	3	5 years	Appointed by president with approval by council of state
Peru	11	Life	Elected by congress from panel submitted by president
Uruguay	5	10 years	Elected by general assembly
Venezuela	10	5 years	Elected by congress

In the Dominican Republic, by Article 19 of the constitution, there is vested in the senate the power of "naming the justices of the supreme court of justice" and those of the other courts.

In some countries, notably in Cuba and Chile, an effort has been made to establish judicial careers. In Cuba, there is an *escalafón* or registry not only for magistrates but for attorneys general (*fiscales*) from which promotions are made in accordance with experience and merit. In

Nicaragua, the idea of a "career system" is stated in Article 253 of the constitution: "The reward of advancement, in each election or appointment of the members of the judiciary, will be for those who have distinguished themselves in the exercise of their functions." The Cuban system is in a limited sense flexible. Judges are to begin their careers by qualifying on the bases of professional training and competitive examination (*oposiciones*) and are to be promoted either by observance of seniority in service or by passing examinations.

In some countries the practice is established of naming alternate or substitute judges (*suplentes*) to take the places of proprietary justices on leave or to fill temporary vacancies. Mexico authorizes the president to nominate "provisional judges," subject to the approval of the senate or, during times of its recess, of the *comisión permanente*. In general, these alternate judges must have the same formal qualifications as the proprietary.

The lower courts vary in number, designation, and structure. Perhaps the nearest to a pattern in the unitary states would be the sequence of local courts (sometimes called the *juzgados de paz*), district courts, and courts of appeals. Taking Cuba as an example, there are *juzgados municipales* (one or more) for the cities; the *juzgados de primera instancia* for the *partidos;* and an *audiencia* for each of the provinces. The states of federal organization have had a dual set of courts—one for the federal jurisdiction and one for the state or provincial. Taking Argentina as an example, there are the following federal courts: (1) *camaras federales,* which are appellate courts, five in number, with three judges for each; (2) *jueces de sección,* which are district courts with one judge, at least one such court for each province; and (3) *jueces letrados,* which are territorial courts with one judge for each court. The provincial courts include (1) supreme courts, (2) appellate courts for some provinces, (3) courts of *primera instancia,* and (4) minor courts of the alcaldes and of the market judges.

Functional courts having special jurisdiction exist in all countries except Mexico, and their number tends to increase. Some of these special courts have a completely separate hierarchy, ranging from trial courts of first instance to intermediate appellate courts and to supreme courts. A variation from this plan occurs where the special jurisdiction operates in lower courts or those of first instance, with appeals going to ordinary tribunals of a higher rank. Even when a separate hierarchy of courts is provided in a field of law, there may be the limitation that cases involving interpretation or construction of the constitution go on appeal to the "regular" supreme court. The proliferation of these special courts might suggest that Latin-American countries are returning to a modified version of the old *fuero* system, and the thought might well give them pause. The immediate reply probably would be that the present aim is to supply functional service through tribunals composed of experts in field law. Granting the propriety of this aim, there is room for difference of opinion—and such difference exists—as to organization, jurisdiction, and responsibility of these special courts. Whether some of these special courts constitute a form of privilege is likely to cause argument.[13]

Some of the special courts are old in origin, such as the military, land and waters (*tierras y aguas*), mines, food supplies (*abastos*), minors, commerce, and taxes and accounts (*cuentas*). Examples of more modern special courts are those in the fields of administrative, electoral, juvenile, labor, and social law. It should be noted here that some of the special fields of law have codes.

Some of the supreme courts always act as a body, e.g., those of Argentina, Chile, and Brazil. Others may operate by divisions, known as *salas* or *cámaras,* and for certain matters, as a whole (*en pleno*). Historically, within the same country, practice from time to time may have varied. For example, the Mexican supreme court, from 1857 to 1900, functioned only *en pleno.* The constituents of 1917 returned to this practice, probably under the influence of Emilio Rabasa, who had urged it. In 1928, under the pressure of business and the multiplication of cases of *amparo* before the court, the membership was increased and the court was divided into three *salas* for cases involving civil, criminal, and administrative law. In 1934, the membership was further increased, and a new *sala* for labor-law cases was created. Cases involving mercantile law are assigned to the civil *sala.*[14]

In Colombia, four *salas* are designated: that for cases under original jurisdiction, that for civil-law appeals, that for criminal-law appeals, and that for "general business." Peru, Bolivia, and Guatemala each have two, one for civil-law and the other for criminal-law cases. Ecuador designates three—civil, criminal, and original jurisdiction. Cuba employs language having a possible reference to five: civil, criminal, administrative, "constitutional and social guarantees," and "government" or general business.

[13] Helen L. Clagett, *The Administration of Justice in Latin America* (New York, Oceana Publications, 1952), pp. 55–115.

[14] Tena Ramírez, *op. cit.,* pp. 379–381.

These divisions, by reason of the fact that some of the *salas* have a constant membership, make it possible for justices to become specialists in one or more fields of judicature.

According to the organic law of the Corte Federal y de Casación, adopted in 1926, in Venezuela, the supreme court, then composed of seven members, was to have three *salas:* the *federal,* that of *casación,* and that for cases and affairs relating to politics and administration. Each of these *salas,* however, had the full membership of the court, at least five members being necessary for the transaction of business.

Recent Trends in Brazil and Venezuela

This section will consider some innovations which have been adopted, at least temporarily, in these countries.[15]

In Brazil, under the constitution of 1937 and during the dictatorship of Vargas, changes were made in the organization of the judicial power. As described in the constitution (Article 90), the court system was to be constituted of the supreme court, the judges and tribunals of the states, the federal district and the territories, and the military tribunals. This plan seemed to eliminate all the local and subordinate federal courts, except for the federal district and territories and for military jurisdictions. State courts became, in the sense of the constitution, instruments of the judicial power for the administration of both state and federal law. Did this mean centralization or the enlargement of the jurisdiction of state courts? It is perhaps unimportant to try to answer the question so far as the Vargas regime was concerned, but it is of significance to ascertain how much of this innovation was retained under the constitution of 1946.

The new charter leaves some issues concerning the judiciary in doubt. For example, the organs of the judicial power, as listed in Article 94, are the supreme court, the court of appeals, military tribunals, election courts, and labor courts. No mention is made of state courts or those of the federal district and the territories. Despite these omissions, the qualifications and tenure of judges of state courts are specified. Provision is made for legal representation of the federal government when cases involving interests of the federal union are being heard in state courts. Clearly the state courts and the local attorney general and staff, constituting the "public ministry," are retained. These state courts have jurisdiction of cases formerly heard in local federal courts. Usually a federal case is

[15] Clagett, *op. cit.,* pp. 22–23, 48–49, 51–53.

transferred to the highest state tribunal, located in the state capital, with appeals going either to the federal court of appeals or the supreme court. The effects and influences of these changes are not as yet evident. It could be reasonably argued that they are a part of the process of centralization and that the state courts, already bound by the federal codes, will increasingly be swayed by federal jurisprudence. On the other hand, they are vastly more important than formerly. However this may be, the state courts, as such, continue to exist and to operate.

In Venezuela, where federalism is nominal, although supposedly supported by tradition and sentiment, more startling changes in judicial organization have occurred. Here by the reforms of 1945 and by the constitution of 1947, the administration of justice and the control of all jails and penitentiaries are placed under federal jurisdiction. No reference is made to any courts or judicial power of the states. This, therefore, is a drastic breach in the theory of the federal system and a break in the continuity of the history of their legal system. Shortly after the legislation was adopted, in 1948, putting this plan into effect, a military junta displaced the government in power and along with it the constitution of 1947. The new government reinstated the constitution of 1936. How much of this new plan of judicial organization will be retained is in doubt.

There were two other innovations adopted by Venezuela in 1947 which should be noted. Authorization was granted for the creation of a "supreme council on the magistracy" composed of representatives from the legislative, executive, and judicial branches, which should seek to promote the independence, efficiency, and good discipline of the judiciary and should study plans for a system of judicial career. Secondly, the solicitor general—an officer named by the congress—was charged with the general duty of watching over the good progress of the administration of justice and seeing to it that the laws, especially in penal cases, were justly administered.[16]

By the constitution of 1953, Venezuela returned to the old system of two higher courts: the federal court, composed of five members; and the court of cassation, of ten members. Members of both courts are elected by the congress. There is little said of state courts, other than the recognition of the state "superior courts" (Article 132, section 4). The move-

[16] Cf. A. Oropeza, *Centralización de la justicia y federación en la evolución constitucional de nuestra república* (Caracas, 1944); Ernesto Wolff, *Tratado de derecho constitucional venezolano* (Caracas, 1945), vol. II, pp. 337–340.

ment toward the nationalization of the administration of justice seems to have been checked.

Fiscales of the Judicial Branch

The legal representative of public interests, the government, and the ministry of justice in the courts is commonly called the *fiscal*. This term does not have a precise equivalent in Anglo-American jurisprudence. It is not adequately translated by any of the terms "attorney general," or "prosecutor," or "solicitor general." While discharging duties of a prosecutor the *fiscal* has the role of technical adviser to the court.

In Cuba, for example, with the exception of the *ministro fiscal* of the supreme court, all the *fiscales* are under civil service and are "career" men. The *ministerio fiscal* in Cuba is charged especially with guarding the fullfillment of the constitution and the law. It is quite generally the practice for the supreme court in any matter concerned with constitutionality to receive an opinion of the *fiscal*. He is representative of "the people" when acting in an advisory capacity and representative of the state when acting in the capacity of prosecutor.

Special Attributes of Supreme Courts

These attributes relate to powers of the initiation or proposal of legislation concerning the judiciary; budgetary responsibilities; disciplinary superintendence and authority over lower courts; nomination or promotion or appointment of members of lower courts; the exercise in some instances of a power to try and decide impeachment cases; and official representation in certain bodies.

The right to initiate legislative measures relative to the judicial branch may be given to the supreme court by constitutional concession or by custom. This right applies to the drafting and oral presentation of such measures. The usual practice is to allow the president of the court, or his representative, privileges of the floor of congress to present and explain the proposed legislation. The matter of new codes, structural changes, additional court services and changes in personnel, increases in salary, and the like usually emanate from the court, whether the right of the expression of such opinions is formally guaranteed or not. This is the case in some countries where the constitution is silent on the matter, as in Honduras, where nearly all such measures originate in the supreme court.

Explicit budgetary responsibilities are granted to the supreme courts with reference to their own expenses and with reference to those of other courts within the "judicial power" by Bolivia, Chile, Nicaragua, El Salvador, and Uruguay. Consultative functions regarding budgets are exercised elsewhere in Latin America. In many countries, the salaries of judges, at least, are entered into what is called the "fixed budget" (*presupuesto fijo*).

González Calderón summarizes the supplementary powers of the Argentine supreme court, stating that it has superintendency over all other federal courts and that it is commissioned to issue suitable regulations in order to obtain the best administration of justice. The supervisory powers of the supreme court include (1) the power to see that its regulations are fulfilled and to impose disciplinary penalties in case of infraction; (2) the power to demand annual reports from lower courts concerning judicial acts of whatever kind; and (3) the power to grant leaves of absence to members of lower courts. In the cases of recurrence of abuses or of negligence in the performance of duty by judges of lower courts, the supreme court will inform the chamber of deputies; and in the cases of failure to perform duty by *fiscales* or other court officials, it will inform the president.[17]

Supreme courts are usually vested with powers of inspection and discipline over other branches of the judiciary. These powers and responsibilities are expressly granted in Bolivia, Chile, Cuba, the Dominican Republic, El Salvador, Mexico, Nicaragua, Paraguay, and Uruguay. The duties are elaborately set forth in Chile's Código Orgánico de Tribunales.

All these disciplinary duties may be vested in the supreme court, or they may be decentralized in that other courts share in the responsibility. These duties, in Cuba, are specified in detail. Periodically, or at the discretion of the court, visits of inspection may be ordered. Local offices of the civil registry, the registry of property, the notarial service, and the local courts are among the services examined. Reports from such visits may be used in determining disciplinary treatment of functionaries. Among possible penalties which may grow out of the exercise of correctional administration are those of fines, suspension from office, and in extreme cases separation from office. Reports of this kind may lead to remonstrances and censure or to suggestions of improvement.

[17] González Calderón, *op. cit.*, vol. III, pp. 416–417.

Independence of the Judiciary

This principle may be formally incorporated in constitutions. In Article 136 of that of Bolivia, the declaration is succinctly made: "Judges are independent and responsible only to the law." The statement of this principle by Panama is: "Magistrates and judges are independent in the exercise of their functions and are subject only to the constitution and the laws."

1. This independence may in a practical sense be safeguarded by tenure—that of a life term or a term longer than that of a single presidential administration. In Mexico a change in judicial tenure of federal judges was made during the time of President Cárdenas from that of life to that of six years, thus bringing, it was thought, the courts more definitely within the orbit of executive control. Later, President Ávila Camacho (1944) successfully urged the adoption of an amendment to restore life tenure.

2. A second way of protection for the courts is found in removing—wholly or partially—the selection of judicial personnel from the power of the executive and establishing a system of judicial career. Some countries have given the supreme court a decisive voice or even complete control of appointments of members of the lower courts.[18]

3. Nearly all countries assure that the compensation of judges shall not be diminished during the term of service.

4. It can be argued that judicial independence has a definite relationship to the power of appointment and the power of removal. The extreme in this matter is to be found in the case of Haiti, where the executive branch appoints members of the judiciary without apparently any requirement of confirmation by the congress. Irremovability, except for a demonstrated cause to be established by formal process, has also been assumed to be a guarantee of judicial independence. In Mexico, despite the fact that judges at present have life terms, removal may be accomplished rather easily. According to Article 111, the president of the republic may request the removal of any member of the supreme court, and of other federal courts, for "misbehavior." "If the Chamber of Deputies, first, and the Chamber of Senators afterwards, shall decide in these cases by an absolute majority of votes that the request is justified, the accused official

[18] Countries in which the personnel of lower courts is named by the supreme court are Colombia, Bolivia, Costa Rica, Guatemala, Panama, Mexico, and Uruguay.

shall be deprived immediately of his position independently of the legal responsibility that may have been incurred, and the executive shall proceed with a new appointment." Although the judge affected has a right to be heard by the president before the request is communicated to the chamber of deputies, there would seem to be no protection of the judge involved in such a proceeding. Many have concluded that under this unusual system of removability, a president and a congress in political sympathy might, with relative ease, purge the courts, and some have likewise concluded that the Mexican court has, for that reason, been timid in holding the political branches to strict constitutional accountability.

A corollary of the principle of independence is the principle that the courts should abstain from the judgment of political matters. Such abstention may be a matter of respect by the judiciary for the principle of the separation of powers. On the other hand, this principle may find expression in legal mandates. For example, the Brazilian constitution of 1937, in Article 94, stated: "It is prohibited that the judicial power take cognizance of matters exclusively political." What is "exclusively political" might be the subject of debate, but Latin-American courts have been slow to take jurisdiction of political questions, although some political functions may be delegated to them. Judges are supposed to abstain from party politics. The present Brazilian constitution forbids court judges "to participate in party politics." In Nicaragua, "The magistrates of courts of justice may not intermeddle in affairs of partisan politics."

It has been a long-established principle in Argentina that the federal courts may not decide political questions. In a well-known case, the supreme court declared:[19]

> If the matter is the affair of the political powers, their decisions in respect of it may not be controverted by the judicial department; the right to decide concerning both the basis and the form of their decisions, as well when the law is passed as when every matter comprehended in their constitutional attributes is resolved, may not be contested. It is an elemental rule of our public law that each one of the high powers which form the government of the nation applies and interprets the constitution by itself when it exercises the powers which that constitution confers on them respectively.

A less formal way of safeguarding the independence of the courts is that of developing a respect for the integrity and a tradition of the in-

[19] Cited by González Calderón, *op. cit.*, vol. I, pp. 437–438. The case was *J. M. Cullen v. B. Llerena, Fallos*, vol. I, p. 58. Cf. *E. Lobos v. D. J. Donovan, Fallos*, vol. 58, p. 180.

dependence of the judicial power. Such an attitude of public opinion is claimed for Brazil, Cuba, and Venezuela. That the judiciary has been able to maintain at least a measure of independence during periods of dictatorship is an extraordinary achievement in the experience of several of these countries.

The legal guarantees of independence and the constitutional or statutory tenures of service have not always been respected; the courts at times have been strongly influenced by political forces. In some states of siege, the jurisdiction of the courts has been suspended concerning issues involving some policies and acts of the government. The supreme court itself may be suspended. This happened in Panama in 1951, and it has happened elsewhere. Not all revolutions have respected existing judicial tenures. Following the Argentine revolution of 1943, some judges were impeached and removed, for political reasons. The treatment of the judiciary at the hands of the Perón government has been severely criticized. If one takes seriously the messages of Perón to the congress and some speeches having to do with this subject, the general grounds on which policy was developed were social and political. Starting with the proposition that the independence of the judicial power is indispensable for "the prosperity of nations," he went on to say that this power should be "efficacious." The ideas and concepts of the judiciary cannot be efficacious if they do not "march along according to the compass set by political sentiment." For the courts to defend the traditional because it is traditional, as they often have, is a "dangerous error." Justice has to be dynamic and not static, otherwise respectable popular desires are frustrated and social development is retarded, with grave injury to the working classes. This reasoning covered a design to change the personnel of the courts and to remove a possible obstacle to the *peronista* program. The device employed was the obscure section 4 of the "transitory dispositions" of the constitution of 1949, wherein it was declared that during the first legislative period following the sanction of the constitution the approval of the senate will be "newly requested" for members of the federal courts. This seems to have meant that judges must be renominated and confirmed. The seats of those judges not satisfactory to Perón were vacated, and a drastic purge was undertaken.

The Use of Juries

It must at once be admitted that little is positively known about the employment of this institution by these countries. Also, little that is informative about the operation of the jury system is to be found in the literature of the countries which have the system, with the possible exception of Brazil. Much was said in the period of struggles for independence and in the decades immediately following about the desirability of adopting the system. The thought of the "jury as the child of the revolution for independence" often lapsed into the idea of it as an orphan or even as an illegitimate offspring. Some countries set it up for use in cases involving the freedom of the press. Others endorsed the system for use in criminal-law cases, but left its inauguration to later action of the congress. A practical usage of a type of jury—as a sort of arbitration board—in mercantile controversies has long been employed in courts of first instance. This usage is more widespread than is commonly supposed. A very general opinion is that the jury system is not well suited to Latin-American systems of law and that, where and when actually tried, it has languished or fallen into disuse.

The constitutions and legislation of Latin America differ sharply in positive action relative to this institution. The Argentine constitution of 1853, in Article 24 and in clause 11 of Article 67, authorized the jury system but left its establishment to the discretion and choice of the congress. This body did not act, and the constitution of 1949 omits reference to the jury.[20]

The constitution of 1830 of Venezuela adopted the jury system, in principle, for criminal as well as some other types of cases. It left to the congress the duty of adopting laws which would apply this principle. Action was taken to set up jury trial in cases involving abuse of the liberty of the press.[21]

On the other hand, in a country in which jury trial has been supposed to be limited to cases involving abuse of the liberty of the press, a very different situation obtains. In Mexico, by mandate of the constitution (1917), the pledge is made in Article 20, paragraph 6, that "there will be judged in public hearing by a judge or jury of citizens, who know how to read and write, and who are residents of the place and district in which the crime was committed, whoever may be punished with a

[20] Austin F. Macdonald, *Government of the Argentine Republic* (New York, Crowell, 1942), p. 273. He shows that the senate did pass a measure establishing the jury system, but the chamber substituted a proposal for a commission to study and report on the matter. The report was rendered in 1874, without any further action being taken.

[21] José Gil Fortoul, *Historia constitucional de Venezuela* (2d ed., Caracas, 1930), vol. II, p. 25.

sentence greater than one year in prison. In every case of crimes committed by means of the press against the public order or the exterior or domestic safety of the nation will be judged by a jury." The jury is formed of seven persons chosen by lot, according to an instruction in the code of penal procedure. The jurors must be Mexican citizens but may not be office holders.[22]

The Paraguayan constitution, in Article 175, states: "Trial by jury is instituted. The law will determine the cases that must be decided by this process." In Nicaragua, according to Article 46 of the constitution, the congress is permitted "to establish a trial by jury in criminal and civil cases." Similarly, by Article 13 of the new constitution (1952), the congress of Uruguay "may establish trial by jury criminal cases." Guatemala and El Salvador make possible the use of juries in cases of the abuse of the freedom of the press. Haiti (Article 24) declares the establishment of jury trials in all cases involving criminal law and political crimes.

Most of these examples refer to countries wherein the jury system is contingent upon implementing legislation. Brazil, on the other hand, is a country in which the jury is of long standing and common use. Article 141, section 28, declares that "the institution of the jury is maintained, with the organization of it that which the law may give to it, provided that the number of the jury shall always be odd and the secrecy of its voting shall be guaranteed, as shall be the fullness of the defense of the accused and the sovereignty of the verdict. The judgment of intentional crimes against life shall obligatorily be within its competence."

The jury in Brazil was instituted during the empire and was sanctioned by the constitution of 1824. Designed to be employed in both the trial of civil and criminal cases, it was never used in civil cases. It was used in both the process of indictment and in the trial of criminal cases. The constitution of 1891 incorporated the system among the guarantees. As applied, the system was to be a feature of both the federal and state processes of law. In the consolidation of regulations concerning the federal juries, which was accomplished in 1898, the institution was to be used in cases involving political crimes, offenses committed by federal functionaries, crimes against public property, infractions of postal laws, violations of electoral laws, and cases of smuggling. Brazilian jurists have carefully appraised the jury system in both theory and practice. Although there are some defenders, probably the greater number condemn it as

[22] Miguel Lanz Duret, *Derecho constitucional mexicano* (4th ed., Mexico, 1947), p. 302.

unsuitable and ineffectual in accomplishing the purposes for which it was established.[23]

Ecuador is sometimes referred to as a country using jury trial for criminal law cases and as having the curious feature that the members of the jury should be lawyers. Although this last requirement is not specified in the present constitution, the idea of a membership made up of lawyers is not wholly original. In Lastarria's well-known treatise on constitutional law, after offering a strong plea for the jury system, he advised that it was necessary to add to the jury "a professor of law, who should explain the law impartially." The jury, however, was not bound to accept this lawyer's opinion either of the facts or of the law[24]

Administrative Law and Its Adjudication

Contributory and originating elements of a body of administrative law may be found in Spanish colonial legislation and practice. These elements include the granting of *fueros,* carrying special courts for certain services and interests; the development of an inchoate system of civil service, including a scheme of "career records" or the *hojas de servicio;* and the use of treasury and taxation courts (*tribunales de cuentas*). The organic instruments for the establishment and operation of institutions, such as the colonial *intendencias* and the *consulados,* were forerunners of the system of administrative law. Far from being a new division of law, it is one of the oldest.

Since independence, countries have had to decide whether the ordinary tribunals should decide cases involving administrative law, or whether they should follow a mixed plan whereby they would set up some functional courts with appeals to be decided by the supreme court, or whether they should create a separate set of administrative-law courts. The last plan has been inspired by influences from France, Germany, Italy, and modern Spain. All three plans are in operation.

In the meanwhile, administrative law has become a distinct branch of studies in law schools, and the ever-increasing number of writings on the subject by Latin-American jurists indicates the growing interest in

[23] Herman G. James, *The Constitutional System of Brazil* (Washington, D.C., Carnegie Institution, 1923), pp. 121–125. He refers to the works of J. T. Bastos, *O jurado na república* (2 vols., Rio de Janeiro, 1909); and J. Barbalho, *Constituição federal brasileira* (São Paulo, 1902).

[24] J. V. Lastarria, *Derecho público constitucional teórico o filosófico,* in *Obras completas,* vol. 1, pp. 138 ff.

public administration.[25] This interest, despite opinion to the contrary, is of long standing, as is evidenced by such works as those of Pereyra and López.[26]

The relations of administrative law to the standard and special codes of law are so numerous and significant that the wisdom of creating a separate system of judicature is seriously in debate. Mexico took a position in opposition to all special courts. For all countries the questions of where to begin and how far to go in this matter have not been consistently answered. Many branches of administrative law—those concerned with revenues and tariffs, penal administration, public lands, conservation of forests and waters, mines, civil registry, property registry, stock exchanges, fairs, and markets, to mention a few of them—show relations and interlocking ties with civil, penal, mercantile, and special codes. The traditional examples, as well as the most commonly persistent examples, of separate courts for special purposes would be the *tribunales de cuentas* and the military courts. Aside from these examples, the most common way of adjusting controversies involving administrative issues is to use the ordinary tribunals, which may have a distinct docket known as the *contencioso administrativo*. Appeals would go to the supreme court and might, as in Mexico, be tried in the *sala administrativa*.

On the other hand, Colombia and Uruguay are examples of countries having separate administrative law courts. In Colombia, appeals go to the council of state for final settlement. In Uruguay, of significance are the special courts of administrative litigation and the electoral court. The

[25] For example, see the following: A. Alayza, *Derecho administrativo general y del Perú* (Lima, 1927), Peruvian; D. Antokoletz, *Tratado de derecho administrativo* (Buenos Aires, 1933), Argentine; A. Aragón, *Jurisprudencia administrativa* (Cali, 1937), Colombian; Rafael Bielsa, *Derecho administrativo y ciencia de administración* (4th ed., 4 vols., Buenos Aires, 1947), Argentine; R. Bullrich, *Curso de derecho administrativo* (Buenos Aires, 1932), Argentine; J. M. Hernández Ron, *Tratado elemental de derecho administrativo venezolano* (Caracas, 1937), Venezuelan; J. E. Malarino, *Tratado de derecho administrativo argentino* (Buenos Aires, 1918), Argentine; L. Mendieta y Núñez, *Administración pública en México* (Mexico, 1942), Mexican; C. Pareja, *Curso de derecho administrativo* (Bogotá, 1939), Colombian; T. E. Tascón, *Derecho constitucional colombiano* (Bogotá, 1934), Colombian; R. Velasco Calvo, *Resumen de derecho administrativo y de ciencia de administración* (Barcelona, 1930), Spanish; A. O. Viveiros de Castro, *Tratado de ciencia da administração e direito administrativo* (Rio de Janeiro, 1914), Brazilian.

[26] Asher N. Christensen (ed.), *The Evolution of Latin American Government* (New York, Holt, 1951), p. 478. The work of R. Pereyra, *Derecho administrativo general y argentino,* was published in Buenos Aires in 1886, and that of Lucio V. López, *Derecho administrativo argentino,* in Buenos Aires in 1902.

tribunal of administrative litigation of three members, having the same qualifications as the members of the supreme court, is a court of "functional autonomy" having jurisdiction of administrative matters in which individuals, private concerns, and public officials may be involved. It encompasses acts of "municipal authorities," the "decentralized services," and the "autonomous entities." It is to be understood that this court judges cases having to do with the application of laws but does not review the laws or adjudge the responsibility of persons. Disputes involving constitutionality are to be decided by the supreme court. The electoral court judges disputed elections—except those of president, vice-president, and members of the congress. It has "corrective, consultative, and economic" supervision over electoral agencies.

In Latin America, there are no systematic codes of administrative law. Nonetheless, there is a vast body of such law, which may be classified, in perhaps an oversimplified manner, as (1) legislation, such as the organic acts, of which the judiciary acts would be an example, and the session laws, of which the budget act would be an example; and (2) *decretos* issued by the executive branch. The decrees of administrative directives are, in theory, derived from a delegation from the constitution or from a legislative act. One encounters in constitutions and in codes the admonition that the executive or his agent might issue a regulation for the "better execution of a statute," "without altering its spirit, purpose and reason." In addition to these chief fountains of administrative law, there are ministerial resolutions, *acuerdos-leyes,* orders, instructions, and ordinances.[27]

Undoubtedly, through the exercise of delegated or assumed powers, expressed in the *decreto* or *reglamento* or some one of the other forms of administrative action, a body of positive administrative law has been assembled in each country. Also, the administrative authorities have been called upon to decide many issues and disputes concerning procedure, authority of administrative officers, and relationship of such officers to

[27] In an old book, the first edition of which was published in 1829, by Baron de Gerando, *Institutes de droit administratif français* (2d ed., 5 vols., Paris, 1842), the attempt is made to assemble the elements of a possible code of administrative law. It is indicated that previous attempts had been made in France to this end, reaching back as far as the time of Louis XIV (vol. 1, p. x). The author warns that administrative legislation by its very essence does not lend itself to true codification and that it is in the nature of such legislation to be adapted to the circumstances of the times in which it was enacted. He did think, however, that existing laws could be collated and classified.

private individuals and groups. This is sometimes called a "jurisdictional power" of the administrative branch. These decisions or *providencias* by administrative organs are usually described as settlements by *vía gubernativa,* i.e., settlements by the same organs as administer the power.[28]

Constitutions may clearly assign to the highest court duties of deciding cases under administrative law having to do with issues that may arise between officials and private persons, and there may be specific grants of power to judge cases concerning contracts, concessions, and the ecclesiastical patronage. In the Venezuelan constitution (1947), Article 220, sections 10 and 12, gives to the court express grant of power to decide administrative litigation.

Defense of the Constitution. In this section the review of legislation and executive acts (decree laws and administrative decrees), regarded as contrary to the constitution, will be considered. This review is predicated on the doctrine of the supremacy of the constitution. This supremacy as a principle is regarded by many Latin Americans "as the cornerstone on which rests the edifice of modern political law."

No uniform practice and no common theory in this important matter have been found. Some countries have the power of judicial review vested officially in the highest court, some grant it to all courts with the supreme court having final decision on appeal, one places this power in a special court, some deny it to the judiciary, and some have constitutions which are silent on the matter. In at least two countries, Guatemala and Peru, the power of review seems to be shared by the congress and the courts. In Ecuador, the basic power to interpret the constitution rests in the congress, although the supreme court has a function to perform. Also the legal effect of a decision that a statute or executive act is unconstitutional varies. It may constitute a nullification. On the other hand, it may be

[28] The term *contencioso administrativo* has the French equivalent of *contentieux administratif.* When referring to jurisdiction, it signifies that judicial instrumentality by which cases are settled which arise from disputes concerned with administration. The term *contencioso,* according to Escriche, is "applied to the judgment which is rendered by a judge concerning rights or things about which contrary parties contest before him." Cf. A. Junco y André, *Derecho procesal civil* (Havana, 1940). In the important work of Eduardo Pallares, *Diccionario de derecho procesal civil* (Mexico, 1952), the term *contencioso administrativo* is defined on p. 111 as follows: "(a)—The jurisdiction which certain organs of the state enjoy of knowing the juridical controversies which arise by reason of the application and execution of the administrative laws; (b)—The process relative to the said jurisdiction or it may be that which takes place in order to decide said controversies."

merely a declaration that the act is inapplicable to a case in question on the ground that it is contrary to the constitution, so that only the case is decided. Some constitutions are silent as to the effect of such a decision.

Undoubtedly much serious thought has been devoted to this subject, considered by many to be a matter of "transcendental" importance. A summary of ideas would include the following:

1. The difference between the constituent power and ordinary legislative powers should not permit the constitution to be altered by statute or administrative decree.

2. If the fundamental law imposes restrictions on governmental organs and authorizes only the exercise of powers delegated to them, acts that are *ultra vires* are invalid.

3. The guarantees and rights in benefit of individuals and groups are limitations upon the encroachment of government, requiring an agency and procedure of enforcement.

Serious attention has been given to the study of historical precedents, ancient and modern, for the exercise of review of legislative and administrative acts with reference to their conformity to the constitution. By way of example, José Manuel Estrada, often regarded as the founder of political science in Argentina, in his teaching referred to the veto powers of the censor and the tribunate of Rome, the role of the *parlement* in the ancient monarchy of France, the institution of the *gran justicia* or *justicia mayor* of Aragon, and the system of judicial review in the United States.[29] Others have studied the various attempts made during the French Revolution to establish a kind of "constitutional jury," the *sénat conservateur* of the Napoleonic period, the decision of the Spanish constitution of 1812 to vest the power of review in the Cortes, the Mexican *supremo poder conservador* of 1836, the plan of the Austrian constitution of 1920, and that of the Spanish constitution of 1931. From these precedents, the agencies were reduced to (1) review by the judicial power; (2) review by a political branch, especially the legislature; (3) review by a combination of the political and judicial branches; and (4) review by a "distinct entity," created for the purpose.

Countries having the federal system have especially felt the need for an agency and jurisprudence of review. A variety of constitutional issues is occasioned by that form of government. There are powers that are delegated to the federal government and are only to be exercised by it,

[29] *Curso de derecho constitucional* (2d ed., Buenos Aires, 1927), vol. III, pp. 316–317.

powers reserved to the states or provinces, powers that are concurrent, powers prohibited to the federal government, powers prohibited to the local governments, and powers prohibited to both state and federal governments.[30]

The principle of the supremacy of the constitution as the "law of laws," to use Alberdi's phrase, is affirmed by a large majority of Latin-American states. The constitutions or laws of 15 states—Argentina, Bolivia, Brazil, Chile, Colombia, Cuba, El Salvador, Guatemala, Haiti, Honduras, Mexico, Nicaragua, Panama, Uruguay, and Venezuela—confer some power of review on some court or courts. A small group of countries confers the power of review on the congress. Cuba has established an "entity," but in fact this entity is an especially created branch of the supreme court.

In the remaining part of this section, some examples of the differences in principle and practice will be given.

In Brazil, Colombia, Costa Rica, Cuba, Panama, and Venezuela, a decision by the court of final jurisdiction that a legislative act or the administrative decree is unconstitutional renders the act or decree in whole or in the part affected null and without further effect. In Chile, Guatemala, Honduras, Uruguay, and presumptively in Argentina and Mexico such a decision has legal effect only in the concrete case to which the decision is directed.

Uruguay is an instance of recent change in practice in this matter of review. The constitutions of 1830 and 1917 had vested the power of interpreting and construing the constitution in the legislative branch. The instrument of 1934 authorized the supreme court to judge all cases of violation without exception.

In Mexico, the "defense of the constitution" has had a long history and a distinctive development. Although granted a constitutional function as to safeguarding the federal system, this power has had little influence in preventing a progressive centralization. Judicial review has not been effectually active in issues concerning the expansion of powers by legislative and executive organs or in those of conflicts between them. The notable exercise of functions of defense has been against abuse of governmental power with reference to rights guaranteed by the constitution to individuals and groups. The process involved is popularly known as the *juicio de amparo,* established initially in the Acta de Reformas (1847), incorporated in the constitution of 1857, and amplified in that of 1917.

[30] Cf. González Calderón, *op. cit.,* vol. I, pp. 424–425.

There have been many thousands of appeals for the writ of *amparo,*[31] and the judgment of *amparo* is known as the "most noble" aspect of Mexican law. As a protection against an abuse of power, involving the claim that the act or decree authorizing the abuse was contrary to the constitution, the *amparo* or protection granted was, according to the interpretation of the famous Justice Vallarta, a protection against the application of a law, not an action against the law itself. Efforts have been made to expand the scope of the *amparo,* and some progress in this direction has been made. But an "*amparo* against laws" (*amparo contra leyes*) is still a subject of controversy.[32]

Mexico has a limited form of judicial review, with important differences from that of the United States. Many Mexican writers, while admitting the limitations of their form, have claimed the merit that under it the court may not "undesirably" interfere in politics or exercise legislative powers.[33]

The Cuban idea of the "defense of the constitution" is predicated upon the principle of the supremacy of the constitution and is noteworthy because of the creation (1940) of a "distinct entity," called the *tribunal de garantías constitucionales y sociales,* as the agency of defense. This device may have been inspired, as some think, by the Austrian constitution of 1920, although the positive imitation is slight. The "distinct entity," after all, is a *sala* or chamber of the supreme court.[34] This chamber, composed for purposes of considering issues of constitutionality of fifteen justices, was to entertain requests for judgments from either public or private sources. The Cuban system of judicial review is one of the most comprehensive in scope, and it will doubtless be watched with interest to ascertain its effectiveness.

Criticism of the Courts. A chief criticism by foreign observers, perhaps, is the assumed weakness of the judicial as compared with the executive

[31] The number of such cases increased so as to cause a congestion of the docket and was the subject of recurrent reports of the court. In 1950, the residue of undecided cases of this kind amounted to 37,881. To expedite action, amendments were adopted in 1950, known as the Reforma Miguel Alemán. Cf. R. León Orantes, *El juicio de amparo* (Mexico, 1951), p. 94.

[32] Cf. Emilio Rabasa, *El juicio constitucional* (Mexico, 1906), and María del Carmen Hernández Ramírez, *Amparo contra leyes* (Mexico, 1954). The trend in recent years seems to be against strict adherence to the Vallarta thesis.

[33] Tena Ramírez, *op. cit.,* p. 413.

[34] J. Garcerán de Vall, *El proceso de inconstitucionalidad* (Havana, 1947); Ramón Infiesta, *Derecho constitucional* (Havana, 1950); Andrés M. Lazcano y Mazón, *Ley del tribunal de garantías constitucionales y sociales* (Havana, 1949).

power. To the citizen, the main criticisms would probably be the slowness in the administration of justice, the prevalence of written as against oral procedure, and the expensiveness of the process of administration.

1. The judgment that the courts are relatively weak depends, of course, upon the factors admitted to the appraisal. Those who would wish the judicial power to act effectively as a curb on the executive branch may seek to make the courts a political check without giving them political power—which means in final analysis control of political patronage, command of the army, and leadership in the dominant political party. Such an investment of courts with political power would be impractical and futile, if tried. If the courts are to be truly independent as a separate organ, if they are not to meddle in partisan politics, and if they are not as courts to judge "political" questions, they are not—as a matter of strict fairness—to be expected to be a political curb on the executive. This charge of weakness would be valid if the courts were constitutionally commissioned to guard the organic law against violations by legislative and executive branches and, having that power, failed to exercise it when cases involving infractions occurred. It must be kept in mind, furthermore, that constitutions have been changed with frequency and ease in some countries, and that executive supremacy and dictatorship may easily be legalized. If constitutional guarantees may be legally suspended and if states of siege, "emergency," "urgency," and "alarm" may be legally declared—with acts committed which are not in all cases subject to judicial review—it is not in logic fair to blame the courts. The issue rather is whether courts, as courts of law, judge cases independently and according to law. Here, too, opinions differ, but opinion favorable to Latin-American courts in some countries can be found. Perhaps the greater weight of opinion would be that they are weak.

Have the courts been slow and even timid in the exercise of powers in cases involving the jurisdictional spheres of other branches—especially the executive? Perhaps an apposite inquiry would be the role of the supreme court of Argentina in the matter of federal intervention in the provinces. This power as exercised by the executive, with or without the assent of the congress, since 1853, has been developed with a frequency of use and a diversity in practice as to signify an expansion of scope beyond that justified by the text of the constitution or by what is known of the intent of the framers. The court, by reason of its own conviction and by use of both commentary and judicial opinion offered in cases before the supreme court of the United States, has held this to be a strictly political question, to be settled by the political branches of government. The Argentine executive, with the acquiescence of the congress, has exceeded the constitutional grant of power in this matter, and the court has adhered to a strict construction of its own legal competency.

It has been charged that the courts have been unduly slow to suggest and to lead in movements for the reform of the legal system and for the revision of codes. This charge may to many observers and students of history seem warranted. At the same time, it should be said that in such fields as criminal law, administrative law, labor and social law, courts as well as commentators have made noteworthy contributions to what were regarded as reform movements.

The study of judicial review will indicate that in some countries courts have actively exercised this high power.

It should be kept in mind that Latin-American courts may be confronted with such complex situations as those caused by revolutions and *de facto* or provisional governments, and they may be the only enduring institution while those extraordinary events and extralegal developments are in process. There might be—and has been—the co-existence of a *de facto* executive and a legal judiciary. The legalization of some acts of a *de facto* government may necessarily occur while a revolution is in progress or in its aftermath. If a revolution is successful, it is inevitable that at least a partial legalization will ensue when stabilization of authority is effected. If the revolution is a failure, legal adjustments may still be made. In neither case is the lot of the judiciary easy and strong, however useful.[35]

In some countries, the judiciary and especially the supreme court have been involved in factional political contests. In Panama, for a part of the period of President Arnulfo Arias, the supreme court was suspended. In that country, while police chief Remón was rising to ascendancy, the court was made a pawn in this political movement. In Guatemala, twice within the last decade actions occurred which demonstrated weakness in the status of the courts. By provisions of the current constitution members of the supreme court and some of the lower courts are elected and are removable by the congress. In 1945, at the beginning of the Arévalo administration, three members of the supreme court were ousted by the congress on grounds of an improper grant of *amparo*. This act occasioned no significant

[35] Cf. R. F. Vázquez, *La corte suprema; su función política* (Buenos Aires, 1946); Segundo V. Linares Quintana, "La Théorie des gouvernements de fait dans la jurisprudence de la Cour Supreme de Justice de la Republique Argentine," *Revue de droit public,* vol. 65, p. 52.

protest. In 1953, the entire membership of the supreme court was dismissed by the congress, following an *amparo* proceeding which involved the application of the new agrarian reform law. In the latter case, the incident led to a strike of lawyers and notaries, a popular riot, and an informal reaffirmation of the principle of the independence of the courts.[36] Despite this support, the status of the courts was considered as insecure.

2. The delays in the judicial process form a very common subject of complaint. It should be remarked that the slowness of some "perpetual" civil cases may be due to the collusion of parties that such cases may be protracted over ten or more years by postponements that are sought and obtained by interested parties. But the charge in its most justifiable and substantial part relates to slowness in the operation of the system itself. The claim is sometimes made that some Spanish American countries have adhered to rules of procedure established by colonial precedents, although Spain may have itself abandoned them.

3. The demand for a change from written presentation of the "book of evidence" to what is called "oral justice" is frequent and strongly supported. Public hearings of witnesses and public presentation of argument by lawyers, it is claimed, would lend greater responsibility to the judicial process, as well as cause greater expedition and less expense.

4. Although comparative studies of the expense of litigation as between such costs in Latin America and elsewhere are lacking, a very common assumption is made that the administration of justice is unduly expensive in these countries. Reference is often made to the fact that in the system of "written justice," the "book of evidence" must be written on stamped, official paper, the costs of which are no small item when such a "book" may run to several thousand pages. It should be said that provision is made whereby the interests of the indigent may be protected at the public expense.

BIBLIOGRAPHY

Aragón, A., *Jurisprudencia administrativa,* Cali, 1937.

Bielsa, Rafael, *Derecho administrativo y ciencia de administración,* 4th ed., 4 vols., Buenos Aires, 1947.

———, *La protección constitucional y el recurso extraordinario,* Buenos Aires, 1936.

Bisán, R., *Derecho constitucional argentino y comparado,* Buenos Aires, 1940.

[36] K. H. Silvert, *A Study in Government: Guatemala* (New Orleans, 1954), p. 46.

Blanksten, George I., *Ecuador: Constitutions and Caudillos,* Berkeley, Calif., University of California Press, 1951.

Cara Escobedo, R., *Los sistemas de defensa de la constitución en el derecho mexicano,* Mexico, 1945.

Clagett, Helen L., *The Administration of Justice in Latin America,* New York, Oceana Publications, 1952.

Franca, G. da, *O poder judiciario no Brasil,* Rio de Janeiro, 1931.

Garcerán de Val, Julio, *El proceso de inconstitucionalidad,* Havana, 1947.

González Calderón, Juan A., *Derecho constitucional argentino,* 2d ed., 3 vols., Buenos Aires, 1923.

Grant, J. A. C., "Judicial Control of Constitutionality of Statutes and Administrative Legislation in Colombia," *Southern California Law Review,* February, 1948.

Hernández Ron, J. M., *La nacionalización de la justicia en Venezuela,* Caracas, 1944.

———, *Tratado elemental de derecho administrativo venezolano,* Caracas, 1937.

Infiesta, Ramón, *Derecho constitucional,* Havana, 1950.

James, Herman G., *The Constitutional System of Brazil,* Washington, D.C., Carnegie Institution, 1923.

Lazcano y Mazón, Andrés M., *La justicia y su administración,* Havana, 1947.

———, *Ley del tribunal de garantías constitucionales y sociales,* Havana, 1949.

León Orantes, R., *El juicio de amparo,* Mexico, 1951.

Lessa, Pedro, *Direito constitucional brasileiro: do poder judiciario,* Rio de Janeiro, 1915.

Macdonald, Austin F., *Government of the Argentine Republic,* New York, Crowell, 1942.

Montagú y Vivero, G. de, "Judicial Organization in Cuba," *Journal of the American Judicature Society,* April, 1949.

Pinto Ferreira, *Princípios gerais do direito constitucional moderno,* 2d ed., 3 vols., Rio de Janeiro, 1951.

Sampaio Doria, A. de, *Direito constitucional,* 3d ed., 2 vols., São Paulo, 1953.

Sarmiento, A., *Organización judicial ecuatoriana,* Quito, 1946.

Tascón, T. E., *Derecho constitucional colombiano,* Bogotá, 1934.

Troncoso Rojas, G., *Organización de los tribunales chilenos,* Concepción, 1949.

Wolff, Ernesto, *Tratado de derecho constitucional venezolano,* 2 vols., Caracas, 1945.

Zeledón, Marco Tulio, *El recurso de inconstitucionalidad,* San José (Costa Rica), 1948.

Chapter 12: LOCAL GOVERNMENT—PROVINCIAL AND MUNICIPAL

The general features of the federal and unitary systems of Latin-American countries as they relate to internal organization have been treated elsewhere. It should be recalled that in the interpretation of the colonial system, especially that of the Spanish empire, emphasis was placed upon the operation of a scheme of checks and balances designed to prevent abuse of power and upon those policies and instructions respecting deviations from pattern and practice which were framed because of the recognition of local conditions, interests, and customs. Much importance was attached to the institutions of municipal government, with the *cabildo* on occasion acting as an agency of petition and protest in representation of local interests. Although the *cabildo* suffered decadence during the later period of the empire, especially in some regions of the Viceroyalty of New Spain, its history and traditions are factors to consider in modern problems of municipal government. It has been pointed out that these several features of the colonial heritage underwent changes during the struggles for independence and thereafter.

In spite of constitutional principles and theoretical implications, federalism in Latin America has not meant decentralization in fact, and the adoption of the unitary system has not always signified excessive central control. Although many proposals have been made by political parties and by individuals in favor of local self-government and although some of them have been placed at least temporarily in operation, the trend in the main has been toward centralization under both systems.

All countries have schemes of the territorial distribution of power, both political and administrative. With the latter—"zones" or "districts" for the administration of judicial, military, fiscal, postal, educational, and statistical services—we shall not here deal. It is with the political units of local government, provincial and urban, that this chapter is concerned. Both these divisions of local government are the subjects of constitutional provisions and of legislation by statute. Of the latter, there are legislative acts known as "organic laws" for the government and administration of provinces and cities respectively. There is considerable literature on local government, including some studies of the principles and practices adopted by foreign countries. Quite commonly, an acknowledgment is made of the pronounced influence of French ideas of local government in Latin America.

Provincial Government

It is often held, especially in countries having the unitary system, that the provinces are artificial institutions, serving as political and administrative agencies of the central government rather than as agencies which represent local interests. Questions about the usefulness of provinces have been raised, as in the convention which framed the Cuban constitution of 1940. The cynical opinion has been expressed that the reason for the continuation of "provinces" or "departments" or the federal "states" is that they provide offices for politicians and staff positions in the civil service. Also, the opinion has been expressed, with no little justification, that the governor or the intendant who is allowed to pursue an independent contructive course is one who is being groomed by the central administration for succession to the presidency of the country. Further, the governor who develops a line of policy without the approval of the central authorities may be establishing the bases for an opposition campaign or a later revolution. Both these lines of conduct are unusual and cannot be thought in accord with the character of the office. These are some of the considerations which cause the treatment of the "province" to be legalistic.

The Federal Countries. Since the constitutional issues have been considered we shall limit the present section to a treatment of institutional structures. Brazil, Mexico, and Venezuela have "states" as the chief unit of local government; Argentina has "provinces." The principal executive official has been called either "governor" or "president." In Argentina Brazil, and Mexico this functionary is popularly elected, although in a few cases this election is indirect. In Venezuela, during the past several decades, the local executive has been appointed by the president of the republic. Usually the elective governors are ineligible for immediate reelection. All the federal countries have for the local units popularly chosen legislatures, authorized to enact measures according to the limitations found in the general and local constitutions. Under the Venezuelan constitution of 1947, state legislatures could by a two-thirds vote remove the governor. There was also the interesting provision (Article 128) that the control of the state administration belonged to the assembly. On the

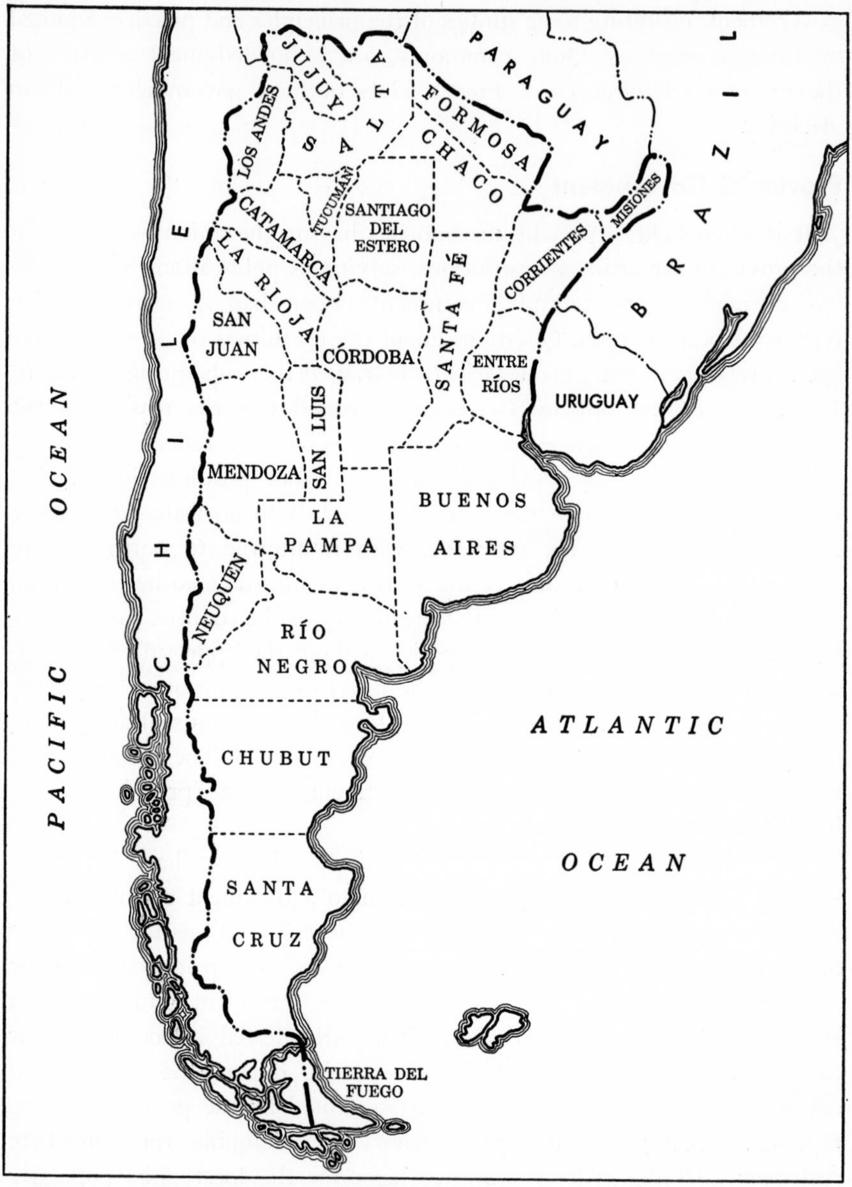

Figure 11. Political divisions of Argentina. SOURCE: A. C. Wilgus, *The Development of Hispanic America,* p. 361. Copyright 1941 by A. Curtis Wilgus. Reproduced by permission of the publishers, Rinehart & Company, Inc.

TABLE 14
PROVINCIAL ADMINISTRATION

Country and chief local unit	Legislative and judicial organs	Executive department
	I. The Federal Countries	
Argentina: provinces	Elective assemblies of either bicameral or unicameral organization; provincial system of courts	Governors popularly elected, but subject to deposition through federal intervention
Brazil: states	Elective legislatures of either bicameral or unicameral organization; separate system of state courts	Governors popularly elected, but states subject to federal intervention
Mexico: states	Elective legislatures of unicameral organization and limitations of reeligibility for membership; separate system of courts	Governors popularly elected; states subject to modified form of intervention by federal authority
Venezuela: states	Elective assemblies	Governors appointed by the president of the country and are his agents
	II. The Unitary Countries	
Bolivia: departments	No elective council	Prefects, subprefects, and corregidors—all appointive
Chile: provinces	Provincial assembly elected by municipalities	Intendants, governors, subdelegates, and inspectors—appointive
Colombia: provinces	Assemblies popularly elected	Governors appointed by the president
Costa Rica: provinces	No legislative bodies	Governors appointed by the president
Cuba: provinces	Provincial council composed of city mayors, ex officio	Elective governors
Dominican Republic: provinces	No legislative bodies	Governors appointed by the president
Ecuador: provinces	Popularly elected assemblies	Governors appointed by the president
El Salvador: departments	No legislative bodies	Governors appointed by the president
Guatemala: departments	No legislative bodies	Governors appointed by the president

TABLE 14 (*Continued*)

Country and chief local unit	Legislative and judicial organs	Executive department
Haiti: departments	An appointive council	Prefects appointed by the president
Honduras: departments	An appointive council	Governors appointed by the president
Nicaragua: departments	No legislative bodies	*Jefes politicos* appointed by the president
Panama: provinces	No legislative bodies	Governors appointed by the president
Paraguay: departments	No legislative bodies	*Delegados* appointed by the president
Peru: departments	Popularly elected councils	Prefects appointed by the president
Uruguay: departments	Departmental boards popularly elected	Plural executive which is elected

other hand, the governor was declared to be the agent of the "national power." These provisions were omitted from the constitution of 1953. In the other countries, the central government exercises a controlling influence through the power of intervention, the suspension of guarantees, the expansion of implied powers, and the grant or withholding of federal subsidies.

The police forces are usually divided into federal, provincial or state, and municipal units. The coordination of these several branches may be the responsibility of a board or junta, as at present in Argentina. Although the use of the federal police may be questioned as to constitutionality, it is in fact the most important in power and rank in a number of countries, as in Argentina.

Territorial Government. In all cases territorial governments are subject to a high degree of centralized control. The appointive governor, as exemplified in Argentina, is responsible to and removable by the president. Despite the provision in Argentina by an act of 1884 for a territorial legislature and for partial self-government, and despite the fact that several territories qualified in terms of population and economic resources for provincial status, these benefits were not granted. Two territories were erected into "provinces" by the Perón administration. The opinion has been expressed that the central government has been tenacious in keeping

Figure 12. Political divisions of Mexico. SOURCE: A. C. Wilgus, *Latin America in Maps*, New York, Barnes and Noble, p. 230.

entire control of territorial affairs in its own hands.[1] Unlike the federal districts, the territories have no voice in the election of president and vice-president. Administratively, "the territories are completely dependent on the federal government."[2]

In Mexico, under present theory and practice, the federal congress and the president of the republic are respectively the legislatures and the executive of the federal district and the territories. The federal judiciary serves as judiciary of the territories.[3] A chief difference is that the territories are not represented in the senate. The territories, which are three in number, are administered by governors, appointed by the president and subject to removal by him. The local divisions of the territory are called "delegations," administered by *delegados*. There is a consultative council, composed of at least seven members.[4] In addition to the territories Venezuela has the "federal dependencies" for the administration of several small islands located off shore in the Caribbean Sea.

The Unitary Countries. This type of internal organization has continued to be the choice of a majority of states. Ultimately, sixteen countries adopted this form. Despite the existence in many of these states of real geographical and political sectionalism or regionalism, centralization in government has been the prevailing fact, although the degree of it has varied. Has this trend resulted in a political system which has become top-heavy or indifferent to the interests of locality? The answer in general would be affirmative. Some developments, looking to a limitation upon centralization, may be noted. Some unitary countries have adopted constitutional statements of principle in favor of provincial and municipal home rule. A greater degree of governmental autonomy for provinces and cities has been promised in Chile, although this pledge has not been redeemed. Perhaps the most significant modifications in centralized government as actually practiced are to be found in Cuba and Uruguay, wherein it might be justly claimed that more local autonomy obtains than

[1] Austin F. Macdonald, *Government of the Argentine Republic* (New York, Crowell, 1942), p. 370.

[2] Segundo V. Linares Quintana, "Algunas cuestiones de derecho público de los territorios nacionales," *Boletín de la Biblioteca del Congreso Nacional,* March–April, 1936.

[3] There is a *ley orgánica del distrito y territorios federales.* The basic law was adopted in 1928. The changes made in 1941 related to the federal district.

[4] See Lucio Mendieta y Núñez, *La administración pública en México* (Mexico, 1942), pp. 141–147; Felipe Tena Ramírez, *Derecho constitucional mexicano* (2d ed., Mexico, 1949), pp. 267–268; and Daniel A. Moreno, *El distrito federal* (Mexico, 1944).

Figure 13. Political divisions of Uruguay. SOURCE: A. C. Wilgus, *The Development of Hispanic America,* p. 444. Copyright 1941 by A. Curtis Wilgus. Reproduced by permission of the publishers, Rinehart & Company, Inc.

in the federal states. As yet, however, for some countries political instability induces authoritarian government, and authoritarian government entrenches itself in power through centralization.

Local government in the unitary countries has been complicated in structure and diversified in terminology. The designations of the largest unit of local government vary. Bolivia, Colombia, El Salvador, Guatemala, Haiti, Honduras, Nicaragua, Paraguay, Peru, and Uruguay have "departments"; whereas the others have "provinces." Some confusion is caused by the fact that some countries have both. Chile has "departments," within provinces; Bolivia and Peru have "provinces" within departments. For the chief administrative agent of the largest unit of local government Chile has the title of "intendant"; Bolivia, Haiti, and Peru have "prefect"; Paraguay has "delegate" (*delegado*); and Nicaragua has *"jefe político."* All others except Uruguay use the title of "governor." In Cuba and Uruguay the local executives are elective, with Uruguay having a collegiate executive. In all other unitary countries this principal officer is appointed by the central authority. In some countries there is a deliberative or advisory body associated with the provincial governor; and in Cuba, Chile, Colombia, Ecuador, Honduras, and Uruguay this council or assembly is elective. In Cuba, the provincial assembly is made up of the popularly elected alcaldes of the cities, sitting ex officio; in Chile, the municipal councils elect the representatives. In the others mentioned, the elections are by direct popular vote.

The main patterns of local administration in the unitary states are two: the "simple," in which there are provinces, districts or cantons, and parishes; and the "complex," in which there are provinces, departments, subdelegations, districts, and parishes. Another scheme may have departments, provinces, districts, cantons, and parishes as units. Peru, Bolivia, and Chile may be classified as "complex."

The provincial governments of Cuba and Uruguay enjoy a large degree of autonomy. The governor in Cuba is popularly elected and serves independently a term of four years. Subject to the limitations of the constitution, the treaties, and the laws of the country, the provincial council with approval of the governor may legislate with reference to local affairs. New taxes must be ratified in referendum by the people. In the constitutional convention of 1940, the opinion was expressed that the provincial council did not serve the interests attributed to it and that it might well be abolished as an institution, but this opinion did not prevail. In Ecuador and Honduras—and in at least a practical and traditional sense in Colombia—a lesser degree of autonomy obtains.

The plan of departmental government in Uruguay under the constitution of 1951 calls for a board or legislative body composed of sixty-five members for Montevideo and thirty-one for other departments, who hold office for four years. A council (*consejo departamental*) composed of seven members for Montevideo and five for the other departments is the executive and administrative branch. Both are to be chosen in popular election under a scheme of proportional representation. The council mem-

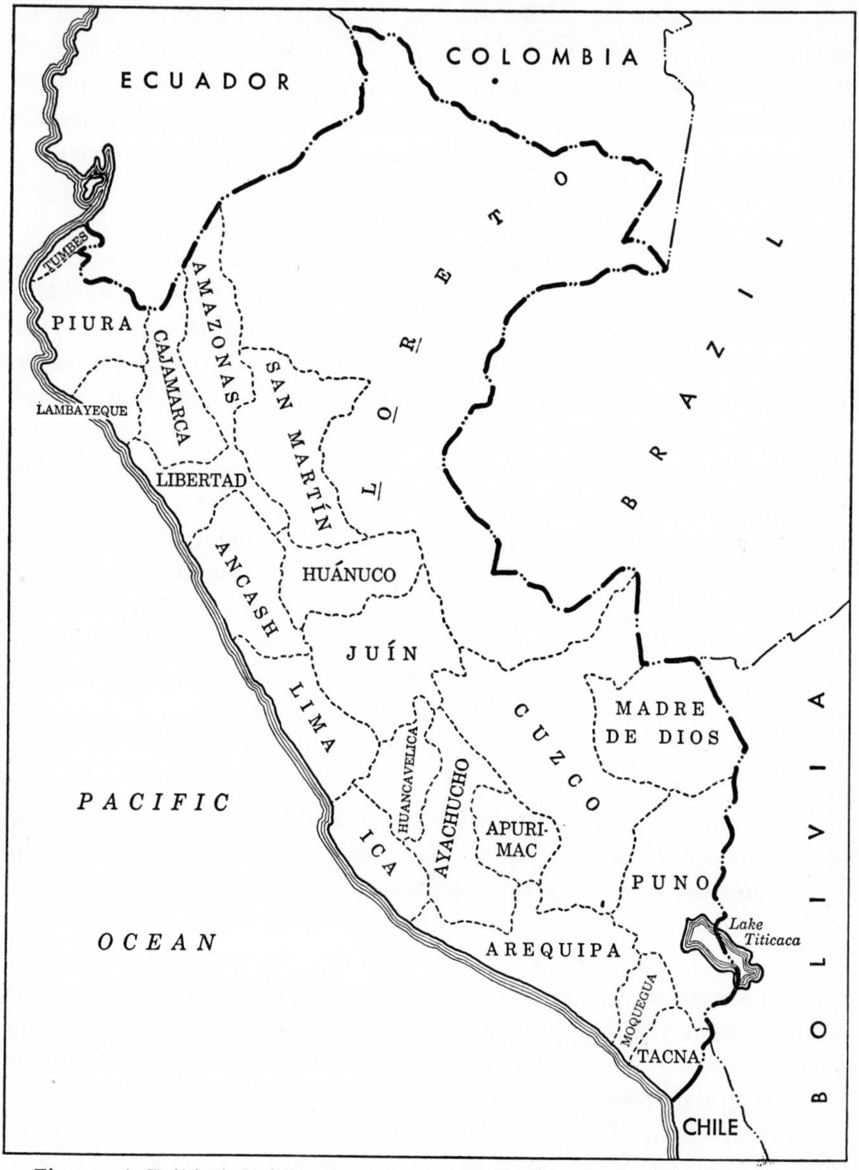

Figure 14. Political divisions of Peru. SOURCE: A. C. Wilgus, *Latin America in Maps,* New York, Barnes and Noble, p. 244.

bers are chosen for four years and may be reelected only once. Included in the legislative powers of the board are those relative to budgetary, taxation, and disciplinary matters. The council or the board may institute suit before the supreme court for any injury to the autonomy of the department. Councilors, but not members of the board, receive remuneration for service. The constitution contemplates the extension of the rights of initiative and referendum to the departments.

In Peru, there is a strong tradition of political centralization; at the same time there is awareness and much consideration of the geographical, cultural, economic, and historical regionalism within the country. The idea attributed to Cecilio Acosta of Venezuela that South America was in need of "political centralization and administrative decentralization" has appealed to some Peruvian thinkers. Several experiments with one or another form of decentralization have been made. One such experiment was with regional congresses, allowing one each for the northern, the middle, and the southern parts. This plan lasted from 1920 to 1931. In the opinion of many writers, it was ineffectual and wrongly conceived.[5] Departmental councils to be elected for terms of four years were authorized by the constitution of 1933 and subsequently provided for by law but were never established.

The Cities

The struggles for independence and the accompanying and ensuing developments of dictatorial and centralized governments destroyed or seriously weakened the town councils or *cabildos.* In the province of Buenos Aires, for example, this institution was abolished by acts of 1820 and 1824. In countries where military necessity of unified administration and command as a needful requirement of fighting a successful war against Spain could not be urged, political interests in centralization brought about this loss of municipal home rule. It was the opinion of Alberdi that the new republics misled by the example of France had unfortunately committed the error of suppressing the *cabildos.* He wrote with reference to Argentina:[6]

[5] J. Pareja Paz-Soldán, *Derecho constitucional peruano* (Lima, 1951), pp. 338–339.

[6] Juan Bautista Alberdi, *Derecho público provincial argentino* (Buenos Aires), part 1, chap. 4.

In the name of the sovereignty of the people, the people were deprived of the ancient power of administering their civil and economic affairs. Out of the old Spanish *cabildo* had been born, May 25, 1810, the republican government of Argentina; but in a few years this government devoured the author of its existence. The parricide was punished with the penalty of a requital, since republican liberty perished at the hands of political despotism, that liberty being without the counterweight of the municipal liberty which opposed tyranny.

Although the Argentine constitution of 1853, under inspiration of Alberdi, sought to assure municipal autonomy and in Article 5 imposed on the provinces the obligation of maintaining a municipal system, as one of the conditions upon which provincial government would be guaranteed by the federal authority, this principle was at best observed in the letter rather than the spirit.[7] Provincial constitutions in general—and the same was true of periods of federal intervention in the provinces—vested the power of naming the *intendentes* or mayors in the governors and restricted the activities and jurisdiction of municipalities to matters of mere administration. It should be said that under the act of 1917 the *intendente* of the federal capital is named by the president, subject to the approval of the senate. It is true that the council of Buenos Aires is popularly elected with use of a scheme of proportional representation.

Despite the political losses suffered by centralizing trends, the cities of Latin America continued to have large territorial areas under their jurisdiction, and some have had their boundaries extended. Many cities have considerable rural territory within their boundaries, some of which is sparsely populated. Such cities have rural problems as well as urban to resolve.

In the second half of the nineteenth century and later, a growing literature appeared in favor of greater municipal autonomy. The ideal of the free city—i.e., the city with a sphere of autonomy and the right through popular election to choose its own officials—was frequently urged. One fruit of this agitation was for municipal government to receive constitutional recognition, as in the Brazilian constitution of 1891. These provisions, however, were contingent upon the adoption by the congress of supporting and implementing legislation. The fact that now all constitutions, federal as well as unitary, have articles dealing with municipal government is indicative of the significance attached to the subject. In

[7] Rafael Bielsa, *Principios del régimen municipal* (Buenos Aires, 1930), pp. 48–60.

seventeen countries the town councils are popularly elected; in nine the chief administrative officials of the city are elected; and in seven the degree of autonomy is supposed to be large.[8]

There was held in Havana in 1940 the first Pan-American Congress of Municipalities, which adopted two resolutions of importance. One declared

> the necessity that in the constitutions of America the city should be recognized as one of the organs of the sovereignty of the people or of the Nation, to the end that the municipal institution should be consolidated and developed, serving at the same time the general structure of the state as a means of greater cohesion and unity.

The second was in favor of

> assuring constitutionally the principle of municipal autonomy, guaranteeing in a special way the election of the city's governing officials, the free collection and appropriation of the city's revenues within its own administrative and financial sphere, and jurisdictional control of its decisions made within its powers and the right of initiative and action in all that is relative to the satisfaction of local needs of a public nature.

Many writers have opposed municipal home rule, although recognizing many new problems of "urbanism"—such as the growth in population, the effects of industrialization, and the need for expert services in the management and operation of the new public utilities. They have been unwilling to go farther than to favor administrative decentralization. They opposed political autonomy, holding that in the cities politics turned upon national rather than local issues, that it was common for the *caudillo* to be a factor in municipal politics, that corruption in elections as well as in administrative practice was frequent, and that elective city officials were all too often unqualified and inefficient. This opposition and the interests in favor of centralization have prevailed in a majority of the countries, with the result that such decentralization as has been permitted has been administrative rather than political. Instruction in the history of municipalities and in the law governing cities has been offered in the universities but is as yet inadequate.[9]

[8] The countries granting a "large" degree of autonomy are Bolivia, Brazil, Costa Rica, Ecuador, Panama, Uruguay, and Venezuela. See Miguel Jorrín, *Governments of Latin America* (New York, Van Nostrand, 1953), pp. 160–161.

[9] There have been many advocates of better education in municipal affairs, such as Francisco Carrera y Jústiz in Cuba and Rafael Bielsa in Argentina.

A leading advocate of municipal home rule was the scholarly, liberal, and austere statesman Lisandro de la Torre, of Argentina. Throughout his career this citizen of Rosario, in the province of Santa Fe, urged reform in city government, despite persistent indifference or opposition in his country. Finally his ideas resulted in action taken by his own province. The much-debated provincial constitution of 1921, of doubtful legality as to its adoption, provided for the organization of cities into three classes, one of which should have the right to determine its form of government and to choose its officials. This experiment was short-lived, being abolished during an intervention by the federal government.

In recent times the prodigious growth of some cities has given rise to many perplexing problems and graver realization of what is called "urbanism." Health and sanitation, the water supply and its purification, housing and city planning, beautification and recreation, crime and vice are receiving increasing attention. The small towns and villages, long neglected, are in line for consideration. Villages of Indians, many preserving aboriginal forms and traditions, have in some countries received formal recognition.

The revival of interest in municipal autonomy, reflected in many constitutions and constituent or legislative bodies, may be indicative of a new trend. However this may be, all too often the municipal executive—*intendente* or *jefe político* or alcalde or other—is an agent of the central government in unitary states. Where this is not true in federal governments, he is likely to be the representative of the state or provincial governor.

In Colombia, despite the shift to the unitary form of organization in 1886, the departments were given important functions and several attributes of autonomy. Among the powers of the departmental assembly was that of erecting new municipalities and determining city boundaries. Cities were to have councils, but their acts were subject to review by the governor on the ground of illegality. These councils have significant powers of local legislation. The towns have alcaldes or mayors, appointed by the governors, having the double character of agent of the governor and of the people. In the amendment of 1945, the mayor's role as agent of the governor was retained, but in addition he became "chief of municipal administration."

In Cuba, a municipality is defined as a "local society politically organized by authority of the Legislative power in a territorial area determined by necessary relations of the neighborhood, on a basis of economic capacity to satisfy the expenses of self government and with juridical personality for all legal effects" (Article 209). It is declared that the municipality is autonomous, invested "with all powers necessary to resolve freely the affairs of local society." Among the special powers granted under the general law are those of owning and operating public services, making public improvements, and of making interurban agreements of cooperation. Among the guarantees are that municipal officers may not be suspended by the president or the governor; that such officers may be deprived of office only by judicial process; that the official acts and resolutions of alcaldes and municipal commissions may be impugned by political authorities only after judicial decision; that municipal funds may not be diverted for provincial or national purposes; and that cities may plead before the supreme court against abuse of power by the national government or the provincial government, alleging violation of municipal guarantees (*recurso de abuso del poder*). There are also guarantees to inhabitants of cities against abuse of power by the municipal government, including the device of recall of officials by local electors. The city may with approval adopt its own charter, providing for one of three systems of local government: the commission form, or the council (*ayuntamiento*) and manager (*gerente*), or the council and mayor (alcalde). In the case of a council and a manager, the office of manager is filled by the council after competitive examination. The examination of persons for the position of town manager is before a body composed of a university professor of municipal government, a public accountant named by the provincial school of commerce, a university professor of administrative law, and two representatives of the town council. An interesting clause of the constitution (1940) provides that a candidate for mayor may not have been in the active service of the armed forces of the republic within two years immediately preceding the election. The metropolitan district of Havana, according to law, offers the possibility of a federation of towns. Although the Cuban congress never passed the enabling legislation putting into operation the clauses relating to the commission form and the plan regarding the town manager, a law did provide for municipal elections to occur at a different time from those for national elections.

In Honduras the constitution provides for a system of municipal government "absolutely independent of other powers," provided that in no case the general laws of the country are violated and provided that local officials are responsible to the courts for any abuse of powers. There is retention of old titles of officials—alcalde, *síndico, regidor*—and of the ancient idea of the municipality as a district of somewhat extended territory rather than a center of population solely. The officials, mayor, councilmen, and the legal representative (*síndico*) serve without salaries, but all are elective. The guarantee of autonomy is sustained in the general law of municipal government, and the cities are active in a wide sphere of local affairs. There are in practice, however, limitations on this autonomy. The superiority of general laws, the requirement in many cases of the approval of the departmental council, the grant of financial assistance with conditions, the requirement that cities petition the congress or the ministry of *gobernación* for permission to act, and the issuance by the central government of many orders or directives restrict the power of cities. Although the importance of municipalities seems to be increasing, centralization of power seems also to be growing. There is not the tradition of municipal independence, and the term of one year—without eligibility of reelection —is too short for such a tradition to be fostered. There are instances of action by the central government because of default on part of the cities which failed to act.[10]

Ecuador is a case of thoroughgoing centralization in a unitary state, but there is a municipal autonomy which "has been a major factor in the history, government, and politics of the republic."[11] To regard the situation as a sort of dualism would be justified if one considers the influence of Quito and Guayaquil in politics and their initiative in local affairs as compared with other cities.

In Panama a much greater degree of autonomy is in law and fact vested in municipalities. Not only are the mayors and the councils or commissions elective, but towns have a voice in the choice of forms of their respective governments. The people may appeal to the devices of initiative and referendum in matters within municipal jurisdiction.

Venezuela, under constitutional guarantee, vests the authority of its cities in the municipal council, which is popularly elected for a term of three years. It chooses the executive officers, and exercises powers under the federal constitution.

In El Salvador, Guatemala, Brazil, Mexico, and Costa Rica the mayors —or those having titles corresponding to that of mayor—and the councils are popularly elected. In Bolivia the mayor is appointed by the president from a list of names submitted by the municipality. In Nicaragua and

[10] William S. Stokes, *Honduras: An Area Study in Government* (Madison, Wis., University of Wisconsin Press, 1950), pp. 151–173.

[11] George I. Blanksten, *Ecuador, Constitutions and Caudillos* (Berkeley, Calif., University of California Press, 1951).

Paraguay all municipal officials are appointed by the national government. In the Dominican Republic, although town councils are elective, little power is delegated to them.

Brazil requires special comment. According to the constitution of 1946, there is the promise of municipal autonomy. The prefects or mayors and the councils are to be elected. Important exceptions are made with respect to prefects. In the federal districts and the territorial capitals, they are to be appointed by the president. In the capitals, resort centers, and strategic seaports of the states they are appointed by the respective governors. There are noteworthy provisions concerning taxation. An allotment of 10 per cent of the federal revenues from income taxes is to be distributed to the municipalities, with one-half this amount to be expended in benefits of a "rural nature." Certain taxes levied by the states are to be shared with the cities. States are permitted to intervene in the cities in order to regularize finances.[12]

In many countries, cities are limited in jurisdiction to administrative and economic matters. In some, the local powers of taxation require approval of either the national or the provincial authority, or both. In some, national politics enter municipal elections, with consequential interference. In still others, centralization has left little or no reality to self-government in municipalities.

BIBLIOGRAPHY

Angulo y Pérez, Andrés, *Cuestiones prácticas de gobierno municipal,* Havana, 1937.

———, *El municipio constitucional en América,* Havana, 1937.

Bielsa, Rafael, *Principios del régimen municipal,* Buenos Aires, 1930.

Bravo, Mario, *La ciudad libre,* Buenos Aires, 1917.

Carrera y Jústiz, Francisco, *La constitución de Cuba y el problema municipal,* Havana, 1903.

———, *La guerra y las ciudades,* Havana, 1918.

———, *Introducción a la historia de las instituciones locales de Cuba,* 2 vols., Havana, 1905.

Cleven, N. A. N., *The Political Organization of Bolivia,* Washington, D.C., Carnegie Institution, 1940.

De la Torre, Lisandro, "Extensión del poder municipal," *Revista de la Facultad de Derecho y Ciencias Sociales* (Buenos Aires), vol. 5, pp. 5–25, 1926.

———, *Régimen municipal,* Buenos Aires, 1889.

[12] Pontes de Miranda, *Comentarios a constituição de 1946* (2d ed., São Paulo, 1953), vol. II, pp. 126–143.

Linares Quintana, Segundo V., *Concordancias del proyecto de ley orgánica de los territorios nacionales del poder ejecutivo 1938,* Buenos Aires, 1940.

———, *Derecho público de los territorios nacionales argentino y comparado,* Buenos Aires, 1937.

Lorca Rojas, Gustavo, *La administración comunal,* Valparaiso, 1943.

Miranda, Pontes dė, *Comentarios a constituição de 1946,* 2d ed., 2 vols., São Paulo, 1953.

Ochoa Campos, Moisés, *La reforma municipal: historia municipal de México,* Mexico, 1955.

Puente Arteaga, Martín, *El municipio en México,* Mexico, 1954.

Zavalia, Clodomiro, *Lecciones de derecho público provincial,* 2d ed., Buenos Aires, 1937.

Chapter 13: POLITICAL PARTIES AND ELECTIONS

The need for responsible parties in a democratic scheme of government is recognized in the voluminous literature concerning Latin-American political parties.[1] And yet, as it is often pointed out, a real party system implies more than the existence of political parties, and it is frequently asserted that Latin America lacks the "climate" necessary for the development of vigorous parties. Some of the faulty elements which are cited include limitations on franchise, not necessarily of a constitutional but of a practical order; lack of availability of political information; socioeconomic patterns which tend to prevent free expression of opinion; and defects of the systems of electoral administration as well as of party organization. These elements undoubtedly produce important flaws in the party picture. Thus, literacy requirements for voting existing in some countries have the effect of disenfranchising a large segment of the population. This is the case in Guatemala, where 72 per cent of the population is illiterate. The voters sometimes are not politically well informed because of restrictions of the freedoms of press and speech, or because of control of all propaganda media. The socioeconomic system, by assuring the dependence of the agricultural worker on the landowner, results in the control by the latter of large blocs of votes, which he can place at the disposal of a particular candidate. Deficiencies in the election systems, antiquated practices such as the printing of the ballots by the parties, and poorly organized election administration also tend to facilitate control of the polling by the group in power.[2] It is obvious that a political environment characterized by these conditions is not favorable to the development of an effective party system.

Characteristics and Weaknesses of Parties

In some countries parties have strength and influence and are in some measure accountable to the rank and file of their membership and to the

[1] Segundo V. Linares Quintana, *Los Partidos políticos: instrumentos de gobierno* (Buenos Aires, 1945), is an example of the excellent quality of Latin-American literature on the subject.

[2] Asher N. Christensen, "The General Nature of Political Parties in Latin America," in Asher N. Christensen (ed.) *The Evolution of Latin American Government* (New York, Holt, 1951), pp. 501–506.

people. However, there are other countries where only one party is legally permitted and still others where, although several parties exist, political factors combine to produce a one-party system. But despite this variety of situations Latin-American parties has in common certain features.

The vices of *caudillismo* and personalism are evils of primary importance in the party system. Because of the strong personalism prevalent in Latin-American politics and a system which makes the executive the effective agent of virtually all political changes, political parties rarely present any concrete platform. They struggle not for the triumph of ideas but for that of certain individuals. Parties tend to split into shapeless factions according to personalities. It is left to the strong leader to establish authority amidst the confusion of rival groups. This cult of the colorful or magnetic personality, the vote for the individual rather than for the platform or the organization, is the most salient feature of the party picture. Party followers are more accurately identified as *callistas, batllistas,* or *irigoyenistas,*[3] after the name of their leader, than by the party title of their affiliation. The organization which followed Juan Perón in Argentina, perhaps in acknowledgment of this reality, was formally known as the Peronista party.

Party programs and electoral platforms are generally received with indifference. They are considered, in good part, as the fulfillment of a formality and not of necessity. Sympathy or antipathy is rallied in the persons of the candidates. In fact, according to political habits, it falls to the candidate to formulate his party's program in speeches and statements after nomination. This practice naturally weakens the candidate's courage to resist pressures from friends, since he cannot invoke in defense his responsibility as executor of the mandate of his party. There is, in addition, a tendency among Latin-American public figures to place personal interests and those of relatives and associates above national or party interests. The practice has even resulted in the coinage of a word used in political jargon: *amiguismo,* meaning, broadly, "government by cronies."

Another common feature is the general lack of discipline in political organizations and the frequent changes of party affiliation. This poses the question of whether there exist, in most cases, real differences among the parties. Although there have existed in the past parties such as the unitary, the federal, the liberal, and the conservative, with their separate factions such as the military, the civilian, the clerical, and the lay, these did not always remain true to their party designations. There have been civilians

[3] Followers of Calles in Mexico, of Batlle in Uruguay, and Irigoyen in Argentina.

who upheld militarism, constitutionalists who consistently ignored the supreme law of the land, and liberals who defended dictatorial rule. Such a situation persists today. The nomenclature of the various parties is still loosely applied and consecrated terms such as "conservative" or "liberal," and other labels such as "socialist," "leftist," "democrat," and "radical" do not carry much meaning. In fact, they are often in contradiction with the ideology of the party which bears them, and their use is completely arbitrary.

Also distinctive of the Latin-American party picture is the aggressive intolerance which is often the prevailing note, each party supporting a leader, a dogma, and considering all others its enemies. For the party in power, the opposition is often a group of corrupt and dangerous subversives, and it follows that for the latter, the ruling party is a government of tyrants. The unwillingness to accept the voters' verdict, what some writers have called lack of "political sportsmanship," is a defect which is found too frequently. According to García Calderón, the Latin Americans, educated in the Roman Church, brought into politics the absolutism of religious dogmas and have no conception of tolerance. The opposition, he added, seldom has the opportunity to fill a place of influence, and often "it is only by violence that the parties can emerge from the condition of ostracism in which they are held by the faction in power, and it is by violence that they return to that condition."[4]

Defects in organization are also characteristic of all parties. The general rule is that of parties controlled by bosses, machines, or an oligarchy. The unregulated convention which is the prevailing nominating scheme results in hand-picked candidates. Since party organization, despite the efforts to impose legal regulation of sorts, is still under almost complete jurisdiction of the party itself, it may easily fall under control of inner groups which dispose of party offices without intervention on the part of the rank and file of party membership. This is a result of the *caudillo* system and the corruption of pressure groups.

A good part of the citizenry in Latin America feels a certain repugnance toward politics and often avoids participating directly in political affairs. To many people, politicians are a special breed of unscrupulous and tainted individuals, a class apart. The mudslinging and intensity of political campaigns cause many able persons to refuse to run for political office and to shun all forms of political activity. Obviously, this attitude

[4] Francisco García Calderón, *Latin America: Its Rise and Progress* (London, Fisher Unwin, 1913), pp. 365–369.

is an added factor which retards the growth of a genuine party system and of democratic processes.

The Traditional Parties

From country to country the nature of the earlier parties was much the same, and it mattered little whether they called themselves liberals or conservatives, centralists or federalists. The alignment was often much more elementary than the myriad of names would indicate. There was the alliance of the landowners, the high clergy, and their followers from the lower classes, defending the Church and the *status quo;* and these were interested, above all, in the preservation of order. On the other side there were the men of more "advanced" ideas: merchants and professional men, who resented the preeminence of the aristocracy and who were also anticlerical. In further simplification we could agree with a Chilean political figure that there existed "two parties in the early period of the political life of Latin America which struggled for power and control. The banner of one of these parties carried the inscription: 'Liberty even if in anarchy' while that of the other read: 'Order even if in despotism.' And in both cases the motto was sometimes inscribed in bloody characters."[5]

The two great issues which determined party alignment during the first half of the century of independence were the separation of Church and state and centralization. These controversies of deep social and political significance divided the ruling and nonruling groups into embittered and hostile factions. All other issues were purely personal and factional. Parties hurriedly organized around one *caudillo* or a nucleus of political chieftains had no degree of permanence beyond the prestige of their leaders.

The Multiparty System

The relatively simple partisan divisions of the early period, following the conventional formula of conservatives and liberals, are now disappearing in some countries and are being supplanted by a system of multiple parties. Cuba, for instance, "came of political age" with only two parties, liberal and conservative, but today the picture is far different, with some six major parties. Chile also furnishes one of the more typical examples. Here the conservative party represented the most powerful of the old landowner class, sometimes tinted with clericalism, and except for

[5] René León Echaíz, *Evolución histórica de los partidos políticos chilenos* (Santiago, 1939), pp. 26–27.

a short period of liberal rule, it dominated the political scene until the 1880s. During this period, the party gradually relinquished some of its so-called principles, since some groups favored various degrees of liberalism. By the turn of the century, Chile had acquired a complex setup of parties, with at least six groups clearly defined. As a result, Chile, like Cuba and other countries, has had to resort to blocs or combinations of parties, thus making coalition governments common.

The minor parties develop from a variety of social groups or issues, with little cohesion or discipline. The shifts and machinations of these political groups almost defy analysis, and at times politics is little more than a struggle for the spoils of office with personal and party interests prevailing over national interests.[6] The creation of fluid organizations in order to achieve short-ranged political objectives is a common occurrence. They are not stable or permanent organizations, and they come into existence only for electoral purposes. It was with reference to this type of party in Bolivia, Ecuador, and Peru that it was said: "In these times, nothing is simpler than to found a political party. To form a political party only three people and one object are necessary: a president, a vice-president, a secretary, and a rubber stamp. The party can get along even without the vice-president and the secretary. . . . There have been cases in which the existence of only the rubber stamp has been sufficient.[7]

The Modern Parties

Today there is more popular participation in the political processes of Latin America than at any other period of its history. This development is closely related to the impact of modern capitalism and technology, and it could be said to have taken place in each country in proportion to the extent to which that impact has been felt. It has involved such factors as the growth of cities, the intimate contact with more advanced nations, the emergence of an incipient middle class and of an industrial proletariat, and the appearance of a new plutocracy of up-to-date industrialists and financiers. These have somewhat weakened the hold of the landed oligarchy over political life. Politics are ceasing to be simple quarrels within the narrow circle of semifeudal landowners, the Church's hierarchy, army officers, and professional politicians. In some countries they are becoming

[6] John Reese Stevenson, *The Chilean Popular Front* (Philadelphia, University of Pennsylvania Press, 1942), p. 19.

[7] Luis Terán Gómez, *Los partidos políticos y su acción democrática* (La Paz, 1942), pp. 50–51. In George I. Blanksten, *Ecuador: Constitutions and Caudillos* (Berkeley, Calif., University of California Press, 1951), p. 70.

class struggles, which take different forms in consonance with the economic and political structures of the country. While it is true that the effects of these developments have been almost negligible in some countries, e.g., in Paraguay or Haiti, it is also true that they have been highly significant in the most economically advanced and most populated countries such as Argentina, Brazil, Mexico, Chile, Cuba, Uruguay, and Venezuela.[8] At the same time, the increased political activity is due, at least partly, to the astounding rise of organized labor as a political force.

The result of this combination of factors has been the formation, in some countries, of parties which seek to correct certain economic inequalities by appealing to the working class, the peasant, and the intellectuals. These new parties are given their strength by a new middle class with political ambitions and by a slowly awakening industrial proletariat. The fact they are competing with the old and strong traditional parties is causing a profound change in the political pattern. In some cases, they are engaged in a decisive struggle with the more conservative groups, a fact which, at least temporarily, may contribute to aggravate the century-old ailment of political instability. In other countries they have been successful in their efforts to capture the reins of power and are attempting to carry out their programs.

Some of these new parties are inspired by European models such as the socialists and the Communists, but the most significant and of greater interest are indigenous and reflect the peculiar economic conditions of specific countries. Among such native new parties are the People's party or Aprista of Peru, which was formally created by Víctor R. Haya de la Torre in 1931 but which actually originated shortly after the First World War; the Cuban Revolutionary party (Auténticos) and the Cuban People's party (Ortodoxos); the Democratic Action party of Venezuela; the National Liberation party of Costa Rica; the Partido Febrerista of Paraguay; the Peronista party of Argentina; the Trabalhista party of Brazil; and the Nationalist Revolutionary Movement (MNR) of Bolivia.

Although all these parties have risen independently in their respective nations, with little or no contact with one another, and their programs developed in response to peculiar domestic conditions, they are nevertheless strikingly similar in development and in ideology. The similarities could well result from the fact that conflicts of social and economic

[8] Arthur P. Whitaker, "A Historian's Point of View," in W. W. Pierson (ed.), "Pathology of Democracy in Latin America: A Symposium," *The American Political Science Review*, vol. 44, no. 1, p. 106, March, 1950.

interests are slowly replacing political or religious issues as a basis of politics in those countries. The emphasis placed by these parties is upon a concept of democracy not exclusively political but socioeconomic, with appeals to nationalism and endorsements of state intervention in the domestic economy. And it should be kept in mind that in this new conception various other social-reform interests should be added to "labor" as motivating forces. Innovations of the new constitutions not only embrace many aspects of labor regulation and protection but extend to assurances of justice in many other areas of social relations, by assertion of principles of social security and by establishment of social-welfare services, protecting the family, promoting cooperative enterprises, and providing low-cost housing.

These new parties have not liberated themselves altogether from personalism and from the "*caudillo* complex," but they give more emphasis to ideology and party discipline than the traditional organizations. Leaders of the new type such as Haya de la Torre of Peru, Grau San Martín of Cuba, Rómulo Betancourt of Venezuela, and Paz Estenssoro of Bolivia are, to be sure, personalities with a devoted following and surrounded by a considerable *mystique.* But although each may dominate his particular organization, his personal leadership is not the only reason for its existence. This weakening of *personalismo,* with the consequent strengthening of party principles, is one of the healthiest developments in the party picture of recent years.

It is characteristic of some of these parties that they rest primarily upon the support of the working class, which was long neglected by political leaders, and which had in these countries, until recently, little or no political organization. In Argentina one of the supports of the Peronista party was the large mass of workers, the "neglected ones" overlooked by politicians, whose support was gained by Perón's labor legislation. In Bolivia through the Nationalist Revolutionary Movement the miners' unions, unorganized until 1943, are a controlling power in support of the administration of Paz Estenssoro in 1955.

The voters to whom these parties make their appeal are approximately the same. The intellectuals and the middle class are faithful followers and in most cases supply the leadership. The urban working class is heavily relied upon, especially if the party has control of the organized labor movement. In Cuba, the agricultural worker, who benefited in large measure from the PRC policies, supplies a considerable bloc of voters, while the Peruvian Apristas make a special appeal to the Indian and mestizo classes. Native industrialists show an inclination to support these parties, while landlords and big merchants generally throw their influence to the opposition.

Some of these parties are labeled by their opponents as left-wingers. It is well to remember that a well-entrenched ruling oligarchy is likely to attach this epithet to any reformist movement regardless of its moderation. Unquestionably some of the leaders of these groups may have been romantically attracted to Russian Marxism at an early stage of their careers, but in any event they are today, with few exceptions, far from being extremists or radicals in any sense. It is very significant that in every country these groups and the Communists are bitter and irreconcilable enemies.

TABLE 15

PARTY MEMBERSHIP, CUBA, 1951

Population	5,526,871
Qualified voters	2,765,049
Recorded party members:	
Partido Revolucionario Cubano (Auténtico)	689,894
Partido del Pueblo Cubano (Ortodoxo)	358,118
Partido Acción Unitaria	227,457
Partido Demócrata	215,179
Partido Liberal	208,745
Partido Nacional Cubano	195,021
Partido Socialista Popular (Communist)	59,900
Partido Republicano	49,388
Partido de la Cubanidad	94,257
Total	2,097,959

SOURCE: *Diario de la Marina*, Dec. 28, 1952, p. 20.

Let us take as an example of these indigenous parties the Cuban Revolutionary party (Auténtico) of Cuba. The party was born in 1934, shortly after the fall of the Machado dictatorship, as a number of revolutionary organizations combined forces. The program, published in 1934, featured political democracy, economic nationalism, agrarian reform, industrialization, social security, and education. From its inception it became the standard-bearer of the "revolution" to carry out a program of economic and social reform.[9] After some vicissitudes the party eventually gained power through an impressive electoral victory in 1944, and it remained in office until the military coup of March, 1952. The PRC while

[9] William S. Stokes, "The 'Cuban Revolution' and the Presidential Elections of 1948," *The Hispanic American Historical Review*, vol. 31, no. 1, part I, pp., 37–79, February, 1951.

in office carried out a considerable part of its program with some success, although it did not live up to the full expectations of its followers. It was a firm exponent of political democracy, and while in power it maintained scrupulous respect for freedom of expression and civil liberties. It attempted, although timidly and much less vigorously than parties of its kind in other countries, some reforms of the agrarian system and some ventures in government planning. It established a firm policy of stabilization of the price of sugar and of better distribution of the wealth derived from this product; and by making efforts to develop other industries, it constructively sought to reduce the dangers of a one-crop economy. It gave impulse to a social security system and generously financed a vast educational program. Economic nationalism is perhaps less evident in this party than others of the new group. The PRC strongly advocated and practiced while in office close relations with the other Latin-American republics and especially with those with regimes which were similar to its own.

The great weakness of the Cuban Auténtico party is the widely alleged corruption and personal dishonesty. In fact, it was this situation which resulted in the rise of a rival party, the Party of the Cuban People (Ortodoxo), an offshoot of the PRC in 1946. The break with the Auténticos was justified by three factors: (1) corruption; (2) slowness in the reform program; and (3) the belief that the party leader, Grau San Martín, intended to hand-pick his successor. By 1951, this offshoot of the PRC, which clearly falls into the class of modern indigenous parties, had become a formidable political force. In 1952, it was making the strongest bid for the presidency. The party's program of "economic independence, political liberty, and social justice" includes also an insistence on keeping the party free from political pacts of any sort. In spite of the radical change introduced by the military *coup d'état* of 1952 and the subsequent one-sided elections of 1954, which legalized the rule of General Batista, these two parties, the PRC and the Orthodox, remain as important forces in the Cuban party picture.

Other parties in the group supply better examples to illustrate different phases of their common ideology. The Peruvian Apristas are significant for their advocacy of agrarian reform and their active defense of the Indian communities.[10] Their short period of participation in the tasks of

[10] For an excellent study of the philosophy and program of *aprismo,* see Harry Kantor, *The Ideology and Program of the Peruvian Aprista Movement* (Berkeley, Calif., University of California Press, 1953).

government in Peru, from 1945 to 1948, was marked by active support of reform measures of this kind. Economic planning by government is given perhaps a more prominent place in the program of the Venezuelan Democratic Action party than in those of others, although the Social Democratic party of Costa Rica has also favored it. Nationalization of industry is not advocated to the same degree by all parties in this category, although some such provision is generally included in their programs. While the issue is not pressed, at least for the present time, by the Apristas of Peru, other parties have carried out nationalization, if they considered it necessary. This was the case in the nationalization of the banks in Costa Rica.[11] On the issue of nationalism, the position of these parties has changed in recent years. It is now somewhat more conciliatory to foreign capitalists, leaning more toward compelling strict observance of the country's social legislation rather than toward outright expropriation and nationalization of foreign property.

These parties, when installed in office, have shown common weaknesses, which, however, are not all to be found in every case. These elements are the lack of effective control over law enforcement, inefficiency in the administrative machine of the government, and extended practices of squeeze and graft, particularly in the second and lower echelons of the bureaucracy. Thus, for instance, the land-reform program of Bolivia's National Revolutionary Movement was jeopardized by land grabbing on such a scale that the government was forced to prosecute the culprits criminally. The success of this measure depended naturally on a much-needed increase in the efficiency of the government. It was reported that once out in the provinces many appointees paid little heed to orders from their superiors. The turnover in officialdom is usually high and its competency low.

The widespread belief that positions of power, especially inasmuch as they may be temporary, should be used for personal gain is a problem of a serious nature. This Latin-American disposition to look after oneself while in political office is an obstacle to honest and efficient government. Although the extent of these peculations is hard to determine, examples of venality abound in every country, and the list of high government officials who have managed to acquire vast wealth while in power is long and impressive. In some countries, such as Mexico and Bolivia, the government has realized the seriousness of this situation and has begun

[11] Robert J. Alexander, "The Latin American Aprista Parties," *The Political Quarterly*, vol. 20, no. 3, pp. 236–247, July–September, 1949.

a "morality campaign." How well a party is able to deal with these problems will determine in a large measure the success it will have in achieving its goals.

Fascist and Profascist Parties. Fascism flourished in some of the Latin-American republics during the 1930s. In Brazil, the green-shirted Acção Integralista Brasileira constituted the largest Latin-American fascist movement. Organized in 1932, it reached a membership of over 200,000 and was reported to be financed with the help of German funds. Its program called for an "integral" nation backed by an "integral society." It denounced liberal democracy and universal suffrage and favored instead a corporative state. With the slogan "God, Country, and Family" it violently denounced Brazil's exploitation by foreign interests. However, the *integralista* movement was swiftly crushed by the government of Getulio Vargas in 1938 after a short-lived but dramatic revolt.[12] The assumption of dictatorial powers by President Vargas in 1937 resulted in the establishment of a regime with some fascist overtones and corporative features. The constitution of the New State (O Estado Novo), as the regime was officially known, broke the constitutional tradition of Brazil by its enthronement of the "leader" principle. However, Vargas's New State, despite its supernationalism and its imitation of Italian Fascist corporations, was not a genuine fascist regime and was closer to a *caudillo* dictatorship of the traditional Latin-American type. The curious constitution of 1937 was largely ignored by Vargas.[13] Some years later his regime became a faithful ally of the democracies in the struggle against European fascism.

An organization of distinctive fascist character appeared in Chile in 1934. Its followers were popularly known as *nacistas* and its uniformed storm troops held military drills in public. Among its leaders and organizers were many German and Italian nationals. A group of similar nature was the Falange de Portales named after Chile's famous strong man of the nineteenth century. Both organizations disappeared after the *nacistas* attempted a coup in 1938 which ended in a massacre of the group and the imprisonment of its leader.[14]

[12] See Federico de Villar, "Life and Death of Brazilian Fascism," *Inter American,* June, 1943, pp. 16–21.

[13] For a study of the Vargas regime, see Karl Loewenstein, *Brazil under Vargas* (New York, Macmillan, 1944).

[14] For the philosophy inspiring this movement, see the works of its leader, Jorge González von Marees, *El problema del hambre* (Santiago, 1937) and *El mal de Chile* (Santiago, 1940).

Fascism in Argentina, although never a unified movement centered around a national "leader," appeared early. In 1919, conservatives groups organized the Argentine Patriotic League (Liga Patriótica Argentina) as a counterforce to militant trade unions. In 1930, the military government of General Uriburu organized an Argentine Civic Legion (Legión Cívica Argentina) with the avowed purpose of defending the military regime and the interests of the landowning aristocracy. During the decade which preceded the Second World War there were in the country some eight uniformed organizations. They were not, however, of any national importance, and functioned only at the provincial level.[15]

Although some dictatorial governments in Latin America may resemble European Nazi and fascist regimes, an important distinction should be made between policies of repression and fascism proper. The fact is that, to the present, Latin-American military dictatorships have not attempted seriously to impose totalitarian control over the economic and cultural life of the country as distinguished from the political. The differences between fascism and Latin-American authoritarianism are significant. The latter emphasizes the privileges and powers of the army and the ruling clique. Its chief support comes from the military rather than from the middle and other classes. There is much less interference in the private lives of the people under a traditional dictatorship than under a genuine fascist regime.

Fascist movements in Latin America have lacked mass support. Their sympathizers have been recruited chiefly from among the younger generation of the wealthy class, government employees, and the families of army officers. Neither in number nor in strength can these groups be compared with the masses of "white-collar" employees and professionals who supplied the backbone of European fascism. In addition, an economic basis for fascism is absent in Latin America. Capitalism in this region is at an early phase of development rather than contracting. Therefore, the analogy that may exist between some Latin-American dictatorships and fascist forms is often one of verbiage and slogans exclusively. At the most, it is possible to speak of "creole fascism" (*fascismo criollo*) as a special variety of fascism, a kind of homespun authoritarianism, which is sometimes encouraged by conservative politicians and by military dictators as an auxiliary force to maintain themselves in power.

[15] For a general account of early fascism and communism in Latin America see Stephen Naft, "Fascism and Communism in South America," *Foreign Policy Reports*, vol. 13, no. 19, Dec. 15, 1937.

Charges of fascist tendencies were frequently made against the Peronista party of President Perón in Argentina. This controversial figure of Latin-American politics was elected in 1946 with the support of the Partido Laborista, an organization established by Perón's followers among labor leaders, and with the assistance of a dissident group in the Unión Cívica Radical, the "grand old party" of Argentina. It was not until after his election that Perón decided to consolidate his supporters in one strong political organization to be composed of the *laboristas,* the pro-Perón Radicals, and the independents. There were serious objections to the proposed liquidation of the Partido Laborista, but Perón's plan was put into effect and the Partido Peronista was formed.[16]

It is generally agreed that the Perón government rested upon three elements: the army, the Church, and organized labor. However, a serious rift later developed between the regime and the Church, apparently caused by the latter's political activities. Faced with a strong popular reaction against its Church policy, the regime toppled in September, 1955, when the armed forces revolted and demanded Perón's resignation. Since these events, the status and future of the Peronista party have been uncertain. Organized labor was the popular strength behind the Perón regime. Whatever Perón and the party did while in power to make the labor movement effective and to consolidate its position—and it was much—came about with a price to be paid: that of subservience to personal rule. A process of ruthless liquidation of anti-*peronista* unions was accompanied by a tightening of a rigid control of the *peronista* labor groups themselves. The fate of the Argentine labor movement was linked, at least temporarily, to the fortunes of the Perón government. Foremost among the problems confronted by the provisional military government established after the fall of Perón was the obvious necessity of eradicating *peronista* control of the powerful Confederation of Argentine Workers.

The question of whether the Peronista party was a fascist group or not cannot be definitely answered. There can be no doubt of Perón's ideological affinity with fascism and Nazism until 1945. Then, as a writer puts it, "the death of the Axis left Perón hanging from an uncomfortable limb," and it became necessary to invent that dubious political theory of *justicialismo*[17] which was advertised as a peculiarly Argentine doctrine.[18]

[16] See Robert J. Alexander, *The Peron Era* (New York, Columbia University Press, 1951), pp. 53–74.

[17] There is no English equivalent of this word. It can be roughly translated as "the era of justice."

[18] For a penetrating analysis of *justicialismo* see George I. Blanksten, *Perón's Argentina* (Chicago, University of Chicago Press, 1953).

The *peronista* philosophy, however, retained only certain features of fascism. There are still remarkable similarities between Italian Fascism (more than German Nazism) and the ideas of Perón. The parallels are easily found in the approaches to such matters as the emphasis on the doctrine of authority or leadership, the disregard of individual liberty, supernationalism, the notion of idealism, and some phases of economics. However, there are also significant differences between Mussolini's fascism and Perón's *justicialismo.* There was no deification of the state in Argentina during the Perón era, and there was no official recognition of an elite or selected group. Some thought of the army as an elite, and others considered the Peronista party in the same position, but the elite doctrine was not officially preached by the regime.

To conclude, there was great resemblance between the policies and techniques of the Peronista group and those of European fascism, but it was in the methods and techniques rather than in the ideology that the resemblance lay. The campaigns of terror in the elections of 1946 and 1951, the irresponsible nationalism, the outrages against the universities and the intellectual class, the browbeating of political opponents, the elimination of the independent press, and the disregard for civil rights were all strongly reminiscent of the practices of Nazism and fascism. At the same time, there was much to make *peronismo* a genuine product of local conditions different from imported totalitarianism. These conditions "give the *criollo* variety of dictatorship in Argentina its own native tinge."[19]

In all fairness one must say that the Peronista group, despite its political perversions, added an impressive new chapter to the social history of Argentina. It is not too much to say that the traditional parties, including the Socialists, have failed so far to attract the worker with an equally positive—although somewhat demagogic—program of social and economic reform. Until another party is able to make an effective appeal to the masses, *peronismo* may remain strong in Argentina.

The *peronista* ideas have been making some headway in Chile, Peru, Bolivia, Paraguay, and Brazil. The National Revolutionary Movement returned to power in Bolivia by means of a successful civilian revolt in 1952 after several years of forced exclusion from Bolivian politics. It was this party which served as the main civilian support of the Villarroel government from 1943 to 1946. This group claims to be representative of the generation of Bolivians who fought the tragic Chaco War (1932–1938) and who returned from the battleground with a desire for reform.

[19] Felix J. Weil, *Argentine Riddle* (New York, John Day, 1944), p. 47.

In the economic field, the MNR challenged the influence of the big tin interests and of the landowning class. The nationalization of the tin mines, effected in 1952, was a highly popular objective of its program.

The political strength of the MNR is closely related to the large mass of tin miners and Indian peasants. The party strives to attract and build up a firm foundation of labor support, just as the Argentine Partido Peronista did, so that it will not be forced to depend exclusively on the support of the young-officer group of the army which first made possible its entry into politics. Charges of fascism, arbitrariness, and irresponsible nationalism have also been hurled in the past against the Bolivian MNR. And again, its rapid rise may be explained by the fact that it seems to offer an attractive program of reform to redress the grievances of a long-forgotten and now restless segment of the nation.

The Communist Parties. An accurate evaluation of Communist influence is difficult because of the tendency of many Latin-American governments to apply this label to any individual or group venturing to oppose or to criticize the *status quo.* Often a Latin-American strong man, faced with opposition against his rule, calls the movement "communistic." In turn, a government undertaking economic or social reforms which affect some powerful vested interests adversely may be the object of similar charges by its opponents.

Active in the labor movement since the early 1920s and having at one time or another influenced labor organizations in some countries, the Communists became a factor of some party significance in the period of the Second World War. For a time they controlled important groups in the labor movements of Chile, Panama, Guatemala, Colombia, Uruguay, Cuba, Brazil, Venezuela, and Ecuador. Latest available figures on Communist party membership indicate the total number in Latin America to be approximately 200,000. This is less than two-tenths of 1 per cent of the people—compared with 1.3 per cent in France and 3.6 per cent in Italy. However, the strength of communism cannot be estimated exclusively on the basis of the number of party members. The electoral strength and influence of these parties is generally superior to what such figures indicate. Thus, the Communist party in Chile, for example, with a membership of about 40,000 has frequently polled a number of votes far exceeding this amount.

The largest Communist groups exist in Argentina, Brazil, Chile, Cuba, and Venezuela. The Brazilian group is the largest single body, with about 60,000 members. Its leader, Luis Carlos Prestes, is also the foremost

Communist figure in Latin America. In Argentina and Chile each there are roughly 40,000 Communists. The Chilean Communist party is among the oldest on the continent. As early as 1918 communism gained there some support among intellectual circles. Numerically Argentina's Communists are only second to Brazil's. Recently, however, there has been an ideological split, with one wing supporting the Perón regime actively. Communist fortunes ran high in Cuba during the early 1940s when they controlled the powerful Confederation of Cuban Workers, but there has been, since 1945, a marked decline in their influence. In Venezuela, the Communists exercise strong influence in the unions representing the workers in the oil industry. Mexican communism has suffered severe setbacks during the last nine years. For a time it was the most influential voice among Mexican intellectuals and it was also powerful in the labor movement. Today it is a weak and scattered group as a result of the policies of Presidents Alemán and Ruíz Cortines. The prestige of Vicente Lombardo Toledano, the powerful labor leader, who although avowedly not a Communist is a consistent follower of the Communist line, has also declined steadily. Lombardo Toledano's Labor Federation is affiliated with the Communist-controlled World Federation of Trade Unions, and his Popular Party (Partido Popular) is generally considered as a Communist front organization.[20]

The development of new political parties such as those which have been already described has been a significant factor in the weakening of Communist influence. Also, the decision of the majority of the Latin-American governments to place the Communist party outside the law has served as a further deterrent to its growth. The party has been declared illegal everywhere except in Mexico, Colombia, Ecuador, Argentina, and Uruguay, but even in these countries it is under control and represents no immediate danger. However, in some countries where the party has been outlawed, a handful of members will operate underground.

Despite their almost insignificant number when compared with other political parties, the Communists have managed in some countries to gain control of organized labor and to occupy key positions in government. Although small in number (about one thousand), through time-honored techniques of front organizations and infiltration the Communists en-

[20] For an appraisal of Communist influence, see Marshall K. Powers, "Communism in Latin America: An Interim Assessment," *World Affairs,* vol. 117, no. 1, pp. 6–10, spring, 1954. See also Víctor Alba, *Historia del communismo en América Latina* (Mexico, 1954).

trenched themselves in important positions in Guatemala during the administration of President Jacobo Arbenz (1951–1954). President Arbenz's land-reform program gave them an opportunity to take over both its administration and its application and to portray themselves as the only party interested in the advancement of the masses. An inept conservative opposition which fought every long-overdue social reform and never advocated a positive idea of its own contributed also greatly to the rise of Communist influence. Non-Communist liberals, confronted with the choice of associating themselves with the Communists or the conservative opposition, did not join either group. The tragic result was that President Arbenz, perhaps without realizing it, found himself relying principally on the Communists to achieve the objectives of his program. This situation led to the invasion of Guatemala by the forces of Colonel Carlos Castillo Armas and the overthrow of the Arbenz regime.

However, forcing out the Communists from positions of power did not automatically solve Guatemala's problems. If the influence of communism is to be permanently uprooted, it is necessary to remove existing conditions which are favorable to its breeding. These conditions are widespread in Latin America. With the growth of urban centers and of industry the narrow class structure of an agricultural society is crumbling. It is generally admitted that, with only some notable exceptions, the oligarchical upper classes have not given much attention to providing opportunities and better life for the large mass of peasants and workers. The nucleus of Communist class-war groups is struggling for the allegiance of the great uncommitted masses—white, Indian, Negro, and mestizo—seeking opportunity. They have some potent weapons in the tremendous appeal of economic nationalism to peoples who feel that they are victims of foreign exploitation, the need for land reform, and the plight of poverty-stricken peasants and miners. From the Communist propaganda line it is clear that their chief target in Latin America is the United States. The second is, quite logically, the large commercial corporations of that nation.

The task of preventing the spread of Communist influence will not be easy. There will be needed keen competition on the part of democratic groups for the favor of the masses. Social and economic reforms are sorely needed. The pleas for justice must be heeded by all other political groups, and a genuinely democratic society must be encouraged. Despite Latin America's economic vulnerability to communism, in countries where strong and dynamic liberal movements exist Communist influence has invariably faded away. It has been shown that where the mass of the people is offered the same advantages by a democratic party as by the Communists, it will choose the former.[21]

TABLE 16
COMMUNIST PARTY MEMBERSHIP IN LATIN AMERICA

Country	*Communists*
Argentina	40,000
Bolivia	2,000
Brazil	60,000
Chile	40,000
Colombia	5,000
Costa Rica	5,000
Cuba	30,000
Dominican Republic	Negligible
Ecuador	5,000
El Salvador	1,000
Guatemala	1,000
Haiti	Negligible
Honduras	Negligible
Mexico	5,000
Nicaragua	Negligible
Panama	1,000
Paraguay	2,000
Peru	10,000
Uruguay	15,000
Venezuela	20,000

SOURCE: *The New York Times*, Mar. 7, 1954, p. 4E.

Although unsolved social and economic problems may tend to make Latin America highly vulnerable to Communist penetration, it must be remembered that there are also factors which may counterbalance such conditions. First, there is the typical individualism of all Hispanic peoples and their inherent hostility to regimentation—so essential a feature of Marxian totalitarianism. Secondly, there is the political idealism of the peoples. It is true that they can violate principles and behave badly, but their political conceptions are ultimately based on high principles and not on expediency. In addition, the majority of the population of these countries is Catholic, and the over-all set of standards and values of the Roman Catholic Church, so diametrically opposed to those of communism, are

[21] An excellent example is provided by Costa Rica. The liberals of President José A. Figueres, elected in 1953, by pushing their own program of credit, education, organization of free trade unions, and agrarian reform have been singularly successful in meeting the threat of communism.

formidable barriers to the propagation of the Communist doctrine. Until recently it was generally believed that, since the economy of Latin America is predominantly agricultural with farm workers outnumbering the industrial proletariat, communism lacked in this area any widespread bases for its development. Such a notion, however, has been shattered by the Communist conquest of China, and there are many who believe that Communist tactics in Latin American will soon reflect the experiences and skills acquired in the course of the Asiatic struggles.[22]

The present world struggle between the Communist bloc and the Free World will affect deeply the destiny of the Latin-American republics. They may at present exert no positive or material influence on the course of that struggle, but they will unquestionably be influenced by its outcome. At this time it is encouraging to note that, despite "economic colonialism" with its fertile breeding grounds for discontent, communism has not been able to influence the masses of Latin America in any considerable degree.

The Socialist Parties. The Socialist party of Argentina is perhaps the most interesting, being the oldest and strongest of the group. Utopian socialism was introduced in the country in 1837 and was developed by the wave of European refugees later. French, Italian, and Spanish socialist groups were organized in Buenos Aires but operated separately until they joined to launch the Partido Socialista in 1896 under the leadership of Juan B. Justo. The influence of Argentine socialism was soon to be felt in many parts of Latin America. After a period of rapid growth in the prewar era the party began to undergo dissension in 1914 and 1915, but it regained strength during the 1920s, and socialists controlled all major labor organizations until 1942. During the same period they scored some major electoral victories, such as winning control of five of the country's largest cities and electing forty-four deputies in the 1931 elections. With the rise of the Peronista party, however, the socialists lost control of labor except for a few unimportant unions. Their electoral fortunes began likewise to decline sharply. This decline may be attributed to the failure of the party to supply leadership to the trade unions and to give attention to long-range objectives. The constant reluctance of the party to take any strong position on important issues that affected labor interests and its responsibility in the so-called bureaucratization of the labor movement have been contributing factors.[23] Whether these views are correct or not, the fact remains that

[22] See Eudocio Ravines, *The Yenan Way* (New York, Scribner, 1951).

[23] A prominent leader of Venezuela's Democratic Action party, who considers himself a socialist, described the present deterioration of the Argentine socialists

Argentine socialism has failed, so far, to afford the type of dynamic leadership and driving force which will be necessary to compete with other parties with any measure of success.

The Democratic party (Partido Democrático) in Chile was a mildly socialist group. This party and the Worker's Socialist party (Partido Socialista Obrero) were rivals of the anarchists in the trade-union movement. A socialist group developed in Peru after the First World War, but it never had much influence except in certain northern communities near the oil fields. After the First World War, some of the Latin-American socialist parties went over to the Communist International, and it was some years before new socialist groups were organized. Gradually organizations arose again in Chile, Peru, Ecuador, Colombia, Uruguay, Cuba, and Brazil. Some contact has existed among these various parties. In 1919 a Socialist Congress was held in Buenos Aires; and in 1940 and 1946 other conferences were held.

It is important to note that a remarkable ideological affinity exists between the new indigenous parties such as the Aprista or Democratic Action previously described and these older types of socialist parties. Although with some differences in emphasis, the programs of the former are in agreement with fundamental socialist postulates, and there is little doubt that if an international grouping of political parties were to be made these new Latin-American parties would generally fall in the class of socialist organizations. In many cases the members of these parties use the term "socialist" as applicable to themselves.

Other Parties. Among the most interesting of the Catholic-Social parties, of which there are only a few in Latin America, is the Falange Nacional of Chile (not connected in any way with the Falange of Franco's Spain). A group of intellectuals with the support of some leaders among the workers has built up in a short time a fighting party which shows promise for the future. Not too far from the European Christian and Social Democrats in its philosophy and platform, this Chilean group is the only party of importance in Latin America which is representative of Catholic political activities. The Roman Church's intervention in almost all other cases is limited to the trade-union movement, with varied results in each country. There is a significant Catholic labor group in Ecuador, an efficient

---

as the result of their failure to keep in touch with the worker and their emphasis on intellectuals and theoreticians. He used the expression "classroom socialism" (*socialismo de cátedra*). (Interview with Rómulo Betancourt, Aug. 23, 1945.)

organization in Colombia which is steadily gaining strength, and an old Catholic labor group in Costa Rica of some prestige and power.[24] On the other hand, the role played by similar groups in Argentina and Brazil is of no great importance.

However, an organization strongly influenced by the Catholic Church and deserving special attention is the controversial Unión Nacional Sinarquista of Mexico, a group which represents an extreme rightist reaction against the "Mexican revolution." It is strongly antiforeign and especially anti–United States. It was originally organized in 1936 by Oscar Schreiter, a German engineer, and it has many typical fascist characteristics such as uniforms, emblems, and salutes. During the Second World War it was pro-Axis and it received encouragement and financial assistance from German sources. With a program which advocates the establishment of a "Christian order" and opposition to "decadent liberalism" and "atheist communism,"[25] the *sinarquismo* (literally: "ruling together," implying cooperation between classes) has recruited considerable support among Mexican peasants, disillusioned with the agrarian policies of the "revolution." The organization is imbued with a curious missionary fervor, but it has failed so far to produce leaders of stature. It represents, however, the most numerous and substantial element among the organized opposition.

There is in Latin America one party which stands in a class by itself. It is the Institutional Revolutionary party (Partido Revolucionario Institucional, or PRI), the cornerstone of Mexico's one-party system. A creation of President Calles in 1928, then called National Revolutionary party (Partido Nacional Revolucionario), it was a combination of regional machines claiming to represent all revolutionary forces in the country. The component parts, labor unions, agricultural leagues, professional organizations, and even military associations retained their identity but were under the authority of a national executive committee. A process of absorption of other parties was immediately begun, and the PNR became a formidable political machine with effective electoral power. President Lázaro Cárdenas (1934–1940) undertook the transformation of the Calles machine into a "functional party" by inducing organized

[24] Such organizations are, in Ecuador, the Confederación Nacional de Trabajadores Católicos and the Confederación Ecuatoriana de Obreros Católicos; in Colombia, the Unión de Trabajadores Colombianos; in Costa Rica, the Confederación de Trabajadores "Rerum Novarum."

[25] *Programa del Sinarquismo* (Mexico, 1944).

laborers and peasants to pour their ranks into the PNR.[26] In March 1939, the PNR was transformed into the Party of the Mexican Revolution (Partido de la Revolución Mexicana, or PRM), and four autonomous sections—labor, peasant, popular, and army—were fused into a single instrument. The army section of the party was later abolished. By including it at first, it was hoped to discourage military coups and to indoctrinate the army in the principles of the "revolution." The fundamental

TABLE 17
MEXICO—SUMMARY OF VOTING BY PARTIES

Party	Popular vote	Percentage
Congressional elections, 1949		
Partido Revolucionario Institucional (PRI)	1,821,781	89.2
Partido Acción Nacional (PAN)	178,952	8.9
Partido Popular (PP)	38,712	1.9
Sinarquistas, Communists (PEP and PCM)	1,847	0.0
Total	2,041,292	100.0
Presidential elections, 1952		
Partido Revolutionario Institucional (PRI)	2,713,419	74.3
Federación de Partidos del Pueblo (FPP)	579,745	15.8
Partido Acción Nacional (PAN)	285,555	7.9
Partido Popular (PP)	72,482	2.0
Unregistered candidates	282	0.0
Total	3,651,483	100.0

SOURCE: Adapted from Howard F. Cline, *The United States and Mexico* (Cambridge, Mass., Harvard University Press, 1953), pp. 328, 331.

task, the PRM stated, was the preparation of the people for the establishment of a worker's democracy as a step toward socialism. Further reconstruction of the party and change of its name to PRI did not really affect the political tradition, although it marked a shift toward moderation in governmental policy. Membership of the party is claimed to be over four million. It includes now all the political and unionist branches of the "revolution," the majority of the rank and file of the army, and the total number of officeholders. The party prepares plans and programs for

[26] Nathaniel Weil and Sylvia Weil, *The Reconquest of Mexico* (New York, Oxford University Press, 1939), pp. 341–369.

the administration. Technicians and specialists study national problems and submit plans which are first approved by the executive committee and then submitted to the party's national convention. Today this formidable electoral machine, vehemently criticized by its opponents as a nondemocratic organ in every sense, makes Mexico effectively a one-party country. While any party may be constituted in Mexico (except religious organizations) with the same legal privileges of the PRI, an opposition party has little chance of electing candidates, and state governors and other high officials are often selected in the PRI national headquarters. However, within the giant PRI there exist wings or factions which, in the internal maneuvering for power, do serve in some measure to mitigate this situation by giving a semblance of the free play of parties in a broader system.

Conclusion. From the preceding discussion it becomes apparent that a number of factors have recently produced a substantial change in the pattern of political activity in Latin America, and that even more novel political alignments may be developing. Among the new factors the most noteworthy are the appearance of new forces in politics, which are competing for power with the older and traditional political groups; the increasing participation of organized labor in politics; the rise of parties which give forceful and dramatic presentation of national socioeconomic problems; the strong nationalistic tone of postwar politics; and the possible weakening of personalism, evident in some cases, with the consequent strengthening of party principles.

Legal Control of Parties

Strongly influenced as they were by the new constitutional current which developed at the end of the First World War, the Latin-American countries became concerned with the problems of legal organization and functioning of parties. Their constitutions had ignored, until this time, the existence of political parties. Now they began to follow a trend of which the first European manifestations were to be seen in the Weimar Constitution of 1919 (Article 124), and the Russian Constitution of 1936 (Article 141).

In accordance with this trend the Latin-American countries have imposed some sort of control upon the organization and conduct of political parties. These regulations commonly prescribe requirements for the legal establishment and recognition of political groups and provide for their extinction under certain circumstances. They are also designed to guarantee the democratic process within the parties and to remedy corrupt practices.

The way in which these aims are achieved through regulation by the state may be shown by some examples.

The Cuban constitution of 1940 deals more extensively than any other with political parties. It states that the organization of political parties and associations is free, but specifically prohibits any political groupings on the basis of race, sex, or class. A political party must meet certain qualifications in order to receive legal recognition. It must be founded by a number of persons equal to or greater than 2 per cent of the corresponding electoral census, according to the national, provincial, or municipal character of such party.[27] A party which, in a general or special election, fails to obtain 2 per cent of the votes loses its legal status. No candidacies may be presented by any party which has failed to hold a new election for its own officers at least six months before each general election. This election of party officers must be held for all the units of a given party on the same day throughout the nation. A party failing to meet this requirement is automatically removed from the registry of parties. A provision safeguards the prerogatives of party conventions by stating that they retain all their powers and may not be dissolved except by legal reorganization. According to this clause, party conventions are the only bodies which can make nominations, and this power cannot in any case be delegated (Article 102). These provisions are supplemented in Cuba by an electoral code (Código Electoral), a remarkable body of laws which covers all electoral matters with considerable minuteness of detail.

Although the constitution of Brazil deals with suffrage, electoral courts, and loss of political rights, it includes only a single clause relating to parties. By it, the organization, registration, and functioning of any party with a program that is opposed to the democratic system is prohibited. Nevertheless, party organization in Brazil is governed by the regulations contained in a decree law of May 28, 1945.

Party Structure

The internal structure of parties in the various countries follows a fairly uniform pattern. The organization of major parties extends from the national level to the provinces, cantons, municipalities, and parishes. The general assembly or convention is the supreme party organ, and local bodies perform a corresponding role for the various smaller units. How-

[27] In Brazil legislation enacted in 1945 established a minimum of 10,000 members. One per cent of the total number of registered voters in the corresponding district is required by Argentina's laws.

ever, the national executive committee (*comité ejecutivo nacional* or *suprema junta,* or *directorio general*) is in most cases the real supreme party authority. The conventions may become rubber-stamp bodies to all practical effects. For parties in power, the formal machinery usually becomes a complacent instrument in the hands of the president.

The local units in the party hierarchy are the precinct committees (*comités de barrio*) and the precinct conventions (*asambleas de barrio*). Elections at the local level are preceded by municipal party assemblies or conventions which select candidates for local offices and delegates to the provincial conventions. The latter, in turn, choose candidates for provincial offices and name delegates to the national convention. It is common for national conventions to meet frequently, in some cases at least once every year, to attend to party business. As has been noted, in Cuba, the law calls for election of party officers prior to every election, and failure to comply causes removal from the official party registry. It was strongly felt that this requirement and the powers granted to the Electoral Supreme Tribunal to intervene in party organization would be effective safeguards of democratic procedures in party matters. Past experiences of control of parties by small cliques during the Machado dictatorship (1925–1933) led to the adoption of these provisions.

Party Primaries and Nominations

Direct primary elections have long been advocated for party offices in Latin America. In general, however, method, mode, and time of elections of party officers are left to the party's own choice provided they are not in contradiction to the laws. With respect to the nomination of candidates for public offices, legislation on parties is generally silent. In Brazil, it is prescribed that registration of candidates must be made fifteen days before the election and that the list of candidates be presented under the party's name.[28] There is no provision, however, concerning the method used by parties in nominating candidates. Likewise, legislation in Uruguay contains no regulations on the selection of candidates but requires official announcement of them.[29] In all these countries candidates for public office are nominated by the national assemblies or conventions. Independent candidacies are permitted in all countries except Brazil, where only candidates registered by parties can participate in elections.

Other aspects of election laws are of some interest. The Argentine laws

[28] Decreto-Ley 7586, May 28, 1945, Art. 40.
[29] Ley Electoral, Jan. 16, 1925, Art. 11.

regulate political propaganda. An interesting feature is one providing that owners of radio stations are obliged to put their facilities at the disposal of the federal electoral courts for one hour a day during the ten days immediately preceding a national election. The courts are supposed to utilize this time to inform the voters concerning their rights. Laws in Cuba and Argentina are counterparts of the Federal Corrupt Practice Act and the Hatch Act of the United States. These laws adequately encompass the various aspects of contributions and accounting of campaign expenses. Expenses of a candidate cannot exceed 10,000 pesos in Argentina (excluding travel, subsistence, mail, and telephone expenses). In Cuba no candidate may spend more than a sum equivalent to one-fourth of the yearly salary assigned to the office. If the post carries no salary, the maximum expense allowed is $500. Individual contributions for a particular candidate may not exceed $100. In the matter of party contributions, a municipal committee may contribute an amount not exceeding $1,000; a provincial committee, $5,000; and the national committee, $10,000.[30]

Electoral Courts

A significant question is that of what governmental body is to be entrusted with the function of enforcing election laws and of exercising legal control over political organization. Three systems have been proposed to this end: (1) to assign this function to the executive branch or to one of its subordinate bodies; (2) to add this task to the function of the judicial branch; and (3) to give these powers to special electoral tribunals which must enjoy the same independence as ordinary courts of justice.[31]

Latin America has favored in good part the establishment of special electoral courts adequately safeguarded by the same constitutional guarantees which apply to the members of the judicial branch. Brazil, Ecuador, Cuba, Nicaragua, Panama, and Uruguay have provided a constitutional basis for the operation of these courts, while in other countries statutory legislation has dealt with their organization and functioning.

The Uruguayan electoral court, for example, has the duties of taking

[30] Código Electoral de Cuba, Art. 354. Enforcement of this legislation has proved difficult. In the Havana municipal elections held in 1950, and in the national elections of 1954, sums amounting to several million dollars were used for campaign purposes. In recent years the cost of campaigning has gone steadily upward. Considering the cost of radio and television, movies, and other modern propaganda media, present ceilings on electoral expenditures appear unrealistic.

[31] Helen L. Clagett, *Administration of Justice in Latin America* (New York, Oceana Publications, 1952), pp. 98–108.

cognizance of all matters relating to elections; of exercising complete jurisdiction over electoral bodies; of deciding appeals and claims; and of judging the elections for all offices. In Ecuador, an autonomous set of courts and boards is charged with the general supervision of elections. Its powers extend to the interpretation of election laws, the investigation of fraud cases, and the counting of votes in presidential elections.[32]

The Cuban system of electoral justice is centered on a Superior Electoral Tribunal composed of three judges of the supreme court and two of the provincial supreme court of Havana (*audiencia*), appointed for a term of four years by the plena of their respective courts. Besides the broad powers which are common to all electoral judiciaries, the Cuban court may, in case of grave disturbance or when it considers that there are not sufficient guarantees, order the suspension or nullification of elections. Although, under the system, jurisdiction over electoral complaints is reserved to electoral courts, appeals in some may be taken to another special court, the Tribunal of Constitutional and Social Guarantees (Tribunal de Garantías Constitucionales y Sociales). An interesting feature of the Cuban plan is a merit system for electoral employees and officials. These officers enjoy tenure and their compensation is fixed by the electoral code.

Suffrage and Elections

The majority of Latin-American opinion favors a concept of suffrage as a public function which involves an irrenounceable duty. This principle is clearly reflected in the constitutions of all countries.[33] In Panama, for instance, suffrage is a right and a duty of all citizens, and in Uruguay every citizen is a part of the sovereignty of the nation and as such he is a voter (Articles 102 and 77, respectively). The Cuban constitution refers to voting as a right, a duty, and a function of all citizens (Article 97).

The present trend is toward compulsory voting. Cuba, Brazil, Argentina, Ecuador, El Salvador, Guatemala, Honduras, Nicaragua, Paraguay, and Peru specifically state in their constitutions the compulsory nature of voting. In Guatemala it is obligatory for citizens who know how to read and write, but optional for women as it is also in Ecuador. In Peru registration and voting are obligatory for men up to the age of sixty years and

[32] Constitution of Ecuador (Arts. 20–25). See also Blanksten, *Ecuador: Constitutions and Caudillos,* p. 72.

[33] For an interesting treatment of suffrage, see Juan A. González Calderón, *Derecho constitucional argentino* (3 vols., 2d. ed., Buenos Aires, 1923), vol. II, p. 321.

optional for those older. In many of the countries voting is restricted to citizens, while in Venezuela it may be extended in municipal elections to aliens who have resided for more than ten years in the country.[34]

The merits of compulsory voting are open to serious question. The law imposes penalties against citizens who fail to cast their ballots, ranging from dismissal from government positions, disqualification for a certain period from public employment, and fines of up to several hundred dollars, but in practice compulsory voting has been effective only in the case of government workers and public office seekers. It has had little or no noticeable effect upon the large mass of voters who stay away from the ballot boxes out of indifference, and who can still do so with relative impunity. Abstention from voting (*retraimiento*) is an electoral practice widely admitted in Latin America. It is used to express the protest of a political party against some manifest coercion, an abusive electoral law, or an arbitrary measure of some sort. By deciding to abstain from participating in an election, the party may serve notice that it refuses to recognize the legal status of a certain administration, and it may justify a further course of action leading to violence on its part. Compulsory voting has not prevented *retraimiento.* After all, it is always possible for anyone who prefers abstention but does not want to risk disqualification from public office to render his ballot ineffective by voting for imaginary candidates.

The age requirement for voting ranges from eighteen to twenty-one. Some countries have established a minimum of eighteen for male voters while requiring twenty-one or twenty-five years for women. In some countries the age is reduced if the person meets certain qualifications, such as being married or owning property. In general the age limit is lower than in the United States.

Compulsory registration of voters is rigidly enforced in some countries because it is a simple way to keep a record of those who, at the same time that they attain the minimum voting age, become eligible for military service. When registration is completed, the voter receives an enrollment book (*libreta de enrolamiento,* or *carnet electoral,* or *cédula electoral*) which generally contains his fingerprints, his signature, and, in some countries, his photograph.

The ballots are still printed by the parties in most countries, subject

[34] Also in Haiti foreigners with a five-year term of residence are entitled to vote in local elections. In Argentina foreigners may vote in local elections in most of the provinces. In Chile a foreigner may participate in municipal elections under certain circumstances.

ordinarily to legal specifications concerning color and size. In several countries the government provides, at its expense, the official envelopes in which the ballot is placed by the voter. In still others the ballots are prepared and printed by the supreme electoral tribunals. The Australian ballot system has been adopted in Mexico, Cuba, Venezuela, Nicaragua, and El Salvador.

Voting is theoretically secret, although voting booths are not always provided. In some countries (such as Ecuador, Honduras, Nicaragua, and Venezuela), in an effort to prevent "repeating," the hands of the voters may be marked with indelible ink. In countries in which ballots are printed by each party it is very difficult to vote a split ticket, but not impossible since the voter may write in other names besides those of his party's candidates. In other countries the voter may choose within the list of his party, but he may not divide his vote among several parties.

The principle of proportional representation is safeguarded by various methods. In Argentina, a system of limited voting is used for the election of members of the lower branch of the congress, by which voters mark their ballots for but two-thirds of the number of seats to be filled. The Brazilian system employs a device for the election of congressmen and state legislators by which each party receives a number of seats on the basis of the vote that favors it. The electoral systems of Chile, Colombia, Ecuador, Venezuela, Uruguay, Nicaragua, and Costa Rica also provide for some method of proportional representation in the legislative branch. The Cuban system has included since 1935 an extension of the principle of minority representation to the upper chamber of congress.

Proportional representation in some countries has not lived up to the expectations of those who advocated it as a device for more effective recording of the popular will. Main defects of the system are the considerable delay caused by a complex method of counting and the loss of popular interest by the time election results are announced. In addition, minority representation has also contributed to a fragmentation of parties which is not desirable, and to the frequent practice of *jugar a la minoría* which literally means "to play the minority game."

Electoral Frauds and Corruption

Despite the enactment of fair laws, election administration in Latin America suffers from vices and fraud, and it is often under complete control of the political group in power. Fraudulent voting and rigged elections have long been known in Latin America, and political history is full of instances in which balloting was a mere farce. There are indeed abundant examples of intolerance and lack of maturity in electoral struggles derived from a tradition of force. Although legal provisions are carefully prepared to ensure freedom in elections, there is no doubt that on the subject of political activity, contradictions exist between law and reality which strikingly illustrate the wide differences between theory and practice. Unfortunately revolution as an instrument of political action, fraud, bloodshed, and illegal activities of various sorts are characteristic of the electoral process in many countries. In others politics and parties are in the hands of small privileged minorities, while the great mass of the people exercise little or no influence on the political process. Elections are still marred in some countries by the practice of *continuismo,* the persistence of *caudillismo,* and the many ingenious devices used by unscrupulous politicians to keep themselves in office.[35]

However, to conclude that these corrupt practices are invariably present in all Latin-American elections would be not only a superficial conclusion but an unjust one. It is possible that observers have been unconsciously inclined to focus their attention on the faulty operation of the electoral system and have failed to record the consistent Latin-American denunciation of and opposition to such dishonest practices. No party leader today dares condone the use of fraud and violence, and political maturity and responsibility are steadily growing. Some recent national elections held in the last decade in Cuba, Guatemala, Honduras, Ecuador, Chile, Brazil, Uruguay, Costa Rica, Venezuela, and El Salvador have been reasonably free and fair. In several of these elections, it is significant that it was the opposition and not the party in control which won the election and that the outcome was accepted without question. More and more the honesty of elections is being better guaranteed by the force of public opinion than it ever was by regulations and laws.

Women in Politics

Some of the constitutions specifically established the principle of equality of political rights of men and women, but in some countries equality has been given by acts of the congress. In Ecuador, the first Latin-American country to recognize the right of women to vote, that principle

[35] For descriptions of electoral trickery in Argentina and Honduras, see Austin F. MacDonald, *Government of the Argentine Republic* (New York, Crowell, 1942), pp. 120–124; and William S. Stokes, *Honduras: An Area Study in Government* (Madison, Wis., University of Wisconsin Press, 1950), pp. 231–264.

of equality first appeared in the constitution of 1929. On the other hand, in Brazil such rights were guaranteed for the first time, not by the constitution, but by means of an executive decree of the federal government in 1932. At present, however, they are included in the constitution. In a few countries women cannot be granted political rights by means of ordinary legislation because the constitution states that the function of suffrage and the right to be elected to office are reserved to male citizens. Such was the case in Colombia, where women were granted this right by action of the Constitutional Assembly of 1954. In Chile, the constitution makes no distinction between men and women with respect to the right to vote. However, it was not until 1949 that women were granted such rights on a national basis by a law of congress, although for some time previously they had voted and had been elected in municipal elections.[36]

At present women enjoy full political rights in sixteen of the countries, but are entitled to participate only in municipal elections in Haiti.[37] In Nicaragua, Honduras, and Paraguay, they are excluded from voting. Two of the countries which have granted rights to vote to women have done so with some conditions peculiar to themselves. For example, in Guatemala, only women who can read and write may exercise the rights of the ballot.

Three countries which have recently established universal suffrage are Mexico, Bolivia, and Peru. By a law of 1946 which amended the constitution, women were given the right to vote in municipal elections in Mexico. As a result, two women were for the first time elected presidents of municipal councils in the state of Hidalgo, and the number of voters increased considerably. Almost 50 per cent of the municipal officers chosen in the first election held after that state recognized woman suffrage were females. In 1952 the Mexican federal congress approved a constitutional amendment establishing universal suffrage in all elections. Such an amendment is at this time in process of ratification by the legislatures of the twenty-nine states of the union. Women also voted only in municipal elections in Bolivia until a decree issued by the executive in 1952 granted them the right to participate in all elections. A bill passed in 1955 granted Peruvian women the right to vote in national elections.

Participation of women in public life was greatly encouraged by grant-

[36] Law 9,292, Jan. 8, 1949.

[37] The Haitian constitution of 1950 stipulates that a law will grant women full voting rights within three years from the date of the first municipal elections in which they participate.

TABLE 18
WOMAN SUFFRAGE IN LATIN AMERICA

Country	*Date achieved*
Ecuador	1929
Brazil	1932
Uruguay	1932
Cuba	1934
El Salvador	1939
Dominican Republic	1942
Guatemala	1945
Panama	1946
Venezuela	1947
Argentina	1947
Chile	1949
Costa Rica	1949
Bolivia	1952
Mexico*	1952
Colombia	1954
Peru	1955
Provincial Suffrage	
Mexico, in the states of	
Yucatán	1923
Chiapas	1926
Guanajuato	1936
Puebla	1939
Michoacán	1939
Municipal Suffrage	
Peru	1933
Bolivia	1945
Mexico	1946
Haiti†	1950

* Pending ratification of constitutional amendment by the state legislatures.

† This confers elegibility to be elected to municipal offices. It further provides that a law must assure unrestricted suffrage and all political rights within a time not exceeding three years after the next succeeding general municipal election.

ing them the right to vote, and at every recent election they have played a role that is increasingly significant. In Argentina women voted for the first time in the national elections of November 11, 1951. Statistics show that about 4,500,000 women and 4,400,000 men cast their ballots. Six women were elected to the senate and twenty-six to the chamber of deputies. In Chile, when women voted for the first time on September 4, 1952, their votes constituted 33 per cent of the 956,000 qualified voters in the entire country. In the municipal elections held in Guatemala in 1945, 90 per cent of the qualified women voters in the capital city cast ballots. In all elections held in Cuba since 1944 the vote of women has been very considerable.

Women are now often elected to congress and to various state and local offices. In the 1952 electoral campaign in Panama, there were eighteen women candidates for congressional seats, and the feminine vote reached over 179,000, indicating a steady increase since 1945. In Uruguay for the first time in the history of the country, a woman presided in 1952 over the sessions of the joint meeting of the congress. Cuban women have had access for some time to seats in both houses of the legislature and have served as provincial governors. Many women have been appointed to top level positions of responsibility in executive departments and in the diplomatic service. Two women were ministers without portfolio in the Cuban cabinet in 1953. In Chile a woman was appointed minister of justice in 1952, and another was heading the ministry of education in 1952. The first woman member of the cabinet was appointed in Nicaragua in 1950. There were 120 women occupying positions in the Mexican Foreign Service in 1952. Women are also finding new opportunities in the administration of justice. They hold numerous judgeships in Venezuela, Cuba, Mexico, Ecuador, Nicaragua, Uruguay, and El Salvador.

BIBLIOGRAPHY

Alexander, Robert J., *Labor Parties of Latin America,* L.I.D. Pamphlet Series, League for Industrial Democracy, New York, 1942.

Astigueta, José M., *Sufragio y partidos políticos. Antecedentes para una mejor legislación,* Buenos Aires, 1940.

Caffarena de Jiles, Elena, *Capacidad de la mujer casada con relacion a sus bienes,* Santiago, 1944.

Comisión Inter-Americana de Mujeres, *Derechos políticos de la mujer de América,* Washington, Pan American Union, 1951.

Echaíz, René León, *Evolución histórica de los partidos políticos chilenos,* Santiago, 1939.

Fabregat, Julio T., *Los partidos políticos en la legislación uruguaya,* Montevideo, 1949.

Linares Quintana, Segundo V., *Los partidos políticos: instrumentos de gobierno,* Buenos Aires, 1945.

Lopes, Alfredo Cecilio, *A racionalização dos partidos políticos,* São Paulo, 1934.

Luna Morales, Clara, *El sufragio femenino en México,* Mexico, 1947.

Matienzo, José Nicolás, "Reglamentación legal de los partidos políticos," in *Nuevos temas políticos e históricos,* Buenos Aires, 1928.

Melo, Carlos R., *Los partidos políticos argentinos,* Cordoba, 1943.

Palacios, Alfredo, *Los partidos políticos: su organización y funcionamiento,* Buenos Aires, 1938.

Pardo Zamora, Miguel, *El sufragio universal en Chile,* Santiago, 1946.

Pivel Devoto, Juan E., *Historia de los partidos políticos en el Uruguay,* Montevideo, 1942.

Roig de Leuchsenring, Emilio, *Los grandes movimientos políticos cubanos en la república,* Havana, 1943.

Rueda Zavalla, Arturo, and Margarita R. Rozada, *Ensayo del gobierno de dos partidos,* Buenos Aires, 1942.

Stevenson, John Reese, *The Chilean Popular Front,* Philadelphia, University of Pennsylvania Press, 1942.

Terán Gómez, Luis, *Los partidos políticos y su acción democrática,* La Paz, 1942.

Chapter 14: LABOR AND SOCIAL LEGISLATION

Labor movements have been in progress in several of the Latin-American countries in one form or another for about fifty years. It was not until recently, however, that trade unions developed as a powerful element in national affairs in countries such as Mexico, Cuba, Chile, and Argentina. In recent decades trade-union membership has grown at an astonishing pace in company with industrial development. Present estimates range from five to nine million organized workers in Latin America. Although such estimates are unreliable, it is commonly accepted that only a small and insignificant portion of Latin America's industrial laborers are not grouped together in some form of organization.[1]

In some countries the greater part of urban workers have been unionized, and trade-union organization has spread to include certain types of workers who, until recent years, had failed to organize because of hostility and resistance of their employers.

Historical Development of Organized Labor

The development of the labor movement has been retarded in Latin America by a variety of causes. The most significant of these are (1) the incipient and late industrial development in countries which hitherto depended on an agrarian economy; (2) the hostile attitude of the employers in some cases; (3) the suspicion and disfavor shown by the governments; (4) the lack of ability and experience on the part of labor's leadership; (5) the economic control exercised by certain enterprises over their workers in some countries; and (6) the strong political tone which has always colored workers' organizations.[2] Each of these factors will be discussed in more detail later in this chapter.

[1] Simon G. Hanson, *Economic Development in Latin America* (Washington, D.C., The Inter-American Affairs Press, 1951), p. 494. It is generally recognized that workers' organizations tend to exaggerate their membership in order to impress potential joiners, their employers, and the government. Employers and regimes hostile to labor often use such distorted claims in justification of their concern at the unions' growth of power.

[2] Moisés Poblete Troncoso, *El movimiento obrero latino-americano* (Mexico, 1946), pp. 23–24.

It may suffice now to say that the late development of industry in Latin America necessarily determined the type of labor organization which has developed. In some countries the labor movement had to struggle bitterly for freedom of organization and for the rights of collective bargaining against the equally obstinate resistance of employers. This struggle lasted many years, and in some cases labor's efforts to gain such rights became identified with the winning of political democracy. The attitude of governments toward labor often resulted in intervention of the authorities in favor of the employers, the persecution and imprisonment of union leaders, the declaration of the state of siege, and the suspension of civil liberties. Mediocre leadership of unions has resulted in frequent abuses of power, irresponsibility, and acceptance of extensive government intervention in labor conflicts. Corruption and mismanagement on the part of labor leaders have at times discredited and weakened their organizations. Lastly, the inclination of unions to engage in political action has exposed their development to the hazards of politics more than in any other region of the world.

The strength derived from friendly relations with sympathetic governments has been a significant factor in the astounding growth of the labor movement in Argentina, Chile, Cuba, Peru, Venezuela, and elsewhere. It is obvious, however, that political identification may have an opposite effect. If and when the friendly party loses control of the government, the new regime may make it appear that the labor movement is nothing but a pretense for subversive political activity, with punitive measures as a consequence. The recent plight of Colombian labor, long identified with the Liberal party in that country, furnishes a good illustration of such a course of events.

A separate treatment by countries would be necessary to present a fair and complete picture of the history of organized labor in Latin America. This, however, is beyond the space limits of this book and, indeed, is scarcely needed since there are available numerous and excellent works dealing with the subject. Therefore, all that will be attempted here is to point out certain lines of development and features which are common to all or to most of the labor movements in these countries.[3]

[3] Among the best with reference to the entire area are: Poblete Troncoso, *op. cit.;* Carlos Moret, *Historia general del desarrollo de las organizaciones de trabajadores* (Buenos Aires, 1933); Robert J. Alexander, *Labour Movements in Latin America* (London, Fabian Publications, and Gollancz, 1947); Ernesto Galarza, *Labor in Latin America* (Washington, D.C., American Council on Public Affairs, n.d.). Numerous studies are available concerning the history of labor in a

Labor organization began in almost every country with the establishment of mutual benefit societies (*mutualidades*). The workers banded together during this period primarily to attend to those immediate needs which arise in case of illness, as well as to those of a "spiritual" character. The *mutualidades* were more than insurance groups, since they served as centers of the workers' activities, providing meetings, lectures, night schools, and libraries. Some of these organizations contributed significantly to the educational improvement of the workers, and their membership is still in some cases impressive. For instance, there are some in Argentina with thirty thousand members. In Chile, where the first *mutualidad* was created in 1853 (Sociedad Tipográfica), there are today about five hundred. In Cuba the powerful Centro Asturiano, Centro Gallego, and others have an estimated membership of 40,000 to 60,000, and in Uruguay La Fraternidad has more than 30,000.[4] Most of the mutual benefit societies were organized on the basis of trades, but often they included laborers other than artisans such as railroad, textile, and maritime workers. Less politically minded than the unions and in general more conservative, these societies still play a significant role in those countries where there is relatively little industrial development. They are well suited to the characteristic individualism of the small artisan who works in a little shop or is his own employer. They remained as the typical form of organization until the appearance of large groups of industrial workers at the turn of the twentieth century.

The next phase of development was marked by the rise of the "resistance groups" (*sociedades de resistencia*). Produced by the newly born economic issues caused by industry's advance, these fighting groups struggled for the improvement of labor conditions and against the influence of the employers. Often they consisted of one or more unions (*gremios*) in the same industry, sometimes organized during a strike. Handicapped by the lack of permanent officers and by inexperience, they were generally short-lived. In Chile, Mexico, Uruguay, Peru, and some other countries these pioneering organizations were controlled by anarcho-syndicalist

---

particular country, such as Tulio Lagos Valenzuela, *Bosquejo histórico del movimiento obrero en Chile* (Santiago, 1944); Moisés Poblete Troncoso, *El movimiento de asociación profesional obrera en Chile* (Mexico, 1945); Edgardo Vargas Serra, *Sindicalismo brasileiro* (Rio de Janeiro, 1939); Moisés Alvarez, *La organización sindical en Bolivia* (La Paz, 1937): and numerous articles published in the *Revue Internationale du Travail* and in *Monthly Labor Review.*

[4] Poblete Troncoso, *El movimiento obrero latino-americano, op. cit.*, p. 20.

groups who were to engage, after the First World War, in a losing battle for influence with the new socialist and Communist elements.

The first groups which were strictly trade unions in the modern sense began to appear at the turn of the century in certain fields of industry where there existed a large labor force under a few employers. Workers in the transportation and textiles industries took the initiative in the broad and rapid expansion of the labor movement which followed. Railwaymen and maritime workers, with older groups of the printing-trade workers and bakers, led the movement in Argentina and Chile. Tobacco workers, railwaymen, and port laborers were among the first to organize in Cuba. Mining and oil workers played a pioneering role in Chile, Mexico, and Venezuela.

With the continued expansion of industry in the interval between the two world wars, trade unions grew to significant proportions. A mass of legislation was enacted in every country setting principles of public policy with respect to the right of association, collective bargaining, wages, hours, compensation, insurance, profit-sharing, protection of women workers, dismissal pay, housing, vacations, and similar subjects. Latin-American workers were guaranteed the eight-hour day at an early date. It existed on a limited scale in Chile in 1908, and it has been applied generally in Uruguay since 1915. Minimum-wage laws were early enacted in many countries, as well as legislation regarding severance pay and working conditions for women.[5]

This remarkable development of labor organization soon showed a tendency, common to all countries, to embrace all categories of wage earners in an effort to eradicate any distinctions between laborers and skilled and professional workers such as lawyers, engineers, and artists (*trabajadores intelectuales*). The "liberal professions" thus became a part of the labor force and, by forming their own organizations, came to receive the benefits of legislation originally designed for the common worker. On the other hand, the idea of allowing government employees to organize has not been generally accepted. Although such a right is recognized in Mexico, it is not granted to public employees in the majority of the countries. Furthermore, this prohibition against forming unions is made extensive in some cases to include workers in the public service industries. Nevertheless, government workers have organizations of an informal or

[5] Henry P. Jordan, "Labor and Social Security in Latin America," *International Postwar Problems,* vol. II, pp. 107–125, January, 1945.

social nature which in practice, as in Chile, serve the interests of those workers as effectively as a union despite the fact that they lack legal status.

Common Features of the Labor Movements

An important common characteristic of the Latin-American labor movements is that they have been identified with political groups. Political inclinations have always been present in the trade-union movement, and all indications are that this tendency will continue to characterize the movement. Naturally this factor may vary in significance from country to country, and even within a single country according to conditions at a given time. However, the opinion that a fully nonpolitical labor movement has never existed anywhere in Latin America is generally accepted.

Identification with political parties has usually been with groups professing a more or less "leftist" ideology. Political action has served the worker as the most effective means of obtaining recognition and protection. Friends of labor have often justified its political activity by arguing that the opposition of employers has driven the workers into compacts with whatever allies they could find.[6]

Anarchist groups exerted a significant influence in early labor groups in Argentina, Uruguay, Peru, Chile, and Mexico. These groups were as political in their control of labor as any political party. Syndicalist influence was strong in Argentina and several other countries, where syndicalists attempted to develop a movement free from interference of anarchists and their rivals the socialists. As has been mentioned before, a socialist party had existed in Argentina since 1896. Socialism extended to most of the countries, and its theories won numerous followers from among the ranks of labor. These groups attained control of many unions. More recently groups who adopted the name, although they may not qualify as socialists by tradition and European criteria, have almost completely dominated the majority of the workers' organizations in Chile, Peru, Colombia, Panama, Brazil, Cuba, and Ecuador.

Communist influence in trade unions did not become important until after 1930 and did not reach its peak until the end of the Second World War. During this period its influence over labor became significant in Bolivia, Chile, Colombia, Cuba, Ecuador, Guatemala, Mexico, Panama, Uruguay, and Venezuela. In more recent years, however, this political influence has consistently and rapidly declined as a result of the rise of

[6] Martin Kyne, *Labor Conditions in Bolivia* (Washington, D.C., Congress of Industrial Organizations, 1943), p. 11.

other political groups of greater appeal. Other political groups such as the *peronistas, apristas,* and Catholic reformist parties took a decisive role in the development of labor organizations in some countries, as was noted in the chapter dealing with party alignments.[7]

The question whether the political inclination of workers' organizations has or has not been beneficial to their development is subject to debate. Without doubt, political action by labor groups has been a significant factor in their growth, as well as in their success in gaining legislation to protect their interests and in winning conflicts with their employers. On the other hand, it seems that labor has paid a high price for political protection. By accepting a close alliance with friendly governments, trade unions have often run the risk of becoming nothing more than political instruments of the government and frequently have also been forced to surrender their freedom of action or accept restrictions of this freedom. In many instances the price has included giving up rights to elect their own officers and to manage their own affairs. It has also had the result that collective bargaining was carried on under the guidance and often the control of the government. The danger of confusing political with labor issues has been serious, and often such confusion has caused labor to split along political lines over questions which did not affect the interests of the worker but rather those of the politician.

In some countries, governments have been prone to support labor groups that were their political allies and to crack down harshly against those that they regarded as hostile. In Argentina unions which did not support the Peronista administration were the victims of severe repression. They saw their leaders arrested, their meetings prohibited, their funds confiscated, and their organizations placed in the hands of government-appointed supervisors (*interventores*). The government exercised control of the machinery for collective bargaining by making it necessary for a union to obtain government recognition (*personería gremial*) before it could negotiate valid collective-bargaining contracts, represent its members, or even make use of the good offices of the Secretariat of Labor. The decree of October, 1945, which introduced this requirement further provided that only a single union would be granted legal recognition in any industry or trade in a given region. Some of the oldest unions in Argentina were refused recognition and were prevented from carrying on their activities, while other organizations that were submissive received government endorsement. The latter were practically guaranteed success in nego-

[7] Chap. 13, pp. 318–336.

tiations with employers. Government control is well illustrated by the fact that in 1946 one-third of the ninety-nine members of the general council of the General Confederation of Workers (Confederación General de Trabajadores) held some position in the government or in congress, or were members of unions either controlled or financially supported by the government. The mechanism of government control consisted in the appointment of a supervisor (*interventor*) who became a director of the union with government power supporting him.

On the other hand, it must be said that *peronismo* gave labor handsome compensation for the loss of its independence. With the strong support of the government the workers of northern Argentina were able for the first time to establish labor unions against the opposition of the landowners and employers. Through decrees enacted by the administration shortly before Perón's election in 1946, the workers made impressive gains: minimum wages and improved conditions were set for agricultural laborers; pension funds were established and government credit given as assurance of payment; minimum-wage standards were raised, annual bonuses provided, a national employment service established, and paid vacations ordered; limitations were imposed on the power of dismissal of the employer, while measures were taken to expand social assistance programs.[8]

The close alliance between labor and government has in a similar manner produced mutually profitable results in other countries. In Brazil, while the labor movement was entirely subjected to the government in the period of the Vargas administration, it received the benefits derived from a series of labor and social laws.[9] In Venezuela the government of Acción Democrática (1945–1948) encouraged labor organizations and made concessions in their favor in exchange for support to its policies. The Cuban Auténticos, after eliminating Communist influence and securing control of the Cuban General Confederation of Workers (Confederación General de Trabajadores), made this organization an important element in winning electoral victories and were always careful to look after the interests of all friendly labor groups.

Mexico furnishes perhaps the best example of a country where close relations exist between organized labor and the government. The trade-

[8] Robert J. Alexander, *The Peron Era* (New York, Columbia University Press, 1951), pp. 20–32. See also Hanson, *op. cit.*, pp. 506–509.

[9] In Brazil, as was the case with Mexico, the workers did not participate significantly in the passage of the laws. They were handed down in both countries without much struggling as a present from the government to the workers.

union movement in that country was indeed a creation of the government, since at the time the constitution of 1917 was promulgated there were no significant labor groups in existence. This constitution, in an effort to develop new sources of political power and to broaden popular support for the government, contained the most elaborate and detailed labor program to be found anywhere at that time. For a country predominantly agricultural and with little industry or domestic capital, as Mexico was in 1917, to adopt such an ambitious labor program was indeed unusual. This is explained by the fact that this new social legislation, while hardly affecting any local interests, was to serve the government as an instrument against foreign capital and foreign control of almost all important enterprises. The labor clauses of the constitution were not politically controversial, since they affected no important native interest, and they were converted into a true nationalist program on behalf of the local workers and against the foreign entrepreneur. The trade unions, now with a definite legal status, were given special rights and privileges, but they were also to become an instrument for government control of the national economy. The recognition of collective labor contract and the creation of special bodies, the Boards of Conciliation and Arbitration, entrusted with the settlement of differences between capital and labor were effective means of control. The resulting partnership between the state and labor has supplied the government with what is perhaps its most significant element of strength.[10]

Evidences of a similar working partnership between government and the employer could, of course, be found in other countries. It would not be too difficult to find cases in which the owners of a certain industry appeared to have rights which the workers did not enjoy. The mine operators in the Bolivian tin industry, for instance, have at times been able to enjoy prerogatives which in reality belonged to the Bolivian government. Dubious practices and peculiar interpretations of the law by the employer have been often condoned and tolerated by the authorities. Wage demands have been considered as disguising political attacks on the government, and often purely labor problems have been identified by hostile administrations with issues involving the preservation of public order.[11] It is fair

[10] Frank Tannenbaum, *Mexico: The Struggle for Peace and Bread* (New York, Knopf, 1950), pp. 113–121.

[11] On one occasion the mining companies demanded that a state of siege be declared in the departments of Oruro and Potosí in Bolivia as a condition to the maintenance of production.

to say, then, that, particularly in the past, the employers have also exerted considerable influence in setting governmental policy. In very much the same way that labor may act today, the employers have frequently acted as a united front, working in full concert with one another and with friendly governments against the interests of the worker.

Along with the strong tradition of nationalism, Latin-American labor movements have had in common an equally strong tone of anti-imperialism, which reached its peak during the 1920s. The newly born organized forces of labor during that period almost invariably were the strongest opponents of foreign capital in the various countries. Banana workers in Central America and Colombia, oil workers of Mexico, miners and railwaymen in Chile, meat-packing laborers in Argentina and Uruguay, or sugar-cane workers in Cuba, were often associated with or led the segments which attacked foreign imperialism. Their struggles for gaining such objectives as higher wages and better working conditions have more often than not been embittered by their intense dislike of the foreign ownership of those enterprises. Such an element of nationalism has been offered as a partial explanation at least for the notable advance of Latin America's labor laws in contrast to the actual backward conditions of labor.[12]

The leader of the Peruvian *apristas,* Víctor Raúl Haya de la Torre, became in the late 1920s the chief advocate of the idea that the large foreign-owned companies were the common enemy of both the workers and the incipient native industrialist class. This theme of domestic unity proved sufficiently attractive to lead to a political class collaboration of sorts, which worked out effectively in some cases. The nationalistic spirit is often expressed in discriminatory taxation and enforcement of the laws with the foreign companies as propitious targets in some countries.

However, there have occurred recently significant changes in this attitude. Beginning with the *apristas* and including nearly all socialists, liberals, and reformist groups, nationalist forces have abandoned the original uncompromising position toward the United States and other foreign-owned corporations and are leaning now toward a more conciliatory attitude. Such factors as the change in the Latin-American policy of the United States and the growing strength and political maturity of the Latin-American states and their recognition of the need of attracting capital from abroad if industrialization is to be achieved are contributory ele-

[12] Robert J. Alexander, *Labor Parties of Latin America* (New York, League for Industrial Democracy, 1942), p. 4.

ments in their new thinking. The fact that antiforeign feeling may be fostered by politicians seeking to promote their own interests does not preclude the existence of responsible groups and leaders who are intent on finding ways to attract outside capital with guarantees of fair and reasonable treatment and at the same time to safeguard their country against any undue economic or political pressures on the part of foreign-controlled interests. Such groups do not fail to realize that, almost without exception, wages are higher and working conditions better in foreign-owned industries than in the rest of the country's labor force. It is also noted that the exploitive attitude characteristic of foreign-owned corporations in the past has undergone a radical change. Outside interests are intent at present on promoting cordial relations not only with the government but with the people of the country as well.

Another common feature of Latin-American labor is the condition of agricultural workers. Although by far the most numerous group, farm workers have until now participated only slightly in the organized labor movement and have received small benefits from the existing protective legislation. It was not until recently that efforts to organize farm labor were launched in Argentina, Chile, Cuba, Mexico, and Uruguay. Workers' organizations have been weak and ineffective, and enforcement of labor laws in rural areas has been difficult and costly. This slow progress made by the agricultural workers is explained in terms of its relation to the crucial problem of land distribution. The landlord class, considering farm labor organization a serious threat to its interests, never hesitates to use all its great political influence upon governments in order to exclude these workers from whatever protection and benefits are received by the industrial laborers.

Agricultural labor cannot be described generally but according to the system, practices, and customs of different localities. Agricultural wages and conditions may vary in accordance with the different forms of ownership and types of production. There may still be found in certain areas a survival of the colonial semiservitude or at least a patriarchial and benevolently feudal type of relationship between owner and laborer. In other regions the agriculture may be centered in large modern industrial farms which operate for a world market. In still other areas there may be vast lands cultivated under a sharecropper system. There are in addition those regions which are under the communal or collective Indian institutions.

Peonage systems in different degrees and varied denominations may still be found in some countries. Workers under this system, called *huasipungos* in Ecuador, *inquilinos* in Chile, *pongos* in Bolivia, or *pisatarios* in Venezuela, still labor under crude conditions of tenant peonage.[13] In some countries, however, through agrarian reform or the industrialization of agriculture these forms of exploitation have gradually disappeared.

The system of debt bondage called *concertaje* or *habilitación* has been difficult to obliterate or even to alter substantially. Under this system farm laborers in some areas of northern Argentina (until only recently), Bolivia, Colombia, Central America, Paraguay, and Peru are engaged under contracts which include their families. These agreements are often preceded by obligations incurred by the laborers through the receipt of advance payments in order to secure supplies, equipment, and household goods. The laborer is ordinarily obligated to satisfy this indebtedness before he can move on to any new employment. This again in principle is justified, but in practice it may, through design, bind the worker to his employer for a period of years. It is a well-established custom, which may be called an unwritten law, that one employer will not employ workers of another without his consent. An important part in this debt-bondage system is played by the stewards of large estates and by local municipal officers who sometimes act as hiring agents, thereby collecting a fee from the peons.[14]

In countries or regions depending upon such crops as sugar, coffee, tobacco, or cotton, frequent and sharp fluctuations of farm income may contribute to aggravating the condition of the agricultural worker. In other areas there still may be found the truck system or payment in scrip which assures that the workers' wages are spent in the haciendas or company stores (*pulperías, tiendas de raya,* or *proveedurías*). By not permitting the peon to buy elsewhere, and in the absence of some form of governmental control, these stores sometimes can make considerable profit at the expense of the workers. Conditions of this kind inspired the inclusion of clauses in many recent constitutions which specifically forbid the payment of wages in other than legal currency.

Large numbers of rural workers have migrated to the urban centers, attracted by the opportunities of industrial employment and the benefits of a social legislation which is largely designed for the benefit of the

[13] Moisés Poblete Troncoso, *Condiciones de vida y trabajo de la población indígena del Perú* (Geneva, International Labor Office, 1938), contains an interesting description of the operation of this system in Peru.

[14] George Soule, David Efrón, and Norman T. Ness, *Latin America in the Future World* (New York, Rinehart, 1945), pp. 90–92.

industrial workers. This migration is one of the factors which has compelled the government to better conditions of farm labor. Organization of agricultural workers is gradually being allowed and, in some countries, Argentina, for instance, specifically promoted by the government. Social insurance programs have been expanded in Argentina, Brazil, Ecuador, Mexico, Paraguay, Chile, Uruguay, and Cuba so as to include the rural workers. These measures may well set a precedent to be followed by other countries, although it is easy to predict that the establishment of an effective rural labor organization will have social repercussions of a serious nature in many of the Latin-American states. This development, however, is still greatly retarded, except perhaps in those countries which have large foreign holdings in agriculture, where it is stimulated by nationalistic policies. Enforcement of legislation protecting the rural worker is made difficult by the lack of transportation facilities, the limited number of trained officials, and the high cost of an effective machinery of administration.

The Latin-American labor movement as a whole has had another common characteristic. This has been the almost exclusive emphasis placed by labor on rights and gains in contrast to a somewhat negligent and uninterested attitude toward its duties. Labor's struggle for its goals seems often to have been almost entirely devoid of awareness of its responsibilities to the public and to its employers. This lack of sense of its duty to society may very well be the greatest weakness of the labor movement and the most vulnerable point of its several organizations. Extenuating circumstances may be found in the fact that there is nothing more difficult than the apprenticeship in the exercise of new freedom and power.

It is also well to remember that Latin-American labor suffered a very serious gap in its historical development. The loss of status and prestige with consequent decline and destruction which was experienced by the colonial guilds (*gremios*) as a result of the emancipation from the mother country interrupted the continuity of a process of development. The gap deprived the labor movement of a steady evolution in which the pride of workmanship and the fine traditions of social responsibilities of labor could have been cultivated. Instead, the labor movement was born out of grievances and carried with it an unfortunate heritage of bitterness. Perhaps this is the key to understanding such common characteristics as instability, a certain flair for politics, and the tendency to grasp for immediate gains rather than struggle for permanent constructive achievements. The long periods during which labor was the victim of ruthless exploitation have engendered hatred and resentment for the future.

The possibility exists, however, that in some cases Latin America's economic development is being retarded by the sometimes arbitrary position assumed by organized labor. In Cuba, for example, despite the prosperity of the country and the presence of many opportunities for investment, only a handful of new enterprises have been undertaken recently by native capitalists. Foreign investors have become increasingly hesitant to embark upon enterprises involving expenditures of imported funds. A report stated in 1952 that 200 million dollars of domestic capital was lying idle, and the National Association of Manufacturers (Asociación Nacional de Industriales) issued warnings that no significant economic development could be expected until labor relations were placed on a more stable basis. Large sums of local capital have gone into rental property—a traditionally safe investment—instead of being channeled into new industries. An official report of the Ministry of Labor issued in September, 1951, indicated that there had occurred in the first eight months of that year 102 strikes, 151 demands for salary increases, and 1,000 meetings held under supervision of the Ministry to settle controversies with employers. Another report made by a special technical mission of the International Bank for Reconstruction and Development stated that the key to Cuba's economic problem rested in labor-management relations, and it proposed a fifteen-point program of improvement.[15]

Under the pressure of a strong and politically minded labor force which rose under the Batista government (1940–1944), the succeeding administrations of Grau San Martín (1944–1948) and of Prío Socarrás (1948–1952) frequently followed a policy of enforcing labor demands by presidential decree, with seizure and administration of enterprises ordered in some instances. Government actions of this kind have tended to increase the reluctance of capital to invest in industrial or agricultural projects with the result of further narrowing the labor market. Thus, in the long run, labor's interests may be adversely affected by the very policies that it has demanded and obtained. The danger of causing a stoppage of capital flow has become real and serious for some countries. It is to be hoped that this situation will be remedied and that the system of relations between employers and workers, while carried out in strict compliance with just labor laws, will be such that any conflict can be

[15] *The New York Times,* Jan. 4, 1952, p. 4

peacefully solved by proper methods where the mutual interests of both are weighed and where issues are resolved with impartiality and justice.

Labor Laws

All Latin-American constitutions contain sections relating to labor. Some of the constitutions, such as those of Cuba, Guatemala, Mexico, Venezuela, and Costa Rica, contain extensive provisions designed to protect the worker. This is also true of the constitutions of Ecuador, Nicaragua, Panama, Uruguay, Bolivia, Honduras, and Brazil. There are no elaborate constitutional bills of rights for the worker in the rest of the countries. In Chile, despite the fact that there is legislation embodying radical principles and general practice regarding labor, there is only a terse reference in the constitution to the protection of labor, industry, and social welfare activities. This is in the section dealing with the constitutional guarantees.

The constitutions of Bolivia, Uruguay, Venezuela, and El Salvador specifically state that labor is under the special protection of the law. In Bolivia such protection is extended to capital or industry as well.

The right of association and organization is guaranteed by clauses in more than half the countries. These provisions include in some cases a requirement that all union officials be citizens by birth, a stipulation designed to prevent foreigners from securing any control of labor groups.

The concept that freedom of labor and work is a right of the individual as well as an obligation to society also appears in most of the laws, although it is expressed in various ways. The social conception of labor is typified by the Uruguayan provision which states that "it is the duty of every inhabitant of the republic, without prejudice to his freedom, to apply his intellectual or physical energies in a manner which will redound to the benefit of the community, which will endeavor to afford him, with preference to citizens, the opportunity of earning his livelihood through the development of some economic activity" (Article 53).

Clauses establishing the right to collective bargaining exist in about ten countries. It is provided by these constitutions that the law shall regulate the system of collective contracts and that they shall be obligatory for both employers and workers. The right to strike is recognized in most countries. A group of states also recognizes the right of employers to the lockout as regulated by the laws (Costa Rica, Cuba, Ecuador, El Salvador, Guatemala, Mexico, and Panama). In some countries the constitution may specifically prohibit strikes in public-service enterprises, as in Venezuela. In Mexico previous approval of the Conciliation and Arbitration Board is required before a lockout can be declared. It should be remembered that collective bargaining, as a result of the strong political tint of the unions, is often carried on under the guidance and control of the government.

The principle of maximum working hours found recognition in Latin America long before it was made law elsewhere. It appears in the constitutions of fourteen countries, and it is regulated in others by ordinary legislation. Some constitutions specifically fix the maximum at eight hours, while others leave this to be determined by law. In most countries, the law establishes exceptions in the case of workers such as household servants, agricultural laborers, and the like. The right of all workers to a maximum working week (usually equivalent to forty-eight hours in pay) and to one month's vacation with pay for every eleven months of work also appears in most constitutions.

In thirteen countries the constitution sets the principle that there will be a minimum wage regulated by law. Minimum-wage laws have spread rapidly during the last twenty years. Although supposedly based upon cost of living studies, wages fixed by law are more likely to reflect the bargaining powers of organized labor and employers.[16] Some legislation allows deductions for housing, supplies, insurance, and other services, and deductions of this kind may amount to a considerable percentage of the formal or contractual wage.

It must be noted that the pay of workers in industry and mining fluctuates from one region to another. For instance, in 1944 the minimum wage in the city of São Paulo in Brazil was approximately $18 a month. In Rio de Janeiro, it was $19, while in places like the interior of the state of Alagoas the minimum wage was set as low as $8.50 a month.[17] Furthermore, Latin-American labor has always had its own "wage aristocrats." Workers in industries requiring high skills such as electric power, transportation, communication, and petroleum are paid wages well above the average for unskilled labor.

Minimum-wage laws generally provide for the establishment of boards which set the minima according to the cost of living and the peculiarities of each region. These boards may be of two types. The first is the mixed

[16] Eugene D. Owens, "Minimum Wage Legislation in Latin America," *Bulletin of the Pan American Union,* vol. 72, no. 7, pp. 223–226, June, 1938.

[17] *Corporations, Labor, and Tax System in Brazil* (New Brazilian Trade Bureau, 1944), p. 9.

commission of workers and employers which is in use in Brazil, Chile, Costa Rica, Guatemala, Nicaragua, Mexico, Uruguay, and Venezuela. The second type of board includes autonomous bodies composed of several members who are not representatives of the interests of either employers or workers and are supposedly placed above any political influences. This is the system employed in Argentina, Ecuador, and the Dominican Republic. The Instituto Nacional de Remuneraciones in Argentina is a typical example.

A number of states have established the principle of obligatory and direct participation of the worker in the profits under the terms and in the manner determined by law. There is little recorded evidence, however, of the successful enforcement of any provision of this kind, and they remain with many other labor clauses as mere statements of goals or objectives which may be attained in the future.

Most laws establish a maximum working period for night work and prescribe the payment of a higher wage than that which is received for day work. In Costa Rica and Guatemala this period may not exceed six hours a day or thirty-six hours a week, while in other countries it is generally specified as seven hours per day. Overtime work must be paid at 50 per cent above the stipulated wage in Costa Rica. However, these provisions are not applicable in certain well-defined cases which are determined by law.

Provisions forbid work for minors under a certain age limit and work in unhealthful industries for women and children; they also regulate the work of minors within a certain age range. In general, children under fourteen years of age are not permitted to work, although the limit is reduced to twelve years in Mexico and Honduras. The work of minors of an age beyond the limit is regulated by acts of the congress, and in every country there is legislation which prohibits the employment of minors for certain tasks. The employment of women in jobs that are dangerous to their health or morality, night work, and other specific cases is similarly forbidden. Women workers are also guaranteed protection during pregnancy and after childbirth. These measures and others put into effect by ordinary legislation usually include special subsidies, prohibition against dismissing the worker without reason, maternity rest, and security in the job. In some countries it is obligatory for the employer to maintain nurseries on the premises.

Eleven countries have included references to accident insurance and workmen's compensation in their constitutions. The general principle is that the employer is responsible for occupational accidents and illnesses that the worker suffers by reason of his work. Some laws, such as that of Cuba, require insurance covering such accidents and diseases under control of the state and at the expense of the employer, so as to assure payment of indemnification to the victim. However, in all countries there are established exceptions to the responsibility of the employers in cases of superior force or acts of God (*fuerza mayor*), accidents intentionally caused by the victim, and (in some laws) accidents due to a state of inebriation of the worker. It is significant that the legal practice is that of considering the employer responsible unless proven to the contrary. However, in most countries employers in certain types of work are exempted from responsibility in case of accidents. Generally included in this category are employers of workers at home and of household servants. Most of the accident laws regulate and classify accidents as a basis for the determination of the worker's compensation.

In a few countries the worker is guaranteed the right to medical assistance, including, in some cases, hospitalization and preventive medicine. In Honduras, by constitutional prescription, all large industrial concerns are required to maintain hospitals in the place of work to assist cases of accidents or illness of their workers.

The general principle of dismissal or severance pay has been adopted in several countries, and in some it has been in effect since 1924 for certain categories of employees. Constitutional provisions prescribing that workers discharged without due cause are entitled to compensation exist in a good number of states. The constitutions of Cuba, Guatemala, and Mexico have in this respect an extensive coverage and are noteworthy for their radical principles.

In Cuba one of the most controversial points in labor relations is that of dismissal. According to the constitution of 1940 no worker can be dismissed except on "proved justified cause" and with the formalities determined by law. The record shows that an attempt to dismiss a worker becomes in practice a long-drawn-out procedure and that the unions have frequently misused their privileges to the detriment of efficient production. The employer may be confronted with severe restrictions on his rights, and dismissal-pay requirements representing several months' wages are usually of considerable proportions.

The Guatemalan constitution of 1945 forced the employer to indemnify the worker with an amount equivalent to one month of pay for each year of service in cases of unjustified dismissal. It further provided that "the worker or employee who ceases to work because of lack of honesty of the employer or bad treatment which is damaging to his dignity as a man" is entitled to the same compensation. The Mexican constitution contains a similarly worded passage but makes compensation in such cases equivalent to three months' wages.

While in most cases the provisions are not so far-reaching as those just mentioned, labor codes and other legislation exist in all Latin-American countries regulating the expiration of labor contracts. These laws generally contemplate a variety of situations which lead to justifiable dismissal of the worker. Among the most common are those that arise from lack of honesty and misbehavior of the worker; damage intentionally caused to machinery, tools, and products; acts or omissions which affect the safety of the establishment and of the workers; failure to fulfill contractual labor obligations; absence from work without cause; and revealing secrets of the industry.

Labor Codes

In a number of countries the accumulation of laws regulating labor relations, often inconsistent and conflicting, produced efforts to compile them in a systematic fashion so as to facilitate their better understanding and enforcement. This tendency toward the codification of labor legislation first appeared in Chile and Mexico where it resulted in the promulgation of codes in 1931, but it has since extended throughout Latin America. At the present time there are labor codes in the following countries: Bolivia (1939), Brazil (1943), Colombia (1951), Costa Rica (1943), Chile (1931), Ecuador (1938), Guatemala (1947), Mexico (1931), Nicaragua (1945), Panama (1948), and Venezuela (1936). Projects of codes are under consideration in Argentina, El Salvador, and Uruguay.[18] In countries where labor codes do not exist some important aspects of labor relations are not regulated at all. This is the case, for instance, in the Dominican Republic with reference to trade-union organization. In other states, notably in Argentina and Cuba, laws relating to almost every labor problem are in operation, although they are not yet compiled in a systematic code.

[18] In Argentina Joaquín V. González drafted the first project of a labor code in 1904, but it was rejected by the congress. Later projects were authored by Alejandro M. Unsaín in 1925, Diego Luis Molinari in 1928, and Carlos Saavedra Lamas in 1933. The last is considered by many experts as the best ever prepared in Argentina. See Carlos Saavedra Lamas, *Código nacional del trabajo* (3 vols., Buenos Aires, 1933).

The two earliest codes, those of Mexico and Chile, have been sources of influence and models for imitation by others in the rest of the continent. The labor codes of Costa Rica, Guatemala, Nicaragua, and Panama have drawn freely from the labor code of Mexico. Those of Bolivia, Ecuador, and Venezuela were obviously inspired by the principles of the Chilean law. In this connection, it is of some interest to note that the Mexican and Chilean codes, despite their many similarities, represent two somewhat different doctrinal approaches. The Mexican law makes no distinction between workers and white-collar employees, and it makes the same regulations applicable to both groups. The Chilean code, on the other hand, distinguishes between them and contains separate provisions which are to be applied to each category.[19]

All these labor codes have expanded constitutional principles on the subject, and they deal characteristically with all the rights or privileges which have already been described.[20] These bodies of law, besides guaranteeing the worker's privileges and rights, may serve in some instances to place organized labor under effective control of the government, as already indicated, by legalizing a tight supervision of union activities and of the processes of collective bargaining. The minute regulation of such matters has become, in fact, the most typical feature of Latin America's labor codes. Labor organizations must be recognized by the government, and they must meet stipulated requirements for such recognition. Unions must have a specified minimum number of members (generally twenty-five) and must be organized at a meeting attended by a government official. Names of union officials elected and proceedings of an organizational meeting must then be submitted to the proper authority. Codes also establish qualifications required of those occupying union offices and may regulate minutely the financial affairs of the unions.

An elaborate procedure for the settlement of collective disputes is also laid down—conciliation and arbitration being the most common methods employed—and the codes generally make it obligatory for representatives of employers and workers to appear before a government conciliation board. The device of arbitration is provided for, but its use is sometimes

[19] The term *empleado* is given a legal definition in the Chilean labor code (in effect since Nov. 28, 1931). According to Art. 2, cl. 2, an *empleado* is any person whose work is predominantly "intellectual" or mental rather than physical. Similar definitions can be found in other codes.

[20] Some codes are of considerable length. The longest is that of Brazil, with 981 articles. Those of Mexico and Panama have 685 and 645 articles respectively. One of the briefest is the Venezuelan, with 236 provisions.

optional. When it is used the parties must abide by the decision of the arbitral body, and penalties are provided for acts in disregard thereof. Only after such procedures are exhausted can strikes or lockouts be legally declared. Among the numerous provisions of the codes there are clauses and articles dealing with the labor contract and with its special varieties; with working conditions; with wages, dismissal, and severance pay; with labor accidents and illness due to occupational cases; with special courts and jurisdiction; and with administrative agencies in the labor field.[21]

Labor Courts

Not all the Latin-American countries have followed a similar course in dealing with jurisdictional questions over labor conflicts. One group of states has favored the system of special or semiautonomous courts or tribunals. Other countries have placed such cases within the jurisdiction of their ordinary judicial bodies. A third group has adopted a system by which special courts or boards decide over labor disputes in first instance only, and appeals from their decisions are brought before the ordinary law courts. Colombia and Brazil are the best examples of countries in the first group. Legislation in both these nations provided for the establishment of a complete labor judicature or hierarchy of courts which consists of trial courts, courts of appeal, and a supreme labor tribunal.

The second group of countries, which do not provide any special jurisdiction or a special set of courts for labor matters, is composed of Cuba, the Dominican Republic, Haiti, Honduras, Paraguay, and Uruguay. However, in some of these, such as Cuba and Uruguay, the practice is followed of setting up conciliation and arbitration tribunals for particular labor cases. These special tribunals are formed by two representatives from each of the parties, plus three others representing the government. In Uruguay special arbitration courts take cognizance of cases affecting public services and utilities.

The third group is composed of those countries where, although there may exist a special labor jurisdiction, this may take an infinity of forms which combine the other two systems.[22] Some examples of these variations follow.

[21] For a comparative study of the labor laws, see María Alvarado Smith and Ariaselva Ruz Durán, *El derecho del trabajo en las legislaciones latino- americanas* (Santiago, 1950).

[22] For an excellent description of these cases, see Helen L. Clagett, *The Administration of Justice in Latin America* (New York, Oceana Publications, 1952), pp. 89–98.

In Argentina, there is no federal legislation concerned with the organization of a labor judicature at the national level. It falls within the powers of the provinces to establish labor jurisdictions of their own. However, a federal law of 1947 regulated the labor courts in the federal capital. Additional legislation enacted after the constitutional reform of 1949 made all local courts of the federal capital an integral part of the national judiciary. There are in the capital forty labor courts of first instance (*juzgados nacionales de primera instancia*) and an appellate court (*cámara de apelaciones*) composed of seven members. In addition, a commission of conciliation appointed by the president functions as a permanent organ of the Department of Labor. The lower courts have jurisdiction in all labor cases except those dealing with social security, over which the appellate court has original jurisdiction. The system is completed by arbitration commissions which are set up on a temporary basis as the need for them arises.

The Chilean labor code has regulated with great care the administration of justice in this field. The lowest units of the labor court system are the labor judges (*jueces del trabajo*), who must be lawyers. Courts of appeal are located in four cities and are empowered to take cognizance of all cases arising from the application of the labor and social insurance laws. Only in rare cases and on specified grounds can an appeal be taken to the supreme court. Since Chilean law makes it obligatory to submit collective-bargaining conflicts to conciliation, it has also provided for the establishment of conciliation boards (*juntas de conciliación*).

The case of Mexico deserves special mention. While the original text of the famous Article 123 of the constitution gave concurrent powers to the national congress and the legislatures of the states on labor matters, an amendment adopted in 1929 restricted considerably the legislative powers of the states and gave the federal congress exclusive authority to enact all laws concerning the greater part of industrial activities.[23]

The federal and state boards of conciliation and arbitration are the significant feature of Mexico's labor courts. These boards, in contrast to those of other countries, have jurisdiction over all cases whether they relate to legal or economic conflicts. Conciliation and arbitration boards in

[23] Such extension of federal powers is defended by Lanz Duret on the grounds that such matters as labor regulation demand a certain uniformity and coordination of principles and practices. He also points out that the reform has served "to avoid the demagoguery of immoral and ambitious state governors." Miguel Lanz Duret, *Derecho constitucional mexicano y consideraciones sobre la realidad política de nuestro régimen* (4th ed., Mexico, 1947), p. 406.

other nations come into play when the point in litigation is one related to wages, work hours, or other conditions of work. The Mexican juntas are not restricted to any type of conflicts and gradually have become endowed with such ample jurisdictional power by the supreme court as to make them true judicial agencies. They have the authority to determine facts of any dispute originating from a labor contract, the interpretation or application of laws, or any related matter. Their decisions are compulsory, and their procedure is not subject to the restrictions of legal proof in ordinary courts of law. Appeals from their decisions can be made only if the latter involve violations of the individual rights guaranteed by the constitution. Such an appeal takes the form of a *juicio de amparo* before the supreme court, one of whose four chambers is exclusively devoted to the consideration of labor *amparos.* It must be noted, however, that an appeal does not result in the suspension of the board's decision in matters of fact or of judgment upon the conflict arising from the collective labor contract. Refusal to submit to a decision of the boards automatically cancels the collective contract and results in financial punishment.[24]

These juntas, including both the federal and the state institutions, are the Municipal Boards of Conciliation, the Central Boards of Conciliation and Arbitration (one in each state capital), the Federal Boards of Conciliation (used in case of failure of the municipal board), and the Federal Board of Conciliation and Arbitration in the national capital.

Labor Administrative Agencies

All countries have developed government agencies which are entrusted with the administration and enforcement of the labor laws. Three institutions are common to all these administrative systems: the ministry or department of labor, with cabinet status; the *dirección general del trabajo,* which is the main agency under this ministry; and a group of labor inspectors. The administration of labor affairs is vested in a separate ministry or executive department by that name in Chile, Colombia, Cuba, El Salvador, Peru, and Venezuela. In another group of states—Argentina, Bolivia, Costa Rica, the Dominican Republic, Ecuador, and Mexico—the department is known as Ministry of Labor and Social Welfare. Labor is combined in one department with justice in Paraguay, with industry in Uruguay, with economy in Guatemala, with public health in Haiti and Panama, with agriculture in Honduras and Nicaragua, and with industry and commerce in Brazil.

[24] Tannenbaum, *op. cit.,* pp. 120–121.

One example will illustrate the pattern of internal structure and organization of these departments. In Chile the Ministry of Labor includes the Labor Supreme Council (Consejo Superior del Trabajo), an advisory and consultative body for labor policy, and another agency to which is entrusted the enforcement of the labor laws (*dirección general*). This agency is composed of four departments in charge of administrative matters, inspection, juridical questions, and labor organizations. Each of these is, in turn, composed of sections or bureaus.

Labor inspectors are charged with the obligation of watching over the enforcement of labor provisions, such as those related to sanitation and safety and all others determined by the collective contracts. Likewise they make all investigations that are needed and submit regular reports to their superiors. They may be empowered, as they are in Ecuador, to impose fines. In Mexico, labor inspectors are state and federal appointees. They are named in the states by the governors and at the federal level by the minister of labor.

Social Security

The development of legislation dealing with social-security programs in Latin America has been similar to that of the labor laws. Chile assumed a pioneering role in the establishment of programs of insurance when it enacted its first laws in 1924, but the movement rapidly extended through Latin America. Today practically every country has a compulsory insurance system which covers the risks of the workers. Although at the beginning these programs were restricted in their coverage to certain groups of workers (usually bank employees, maritime workers, railwaymen, and journalists), other groups have come gradually to be included in them. At the present time highly expanded systems of social security have resulted in some countries in the development of a complex structure of agencies and various funds. Constitutional provisions stating principles of policy related to old age, illness, disability, death, and maternity benefits can be found in a number of countries. Risks covered by insurance systems in operation are the same as those that are included elsewhere, although some are expanded to a significantly broad scope and there are a few features that may be considered novel. Thus, in Chile the Preventive Medicine Act of 1938 extended socialized medicine to cover benefits of preventive treatment, and other laws give mothers free medical assistance from the first examination preceding childbirth until the child is two years old.[25]

[25] Jordan, *op. cit.*, p. 116.

Twelve countries had in 1949 compulsory contributory insurance plans covering old age, invalidity, and survivors' insurance. Argentina and Uruguay have national pension or assistance plans supplementing such insurance for old age, and a group of countries provide supplementary insurance for invalidity and survivors. In all countries but three, there exist plans for workmen's compensation. Chile and Uruguay had in addition unemployment-insurance programs, and Brazil, Chile, and Uruguay family-allowance systems.[26]

These plans are financed by contributions of employers and workers at widely varied ratios, but in many cases the government also contributes a substantial amount or guarantees payment of benefits with a special fund. Workers' contributions vary between 3 and 6 per cent of the wages and in most countries are compulsory only for income groups up to a certain maximum. Higher-income groups may participate on a voluntary basis. Employers' contributions are usually considerable.

Retirement plans based on lower estimates of average life expectancy than in other parts of the world make it possible for the worker to claim benefits on reaching an age lower than that required in other countries. In Argentina and Uruguay, for example, retirement age for railway workers is set at fifty-five.

Enforcement and administration of social-security legislation has met, in general, with serious difficulties. In many instances the purpose of this legislation has not been attained because of defects in the administrative machinery. Difficulties of communication and transportation provide physical handicaps, while insufficient funds and the lack of a corps of trained officials are obstacles at the governmental level.

In conclusion, it must be reiterated that much of the labor and social legislation which has been described in this chapter has not been fully carried into effect for various reasons. In fact, much of this legislation represents only a setting of desirable goals and an expression of aspirations rather than concrete achievements. The proliferation of laws without effective administration reflects the lack of a sincere and realistic understanding of labor and industrial relations on the part of the effective political leadership, and it is to be deplored. Furthermore, legislation enacted at the urgent and pressing demands of the workers has often failed to produce better conditions because of the lack of a well-trained force of public serv-

[26] U.S. Federal Security Agency, *Social Security Legislation throughout the World* (Washington, 1949), pp. 2–5. For an account of the impressive development in legislation during the period from 1939 to 1949, see Hanson, *op. cit.*, pp. 510–513.

ants. Enforcement of legislation may also depend, as has been mentioned above, upon the influence that the labor or employer groups may have with a certain administration and may also be related to nationalistic policies. If the latter is the case, one is likely to find strict enforcement against foreign-owned enterprises while domestically controlled concerns, which have obligations to conform to the laws, are usually able to find ways to evade them.

Economic conditions in each country also have a great deal to do with the problem of attaining a real betterment of the standard of living of the worker. The failure in this field is, in many instances, due to the inability of the employer to meet the expense involved or to the fact that the government does not have sufficient means to establish all the social services created by law. These economic factors have inevitably restricted the standards which may be effectively established. They make it logical to wonder whether labor's efforts should not have first concentrated on securing higher wages before gaining social security and welfare laws. Such a reversal of objectives may become a permanent obstacle to solving the basic problem of the low purchasing power of the average wage earner. Economic experts consider it disturbing that enjoyment of social security, so urgently demanded by labor, may very well prevent the expansion of capital accumulation which is necessary in order to promote a higher standard of living.[27]

A strong criticism of this situation[28] was made by a Chilean industrialist who considered the problem as one of an

> excessive, badly studied social legislation which pretends to a miracle beyond the economic capacity of the country by creating wealth through higher returns to labor and lower production. . . . We have . . . [enacted] innumerable laws which pretend to assure protection in all cases of emergency, accidents, old age, sickness, dismissal, retirement, etc. We have so increased the cost of production and the cost of living in favor of the trappings that we have neither the time nor the money to solve the fundamentals.

This statement coming from an interested party may not represent an entirely impartial and unprejudiced view of the problem, but it certainly is indicative of the discouragement of employers at the staggering implications of the responsibilities which are continuously being thrust upon them by the social and labor laws.

[27] Hanson, *op. cit.,* pp. 497–498.
[28] *Ibid.,* p. 496.

It must be kept in mind that much of Latin America's legislation is progressive, moderate, and in keeping with principles of labor and social relations that have been fairly generally accepted by people who have experienced industrial development. If, unfortunately, until the present, part of this legislation has failed to produce the desired results, it is a result of the fact that the designs of irresponsible union leaders and employers as well as the ambitions of politicians have much to do with its application. Furthermore, there must be taken into account the natural difficulties of introducing just and moral reform in an environment not wholly prepared for such innovations.

Women before the Law

In the last few decades, the women of Latin America have moved a long way from the traditional position that they occupied for centuries. A kind of feminine "revolution" which began in some countries about thirty-five years ago, and which received great impetus as a result of the two world wars, has resulted in a considerable enlargement of their opportunities for work and participation in public affairs. There is no doubt that, at the present time, women are becoming increasingly important in the development of their countries economically, politically, and socially, and are having more opportunities to prove their ability. These changes in the social reality have forced modifications of great significance in legislation, so as to erase discriminatory provisions which affected the status of women before the law and their rights to participate in politics.

The movement for the recognition of women's rights began at the Fifth Pan-American Conference, at Santiago, Chile, held in 1923, with a motion presented before that Assembly by the Chilean delegate, Manuel Rivas Vicuña, and by the delegate from Guatemala, Máximo Hall, recommending a study of means of abolishing discriminations for reasons of sex. It received new impetus from the creation of the Inter-American Commission of Women, by the Sixth Pan-American Conference of Havana, in 1928. On that occasion the Commission presented a study of comparative legislation in twenty-one volumes. This pointed out the discriminatory features of most of the codes and laws then in effect. The culmination of the movement occurred in 1948 when, at the Ninth Pan-American Conference held in Bogotá, twenty countries signed the Inter-American Convention on the Granting of Civil Rights to Women, and fourteen states signed a similar convention concerning political rights.

The status of women before the law had been affected in the past by principles which restricted chiefly (1) their legal capacity; (2) their rights of representation and administration in regard to the property of children and custody or guardianship of the same; and (3) their control over their property.

Changes and revisions made in the civil, penal, and procedural codes in the various countries eliminated such inequalities. Some of the new constitutions have included among their provisions clauses prohibiting restrictions based on differences of sex in the enjoyment of all civil rights. The following common tendencies are to be observed in recent legislation:

1. To grant to women legal capacity to engage freely in any industry, business, profession, employment, or occupation, to contract, and to accept or to reject inheritances and donations
2. To permit women to act as guardians, administratrices, executrices, and to testify in court procedures under the same conditions as men
3. To accept the principle that women do not lose their legal capacity because of marriage and that they should, consequently, retain their full capacity to engage in the activities and to carry out the duties referred to in (1) and (2)
4. To recognize the right that every married woman has, jointly with her husband, of representing their common children and of administering their property and that, in the event of disagreement and in cases of legal separation, such representation and administration should be exercised by a person selected jointly by the husband and wife
5. To recognize that the custody or guardianship of children should be exercised in common by the father and mother
6. To permit a widow or divorced woman who remarries to retain her parental authority (*patria potestad*) and the guardianship of her children by a previous marriage[29]

The trend toward equalization of the status of men and women in the enjoyment and exercise of civil rights has, of course, not been uniform. While in El Salvador, Guatemala, Uruguay, Cuba, the Dominican Republic, Costa Rica, and Peru women have been granted equality as to civil status and enjoy most if not all of the rights that have been enumerated, in other

[29] The term *patria potestad* is difficult to translate. It implies more than the expression "natural guardianship," i.e., the legal right of the parents over the persons of their minor children. The *patria potestad* includes the total rights that the law gives parents over the person and the property of their children. Chile is the only country which restricts the scope of this power to the control and administration of property.

countries they may be restricted as to some. Moreover, although equality may have been established by law, it has not been implemented by the necessary reforms of civil and procedural codes. Uruguay, Cuba, and Guatemala are perhaps the three countries which have made the most complete revision of their legislation. In Chile, on the other hand, despite the fact that women are particularly active in all fields of endeavor, certain discriminatory legislation still persists.

With regard to nationality, recognition of equality of rights of women came as a rather rapid development. In 1933, only four countries recognized equality in this respect: Argentina, Chile, Paraguay, and Uruguay. By 1938 Brazil had moved in the same direction and three other countries, Colombia, Guatemala, and Panama, were about to follow. At the present time, there is not a single country in which women lose their nationality automatically when they marry.

Legislation Concerning the Home and Children

The protection of the family, of marriage, and of maternity and children are matters which in the past were regulated only by legislation. Today, however, practically all the Latin-American countries, following the precedent established by some of the European nations in the period following the First World War, have given constitutional recognition to these precepts. The trend has continued with new impetus in the period of constitutional growth which followed the Second World War. The result is that, while in 1942 only a few countries—Cuba, Brazil, Uruguay, and Panama—dealt at any length with the subject in their basic laws, at the present time the great majority, if not all, of the constitutions include provisions dealing with these matters, in full accordance with the new emphasis on society rather than on individuals.

Fourteen of the constitutions specifically provide that the family is entitled to receive special protection from the state. The same fourteen countries extend similar formal protection to maternity. A few of them, such as Uruguay, Ecuador, and Venezuela, stipulate that protection is to be given by the state regardless of the condition or civil status of the mother and guarantee her right to the assistance of society in case of destitution or desertion. State protection is also to be given to marriage, which in some constitutions is described as the essential basis of the family. A few of the laws establish the juridical equality of husband and wife, and the constitutions of several countries recognize the common-law marriage (*matrimonio de hecho*) with some qualifications. In Bolivia, this kind of union is recognized after two years of living together or by the birth of a child, provided the parties have legal capacity to marry. In Panama, a common-law union between persons legally able to marry, if maintained during ten consecutive years, has all the effects of civil marriage.

The care and education of the children are the main duty and right of the parents in some countries, with the state sharing the responsibility in a subsidiary manner. Other countries, however, consider the protection of the physical, mental, or moral health of the child to be a primary duty of the state. In Uruguay, legislation provides the necesssary measures for the protection of children against physical, intellectual, or moral neglect by their parents or guardians, as well as against exploitation and abuse of them. There exists a Child Code (Código del Niño), which comprises an extensive body of laws related to the protection of mothers, investigation of paternity, desertion, allowances, labor conditions, and other matters affecting children's welfare. In Ecuador, the Ley Orgánica de los Hogares de Protección Social provides special protection for foundlings. Chilean legislation designed to protect the family is voluminous, although no elaborate provisions dealing with the subject are to be found in the constitution.[30]

Approximately half the constitutions provide that parents have the same duties toward children born outside of wedlock as toward those born within it, or specify that these children have the same rights and duties as others. A recent trend in legislation, probably begun by the Cuban constitution in 1940, is the incorporation of the right of children to know who their parents are (*derecho de investigar la paternidad*) and the abolishment of any qualifications on the nature of filiation. According to this principle no statement can be made in any registry of baptism or birth certificate making any distinction between births on the basis of civil status of the parents. Some laws may establish exceptions to the principle of equality of rights of legitimate and illegitimate children in the case of inheritance.

Assistance to families with numerous offspring is provided for in some of the countries, and such families may be entitled to special subsidies based on the number of children. In Guatemala, for example, fathers of six or more minor children are entitled to receive protection from the state, and have preference in equal circumstances to holding government positions.

[30] With that of Chile, the constitutions of Colombia, the Dominican Republic, and Paraguay are the only ones in Latin America which make little or no reference to the family.

Recognition of the homestead or place of family abode (*bien de familia or patrimonio familiar*) is made by the great majority of the countries, and it is accompanied by protection against the claims of creditors and by declaration of its inalienability. Special legislation determines the nature and amount of property which will constitute it.

BIBLIOGRAPHY

Academia de Ciencias Económicas, *Las cláusulas económico-sociales en las constituciones de América,* 2 vols., Buenos Aires, 1947–1948.

Aichele Hohmann, María Luisa, *Breve estudio comparativo de las legislaciones del trabajo de Chile y Uruguay,* Santiago, 1950.

Bernaldo de Quirós, J., *El seguro social en Iberoamérica,* Mexico, n.d.

Bezerra de Menses, Gerardo, *Política sindical brasileira,* Rio de Janeiro, 1943.

Bianchi Rosas, Alvaro, *Breve estudio comparativo de las legislaciones del trabajo de Chile y México,* Santiago, 1946.

Bush, Archer C., *Organized Labor in Guatemala,* Hamilton, N.Y., Colgate University Press, 1950.

Clark, Marjorie R., *Organized Labor in Mexico,* Chapel Hill, N.C., The University of North Carolina Press, 1934.

Gaete Berrios, Alfredo, and Ezequiel Figueroa Araya, *Tratado elemental del derecho del trabajo,* Santiago, 1949.

González, G., *El problema de la implantación del seguro social en México,* Mexico, 1950.

Granados Aguirre, Jesús, *Legislación del trabajo en Venezuela,* Caracas, 1944.

López Aparicio, A., *El movimiento obrero de México: antecedentes, desarrollo y tendencia,* Mexico, 1947.

Pinto J., Antunes, *O sindicalismo brasileiro,* São Paulo, 1940.

Poblete Troncoso, Moisés, *El movimiento de asociación profesional obrera en Chile,* Mexico, 1945.

Sanguinetti Freire, Alberto, *Legislación social del Uruguay,* 2 vols., Montevideo, 1949.

Treviño, R., *El movimiento obrero. Su evolución ideológica,* Mexico, n.d.

Chapter 15: THE ECONOMY AND PUBLIC FINANCE

The distinguishing features of the Latin-American economy have been of primary importance in determining and shaping many of the political and social institutions in the area. Economic factors have combined to make the kind of environment in which it is difficult to found and to maintain democratic political institutions. With low standards of living, sometimes below the subsistence level, and control of all chief means of production in the hands of a privileged few, most of the Latin-American republics must cope with varied and complex problems of government. Some of these conditions have been already described in Chapter 1. The emphasis in the discussion that follows is on the direct effects of economic factors upon the social and political structure and ideas.

The System of Land Tenure

Most experts agree that, among the economic maladjustments that beset Latin America and retard its political progress, the one which stands out over all the others is the system of land ownership.[1] Ownership of land is regarded as the major economic basis for the exercise of power and as one of the basic conditioning factors of government, because in Latin America, perhaps more than in any other region of the world, the people depend directly for their living on agricultural and pastoral pursuits. In fact, more than two-thirds of the total population is dependent upon agriculture as a chief source of income. Despite this fact, the main characteristic of the agrarian system is the high degree of inequality in land ownership. Monopolization of land has been in the past and is today the chief source of political power. The large estate or *latifundio* is the prevailing form of land ownership in most countries, although small independent farms have long existed in parts of Colombia, Haiti, Costa Rica, and other areas. Concentration of land ownership in the hands of a small group of absentee landlords, native gentry, or foreign corporations is the

[1] For a masterly analysis of these maladjustments see Sanford A. Mosk, "An Economist's Point of View," in W. W. Pierson (ed.), "Pathology of Democracy in Latin America: A Symposium," *The American Political Science Review,* vol. 44, no. 1, pp. 129–142, March, 1950.

persistent agrarian pattern. Thus, for example, in Chile large holdings include 62.8 per cent of all farm land, while constituting only 1.4 per cent of all holdings.[2] In Bolivia, the 1950 census disclosed that 4.5 per cent of the rural landowners possessed 70 per cent of the private landed property.[3] Despite large-scale programs of land redistribution which have been carried out in Mexico since the revolution of 1910, in lands not under the communal or *ejido* system, 0.8 per cent of all holdings constitute 79.5 per cent of the farm area.[4] Large agricultural holdings persist in Cuba, Venezuela, Ecuador, Peru, and Argentina.

The concentration of land ownership dates from the colonial era, but it is important to emphasize that, far from disappearing or at least from being attenuated with the advent of independence, it became more extended and refined as a result of new trends of economic development in the middle of the nineteenth century. In the colonial period the social structure was chiefly an outgrowth of the system of land tenure which called for compulsory service from Indian labor and for the introduction of Negro slaves. Institutions and practices such as the encomienda or the *repartimiento* became rooted because they served the interests of the *latifundio.* Colonial society, rigid and stratified, was characterized by a small ruling class at the top and a large group at the bottom. A middle group was almost nonexistent. An effect of the concentration of land ownership was the establishment of a quasi-feudal relationship which tied the members of the lower group by personal bonds to the dominant class. In time the encomienda and the *repartimiento* were replaced by peonage. In this system, as we have seen, although theoretically the Indian was a hired laborer, he became permanently attached to this employer through a debt relation.

Political independence did not bring any important change in this social structure. On the contrary, there occurred an extension of the basic elements of the colonial economy as a consequence of the great technological developments of the nineteenth century which affected the nature and functioning of the world economy. The demands of the latter caused Latin America to give emphasis to production for markets in place of production for subsistence. The strong impulse given to economic activities by the growth of foreign markets was also felt in the domestic markets, and these, in turn,

[2] United Nations, Department of Economic Affairs, *Progress in Land Reform* (New York, 1954), pp. 42–43.

[3] *Ibid.,* p. 40.

[4] *Ibid.,* p. 39.

expanded also in most of the countries. This expansion of both foreign and domestic markets stimulated the extension of the system of large landholdings. New large estates were carved out of lands which had remained as public property and were unexploited but which were now attractive to private owners in view of the accelerated pace of economic activity. The government was willing in most countries to grant or to sell large tracts of public domain to private individuals or to companies, supposedly in payment for services rendered or for the purpose of promoting the development of sparsely populated areas. At other times, lands were auctioned off at small prices to influential persons or leased as long-term concessions to foreign companies. In Argentina, grants involving vast areas were given out for service in the Indian wars. The colonization company also played a prominent role in the partition of public lands. It was perhaps in Mexico, more than in any other country, that the procedure was most abused during the long rule of Porfirio Díaz, who was inclined handsomely to reward his supporters in this manner. The extravagance of such handouts after 1883 indeed set new records. Thirty million acres of public domain in Chihuahua were given to seven individuals; in Durango, two persons owned five million acres.[5] Further concentration of land was achieved in Mexico, during the same period, by depriving the Indian communities of their lands through the use of legalistic revisions of the confusing systems of title deeds. Often the property still held communally by Indians was expropriated through the use of sheer violence and military force. Indian villages in Bolivia, Peru, and other countries were similarly victimized, and their lands became the property of wealthy landowners. It has been said that "fully as much public domain and Indian communal land was alienated into the hands of a few aristocratic families, military officers and foreign companies and individuals between 1830 and 1920 as during the three centuries of Spanish domination."[6]

Simultaneously with this expansion of large holdings, the relationship between landowner and peon underwent a significant change. Rather than increasing productivity through greater efficiency in order to obtain the desired profits, the landowner resorted to the devices of peonage and low wages. The feudal characteristic of mutual rights and obligations and the softening influence of paternalism of colonial times, because of the nominal wage paid, gave way to much more formal relations between employer and

[5] Mosk, *op. cit.*, p. 133.

[6] George Soule, David Efrón, and Norman T. Ness, *Latin America in the Future World* (New York, Rinehart, 1945), p. 66.

worker, with some oppressive stipulations. Peonage became more common and was practiced more intensively. In some countries legislation was enacted which had, in practice, the effect of keeping the Indian in a state of semiservitude. Thus, the commercialization of the economy caused by

TABLE 19
INDEX OF THE VOLUME OF AGRICULTURAL PRODUCTION IN LATIN AMERICA, PREWAR COMPARED WITH POSTWAR
(1935–1939 = 100)

Country	1949–1950	1950–1951	1951–1952	Per capita 1949–1950
Argentina	68	84	57	50
Bolivia	174	170	181	154
Brazil	127	132	129	104
Chile	107	111	118	84
Colombia	163	143	162	130
Costa Rica	161	156	168	122
Cuba	191	196	242	150
Dominican Republic	120	123	136	89
Ecuador	140	178	162	130
El Salvador	127	129	137	116
Guatemala	122	117	119	99
Haiti	131	129	144	109
Honduras	146	153	148	112
Mexico	179	186	214	129
Nicaragua	166	163	190	151
Panama	149	157	142	98
Paraguay	117	114	114	80
Peru	128	134	129	106
Uruguay	119	155	143	106
Venezuela	112	129	143	74
All Latin America	119	127	125	94

SOURCE: U.S. Department of Agriculture, *Foreign Agriculture*, November, 1952.

the expansion of markets, instead of bringing about more personal freedom, had the opposite effect.

The outcome of these developments was the strengthening of the economic power of the landed class and, inevitably, the establishment of a political oligarchy. The changes in land tenure and the development of peonage and tenancy fortified the existing social pattern and concentrated political power in the hands of the landowners. Whether or not one of their class was actually in office, the landowners constituted the most influential group in the political life of every country. Through their vast political power they have succeeded in keeping rural property almost free from any taxation burden to this day.

Many governments have tried to broaden the basis of land ownership, but their efforts, in most instances, have been unsuccessful. Land redistribution has been probably more effectively carried out in Mexico than in any other country. Land reform became the key to the program of social and political change of the Mexican Revolution and the primary plank in its platform. According to President Cárdenas, if Mexico was to have peace, the fundamental demand of the revolution, that of agrarian reform, had to be satisfied. The implementation of the agrarian laws has had a profound effect upon the economy, the society, and the political institutions of the country. It has also caused a variety of opinions to arise concerning the methods and techniques used by the government. Regardless of the judgment that may be passed upon the wisdom of the policies adopted, the fact remains that very considerable tracts of land have been redistributed. Through the *ejido* system under which lands are granted to villages and are held collectively, and through the breaking up of large holdings, some 49 million acres were divided between 1915 and 1938. This is approximately one-fifth of Mexico's estimated total of agricultural land.[7] Despite the impressive achievements of the land-reform program, no Mexican would claim today that the country has solved its agrarian problem, for land distribution alone is not the answer. It is not enough to give the peasant a piece of land; he must also have credit to be able to acquire the equipment which he needs if he is to take advantage of modern farming techniques. Otherwise, land redistribution can very well result in a decrease of agricultural production, as has been the case in some areas. Interesting experiments with systems of rural credit have been conducted in Mexico such as the establishment of national financing institutions exemplified by the National Bank of Ejido Credit. The program of land distribution and credit extension has been supplemented with the organization of *ejido* or village communities and with vigorous efforts toward the reeducation of the rural masses. Expediency and the effects of the Second World War caused a "freeze" of further subdivision of

[7] For an excellent study of Mexico's agrarian problem see Eyler N. Simpson, *The Ejido: Mexico's Way Out* (Chapel Hill, N.C., The University of North Carolina Press, 1937). A recent report is found in Henrik F. Infield and Koka Freir, *Peoples in Ejidos* (New York, Frederick A. Praeger, 1954).

Mexico's land during the administration of Ávila Camacho (1940–1946), who promised "no nationalization" to the remaining private owners. In addition on *ejidos* the peasants were given the choice of holding and tilling the land communally or having it distributed among heads of families who could utilize it as they wished. The government's interest shifted from distribution to land and agricultural improvements, but the fact remains that Mexico, by the time this change of emphasis took place, had taken longer strides than any other country toward democratization of land.[8]

There are formidable obstacles in the way of solving the land problem. Inevitably, programs of land redistribution arouse the hostility and militant opposition of the landed aristocracy which still exercises almost absolute power in some countries. In the struggle to block agricultural reform other great vested interests, such as the Church and the army, have not failed to support the landowners. And it is not too surprising to discover that two of the most persistent motives for revolutions in Latin America have been the desire for land reform on the one hand and, on the other, the opposition to such action.

One-sided Economies

Other characteristics of the "colonial economies" of Latin America are dependence upon exports to the markets of the industrialized nations and an extreme specialization upon a few products. Latin America's main economic activity is the production of foodstuffs and raw materials for export. In Argentina and Chile, for example, approximately one-third of the national production goes into the foreign market.[9] There is not a single country that does not rank high in order of dependence on exports. Such a dependence on foreign markets, together with the tendency to rely upon foreign sources of capital for the investment needed to produce and export primary products, exposes Latin America to serious dangers. Whenever the prices of foodstuffs and raw materials fall in relation to prices of manufactured goods, these countries are placed at a disadvantage. Events which take place abroad and over which they have no control often have disastrous effects upon their economies. Thus, when the world economy broke down as a result of the depression of the 1930s, the total value of exports from all the Latin-American countries dropped by approximately two-thirds in the period from 1929 to 1932, and the inflow of foreign capital during

[8] Howard F. Cline, *The United States and Mexico* (Cambridge, Mass., Harvard University Press, 1953), pp. 290–291.

[9] Soule, Efrón, and Ness, *op. cit.*, p. 104.

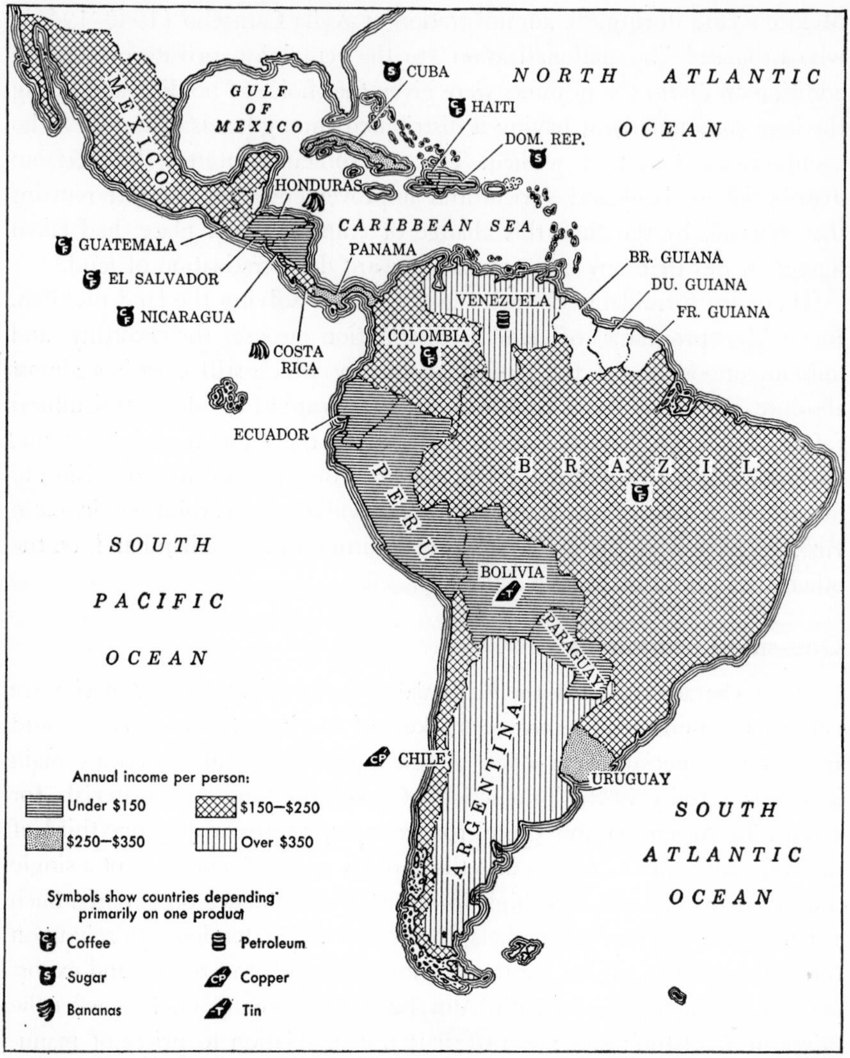

Figure 15. Latin America's troubled economics—two key factors. SOURCE: *The New York Times,* Nov. 28, 1954.

that same period came to a stop.[10] The economic depression was severely felt in Latin America because of these circumstances. Recovery was slow and painful as a result of its disadvantageous position in bargaining with industrialized nations.

The risks that are inherent in dependence on foreign markets are in-

[10] Mosk, *op.cit.,* p. 138.

creased by the extreme degree of economic specialization. A single product represents half or more of the total value of exports in many countries. "Monoculture," as it is generally designated in Latin America, has been the case with sugar in Cuba, coffee in Brazil, copper and nitrates in Chile, and tin in Bolivia. Coffee amounts from 50 to 60 per cent of all Brazilian exports; it represents 80 per cent of the exports of El Salvador, more than 70 per cent of Guatemala's, and 73.2 per cent of Colombia's for 1953.[11] Three-fourths of the total value of Cuban exports consists of sugar.[12]

Monoculture produces extreme vulnerability to the viscissitudes of fluctuations in the exchange rates whenever there is a drop in world prices as well as to competition from other countries. A change in tariffs, the adoption of a quota system, world overproduction, development of a synthetic substitute, or the appearance of a new and competitive source of supply are all events which may bring economic ruin upon particular countries. In addition, almost all the products involved are subject to cyclical fluctuations. Consequently, the economic pattern of some countries is a series of wonderful one-product export booms, invariably followed by abysmal busts. These cyclical variations affect, at times, the entire area, since, because of the basic uniformity of Latin America's export products, it often happens that a recession affecting one product is reflected upon almost all the others. Cuba, with its economy largely dependent on the price of sugar, is an excellent example of a one-crop nation. The prices of sugar since 1920 has ranged from 22 cents a pound to less than 1 cent.[13] Consequently, Cuba has enjoyed periods of great prosperity but has also suffered others of acute depression. Generally, since sugar and its by-products, such as alcohol, are vital war materials, Cuba enjoys high prosperity during wartime. The most prosperous period in the history of the country was during the First World War, when sugar prices jumped to unprecedented levels. This period, which Cubans now refer to as the "Dance of the Millions," was followed by an almost tragic collapse of Cuba's economy. Cubans, in obvious reference to the Biblical story of the interpretations by Joseph of the Pharaoh's dreams, often refer to the cyclical variations of their economy as the "fat-fleshed kine" and the "lean fleshed kine."

[11] United Nations, Department of Economic Affairs, *Economic Survey of Latin America, 1953* (New York, 1954), pp. 54, 56.

[12] International Bank for Reconstruction and Development, *Report on Cuba* (Washington, D.C., 1951), p. 7.

[13] Austin F. Macdonald, *Latin American Politics and Government* (New York, Crowell, 1954), p. 552.

TABLE 20
VALUE OF LATIN-AMERICAN EXPORTS AND IMPORTS
(In millions of dollars)

Country	1937	1948	1950	1952
Exports				
Argentina	$ 757.0	$1,700.0	$1,100.0	$ 670.0
Bolivia	46.2	112.8	94.0	139.0
Brazil	350.0	1,172.7	1,346.5	1,408.8
Chile	186.0	328.0	282.0	454.0
Colombia	86.0	289.0	396.0	473.0
Costa Rica	10.8	45.9	55.6	73 3
Cuba	186.0	709.8	642.0	675.3
Dominican Republic	17.9	82.8	86.8	115.0
Ecuador	12.5	46.3	65.5	79.3
El Salvador	15.5	45.6	69.5	88.2
Guatemala	16.1	50.1	67.6	87.4
Haiti	8.9	29.8	38.6	52.0
Honduras	9.6	22.1	22.6	61.4
Mexico	247.9	477.1	501.6	726.3
Nicaragua	6.1	18.7	26.5	42.4
Panama	4.0	10.5	10.6	12.0
Paraguay	8.2	28.1	33.0	31.2
Peru	86.4	156.8	189.9	234.1
Uruguay	65.6	178.1	254.3	208.1
Venezuela	183.0	1,114.0	1,248.0	1,552.0
Total	$2,303.7	$6,618.2	$6,530.6	$7,182.8
Imports				
Argentina	$ 482.0	$1,485.0	$ 930.0	$ 860.0
Bolivia	21.1	68.7	55.8	64.3
Brazil	334.6	1,134.2	1,097.9	2,009.5
Chile	89.0	269.0	248.0	371.0
Colombia	96.0	337.0	364.0	416.0
Costa Rica	11.9	42.3	46.0	67.9
Cuba	129.5	527.4	515.0	618 3
Dominican Republic	11.7	65.3	43.6	79.4
Ecuador	11.3	49.7	41.6	56.5
El Salvador	10.4	41.5	47.2	67.7
Guatemala	16.7	68.4	71.2	75.7
Haiti	9.2	30.8	37.8	52.9
Honduras	10.3	35.6	34.2	57.6
Mexico	170.5	528.6	509.0	807.6
Nicaragua	5.6	24.1	24.7	39.7
Panama	21.8	63.7	67.0	75.9
Paraguay	8.4	24.3	19.0	37.0
Peru	59.4	167.7	175.1	287.5
Uruguay	66.3	199.7	199.6	236.6
Venezuela	89.0	839.0	537.0	723.0
Total	$1,654.7	$6,002.0	$5,063.7	$7,004.1

SOURCE: Reproduced from *Selected Economic Data on the Latin American Republics* (Washington, D.C., Pan American Union, 1954).

TABLE 21

AREA DISTRIBUTION OF LATIN-AMERICAN EXPORTS AND IMPORTS

(Percentage of total)

Country	United States and Canada		Latin America		Sterling area		Continental EPU countries and dependencies		Rest of the world	
	1937	1952	1937	1952	1937	1952	1937	1952	1937	1952
Exports										
Argentina	16	26	8	16	30	14	42	34	4	11
Bolivia	7	68	3	1	60	26	30	5		
Brazil	37	53	7	9	10	4	38	28	8	6
Chile	23	57	4	15	20	5	29	17	24	6
Colombia	63	84	1	1	...	1	34	13	2	1
Costa Rica	44	72	3	8	20	...	29	18	4	
Cuba	81	63	1	3	11	9	6	15	1	10
Dominican Republic	35	43	1	...	31	39	29	8	4	10
Ecuador	33	55	7	9	2	7	41	19	17	11
El Salvador	64	85	3	3	1	1	28	11	4	
Guatemala	65	84	1	2	1	2	30	12	3	
Haiti	28	55	...	1	16	...	52	43	4	1
Honduras	89	85	1	11	...	...	7	3	3	
Mexico	56	83	2	3	13	2	22	5	7	7
Nicaragua	56	53	4	14	...	13	33	17	7	3
Panama	93	87	...	10	...	...	3	2	4	1
Paraguay	7	25	21	42	10	3	33	27	29	2
Peru	29	30	15	31	23	9	27	26	6	4
Uruguay	21	25	7	15	26	17	28	39	18	4
Venezuela	14	35	1	8	4	4	64	51	17	2
All Latin America	46	62	4	8	14	6	28	19	7	5
Imports										
Argentina	18	19	9	22	26	8	39	37	9	14
Bolivia	29	54	31	19	8	9	24	17	8	1
Brazil	25	44	16	9	14	12	42	35	3	2
Chile	30	54	16	21	12	10	35	13	7	2
Colombia	49	69	3	4	19	5	26	18	3	4
Costa Rica	42	67	6	4	9	6	31	21	12	2
Cuba	69	78	3	3	8	7	14	10	6	2
Dominican Republic	54	71	1	2	9	6	17	17	19	4
Ecuador	39	66	6	6	10	8	36	19	9	1
El Salvador	40	65	6	11	11	5	38	17	5	2
Guatemala	45	66	4	9	8	6	38	17	5	2
Haiti	52	76	...	2	17	5	17	15	14	2
Honduras	59	75	4	8	3	3	17	13	17	2
Mexico	63	86	2	1	5	3	26	9	4	1
Nicaragua	54	73	7	7	7	5	22	15	10	
Panama	52	68	2	5	6	7	12	7	28	13
Paraguay	7	28	44	31	8	11	21	27	19	2
Peru	38	63	11	7	13	12	31	17	7	1
Uruguay	23	26	11	25	21	13	34	30	11	6
Venezuela	53	73	1	1	9	7	31	13	6	6
All Latin America	44	61	9	7	11	9	30	21	6	2

SOURCE: Reproduced from *Selected Economic Data on the Latin American Republics* (Washington, D.C. Pan American Union, 1954).

Brazil's national economy is also a boom-and-bust affair. In the seventeenth century this Portuguese colony was for a time the greatest exporter of sugar. Then came the discovery of gold and diamonds. While the gold rush lasted Brazil produced more than 40 per cent of all the gold mined in the eighteenth century. With the advent of the automotive age, the gold rush was followed by a great rubber boom. Before the decline of rubber exports, caused by the rise of competitive new sources and the development of synthetic rubber, Brazil became the world's first exporter of coffee. As one Brazilian official once put it, "Brazil walks on one leg, and the leg now is coffee."[14] The trouble is not only that this leg is wobbly, but that it might some day wither altogether. Coffee might go the way of sugar, gold, and rubber.

This economic instability has an important bearing upon politics. Taxes on export products constitute the largest fraction of the revenues of some Latin-American governments. In other countries royalties on mineral production are the main source of public income. The latter case is well exemplified by Venezuela, where approximately one-third of the total budget receipts consists of oil royalties alone.[15] Thus, any alteration or upset of foreign markets necessarily has damaging effects upon government finances, and a severe and prolonged decline in foreign trade may easily bring national bankruptcy.

Latin-American leaders have long been aware of the inherent evils in their one-sided economies and consequently have been searching for remedies. Logically, the most desirable solutions are diversification of production, expansion of industrial activity, and the attainment of greater economic self-sufficiency. However, the transition from an agricultural economy based on production for export to a diversified economy based on production for domestic use is a difficult one. Reconstructing the economy involves many complex problems of policy making, so progress necessarily must be slow. Furthermore, economic development is often hindered by an acute shortage of experts and technicians as well as by lack of much-needed financing means. Agricultural diversification is opposed in some countries by foreign corporations and powerful native interests. These groups have obstructed diversification by the tendency to keep large

[14] *Time,* Dec. 6, 1954, p. 50.

[15] More than 60 per cent of the revenue of the Venezuelan government is contributed, in one way or another, by the petroleum companies. See United Nations, Department of Economic Affairs, *Public Finance Surveys: Venezuela* (New York, January, 1951).

TABLE 22

PRINCIPAL EXPORTS OF LATIN-AMERICAN COUNTRIES

(Percentage of total exports of each country)

	1937	1952*
Argentina:		
Corn	26	8
Wheat	21	1
Meat	10	15
Wool	7	16
Hides and skins	6	9
Quebracho	2	7
Others	28	44
Total	100	100
Bolivia:		
Tin	63	59
Lead	6	8
Tungsten	4	10
Zinc	4	9
Others	23	14
Total	100	100
Brazil:		
Coffee	42	74
Cacao	5	3
Cotton	19	2
Others	34	21
Total	100	100
Chile:		
Copper	56	63
Nitrate	19	13
Others	25	24
Total	100	100
Colombia:		
Coffee	65	82
Petroleum	23	16
Others	12	2
Total	100	100
Costa Rica:		
Bananas	54	59
Coffee	36	34
Others	10	7
Total	100	100

TABLE 22 (*Continued*)

	1937	1952*
Cuba:		
Sugar	78	85
Others	22	15
Total	100	100
Dominican Republic:		
Sugar	60	45
Cacao	14	13
Coffee	10	23
Others	16	19
Total	100	100
Ecuador:		
Bananas	4	27
Cacao	34	22
Coffee	17	26
Others	45	25
Total	100	100
El Salvador:		
Coffee	95	88
Others	5	12
Total	100	100
Guatemala:		
Bananas	25	5
Coffee	68	82
Others	7	13
Total	100	100
Haiti:		
Sugar	9	6
Coffee	52	66
Others	39	28
Total	100	100
Honduras:		
Bananas	77	66
Coffee	3	26
Others	20	8
Total	100	100

TABLE 22 (*Continued*)

	1937	1952*
Mexico:		
Coffee	4	8
Cotton	1	23
Copper	7	6
Lead	15	13
Zinc	11	8
Others	62	42
Total	100	100
Nicaragua:		
Bananas	16	1
Coffee	50	51
Cotton	9	18
Others	25	30
Total	100	100
Panama:		
Bananas	68	38
Cacao	20	13
Others	12	49
Total	100	100
Paraguay:		
Hides and skins	9	10
Cotton	37	34
Quebracho	19	18
Others	35	38
Total	100	100
Peru:		
Sugar	9	14
Cotton	25	34
Petroleum	34	8
Copper	15	6
Lead	4	11
Zinc	1	6
Others	12	21
Total	100	100

TABLE 22 (*Continued*)

	1937	1952*
Uruguay:		
Meat	16	14
Hides and skins	14	11
Wool	46	33
Others	24	42
Total	100	100
Venezuela:		
Petroleum	89	95
Others	11	5
Total	100	100

* For Peru, 1951.

SOURCE: Reproduced from *Selected Economic Data on the Latin American Republics* (Washington, D.C., Pan American Union, 1954).

areas of land in idle reserve. These potentially productive lands are hoarded in expectation of demand increases for products now being exported. In addition, the landowner is generally reluctant to enter into any kind of contract with tenant farmers which might restrict his freedom to adjust quickly to fluctuations in foreign demand.[16]

Low Standards of Living

As a result of the system of landownership the average income for the masses has always been extremely low in Latin America. For centuries the largest portion of the national income has gone to a small minority, while the bulk of the population lives under low-level conditions. Considerable segments of the population are physically undernourished or suffer from infectious or deficiency diseases. In many countries the Indian laborer remains "unincorporated," i.e., apart from the economic and social systems, and his consuming power is generally insignificant. Living conditions are peculiarly unstable because of dependence on fluctuations of foreign markets, and in general they are far below those of the United States or Western Europe. Despite the amazing advances made in recent years, the income of all Latin America is only one-eighth of that of the United States. As a result of the high inequality in the distribution of income there are

[16] Soule, Efrón, and Ness, *op. cit.*, pp. 68–69.

many very poor, a small number of very rich, and in many countries almost no middle class. Malnutrition and poor housing constitute obstacles to improving the health and productivity of the Latin-American people.

In all fairness, it must be said that the system of land tenure is not solely responsible for these conditions. Other factors, such as deficiencies in natural resources and unfavorable climatic conditions, by restricting productivity, have determined in part the low standards of living.

The effect of low standards of living on political institutions seems obvious. It is easy to understand how the operation of representative government may be seriously handicapped by these conditions. Poverty and illiteracy contribute greatly to the strength and perpetuation in office of the political oligarchy. Conversely, a significant rise in average standard of living would foster the growth of democratic institutions. It may be assumed, therefore, that, generally speaking, the Latin-American oligarchs, despite their protestations to the contrary, are opposed to measures of reform designed to raise the standards of living of the people. If the majority of the population should succeed in securing freedom from material want, it would develop a sense of responsibility and a desire to share in the conduct of public affairs. In this case, the privileged position of the ruling minority would be challenged and its hitherto undisputed control could come to an end.

Large Foreign Investments

Another economic factor which has an important influence in politics is the existence of large foreign investments. In many of the Latin-American countries a substantial part of the economic activity is controlled by business concerns located abroad. In Chile, for example, over 90 per cent of the total copper production is owned by foreign enterprises. Of a total of 351,000 tons of copper mined in 1953, more than 325,000 tons were produced by large United States–owned companies.[17] The foreign-owned Cerro de Pasco Corporation of Peru produces about two-thirds of the copper output of that country.[18] The case of Venezuela and its petroleum industry is typical. Oil represents about 95 per cent of Venezuelan exports, but this product is almost entirely in the hands of foreign-owned corporations. One company, a subsidiary of a large United States oil firm, owns

[17] United Nations, Department of Economic Affairs, *Economic Survey of Latin America, 1953,* p. 185.

[18] *Ibid.,* p. 187.

almost half the total production. Capital investment is estimated at about two billion dollars, of which nearly one billion and a half comes from the United States.[19]

This situation has often led to charges of "economic imperialism," hurled particularly against the United States. In some cases, it has turned large foreign concerns into political scapegoats. An objective appraisal of such charges is a formidable task because of the elusiveness of the evidence, and it is rendered even more difficult by the fact that fervent nationalism is prone to exaggerate the power of foreign interests. However, it is undeniable that (1) such interests often intervene in politics, and (2) they have more often thrown their weight on the side of dictatorship than in support of democratic groups. More than a few Latin-American strong men have owed their power to the constant support of foreign interests in exchange for favorable treatment and protection of their investments.

Even more important than intervention in politics may be the fact that most foreign investments, because of their nature, have coincided with the interests of the landowning aristocracy. It has been pointed out that in agricultural enterprises foreign corporations have, in most cases, acted toward their laborers in identical fashion as the native aristocracy, and they have made skillful use of local methods of exploitation. Also, as it was explained in our introductory chapter, a great amount of foreign investment has gone into the kind of developments which stimulate exports, and therefore it has strengthened the economic power of the big landowner. In mineral production, although such community of interests between the foreign companies and the landholding class is not present, the foreign mining corporation has not shown in the past much concern with the average purchasing power within the country or with standards of living.[20]

Industrialization

Many leaders and governments in Latin America are convinced that the panacea that would cure all economic ills and that would lead to the wealth and eminence they desire for their nations is industrialization. However, industrial development is not uniform over the area, and there are notable variations from country to country. At present industry has attained a firm hold in some countries, such as Argentina, Brazil, Chile, and Mexico; it

[19] Donald W. Beatty, "Venezuela: Rich Abroad—Poor at Home," *Current History,* vol. 24, no. 139, p. 153, March, 1953.
[20] Mosk, *op. cit.,* p. 140.

has made considerable progress in Cuba, Colombia, and Peru; while in other countries it is reduced to scattered small-scale manufacturing plants which employ only a few workers. Despite its unevenness, the rapidity with which industrialization is taking place is perhaps the most far-reaching event in Latin America's recent history.

TABLE 23

CUBAN POPULATION AND INCOME

Year	Estimated population, thousands	National monetary income	
		Total, millions of pesos	Per capita
1937	4,165	614	141
1938	4,228	468	106
1939	4,253	488	108
1940	4,291	431	94
1941	4,236	678	146
1942	4,372	710	150
1943	4,779	933	194
1944	4,784	1,212	248
1945	4,913	1,074	216
1946	4,968	1,259	251
1947	5,052	1,674	329
1948	5,199	1,697	329
1949	5,308	1,570	300
1950	5,415	1,683	318
1951	5,527	1,971	368
1952	5,745	1,962	342
1953	5,825	1,701*	292*
1954	5,906		

SOURCE: Banco Nacional de Cuba. Reproduced from *Cuba: Facts and Figures* (Havana, The American Chamber of Commerce of Cuba, 1955).

* Tentative

Industrialization, by challenging the old economic forces of colonialism, should bring profound changes in social and political patterns. Even now, before it is fully developed, it has already brought into play new political elements. The amazing rise of labor as a force in politics, the appearance of a new industrialist class, and the proliferation of social and labor legislation are suggestive enough of the potential impact of industrialization upon Latin-American society. As Professor Mosk says, "Industrialization is never solely a technical and economic development. It is a social and cultural process as well, and in underdeveloped countries nowadays it is also likely to have profound political repercussions."[21] He further claims, and the authors are inclined to agree with him, that the new blocs of economic power (i.e., the industrialists and the trade unions) in the prevailing structure are bound to be prodemocratic forces. If this proves to be correct, the resulting boost for the cause of democracy will have many beneficial effects upon the political stage.

It should be remembered, however, that Latin America is at an early stage of industrialization. These countries lack the huge financial means and the techniques which are needed for the development of heavy industries, and they are still dependent upon foreign sources of capital.[22] The leading industries, generally speaking, are textiles and foodstuffs. Most countries continue to import much of their machinery, transportation facilities, and manufacturing equipment. A disturbing factor is a reported slackening in the rate of industrialization since 1950.

Some Contemporary Economic Problems

Since the end of the Second World War, new factors have appeared which further complicate the already complex economic situation of Latin America. One of these has arisen from the truly spectacular growth of the population which, according to some, may possibly give Latin America as many people to feed by the end of this century as China now has, i.e., about 600 million. This population growth means, of course, that production gains are being absorbed disproportionately in feeding more mouths. Moreover, unemployment is an inevitable corollary of the increase in population.

Another important problem arises from overzealous efforts for rapid economic development, and especially from plans for industrialization. It is represented by the decrease in the production of food and raw materials relative to growing needs of some rich agricultural countries which have

[21] *Ibid.,* p. 142.

[22] Latin America has often resorted to the Export-Import Bank of Washington for funds. This institution supplied about half the capital that was needed for the steel plants at Volta Redonda (Brazil) and Huachipato (Chile). In other instances, loans have been received from the International Bank of Reconstruction and Development. These loans, however, represent but an insignificant fraction of the enormous capital that is needed for Latin America to fulfill its goal of industrialization.

TABLE 24
PRICES OF LEADING LATIN-AMERICAN EXPORT COMMODITIES
(In dollars per 100-lb. in the United States, except as otherwise indicated)

Commodity	1938	1948	1950	1952	1953 (Oct.)
Bananas	6.70	15.50	15.40	15.22	15.30
Beet (100 lb. in Argentina)	7.99	12.67	16.35	17.22	21.75
Coffee	7.80	26.83	50.91	54.12	60.00
Cacao	5.30	39.78	32.05	35.40	40.00
Copper	10.22	22.32	21.61	24.50	29.50
Lead	4.74	18.04	13.30	16.52	13.50
Linseed oil	9.00	29.60	18.40	*	16.00
Nitrate (short ton)	29.00	49.40	51.50	57.00	53.00
Petroleum (barrel)	1.12	2.51	2.51	2.51	2.76
Quebracho	n.a.	12.22	8.32	11.50	11.50
Sugar	2.04	5.57	5.92	6.27	6.40
Mutton (100 lb. in New Zealand)	14.34	18.79	15.88	19.19	21.50
Tin	42.30	99.20	96.00	120.40	80.30
Zinc	4.98	14.20	14.58	17.11	10.50
Cotton	9.00	33.80	36.20	38.70	32.60
Wheat (bushel = 60 lb.)	0.78	2.41	2.23	2.39	2.23
Wool (greasy, Uruguay)	20.10	57.80	83.90	61.20	72.40

* Not available.

EXPORT PRICE INDEXES, LEADING EXPORT AREAS
(January–June 1950 = 100)

Area	1938	1948	1950	1952	1953
Latin America	33	88	108	118	116 (Aug.)
United States	55	114	102	116	116 (Sept.)
United Kingdom	68	137	102	126	120 (Oct.)
Continental EPU countries	56	129	102	130	121 (Aug.)

SOURCE: *International Financial Statistics* (International Monetary Fund, January, 1954), pp. 35.

COST-OF-LIVING INDEXES
(1948 = 100)

Country	Type of index	1938	1950	1952	1953
Argentina	Capital city	49	165	312	320 (Sept.)
Bolivia*	Capital city	19	149	247	396 (May)
Brazil	São Paulo	23	104	133	165 (Sept.)

TABLE 24 (*Continued*)

Country	Type of index	1938	1950	1952	1953
Chile	Capital city	23	137	204	318 (Nov.)
Colombia	Capital city	40	129	137	153 (Nov.)
Costa Rica	Capital city	47	119	122	121 (Nov.)
Cuba	Food at retail, Havana	37	84	94	92 (Sept.)
Dominican Republic	Capital city	79 (1945)	96	106	102 (Oct.)
Ecuador	Food at retail, Quito	26 (1939)	97	112	111 (Aug.)
El Salvador	Food at retail, San Salvador	42	99	†	†
Guatemala	Food at retail, Guatemala City	42 (1939)	116	126	125 (Sept.)
Haiti	Food at retail, Port-au-Prince	†	†	109	99 (Mar.)
Honduras	Capital city	60	111	120	121 (Sept.)
Mexico	Retail prices, Mexico City	31	112	144	142 (Oct.)
Nicaragua	Food at retail, Managua	19	114	138	152 (Mar.)
Panama	Food at retail, Panama City	50‡	91	96	96 (Sept.)
Paraguay	Capital city	24	231	687	1180 (Aug.)
Peru	Capital city	30	129	152	169 (Sept.)
Uruguay	Capital city	55	101	131	144 (Oct.)
Venezuela	Food at retail, Caracas	49	97	98	96 (Sept.)
United States	General	46	109	124	112 (Oct.)

* Annual data refer to December.

† Not available

‡ October, 1939, to June, 1940.

SOURCE: Reproduced from *Selected Economic Data on the Latin American Republics* (Washington, D.C., Pan American Union, 1954).

neglected agriculture so as to stimulate industry. A third element, which is again the result in part of overambitious development programs, is inflation. Inflation is partly a spiraling upward of wages and prices, and partly the necessity of meeting deficits, industrialization costs, and public-works projects by printing money. Manufacturing money has been in most cases the only solution to fill the gap between savings and investments. This gap is caused by the tendency to concentrate on investments, the total of which exceeds nearly three times the amount of savings, and by the fact that foreign loans have contributed little toward investment requirements. Inflation has been the cause of discontent as well as financial and economic crises and irksome economic controls.

It may then be said that, unfortunately, programs for economic development have had some harmful effects. In addition to inflation other adverse consequences have been the higher cost of producing locally what can be purchased more cheaply abroad, and what is more important, the unfavorable effect on the balance of international payments. Because incomes are increasing and prices are high, some Latin-American countries export less and import more than they used to. An inevitable consequence of this situation is a depletion of foreign reserves with the resulting establishment of minute government controls of foreign exchange, prices, and trade. At present, government economic controls are more evident in Latin America than in any other region of the world.

It seems obvious that the political results of inflation and an unfavorable trade position can be very serious. If Latin America is to cope successfully with these problems it needs technical help and financial assistance. The question of the role that the United States, as the leading country in the Western Hemisphere, should play in Latin America's economic development is a very important one. Economically the United States is more than ever dependent upon Latin America for stategic and raw materials; politically, it shares with the nations to the south its political ideals of individual freedom and representative government. Economic assistance may well be translated into political progress and stability; by giving aid the United States may, indirectly, be fostering the development of Latin-American democracy.

A leading economist, after taking a new and hard look at the relations between the United States and Latin America, maintains that the former has failed to fulfill the responsibility of a creditor nation, namely, to lend adequately. He points out that out of a total of eighty billion dollars of United States government foreign aid since 1940, Latin America received but 1 to 2 per cent. He also cites United States trade restrictions as another source of concern and criticizes the apparent unwillingness to take measures to stabilize the prices of Latin-American exports. In his opinion, the United States must contribute to a solution of Latin America's economic troubles in four different ways: providing government loans at low rates of interest; furnishing adequate technical assistance; protecting Latin-American exports against dangerous price declines; and, lastly, opening up the United States markets to Latin-American products.[23] There is little doubt that all these are sound suggestions. It may be added, to conclude, that the ultimate goal of the United States in Latin America should continue to be to promote its economic growth but that priority should be given to those measures which, by benefiting the bulk of the population, can most effectively contribute to fostering a democratic political society.

Government and the Economy

A cursory examination of the economic activity of the countries of Latin America will show that their governments are taking an increasingly larger share of participation and assuming more and more responsibilities in that sphere. This is not solely a Latin-American phenomenon, but it is nevertheless striking in view of its recent and rapid development. According to an economist, the governments were responsible in 1950 for more than one-fourth of the economic endeavors in those countries, and even this figure did not accurately represent the degree of influence exercised by the governments in the economic field. He further noted that, as a rule, government expenditures amounted to from 15 to 25 per cent of the national income in each country, and that the rate showed a tendency to increase at a faster pace than the national income.[24] Such a remarkable expansion of government activity, beyond the normal functions of the state, is explained in terms of the need of governmental intervention to supply services, the reluctance of private capital to invest in certain industries, the political expediency of building up prestige for the administration both at home and abroad, the elimination of foreign enterprise as an aim of nationalistic policy, or the mere fact that only the government is financially able to undertake the particular enterprise. Government participation, however, is not limited to the industrial field. Its arms are extending more and more into finance, foreign trade, and formal planning, setting up a growing system of credit and banking institutions, trade-control devices, and ambitious "plans" of assorted kinds.[25]

[23] Seymour E. Harris, "How Good Is Our Good Neighbor Policy?" *The New York Times Magazine,* Nov. 28, 1954. With reference to the need of opening United States markets, the author mentions that Latin America had about 135 bilateral agreements in 1953, and that four-fifths of Argentina's trade was thus being covered. He found it alarming that, whereas there were only seven of these agreements with countries within the Soviet orbit in 1952, by the following year there were thirty-two.

[24] Simon G. Hanson, *Economic Development in Latin America* (Washington, D.C., Inter-American Affairs Press, 1951), p. 456.

[25] *Ibid,* pp. 456–458.

Although it is not within the purpose of this book to make any appraisal of the success or failure of government ventures for economic development, it must be noted that some formidable obstacles, difficult to remove, have impaired, and probably will impair for a long time to come, the effective attainment of whatever objectives are pursued by such government activities. The lack of a well-trained staff of experts with high standards and technical knowledge of subjects involved is an important factor. The long-existent corruption and mismanagement, which have been traditional evils of public administration in almost every country, are serious barriers, since they undermine such efforts. They cause lack of faith on the part of the people and lack of that popular support which is almost indispensable for successful development activities. This situation has been slow to change. Political instability and the spirit of expediency also are important factors in explaining the difficulties encountered by most Latin-American governments when they undertake any detailed planning of the economy.

If one applies systematic criticism and appraisal to Latin-American economics, many inconsistencies will be found. One student of the subject enumerates the common objectives of economic policies now in vogue in Latin America and points out their inconsistencies. He finds a common objective to be that of greater production, but in pursuing this goal "the national aspirations for industry regardless of cost cause excessive protection to be given to politically powerful industrialists, with corresponding discouragement of efficiency." Nationalism may discourage or prevent the entrance and establishment of foreign enterprise, although the need for outside capital is not denied. Agrarian reform plans may often reduce agricultural productivity. The object of attaining a more nearly equal economic opportunity and status for the people was thought by many statesmen to be enhanced by a graduated income-tax system. This aim was doomed to defeat because of the stubborn opposition to any such taxation system on the part of persons with large property interests. This relatively simple conflict was complicated, first by the fact that the proponents of tax reform were leaders in the adoption of policies of protection to new industries and, secondly, by the fact that the protected new industries became holders of wealth and in turn opponents of income taxes having graduated rates. An objective of extending government services into new fields of activity is handicapped by the weight and expense of old activities and vested obligations such as an enormous bureaucracy and the burden of the military budget. The policy toward greater productivity is seriously affected by the social and welfare legislation enacted by most countries.[26] In this connec-

[26] *Ibid.*, pp. 459–461.

tion it may be said that Latin America has been anxious to enjoy the benefits of economic development before it has made the necessary sacrifices implied in such development and before it is in a position to afford them. In accepting the costly social and welfare standards of industrialized nations Latin America often faces the dilemma either of not attempting any rigid enforcement of its social legislation and merely letting it stay on the books, or of enforcing it and thereby causing retardation in the general development of industrialization.

There are two main facts to be considered in relation to the problem of government expenditures. Both of these have an adverse effect on the national economy. The first is the disproportionate size of the bureaucracy in all the countries and the failure to maintain high standards of selection and efficiency in the civil service. It is estimated that approximately 8 to 12 per cent of the total number of persons employed in Latin America are public servants. In Cuba, for example, the government in 1953 expressed serious concern that some 50 per cent of the total national expenditure was paid to public officials and civil servants, a group which exceeded 100,000 in number. The second fact to be noted is the high cost of the military establishments which is a major drain on foreign exchange resources. Of a total budget of approximately 300 million dollars, the estimated military expenditures of Cuba in 1953 amounted to about 50.5 million.[27] In Argentina in recent years, more than 40 per cent of the public expenditures has been devoted to military purposes.[28] Such a mounting burden results generally in an enlargement of the public debt. This situation is particularly serious for two reasons: (1) a sound revision of the taxation system is unpopular, (2) a strict inspection of government expenditures and a retrenchment policy are politically unacceptable. Fortunately, there has been a noticeable decline of foreign-held debt as against the locally held, but despite this fact, Latin-American governments still experience some difficulty in disposing of public securities in view of the general distrust of government bonds and securities as safe investments. Also government securities have to compete with the traditionally more attractive investments in real property.

Government and Industrialization

Governments are very much involved in all Latin-American efforts for industrialization. They have supplied in most countries the necessary stimu-

[27] *Bohemia,* Mar. 1, 1953, p. 69.
[28] Hanson, *op. cit.,* p. 463.

lus to industrialize, and credit and development agencies created by governments have participated in the planning, establishment, and operation of new industries. A very important part has been played in the economic expansion of the various Latin American countries by these state-controlled industrial and commercial corporations. A series of developmental and financing establishments have been set up as an answer to the problems of certain types of industry. Many of these agencies were established as a result of the war, but the basic objective of all is that toward a long-range development of the national economy.

Significant in the new trends of modern Latin-American constitutionalism is the inclusion of principles regulating the establishment and operation of agencies of this kind. Special chapters are devoted in the recent constitutions of Costa Rica, Nicaragua, and Uruguay, to the treatment of the autonomous entities and decentralized services (*entidades* or *entes autónomos y servicios centralizados*). These constitutions provide for the administration of the various state-controlled industrial and commercial services by autonomous councils or boards of directors. In Uruguay, such boards consist of five or seven members, appointed by the executive branch and confirmed by the senate. In Nicaragua, they are composed of not less than three members appointed by the president in cabinet session. A special provision guaranteed the participation of minority parties in their membership. The law regulates the way by which private capital may be invested in such enterprises and declares the manner of participation by shareholders in their administration and management. It always stated, however, that the amount of private capital shall never be greater than that invested by the government. Special majorities are necessary in the congress when such agencies are created by legislative action.[29]

The oldest and most influential of the development agencies in Latin America is the famous Chilean Development Corporation (Corporación de Fomento de la Producción), established in 1939 with the following basic aims: (1) to raise the standards of living; (2) to improve the balance of trade; (3) to draw general plans aimed at more effective and larger production; (4) to develop locally the national resources; and (5) to coordinate the development of industry with that of mining, agriculture, and commerce. The corporation is managed by a board of twenty-one members which includes representatives of the government, business, and labor. The chairman is the minister of the treasury. It is divided into six

[29] Costa Rica (Arts. 188–190); Nicaragua (Arts. 271–275); Uruguay (Arts. 185–203).

departments: agriculture, trade and transportation, industries, mining, electricity and fuels, and finances. The corporation operates with great flexibility, since it is authorized either to do its work directly or to invite participation of private enterprise. It is able to finance existing or proposed industries by a variety of methods. It may acquire part of the stock of a private industry and participate in its management. It exercises practical supervision over all industry, since no new industrial operation or plant expansion is permitted if not authorized by the corporation. The agency was in 1949 the co-owner of some sixty enterprises of the most varied nature. A basic principle of policy is for the corporation to discontinue its support and share of control of enterprises as soon as they can dispense with its aid.[30]

In Colombia, the creation of the Autonomous Regional Corporation of the Cauca in 1955 followed the lead of a study made by D. E. Lilienthal, former chairman of the Tennessee Valley Authority, at the request of the Colombian government. The Cauca corporation, like the TVA, is designed to develop an entire region—the 18,000-square-mile valley of the Cauca River, which has a population of some two million. This is to be done through the generation and distribution of electric power, through the coordination of existing power systems, and through flood control, irrigation, reclamation of swamp land, soil conservation, reforestation, and improvement of river courses. Proper use of lands for farming and livestock will be stimulated by the corporation in such a way as to encourage private initiative and create new opportunities for private participation. Financing is to come through the national government and state appropriations, and the sale of electric power and other products and services. Both Mr. Lilienthal in his report and the Colombian Council of Ministers in its decree creating the Cauca corporation stressed its basic aim: to improve the living conditions of the people of Colombia. The new corporation may well prove to be of considerable historical importance—both to Colombia and also to the United States in its relations with Latin America. To improve living conditions is not only worthy in itself; it is also the most effective way of making the people of Latin America immune to communism.

Other development (*fomento*) organizations of significance in Latin America are the Instituto de Fomento Industrial in Colombia; the Société

[30] Soule, Efrón, and Ness, *op. cit.*, pp. 273–276. See also Hanson, *op. cit.*, pp. 479–485, and Herman Finer, *The Chilean Development Corporation* (Montreal, International Labour Office, 1947).

Haïtienne-Américaine de Développement Agricole in Haiti; the Comisión de Fomento Nacional in Cuba; the Ecuadorean Corporación Ecuatoriana de Fomento; the Corporación Peruana del Amazonas; and the Bolivian Corporación de Fomento. None of these institutions may conduct any business foreign to that specifically assigned to it by law, nor may it devote any of its resources to purposes other than its normal activities. They are required in all cases to publish periodic statements which clearly indicate their financial condition.

Tax Systems

The acceptance by the governments in Latin America of responsibility for providing a new and growing body of services has made it necessary to undertake a reappraisal of revenue systems with a view toward scientific readjustment to make it possible to meet the costs involved. Such a readjustment, however, is proving to be a difficult task in most of the countries and has not yet been seriously attempted in any of them. Taxes in Latin America continue to be, as in the past, mostly regressive in nature and are heavily centered upon consumption levies. Income taxes, although adopted in the 1930s in some countries, tend to be at relatively low rates on the upper brackets, and evasion is not effectively prevented. Excise taxes, on the other hand, generally account for a considerable part of revenues.

Customs duties have long been the major source of government revenue in Latin America and were always preferred because they were more productive than any other tax and easier to administer. Customs duties and related levies were in practice imposed on articles of basic necessity, and no serious effort was made to distinguish technically between luxury items and mass-consumption goods. Import duties were an important source of revenue in all the countries until they declined as a result of the world depression.

Income taxes, as has already been indicated, were not adopted until the drop in customs revenues occurred after 1929. They are generally levied not only upon salaries and wages but upon other incomes, such as those from rural and urban lands in Argentina. The rate progression stops at much lower points than those used in the United States. In Mexico, the rate was 30 per cent on income from commerce, industry, and agriculture in excess of $100,000, and a person with a $8,000 salary pays less than 5 per cent tax; in Venezuela, 26 per cent marks the top bracket. However, it is possible for persons in a low bracket to receive tax treatment which is more burdensome than that borne by persons with a higher income.[31]

Inheritance tax laws exist in some of the countries, but in general they impose mildly progressive rates. Federal legislation in Argentina in the 1940s established a maximum of 30 per cent for the largest fortunes.[32] Another common source of government revenue is the stamp tax, which may apply to all judicial transactions, deeds, contracts, bills of exchange, postal money orders, drafts from banks, and many other similar documents. Taxes on gasoline, tobacco, alcohol, and liquid combustibles represent a substantial amount in some countries. Exchange taxes are to be found everywhere. Tax receipts are supplemented by property transfer taxes, imposts on industries and professions, and business licenses. Rural and urban land taxes, although they exist in some of the countries, have contributed only negligibly to the cost of government. Such a policy, dictated by the political influence of the landowning class, has long been criticized as one of the major defects of Latin America's revenue systems.

Double taxation has been avoided in many of the Latin-American countries. In some, such as Brazil, constitutional provisions may prescribe that a federal tax shall exclude an identical state tax. In Argentina, the practice of federal subsidies (*subsidios*) to the provinces has long been established. Authorized by the constitution, these subsidies are extended to those provinces "whose revenues, according to their budgets are insufficient to meet their ordinary expenses.[33] Although such grants were contemplated theoretically to be used in periods of emergency only, they have become established practice over the course of time. Some of the federal tax revenues are also shared by the Argentine provinces, as is true in the case of income tax and sales tax, 17½ per cent of the proceeds of both of which are apportioned among the provinces and the federal capital, with no conditions attached. Proceeds of the combined internal taxes have also been apportioned among the several provinces since 1934. Legislation enacted that year provided for the unification of such taxes, and prevented the situation which existed until that date, in which federal, provincial, and municipal governments were imposing taxes on the same articles. Although these taxes were not high they varied sharply from province to province and resulted in unjust discrimination. Under the system of

[31] Hanson, *op. cit.,* p. 466.

[32] Austin F. Macdonald, *Government of the Argentine Republic* (New York, Crowell, 1942), p. 295.

[33] Art. 68, cl. 8.

1934, the federal government undertook the obligation of compensating the province for the loss of such taxes voluntarily renounced by them, and the provincial legislatures were requested to agree not to levy taxes on items already subjected to federal taxation. The effects of these reforms were immediately apparent. They successfully prevented any damaging economic competition among the provinces by concentrating in the hands of the federal government the collection and administration of internal taxes, and they eliminated some of the acute inequalities of the old tax system.[34]

The system of subsidies has also been used in Venezuela for a long time. In this country the national budget must include an item for this purpose, equivalent to at least 25 per cent of the total revenues. This percentage is established annually on the basis of the total receipts for the preceding year. It is to be distributed among the various states, the federal district, and the territories acording to this formula: 30 per cent is divided equally and 70 per cent according to population. In turn, at least 20 per cent of the share belonging to each state is allocated for distribution among the municipal districts in the same manner.

The Budget

Budgetary policies and procedures are among those aspects of government in Latin America which are most defective and most needful of careful scientific reform. Chronic failures to achieve a balanced budget, to provide an accurate appraisal of the financial state of the nation, and to centralize fiscal control are serious faults of public finance. There has been for some time in Latin America an awareness of the damaging effects of such unsound practices, and some constructive efforts are being made toward more careful financial planning, as evidenced by the most recent constitutions. The current constitutions of Brazil, Costa Rica, Cuba, Ecuador, Guatemala, Nicaragua, and Uruguay include lengthy sections and special chapters designed to achieve objectives such as the preservation of the unity of the budget, limitations of the power of the executive to shift funds, or restrictions against the authorization of new expenditures.

In all the countries the executive branch is charged with the preparation of the budget, which must include all probable revenues and all authorized expenditures of the government during the fiscal year. This duty of the executive is carried out in some countries through specialized departments

[34] Macdonald, *Government of the Argentine Republic,* pp. 284–289.

TABLE 25

CUBA—GOVERNMENT BUDGET FOR THE FISCAL YEAR, 1952–1953

(In millions of dollars)

Receipts	
Imports	$ 87.4
Capital	9.7
Personal income	21.7
Profits	48.3
Interest and capital gains	11.6
Special taxes	4.2
Mining	1.5
Livestock industry	0.1
Transportation	2.9
Various industries	2.4
Property transfer and transactions	97.9
Consumption	31.9
Games and events	3.3
Fees	6.7
Transfer from other government agencies	1.2
Fines and penalties	0.3
Nontax receipts	6.1
Miscellaneous	5.1
Total	$336.3
Expenditures	
Judicial	$ 10.9
Legislative	4.4
Presidency	1.4
Advisory council	0.7
State	3.7
Justice	0.9
Interior	21.3
Finance	17.4
Public works	36.3
Agriculture	5.7
Commerce	2.3
Labor	2.6
Education	83.5
Health	21.4
Communications	12.8
Defense	56.5
Information	0.8
Pensions	42.3
Habana University	2.8
National debt	8.6
Total	$336.3

SOURCE: Reproduced from *Fiscal Receipts, Expenditures, Budgets and Public Debt of the Latin American Republics* (Washington, D.C., Pan American Union, n.d.).

and in others through the minister of finance who submits the budget to congress. In Costa Rica, this duty is performed by a special agency, the head of which is appointed by the president for a term of six years. This department has authority to reduce or even to suppress any items in the proposed budgets drawn up by the heads of the executive departments and by the legislative and judicial branches. In the event of a controversy, however, between this agency and the other departments, the president is authorized to make a final decision. A technical committee of the budget performs similar functions in Ecuador. This committee is composed of the minister of finance, the minister in charge of the national economy, one legislator designated by the full congress, and a representative of the national council of economy designated from among its members. A director of the budget acts as secretary of the committee. In Peru, a special department was created for control of the execution of the general budget and the administration of agencies collecting revenues.

The bill for the budget law must be presented in most countries within a specified period of time, together with the appropriations bill. The congress has similarly a fixed period of time in which to consider and approve the project.

In spite of these precautions it is not altogether rare for the budget to be extended from year to year as a result of inaction on the part of the legislature or failure of the executive and legislative branches to come to a political compromise on financial plans. Such a situation is met in various manners by the several countries. In Bolivia, if the legislature fails to sanction the budget for two years, the last executive project not approved goes into effect for the following year. In Chile, the bill presented by the president becomes effective at the expiration of the period allowed for consideration. In Colombia and in Guatemala, in such a situation, the previous budget continues in force, and the administration may alter it when the estimates of revenues of the new fiscal year make it advisable. The Cuban and the Nicaraguan systems provide that, if the budget law is not voted before the beginning of the new fiscal year, the old budget remains in force for a three-month period. In Ecuador, if it is not enacted, the original draft of the executive will enter into effect.

There is a common trend toward considering all public revenues as a common, indivisible, and single fund and therefore having them all included in a common aggregate. However, some countries still separate certain funds from the general budget items, and they further disrupt budgetary unity by the establishment of numerous special funds or the allocation of some taxes to certain specific expenditures.[35] Some countries follow the established principle of distinguishing between two parts in the budgeting of expenses. In Brazil, a fixed part of the budget may not be altered except by virtue of previous legislation to that effect, and another part is variable and not subject to strict specialization. The Cuban law, perhaps the most elaborate of its kind in Latin America, provides for a fixed portion of the budget which includes the expenditures of the legislative and judicial branches, and the tribunal of accounts, the interest and amortization of loans, as well as the revenues by which they are covered. This fixed budget is in force until revised by special laws. Similar expenditures or taxation prescribed in general or special laws are also considered a fixed part of the budget in Chile. All other variable expenditures may be modified by the congress, but in most countries the initiative for increases or for altering the estimate of receipts belongs exclusively to the executive branch, and the congress cannot approve any new expenditures chargeable to the national treasury without at the same time creating or indicating the sources of revenue necessary to provide for those expenditures.

It has not been uncommon in the past, in some of the countries, for the budget to deal with matters other than those strictly financial. Important policy measures may be attached by the executive to the budget as a means of obtaining their enactment more rapidly. In Argentina, measures such as a minimum-salary law for federal employees and legislation reorganizing the court system have been adopted as "riders" to the budget bill.[36] Some of the recent constitutions include provisions intended to correct this situation, by establishing an absolute prohibition against the inclusion in the budget bill of legislative or administrative reforms of any other kind.

The relative facility with which funds can be shifted by the executive and the extensive use made of special appropriation laws have always been characteristic of the Latin-American budgetary systems. These practices have probably contributed more than any others to diminishing the effectiveness and usefulness of budget laws. Although perfectly justified in cases of emergency, the enactment by congress of increases on appropriations already voted and special ones for services not provided by the budget (*créditos suplementarios* and *créditos extraordinarios*) and the executive

[35] A special highway treasury, independent of the general treasury and with revenues determined by law, is in existence in Honduras.

[36] Macdonald, *Government of the Argentine Republic*, p. 307.

practices of authorizing expenditures by decree without legislative authorization, and of shifting funds, necessarily create serious fiscal problems. The exercise of such authority, however, is constitutionally granted and regulated in most countries. The president may, with the approval of his cabinet, decree payments not authorized by law under certain circumstances and when the congress is not in session. His authority may also extend to the transfer of funds by decree. The emergency cases in which the president can exercise these powers are the following: (1) war or imminent danger of war; (2) grave disturbance of public order; and (3) public calamities. Of course, in all countries the congress must subsequently give its approval to the president's actions. In some cases, the respective executive decree automatically implies convening the congress into special session so that it may act upon it. The total of expenditures that can be made by decree cannot exceed a certain percentage of the amount of the expenditures authorized by the general budget law.

In spite of all constitutional limitations, the chief executive, in practice, is not always restrained in the use of these powers in the situations mentioned by the law. He frequently orders payments from the treasury for a wide variety of purposes, taking advantage of legislative recesses. During the Second World War, the freedom with which Latin-American executives exceeded budget authorization, by means of the exercise of emergency powers, resulted in a significant decrease of congressional authority concerning fiscal policies.

The Tribunal of Accounts and the Comptroller General

Most of the countries have established by law special agencies whose main function is to supervise the revenues, expenditures, and other financial interests of the state, and to examine and audit accounts of all departments. In some countries these agencies may be entrusted in addition with judicial powers in matters concerning accounts, and in a few they may function as a component part of the national judiciary. In all countries these auditing agencies are given an autonomous status.

A tribunal of accounts (*tribunal de cuentas*) has been established in the following countries: Argentina, Brazil, Cuba, Guatemala, Honduras, the Dominican Republic, El Salvador, Nicaragua, and Uruguay.[37] In Argentina, the general accounting agency is composed of three chief auditors, six as-

[37] For a typical example of "organic laws" regulating the functioning of these tribunals, see Ley Orgánica del Tribunal de Cuentas, no. 14, Dec. 20, 1950, *Gaceta Oficial Extraordinaria* (Havana, Dec. 28, 1950).

sociate auditors, and two secretaries. The chief auditors compose the "tribunal" which honors orders for payment. However, the president can overrule decisions of this body on matters which affect the departments under his control. Somewhat different in structure and scope of authority is the *tribunal de cuentas* in the other countries. In Brazil, it is composed of officials with the same rights and privileges as judges of the federal court of appeal, who are appointed by the president with the consent of the senate. In Cuba, it is composed of seven members, four of whom are attorneys and three public accountants or professors of commerce. Two of them are appointed by the supreme court, and two by the senate and president respectively. One of the three public accountants is designated by the council of the University of Havana, one by the senate, and one by the president. They are in office for eight years and cannot be removed except by the Tribunal of Social and Constitutional Guarantees. The Guatemalan tribunal is composed of five members, appointed for four-year terms, and with the same guarantees and prerogatives as members of the supreme court. In El Salvador, the Corte de Cuentas is divided into one chamber of second instance (appeal), composed of a president and two judges elected for three years, and several chambers of first instance whose judges are appointed by the first chamber. In Uruguay, it is composed of seven members, with the same qualifications as senators, appointed by the congress by a two-thirds vote of the entire membership. Their terms end when the general assembly makes appointments for a new period.

The powers most commonly enjoyed by these courts of audit are the following: to follow and to control the execution of the budget; to pass upon the legality of contracts, retirements, removals, and pensions; to pass upon the accounts of those officials responsible for funds and other public properties, and those of the autonomous entities; to register all contracts which affect receipts of expenditures or any act of administration which results in obligation of payment by the treasury; to inspect, in general, all expenditures and disbursements for public works of the national, state, and local governments; to ask reports of all departments and to appoint special delegates to conduct investigations; to supply information to the president and to the congress when requested; to give annual reports on the condition and administration of the public treasury, the national currency, the public debt, the budget and its liquidation; and to receive statements under oath of citizens appointed to public office concerning their private incomes. In Brazil, the tribunal gives prior opinion, within sixty days, upon the accounts that the president must render annually to the congress. In Guatemala, it pronounces upon the constitutionality and legality of decrees that may authorize expenditures or establish revenues, returning them for reconsideration by the executive or the congress, as the case may be, within ten days counted from their receipt. However, in such cases, the executive may issue a decree of insistence with the approval of the cabinet, and the tribunal must accept his decision.

As has been noted, these boards are both administrative and judicial bodies, with special jurisdictions in the tax and customs fields. They not only may be custodians of all national property and the supervising agencies of the budget, but they may also have jurisdiction over all cases concerning financial legislation. The Fiscal Tribunal (Tribunal Fiscal) of Mexico is an interesting example of a special court designed to take cognizance of tax cases and other matters related to financial legislation.[38]

Other countries have established the office of comptroller general for the supervision of the fiscal management of the government. In Panama, it is considered an independent department in the executive branch. The comptroller and subcomptroller are appointed for a four-year term by the congress and cannot be removed except by the supreme court. The Bolivian comptroller is appointed by the president from a panel submitted by the senate, receives the same remuneration as a cabinet member, and has tenure as a supreme court justice. The Contraloría General functions in Costa Rica as an auxiliary agency of the congress, but it also has some functional autonomy. The comptroller and his assistant are appointed by the congress two years after the beginning of a president term for a period of eight years and are responsible to congress, which may remove them by a vote of not less than two-thirds of its membership. In Ecuador, the comptroller general is elected by the legislature every four years and is an ex officio member of the council of state. Supervision of the fiscal management of the government is also entrusted to this official in Colombia, Venezuela, and Chile.

The functions performed by the comptroller general include part of those assigned in other countries to the tribunals of accounts: to conduct the general accounts of the nation, to revise and to close accounts of those responsible to the treasury, to denounce before the proper authorities any irregularity which may be observed in the management of public funds, to countersign orders for payment, to request information from the various agencies, to report to the congress annually, and in some countries to

[38] Helen L. Clagett, *Administration of Justice in Latin America* (New York, Oceana Publications, 1952), pp. 75–78.

advise the executive on the practicability and legality of extraordinary appropriations.

BIBLIOGRAPHY

Behrendt, R. F., *Economic Nationalism in Latin America,* Albuquerque, N.M., School of Inter-American Affairs, University of New Mexico, 1941.

Gómez, Eugenio J., *Ideas económicas y fiscales de Colombia,* Bogotá, 1949.

Gondra, L. R., and others, *El pensamiento económico latino americano,* Mexico, 1945.

Gordon, Wendell C., *The Economy of Latin America,* New York, Columbia University Press, 1950.

Hanson, Simon G., *Economic Development in Latin America,* Washington, D.C., The Inter-American Affairs Press, 1951.

Harris, Seymour E. (ed.), *Economic Problems of Latin America,* New York, McGraw-Hill, 1944.

Horn, Paul Valentine, and Hubert E. Bice, *Latin American Trade and Economics,* New York, Prentice-Hall, 1949.

Magill, Roswell, and Carl Shoup, *The Cuban Fiscal System* [n.p.], New York, 1939.

Mosk, Sanford, *Industrial Revolution in Mexico,* Berkeley, Calif., University of California Press, 1950.

Prebisch, Raul, *The Economic Development of Latin America and Its Principal Problems,* United Nations Document C/CN, 12/89/ rev. 1, 1949.

Rippy, J. Fred, *Latin America and the Industrial Age,* New York, Putnam, 1944.

Rubio Rubio, Carmelo, and Antonio Riva Maruri, *El tribunal de cuentas y sus funciones,* Havana, 1952.

Silva Herzog, Jesús, *El pensamiento económico en México,* Mexico, 1947.

Viana, Arizo de, *Budget-making in Brazil,* trans. by Harvey Walker, Columbus, Ohio, Ohio University Press, 1947.

Wythe, George, *Industry in Latin America,* rev. ed., New York, Columbia University Press, 1950.

———, *An Outline of Latin American Economic Development,* New York, Barnes & Noble, 1946.

Chapter 16: EDUCATION

Public education, administered and conducted by laymen, was a product of political independence. But its development has been neither uniform nor consistent. In respect of the public-private basis of support and control, Latin America has had three distinct systems: (1) that in which all education is subject to a moral emphasis, with the church having influence over it, Colombia being the chief current example; (2) a dual system, with public and private schools in operation at one or more or all scholastic levels—examples being Argentina, Brazil, Chile, Cuba, Peru, Panama, and Costa Rica; and (3) that in which elementary and secondary education is exclusively the function of the state, as in Mexico, but where private colleges and technological schools of nonsectarian affiliation may be permitted under special incorporation.

Children, usually between the ages of six and eight, enter the primary or elementary school, where they remain for five to eight years. The secondary school, which is most commonly known as the *colegio* or *liceo*—with some given the name of *gimnasio* (Brazil) or *instituto* (Cuba)—has a period of four to eight years. Those successfully completing the program of studies are usually awarded a diploma, commonly the *bachillerato* or bachelor's degree. In some countries this degree is not then awarded but is delayed until the student has completed a program of studies in a university. Such students are eligible to apply for admission to "higher education" and are ordinarily from seventeen to nineteen years of age. In the university or the professional schools, they remain according to the program pursued from one to seven years. Usually the program in medicine requires seven years, those in law and engineering five, and that in pharmacy three.

There are primary and secondary schools of shorter duration than the time limits mentioned above. Many of these are vocational in emphasis, and many are terminal so far as the educational objective of the student is concerned. There are stages at which students may digress from this regular sequence in order to enter special schools, such as the normal, industrial, and trade schools. Normal or teacher-training schools are sometimes divided into "inferior" and "superior" categories, with the former often used as a substitute for the *colegio* and with the latter sometimes being classified as "higher education."

The most common experience of an educated person, perhaps, is that of six years for the student in primary school, six in the *colegio,* and three to seven in the university.

Private schools which prepare students for admission to the universities conform to this plan, just as they do in the matter of curriculum, by including the required subjects offered in the public schools. Such schools are in general subject to inspection by representatives of the ministry of public instruction, and very commonly their students must take examinations in the framing and appraisal of which the public school authorities have a voice.

Constitutional Provisions

Education has received recognition, often under the theory that it is a fundamental and original (*primordial*) function of the state, in all constitutions. In some, the statement is brief and may be confined to a single article, as in that of Colombia (Article 41). In that article there is a guarantee of the liberty of instruction, the declaration that primary education is gratuitous (in public schools) and compulsory, and the assertion that all education—public and private—is subject to inspection by the state. In others, especially those adopted recently, the statement is far more elaborate and is in some instances embodied in a separate chapter. Consistently, there is the guarantee of the freedom of instruction, without prejudice to the right conferred on the state to inspect and regulate. Very common, too, is the pledge that primary education shall be gratuitous in all schools operated under public authority and support. Many countries declare that education at this stage is compulsory, but this requirement may be met in different ways, either by attending approved private schools, where permitted, or in special schools, some of which are of shorter duration than that prescribed for the full course of primary studies. Quite common is the declaration that education is a function of the state, and, given this function, the authority is granted to regulate the system and to determine and administer criteria of competence in the teaching profession. The statute giving application to the constitution is usually called the *ley orgánica de educación* or *ley orgánica de instrucción,* sometimes designated as a code. Some examples of these lengthy provisions in constitutions will be given.

Brazil, which makes primary education obligatory and gratuitous (in public schools), requires the instructional use of the national language. Religious instruction is required, outside the hours for regular instruction and according to the religious affiliation of the pupil or the preference of parent or guardian. Teachers in the secondary system have tenure. The federal government shall expend on education not less than 10 per cent of the revenues derived from taxes for "the maintenance and development of teaching," and the states, the federal district, and the municipalities not less than 20 per cent. Federal aid to supply deficiency in funds, especially to primary education, may be provided. The federal government, also, shall promote research institutes in connection with higher education.

Cuba (1940) in its lengthy chapter makes all education from kindergarten to the *institutos,* when operated by the state or the municipalities, gratuitous. In such *institutos,* classified as pre-university, there will be a "reasonable" tuition. In institutions where tuition charges exist, the state will create, in so far as possible, fellowships for the benefit of persons of high qualifications who do not have sufficient resources of their own. The state shall support special schools for adults in order to overcome illiteracy. It shall also conduct special vocational schools for rural areas, for training in agriculture, in manual arts, and in industries. All these will be gratuitous. The law shall establish the professions and occupations for which academic degrees are required. The constitution sets forth the idea of an educational system as having an "organic form" in which there will be an "adequate articulation and continuity between its divisions, including the superior." The budget for the ministry of education shall not, except in time of emergency, be less than that of any other department, and the monthly salary of a primary school teacher shall not be less than a millionth part of the total budget of the state.

The Mexican constitution (1917 with amendments of 1921, 1934, and 1946) grants to the federal government complete control of education, with authority to distribute functions to the states and municipalities. This control extends to all stages and to associated activities. In basic principles, there is a continuation of the ideas of Juárez that elementary education should be compulsory, that all public instruction should be gratuitous, and that there should be no religious instruction in public schools. This last principle is stated as follows: "Education will be maintained completely foreign to any religious doctrine whatever and, based on the results of scientific progress, will struggle against ignorance and its effects, the servitudes, the fanaticisms, and the prejudices." In the well-known amendment of 1934, it was ordered that the education imparted by the state "will be socialistic." This special emphasis, controversial in itself, during the twelve years of its duration was not, it has been claimed, established in fact as a rule of practice. It has been said to have been "one of the least fortunate" ventures.[1] Reference should be made to the transformation of education into a missionary character, beginning in 1920 with the appointment of José Vasconcelos as Rector of the National University and later as a member of President Obregón's cabinet. In the ministry of education, his leadership and cooperation in reforms and innovations in popular education, with the remarkable movement in rural education, with the "incorporation" of the Indian in Mexican society, with volunteer teachers in special schools, and with the establishment of many local libraries, marked the beginning of the new era. The credit is shared by such men as Rafael Ramírez, Moises Sáenz, and Manuel Gamio.

An amendment in 1946 eliminated the requirement of socialistic emphasis and declared that education "will be democratic, considering democracy not only as a juridical structure and a political regime, but as a system of life founded in the constant economic, social, and cultural improvement of the people."

Costa Rica in its new constitution (1949) states that public education is an integral process correlated in phases from the preschool period to the university. Both primary and secondary instruction are free of tuition charge, and study in the primary school is compulsory. The state will provide "food and clothing for indigent pupils" and will supply scholarships and assistance to the well-qualified who are lacking in resources to pursue higher education. It will also provide support for private initiative in "scientific and artistic progress."

The Bolivian constitution of 1948 declares that education is the highest function of the state. Teachers are not removable (*inamovible*) from their positions except for cause. This country will give economic assistance to capable students who lack resources of their own and who would thereby be denied access to higher education (*ciclos superiores*).

The constitution of Argentina of 1949 gave sanction to what was already a definite trend—the federal control and support of public education at all stages. The participation of provinces in the support and control of primary schools was no longer mentioned. Attendance in the primary school was compulsory, and instruction was gratuitous in the public schools of that class. Special objectives were set for the rural schools, and the state was to establish the institutes to prepare teachers for this type of school. This instrument is of particular interest in the mandate given to the six

[1] José E. Iturriaga, *La estructura social de México* (Mexico, 1951), pp. 155–156.

universities. The territory was divided into institutional regions (*regiones universitarias*) within each of which one university was to exercise its functions. Each was to lead the youth to "cultivate the sciences in service of spiritual ends and the aggrandizement of the Nation. . . . The Universities have the right of governing themselves with autonomy, within the limits established by a special law which will regulate their organization and functioning." Each was, in addition to giving instruction in universal knowledge, to attempt to deepen (*profundizar*) the "study of literature, history and folklore of its zone of cultural influence" and promote the technical arts and applied sciences. Courses were required in all faculties, with the object that every student may "know the essence of the Argentine, the spiritual, economic, social and political reality of the country, the evolution and historical mission of the Argentine Republic, and in order that each student may acquire consciousness of the responsibility which he must assume in the enterprise of obtaining and guaranteeing the ends recognized and fixed in this constitution." This was to be the "political formation" of the student. With the overthrow of Perón and the restoration of the constitution of 1853, these innovations were discontinued and the reestablishment of autonomy in university government was promised.

Education in federal states is plainly undergoing a long-standing trend toward control by the central authority. In Argentina and Venezuela, all vestiges of provincial or state participation tend to disappear. In the former, the provinces had a constitutional and an actual function (1853) with respect to primary education, but federal subsidies became available as early as 1857. The role of the federal government became increasingly significant in both economic and regulative aspects. This development was due to the neglect of responsibility by the provinces, to inability to provide funds, or to corruption in administration of the funds allocated by the federal government.[2] In 1897, the requirement was enacted that the provinces should devote at least 10 per cent of their revenues to elementary education. Earlier, in 1884, an important law had been adopted concerning primary education which established regulations governing the organization, administration, and the curriculum of this type of school in the federal district and the territories. It also dealt with the qualifications of teachers. This law, although subsequently amended, is of historical importance in that it became the norm and guide for provincial legislation

[2] Austin F. Macdonald, *Government of the Argentine Republic* (New York, Crowell, 1942), pp. 320–323.

and for the establishment of inspection services. Later when the federal government took the decisive step of establishing primary schools in the provinces or of incorporating some provincial schools in its own system, the provisions of the laws of 1884 were made applicable. Under the new constitution (1949), all features of dualism were removed.

In Mexico, as has been remarked, the role of states and municipalities in education is by way of permission and assignment—although of itself this part is significant.

Brazil has an educational system which deviates in some respects from the foregoing. It has been slow in evolving the present structure. There is, since 1930, a ministry of education and health, a national council of education, and an extraordinary number of divisions, services, committees, and institutes which comprise the complex federal organization. Secondary and higher education are legally under the control of the federal government; primary education, under that of the states or municipalities—thus conforming to the idea of the Argentine plan of 1853. Since 1922, the federal authority has entered the field of primary education and has exercised an increasing influence and control of it. The federal government, the states, the municipalities, and private institutions operate in education at all levels. The number of federal establishments at present is far less than that of establishments of other classification. It is possible that variation from the Spanish American type of organization was in part due to the fact that Brazil opened its first university in 1920.[3] Functional demarcation has been less sharply defined during the past thirty years while education has undergone remarkable expansion. The basic course of studies in the Brazilian secondary schools requires five years. In the federal district, two additional years organized in three categories respectively for future students in law, medicine and pharmacy, and engineering and architecture are usually required for admissions to university studies in these branches.[4] It has been a requirement that students seeking admission to the Facultad de Filosofía should also have had two extra years in the district's preparatory school (Colegio Universitario).

All countries now conduct and support institutions designed in purpose for the preparation of teachers in primary, secondary, and some of the special schools.[5] These normal schools, of a varied designation, are separate

[3] Lourenço Filho, *Tendencias da educação brasileira* (São Paulo, 1940).

[4] See the public document *Opportunidades de educação na capital do país* (Rio de Janeiro, 1941).

[5] The movement for establishment of normal schools, usually regarded as one of

operations, although they sometimes overlap other schools in curriculum. They are at times used as a substitute or alternative for the customary manner of preparation for "higher education" in the university. It would be difficult to decide, in the multiform changes in curriculum, whether the functional character of these institutions has been maintained. Most of the normal schools cover the age span occurring in the *colegios,* with those classified as "superior" extending two years beyond. In some universities, of the present time, there is a "pedagogical institute" or a "faculty" with some members occupied with professional education. Some countries have established a "teaching career" (*carrera del magisterio*), with tenure and retirement compensations.

Institutions of Administration

Every country now has a ministry of education, although this ministry may not be solely occupied with this subject and although all education may not be administered by it. In some countries, the ministry is that of education and justice, as in Argentina and Peru. The cabinet offices having to do with military affairs may administer institutions which train officers for the armed services, the ministry of the interior may administer education in correctional institutions, and education in special schools for agriculture and commerce may be administered in ministries other than that of public instruction. But all public education may be administered by a single ministry of the president's cabinet.

With the minister is usually associated a general council which is appointed by the chief executive. Subordinate to the minister and his advisory council, there is usually a variety of administrative services organized with varying designations. In Chile, for example, the chief divisions are those of elementary education, secondary education, normal schools and pedagogical institutes, higher education, and commercial education, each headed by a director general. Under them are directors, supervisors, and inspectors.[6]

---

the significant steps in public education, was the work of many individuals and was associated with proposals having to do with other aspects of education. Credit for it is in greatest measure, perhaps, given to the distinguished educator and statesman of Argentina, Sarmiento, who contributed to the foundation and was the director of the first normal school of Chile (1842). See M. A. Ponce, *Sarmiento y sus doctrinas pedagógicas* (Valparaiso, 1890); and Amanda Labarca Hubertson, *Historia de la enseñanza en Chile* (Santiago, 1939).

[6] The Ministerio de Educación Nacional had under the Ley de Ministerios of 1936 in Venezuela the following branches: (1) primary education—private ele-

This summary of organization, which is typical as to lines of authority, shows a high degree of centralization. In this respect, it is generally thought that the Latin-American countries have adopted the French educational system.[7] This fact has led to many criticisms and warm defense. The critics, while admitting that uniformity and centralization may result in a relative efficiency, contend that they tend to cause inertia on the part of staff, to discourage experimentation, and to impede adaptation to local circumstance and condition. On the other hand, it may be claimed that the system rests on the principle of the freedom of teaching and is no more calculated to cause inertia than other systems, that experimentation has occurred, and that adaptation to local conditions is a feature of the special schools. The criticism does not take into account the significant merit of affording the means and the opportunity of keeping functional institutions within the bounds and metes of their functions. Thus the idea that, for the person planning to undertake studies in a university, the *colegio* or *liceo* has as a basic purpose the provision of an academic course of studies, qualifying a graduate for admission to institutions of higher education, has been considered a sound one.

Special Orientations

Allusion has been made to the requirements Argentina has made that higher education should give instruction in such themes as "the essence of the Argentine" and in folklore and to that of Mexico (1934–1946) that all education "will be socialistic." It remains to be seen what the demand, constitutionally made in 1946, that education "be democratic" will mean. Another type of required emphasis is that designed to inform the student, especially in the secondary schools, of the history, geography, resources, and constitutional system of the country. Of particular interest is the requirement in Cuba that the student shall be instructed by Cubans in *cubanidad,* the history, geography, and constitutional law of the country,

---

mentary schools, urban and rural, physical education, institutes of physical education; (2) secondary—*colegios* and *liceos, institutos* associated with them, normal schools (primary and superior), special and technical schools (industrial, commerical, "psychotechnical," institutions for the abnormal, blind, and deaf-mutes, reformatories, special schools of arts and applied arts; (3) universities—higher education, museums, academies, university extension services; (4) general—official inspection of instruction, mission schools, textbooks, statistics. See J. M. Hernández Ron, *Tratado elemental de derecho administrativo* (Caracas, 1937), p. 257.

[7] I. L. Kandel, *Comparative Education* (Boston, Houghton Mifflin, 1933), p. 210.

from textbooks written by Cubans. It is easy to see how under such mandate and authority, however meritorious some of them may be, education can be made the instrument of political action. The freedom of teaching under some circumstances may be circumscribed, despite guarantees.

Higher Education and the Universities

If the administrative structure as relates to the primary, secondary, and special schools has predominantly been influenced by France, despite many changes, reorganizations, and reforms, higher education in Spanish America remains, also despite many changes, the subject of influence by the mother country. Since the First World War, much influence has been ascribed to the United States. Higher education in Brazil and Haiti has not experienced a corresponding influence. The Spanish American universities still look to the example and feel the inspiration of Salamanca. In 1949, a graduate of San Marcos—a professor and one-time rector of that university—who was widely acquainted with institutions in many Latin-American countries by reason of professional and academic ties, described their distinctive features as follows:[8]

1. The Latin-American university not only tries to produce teachers and investigators and to preserve, augment, teach, and propagate human knowledge in all fields, but fundamentally it tries to serve its people and the state.

2. This university, although in general it enjoys or tries to enjoy autonomy, has directly to concern itself with public needs and does try to serve them.

3. It is looked upon with indifference, if not enmity, by the monied classes, which rarely lend it economic support.

4. It is viewed with jealousy, if not opposition, by political regimes in general, especially by the dictatorial and oligarchical ones; therefore it is naturally rebellious.

5. It has tried to restore or has restored the classical concept of being an association or fraternity of professors, graduates, and students.

6. It still practices the system of theoretical and classical teaching with little practical application.

7. It tries to create a professional class with tenure, but failing in that it endeavors to correct academic bureaucracy with a limited term of the professorship.

[8] Luis Alberto Sánchez, *La universidad latinoamericana* (Guatemala, 1949), p. 7.

8. It faces the arduous problem of many students coming from the proletariat who must work in order to live and to study.

9. It enjoys insufficient revenues for its most elemental objectives.

10. It is isolated from the general educational system; it must recover its participation and activity in this process.

Yet, as this writer with much evidence shows, there are significant differences among these institutions. They differ in the degree of autonomy and the extent of control exercised by the state, in plant and material resources, in the powers and the manner of choice of the rector, in the number and organization of the faculties and schools, and in student participation in university government. Perhaps more significant, but less easy to demonstrate, are the differences in spirit and tradition, in the research power and quality of faculties, and in the cultural influence on the community.

Several of the universities are affected by constitutional provisions giving to them status, rights, and duties. All of them are immediately governed by laws which significantly have different origins. Some of these are *leyes orgánicas* or *estatutos* adopted by the congress, some are *decretos* drafted by the executive branch in carrying out a resolution of the legislative power, and some are *decretos-leyes* which are executive acts with or without antecedent influences from other sources. These acts currently operative are in almost every case of recent date, which means that this sort of regulation is frequently changed.[9]

It is proper to say that not all these changes indicate instability or drastic alteration of practice and educational policy or radical reforms and deviations from tradition. They could signify one or more or all of these changes. A possible act of government—and one which has occurred in some countries more than once—is that of suspending of university activities altogether.

A valued part of the colonial heritage was that of the autonomy of universities, without royal or governmental interposition in the choice of rectors, the selection of faculty personnel, and the determination of curriculum. Although this tradition will not bear too close a scrutiny if one seeks evidence that it was evenly sustained in fact, it is an asset to the Spanish American university—perhaps the most valuable one it has. Interference by political authorities in universities occurred during the struggles for independence when both faculties and students took a part in the issues of that series of crises. Following independence, many

[9] *Ibid.*, p. 9. Sánchez remarks: "Many of our Universities have had as many statutes as Rectors or as Presidents of the Republic."

such interferences have occurred because faculties and students, especially the latter, from time to time took sides in internal disputes and because governments under some regimes sought to make of universities instruments of political action.

An interesting phase of the autonomy enjoyed by many universities is the custom and sometimes the legal provision that institutional grounds are "out of bounds" for the police and for soldiers. This exemption, which might be called a right of asylum, has sometimes been abused, as was reported to have occurred recently in Cuba.[10]

Usually the law confers on universities a juridical character or capacity (*personería* or *capacidad jurídica*) which enables them to acquire rights and contract obligations.[11] A classification of institutions as to the autonomy enjoyed or allowed would be hazardous; if made historically it might show that in one period such autonomy had been enjoyed but that it had been limited or withdrawn at another time. Some would argue that the independence and autonomy of the university are contingent and are conditioned by multiple factors produced by the general political circumstance within the country involved. Extreme instances of state intervention occur when the executive power names both the rector and professors and when faculty members may be dismissed without cause of a professional and moral nature.

Argentina is a country with a proud tradition of university autonomy, but since 1943 and especially under the administration of President Perón, it suffered interference and a change of status. An old law (No. 1597)

[10] The reference is to a report that students taking refuge in university grounds fired upon soldiers and police representing the authority of the Batista government.

One of the authors was in Chile in 1924 during the regime that is known as the "military junta." One night a minor disturbance occurred on the Alameda immediately in front of the University. The next morning, a professor approached the entrance to the University with the idea of meeting his class. The door was open, but a soldier was stationed beside it. The professor inquired if the University was closed and was told, "No, *señor,* do you not see that the door is wide open?" Turning away to return to his home, the professor remarked: "No university door is sufficiently wide open for a teacher to enter if occupied by a soldier."

[11] Sánchez, *op. cit.,* p. 55. He presents a classification of countries as to autonomy of universities (1949):

Complete autonomy: Bolivia, Costa Rica, Cuba, Ecuador, Guatemala, El Salvador, Mexico, Peru.

Partial autonomy: Chile, Colombia, Brazil, Uruguay, Venezuela.

"Attenuated": Argentina, Nicaragua, Honduras.

No autonomy: Haiti and Paraguay.

He was unable to secure data concerning the University of Santo Domingo. Panama is absent from this chart, without explanation. On p. 52 it is stated that the University of Panama has a "certain" autonomy.

adopted in 1885 in the time of Avellaneda provided for a "university interventor" to be appointed by the executive power in case of institutional crisis.[12] There have been instances of the use of this curious institution, since 1946, as a standing representative of the federal government at each of the six national universities. Reports of conditions at these institutions, under the Perón administration, showed arbitrary intervention, the dismissal of professors for political reasons, and the dismissal of thousands of students because of opposition to the government.[13] With the new constitution emphasizing a reorientation of educational objective, with a new law giving the executive power to appoint rectors and staff, with a wide distribution of scholarships calculated to appease and silence student criticism, and with the projected revamping of the curricula, Argentine universities were reduced to servility during the Perón era.

A feature of the university, also variable as to time and place, is the role of the student in institutional government, e.g., in the choice of rectors and the determination of some policies.[14] This participation usually takes the form of membership, through election, in the administrative council (*consejo directivo*) and in the councils of the respective faculties. At present the trend is in favor of student participation in the decision of administrative matters and in the choice of certain of the staff.

It is well known that Latin-American students in universities are politically self-conscious and that student groups are often active politically by way of protests, demonstrations, resolutions, declarations, and strikes. These activities, when adverse to the government in power, sometimes lead to the closing of the institution.

Latin-American universities depend in large part upon public appropriations. One estimate is that "in general 70 per cent of the funds comes from the budget of the state."[15] Where university education is gratuitous (Venezuela and Argentina), all is so derived, either from the state or

[12] Cf. *Constituciones de la Universidad de Córdoba* (Córdoba, 1944), pp. 507–515. Herein are given the documents concerning three interventions in that institution during the period known as the "reforms of 1920." They occurred in 1918, 1922, and 1923. In all these uses of the power of intervention an outside person was sent to intervene, as was the eminent scholar, José N. Matienzo, in 1918. This intervention followed a famous strike of students. After serious disturbances caused by students, in 1923, the interventor decreed that students be given representation on the university council.

[13] Robert J. Alexander, *The Peron Era* (New York, Columbia University Press, 1951), pp. 133–140.

[14] Gabriel del Mazo, *Estudiantes y gobierno universitario* (Buenos Aires, 1946).

[15] Sánchez, *op. cit.*, p. 183.

from endowments. Charges to the student in the way of tuition and incidental fees may represent an amount as low as 10 to 15 per cent of the institutional income. Tuition charges are comparatively low, being only $20 to $30 per annum. In some countries where this fee is charged, it may be waived on grounds that a student is indigent. Some countries may fix a certain ratio of their revenues for appropriation to universities, as in Cuba and Venezuela. Others set aside the products of specified taxes or imports for this purpose. In the case of the National University of Mexico, in 1933, it was decided to endow it with ten million pesos, which would be the contribution of the state to that institution. This plan was not fully carried out, and subsequent appropriations have been made. Some countries allow some minor privileges of economic significance: franking privileges for mails and telegraph as in Bolivia, Guatemala, and Mexico; and exemption from import taxes and building imposts.

A "reform movement," as it was generally called, started in 1918 as a consequence of a student strike at the University of Córdoba in Argentina, which had repercussions in many, perhaps in all, countries. Immediately affecting universities, it came to embrace in one way or another all education. The reform, as it spread, assumed varying manifestations and had different effects. Reforms quite often were supplanted by counterreforms. As to institutions of higher education, the reform was to alter university government and to give students a voice therein, to modify and broaden the curriculum, and in general to signify an interest in popular education. In some countries, an effort was made to adopt some of the university procedures and principles in vogue in the United States.[16] Another phase of this reform was the effort to provide for student welfare and health (*bienestar estudiantil*), to which large sums have been devoted as well as earnest care. Efforts were made, sometimes with public support, to reduce *analfabetismo* or illiteracy; sometimes these efforts were made by informal "universities" with volunteer teachers.[17] Although these informal "universities" did not originate in this so-called reform movement, their spread and greater activity may have been stimulated by it. These institutions charge no fees, grant no degrees, and give no examinations. They have no plant of their own, but hold classes in quarters that are rented or donated. The teachers are often students in local or nearby universities.

[16] R. Carrancá y Trujillo, *Panorama crítico de nuestra América* (Mexico, 1950), p. 223.

[17] An example is that of the Universidades Populares González Prada of Peru, in which Haya de la Torre, the founder of the Aprista party, took a leading role.

In Chile, this "institution" is called the Universidad Lastarriana, founded prior to 1918; in Panama it is named after Justo Arosemena and in Cuba after Martí. The subjects taught cover a wide range, elementary or advanced, according to demand and to ability to secure teachers.

In Latin America, the early universities occupied a restricted space, usually not more than a block, in the city of its location. In the course of its development, some faculties were established in buildings located apart and possibly in a different section of the city or in a different city. There was, and in some cases there is, no campus in the sense known elsewhere. Few provided residence halls for students, and if any such halls existed, they were usually for members of the religious orders or clergy. Few, if any, provisions were made for extracurricular activities of students. The increase in students and the widening of educational opportunity made such establishments inadequate. One of the first countries to realize the need for new and larger and different plants was Cuba. What has come to be called the movement for the "university city" was undertaken there, and the result is a modern university of many beautiful and functional buildings. This movement has during the past generation spread in Peru, Brazil, Mexico, Venezuela, Panama, and Colombia. Some of the "cities" have many buildings constructed on spacious grounds, according to effective plans and with beautiful landscaping. There is the example of classical architecture at Havana, that of colonial style at Arequipa, that of Indian mestizo and modern style at Mexico City, and that of modernistic style at Panama. All are expensive, with that at Mexico City being popularly estimated at fifty million dollars. Most of these university cities have stadia and extensive facilities for physical education and athletics. It is assumed that with the creation of these centers, there will be a strong effort made to secure and retain faculties whose members devote full time to academic service. With increased costs of maintenance of these expensive plants and with the inevitable increase in faculty salaries if full-time services are rendered, the budgets provided to such universities must be increased substantially—with funds coming either from the state or the students.[18]

Some Conclusions

The distinctive developments in Latin-American education during the present generation have been as follows:

[18] A late venture is that of Brazil. Using nine small islands in the Bay of Rio de Janeiro and filling in the intervening space, creating a single island thereby, a "university city" will be erected which will afford facilities for 30,000 students. Of these, 10,000 will be accommodated in residence halls.

1. The "reform movement," beginning about 1918, related to many matters of administration, objectives, and emphasis. It increasingly gave regard to popular education as a public responsibility, and included student participation in university government usually by means of student representation on university councils and on the councils of faculties in some institutions.

2. A contribution of high importance and great influence was the Mexican rural school—mission and normal—which had chief concern with village and community affairs and only incidental emphasis on formal studies.

3. Vastly larger percentages of students from social groups hitherto sparsely represented in student bodies are securing education in several countries through financial aid granted to exceptionally qualified or needy students.

4. Most countries have financially supported programs of instruction for adults to reduce illiteracy.

5. Some states have made efforts to improve the status of teachers in primary and secondary schools by providing better salaries, establishing security in positions, and granting retirement benefits.

6. The number of women enrolling in universities and professional schools has greatly increased in recent years.

7. There is a high degree of centralization in all countries. In countries with a federal form of government the control of education is usually granted to the central authority.

8. In such countries as Cuba, Colombia, Brazil, Panama, Mexico, Peru, and Venezuela the movement for "university cities" occurred, which will inevitably have very profound influences on education at all levels.

9. The establishment of gratuitous education in universities in some countries, such as Argentina and Venezuela, was an innovation, but in higher education in general low tuition charges have been the prevailing rule.

BIBLIOGRAPHY

Alexander, Robert J., *The Peron Era,* New York, Columbia University Press, 1951.

Apstein, Theodore, *The Universities of Mexico,* Washington, Pan American Union, 1946.

——— and Theodore R. Crevenna, *The Universities of Paraguay and Uruguay,* Washington, Pan American Union, 1947.

Aragón, Arcesio, *La universidad del Cauca,* Popayán, 1925.

Bielsa, Rafael, *La autarquía de las universidades,* Buenos Aires, 1926.

———, *Cuestiones universitarias: política y cultura; administración y jurisdicción,* Buenos Aires, 1928.

Bunge, Carlos O., *La educación,* 3 vols., Buenos Aires, 1920.

Carrancá y Trujillo, R., *Panorama crítico de nuestra América,* Mexico, 1950.

Chávez Orozco, Luis, *La escuela y la sociedad mexicana,* Mexico, 1940.

Ebaugh, Cameron D., *Education in Ecuador,* Washington, U.S. Office of Education, 1947.

———, *Education in El Salvador,* Washington, U.S. Office of Education, 1947.

———, *Education in Guatemala,* Washington, U.S. Office of Education, 1947.

———, *Education in Nicaragua,* Washington, U.S. Office of Education, 1947.

———, *Education in Peru,* Washington, U.S. Office of Education, 1946.

Filho, Lourenço, *Tendencias da educação brasileira,* São Paulo, 1940.

Fuenmayor, Alejandro, *Programas metodológicos de los tres primeros grados de la educación primaria,* Caracas, 1937.

Furbay, John H., *Education in Colombia,* Washington, U.S. Office of Education, 1946.

Grummon, S. E. (trans.), *A Sarmiento Anthology,* Princeton, N.J., Princeton University Press, 1948.

Hernández Ron, J. M., *Tratado elemental de derecho administrativo,* Caracas, 1937.

Iduarte, Andrés, and James F. Shearer, *Sarmiento a través de sus mejores páginas,* New York, Dryden, 1949.

Iturriaga, José E., *La estructura social de México,* (Mexico, 1951).

Labarca Hubertson, Amanda, *Historia de la enseñanza en Chile,* Santiago, 1939.

Logan, R. W., *Education in Haiti,* Washington, U.S., Office of Education, 1930.

Mazo, Gabriel del, *Estudiantes y gobierno universitario,* Buenos Aires, 1946.

Oportunidades de educação na capital do pais (government publication), Rio de Janeiro, 1941.

Pensamiento y destino de la ciudad universitaria de México (*discursos* of Alemán, Ruiz Cortines, and others), Mexico, 1952.

Ponce, M. A., *Sarmiento y sus doctrinas pedagógicas,* Valparaiso, 1890.

Potter, G. L., and C. D. Ebaugh, *Education in the Dominican Republic,* Washington, U.S. Office of Education, 1944.

Sánchez, George I., *Mexico, A Revolution by Education,* New York, Viking, 1936.

Sánchez, Luis Alberto, *La universidad latinoamericana,* Guatemala, 1949.

Smith, Henry L., and Harold Littell, *Education in Latin America,* New York, American Book, 1934.

Chapter 17: RELATIONS OF CHURCH AND STATE

The Roman Catholic Church is by decisive odds the leading church in membership throughout Latin America. From a broadly similar heritage and establishment have arisen relationships between Church and state in contemporary Latin America so radically different as to be contradictory. Four main classes of such relationship exist: (1) an officially established church, on generally harmonious and friendly terms with public authority; (2) official establishment, but with the Church restricted and regulated under public law in a manner which might be described as unfriendly; (3) separation of Church and state, under the principle of a "free church in a free state"; and (4) separation, but with the Church suffering regulatory restraints which might be regarded as hostile. Some would add a fifth classification under which the status of the Church is uncertain and debatable.

In every country, since 1810, there has been a partial but progressive liquidation of the colonial heritage in the matter of the Church. Some steps in this process were immediate products of the movement for independence, such as the abolition of the Inquisition, the removal or limitation of ecclesiastical participation in censorship, and the partial loss of clerical leadership in the field of education. Other steps were of slower development, commonly attended by bitter controversies.

The new countries had difficult problems to resolve concerning relations with the papacy, the decision as to whether or not the rights of Real Patronato were to pass on to the new states by way of succession, the determination of the civil status of the Church, and the decision of what degree, if any, of toleration of dissident faiths would be allowed.

In the matter of the toleration of religious dissent, for example, fidelity to the traditional idea of unity might lead, as it did in some cases, to the constitutional recognition of a single faith. This declaration of exclusion, however, might be accompanied by a denial to government of the right to coerce opinion. The disallowance of corporate status to dissenting churches might lead to the compromise position of prohibiting the public celebration of the rites of a dissenting faith and cause perplexing issues as to what constituted "public," in contrast to "private," worship. What outward symbols of dissident faith, if any, could be employed was a question that caused embarrassment. The conflict between the ideal of religious and ecclesiastical unity and the desire for immigration, commerce, and toleration led to many subtle accommodations, some treaty stipulations, and some public efforts to restrain intolerance.[1] Slowly and with some reversals of policy and practice, the idea of toleration won acceptance.

The right of nomination or presentation, which is the essential power of "patronage," was conceded during the colonial period to the crown. It was exercised by the king, who named persons for high clerical positions to the pope for canonical installation. Nominations for lesser benefices were made to local archbishops or bishops either by the crown or by its representative, the vice-patron. This right of patronage, even then, caused issues full of complexity and contention. Likewise, it has done so after independence. Many of the new states promptly claimed the rights which formerly belonged to the crown.[2] To secure a recognition of this claim by the papacy was even more difficult than to securing political recognition. In practice many of the new republics acted as if the claim were well founded. The congress of Gran Colombia embodied in the famous law of 1824 the claim that ecclesiastical patronage inhered in the state. In Argentina, as early as 1819, patronal rights were claimed for the government, but their exercise was uneven during the next several decades. In several countries efforts were made to negotiate concordats with the papacy whereby these rights would be recognized and other important relations of Church and state regularized. Despite repeated efforts, such agreements were not concluded until the middle of the century, the first being by Guatemala in 1852. This concordat conceded the right of patronage, but a new one negotiated in 1884 surrendered it.[3] The concordat with Colombia

[1] The long struggle for toleration in Chile, for example, is well told by Ricardo Donoso, *Las ideas políticas en Chile* (Mexico, 1946), pp. 174–326.

[2] For a comprehensive study, see J. Lloyd Mecham, *Church and State in Latin America* (Chapel Hill, N.C., The University of North Carolina Press, 1934). For commentaries of Latin-American writers, see Lucas Ayarragaray, *La iglesia en América y la dominación espãnola* (Buenos Aires, 1920); C. Chacaltana, *Patronato nacional argentino* (Buenos Aires, 1885); J. M. Estrada, *La iglesia y el estado* (Buenos Aires, reprint of 1929); F. J. Legón, *Doctrina y ejercicio del patronato nacional* (Buenos Aires, 1920); P. Leturia, *La acción diplomática de Bolívar ante Pio VII, 1820–1823* (Madrid, 1925); J. P. Restrepo, *La iglesia y el estado en Colombia* (London, 1881); D. Vélez Sarsfield, *Relaciones del estado con la iglesia en la antigua América española* (Buenos Aires, 1889).

[3] Other concordats were negotiated for Costa Rica (1852; revoked, 1884); Haiti (1860); Ecuador (1862; suspended, 1870; new ones, 1891 and 1890; termi-

(1887) recognized no patronal rights, but did agree to give precedence to the government's recommendations. Although the papacy did not formally recognize the right of patronage as inhering in sovereignty, the exercise of it in practice was allowed in some cases and conceded in some others. It is noteworthy that political recognition by the papacy preceded all this. The independence of New Granada was recognized in 1835, and it was the beginning of a series of such acts.

Despite the fact that some of the early constitutions might have had no formal declaration to that effect, all the Latin-American countries had state churches. There were individuals who entertained thoughts of the separation of Church and state. Some of them had had European experience, and many were acquainted with anticlerical writings in eighteenth-century European literature and were influenced by the legislation of the French Revolution. In general, however, they yielded to the overwhelming weight of history and tradition, to the immense prestige of the Church, and accepted establishment. Among these were Bolívar and some of the other prominent leaders.

The Anticlerical Movement

In the course of the nineteenth century, however, anticlerical measures, either by legislative or constitutional action, embraced such fairly common features as (1) abolition of the ecclesiastical *fueros;* (2) discontinuance of the public collection of tithes and some other ecclesiastical fees; (3) secularization of many activities such as banking, recreation services, and education; (4) civil control of cemeteries, either partial or complete; (5) civil registry of vital statistics, wills, deeds, and contracts; (6) civil marriage; and (7) abolition or restrictive regulation of the regular orders of the clergy. In some countries, there was expropriation or nationalization of certain church properties. Some limited or forbade the participation of the clergy in political affairs. These measures, country by country, varied in the order enactment and in detail. The political achievement of such a body of legislation was not easy or peaceful, but the opposition differed sharply in sustained determination and in disposition to resort to violence.

The legislation which has just been outlined abolished some rights, but in the main it authorized the state to do what had previously been done by the Church. Some of these measures were thought of as successes for the cause of anticlericalism. What is the explanation of anticlerical movements

---

nated, 1900); Honduras (1861; revoked, 1860); Nicaragua (1862; dissolved, 1894).

in countries predominantly Catholic? The answer or answers, to the fair-minded person, would be peculiarly difficult. Perhaps no single explanation would be adequate for any country, nor would any combination of answers be likely to have the same order of importance for any two countries. Personalities would often be factors of as great importance as principles and conditions. Political controversy over religion seemed to generate a heat that fed upon itself. It carried opposing factions and individuals to extremes of partisanship and to acts of retaliatory vengeance. On the other hand, as against situations in which there was no compromise, one may find cases of peaceful solution. Although the matter is so complex that each country deserves a commentary for itself, the following reflections are offered as having a wide, though not necessarily a comprehensive, application:

1. At the end of the colonial period, the Church was a vested power in society with a diversified set of activities—ecclesiastical, intellectual, economic, social, and political. Participating in affairs involving all these interests and assumed responsibilities, it inevitably became a party in the contests which evoked revolutionary changes—even if the clergy was not always united. In the course of time, the opposition of the Church—alleged or real—to social and economic changes was made the occasion of attack upon the social activities of the clergy and upon the economic resources of the Church, which led to a denial to the clergy of the right to engage in political activity.

2. Some intellectuals, like Francisco Bilbao of Chile, González Prada of Peru, and Ignacio Ramirez of Mexico, attacked the Church not only as an agency for the preservation of the colonial heritage, but as a spiritual and social force. Others, like Florentino González, attacked the Church, as such, on the ground that it was an obstacle to the realization of democracy.

3. In the nineteenth century, all states adopted legislation whereby certain temporal activities of the Church were secularized in whole or in part. The proponents generally professed that such acts were not attacks on religion. Some claimed that the secularization of such services and controls would free the Church so that it might occupy itself more completely and without diversion of energy with its spiritual mission. The claim was in general combated by the clerical party as false and insincere. Anticlericalism as a series of movements to give the state control of activities and affairs regarded as secular or temporal, therefore, was professedly not an attack on religion.

4. The Church as the holder of wealth and property was open to the charge of being in sympathy with the lay owners of large estates and riches. As anticlericalism grew in strength and the lines of propaganda were drawn, the argument was offered that the Church was the active ally of the conservative faction and was an obstruction to progress. Undoubtedly many acts designed to force church property into private or public ownership were confiscatory, and often for one reason or another they failed to achieve the ends of public welfare which had been proclaimed. Some of the acts were those of despoilation. Whatever the motive, through action of government in countries such as Mexico, Guatemala, Honduras, Haiti, Colombia, Venezuela, Ecuador, and Paraguay the Church has lost much, and in some all, of its property. On the other hand, in Brazil, Chile, Bolivia, Peru, Cuba, Panama, and El Salvador it has retained its holdings in large part.

5. Anticlericalism has a curious and not always clear relation to the issue of union or separation of Church and state. In the first half of the nineteenth century, the prevailing thought was that union of Church and state was best for both, that the Church would enjoy greater power and prestige with establishment, and that separation would be a humiliating defeat for it. No law of separation was enacted before 1853. Unquestionably great interest—emotional, religious, and political—was attached to choices in policy. The advocates of separation have commonly been thought of as extreme critics of the Church, and some of them have been. But separation has not necessarily carried adverse consequences, and establishment as a state church has not necessarily meant the enjoyment of privilege. Indeed, the established church in some countries, like Venezuela, fared worse than in some where it was separated. To be sure, separation in Colombia (1853–1887) and in Mexico (1873) was a partisan triumph, achieved in civil war and in a spirit of hostility. Considering the passion of controversy in these countries, it was quite remarkable that separation could be effected peacefully in Brazil (1890), Cuba (1902), Panama (1904), Uruguay (1919), and Chile (1925). It is the claim of many students of the subject that in these countries the Church benefited from separation, although advocacy of separation had been generally associated with anticlericalism.

Legislation Concerning the Church

The withdrawal of the administration of many secular activities from the Church and its transfer to the state was a slow process and is still incomplete. It was not necessarily accompanied by controversy as to jurisdictional control but was a part of the gradually expanding police power of the state. Within some countries, the old regime of society, economic relations, recreational practices and customs, and guardianship of welfare have persisted in remoter and rural parts, whereas in urban areas changes may have occurred.

In addition to the legislative enactments demanded by the so-called liberal factions in Latin-American politics, other legal measures of a more radical nature were enacted, some in the nineteenth century, but mainly in the twentieth. Some states denied the right of the Church to receive entailments and bequests. With properties expropriated, with fees unenforced or limited or disallowed, and with bequests forbidden, the Church might be reduced to financial straits. Some states responded by granting subventions, but such subsidies were rarely generous or adequate. Some countries which previously enforced laws against the acquirement of property have since repealed them. Such is the case in Venezuela, where the Church had been impoverished. During the Gómez regime it was permitted to receive entailments and bequests. The majority of countries, whatever the former policy may have been, now permit such acquisition.

Some countries limited eligibility to membership in the clergy to nationals. This action may be thought of as both nationalism and anticlericalism. There were other means, direct and indirect, of reducing the personnel of the clergy: nationalization of church property; prohibition of entails and bequests, thereby causing a lack of resources; decline in the construction of church buildings; and the expulsion of and antagonism to the regular orders, especially the Jesuits. This decline in the number of the clergy was abetted by legislation imposing limits.[4] In some countries the number of the clergy was insufficient for the performance of the customary pastoral services.

The vicissitudes in the fortunes of the Church involved its services in the field of education, in which originally it had had what approached a monopoly. The extremes of effort at secularization carried some countries to the exclusion of church schools—as in Mexico. At the other extreme, the Church was able to maintain a complete educational system from the

[4] Professor Mecham (*op. cit.,* p. 484) gives a list of quotas prescribed in 1926 by the Mexican states. Examples are Aguascalientes, one priest for each 5,000 inhabitants; Tamaulipas, twelve for all the state; Sonora, one for each 10,000 inhabitants; Yucatán, forty for all the state; Tabasco, six for all the state. Some of the states were more generous, such as Coahuila, San Luis Potosi, and Michoacán.

primary school through one or more universities—as in Chile and Colombia. Between these extremes, great variation occurs—in educational plant, quality, subjection to public inspection, scope of education covered, and prestige of effort. Likewise there is variance of practice in permitting religious instruction in public schools. Some countries permit it and compensate for it, some make it optional on choice of parents or guardians, some require that it be given at hours other than those in the school schedule, and some do not permit it under any circumstances in public schools. The retention of private church schools where it is allowed is due in part to the fact or the assumption that the number and distribution of public schools are insufficient to serve the educational interests of society.

Other laws restricting the Church included the following: reduction of the number of holidays having ecclesiastical justification; abolition of a religious oath for those assuming office and for many other occasions wherein such oaths were formerly required; exclusion of the Church from participation in the administration of certain charitable services and institutions; adoption of divorce laws, including in some countries provision for absolute divorce; prohibition of the wearing of clerical garb and special insignia outside church buildings or places where religious ceremonies are officially held; prohibition that the clergy, in their ecclesiastical capacity, criticize the laws of the state or the administration thereof.

Church and State in Mexico

One of the most persistent, bitterly contested, bloody, and ruinous issues in Mexican politics and society has been that of the relations of Church and state. In contrast with the capacity of the Church and of the state for the adjustment of these relations as shown in some other Latin-American countries, here the issue has often been joined in frontal attack and counterattack. In a formal and legal sense, despite some reversals in policy and law, the Church has step by step lost this fight. The abolition of the ecclesiastical *fuero;* the secularization of many controls such as those relative to marriage, registry, cemeteries, and education; separation of Church and state, under the supposed principle of independence of the one with reference to the other; prohibition of political activity and participation of the clergy, denial of the right to the clergy of public criticism of the government in office, and the declaration of their ineligibility to hold secular office; nationalization of all church property and denial of rights to entailments and bequests; supremacy of the state in all matters concerning civil and political life of society; and the exercise of police power by the state to ensure order in the public celebration of religious ceremonies—all these have been so many stages in the victory of the state.

Separation of Church and State

Separation of Church and state in Mexico occurred by means of constitutional amendment on October 5, 1873. Along with this principle, certain of the "reform laws" fought over during the preceding twenty-five years were incorporated in the constitution. They were civil marriage, as the only legal form; invalidation of the right for religious institutions to acquire real property or to receive revenues from it; substitution of an affirmation (*protesta*) for the religious oath; and the illegality of religious vows. The legislation which was designed to carry into effect the separation forbade any religious instruction in any public institution, any religious act to be performed outside a church building, the wearing by priests of distinctive clothing outside church premises, and the ringing of church bells except as a call to religious service. Notice has already been taken of the fact that separation was attended by state regulations and of the fact that in the conflicts which were to develop, 1923–1935, the Church, denied corporate recognition, was not free to manage its own affairs.

These achievements in law may be assumed to represent the juridical bases of the proper relations of Church and state, according to "liberal" opinion and theory. In the judgment of Lanz Duret, the constitution of 1917 expressed in Article 24 the high and noble principles that every man "is free to profess the religious belief which most pleases him and to practice the ceremonies, devotions, or rites of the respective faith in churches or in his private domicile, provided they do not constitute a crime or misdemeanor punishable by the law." Lanz Duret holds this article to be a guarantee of liberty of conscience in religion. He goes on to maintain that other guarantees, found in Articles 6, 7, and 9, having to do with the freedom of thought, writing and publishing, and association are solemnly proclaimed by the constitution. Do they supplement and support the guarantee of liberty of conscience? Under Article 130, the state denied to the Church juridical personality. Under it and the statutes and decrees subsequently issued, the Church became a simple private association, and the clergy became professional practicioners subject to regulation and to certain civil and political disabilities. Article 130 and the laws and decrees later issued to implement and develop it have been regarded as inconsistent with Article 24 and contradictory of the principle of separation.[5]

[5] Miguel Lanz Duret, *Derecho constitucional mexicano* (4th ed., Mexico, 1947), pp. 417–427. Cf. Mecham, *op. cit.,* pp. 456–501.

It is not pertinent to try to tell the history of the last twenty-five years of religious strife in Mexico. It would include many crises, incipient and bloody civil wars, much vehement criticism and recrimination, the complete cessation (1926–1929) of religious services under priestly guidance, the deportation of many of the clergy, the initiation and unsuccessful promotion of a schismatic church, many allegations of persecution, and many efforts at reconciliation. No judgment need here be made of controversies about consistency, about indiscretion in precipitating the conflict, or about whether or not the conflict was irrepressible. The record suggests that the Church and those in sympathy with it did not—and, under the circumstances pertaining to military strength in Mexico, could not—mobilize forces enough to win, nor did the opponents of the Church destroy the loyalty of the faithful to the ancient religion. It was noted that even during the cessation of religious services churches were often full of worshipers. In this strife, both sides went too far in their partisanship. From the time of President Portes Gil progress was made by slow stages toward a *modus vivendi.* The bases of such a settlement as seems to have been reached or in process of being reached are tacit and implicit acceptance of the juridical personality of the Church, whereby it may control its own organization; neutrality of the Church in all matters of politics and abstinence from political activity, whatever its lay members in their capacity as citizens may do; and noninterference by the state in the performance of spiritual and pastoral duties. In 1952, President Ruiz Cortines and the archbishop, on the occasion of the dedication of the Plaza de la Virgen de Guadalupe, publicly exchanged a cordial embrace!

The separation of Church and state in the rest of Latin America, with which we are now concerned, is a further example of complexity in causation and of variation in settlement.

Colombia. In Colombia, the clerical interest had been a leading factor in political contests from the beginning, and that interest experienced the radical changes characteristic of politics in the history of that state. Under the relatively friendly administrations of the Conservative party, the Church was subjected to some limitations, suffered some loss of property, had a few convents suppressed, and had some services secularized. Prior to 1853, under the Liberal party, a less friendly policy was followed. Perhaps the most important anticlerical measures adopted, under these auspices, were the legalization of divorce, the extension of the privilege of *fuero,* the radical step of conferring on the supreme court of jurisdiction of cases concerning "the improper exercise of their functions" by the clergy, and the restriction of the right to educate candidates for the priesthood. In

1853, with a new constitution which had released the government from restraints in the matter, Colombia by legislative statute became the first Latin-American country to disestablish the Church. Any exercise of the rights of patronage by the state was to cease; there was to be no intervention in the exercise of the Catholic religion, or any other, by the civil authority; and ownership of the church buildings was to be vested in the resident Catholics of the parish or diocese.

Although relations of the "independent" Church and the state were for a time harmonious and improved, they became hostile after 1860, especially during the administration of Tomás Cipriano de Mosquera, when the Church was placed under the rigorous regulations, most of the property was confiscated, all orders of the regular clergy were suppressed, and many of the prelates were either imprisoned or banished. Under the pretense of protection (*tuición*), the government through active persecution and inspection reduced the Church to servitude. Despite the federalism of the constitutions of 1853 and 1863, anticlerical policies and results were almost uniform. These influences continued until the retirement of Mosquera in 1867.[6] There was some abatement of the rigor of state action in succeeding administrations, but the fortunes of the Church did not greatly improve until the "conversion" of Rafael Núñez from Liberal to Conservative party affiliation and "faith." Although such a political about-face in Colombian history was not unknown, this one was to have revolutionary consequences which have, so far, been enduring.[7] After having served as president, 1880–1882, Núñez was again chosen in 1884, organized a new

[6] Enrique Pérez, in his *Vicios políticos de América* (Paris, n.d.), pp. 109, 122–123, holds that in Latin America two fanaticisms have often been at war, arising out of the situation when the clergy take part in political matters and when politicians intervene in affairs of a religious character. Both are deplored as becoming uncompromising. He comments: "In our inter-tropical America, the reactions of religious fanaticisms are fruitful in disasters. Exploited with ends of a merely political character, religious sentiment reaches its maximum of exaltation, and that exaltation provokes inexplicable conflicts among political leaders; and we say inexplicable because all profess with more or less zeal a common religion. The evil is in having mixed politics with religious beliefs; and that is what we must combat, that is what we must condemn."

[7] Under the circumstances, the character and conduct of Núñez called forth quite divergent interpretations. Reference should be made to his own work, *La reforma política en Colombia* (Bogotá, 1885). Important documentary materials are to be found in Manuel A. Pombo and José J. Guerra, *Constituciones de Colombia* (2 vols., Bogotá, 1911). A contemporaneous biography is that of Marco F. Suárez, *Rafael Núñez* (Bogotá, 1894). For a fiercely critical view, see J. M. Vargas Vila, *Los divinos y los humanos,* in *Obras completas* (Barcelona, n.d.), pp. 57–75.

party—a coalition called Independents—crushed the opposition in a brief civil war (1885), and led the movement for a new constitution (1886). This victory placed Núñez in a position of leadership, regarded by many as dictatorship.

The new constitution embodied the principles which had of late been urged by Núñez: the adoption of the unitary form of government, an independent church with many rights restored, and the strengthening of powers of the executive, to whom a term of six years was granted. The trend of this movement was proclerical, and the "independent" church was in reality to be an established church. A concordat with the papacy was negotiated (1887), by which the Church was recognized as "an essential element of the social order" to be protected and respected while enjoying "its rights and prerogatives, without any intervention of the civil power in the free exercise of its spiritual authority and jurisdiction." Having juridical personality, the Church was to have the right to acquire property, which was to be subject to taxation, except such buildings as were to be used for religious exercises and for episcopal and pastoral residences. Regular orders of the clergy and religious associations of both sexes were to be allowed. Education, at the several stages, "was to be organized and directed in conformity with the dogmas and morals of the Catholic religion." Patronal rights belonged to the papacy, but the wishes of the Colombian president would "take precedence." Indemnification for properties that had been expropriated was promised. Ecclesiastical marriage for members of the Church was recognized, with a civil functionary witnessing the ceremony. Cases affecting the bonds of matrimony and the validity of betrothals were to be under the exclusive jurisdiction of the clerical authority. Subsequently, in 1892, important supplements were adopted relating to the manner of trial of civil and criminal cases involving clerics, church administration and control of cemeteries for Catholics, and clerical administration of the registry of births, deaths, and marriages. Other minor supplements were adopted, but they were additions, rather than changes. The Church regained economic competence, social and political influence, and many ecclesiastical privileges.[8]

Other Countries. In Central America, anticlericalism appeared early, and strife over the Church was one of the causes of the disruption of the confederation in 1839. The individual countries were to have extreme differences in policy and practice with reference to the Church. Church and

[8] Clarence H. Haring, *South American Progress* (Cambridge, Mass., Harvard University Press, 1934), pp. 183–213.

state are definitely separated in Honduras (1880) and El Salvador (1886). In both exist a body of anticlerical laws in which there are similarities, such as the restrictions on ownership of real property other than churches and residences, religious instruction in the public schools, and religious orders. The social status and influence of the Church in the two countries radically differ, with the Church having a more favorable position in El Salvador. The status of the Church in Guatemala might be debated. It was described by Professor Mecham as being "theoretical separation." There are severe anticlerical laws and interference in church government and choice of prelates. It is open to question whether the laws restricting the Church, long on the statute books, are enforced evenly and effectively. In Central America, two states have definite separation: one, Guatemala, has "theoretical" separation; one, Nicaragua, has "nominal" separation. One Central American state, Costa Rica, has union. In Costa Rica the Church is a state establishment (Article 76, constitution of 1949), and the relations of Church and state, in spite of some periods of minor antagonism, have been harmonious. Although the status in Nicaragua is sometimes described as separate, the state "recognizes" the exercise of this religion and grants the Church many privileges. The Church has a relatively strong position, and relations with the government are in general harmonious. The same is true in El Salvador.

Brazil has had a specially important contribution to make to this subject. Under the empire, with patronal rights passing after brief delay from the Portuguese crown to the Emperor, the Church enjoyed prosperity and great influence in education and society. It was attacked by republicans, theoretical socialists, and positivist thinkers, and it on its part attacked the Masons. There is ground for dispute as to the responsibility for the beginning of the dispute over Masonry. Also much disputed as causes of the fall of the empire are the liberality of the Emperor toward current intellectual movements, the supposed conservatism of the heiress apparent, Princess Isabella, the influence of the traditional church, and the harshness of treatment of certain offending prelates. It is clear that during the late empire, several anticlerical measures in favor of civil marriage and the secularizing of some of the church activities indicated a drift of opinion. The positivists, who exercised a strong influence, considered the state church an obstruction to the intellectual emancipation of the country and boldly urged separation.[9] Their attitude was temperate and detached from

[9] F. Freire, *Historia constitucional de república dos estados do Brazil* (3 vols., Rio de Janeiro, 1894); P. A. Martin, "Causes of the Collapse of the Brazilian

the passions of controversy, but they did insist that separation was a condition of spiritual liberty—as much for the Church as for the citizen. When the empire fell, one of the proposals was for separation of Church and state, and this was decreed January 7, 1890, by the provisional government. This decree was confirmed by the constitutional convention, and separation thus became a part of the fundamental law on February 24, 1891. The spirit of this decision was that of a "free church in a free state," as one of the members of the convention put it. The Church was granted full ownership of all its properties, with all buildings used solely for religious purposes exempt from taxation. There was to be no restriction on the right to acquire property. On the other hand, the state was to make no financial contribution to the Church, with the exception of that to the missions among the Indians. Public instruction was secularized, but instruction in religion might be given outside the school hours. No limitation was placed on the right of the Church to conduct schools of its own. The same freedom applies to charitable activities. Existing religious orders, including the Jesuits, were allowed to continue, but new ones were prohibited. The clergy, with the exception of members of the regular orders, were given political rights, including that of officeholding. The peaceful adoption of these measures must be regarded as a remarkable achievement.

In Uruguay, the relations of the Church to public authority had never been a significant political issue, and those relations had become by the twentieth century quite tenuous. Immigration and the influences of the re-Europeanization process probably contributed to reduction of the percentage of the total population who were members of the Church to the lowest figure among the Latin-American states. Although Uruguay had expropriated some church property and had adopted some of the more common laws secularizing church activities, the political contests between the leading parties had rarely turned upon religious issues. Separation was the result of an evolution in opinion and politics, in which modernism and religious indifferentism, the genuine spirit of toleration, and the relative modesty of the ecclesiastical plant and effort were factors.[10] in the constitutional convention of 1917, separation was adopted peacefully and in good spirit. The Church retained all the properties it possessed as of 1919,

---

Empire," *Hispanic American Historical Review,* 1921; Mary W. Williams, *Dom Pedro* (Chapel Hill, N.C., The University of North Carolina Press, 1937).

[10] Mecham, *op. cit.,* p. 339, states that in 1924 there were only eighty-five churches and chapels in the entire country. There were 200 priests, regular and secular, and 150 nuns. Only 500,000, out of a population of two million, were communicants.

which were to remain untaxed. Properties acquired after that date would be taxed according to common law. Granted the recognition of juridical personality, the Church could receive entailments and bequests. It was to have entire and free control of its own organization. No restrictions were placed on social services and activities, and in consequence the Church has developed at all levels its own educational system, although no religious instruction is given in public institutions. The same liberties are extended to any other religion.

The outcome in Chile was similar, but the background was quite different. There political issues concerning the Church were of great significance and bitterness, the Church possessed large properties, enjoyed great prestige, social and political, and had a leadership—both lay and clerical—of distinction and energy. The anticlerical legislation, which has been classified as "fairly common," was adopted in Chile, but only after long and vigorous opposition. Separation, however, was a "liberal" principle. Its proponents sometimes used the statement of a prominent churchman, made while he was a bishop (1859): "When ministers [i.e., clergymen] become affiliated with political groups, they compromise the sacred interests of their charge. The future of the church, the most precious interests of religion, are then tied up to the fortunes of a party."[11] It is to be noted that in 1925 separation was not opposed by the Church and further that when separation was adopted its advocates were careful not to give offense to the Church, acting with awareness of its immense prestige. It was granted complete control of its own organization, the title to all its properties, the right to conduct its own educational system, and a generous subsidy over a period of five years of transition. There was to be no taxation of churches and accessory property, but other properties were to be taxed at the ordinary rates. No limitation was placed on the right to receive bequests and entailments. This, too, was a notable achievement in the resolution of a delicate problem, with praiseworthy conduct and forbearance on the part of all concerned.

Separation in Cuba and Panama was incidental to or consequential upon independence, but its terms differ in details. Cuba declared separation in 1902. The existing property of the Church was retained, but subject to taxation, with the exception of buildings used for religious purposes. Compensation was granted for some properties expropriated during the Spanish control. Civil marriage only is legally recognized (1918). Absolute divorce

[11] Quoted in a message to the congress by President Alessandri, 1923. The words were by Bishop Valdivieso. Mecham, *op. cit.,* p. 268.

is obtainable. No religious instruction is permitted in the public schools, but the Church is at liberty to conduct schools of its own. The relations of Church and state have not been an important issue in Cuban politics since 1902.

Panama is commonly classified as having no established church. Constitutionally, "it is recognized that the Catholic religion is that of the majority" of the people. Just what this "recognition" means in law is perhaps not important to determine. It means practically that the position of the Church is favorable. Religious instruction in public schools may be given by clerics. The Church may maintain its own schools, to which public subventions are sometimes given. There is civil marriage, but religious marriage is recognized provided the persons involved register with the proper civil authorities. Missions to the Indian tribes are subsidized. Religious associations are granted juridical capacity and may receive entailments and bequests. Members of the clergy may not occupy public office, except those related to social welfare and public instruction. The status of the Church has not been an active political issue since 1904.

Ecuador is a country in which the status of the Church is debatable. Formally, the Church was disestablished in 1906, but it is the subject of regulation. Many issues concerning religion, foreign priests, education, and property claims have caused bitter contests and sometimes extreme measures.

The countries having separation are Brazil, Chile, Cuba, Ecuador, Guatemala, Honduras, Mexico, Nicaragua, Panama, Uruguay.[12]

Nine of the states are classified as having an established church. In Bolivia, Colombia, Costa Rica, the Dominican Republic, Haiti, Paraguay, and Peru, the relations are on a basis that is mutually satisfactory and harmonious. Political issues of gravity are possible, but custom and tradition would suggest that no change is likely to occur in the near future. A technical reservation as to this classification might be made as to the status of the Church in Argentina and Colombia. The question has been argued as to establishment of the Church in strict law. The Church is formally described as "independent" in Colombia, with the state exercising no rights of patronage in a legal sense. The Church is active in many affairs of the state, rather than the state exercising control or meeting responsibilities in the Church. The state respects rights which are exclusively enjoyed by the Church. Likewise, a point at law could be made as to the status of the

[12] Separation in Ecuador is "open to question." As has already been stated, in Guatemala it is "theoretical" and in Nicaragua it is "nominal."

Church in Argentina, but the realities of the situation have led students of the subject to classify Argentina as having a state church.

One of the latest developments in the relations of Church and state in Latin America occurred during the closing months of the Perón regime in Argentina. General Perón had in 1954 charged that the Church was making an effort to undermine his government and to encourage opposition to it. Church leaders denied these charges. Some priests were arrested, some were banished; some church buildings in Buenos Aires were attacked by mobs and partially wrecked. Measures were introduced which were designed to effect definitely the disestablishment of the Church and to withdraw from it certain guarantees and privileges. After one of the attempts to overthrow Perón had failed, tentative peace was negotiated between him and the Church. Whether the Church was or was not originally active in the encouragement of opposition to Perón, it was by force of circumstances to become a factor in that opposition. Perón's attack on the Church has been regarded as a political blunder, and it is held to have been one of the contributing causes of his downfall in September of 1955. It is also thought that the Church emerged from the revolution with greatly increased prestige.

The situation in Venezuela has often been described as unique. A state church, which has lost much of its property and had been denied the right of obtaining resources for a long time, was weak and discredited as a spiritual force and was powerless in politics, although the clergy retained rights of political participation. This was the plight of the Church from the times of Guzmán Blanco until well into the period of Gómez. It was an uphill fight of the Church leaders to regain a respected position in society, culture, and spiritual ministry. Some of the country's thinkers—many of whom were indifferent personally to religion—came to the conviction that the state's victory had been carried too far.[13] In consequence, morals had suffered. Since then, the position of the Church has improved. Materially, the economic resources have increased. Four bishoprics have been added, and one bishopric *in partibus* to administer missions to the Indians. Seminaries have been allowed for the education of aspirants for the priesthood, and private schools have been conducted under super-

[13] Mary Watters, *A History of the Church in Venezuela, 1810–1930* (Chapel Hill, N.C., The University of North Carolina Press, 1933), pp. 214–221. Two intellectuals who have urged a restoration of the social influence of the clergy are Pedro M. Arcaya and Laureano Vallenilla Lanz. See the latter's *Críticas de sinceridad y exactitud* (Caracas, 1921), pp. 415–425.

vision of the public authority. Some orders of regular clergy have been allowed, although their status is informal. Missions to the Indians have been promoted, especially by the Spanish Capuchins.

BIBLIOGRAPHY

Alessandri, Arturo, *Reformas constitucionales,* Santiago, 1925.

Ayarragaray, Lucas, *La iglesia en América y la dominación española,* Buenos Aires, 1920.

Callcott, Wilfrid H., *Church and State in Mexico, 1822–1857,* Durham, N.C., Duke University Press, 1926.

———, *Liberalism in Mexico, 1857–1929,* Stanford, Calif., Stanford University Press, 1931.

Donoso, Ricardo, *Las ideas políticas en Chile,* Mexico, 1946.

Gruening, Ernest, *Mexico and Its Heritage,* New York, Appleton-Century-Crofts, 1928.

Haring, Clarence H., *South American Progress,* Cambridge, Mass., Harvard University Press, 1934.

Lanao Loaiza, José R., *La cuestión religiosa en Colombia,* Manizaldes, 1935.

Lanz Duret, Miguel, *Derecho constitucional mexicano y consideraciones sobre la realidad política de nuestro régimen,* 4th ed., Mexico, 1947.

Legón, F. J., *Doctrina y ejercicio del patronato nacional,* Buenos Aires, 1920.

Mecham, J. Lloyd, *Church and State in Latin America,* Chapel Hill, N.C., The University of North Carolina Press, 1934.

Puig Casauranc, J. M., *La cuestión religiosa en relación con la educación pública en México,* Mexico, 1928.

Restrepo, J. P., *La iglesia y el estado en Colombia,* London, 1881.

Vasconcelos, José, and Manuel Gamio, *Aspects of Mexican Civilization,* Chicago, University of Chicago Press, 1928.

Vélez Sarsfield, D., *Relaciones del estado con la iglesia en la antigua América Española,* Buenos Aires, 1889.

Watters, Mary, *A History of the Church in Venezuela, 1810–1930,* Chapel Hill, N.C., The University of North Carolina Press, 1933.

Zum Felde, A., *El proceso histórico del Uruguay,* Montevideo, 1919.

Chapter 18: LATIN AMERICA IN WORLD AFFAIRS

With its incipient but rapidly increasing industrial development and its spectacular population growth,[1] Latin America is destined to play an important and independent role in world affairs. Its enormous material and human potential resources, which have been hardly tapped, make it one of the regions which—given education, decent standards of living, and opportunity—could play a major role in the world of the future. Latin America is awakening. It is no exaggeration to say that these last twenty-five years have witnessed in this area the most important changes in its economic, social, and political institutions that have taken place since these countries attained their independence. Latin America's international importance has grown accordingly, and events in this region should today be as much the concern of the rest of the world as of the Western Hemisphere. Although somewhat remote geographically from the focal points of world conflict at present, it is inextricably involved in the struggles of modern world politics. It is significant that the twenty Latin-American countries compose the largest single group among the sixty members of the United Nations. The voting strength of this group is clearly great, but not entirely out of proportion to its rising power potentialities. The experience of the Latin-American states in world politics, together with their contributions to international attitudes and institutions, must then be reviewed in the light of the significance that the area may have in any future balance of power as well as in consideration of present-day problems.

Latin-American Contributions to International Law

Although, in contrast to the relatively small educated class, the great masses of Latin America have neither knowledge of foreign affairs nor an interest in world politics, these countries have demonstrated throughout their history notable talents for statesmanship and diplomacy. This is even more remarkable when considered in terms of the rudimentary political development which has characterized many of these nations. Whatever the

[1] For a recent report see Robert C. Cook, "Latin America: Area of Population Explosion," *Population Bulletin,* vol. 9, no. 6, p. 65, October, 1953.

TABLE 26

IMPORTS AND EXPORTS OF LATIN AMERICA AS A PERCENTAGE OF ENTIRE WORLD AND ENTIRE WESTERN HEMISPHERE, 1913–1950

Year	World		Western Hemisphere	
	Imports	Exports	Imports	Exports
1913	6.5	7.9	35.5	34.5
1929	6.8	8.9	28.7	30.2
1938	6.3	7.9	31.6	28.7
1947	11.3	12.2	36.7	23.9
1948	10.0	12.1	33.5	28.2
1949	9.0	10.2	31.8	26.2
1950	8.6	11.4	26.4	31.5

INDEX OF GROWTH OF IMPORTS AND EXPORTS OF LATIN AMERICA AND THE WORLD, 1950
(1913 = 100)

Area	Imports	Exports
Latin America	366	406
Europe*	193	190
Western Hemisphere	494	444
World	276	283

* Consists of Belgium, France, Germany, Italy, Netherlands, Sweden, and the United Kingdom.

POSITION OF LATIN AMERICA RELATIVE TO WORLD TOTAL COMPARED WITH EUROPE AND THE UNITED STATES

Area	Imports, % of entire world		Exports, % of entire world	
	1913	1950	1913	1950
Latin America	6.5	8.6	7.9	11.4
Europe	62.5	42.5	56.3	39.9
United States	8.3	16.9	12.3	18.2

SOURCE: Reproduced from *The Foreign Trade of Latin America since 1913* (Washington, D.C., Pan American Union, 1952).

reasons, Latin America possesses a distinguished record in world affairs of which it is justly proud. An impressive list can be made with the names of its many great diplomats and jurists. Figures such as Rio Branco and Ruy Barbosa of Brazil, Alejandro Alvarez of Chile, Antonio Sánchez de Bustamante of Cuba, and many others were men of world-wide reputation and prestige who made significant contributions to the development of the law of nations.

In matters such as pecuniary claims, the recognition of new governments, and the peaceful settlement of international disputes, Latin-American contributions to international law have been greatest. It is apparent that these are reflections of historical, geographical, social, and economic factors. These countries, being dominated economically by foreign capital and subjected to political convulsions, were frequently engaged in controversies with other governments concerning claims of their citizens for damages to their persons and property. Although these claims were often grossly exaggerated and frequently lacked serious foundation, important doctrines resulted from them.

The most important of these doctrines are those associated with the names of Carlos Calvo and Luis M. Drago, both of whom were distinguished Argentine jurists. The Calvo Doctrine, in essence, laid down the principle that a government is not responsible for losses or damages suffered by foreigners by reason of internal disturbance within its jurisdiction; that to admit responsibility in these matters would be to create an unjustifiable inequality between nationals and foreigners; and that the collection of debts and the support of private claims do not justify the armed intervention of governments. Later, Luis M. Drago gained world-wide support for his dictum that "the public debt of a state cannot give rise to armed intervention, and much less to a material occupation of the territory of American nations by the creditor state." This doctrine secured the support of the most famous internationalists and attained final and universal sanction at the Second Peace Conference held at The Hague in 1907.

The chronic instability of governments makes the question of recognition a problem of great interest in Latin America. The evils caused by revolutions gave rise in some countries to a movement favoring the standard of legality. The five Central American states signed in 1923 an agreement by which they bound themselves not to recognize any regime arising from a triumphant revolution against a legitimate government. Although the treaty was subsequently denounced and is no longer in force, the idea that it embodied had been advocated in 1907 by Carlos Tobar, Minister of Foreign Affairs of Ecuador, who suggested it as an effective remedy against the curse of revolutions.

More recently, a significant contribution to the theory and practice of recognition originated in Mexico with the doctrine formulated in 1930 by Genaro Estrada. In accordance with the Estrada principle, nations should not explicitly recognize new governments, considering that the sovereignty of a nation is infringed when other governments set themselves up as judges of its internal affairs. The Estrada formula prescribes that a country limit itself to maintaining or retiring its diplomatic representatives and to accepting or maintaining those accredited by the other nation, without judging the right of others to change their governments or their authorities.

In the field of peace, Latin America has a most remarkable record. The development and use of arbitration and other peaceful means for the solution of controversies is perhaps the greatest contribution of these countries to international law. They were the first in the world to establish permanent arrangements for the arbitral settlement of international disputes, albeit initially on a bilateral basis. Treaties negotiated by Colombia, Peru, and Chile as early as 1822 contained provisions for arbitration of disputes. These were followed by many similar agreements among other Latin-American states. In addition, some of the early constitutions embodied general principles of pacific settlement and provisions stating that war should be declared only when arbitration had failed to settle a controversy. Since they became independent the Latin-American countries have concluded about one hundred bilateral treaties of pacific settlement, and, what is even more significant, they have successfully settled about the same number of disputes by arbitration and conciliation.[2]

It is not very well known that the first permanent international court of justice was established in Latin America. This was the Central American Court of Justice created by Costa Rica, Guatemala, Honduras, Nicaragua, and El Salvador under a treaty signed in 1907. Although it lasted only until 1918 and was not particularly successful, this court established valuable precedents on the organization and administering of an international judiciary.

Numerous multilateral treaties, conventions, protocols, and declarations, to many of which the United States was also a signatory member, comprised the machinery for the settlement of international disputes until

[2] Ricardo J. Alfaro, "American Contributions to International Law," *Bulletin of the Pan American Union,* September, 1941.

1948. In that year, as a result of efforts to coordinate or codify existing peace treaties, a single treaty of pacific settlement known as the Pact of Bogota was signed at the Ninth International Conference of American States held in the Colombian capital. This treaty established a variety of procedures covering every method of peaceful settlement: investigation, conciliation, arbitration, good offices and mediation, and judicial settlement.

Latin America has also given practical demonstrations of its desire to maintain peace. The change from colonies to independent states left practically all these nations with vague and undefined boundaries, which became an inexhaustible source of conflict and strife. However, most of the boundary questions were settled by orderly and peaceful processes. Brazil, bordering on every one of the other South American republics except two and touching the European Guianas, affords an excellent example of the application of pacific methods to the settlement of boundary conflicts. This nation definitely determined its present frontiers through a remarkable series of successful and peaceful diplomatic negotiations. A valuable guiding rule which served these countries to define boundaries on a general and fair basis was the principle of *uti possedetis,* under which the administrative divisions of the mother country in existence at the time the independence movements broke out in the former colonies were recognized and adopted as the boundaries of the new nations.

Major Latin-American Wars

The foregoing statements are not meant to imply that peaceful coexistence has always been the case in this region. There have been international wars in Latin America—some, in fact, as costly and bloody as armed conflicts in other parts of the world. These, however, were isolated exceptions in the extraordinarily peaceful record of the area.

Among these wars was the armed conflict between Argentina and Brazil from 1826 to 1828, which was fought over the question of Uruguay. Anarchical conditions in the Banda Oriental, as the province was then called, resulted in invasion by the Portuguese in 1817 and annexation to the United Kingdom of Portugal, Brazil, and the Algarves, under the name of "Cisplatine Province." Portuguese domination did not last long. Uruguayan patriots fought the foreign intruder with success and requested incorporation of their land with Argentina. Acceptance of this incorporation by the general congress of the United Provinces of the River Plate meeting in Buenos Aires brought war with Brazil as a consequence. This conflict ended with a treaty of peace which provided for the recognition of the independence of Uruguay by both countries. This new country was established as a buffer state between the two largest South American powers as regards the La Plata estuary.

Another major conflict broke out between Chile on one side and the Peru-Bolivian Confederation on the other. The confederation had been declared by Andrés Santa Cruz in 1835. This new political scheme, which united Peru and Bolivia under a confederation with Santa Cruz as "supreme protector," was destined to be short-lived. Chile, then under the strong rule of Portales, considered the formation of the new state a threat to the balance of power in the South Pacific. Chile, with the initial diplomatic support of Rosas, the Argentine dictator, but acting militarily alone, sent armies to destroy it. Although at first the invaders were defeated and the struggle almost ended, it was resumed in 1839 with more vigor by Chile, whose armies defeated Santa Cruz and broke up the confederation.

The acquisition of Texas by the United States in 1845 was shortly followed by the war between this country and Mexico of 1846–1848, which in turn resulted in additional losses of territory for Mexico. The main causes of this war were Mexican resentment over the loss of Texas; a controversy as to where the true southwestern boundary line of Texas lay; the Mexican failure to pay certain damage claims of citizens of the United States; and President Polk's determination to acquire California at any cost. As a result of this war Mexico lost about half a million square miles, approximately half of her natural territory, and the United States secured the Rio Grande boundary, Upper California, and the vast intermediate area then known as New Mexico. Many people in the United States, including members of Congress and of the cabinet, favored even harsher terms, and some even urged annexation of all of Mexico. The idea of "manifest destiny" spurred the great expansionist sweep which gained for the United States an increase of territory of over 66 per cent and turned this nation into a Pacific power. Understandably, the memories of this war embittered for many years the relations between the two countries.

A large-scale war broke out in the Río de la Plata area in 1865 as a result of the extensive military preparations and imperialistic intents of Francisco Solano López, dictator of Paraguay. The conflict arose over Uruguayan politics and involved an alliance of Brazil, Argentina, and Uruguay against López. The Paraguayan War, as it is called, lasted six years, owing to the determined resistance of the Paraguayan people. The allied troops penetrated well into the interior of Paraguay and finally defeated the remnants of López's army in the northern region in 1870. The dictator was killed in the final battle. By this time, the population of Paraguay had been reduced to about half by war, starvation, and pestilence.

Another war of grave consequences was the so-called War of the Pacific between Chile on one side and Peru and Bolivia on the other. The dispute arose when Bolivian authorities, despite the protests of the Chilean government, imposed new taxes upon nitrate exports and seized the property of Chilean concessionaires when they, considering the impost illegal, refused to pay it. Chilean troops took possession of Antofagasta in 1879, and the war started. Peru came to the support of Bolivia in fulfillment of a treaty of alliance which existed between the two countries. Chile occupied the Atacama region and also the Peruvian provinces of Tarapacá, Tacna, and Arica, and by 1881 the capital city of Lima was taken. Peru signed a treaty of peace with Chile in 1883 under which it ceded Tarapacá to Chile and consented to Chilean occupation of Tacna and Arica for ten years. At the end of this period a plebiscite was to determine ownership. Bolivia was forced to sign a truce in 1884. Because of their defeat the Bolivians were confined to their Andean tableland and lost their rich *litoral* to the victor. A treaty, signed in 1904, ended the indefinite truce but left Bolivia in its landlocked position. The hope of the Bolivian people of recovering at least part of their coastal territory is still very much alive, but for the present there seems to be no prospect of such recovery. The Tacna-Arica question in time became one of the thorniest problems in Latin-American international relations. It was settled in 1929, under the terms of a proposal submitted by President Hoover giving the province of Tacna to Peru and leaving Arica to Chile. Peru received in addition an indemnity of six million dollars.

The last of Latin America's conflicts was the Chaco War, fought by Paraguay and Bolivia over the territory of that name. A clash between forces of these two countries in 1928 led eventually to a full-scale war in 1933. Two years later Paraguayan troops occupied most of the area in dispute, but fighting continued until 1938. In that year, through the mediation of other countries, a peace treaty was signed and the Chaco territory divided between the belligerents.

European Interventions in Latin-American Affairs

The Latin-American states that achieved independence at the dawn of the nineteenth century were weak nations, in a military sense, with scanty populations scattered over vast territories, few and rudimentary means of communication, little or no industry, and practically no experience in self-government. Consciousness of this weakness kept them in constant alarm at the possibility of reconquest by Spain or of aggression by other European powers. Consequently, they sought security against foreign domination of any sort, and, in general, agreed with the United States in the policy of opposing European interference in Western Hemisphere affairs. Fear of foreign intervention was, indeed, not groundless, for on frequent occasions and under various pretexts several European powers attempted to extend their control over parts of Latin America. Several of these encroachments on the sovereignty of the Latin-American states are of sufficient importance to require brief attention here.

A Spanish expedition landed in Mexico in 1829 to restore Spain's control over the country, but it was defeated by Mexican troops commanded by General López de Santa Anna. In 1833, a British ship landed troops on the Argentine-owned Falkland or Malvinas Islands in the South Atlantic and declared them occupied by Great Britain. Although the government of Argentina protested vigorously against this action, the British continue to occupy the islands to this day. Interventions by France and Great Britain in the Río de la Plata estuary at Buenos Aires and Montevideo occurred from time to time during the period between 1838 and 1850. Interference on these occasions involved blockades and even the landing of troops.

The most serious intervention on the part of a European country was the French attempt to establish a puppet empire in Mexico. This arose from Mexico's suspension for two years of payments on its foreign debt in 1861. England, France, and Spain decided then to intervene jointly in Mexico and to seize some of its ports in order to protect the interests of their nationals. After the port of Veracruz was occupied jointly and subsequent negotiations with the Mexican government had failed to bring results, the British and Spanish forces withdrew, it having become obvious that France intended more than a mere collection of debts. The French forces, supported by a native minority, fought their way into Mexico City and forced the legitimate government of Benito Juárez to flee. An assembly under French auspices adopted a monarchical system and offered the crown to the Austrian Archduke Maximilian. Eventually, this French adventure ended in disaster. Maximilian's regime, already weakened by Mexican resistance, collapsed after Napoleon III ordered the withdrawal of the French troops. Captured by republican forces, Emperor Maximilian was tried and executed in 1867. This marked the end of French dreams to establish a great Catholic empire in America which could serve as a bulwark against the expansion of the United States and as a plentiful source of raw materials for France.

Spain reestablished its power over a former colony in 1861, when dictator General Santana of the Dominican Republic invited the mother country to return. Santana became governor general of the restored colony. However, Spanish domination lasted only until 1865. Dominican patriots rose in revolt, drove the Spanish forces from the island, and reestablished the republic.

In 1864 Spain, in reprisal for alleged ill-treatment of Spanish subjects, seized the Chincha Islands off the coast of Peru. This action led to a state of war between Peru and Spain. The latter had not yet recognized Peruvian independence. The conflict—during which Peru received the support of its neighbors Ecuador, Bolivia, and Chile—lasted only a few months. Under the peace terms Peru settled the Spanish claims, and Spain returned the Chincha Islands.

Latin America and Europe

Although opposed to the establishment of any political connections with Europe, the Latin-American countries have always been eager to develop trade and cultural contacts with the Old World. In general, they have been also less reluctant than the United States to participate in European affairs. At the beginning Latin America lingered "on the margin of international life," absorbed in its own problems and almost unnoticed by the rest of the world. When given a chance to participate in world intercourse, however, it responded with enthusiasm and revealed its gifts for diplomacy.

England is the only European state which has enjoyed in relation to Latin America that privileged position which is now occupied by the United States. Latin-American relations with Great Britain have been mostly of an economic nature. British trade with these countries increased very rapidly after their independence was won. This increase was accompanied by the growth of British investments, which by 1830 amounted to almost 200 million dollars. English influence in Latin-American trade remained unchallenged almost throughout the nineteenth century. It was not until the United States emerged as an industrial power that Britain was to encounter any serious competition. During this period and particularly after 1850, Great Britain played the role of investment banker to Latin America. While British banking concerns sometimes made direct loans to governments, most of the flow of private capital went directly into the economies of the several nations for basic development.

Although Argentina was preferred by British investors, they contributed to the development of South America as a whole. In Argentina, British investments were made in railways, meat packing, livestock ranches, commercial banks, mortgage, loan, and trust companies, shipping concerns and port facilities companies. Of the total amount of British capital invested in Latin America, Argentina received more than one-third. It was, furthermore, consistently the best customer for British manufactured goods, and Great Britain, on its part, has remained dependent upon Argentina for almost half its beef consumption. In general, British investment in Argentina, as late as 1927, still surpassed by a wide margin that of any other country and was four times the value of United States investment.

During the mining boom of the 1880s, British capital was invested chiefly in gold and silver in Mexico, Venezuela, and Colombia. The most profitable mining investments were made in Chilean nitrates.

The peak year of British investments in Latin America was 1913. Despite the First World War, Great Britain was able to maintain its economic position in this area. It was purchasing almost 21 per cent of Latin America's exports in 1913 and about 18 per cent in 1925, while selling nearly 24 per cent of the region's exports in 1913 and about 18 per cent in 1925. In 1924 the value of Britain's Latin-American trade was almost 900 million dollars.

The Second World War had serious effects upon this trade, which had been already declining. At the end of hostilities, Latin America's purchases from England were only approximately 10 per cent of their total value on the eve of the world conflict. Today, although still greatly respected and admired, Great Britain has lost much of her influence in Latin America. Many British holdings have been sold and some have been expropriated. The expropriation in 1938 of the oil companies in Mexico and the nationalization of the railways in Argentina substantially reduced Britain's economic stake in this area.[3]

The interest of France in Latin America has been confined to economic and cultural matters, with the exceptions of the interferences in the Río

[3] For details concerning British investments in Latin America, see a series of articles by J. Fred Rippy in *Inter-American Affairs.* See also Richard W. Van Alstyne, "Britain in Latin America after 1865," *Current History,* vol. 28, no. 163 pp. 148–153, March, 1955.

de la Plata in the 1840s and the fiasco of Maximilian's empire in Mexico. In 1928 France had a 323.6-million-dollar trade with South America. Although this dropped to 143.2 million dollars at the outbreak of the Second World War, French trade reached its highest mark in 1951 when French imports totaled 337 million dollars and exports were 297.7 million dollars. Brazil is now France's greatest supplier and greatest buyer, having taken the place that Argentina occupied in French trade prior to the last war.

The intellectual influence of France has always been very significant, and it has remained extensive to this day. Most of the educated people in Latin America have a knowledge of French, and they look upon this nation as the cradle of liberty and the abode of civilization. Ideas from France provided the ideological structure and emotional appeal for Latin-American independence. French cultural influence remained strong throughout the nineteenth century, as exemplified by the profound effect of the political and social philosophy of Auguste Comte's positivism in many countries. It may now have been relegated to a position of somewhat less prestige by the increasing importance of the English language in trade matters and the preponderant economic influence of the United States. Nevertheless France continues to exercise some influence upon the intellectual life of Latin America.

Spain did not recognize the new status of its former colonies until long after their independence was a fact. Mexico was recognized in 1836 and Ecuador in 1840, but Uruguay and Honduras, for example, were not recognized until 1882 and 1894 respectively. After the heritage of resentment and hatred left by the wars of emancipation began to fade, Spain started to promote a *rapprochement* with its former colonies. This movement, which some called Pan-Hispanism, was based upon the idea of a kindred race and the community of language and culture. Spain's shock at its defeat in the Spanish-American War and the final liquidation of its once-great empire caused a distinguished and capable intelligentsia—now often referred to as "the generation of 1898"—to ponder upon the reasons for Spain's national decline. Part of their reappraisal of Spain's historic role included a strong support for the idea of solidarity of the Hispanic community of nations. Since the Spanish Civil War, Pan-Hispanism has taken a new turn and become the export product of Spanish fascism (*falangismo*) with strong stress on political propaganda and objectives. This brand of "Hispanicism" has had only limited success.

Hundreds of thousands of Spanish emigrants became part of the population of Latin America in the early part of the twentieth century. The number who settled there permanently is estimated to be about three million. They are found in the largest numbers in Argentina, Cuba, and Mexico. A new wave of emigration occurred in 1939 at the end of the Civil War in Spain. These new emigrants—professionals, businessmen, and intellectuals, for the most part—have played an important role in Latin America's recent economic and cultural development.

Many Portuguese migrated to Brazil when this nation became the economic heart of the Portuguese world. By 1857 as many as 54,000 Portuguese had been attracted to Brazil, and between 1884 and 1939, a total of over one million of them settled there. Portuguese-Brazilian relations offered an interesting contrast with those between Spain and Spanish America. While the Hispanic countries remained to some extent culturally dependent upon the mother country, Brazil, because of the intellectual decline of Portugal—a tiny country exhausted by its efforts to hold an empire—became the leader of the Portuguese-speaking world in all fields of intellectual endeavor.[4] Nevertheless the number and influence of the highly assimilable Portuguese immigration have been such that it should be credited with having made a notable contribution to modern Brazil.

Germany has played an important role as investor and trader in Latin America. German nationals have also settled in large numbers in some countries such as Argentina, Brazil, and Chile, and on a smaller scale in Mexico, Guatemala, and Venezuela. It is estimated that about 1896 there was a colony of 400,000 Germans in Latin America. In 1913, Germany's trade in the area was approximately 470 million dollars and its investments reached two billion dollars. The German population had increased, by this time, to 700,000 people. The First World War then isolated Germany from Latin America, and its trade disappeared almost completely. During the period between 1919 and 1933, Germany was not able to recover as an investor, but its efforts as a trader were crowned with success. By 1938 German trade in Latin America was valued at about 13 per cent of the total foreign trade of these countries. The Second World War once again disrupted German relations with Latin America. However, at present, with the rapid economic rehabilitation of West Germany, German trade with Latin America has spectacularly risen, and it stands in competition with England, the United States, and Japan. German exports are chiefly composed of machinery, electrical equipment, vehicles, and chemicals. In

[4] J. J. Johnson, "Portugal in Latin America," *Current History*, vol. 28, no. 163, pp. 137–142, March, 1955.

1951 these exports to Latin America amounted to 441.6 million dollars. Germany is showing considerable interest in the underdeveloped areas of Latin America, and its trade-expansion programs contemplate the inclusion of technical aid in German treaties of commerce. German organizations plan to cooperate in various Latin-American development projects by rendering technical advice and training personnel.[5]

The political relations between Germany and Latin America, with a few exceptions, were amicable until the First World War. However, with the advent to power of Hitler, the Nazis made attempts to win the Latin-American countries by persuasion in some instances and by infiltration and subversion in others. The large colonies of German nationals became in some countries a positive threat, and local pro-Axis movements, financed or promoted by Nazi Germany, sprang up in Argentina, Chile, Bolivia, Brazil, and Paraguay. Nazi propaganda during the war was chiefly aimed against the United States and against the inter-American system of security.

The influence of Italy is felt in Argentina and Uruguay, where a large segment of the population is of Italian birth or ancestry. A fairly large number of Italian immigrants have settled in Brazil, especially in the industrial southern state of São Paulo. In the rest of South America, with the exception perhaps of Peru, and in the Caribbean area, Italian migration is not numerous, and therefore its influence is almost insignificant.

The influence of the Soviet Union has been limited to interest in the development of local Communist parties. After a brief period of cordial relations during the Second World War, the Soviet Union became unpopular again with the governments of Latin America. These countries do not maintain, at present, diplomatic relations with the U.S.S.R. with the exceptions of Argentina, Mexico, and Uruguay. As it has been previously explained, only a handful of countries recognize the Communist party as a legal organization. However, the lack of intimate ties with the Soviet Union should not be taken as minimizing the threat of communism to an important degree. As long as Latin America's social and economic maladjustments persist, the danger of Communist extension is a real one.

Latin America and the League of Nations

Eight of the Latin-American countries joined the Allied camp in the First World War: Brazil, Cuba, Costa Rica, Guatemala, Haiti, Honduras,

[5] Herbert Dorn, "Germany in Latin America," *Current History,* vol. 28, no. 163, pp. 168–176, March, 1955.

Nicaragua, and Panama. Five others broke diplomatic relations with Germany: Peru, Bolivia, Uruguay, Ecuador, and the Dominican Republic. The seven countries which remained neutral were Argentina, Chile, Colombia, Mexico, El Salvador, Venezuela, and Paraguay. It is interesting to note that, of the countries which declared war, all except Brazil are located in the Caribbean region, well within the direct area of influence of the United States. It should also be mentioned that three out of the four strongest countries preferred to stay out of the conflict, namely, Argentina, Chile, and Mexico. The position of Mexico was partly due to hostility toward the United States, arising from past interference of this country in Mexican affairs. Colombia's neutrality was also partly due to resentment against the United States for the part it allegedly played in the events leading to the independence of Panama.

Of the belligerents, only Brazil and Cuba participated actively, and the military contributions of these two countries were exceedingly modest. However, all the participating states contributed commodities which were essential to the conduct of the war. An important factor was the increased international prestige won by Latin America as a consequence of its participation in the world conflict.[6]

Thirteen of the Latin American nations participated in the Versailles Peace Conference. Eleven signed the treaty, and ten, by ratifying it, became charter members of the League of Nations.[7] Six of the seven countries which remained neutral also became original members by adhering to the League's Covenant within two months. Mexico, the only neutral not invited to do so, was greatly offended and did not join until 1931, and then only after express invitation of the Assembly. Most of the Latin-American states were thus members of the League by 1920, and all eventually joined.[8]

The League of Nations had a strong appeal to Latin-American idealism, but perhaps its greatest attraction was the fact that it afforded a platform or forum for Latin America on which to voice its grievances. At a time when domination of the United States was strongly feared, the League afforded the Latin Americans possible protection against encroachments by the "colossus of the North." In addition, the new society of nations offered

[6] For a good treatment of Latin America's role in the First World War, see Percy Alvin Martin, *Latin America and the War* (Baltimore, Johns Hopkins Press, 1925).

[7] Ecuador failed to ratify it, and did not become a League member until 1934.

[8] J. Fred Rippy, *Latin America in World Politics* (New York, Appleton-Century-Crofts, 1942), pp. 267–268.

them an opportunity to participate actively in international life and to display their talents.[9]

The League of Nations was able to settle in 1934 the difficult Leticia dispute between Colombia and Peru. In general, the technical organs of the League, like the International Labor Office, were more successful in Latin America than elsewhere. Two Latin Americans served as presidents of the Assembly; delegates from Brazil, Uruguay, and Colombia presided over the Council. Among the seven justices of the Permanent Court of International Justice were two distinguished Latin-American jurists: Antonio Sánchez de Bustamante of Cuba and the Brazilian Ruy Barbosa.[10] After 1926, the Latin-American states always occupied three seats on the Council. However, as the power and prestige of the League declined, Latin Americans lost interest in it, particularly when the League turned to questions in which these countries were not directly concerned. During the 1930s there were numerous withdrawals of Latin-American member nations.

Latin America and the Second World War

The war of 1939 to 1945 presented the Latin-American nations with new opportunities but also with heavy responsibilities. The outbreak of the conflict in Europe prompted the calling of the First Meeting of Consultation of Foreign Ministers of the twenty-one American republics in Panama. Measures for economic cooperation and continental solidarity were approved. The American nations solemnly proclaimed their intentions to prevent involvement in the war and to safeguard neutrality. They also agreed to establish a "neutrality zone" around the Western Hemisphere and to take measures designed to cushion the economic consequences of the war. Soon after the fall of France, the second consultative meeting was held at Havana in 1940. This conference passed measures looking toward prevention of the transfer of European colonies in America to other non-American countries, and it also recommended procedures for placing those colonies under the provisional administration of American states in case an attempt to transfer control should be made. Thus, the implementation of the Monroe Doctrine became a reality. The meeting also passed a resolution accepting the principle that an attack against any American country would be regarded as an attack against all the signatory countries.

[9] See Warren H. Kelchner, *Latin American Relations with the League of Nations* (Boston, World Peace Foundation, 1930), pp. 12–14.

[10] Rippy, *op. cit.,* p. 269.

The attack on Pearl Harbor clearly revealed the progress of hemispheric solidarity. Nine Latin-American countries declared war against the Axis within three days: Nicaragua, Honduras, El Salvador, Guatemala, Haiti, the Dominican Republic, Panama, Costa Rica, and Cuba. A third Meeting of Consultation of Foreign Ministers was held at Rio de Janeiro in January, 1942. Among its political decisions was the recommendation that all the American republics should break diplomatic and commercial relations with the Axis powers. This meeting also elaborated a series of economic arrangements which committed the American community of nations to a policy of full economic cooperation.

By the end of the Rio meeting all the Latin-American states except Chile and Argentina had broken off relations with the Axis. All ultimately became belligerents, and a Brazilian expeditionary force participated in 1944 in the Italian campaign. Through a series of bilateral military agreements the United States acquired the use of important military and naval bases in Latin America. Essential war materials were made available to the United States in huge quantities. Tin ore from Bolivia, manganese from Brazil and Cuba, tungsten from Bolivia, Mexican lead, and other mining products flowed in ever-increasing volume for military production. Cooperation on a hemispheric basis eliminated Nazi propaganda, espionage, and sabotage. This solidarity of the hemisphere proved to be the greatest element of safety that the United States possessed at the time of the attack upon Pearl Harbor.

Near the end of the war, in January, 1945, the American republics met again in Mexico City for a special conference on war and peace problems. This time, however, Argentina was absent. The United States and many of the Latin-American countries were no longer in normal relations with the *de facto* military government which ruled Argentina. Besides reconciling Argentina with its sister republics, the conference produced the Act of Chapultepec, which went farther than any other inter-American agreement. In addition to declaring that an act of aggression against an American state should be considered as an aggression against all American nations, it provided sanctions which included even the use of armed force.

The Mexico City conference also gave the Latin Americans an opportunity to express their views concerning plans for an international organization. Although consultation was supposedly the main feature in inter-American relations, the fact was that Latin America had not been consulted about its ideas on world organization. The Dumbarton Oaks proposals represented agreements on the part of the United States, the United Kingdom, Russia, and China on some of the major points to be ultimately submitted to the United Nations Conference at San Francisco. During the Chapultepec meeting, these proposals were severely criticized by the Latin Americans, many of whom considered that the plan envisaged an organization dominated by the big powers and that it did not represent any improvement over the old League of Nations. However, at Mexico City all proposals on this subject were referred to the forthcoming San Francisco Conference. In fact, almost every action that was undertaken by the conference regarding the relationship of the inter-American system to the projected organization was subject to revision by the San Francisco assembly.

Latin America and the United Nations

The United Nations Conference was held at San Francisco from April to June of 1945. According to the voting system of "one state, one vote," the Latin-American group had close to a majority, since out of a total of forty-six participating states, twenty were Latin-American. The chief contribution of these nations consisted in aiding greatly to improve the plan of world organization made at Dumbarton Oaks. Among these improvements were provisions dealing with principles and purposes of the organization, defining its powers more clearly, and providing international protection of human rights. Thus Latin America contributed, together with other countries in the small-power category in liberalizing the Dumbarton Oaks plan and making it more democratic.[11]

Eight of the twenty-nine nations which first ratified the United Nations Charter were Latin-American states: Argentina, Brazil, Chile, Cuba, El Salvador, Haiti, Nicaragua, and Panama. The other twelve deposited their ratifications in short order. Thanks to the principle of geographical distribution of posts, Latin America is well represented in all United Nations organs. In 1955 Brazil (1956) and Peru (1957) occupied two of the six nonpermanent seats in the Security Council. Four of the eighteen members of the Economic and Social Council are Venezuela (1956), Ecuador (1957), Argentina (1958), and the Dominican Republic (1958). The fifteen-member International Court of Justice included distinguished jurists from Mexico (1964), El Salvador (1964), Argentina (1964), and Uruguay (1961).[12]

[11] Arthur P. Whitaker (ed.), *Inter-American Affairs, 1945* (New York, Columbia University Press, 1946), p. 23.

[12] Dates in parentheses indicate the year in which the terms for which they were elected would expire.

The Latin-American nations in general have played a secondary role in major political questions that are related to other areas of the world, but they have always participated in the debates of such questions and occasionally have even taken the lead. Their voting behavior has not been according to any consistent pattern, and as a rule they have shown remarkable independence of position. On fundamental issues dividing East and West they have aligned themselves with the United States, but they have also opposed it on other occasions, particularly when the issue of small versus big powers was involved. In summary it may be said that Latin America has taken a genuine interest in the United Nations from its start; that it has contributed in some ways to the liberalization of the Charter; that it has played a fairly prominent role in UN deliberations; and that, far from forming a voting bloc either by itself or together with the United States, it has often maintained an independent position.

BIBLIOGRAPHY

Alvarez, Alejandro, *Le droit international américain,* Paris, 1910.

Arciniegas, Germán, *The State of Latin America,* New York, Knopf, 1952.

Brum, Baltasar, *The Peace of America,* Montevideo, 1923.

Daniel, James, *Red Design for the Americas: Guatemalan Interlude,* New York, John Day, 1954.

Daniels, Walter M., *Latin America in the Cold War,* New York, H. W. Wilson, 1952.

Gaston, Gaillard, *Amérique latine et Europe occidentale,* Paris, 1918.

Kelchner, Warren H., *Latin American Relations with the League of Nations,* World Peace Foundation Pamphlets, Boston, 1930.

Kirkpatrick, F. A., *South America and the War,* Cambridge, Mass., Harvard University Press, 1918.

Lavalle, Juan Bautista, *El Perú y la Gran Guerra,* Lima, 1919.

Martin, Percy Alvin, *Latin America and the War,* Baltimore, World Peace Foundation, 1925.

Quintanilla, Luis, *A Latin American Speaks,* New York, Macmillan, 1943.

Rippy, J. Fred, *Latin America in World Politics,* New York, Appleton-Century-Crofts, 1942.

Urrutia, Francisco J., *La evolución del principio del arbitraje en América,* Madrid, 1920.

Webster, C. K., *Britain and the Independence of Latin America,* New York, Oxford University Press, 1944.

Chapter 19: LATIN AMERICA AND THE UNITED STATES

The general interests and objectives of the United States in Latin America are centered, as elsewhere, on security and trade. From the strategic viewpoint the hemisphere is a single unit; Latin America with its approximately 170 million people and its vast natural resources might be used as a base against the United States by a hostile power. Naturally not all of Latin America is of the same strategic importance. Mexico and the Caribbean area are more vital than the South Atlantic countries because of their geographical proximity to continental United States and to the Panama Canal. Consequently, United States influence is greater in this part of the continent than in countries farther removed. Despite this distinction, it can be said that, in general, the peace and safety of the United States are closely linked with the peace and safety of Latin America.

As far as trade is concerned, "Latin America is as important to the United States, in terms of an export market, as all of Europe and more important than Asia, Africa, and Oceania combined. As a source of United States imports the Latin American republics have even greater relative importance, standing well ahead of Europe or the other continents."[1] According to Lleras Camargo, former Secretary General of the Organization of American States, the trade between the United States and Latin America amounted in 1953 to 3 billion dollars in United States exports and 3½ billion dollars in imports. He stated that these figures have more meaning when compared with the volume of exports and imports with the members of the North Atlantic Organization: Belgium, Canada, Denmark, France, Great Britain, Greece, Holland, Iceland, Italy, Luxembourg, Norway, Portugal, and Turkey. The total value of United States exports to this group of countries was approximately 5 billion dollars in 1953, and that of imports was less than 4 billion dollars. However, out of this group, Canada alone accounted for more than 3¼ billion dollars of the exports and for almost 2½ billion dollars of the imports.[2] It should also be mentioned that the U.S. Department of Commerce estimated that United States

[1] Quoted from Milton Eisenhower's report on Latin America in Alberto Lleras Camargo, "The Two Americas," *The Lamp,* vol. 36, no. 3, p. 2, September, 1954.
[2] Lleras Camargo, *ibid.,* p. 3.

capital investments in Latin America amounted in 1950 to 4.7 billion dollars in some two thousand enterprises controlled by United States companies.[3]

A series of factors have bearing upon the relations of Latin America with its northern neighbor. There is, in the first place, the heritage of some bitter memories over past United States policies, such as tariff walls, landing of troops and occupation in some Caribbean countries, financial imperialism, and general interventionism. On the other side of the ledger, there is occasional maltreatment of United States citizens and confiscation and expropriation of their property, default on financial obligations, and the many business hazards which derive from political instability. Lack of general knowledge about the social and political problems of Latin America, combined at times with irresponsible and oversimplified reporting on both sides, have often distorted actions and misinterpreted motives. Outside government circles, some business organizations, and academic institutions, the majority of the people have only superficial or inaccurate notions about their neighbors. These factors, often accentuated by language and cultural barriers, are at work on both sides against a sound foundation for policy.

In addition, the United States has often reflected in its diplomacy that sense of superiority which is inevitably produced by wealth, general well-being, and successful political institutions. In contrast, the Latin-American countries as a whole are poor, weak, and backward. They often manifest a mixture of fear and envy over the wealth and power of the United States as well as resentment over the fact that they are economically dependent upon their prosperous and mighty neighbor. Latin America's political instability is unjustly regarded, sometimes with superficial judgment, as a demonstration of lack of maturity and more often as congenital weakness. Out of this situation arose the conflict between United States investments and Latin America's new and intense nationalism. Other products have been the attempt to dictate on one side and, on the other, the irresponsible exploitation of antiforeign sentiment for political advantage.[4]

The Monroe Doctrine

In 1822 the United States was the first important power to recognize the independence of Latin America. This nation was at that time a young

[3] *The New York Times,* Oct. 18, 1953.

[4] Lawrence H. Chamberlain and Richard V. Snyder, *American Foreign Policy* (New York, Rinehart, 1948), pp. 702–704.

and comparatively weak country which still spoke with a small voice in world councils. It was also the standard-bearer of a political system which was considered revolutionary by almost the entire world. The Monroe Doctrine, denying the extension of European power and influence in the New World,[5] when declared in 1823 was a unilateral statement of the policy of the United States, put forth to meet a certain emergency. This situation concerned the threat of the so-called Holy Alliance to regain for Spain her lost colonies, and the menace of Russian expansion on the American Northwest. Although partly a gesture of sympathy toward the newly born republics of Latin America, the Monroe principle was chiefly a measure of national security. It was also partly designed to assert the political preponderance of the United States within the hemisphere and thus indirectly to secure its economic interests.[6] It embodied the fundamental conviction that the extension of the power and influence of the "political system" of absolute monarchies of Europe would endanger the safety of the United States.

Although the danger of intervention by the Holy Alliance was past at the time the doctrine was stated, the important thing is that it became the most celebrated and frequently invoked postulate of American foreign policy. In reality the great deterrent against European intervention in Latin America was the naval power of Britain. Nonetheless, Latin America had been threatened by European encroachments from the moment it became independent, and the significance of the Monroe Doctrine was that it represented the beliefs and the sentiments of the American people as well as their concern with the fate of the newly born republics.

During most of the nineteenth century the Monroe Doctrine was not upheld with consistency. The United States invoked it only when it was able and when it saw fit to do so. It did not try to vindicate it in all cases and allowed it to be violated on numerous occasions. The United States made no protest when the British seized the Falkland Islands, and also made none on the occasions of the French and British interventions in the Plata region. It permitted reannexation of Santo Domingo and seizure of the Peruvian Chincha Islands, although it protested vigorously in both these cases. Absorbed in the War between the States, the United States was not able to take a firm stand against the French in Mexico until Maximilian's empire had almost collapsed.

[5] See Chap. 4, pp. 95–96.

[6] Robin A. Humphreys, *The Evolution of Modern Latin America* (New York, Oxford University Press, 1946), p. 126.

However, by the last decade of the nineteenth century, United States foreign policy began to reflect a growing strength, and Monroe's principles were now proclaimed with new vigor. This opened a new era in the relations of the United States with Latin America. The former was now a closely knit nation which had advanced its borders to the Pacific Ocean in the west and to the Caribbean in the south. Its industry was seeking foreign markets; its capital was also looking for investment opportunities abroad. With all these changes the message of Monroe was to be transformed from a negative into a positive and even aggressive doctrine. Thus, when a dispute arose, in 1895, between Great Britain and Venezuela concerning the boundary of British Guiana, the United States invoked the doctrine and insisted upon settlement by arbitration. And Secretary of State Olney wrote his famous note to Great Britain: "Today the United States is practically sovereign on this continent, and its fiat is law upon the subjects to which it confines its interposition." As one writer puts it, "for Latin America as well as Europe the signs were plain for all to read.[7] A remarkable process of extension and reinterpretation of Monroe's principle had begun.

Latin America wondered if the signs meant that the United States was ready to make them into protectorates and to annex more territory. At the inception of the doctrine in 1823, Latin America had received it with enthusiasm. Several of the new states proposed alliances with the United States and offered to share responsibility for its enforcement. These offers were declined by the United States, which carefully avoided commitments that could impair future interpretations of the declaration. But now, in later years, Latin Americans became very critical, not of the original message of Monroe, but of the subsequent interpretations and even distortions of its text. They felt that the Monroe Doctrine, far from protecting them, was preventing them from establishing closer relations with Europe, and they came to fear the United States more than the Old World.

The Roosevelt Corollary

The southward expansion of the United States received new impetus at the close of the century. The Spanish-American War resulted in acquisition of Puerto Rico and of bases and the right to intervene in Cuba, now free from Spain but under tutelage of the United States by virtue of the Platt Amendment (1902).[8] Great Britain, which after 1856 had already begun

[7] *Ibid.,* p. 128.

[8] The Platt Amendment, embodied in the treaty of 1903 which regulated relations between the two nations and attached to the Cuban constitution of 1901 at

to recede from the Caribbean area, now virtually recognized that the political interests of the United States were paramount in Latin America, reduced its naval strength in America, and ceased objecting to the Monroe Doctrine. While it did not completely withdraw—it kept its colonies and maintained its strong economic ties—there was an essential conformity of views with the United States concerning Latin-American affairs. Through the nineteenth century Britain's position had been unrivaled. Even now, at the opening of the new century, Britain was still the only power that was able to challenge the United States in the Western Hemisphere, but it was willing to accept the political hegemony of the latter over the Caribbean area. This action contributed perhaps more than any other to the strengthening of Anglo-American friendship.

The question of forcible collection of debts brought the most important change in the meaning of the Monroe Doctrine. On several occasions there was threat of armed intervention by European powers to compel Latin-American governments to repay loans. In this connection, Theodore Roosevelt in his message to the Congress in 1901 asserted that "we do not guarantee any state against punishment if it misconducts itself, provided that punishment does not take the form of the acquisition of territory by any non-American power."[9] However, when Germany, England, and Italy blockaded the coast of Venezuela in 1902 to enforce collection of debts, President Roosevelt acted upon his "speak softly and carry a big stick" theory and threatened to use the American navy to prevent the blockade, whereupon Germany, the leader of the blockading powers, backed down and agreed to arbitration. This case and the seemingly chronic financial difficulties of the Dominican Republic posed the question whether, if the United States would not permit foreign creditors to collect debts in Latin America, it should not assume the responsibility itself to require these countries to meet their financial obligations.

Roosevelt's formula to remove all excuse for European intervention in the New World was announced in his annual message of December 6, 1904. The Roosevelt Corollary, as it came to be known, read as follows:[10]

---

the insistence of the United States, guaranteed the right of this country to intervene in Cuban affairs at any time for the purpose of safeguarding Cuban independence or maintaining a stable government. It also gave the United States rights to lease land for naval bases and to land troops on the island.

[9] Quoted in Dexter Perkins, *Hands Off: A History of the Monroe Doctrine* (Boston, Little, Brown, 1941), p. 87.

[10] Quoted in Hollis W. Barber, *Foreign Policies of the United States* (New York, Dryden, 1953), p. 246.

> If a nation shows that it knows how to act with reasonable efficiency and decency in social and political matters, if it keeps order and pays its obligations, it need fear no interference from the United States. Chronic wrongdoing, or an impotence which results in a general loosening of the ties of civilized society, may in America, as elsewhere, ultimately require intervention by some civilized nation, and in the Western Hemisphere the adherence of the United States to the Monroe Doctrine may force the United States, however reluctantly, in flagrant cases of such wrongdoing or impotence, to the exercise of an international police power. . . .
>
> It is a mere truism to say that every nation, whether in America or anywhere else, which desires to maintain its freedom, its independence, must ultimately realize that the right of such independence can not be separated from the responsibility of making good use of it.

Roosevelt transformed the whole tenor of Monroe's principle from a passive into a positive and active doctrine which proclaimed United States assumption of the role of international policeman for Latin America. The justification of the Roosevelt Corollary was that the United States would intervene in Latin America in order to do for the European governments what it did not want them to do for themselves. It was a policy that was to breed bitter resentment and hostility in Latin America until it was disavowed twenty-five years later. The Latin-American countries felt that the Roosevelt Corollary made a legal claim to a potential United States dictatorship on the hemisphere. As the corollary was subsequently applied to situations in the Caribbean area, Latin America concluded that, under the pretext of preventing European intervention, the United States had embarked on a program of economic imperialism and self-aggrandizement.

The first practical application of the new doctrine came in 1905, when the United States, under an executive agreement with the Dominican Republic, established supervision of that country's finances. An American general receiver of customs applied part of the revenues to debt service and turned the remainder over to the Dominican government. This receivership, however, led to more drastic intervention later and to the establishment of military controls, and in 1916 United States troops were landed to maintain order. These troops remained in the Dominican Republic until 1924, when self-government was restored.

The Panama Canal Affair

The events connected with the construction of the trans-Isthmian canal are important to the student of United States–Latin-American relations. They resulted in the creation in 1903 of a new independent state in territory formerly belonging to Colombia. The affair also aroused a great deal of wrath and suspicion against the United States among the Latin-American countries.

Speculation about the construction of a waterway across Panama had existed since the early days of Spanish colonization. It was not, however, until the early part of the nineteenth century that the project was seriously considered by several nations. The first diplomatic step of importance taken by the United States was the negotiation of a treaty with Colombia (then called New Granada) in 1846 by which Colombia guaranteed to United States citizens (although not to them exclusively) the right of transit across the Isthmus of Panama and the United States, in turn, guaranteed the neutrality of the isthmus and the sovereignty of Colombia over it.[11] The territorial expansion of the United States and the events of the Mexican War had some influence upon subsequent development. The territory of the United States was now much nearer to Panama. There was Anglo-American rivalry about the canal and other territorial rights in Central America, but in 1850 the United States concluded with Britain the Clayton-Bulwer treaty, by which any future canal route in Central America would be placed under joint control of both nations. This treaty later blocked the way for the construction of a canal solely by the United States.

The dramatic episode of the dash of the battleship *Oregon* from San Francisco to Cuba in sixty-eight days, by way of Cape Horn, during the Spanish-American War of 1898, revived United States interest in an interoceanic canal. Finally, after some wrangling, Britain consented to the Hay-Pauncefote treaty of 1902, which superseded the Clayton-Bulwer agreement. Under the terms of the new treaty the United States was free to build a canal under its own exclusive control.

The French canal company which had secured from Colombia the concession for the construction of the canal in 1878 went into bankruptcy after eight years of work and a political scandal that rocked the French Republic. The concession, which was to have expired in 1904, was now offered by the French company to the United States. Through approval of the Spooner bill, the President was authorized to secure the rights of the French company for forty million dollars and to acquire from Colombia

[11] The text of the Bidlack-Mallarino treaty of 1846 is reprinted, together with other documents related to the canal affair, in Ruhl J. Bartlett (ed.), *The Record of American Diplomacy* (New York, Knopf, 1947), pp. 251–252.

control of a strip of land for the construction of the canal or, if this could not be done on satisfactory terms, to secure a corresponding grant in Nicaragua.

The Hay-Herrán Treaty between Colombia and the United States was signed on January 22, 1903. By its terms the United States was to pay Colombia ten million dollars upon exchange of ratifications and an annuity of $250,000 beginning nine years thereafter. The United States should have exclusive rights to construct, operate, and control a canal and to use and control a strip of land 5 miles wide across the isthmus. Colombia had been torn by civil war from 1899 to 1902, and even now there prevailed a great deal of fractional strife. President Marroquín, aging and vacillating, attempted to shift responsibility for the treaty to the Colombian senate. The terms negotiated were met with strong opposition in Colombia, where public opinion considered the financial compensation offered totally inadequate especially when compared with the amount that the United States was paying for the nearly worthless holdings of the French company. A special committee of the Colombian senate recommended approval of the treaty subject to nine modifications, but when the United States threatened in a series of peremptory notes with actions "which every friend of Colombia would regret," the enraged legislators rejected the treaty by unanimous vote on August 12, 1903.

On November 3, 1903, a revolt broke out in Panama. Planned by a group of Panamanians and fomented by Philippe Bunau-Varilla, a former canal chief engineer and fabulous entrepreneur who owned substantial shares of the French company, the revolt succeeded without bloodshed. United States warships, dispatched earlier to both sides of the isthmus, prevented the landing of Colombian troops to suppress the long-awaited rebellion. Three days later the United States recognized the new republic. A treaty with Panama was signed on November 18, by which the United States received "in perpetuity the use, occupation and control" of a 10-mile-wide strip of land and all sovereignty rights over it. Panama received the financial compensation that had been previously offered to Colombia. Years later Theodore Roosevelt publicly made his famous boast: "I took the Canal."

The circumstances surrounding the Panama revolt and the obscure role played in it by the United States created bitter indignation not only in Colombia but in every Latin-American country. A segment of opinion in the United States, represented by some influential newspapers, was also critical of Roosevelt's action. *The New York Times* referred to it as "the path of scandal, disgrace, and dishonor."[12]

In 1921, two years after the death of Theodore Roosevelt, the United States agreed to a treaty giving Colombia twenty-five million dollars as compensation for the loss of Panama. Even this tacit admission of wrong-doing on the part of the United States failed to dissipate completely Latin-American resentment, and the bad memory of the Panama revolution lingered on for more than a quarter of a century.

The Interventionist Era

The Roosevelt Corollary had the practical effect of distorting the Monroe Doctrine into the opposite of its original meaning. According to this new interpretation, the doctrine now protected Europe against Latin America's misbehavior, and it asserted the right of the United States to exercise an unrestricted police power over the internal and external affairs of its neighbors. For a period of nearly thirty years after the corollary was enunciated, the United States intervened repeatedly in the small nations of Central America and the Caribbean. This intervention took several forms: political "protection," economic pressure, financial control, and in some cases military occupation. The decision to interfere always rested solely with the United States. There was never consultation with other powers.

The Caribbean policy of the United States during this period was determined by this country's search for security. In support of the United States' moving down into the Caribbean and beyond was the general theory that the security of the United States demanded control of areas which other powers might use as footholds on the Western Hemisphere. This theory was implemented by unilateral intervention.

The interventionist policy, however, reflected more than strategic and military interests. In a lesser degree it was also motivated by economic interests. Security was only a secondary motive in some interventions. United States trade in the Caribbean area had increased considerably, and there were considerable dollar investments throughout the region. President Taft on one occasion expounded the idea that United States diplomacy might "include active intervention to secure for our merchandise and our capitalists opportunity for profitable investment."[13]

[12] Quoted in Julius W. Pratt, *A History of United States Foreign Policy* (New York, Prentice-Hall, 1955), p. 410.

[13] J. W. Garner, *American Foreign Policies* (New York, New York University Press, 1928), p. 39.

The principal countries which experienced United States intervention, in addition to the Dominican Republic, were Cuba, Panama, Nicaragua, Haiti, and Mexico. All these countries, with the exception only of Mexico, became at one time or another virtual American protectorates. A United States military government was formed in Cuba between 1906 and 1909. A practical protectorate was established in Panama, where United States intervention was especially needed in time of elections. American troops occupied several Panamanian cities in 1918 and 1925 and an entire province in 1918–1920, to keep order and to protect the lives and property of United States citizens. Intervention in Nicaragua was begun during the administration of William Howard Taft by his secretary of state, Philander C. Knox. It is often cited as an example of the "dollar diplomacy" with which that administration is usually identified. The "dollar diplomacy" involved two methods: the use of diplomatic means in order to promote and defend American investments abroad, and the use of dollars to advance the objectives of American diplomacy.[14]

An American customs receivership was established in Nicaragua, and a treaty was signed which gave the United States a perpetual monopoly of the canal route across that country and the right to certain naval bases. United States marines were landed in 1912 to support a friendly government, and they remained, except for a brief interval, until 1933. Financial intervention in Haiti began in 1914, troops were landed in 1915, and fiscal and military controls were also established in that year. The troops did not depart from Haiti until 1934. In Mexico, there were instances of intervention during Woodrow Wilson's administration. In 1914 American forces occupied the city and port of Veracruz. In 1916 a punitive expedition under Brigadier General Pershing marched into Mexican territory in pursuit of the bandit Pancho Villa, and once more these two countries came close to an armed conflict.

It should be remembered that when the United States intervened in these countries it was exercising rights which were embodied in treaties, no two of which were identical. Also, in some cases, intervention was requested by Latin-American governments, and in others it was the result of a chronic condition of armed revolution.

Intervention in Mexico was conditioned by factors different from those operating in the other countries. Paradoxically, President Wilson, a professed anti-imperialist who had taken pains to reassure Latin America that the United States had no aggressive designs, was responsible for the policy

[14] Pratt, *op. cit.*, p. 420.

of denying recognition to governments which attain power by revolution. This policy was a radical departure from the traditional practice of the United States of recognizing any government, regardless of origin, that was firmly established and capable of performing its duties. The Wilsonian policy of recognizing only "constitutional" governments was first applied to Mexico in 1913 when an army revolt led to the accession to power of Victoriano Huerta and the assassination of his predecessor Francisco I. Madero. In Mexico, the nonrecognition policy, despite Wilson's good intentions, resulted in bickering, threats, and danger of war.[15] In general, the new recognition policy, designed to deter Latin-American revolutionary habits, became a powerful political weapon in the hands of the United States. Recognition was promptly given to governments that were friendly to the United States and denied to those which were hostile. Consequently, the doctrine of "constitutionalism," with its denial of the right of revolution, was denounced by Latin America as a new and more subtle form of interference: "negative intervention."

Harding's administration and most of Coolidge's were characterized by a continuation of the vigorous Latin-American policy of Roosevelt, Taft, and Wilson. The right of revolution was denied, the five Caribbean protectorates were retained, and United States property and lives were protected by strong diplomacy and by armed force.

Latin-American reaction to the events of the interventionist period was strong and bitter. A wave of anti–United States feeling or "Yankeephobia" spread throughout the continent, producing in some countries numerous volumes of "anti-Yankee" literature. A Brazilian writer, Eduardo Prado, wrote a book, *A Ilusão Americana* (1903), with the thesis that the Monroe Doctrine had served not against European intervention but as a cloak for aggression for the United States. Another writer, Manuel Ugarte of Argentina, after making a tour of the Latin-American countries in 1913, denouncing the United States, made a dramatic appeal to President Wilson by means of a public letter in which he voiced the hopes of Latin America and demanded equality and respect for all nations. These and other books on the same theme were widely circulated and read throughout the area.

The relations of Latin America with the United States had, by the late 1920s, reached the lowest ebb in history. When the Sixth International

[15] It is indeed curious that interventionism, while having different tones and motivations, would reach its peak of development under a president who believed that intervention was morally wrong.

Conference of American States met at Havana in 1928, a bloc of Latin-American states, led by Argentina, made a direct attack against the United States and proposed a resolution denouncing all forms of intervention. Although the Secretary of State succeeded in blocking this resolution, resentment toward the United States reached a new high after the conference, and many observers predicted the dissolution of the Pan-American movement.

The Good Neighbor Policy

Despite the failure of the Havana Conference, there was some evidence toward the end of the long period of Republican dominance in Washington that the United States was adopting a more conciliatory attitude with regard to its neighbors. The Coolidge administration retreated from the extreme position that it had assumed in the long-drawn-out conflict with Mexico and wisely appointed Dwight W. Morrow as ambassador to that country. Morrow proved to be an able diplomat and laid the foundations of a cordial relationship between the two countries. American occupation forces were removed from the Dominican Republic in 1924. A process of revision of the Monroe Doctrine was under way in order to make it more palatable to Latin Americans. The famous Clark Memorandum was prepared by Under-Secretary of State J. Reuben Clark in 1928 and printed in 1930. It made a review of the historical development of the Monroe Doctrine and directly disavowed the Roosevelt Corollary.

Herbert Hoover made a good-will tour of Latin America soon after his election. His administration also took some significant steps. It abandoned the legitimist doctrine of nonrecognition of revolutionary governments with the exception of Central America, where it was still to be applied in view of previous commitments. Most of the troops were withdrawn from Haiti by 1931, and the last marine forces were out of Nicaragua by January, 1931. The Hoover-Stimson policy toward Latin America was in striking contrast with the days of Roosevelt or Taft, and these events were a portent that a significant change in American foreign policy was in the making.

These changes, however, were made piecemeal, without a motivating political philosophy, and, as it has been said, were "hesitantly, almost surreptitiously introduced."[16] Although there had been a recession from the interventionist practices, the right of intervention was still unre-

[16] Samuel F. Bemis, *The Latin American Policy of the United States* (New York, Harcourt, Brace, 1943), p. 202.

pudiated. It was left to the new administration of Franklin D. Roosevelt to put an end to the period of distrust and to launch a new era of reconciliation based on the Good Neighbor policy. In his inaugural address Roosevelt made his famous pledge: "In the field of foreign policy I would dedicate this Nation to the policy of the good neighbor—the neighbor who resolutely respects himself and, because he does so, respects the rights of others."[17]

This declaration was followed on December 28, 1933, by an even more significant statement made at a Woodrow Wilson Foundation dinner, by which the Monroe Doctrine was transformed from a unilateral into a hemispheric policy. On this occasion the President announced:[18]

> The definite policy of the United States from now on is one opposed to armed intervention. The maintenance of constitutional government in other nations is not a sacred obligation devolving upon the United States alone. The maintenance of law and orderly processes of government in this hemisphere is the concern of each individual nation within its own borders first of all. It is only if and when the failure of orderly processes affects the other nations of the continent that it becomes their concern; and the point to stress is that in such an event it becomes the joint concern of a whole continent in which we are all neighbors.

Two days before the President's speech, the delegation of the United States at the Seventh International Conference of American States at Montevideo had accepted the Latin-American position on intervention and had signed a convention embodying the principle that "no state has the right to intervene in the internal or external affairs of another." A new spirit began to inspire the Latin-American policy of the United States, and mutual confidence was its natural outgrowth. By accepting the principle of nonintervention, the United States changed an atmosphere of ill-will into one of cordiality, and much of the past distrust was removed.

The Roosevelt administration followed these declarations by positive actions to liquidate those protectorates where American intervention had been frequent. It did not intervene in Cuba when serious disorders took place on that island in the summer of 1933, although it withheld recognition from *de facto* governments which it did not trust. However, it signed a treaty with a new Cuban government in 1934 which, by abrogating the odious Platt Amendment, gave fuller sovereignty to that country. From

[17] B. D. Zevin (ed.), *Nothing to Fear: The Selected Addresses of Franklin Delano Roosevelt, 1932–1945* (Boston, Houghton Mifflin, 1946), p. 16.

[18] James W. Gantenbein, *The Evolution of Our Latin American Policy* (New York, Columbia University Press, 1950), p. 166.

that moment there was no further interference in Cuban affairs. It removed the exception of Central America from application of the nonrecognition formula when it recognized revolutionary governments in El Salvador (1934) and in Nicaragua (1936). It ordered the withdrawal of the last troops from Haiti in August, 1934. It signed a new treaty with Panama, surrendering United States rights to intervene in the Isthmian republic and providing for fairer treatment of its interests in the canal. A new treaty with Mexico was signed in 1937 by which the United States relinquished the rights secured after the Mexican War to protect with military forces the railway across the Isthmus of Tehuantepec. Financial controls over the Dominican Republic were gradually abrogated, and the last vestiges of the former protectorate disappeared with the total liquidation of the Dominican debt in 1947.

The Good Neighbor policy was put to an acid test when President Lázaro Cárdenas of Mexico in 1938 ordered the expropriation of the properties of foreign oil companies. But even then there were no threats of armed intervention or economic sanctions. President Roosevelt held firmly against pressures for intervention and insisted that the American companies negotiate directly with the Mexican government. With war clouds rising in Europe, the international situation was conducive to compromise. An agreement signed in 1941 settled the controversy, and by 1949 the American oil claims had been paid. Settlement with expropriated British companies did not come until 1947, after the war had been concluded.

The Good Neighbor policy was based on principles of equality and partnership. These principles are indivisible, and a true partnership between the United States and Latin America was not possible without recognition by the former of the juridical equality of all states, large and small. Latin America's trust was won by the sincere repudiation of intervention on the part of the United States.

A feature of the new policy was the practice of consultation among the American nations on matters of joint interest. This idea also included joint hemispheric action, with each country participating according to its ability. The general objectives of the Good Neighbor policy were chiefly the establishment of inter-American responsibility for the security of the Western Hemisphere and the promotion of democratic government. The first goal was to be achieved not on an isolationist basis but as part of the world order; the second, through all kinds of measures, chiefly economic and educational, tending to raise the standard of living of all people. Three men contributed particularly to its success: Secretary of State Cordell Hull, patient negotiator; Assistant Secretary Sumner Welles, a man of extraordinary ability and insight; and President Roosevelt, who, in 1928, some years before reaching the presidency, had felt that the United States "should renounce for 'all time' its practice of 'single-handed intervention in the international affairs of other nations.' "[19]

Naturally not all the underlying motives of the radical change in the Latin-American policy of the United States were entirely devoid of selfish interest. The reappraisal which began in the early 1930s was partly stimulated by the world economic depression of 1929 and the imperative need for the United States to expand her foreign markets. But also important was the realization that the sentiments of the people of the United States were basically against unjust and undemocratic treatment of other nations, and that the Latin-American people in particular had the right to work out their own destinies without foreign interference. Furthermore, Latin America was now showing increased political stability, economic development, and ability to manage its own affairs. Whatever the motives, the policy was successful, and the suspicion and hostility which had been so widespread and intense gave room to surprising understanding and cordiality. Thus, the United States was able to assure the support of the Latin-American countries in the impending world conflict.

In conclusion, it should be said that, despite the mistakes and excesses of the past, and considering the enormous disparity between the power and wealth of the two Americas, North and South, the United States has shown notable restraint and moderation in using its coercive powers over its weaker neighbors. It should also be emphasized that there has been almost always an ideological element mixed with self-interest in the policies of the United States toward Latin America. If it is true that these policies have reflected interest for political security and economic advantages, it is equally true that they have also contained a measure of idealism. This ideological element was present again in the Good Neighbor policy, which in some measure was the true heir of Wilson's idealism.[20]

THE INTER-AMERICAN SYSTEM

The Pan-American Movement

Pan-Americanism is a vague term and even a misnomer, since the movement little resembles other "Pan" movements such as the Pan-German and Pan-Slav ideas. In contrast with these, Pan-Americanism does not imply

[19] Pratt, *op. cit.*, p. 609.
[20] Humphreys, *op. cit.*, pp. 134–135.

any idea of political unification or even loose confederation. It can be best described as an effort to secure international harmony and cooperation among the group of independent countries of the Western Hemisphere. In its origin, it was exclusively a Spanish American movement, but it became hemispheric in scope when in 1890 the United States assumed leadership. The First International Conference of American States of 1889–1890, held at Washington, marked the beginning of the modern Pan-American movement.

Two periods can be distinguished in the earlier history of Pan-Americanism: one comprising the inter-American political conferences held between 1826 and 1864, the other including the juridical congresses that met between 1864 and 1888. Among the first group were the Congress of Panama (1826), the American Congress of Lima (1847), the Continental Congress of Santiago, Chile (1856), and the second American Congress of Lima (1864). These early conferences were essentially political, and their main task was to consider measures for the common defense and mutual protection of the participating states. For many years after these countries became independent, rumors and threats of European aggression were rife, and their leaders recognized the need of uniting forces so as to resist any attempt to encroach on their sovereignty. That their fears were well founded is proved by the various European interventions which actually occurred. Some of these instances of European interferences were described earlier in this chapter. The dominant theme of these gatherings was, therefore, the question of national safety. The United States was seldom asked to participate in these earlier conferences.

The first conference, the famous Congress of Panama of 1826, had been the dream of Simón Bolívar, the Liberator, who envisaged the possibility of a vast confederation embracing all the former Spanish colonies and acting through a central government. But the results of the Panama meeting as well as those of the subsequent conferences were meager. Few of the treaties signed were ratified, and none was carried out in its entirety. Reasons for the failure to implement these agreements after they had been signed were the "enormous distances which separated the countries, the instability of the early governments, the exaggerated regional spirit of independence, boundary disputes, and civil wars."[21] Yet these early conferences were not entirely without result, because they inaugurated a series of traditions and precedents of the highest value. Many of the fundamental features of the inter-American system of today, such as the

[21] Alejandro Alvarez, *Le Droit international americain* (Paris, 1910), p. 60.

principles of equality of all nations, of nonintervention, of territorial integrity, and submission of international disputes to arbitration were affirmed at these gatherings.[22]

The juridical congresses of the period between 1864 and 1888 were of some value also, but in another way, since the threat of reconquest had disappeared by this time. The purpose of these meetings was to work out an acceptable and appropriate legal basis for the relations of the sovereign states of the area. The conferences, held in Lima in 1877 and at Montevideo in 1888, resulted in the signing of important treaties dealing with principles of international law applicable in the countries of Latin America.

The scope and direction of Pan-Americanism changed when the United States became interested in the movement. When, at the invitation of the United States, all the independent states of America met in Washington on October 2, 1889, the agenda before them emphasized the commercial and economic, rather than the political, aspect of inter-American relationships. This suggested that the motives which had prompted the United States to take the Pan-American movement under its wing were mainly economic—trade and new fields for capital investments and business enterprises.

The Inter-American Conferences

The modern movement was carried on by instruments of two distinct types: the International Conference of American States (better known as Pan-American Conferences), with a large number of special or technical conferences, and the Pan American Union and other permanent agencies which were established. This system took permanent shape with the signing in 1948 of the Charter of the Organization of American States at Bogotá. The old Pan American Union became then the Secretariat of the new organization. A detailed consideration of the large number of conferences that were convened since the launching of the new Pan-Americanism in 1889 would transcend the scope of this chapter. A very brief survey of the regular Pan-American Conferences must suffice.

Up to the present, ten of these conferences have been held. The second took place in Mexico City in 1901–1902, and since then conferences have been held about every five years, with the exception of the periods during the two world wars. The second conference reorganized the International Bureau of American Republics, founded at the Washington conference,

[22] See J. M. Yepes, *El panamericanismo y el derecho internacional* (Bogotá, 1930).

and the secretariat of the then "Union of American Republics." The third assembly met in Rio de Janeiro in 1906, the fourth in Buenos Aires in 1910, and the fifth in Santiago in 1923. All these conferences were confined mainly to economic and cultural matters and to the peaceful settlement of international disputes.

When the sixth general conference met at Havana in 1928, Latin-American reactions against United States interventions in the Caribbean area came close to causing the collapse of the Pan-American movement. However, the Latin-American bloc, led by Argentina, failed in the attempt to condemn intervention, and all other political questions were postponed until the next conferences. This gathering, the seventh of the series, was held in 1933 at Montevideo, and it proved to be a momentous one in the history of inter-American relations, for during it, as we mentioned before, the United States agreed to the principle of nonintervention which had been vigorously advocated by Latin America.

A special meeting took place in the interval between the seventh and the eighth Pan-American Conference. This was the Buenos Aires Conference of 1936, which laid the cornerstone of the hemispheric security system by agreeing to consider a threat to the security of one American state as a threat to all, and to consult together in the event of such a threat. Two years later the eighth regular conference met at Lima at a time when the world situation had become critical. This time the Declaration of Lima was adopted, by which the American nations reaffirmed their continental solidarity and their intention to consult with one another to meet any threats to their peace or territorial integrity. A new type of meeting was authorized for this purpose: the Meetings of Consultation of Foreign Ministers of the American Republics. The part that these special meetings played during the emergencies of the Second World War has been previously described. A fourth Meeting of Foreign Ministers was held in Washington in 1951, at a time when the "cold war" was already in progress, in order to deal with the threat of Communist infiltration in the Americas.

Another important special gathering in the postwar era was the defense conference at Rio de Janeiro which met in 1947 and resulted in the creation of the Inter-American Treaty of Reciprocal Assistance, commonly called the Rio Treaty. This instrument, described by Senator Vandenberg as "the greatest advance ever made in the business of collective peace,"[23]

[23] Quoted in Arthur P. Whitaker, "Development of American Regionalism," *International Conciliation,* no. 469, p. 134, March, 1951. This is an excellent history and analysis of the inter-American system.

created a permanent defensive alliance. It pledges every American state to assist in meeting an armed attack upon another American state. It also stipulates reciprocal assistance in case of an aggression or threat of aggression other than an armed attack. No distinction is made in the treaty between American and non-American aggression, and its provisions apply to all regardless of source. In the event of aggression, the nature of the action to be taken is determined by a meeting of foreign ministers called without delay for this purpose. Measures ranging from severance of diplomatic relations through economic sanctions to armed force are adopted by a two-thirds vote of the foreign ministers' meeting, but no state can be required to use armed force without its consent. The Rio Treaty, which went far beyond any previous security arrangement, served later as the model for other regional and collective security pacts in other regions of the world such as the North Atlantic Pact.

The Organization of American States

The ninth regular Pan-American Conference was held at Bogota, Colombia, in 1948. This conference was notable for producing two other agreements which, with the Rio Treaty of 1947, constitute today the pillars of the American regional system. One was the American Treaty of Pacific Settlement (Pact of Bogota) which coordinated all the existing treaties of pacific settlement. The other was the charter or constitution of the Organization of American States, as the formerly loosely knit association of American nations was now baptized. The new organization was an improved version of the old and not a new creation, but it represented some departures. The powers and duties of the OAS were, for the first time, defined, and although this necessarily implied a restriction of its scope, it also rendered its actions more effective in the future.

A very significant feature of the OAS is the equality of all members. In contrast with the United Nations Security Council, there is neither a great-power veto nor a distinction between permanent and nonpermanent membership in its Council. Every American state is represented in every organ of the OAS; each country has one vote; and, although in some cases a two-thirds vote is required, a majority vote is sufficient for most decisions. But the paramount feature of the system is the nonintervention principle which prohibits all forms of intervention with the exception only of the enforcement measures required by the Rio Treaty for defense in the event of aggression. This is again in contrast with the United Nations, which rules out only intervention in internal affairs.[24]

[24] *Ibid.*, p. 138.

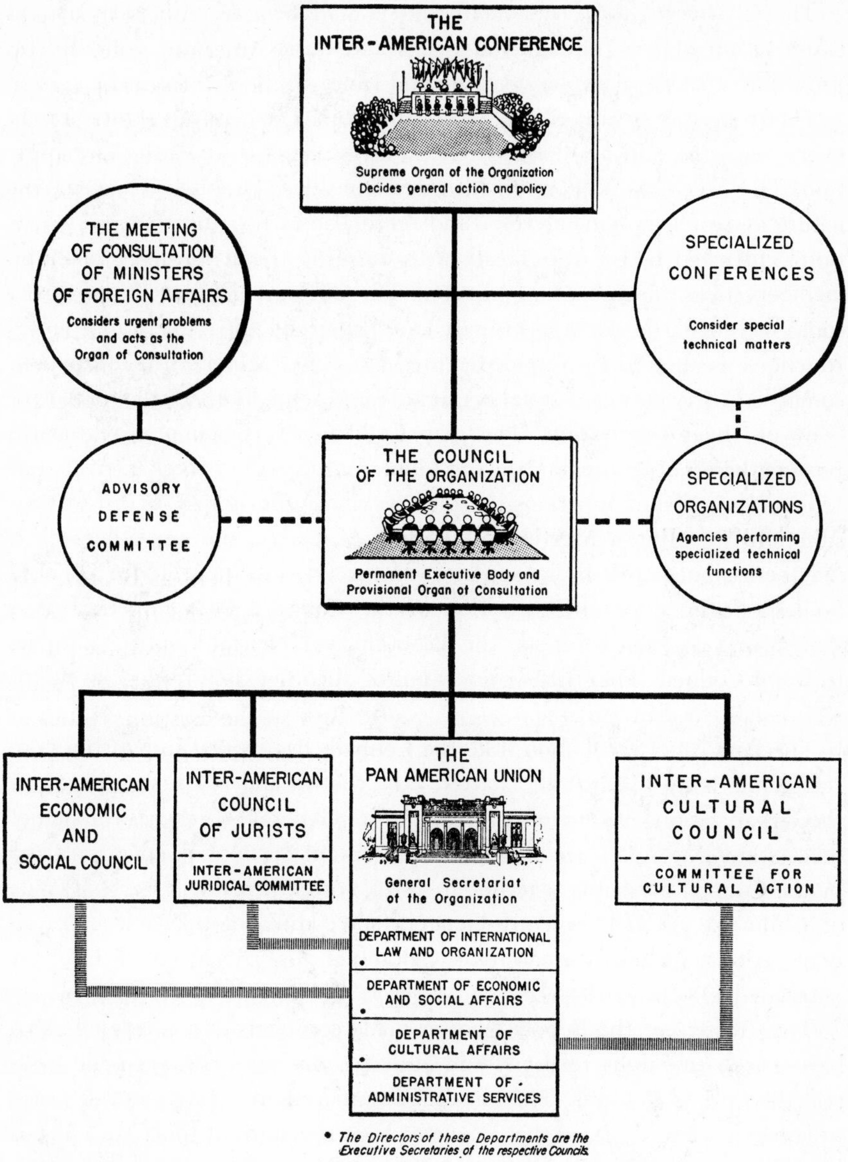

Figure 16. Organization of American States. SOURCE: The Pan American Union, Washington, D.C.

The Charter of the OAS opens with a statement of principles and an enumeration of the fundamental rights and duties of states, followed by provisions that regulate the structure and functioning of the organization.[25]

The supreme organ is the Inter-American Conference, which meets every five years and decides the general action and policy of the Organization. The Meetings of Foreign Ministers consider "problems of an urgent nature and of common interest" and serve also as the "organ of consultation" entrusted by the Rio Treaty with deciding the action to be taken by member states in case of aggression. The advisory Defense Committee, composed of "the highest military authorities of the American states," functions as an adjunct to the Meeting of Foreign Ministers. The Council, composed of twenty-one members, one from each country, is the executive body of the Organization. The new Council was given more extensive powers than its predecessor, the old Governing Board of the Pan American Union. Its political functions are to serve as a provisional "organ of consultation" pending a Meeting of Foreign Ministers, and any other which may be assigned to it by its superiors in the Organization. Three advisory bodies operate under the direction of the Council. These are the Inter-American Council of Jurists, the Economic and Social Council, and the Cultural Council. The first two grew out of already existing agencies which were established in wartime.

The Pan American Union, like the Council, has its seat in Washington. It became, according to the Charter, "the central and permanent organ of the Organization of American States and its General Secretariat." Its chief officers are a Secretary General and an Assistant Secretary General, elected by the Council for ten-year terms. In 1954, former President Carlos Dávila of Chile was elected Secretary General, succeeding another former president, Alberto Lleras Camargo of Colombia. José A. Mora of Uruguay succeeded Dávila in 1956.

The drafters of the Bogota Charter made conscious efforts to establish a basis for harmonious relations and fullest cooperation between the OAS and the United Nations. They included numerous references to the world organization and declared that "none of the provisions of this Charter shall be construed as impairing the rights and obligations of the member states under the charter of the United Nations." Moreover, to use again the

[25] For a complete text of the Charter, see William Sanders, "The Organization of American States: Summary of the Conclusions of the Ninth International Conference of American States, Bogota, Colombia, March 20–May 2, 1948," *International Conciliation,* no. 442, June, 1948.

words of the Charter, "Within the United Nations, the Organization of American States is a regional agency." Obviously a reciprocal relationship between the two agencies was intended, but it is equally clear that the OAS, embodying a regional system that has had a long and relatively successful life, intends to preserve its identity and status, and to continue to function even should the United Nations cease to exist.

Problems in Inter-American Relations

Relations between the Latin-American group of countries and the United States began to deteriorate during 1944 as a result of changes in the foreign policies of the latter. Events which took place some time earlier had already forecast a change in the attitude of the United States toward Latin America. In 1943, Sumner Welles resigned as Under Secretary of State. His resignation, due to personal differences with Secretary Hull, was a loss for Latin America of a powerful advocate and friend in the United States government. The State Department official in charge of Latin-American relations changed four times between 1943 and 1945. Other symptomatic events were the publication of the Butler and Merritt reports, the former being an attack by the Senator of that name against the Good Neighbor policy, and the latter the work of a subcommittee of the House Military Affairs Committee which recommended that the United States procure permanently the use of air bases built for wartime purposes in Latin America.

By 1944, a separation rather than an estrangement had become noticeable. It was chiefly caused by the priority given by the United States to great-power relationships in Europe and Asia with the consequent neglect of hemispheric regionalism. The idea of globalism, as contrasted with regionalism, had grown steadily after 1942, and many people came to consider the inter-American system as an obstacle to the establishment of a general international organization. With the changing face of the war, United States planning was concentrated on the occupation of enemy countries, the rehabilitation of Europe, and the building of a world organization, and there was little time devoted to relations with Latin America. Moreover, United States condemnation of the government of Argentina throughout the war for its complacency toward Axis activities caused a serious rift between the two countries. Argentina's failure to fulfill inter-American commitments and to combat Nazi influences made this problem one of the touchiest and most difficult for the United States to solve. Vacillations on the one hand and attempts to interfere in the local politics of

Argentina on the other contributed to a weakening of United States hemispheric leadership and laid this country open to charges of interventionism. Moreover, it was felt by many Latin Americans that, although the United States outwardly adhered to the practice of consulting with the other countries on important problems, it was in reality pursuing a unilateral policy which it expected them to follow.

An outbreak of anti–United States feeling marked the end of the Second World War. Revolutions, followed by changes of government, took place in several countries. The Caribbean area, beginning in 1945, was disturbed by plots and counterplots, and at times the entire region approached a state of political turmoil. Serious incidents occurred between the Caribbean countries, and international intrigue became characteristic of the area as hostility arose between dictatorial and democratic governments. In Argentina the course of United States policy changed several times, and the feud continued until 1947, after the Argentine elections had given constitutionality to the Perón regime. But the basic problem in postwar inter-American relations has been related to economic policy. Latin America turned after the war to economic nationalism, while the United States became the leading advocate of freer trade, which is the most advantageous policy for a country which emerged from the war with its economy intact and its industrial productivity at a new high. This divergence of economic views has been the chief source of friction in recent years.[26]

Furthermore, Latin America witnessed the application of unprecedented relief measures designed for the benefit of Europe. Many of the receiving nations were enemies of the United States in the war, and yet they received immense benefits from generous programs for rehabilitation. The Latin-American countries, neighbors and allies, felt that they were unjustly neglected. In their opinion, the material devastation of war areas was not much greater than the economic distress with which Latin America was afflicted, and they resented being left to a "straight across the table" bargaining. They lamented the fact that the United States seemed unwilling, or at best reluctant, to lend a helping hand in their industrialization. They also felt abused when their dollar reserves, accumulated during the war, whittled down when peace came as a substantial rise in price levels took place in the United States.

A special conference of Ministers of Finance or Economy, meeting at Petrópolis, Brazil, in December, 1954, was an attempt to improve hem-

[26] See William L. Neumann, "Economic Conflict in Inter-American Relations," *Inter-American Reports,* no. 3, July, 1948.

ispheric economic relations. The United States, however, could not agree with Latin-American demands for an inter-American stabilization and development fund and for guaranteed or fixed prices for their raw materials, such as mineral ores, coffee, sugar, and bananas. The delegation of the United States restated the position which favors private over public investment, and it emphasized the need for Latin America to create conditions to attract foreign private capital. It also promised to recommend to its government a more liberal loan policy and a formula to reduce taxation on private foreign investments. The results of the conference were disappointing to most Latin-American countries, and little progress was made toward solutions to longer-range problems in the economic sphere.

The sessions of the tenth Pan-American Conference, held at Caracas, in March, 1954, were dominated by discussions of the problem of encroachments of international communism in the Western Hemisphere. The efforts of the United States were directed toward securing agreement on an anti-Communist declaration, although other topics such as human rights, anticolonialism, and fair economic treatment were also discussed. After heated debates between the United States delegation headed by Secretary of State Dulles and the representatives of Guatemala, the Caracas Declaration was approved by the conference by a vote of 17 to 1. Its essential passage declared that domination or control of the government of any American state by the international Communist movement constituted a threat to the sovereignty and political independence of the other republics, endangering the peace of America, and would call for a meeting of consultation to consider appropriate action. Within a few weeks after the Caracas Conference ended, the Communist-infiltrated government of President Arbenz of Guatemala was overthrown by an invasion of Guatemalan exiles from Honduras. Arbenz formally complained of aggression to the United Nations Security Council, but his regime fell before any action was taken, and before the Foreign Ministers of the American Republics could meet. Whether the Guatemalan revolutionists received direct help and encouragement from the United States is not known; but sympathy with their purpose was publicly expressed by responsible United States government officials, and the new *de facto* government was recognized without delay.

The Guatemalan revolution gave rise to some uneasiness and suspicion among Latin-American circles. There were many who felt that the United States, after securing Latin-American endorsement for multilateral action at Caracas, had taken the situation in its own hands.[27] Some Latin Ameri-

[27] Arthur P. Whitaker, *Foreign Policy Bulletin,* Sept. 1, 1954.

cans wondered whether United States preoccupation with the threat of international communism might not lead to future interference in their internal affairs.[28] Though all these countries are basically anti-Communist, they are also intent on maintaining each country's right to regulate its own internal affairs.

Another source of ill feeling lies in what has been called the "democracy-dictatorship-nonintervention tangle." The question of recognition has always been a delicate problem for the United States. Return to the traditional Jeffersonian policy of recognition of all established governments, regardless of origin, in the 1930s prevented the charges of "negative intervention" which had been hurled against Wilson. This policy, however, is also criticized, since many of the Latin-American governments recognized by the United States are dictatorships. This had led to the belief among some Latin-American groups that the United States is bolstering local dictatorships and opposed to popular rule.[29] These critics would claim that the United States is chiefly concerned with the problem of security and that it prefers to deal with dictatorial governments, which by their nature are able to make prompt decisions, rather than with true democratic regimes with their slow-moving procedures. This poses a serious dilemma from which there is no escape, for if the United States attempts to foster democracy by withholding recognition from dictatorial regimes, it would lay itself open to charges of intervention. In addition, it would be passing judgment upon the democratic claims of every government, and therefore almost inevitably its motives would be questioned. Despite its shortcomings, the safest course appears to be that of recognizing all established governments, revolutionary or constitutional, that meet their international obligations. If and when a government is recognized under these circumstances, this act of recognition need not be taken to imply approval of it or its policies.

These problems illustrate the difficulties involved in the effective operation of the inter-American system under present international conditions. The dual relationship of the United States with the regional system and the world organization must also be taken into consideration. In the inter-American system, the Latin-American countries are on a footing of equality with the United States, while within the United Nations the United States

[28] See, for instance, Jorge Mañach, "Un Drama Americano," *Bohemia,* Aug. 17, 1954.

[29] See "Latin American Dictatorships and the United States," *Foreign Policy Reports,* Dec. 1, 1949.

belongs to the privileged group of great powers. In addition, the difficulties for the United States of carrying the burden of hemispheric leadership, at a time when its world responsibilities are constantly increasing and when a new kind of political struggle is being waged, are serious. To solve the problems ahead there is need of good will, understanding, and patience on the part of all the American states, for they are bound together for better or for worse.

BIBLIOGRAPHY

Bemis, Samuel F., *The Latin American Policy of the United States,* New York, Harcourt, Brace, 1943.

Callcott, W. H., *The Caribbean Policy of the United States, 1890–1920,* Baltimore, Johns Hopkins Press, 1942.

Cline, Howard C., *The United States and Mexico,* Cambridge, Mass., Harvard University Press, 1953.

Dávila, Carlos, and Clarence Senior, *Latin America and the Good Neighbor Policy,* New York, New York University Press, 1944.

De Conde, Alexander, *Herbert Hoover's Latin American Policy,* Stanford, Calif., Stanford University Press, 1951.

Duggan, Laurence, *The Americas: The Search for Hemispheric Security,* New York, Holt, 1949.

Fenwick, C. G., *The Inter-American Regional System,* New York, Declan X. McMullen Company, Inc., 1949.

Fitzgibbon, R. H., *Cuba and the United States,* Menasha, Wis., Banta, 1935.

Gallardo Nieto, Galvarino, *Panamericanismo,* Santiago, 1941.

Guerrant, E. O., *Roosevelt's Good Neighbor Policy,* Albuquerque, N.M., University of New Mexico Press, 1950.

Hill, H. C., *Roosevelt and the Caribbean,* Chicago, University of Chicago Press, 1927.

Jones, C. L., *The Caribbean since 1900,* New York, Prentice-Hall, 1936.

Mack, Gerstle, *The Land Divided: A History of the Panama Canal and Other Isthmian Projects,* New York, Knopf, 1944.

Masters, Ruth D., *Handbook of International Organization in the Americas,* Washington, D.C., Carnegie Endowment, 1945.

Miner, D. C., *The Fight for the Panama Route,* New York, Columbia University Press, 1940.

Munro, D. G., *The United States and the Caribbean,* Boston, World Peace Foundation, 1934.

Perkins, Dexter, *Hands Off: A History of the Monroe Doctrine,* Boston, Little, Brown, 1946.

———, *The United States and the Caribbean,* Cambridge, Mass., Harvard University Press, 1947.

Planas-Suárez, Simón, *La solidaridad americana,* Caracas, 1945.

Quintanilla, Luis, *Pan Americanism and Democracy.* Boston, Boston University Press, 1952.

Smith, O. E., Jr., *Yankee Diplomacy: United States Intervention in Argentina,* Dallas, Tex., Southern Methodist University Press, 1953.

Stuart, Graham H., *Latin America and the United States,* 5th ed., New York, Appleton-Century-Crofts, 1955.

Whitaker, Arthur P., *The United States and Argentina,* Cambridge, Mass., Harvard University Press, 1954.

———, *The United States and South America. The Northern Republics,* Cambridge, Mass., Harvard University Press, 1948.

———, *The Western Hemisphere Idea: Its Rise and Decline,* Ithaca, N.Y., Cornell University Press, 1954.

———, (ed.), *Inter-American Affairs,* New York, Columbia University Press, published annually, from 1941 to 1945.

Williamson, René de Visme, *Culture and Policy: The United States and the Hispanic World,* Knoxville, Tenn., University of Tennessee Press, 1949.

GLOSSARY*

Acordada. A judicial pronouncement or order, sometimes issued as an advisory opinion or as a statement of principle, without a case between parties before the court.

Acuerdo. A resolution or agreement. In colonial times, the term referred commonly to resolutions of a quasi-legislative character adopted by the *audiencia.*

Alcalde. In modern times a municipal official, comparable to that of mayor. In the Spanish colonies the *alcalde ordinario* was a member of the town council and a local judge of first instance. The *alcalde mayor* was usually a district or provincial judge or a provincial executive.

Alcalde mayor. See **alcalde.**

Alcalde ordinario. See **alcalde.**

Amparo. Protection against abuse of power or violation of guaranteed rights. *Juicio de amparo* or *recurso de amparo* the judgment of a proper and competent court in an action; these terms also refer to the procedure in securing such judgments.

Audiencia. In the Spanish colonies the term referred to the highest tribunals located therein, although functions other than judicial were assigned to them. In modern times, as applied to courts, it designates tribunals of lesser rank, such as the provincial courts of Cuba.

Ayuntamiento. City hall or council.

Bandeira. Literally, "banner" or "flag." In Brazil the term referred to groups of frontiersmen (*bandeirantes*) who in bands hunted slaves, explored, and settled the hinterlands.

Bandeirante. See **bandeira.**

Barrio. A municipal division or ward.

Cabildo. City hall or council. The *cabildo abierto* was an "open" meeting to which the local citizens were called in contrast to the usual "closed" (*cerrado*) meeting.

Cacique. Literally, the chief of an Indian tribe. *Caciquismo* signifies the strong personal and political influence of certain leaders of the people. A type of "boss" rule.

* Spanish and Portuguese terms either used in the text or in the literature cited. For constitutional terms, see Russel H. Fitzgibbon, "Glossary of Latin American Constitutional Terms," *The Hispanic American Historical Review,* vol. 27, no. 3, pp. 574–590. August, 1947.

Caciquismo. See **cacique.**

Capitão mor. Official responsible for defense matters in colonial Brazil. Also an official in charge of local government.

Capitulación. A contract or convention, such as the articles of agreement between the crown and an explorer.

Casa de Contratación. Literally, "house of trade." The institution for the administration of trade between Spain and the colonies and for the execution of the laws concerning commerce or other matters committed to it.

Casación. Cassation, appeal, the act of annulling or repealing a law or reversing a judicial sentence. *Tribunales de casación,* courts of appeal to consider requests for annulment or reversal of a decision by a lower court.

Caudillo. Sometimes used synonymously with *cacique* and meaning "chief" or "leader." *Caudillismo,* the political regime in which the *caudillo* exercises a dominant personal influence, has no precise equivalent in English. The word in usage often carries a sinister connotation of dictatorship.

Caudillismo. See **caudillo.**

Cédula. An official paper, such as a card of identification or a letter of credit. In colonial times a *cédula real* was a royal order of general character or an announcement of a law or the grant of some request.

Colegio. Institution of education, comparable to high school or junior college; also, a corporation or society of members of the same profession. Synonymous terms are: **liceo; instituto; gimnasio.**

Consejo Real y Supremo de las Indias. Body which held supreme jurisdiction in Spanish colonial affairs under the king. Its powers included the whole range of government—legislative, judicial, and executive.

Consulado. Literally, "consulate." During the colonial period the term referred to the organization, identified with a city, of merchants, importers and exporters, occupied with such matters as shipping, the settlement of mercantile disputes, and promoting prosperity.

Corregidor. Provincial executive responsible to the *audiencia* in matters of justice and to the viceroy or captain general in administrative affairs. *Corregidores de pueblos de indios,* officials ruling over districts composed of Indian villages and towns.

Cortes. An assembly or parliament. Also, the courts.

Decreto-ley. Literally, "decree law." Legislation by the executive department. Restrictions may limit the exercise to occasions of emergency.

Some countries may require either the prior or the subsequent validation of such legislation by the congress.

Designado. An individual elected by, and often from, the legislative branch to succeed the president in case of vacancy. Some countries have more than one *designado.*

Donatario. A receiver of a territorial grant (*capitania*) in colonial Brazil by royal favor, who was endowed with ample economic and political privileges.

Ejido. Communal land. A tract of land owned and worked in common by a community. Used extensively in Mexico as a feature of the agrarian redistribution program. In colonial times, the municipal commons served several purposes.

Encomendero. See **encomienda.**

Encomienda. Literally, "trust." Grant in trusteeship of a group of Indians with services to be rendered by both the holder (*encomendero*) and the Indians.

Estancia. Farm for grazing cattle; landed property.

Fallo. See **juicio.**

Feitoría. Portuguese trading post.

Flota. Fleet. In the seventeenth century the fleet which was dispatched each year from Spain to Mexico became specifically the *Flota,* while the one which was sent to Panama came to be known as the *Galeones.*

Fuero. Charter of an institution; guarantee of liberties; grant of exemptions or privileges, such as that of a separate court for consideration of ecclesiastical or military cases.

Gobernador. An executive official in charge of one of the smaller political jurisdictions into which each viceroyalty or captaincy general was divided.

Gremio. Body, society, corporation. In colonial times, guilds of tradesmen who enjoyed special privileges (*fueros*).

Hacienda. Estate, farm, finances, funds. *Real hacienda,* Royal Exchequer. *Departamento de hacienda,* department of finance, treasury. *Hacienda pública,* public treasury, finances.

Intendencia. Intendancy. In the Spanish colonial system, an institution primarily concerned with the collection, safekeeping, and disbursement of public money. In modern times, usually the district ruled by a municipal officer, the counterpart of mayor, or by a provincial executive.

Jefe político. An official who in a local jurisdiction, e.g., province or city, represents the central government.

Juicio. In a general sense, a case at law and its consideration and decision by a court. Many varieties of *juicio* bear distinctive designations. The terms *sentencia* and *fallo* are those most commonly used for the "opinion and decree" of a court.

Junta. Committee, board, commission. Sometimes, a meeting of such a body. *Junta de gobierno,* a collegial or plural executive, usually provisional or temporary.

Jurado. Jury. *Gran jurado,* grand jury. In Mexico, when the chamber of deputies decides, as in impeachment cases, whether there are sufficient grounds for proceedings against a government official it is acting as a *gran jurado.*

Juzgados. Local courts. Principal courts of first instance.

Latifundio. A great landed estate. *Latifundia,* system of land tenure under which the large estate is the prevailing form.

Letrado. Literally, "lettered" or "learned." Lawyer, advocate, counselor. In colonial times, a man trained in the civil law.

Ley orgánica. An act of the legislative body, implementing the constitution, which regulates the organization and functioning of a branch of the government. For example, in all countries constitutional provisions respecting the judicial branch are supplemented by a judiciary act or *ley orgánica del poder judicial.*

Llanos. As a geographical term, it refers to the extensive plains in Venezuela, north of the Orinoco River.

Mandado. In Portuguese, a writ. An order from competent judicial or administrative authority. *Mandado de segurança,* a writ used in Brazil to protect personal and even property rights.

Mayorazgo. Family estate, which devolves to the eldest son, by right of inheritance; an entailed estate.

Mestizo. The offspring of an Indian and a European. In some countries, applied to any person of mixed blood.

Ouvidor geral. Chief justice. Official in charge of the administration of justice in colonial Brazil.

Padrinazgo. Compaternity, or the system of extralegal and extranatural kinship which is represented in part by the title of "godfather."

Patronato. The right of presentation; the right or power of civil officials to nominate clerics for appointment to high ecclesiastical offices. Also means patronship, foundation of a charitable or pious establishment.

Peonaje. Peonage. System under which the laborer is bound to the farm or mine by placing him in debt to his employer.

Provedor môr. An official charged with the general supervision of finances in colonial Brazil.

Recopilación. Compilation. Applied to a compilation of colonial legislation (exact title, *Recopilación de leyes de los reynos de las Indias*) published in 1681.

Recurso. Recourse, resort, petition, appeal (law). In law, *recurso* refers not only to the right of appeal—to the court rendering the judgment or to a higher court—but to the procedure to be followed.

Regidor. Alderman or councilman of a city.

Reglamento. Literally, "regulation." As used in this book, it refers to an administrative directive or to a collection of them issued by an executive.

Residencia. Review of the conduct of an official at the end of his term. The court of *residencia* had relative freedom in procedure.

Sentencia. See **juicio.**

Sertão. Backlands or interior of Brazil.

Sindicato. A corporation or a labor union. Other organizations—of agriculturists, merchants, and professional people—are often so designated.

Síndico. Person chosen to represent or defend or guide an organization, e.g., the *síndico* of the *consulado.* A local official with legal and sometimes financial duties.

Visita. Literally, "visit." In this book the term refers to official visits of inspection or investigation in colonial times. Some *visitas* instituted reforms and exercised governmental powers.

Zambo. Offspring of a Negro and an Indian.

INDEX

NORTH ATLANTIC OCEAN
GULF OF MEXICO
MEXICO
Chihuahua
Monterrey
Guadalajara
Mexico City
Puebla
Veracruz
Mérida
Havana
CUBA
Santiago
DOMINICAN REPUBLIC
Port-au-Prince
Ciudad Trujillo
HAITI
BR. HONDURAS
Belize
HONDURAS
Tegucigalpa
GUATEMALA
Guatemala
EL SALVADOR
San Salvador
NICARAGUA
Managua
COSTA RICA
San José
PANAMA
Panamá
CARIBBEAN SEA
Maracaibo
Cartagena
Caracas
Barquisimeto
Ocaña
Mérida
VENEZUELA
Georgetown
Paramaribo
Cayenne
GUIANA
BR.
DU.
FR.
Medellín
Bogotá
Cali
Popayán
COLOMBIA
Quito
ECUADOR
Guayaquil
Cuenca
GALAPAGOS IS. (Ecuador)
Manaus
Belém
BRAZIL
Recife (Pernambuco)
Trujillo
PERU
Callao
Lima
Ayacucho
Cuzco
Arequipa
Baía (São Salvador)
SOUTH PACIFIC OCEAN
BOLIVIA
La Paz
Cochabamba
Santa Cruz
Sucre
Potosí
Arica
Belo Horizonte
PARAGUAY
Rio de Janeiro
São Paulo
Santos
Antofagasta
Tucumán
Asunción
Villarica
CHILE
Porto Alegre
Córdoba
Santa Fé
Valparaíso
Mendoza
Rosario
URUGUAY
Santiago
Colonia
Buenos Aires
Montevideo
Concepción
Bahía Blanca
ARGENTINA
SOUTH ATLANTIC OCEAN
FALKLAND IS. (Malvinas)